Manual for Teaching

the Third Reader — 1

REVISED EDITION

By DAVID H. RUSSELL

GRETCHEN WULFING

and ODILLE OUSLEY

Assisted by Eleanor Robison

GINN AND COMPANY

| BOSTON · NEW YORK · CHICAGO · ATLANTA |
| DALLAS · PALO ALTO · TORONTO · LONDON |

ACKNOWLEDGMENTS

Grateful acknowledgment is made to the following authors and publishers for permission to use the copyrighted materials:

Abelard-Schuman, Ltd. for the poems "A Dog" and "Riding Horseback," by AILEEN FISHER. Reprinted by permission of the publishers Abelard-Schuman, Ltd., from *Up the Windy Hill*, by Aileen Fisher. Copyright 1953.

Marie Louise Allen for her poem "Sneezing," from *A Pocketful of Rhymes*, by MARIE LOUISE ALLEN, published by Harper & Brothers, 1957.

Board of National Missions of the Presbyterian Church for the poem "Dahlias," from *The Songs of Marcelino*, by EDITH AGNEW, copyright, 1953, by Board of National Missions of the Presbyterian Church.

The Bobbs-Merrill Company, Inc., for the poem "The Funniest Thing in the World," from *Rhymes of Childhood*, by JAMES WHITCOMB RILEY. Published by The Bobbs-Merrill Company, Inc., 1891.

Paul Burlin for the poem "Corn Grinding Song," from *The Indians' Book*, by NATALIE CURTIS BURLIN, published by Harper & Brothers, 1937.

Doubleday & Company, Inc., for the poem "Night Magic," from *Hearts Awake*, by AMELIA JOSEPHINE BURR. Copyright, 1919, by Doubleday & Company, Inc.

Harper & Brothers for the poem "Red Hen," from *I Know Some Little Animals*, by JAMES S. TIPPETT. Copyright, 1941, Harper & Brothers.

Charles Scribner's Sons for the poem "The Monkey's Baby," from *Open the Door*, by MARION EDEY and DOROTHY GRIDER, copyright 1949, by Marion Edey and Dorothy Grider, and reprinted by permission of Charles Scribner's Sons.

ii

MARCHETTE CHUTE for her poems "Horses," from *Rhymes about the City*, "My Dog," from *Rhymes about Ourselves*, and "Newness," from *Rhymes about the Country*, all published by The Macmillan Company.

NONA KEEN DUFFY for her poem "Young Cowboy," reprinted from *Grade Teacher* magazine, February, 1955.

AILEEN FISHER for her poem "December," from *That's Why*, published by Thomas Nelson & Sons, 1946.

Follett Publishing Company for the poem "Broomstick-Time," from *Songs from around a Toadstool Table*, by ROWENA BENNETT. Copyright 1930, 1937, by Follett Publishing Company, Chicago, Illinois.

ETHEL ROMIG FULLER for her poem "Wind Is a Cat," from *White Peaks and Green*, published by Binfords & Mort, Publishers, copyright, 1928, by Ethel Romig Fuller.

Houghton Mifflin Company for the poem "The Fairy Book," from *A Pocketful of Posies*, by ABBIE FARWELL BROWN, copyright, 1902, by Houghton Mifflin Company.

Mary Britton Miller for her poem "Cat," from *Menagerie*, by MARY BRITTON MILLER, published by The Macmillan Company.

Macrae Smith Company for the poem "Topsy-Turvy World," by WILLIAM BRIGHTY RANDS, from *One Thousand Poems for Children*, compiled by ELIZABETH H. SECHRIST. Copyright, 1946, Macrae Smith Company.

ILO ORLEANS for his poem "First and Last," reprinted from *The Instructor*, September, 1952.

G. P. Putnam's Sons for "Supper for a Lion," from *All Together*, by DOROTHY ALDIS; copyright 1952, by Dorothy Aldis.

Rand McNally & Company for the poem "Columbus," from *The Peter Patter Book*, by LEROY F. JACKSON. Copyright 1918, renewal copyright 1946, by Rand McNally & Company, publishers.

H. Langford Reed for the poem "There Was a Young Lady of Niger," by COSMO MONKHOUSE, from *The Complete Limerick Book*, by LANGFORD REED. Published by G. P. Putnam's Sons, 1925.

Sidgwick & Jackson Ltd. for the poem "Choosing Shoes," from *The Very Thing*, by FFRIDA WOLFE.

NANCY BYRD TURNER for her poem "Dark Eyed Lad Columbus," from *Sing a Song of Seasons*, compiled by SARA and JOHN BREWTON, published by The Macmillan Company, 1955.

The Viking Press, Inc. for permission to use and set to music an excerpt from *In My Mother's House*, by ANN NOLAN CLARK. Copyright 1941, by Ann Nolan Clark. Reprinted by permission of The Viking Press, Inc., New York.

Every effort has been made to contact the copyright owner of the poem "My Valentine," by MARY CATHERINE PARSONS, from *Let's Read-Together Poems*, compiled by HELEN A. BROWN and HARRY J. HELTMAN, published by Row, Peterson and Company, 1949.

Contents

USING THIS MANUAL EFFECTIVELY

This manual is a guide and a friend. It offers a sound philosophy of reading instruction, recommendations for individual lessons, and hundreds of suggestions for activities. From this program a teacher or a guided group of children may choose what to do in reading.

For General Helps

1. See the description of a modern developmental program in reading in Chapter I.

2. Note how Chapter II makes reading a continuous all-school task.

3. Read Chapter III for an overview of the program for this grade level.

4. Note how examples of charts, word games, informal tests, and skill-builders are scattered throughout Chapter IV.

5. Discover hints for dramatizations, music, recordings, films, filmstrips, and follow-up activities throughout the lesson plans.

6. Make constant use of the suggestions for Stories to Enjoy, and Poems to Enjoy.

7. Refer to the Index of Word-Study Skills whenever the group or a child needs special help.

For Specific Helps

1. Read through the stories in the Reader and their accompanying plans outlined in the Manual.

2. As you read the suggestions in the Manual, check those which seem to fit the needs of the group.

3. On your chart of daily or weekly plans, note the manual page numbers for the suggestions you intend to use with the group.

4. If a few children need special help, list their names followed by numbers of manual pages which offer specific aids.

5. List necessary materials which may be brought from home by the children, borrowed from the public library, or obtained through other sources.

6. At the end of the week, make a brief note about the progress made on any activity which runs through a whole unit or is a culmination of it. Add suggestions for children's work to be emphasized during the following week.

Planning in this manner gives point to each day's reading activities and assures balance and continuity in the year's program.

Manual for Teaching

Finding New Neighbors

Reading competence is needed by children, youth, and adults.

I

A Basic Reading Program

Learning to read is one of the most urgent and crucial tasks of a lifetime. The undertaking ranks in importance with such developmental tasks as being a member of a family or getting along with peers in a school group. Reading abilities are not fully acquired in the primary grades or in the elementary school, but the foundations for reading competence laid during these school years will determine much of a person's future success and happiness. Failure or partial failure in reading may handicap an individual's work in school as well as his total adjustment. Success will contribute to his personal needs, the requirements of his job, and his relationships with others. Reading abilities are needed by all children, youth, and adults.

A Series Designed for Children

A basic reading program is designed for children. It concentrates on the development of reading abilities, but at the same time contributes to the total growth pattern of the child. As they learn to read, children discover that reading is thought-getting and book-using, not merely word-calling. As they grow *in* and *through* reading, children find that learning to read is a complex undertaking. A basic reading program helps children develop the essential abilities, habits, and attitudes needed in this subtle and intricate process.

In a good basic reading program, certain characteristics are evident.

Every child learns to read to the best of his ability.

Every child develops reading habits and skills at his own learning rate.

Every child is taught by methods best suited to his particular needs and abilities.

3

Every child becomes increasingly aware of the purposes for which he reads and of his own progress in reading.

Every child becomes more independent in his use of reading materials.

Every child participates in a balanced and varied program of reading activities.

The above-mentioned characteristics of children who are learning to read do not develop automatically or inevitably. They must be provided for and nourished in a well-planned reading program. About one half of the adult population of the world have never learned to read, and even in countries where literacy is high, one tenth or more of the adults cannot read well enough to enjoy and use their reading. Children need the stimulation, support, and organized approach of a comprehensive and thorough reading program if they are to enjoy and use reading in childhood and in adult life.

Such a program is provided by the GINN BASIC READERS. These books, with their accompanying manuals, workbooks, tests, word cards, and enrichment materials, comprise a complete and well-rounded offering of reading materials. The materials provide opportunities for children to develop specific as well as general reading abilities and they offer teachers a planned and co-ordinated program for aiding such development. The program especially stresses four interrelated phases of reading-in-action.

The Developmental Program. This phase involves systematic group and individual instruction to develop basic habits and skills in reading. It includes use of the basal text with suggestions from the accompanying teachers' manual and related materials. It helps answer the question "What is Bill doing in reading?"

The Recreational Program. This phase includes the development of positive attitudes toward reading and the enjoyment of varied reading materials. It means finding good books, reading them, and liking them. It lays a foundation for habits of turning to books, magazines, and newspapers all through one's life. It helps answer the question "How is Bill enjoying reading?"

4

The Functional Program. This phase is concerned with putting reading to work. It means using printed materials as aids in accomplishing worth-while tasks in and out of school. It includes not only fact-finding, but the interpreting and organizing of facts for use in a variety of situations and in answer to various needs. This phase of the program utilizes basal readers, textbooks in the content areas, and such reference materials as dictionaries and encyclopedias. It helps answer the question "How is Bill using reading?"

The Enrichment Program. This phase assures that the basic reading program will add meaningful ideas to the child's life, enlarge his horizons, and stimulate his thinking. It includes the child's creative activities growing out of reading, his development of a sense of self, and his added insights into his relations with other people. It is reading applied to personal needs and deeper understandings. It is the part of the program involved in the question "What is reading doing to Bill?"

All four of these main phases of a modern reading curriculum are emphasized in the GINN BASIC PROGRAM. The readers, the workbooks, and the suggestions in the accompanying teachers' manuals stress one or more of these aspects of the whole program. Suggestions are made in the manuals for the use of other materials to strengthen parts of the program, such as juvenile books, reference books, newspapers, and children's own writing. Most reading lessons and related activities involve all four phases, but vary in emphasis on each of the four, with changes from day to day and from selection to selection. Some children need more help in one area than in others. The wise teacher is the best judge of what phase shall be stressed in each story, article, or poem for each child or group. The breadth of selections in the readers and the wide range of suggestions in the manuals enable the teacher to select the phase or phases of the four parts of the program which will best help a particular group of boys and girls.

Some Principles in a Basic Reading Program

The GINN BASIC READING PROGRAM is constructed on a firm foundation of research and good practice expressed by the principles listed below.

1. A systematic, co-ordinated program of reading instruction is needed throughout the elementary and the junior high schools.

2. Incidental reading instruction at any grade level, including the upper grades, does not produce the same results as a planned program.

3. A basic reading program should provide a gradual approach in the difficulty of the materials used.

4. A basic reading program should be closely related to other curricular activities and should contribute richness and depth to other learnings.

5. A basic reading program should emphasize understanding, interpretation, and use of the materials read.

6. All useful reading skills and habits cannot be taught in grades one, two, and three.

7. Reading skills taught in the primary grades must be maintained and extended in the later grades.

8. As children grow into later childhood and early adolescence their changing interests and activities, as well as the demands of the total curriculum, require a broader and deeper pattern of reading experiences.

9. Because children are different and the reading process is complex, no single method of reading instruction is sufficient for a well-rounded program. A combination of methods, with varying emphasis as needed, is the best "system" of teaching reading.

10. A basic reading program may be described horizontally in terms of activities planned for the first or the fourth grade, but it must also be planned in terms of a sequential, vertical organization for all grades. Teachers, principals, and textbook makers should consider both horizontal and vertical aspects of child growth in the development of reading abilities.

Thus the GINN BASIC PROGRAM is built on careful research in child development and in the psychology of learning to read as translated into the ten principles stated above. The succeeding pages in this manual illustrate the ways in which the GINN BASIC PROGRAM provides for (1) continuity in growth of abilities, (2) variety of activities, (3) organization of experiences, and (4) content of important ideas.

The Psychology of a Basic Reading Program

At least ten thousand worth-while articles on the teaching of reading and several hundred detailed researches on the psychology of reading have been published in educational and psychological journals. Any summary of these articles must necessarily be an over-simplification. The subtleties of the reading process require detailed study, a description of which cannot be given in full in a manual designed as a practical aid to teaching. Many school people will want to make a detailed study of the research on reading for themselves; others may be content with a summary of such researches. Accordingly, this chapter concludes with a brief look at the research evidence related to reading, particularly as it affects a basic program. The following points have been used as guides by the authors of the GINN BASIC READERS in their selection of materials and in the detailed suggestions for teaching procedures given in the next three chapters and appended references:

The Reading Act Is a Complex Process. Scores of studies have been made of eye movements alone, and these involve only one part of reading behavior. One way of illustrating the complex of reading activities in simplified form is shown below.

		READING =		
CLEAR PERCEPTION OF SYMBOLS	+	UNDERSTANDING OF WORDS, SENTENCES, AND PASSAGES	+ INTERPRETATION OF MEANING +	USE OF PRINTED MATERIALS

This means that, when children read, they must (1) see words clearly, noting the difference between *b* and *d* or between *hand* and *hard*; (2) have experiences which enable them to understand the ideas expressed in a sentence or paragraph, as when they decide whether the word *band* refers to an elastic binder, a musical organization, or a group of outlaws; (3) go beyond the literal understanding of printed symbols and sense new relationships of ideas, such as making deductions about character or inferences about right and wrong; (4) be able not only to understand and judge, but also to put reading to use in some way, such as creating a new outcome in dramatization, preparing a report, or simply enjoying a good laugh.

These simultaneous processes in the reading act suggest that reading in basic books is something more than one silent reading of a selection and greater than "oral reading around the class."

A Basic Reading Program

"The band of outlaws..."

Pete's red hot band !

rubber band

Choosing the correct meaning for a word to fit the idea expressed in the sentence or paragraph is only one part of reading behavior.

Learning to Read Is Learning to Communicate. Reading is one of the language arts, that important group of human activities concerned with the communication of ideas. Communication involves giving ideas to others as in speaking, oral reading, and writing. It also involves receiving ideas from others, as in listening, observing, and reading silently. Reading, then, involves both the giving and the receiving of ideas. The effectiveness of oral reading may be measured by how well the audience understands the oral reading of a story, poem, or passage; the adequacy of silent reading may be measured by the speed and exactness with which one gets the facts, the main ideas, or the implied outcomes from the printed page. As one of the language arts, the child's reading is closely connected to his oral language, his writing, and his other work with words.

Learning to Read Takes Place in Several Different Ways. Educational psychologists of yesterday and today have attempted to explain the process of learning by a number of different theories including the association theories of connectionism and behaviorism, stimulus-response mechanisms, insight solution, and Gestalt psychology. It seems probable that no one psychological theory is adequate to explain all the learning that takes place in the acquisition of skills and habits involved in the complex process of learning to read. Accordingly, successful teachers no longer rely on one specific method of teaching such as the look-say, the phonetic, or the experience method. Rather, the skilled teacher combines aspects from a number of systems for learning to read, varying the method in relation to the specific purpose back of the learning.

True Learning in Reading Must Be Meaningful to the Child. The various parts of the modern school curriculum emphasize the role of meaning in learning. Arithmetic is taught not as meaningless drill but as understanding of quantity and system; social studies and science emphasize the growth in children's concepts or understanding of such social and scientific terms as *conservation* or *energy.* So too with reading. The content of a child's book must be connected to or grow out of his interests and his concerns in and out of school. The ideas met in reading must be supported by related activities and by kindred thoughts met in other reading. Accordingly, the books of the GINN BASIC SERIES contain stories and other materials organized into units around central themes which are closely related to the interests and experiences of children. As the child reacts to a planned pattern of related skills and concepts, learning is swifter and faster because the reading materials have meaning for him.

Different Kinds of Learning in Reading Proceed Together. The principle of what psychologists call simultaneous learnings may be applied to reading at all stages of the child's development. The teacher may be concentrating on word study but the child may at the same time be learning to like or dislike dog stories or to find the main idea of a paragraph. While no teacher can control all the learning that goes on, a good reading program is so planned that different reading abilities are used to strengthen one another. Phonetic and structural analysis of words augment one another, and both in turn can be combined with the use of context clues to strengthen the child's word-identification and recognition abilities.

The skillful teacher capitalizes on the principle of simultaneous learnings by the use of several different approaches to reading problems. A combined auditory, visual, and kinesthetic approach to new words in the beginning stage of learning to read may assure, for most children, success in the important task of recognizing words. A group of fourth-graders may express their reactions to an exciting story through a spirited discussion, individual paintings, a group diorama, or plans for a dramatic production in several scenes. Better still, the group may react in several of such ways, each way contributing to the others.

9

Motivational Factors Affect the Efficiency of All Learning in Reading.
Learning to read is not purely an intellectual process. When a child comes to school, he brings his hopes and fears, his satisfactions and his frustrations. All of these he brings to the reading group. If the introduction to a new story captures his interest, he is likely to read more efficiently than if he is bored or tired. If he has deep-seated personality difficulties, the teacher's best efforts may come to naught. In general, learning to read proceeds more satisfactorily in a pleasant environment without undue pressure on the child. Because it is important for the teacher to stimulate interest and to encourage learning, this manual contains many and varied suggestions for setting the stage for the reading of a selection. The teacher is successful in motivating a lesson to the degree that he knows each child in the group—his interests, his wishes, and his special needs. No teacher can control all the varied emotional and personal factors in a group of children, but he can utilize knowledge of these forces to some extent in stimulating individual and group learning.

The Rates and Methods of Learning to Read Vary Widely with Different Children. The principle of "individual differences" applies as strongly to reading as to all school learnings. Not only do children vary greatly in their motivational needs, but they are different in every attitude and ability relating to reading. When they first come to school, children differ in such areas as language backgrounds, familiarity with stories, and powers of visual perception; the effect of school experiences is, on the whole, to increase these differences. The thousands of researches that have been done in child development all suggest that a class of six-year-olds or a group of fifth-graders are much more different than alike in reading as in other abilities. All of the fifth-graders, for example, may be going through the same pattern in the development of reading abilities, but all children will not be at the same stage in the development of any one of the specific phases of the reading program at the same time.

There is no prospect of teaching any class of children as if they were all alike. The further the children go through school, including the high school, the wider will be the range of differences in reading abilities. Teachers must plan for many ways of providing for these differences. This manual offers such suggestions not only in the succeeding chapter but also in the specific lesson plans designed to accompany the reading of the text.

Readiness Is a Factor in Learning to Read at All Levels. The factor of readiness is closely related to the principles of motivation and of individual differences. Giving an important place to readiness is an outgrowth of the child

**Most children go through the same developmental
reading patterns, but they progress at different rates.**

study movement, one of the most important influences on educational planning since 1915. The study of the "whole child" suggests that there is a time in the child's life at which he is able to acquire a particular skill or a certain proficiency with reasonable ease and assurance. Before that time, his efforts to learn the particular competence will often meet with frustration and defeat. Before a child is ready for the initial stage of translating symbols into words and meanings, he must possess a certain combination of physical, social, and psychological characteristics which make him capable of achieving success in beginning reading. At later stages he must be "ready" for understanding the concepts in the fourth reader or for acquiring the ability to outline a passage.

Whether at first-grade level or at later grade levels, readiness for particular reading tasks must be regarded as a complex combination of natural growth and learned factors. There is probably no one single test or index of readiness. Most teachers can do little about inherited factors, but they can stimulate the development of acquired abilities which often constitute a large part of readiness. In succeeding chapters, this manual gives specific help to the teacher about items which can be learned. Chapter II gives detailed information about readiness and the lessons in Chapter IV give scores of suggestions for developing readiness for the acquisition of reading skills and for the understanding of ideas met on the printed page. These suggestions are nicely graded to the maturity level of the children for whom they were planned, whether at a second-grade level or a seventh-grade level.

11

Continuous Evaluation of Progress Is an Important Part of Learning to Read. Self-evaluation by the child is more important than most forms of extrinsic evaluation imposed by such an outside agency as an adult or a question in

As the child grows in ability to assess his own reading abilities and tastes, he achieves readiness for further progress in reading.

a test. What may be a reading challenge to a teacher or adult may be a matter of complete indifference to an older child. As the child gains interest in reading materials and understands the uses of reading, he can begin to appraise some of the reading skills and abilities which he already has and those which he needs to acquire. Primary children are often willing to take the teacher's judgment of what should be tested, but even young children with the teacher's help can develop standards of their own about materials and methods of reading. As children grow in ability to assess their own achievements and tastes, they will achieve readiness for further progress in reading.

Evaluation should encompass the content as well as the method used by a child or a group. It is not enough to be a skillful reader if one never reads or reads only trash. One of the best tests of a reading program is whether the children, in their spare time, go to the library table or bookshelf and settle down with a good book. If so, they are building reading habits and an interest in books which may last a lifetime.

Evaluation should also determine whether the children are acquiring the skills necessary for competent reading. Can they work out a new word for themselves, skim to find a specific fact, and grasp the meanings of a longer paragraph or passage? These abilities are tested more frequently than reading tastes are evaluated in the usual standardized reading tests. The testing program that accompanies the GINN BASIC READERS includes both readiness and achievement tests at all levels in the first six grades. These tests have much more value for diagnostic purposes than the usual standardized tests. In addition, there are many detailed suggestions throughout this manual for appraising a child's grasp of a particular selection, his interpretation of materials read, and his attitudes toward reading.

Learning to Read Is a Continuous Process Spreading over Many Years in a Child's Life. The modern school curriculum typically provides a certain learning experience, not at one specific month in a child's school life, but stretching the period of learning over several years. Learning such skills as the use of capitalization in writing or the use of context clues while reading does not occur all at once. Good curriculum planning reflects this fact. A well-planned program includes readiness activities leading to certain skills or abilities, motivated practice on the ability over a period of time, and spaced reviewing of the skill to encourage permanent learnings. As a child grows older, he becomes capable of broader and deeper vocabulary knowledge; he has more experience with which to judge and interpret his reading materials; he finds new uses for the material read. Thus a basal reading program does not introduce a skill and drop it. Rather, the program provides over the years for gradual and continuous development of important reading achievements. Because children grow at different rates and are ready for particular learnings at different times, the well-planned program offers opportunities for such learning on different occasions and in different settings.

The GINN BASIC READING PROGRAM offers many opportunities for such gradual and continuous growth of reading abilities. For example, word-attack techniques introduced in one grade may be maintained and strengthened throughout several grade levels. Practice in reading for sequence of ideas may extend, in various forms, throughout all the elementary grades. In other words, the program is constructed not only in terms of *horizontal* levels, such as a pre-primer plan or a fifth-reader program, but also in terms of *vertical* development, stretching through all the first eight years of school. It is based, not on a particularly good set of activities and materials in the first year or the sixth reader, but on careful provisions for all phases of reading ability developing gradually over the years. Chapter II enlarges upon the various parts of such a vertical program of gradual growth in reading abilities.

Reading is essential to a child's wholesome development. Children and books are close together and, like the *New England Primer*, the child may say:

My Book and Heart
Must never part.

To accomplish this aim, the basic reading program has four interrelated phases—the developmental, recreational, functional, and enrichment programs. These are based on sound principles, ten of which have been listed in this chapter. Research and good practice have also been summarized into ten canons which are guides to reading instruction in modern schools.

II

Continuous Growth in Reading

A school year in a child's life is a product of all that has gone before and a portent of years stretching ahead. The activities of two months in the second grade, or the work of six months or a year in the eighth grade, are small parts of the child's total life as he grows from infancy, through childhood and adolescence, into adulthood. One reading lesson, or even the reading activities of one month or of one year, are links in a long chain.

The reading a child does in the first or in the fifth grade is closely connected with past experiences and with future activities; it cannot stand alone. His reading activities must be projected in a continuous sequential way, and a basic reading program must have a developmental plan, an on-going or vertical structure. A reading lesson must be of value not only in its own right but in terms of total and gradual development of reading skills and habits over a period of time. Reading abilities are long a-growing. Accordingly, the GINN BASIC SERIES is planned as a continuous program stretching over successive years in the child's life. Each teacher contributes something to the sequential vertical aspects of the child's reading development.

The horizontal structure of the GINN BASIC PROGRAM may be described in terms of grade levels, such as the fifth-grade program, or of book levels, such as a second-reader level. At any one level, the program has both breadth and depth. It contains a wide variety of reading and language activities and it provides for permanent learnings and thorough understanding of the ideas presented. The keynotes of the program are *abundant variety* and *meaningful repetition*. These are obtained at any one level through provision for (1) systematic introduction and repetition of vocabulary and concepts, with enrichment of ideas at each succeeding stage, (2) unit arrangements of material with stories, selections, and poems centering around an important theme, and (3) workbooks and manuals, which clarify and reinforce the ideas of the

Each teacher and each reading lesson contributes to the total and gradual development of reading skills and habits over a period of time.

basic books. Thus children achieve breadth and depth in reading activities at any one *horizontal* level.

But in addition to breadth and depth a basic reading program must be concerned with height. It must be planned to cut across grade lines and to emphasize the continuity of growth in reading abilities from year to year. It is not enough for a school to have a well-developed reading design at the third-grade level. In addition it must have a continuous program stretching through all elementary grades. The third-grade program can be planned only in terms of what has gone before and what will probably come after; the same is true of the other grade levels. The well-planned reading program has a *vertical* as well as a horizontal structure for its hundreds of activities.

Research and successful school practice indicate that there is no such thing as a single reading ability that covers all reading situations. Instead, there are many different reading abilities which children learn to use and which they can apply as needed in a variety of specific situations. Children in the primary grades learn several methods of word attack, such as phonetic analysis, structural analysis, or the use of context clues, and they apply the method or methods that seem most useful in unlocking a particular word. Similarly, children in the intermediate grades acquire new reading interests and study skills. They learn to use different types of comprehension skills, such as getting a general impression, noting the details, or determining the relationships of main and subordinate ideas. The successful reader possesses not one reading skill but a composite of abilities and habits which contribute to reading success. The GINN BASIC PROGRAM provides for the development of these many abilities in a continuous and interrelated way.

Though basic readers with accompanying materials have an important place in the reading program of a modern school, they do not constitute all of the materials used in a full-scale plan for reading activities, but are ordinarily supplemented by the materials presented below.

Supplementary readers
Library books of fiction and nonfiction
The children's own writings or dictated stories
Charts of various types
Newspapers and magazines
Picture dictionaries, dictionaries, and encyclopedias
Captions on filmstrips

These and other materials contribute to one or more of the developmental, recreational, functional, and enrichment facets of the reading program and to many of the phases of vertical planning emphasized in the GINN BASIC PROGRAM.

The Vertical Organization

The GINN BASIC PROGRAM for continuous growth in reading is organized around ten major strands running through the first eight grades. These ten vertical strands, which are described in this chapter, are interrelated and contribute to one another. These phases of reading are divided into the two categories of children's competences and instructional problems. Although the subdivisions in both categories overlap, they are stated in this manner because of the emphasis given to them in the manuals which accompany the readers. Chapter IV in this manual and suggestions to teachers in all other manuals of the series make some reference to these strands, not occasionally in one or two units, but for nearly every selection in the basic books. Teachers may use these suggestions for specific guidance in developing the ten strands within the larger program in terms of the needs of children.

17

The psychology of reading outlined in Chapter I indicates the need for vertical planning. There are at least five reasons for the emphasis given such developmental programs throughout the GINN BASIC SERIES:

1. Most reading abilities grow, not all at one time, but in continuous fashion year after year.

2. Most children acquire reading abilities more efficiently if they have a chance to practice them in new settings at planned intervals.

3. Many courses of study, not only in language arts, but in other curricular areas, reintroduce specific learning experiences in several successive grades rather than listing them for one grade level only.

4. The different abilities that make up reading competence may develop unevenly for any one child. Vertical planning enables the teacher to provide readiness for the competence at a particular level, to guide actual learnings of it at a later level, and to give such practice as is necessary for mastery at a higher level.

5. Children differ widely in their ability to profit from instruction at any one age or grade level. Suggestions for readiness, learning, and practice not only apply to an individual child but also allow for adaptation to the needs of different children within a group.

This need for continuous development is met in the GINN BASIC PROGRAM in a variety of ways, some of which are listed here.

Through ease of approach and gradual transition to more mature materials in each of the successive books. Such factors as vocabulary control, gradual introduction of new concepts, and changes in format all contribute to gradual growth in reading ability without presenting severe obstacles to be hurdled.

Through methods and materials suggested in the manuals and workbooks of the series. Suggestions for individual lessons differ with the content of the lesson, but there is a uniformity of approach to lessons which will help both teacher and children become accustomed to certain procedures and feel secure in what they are doing.

Through the content of important ideas in the books. Although meanings may be forgotten, the specific way one arrived at them will not necessarily be forgotten. Successive books and manuals help deepen the children's understandings of some of the fundamental factors in their lives and in modern society. Such ideas as co-operative family living, community organization, conservation, courage in the face of danger, and life in regional America are repeated at different levels in the units and stories of the books.

Through the ten major vertical strands of the program. These strands may be conceived as developmental aspects of an all-round reading ability or as planned attacks on instructional problems which teachers and children meet at all grade levels. (See figure below.) Suggestions which involve the development of these strands are given in detail in Chapter IV. The following material outlines a vertical program with which a curriculum committee, a principal or a supervisor, and each teacher must be familiar if a school is to have a well-planned reading program.

Grades	Readiness—	Word-Study Skills—	Comprehension and Study Skills—	Creative Reading Abilities—	Reading Interests—	Related Language Abilities—	Providing for Enrichment Activities—	Relating Reading Activities to Other Areas of the Curriculum—	Evaluating Growth—	Providing for Individual Differences—
8										
7										
6										
5										
4										
3										
2										
1										
Grades	Reading Abilities Needed at All Developmental Levels						Instructional Problems at All Grade Levels			

The Vertical Programs of the Ginn Basic Series

Specific Vertical Programs

Readiness for Reading

Readiness for reading is an important factor not only at the first-grade level but throughout all the grades. Just as children may or may not be ready for reading a pre-primer or primer, so they may or may not be ready for a fourth reader or seventh reader. Readiness may refer to general maturity or to specific preparation for reading a certain selection in one of the readers.

19

Suggestions for studying general readiness for reading are given in this manual and in the manuals and answer keys for the readiness tests which are part of the testing program for each grade through the sixth. Suggestions for developing specific readiness for a particular story or article are given in the lesson plans to accompany each selection in the basic books. From the first lesson plan for the first pre-primer to suggestions for the last lesson in the eighth reader these two main factors in readiness have been considered in the GINN BASIC PROGRAM.

The readiness of every pupil at each successive stage must be diagnosed and, if found wanting, must be carefully developed. As they advance through the school program, children meet new words, encounter widened concepts of old words, cope with more complex organization of materials, and develop new needs or purposes in reading. Thus, in a very real sense, the child is always beginning and, therefore, always in need of readiness.

Accordingly, at every grade level, the teacher using the GINN BASIC SERIES is given help in planning the readiness procedures listed here.

1. Making sure that the children have a basis of reading habits and skills as a foundation for the activities required in the reading task

2. Stimulating interest in what is to follow by relating it to the experiences of children in the group or by appealing to the children's interests

3. Building a background of concepts or key ideas that are related to or occur in the reading materials

4. Providing a mental set for the material to be used, particularly in terms of the author's mood or purpose

5. Helping to develop a systematic attack by making sure the children understand the purpose for which they are to read

Word-Study Skills

Children have four distinct but overlapping vocabularies: (1) a listening or meaning vocabulary, (2) a speaking vocabulary, (3) a word-recognition or reading vocabulary, and (4) a writing vocabulary. When they enter school, the above order indicates the size of their vocabularies from large to small. At six years the child usually understands thousands of different words, but he reads or writes few words or none at all. During the primary grades, the child's recognition vocabulary and even his writing vocabulary grow very rapidly. The writing vocabulary almost always remains the smallest. Somewhere around the fourth- or fifth-grade level, the child's reading vocabulary ordinarily overtakes and passes his speaking vocabulary. At all grade levels, the teacher of reading is especially concerned with word-recognition skills but is aware that the various vocabularies are involved in all reading activities. The teacher at the intermediate-grade level has a responsibility to bring the child's reading or recognition vocabulary up to the level of his listening vocabulary. At times the reading vocabulary may contribute to an increase in the listening vocabulary as the child meets new words in a meaningful reading situation and incorporates them into his total understanding vocabulary. Similarly, words heard during planned listening experiences are more easily recognized when the child meets them in print.

In the wider sense, the study of words means the development of understanding, reading, speaking, and writing vocabularies. Since these are all interrelated and contribute to one another, a basic reading program must provide opportunities for many experiences in the various language arts which are designed to develop the four vocabularies. Suggestions for such experiences will be found in all lesson plans in the manuals for the GINN BASIC READERS.

In each of the primary, intermediate, and upper grades the teacher and the pupils are concerned with the development of the interdependent abilities of word understanding and word recognition. In each lesson plan a section on

Children learn to use many methods to attack unfamiliar words.

Continuous Growth in Reading

"Word-Study Skills," included in the area for "Building Essential Habits and Skills," gives specific suggestions for developing word-attack skills.

The program of the GINN BASIC READERS, as outlined in the primary manuals of this series, does not depend upon any one method of attack on words. The identification and recognition of words are thoroughly developed in the primary grades through a variety of methods.

1. Recognition through general configuration or unusual characteristics of the word
2. Recognition through similarities to known words—common elements
3. Use of picture clues
4. Use of phonetic analysis
5. Use of context clues
6. Use of structural analysis

In the intermediate and upper grades the last three of the above-mentioned methods are used most often and are further developed in precision and scope. In addition, the following methods of developing word-study skills become useful:

7. Use of the glossary and dictionary
8. Wide reading

Because the five methods of word attack mentioned last are more complex and become increasingly useful as the child advances through school, they are described briefly below.

Phonetic Analysis. One of the outstanding features of the GINN BASIC PROGRAM is the systematic plan for the use of phonics throughout the manuals and workbooks to aid the child in the recognition and identification of words. This plan makes activities designed for the phonetic analysis of words an intrinsic part of the entire word-study program. The system introduces important phonetic elements and teaches certain phonetic principles and their application in unlocking unknown words. The program is carefully graded from phonetic-readiness work, such as listening for initial consonant sounds and rhyming elements; through using initial and final consonants, consonant blends, and digraphs in the first grade; noticing vowel differences in the second grade; syllabication in the third grade; to diacritical marks and the use of a dictionary in the middle and upper grades.

All phonetic elements are introduced through the use of known words, and most lessons are concluded with an activity in which the child is asked to use the new phonetic element to identify an unknown word in a familiar context.

Unfamiliar words identified in the final step of the lesson are usually words which will occur later in the text of the readers.

Frequent consideration is given to spelling, not only for its use in written composition but also for its help in the identification of words.

Syllabication involves a knowledge of phonics and the application of principles of phonetic analysis. Phonetic readiness for syllabication is developed in the lesson plans and workbooks of the third-grade program of the GINN BASIC READERS. Attention is given at that level to the number of vowel sounds in words, to the long and short vowel differences, and to accent. In the intermediate and upper grades there is a graded vertical program for increasing and refining these abilities and for practice in applying them in conjunction with other word-attack skills. Children are helped to understand that a syllable contains one speech sound and that a syllabic unit is a pronunciation unit. Practice in dividing words into syllables is provided at increasing levels of difficulty both as an aid to the pronunciation of words and in the division of words at the end of a line. The respelling of words in the glossary and in the dictionary further acquaints children with the syllabic characteristics of words and provides motivation for understanding these characteristics.

Structural Analysis. This method of attack refers to practice in the careful scrutiny of words to note elements related to their structure. It involves identifying basic words in such compound words as *snowman*; recognizing the parts of such a hyphenated word as *cement-mixer*; noting root words and their common variants, as in *rushed*; and understanding such contractions as *didn't*. In the intermediate grades, increased skill in noting the structural parts of words is developed. Contractions which omit two or more letters and variant forms of root words with both prefix and suffix are developed. Syllabication, one type of structural analysis, is important at the intermediate-grade level and deserves special mention because it often becomes one of the most valuable clues to word recognition used by mature readers in the elementary school and by adults. If a sixth-grade pupil or an adolescent meets a word like *anticipation* or *eligible* for the first time in his reading, skill in dividing the word into syllabic units, which he can easily attack phonetically, will ordinarily enable him to recognize it.

The Use of Context Clues. The use of context clues may be enlarged to include picture clues and any reading activity which involves an active attack on words with emphasis upon meaning of the whole sentence or paragraph in which the words are imbedded. The use of context clues should be combined with phonetic and structural analysis, for each acts as a check on the accuracy of the other. The manuals to accompany the GINN BASIC READERS provide practice in the use of seven types of context clues which are illustrated below.

1. DEFINITION. The unknown word is defined. "The long climb had made Jack *hungry*. So he went to the castle to ask for food."

2. EXPERIENCE. The unknown word is predictable from the child's life experience. "Soon Abel had planted the last *seed* in the very last hill."

3. COMPARISON. Contrast in meaning gives a clue to the unknown word. "The little woman missed the noises of the big city. . . . It was very *quiet* on the farm."

4. SYNONYM. The clue is a known synonym for the unknown word. "Mary and Jerry liked to ride in the little *caboose*. The caboose was the last car on the train."

5. FAMILIAR EXPRESSION OR LANGUAGE EXPERIENCE. This clue requires an acquaintance with everyday expressions. "The big horse was as *gentle* as a lamb."

6. SUMMARY. The unknown word sums up the ideas that precede it. "From the grandstand, Bob saw the riders line up. He watched cowboys rope and ride wild horses. He laughed at the cowboy clown. Bob thought the *rodeo* was great fun."

7. REFLECTION OF A MOOD OR SITUATION. The unknown word fits a situation or mood already established. "There were no sheepskins on which to sit. There was a furnace, but no fireplace. There were chairs and tables. The place was not like home. Everyone was very kind, but Blue Cornflower was *homesick*."

The Use of the Glossary and Dictionary. Each of the fourth, fifth, and sixth readers of the series contains a glossary, which is useful in its own right for developing word recognition and meaning, and which also serves as an introduction to the use of a larger dictionary. In the third-grade program, the child has had an opportunity to develop specific skills related to readiness for use of the glossary—for example, alphabetizing and recognizing certain common syllabic units, such as *ed* and *ing*. In the intermediate grades he develops other skills needed for the use of a dictionary, such as alphabetizing to the third or fourth letter, using guide words, using the pronunciation key, interpreting pronunciation symbols, and selecting meanings appropriate to context.

Wide Reading. Research studies show that opportunities to read widely in varied types of materials strengthen and enlarge the child's recognition and meaning vocabularies. Accordingly, this manual contains literally hundreds of suggestions for extending the reading activities of the children

using the GINN BASIC READERS. Specific references are given to such basic materials as the ENRICHMENT READERS and to that body of children's literature which deals with related topics. The lesson plans are designed as contributions, not only to the developmental and functional aspects of reading, but also to the recreational and enrichment aspects which are essential to a balanced program.

The preceding paragraphs have emphasized methods for developing a recognition vocabulary, but at all stages the child develops and practices word recognition and word meaning at the same time. It will not help him to work out laboriously the pronunciation of a word such as *muskrat* if he has no concept of what the word means. Unless a word has meaning for the child, it will soon be forgotten. Moreover, as the child learns to identify the word and then to recognize it again in a number of different contexts, its meaning becomes clearer to him.

Comprehension and Study Skills

Reading is for something. It is a key that unlocks doors. It is "Windows on the World" of people and things as well as the world of books and magazines. One of the main phases of the basic reading program is that of functional reading in which all children learn how to put reading to work.

The GINN BASIC READERS and accompanying materials provide a careful gradation of comprehension and study skills with many opportunities for reteaching and maintenance. In the first grade the teacher may ask such simple work-type questions as "On what page does our story begin?" The third-grade teacher asks a group to check the table of contents to find a story about Indian children. A sixth-grade pupil uses several reference sources in compiling a report or in finding facts for arguments on both sides of a controversial issue. In all grades, children may learn to *use* reading as a tool more efficiently. No one set of basic books can give the child the functional reading practice he needs to get from signs, newspapers, how-to-do-it books, and other reference materials. However, a basic reading program can lay the foundation for useful reading skills. This foundation is laid in the GINN BASIC SERIES by putting reading to work in many ways. In the sections "Building Essential Habits and Skills" and "Rereading for Specific Purposes" of each lesson plan the child is asked to do something about what he reads. The language arts and enrichment strands described in this chapter contain many suggestions for using reading in creative ways.

In the development of study skills the purpose of the pupil, rather than the nature of the material, should have first emphasis. A story about buried gold may be read for the sequence of the story or geographical facts about tropical islands. Not until his purpose is clear is the child able to turn to suitable materials or apply proper reading techniques. The teacher has a twofold function of helping pupils understand the purposes for reading and at the same time making sure that specific study skills are developed to make it possible for him to fulfill the purpose.

The following analysis of comprehension and study skills lists the various skills and abilities needed in work-type reading. The main headings show in sequence the abilities required in any situation where reading is being used. The subheadings are not in sequence, nor are all those listed under any one main heading likely to be used in a single reading situation.

Study Skills Needed for Work-Type Reading

    I. Ability to define a specific purpose for reading

   II. Skill in locating information
       A. Skill in using the table of contents
       B. Skill in using the index
       C. Skill in using the dictionary or glossary

D. Skill in using an encyclopedia
E. Skill in using a card file and other library tools
F. Skill in using pictures, maps, graphs, charts, and tables
G. Skill in skimming
H. Skill in using headings and other typographical aids

III. Ability to comprehend and organize what is read

A. Ability to find the main idea
B. Ability to see the sequence of ideas
C. Ability to find details
D. Ability to draw conclusions, see relationships, and make inferences

IV. Ability to select and evaluate information

A. Ability to select suitable sources of information
B. Ability to distinguish between relevant and irrelevant
C. Ability to recognize the difference between fact and opinion
D. Ability to judge the validity of one's information
E. Ability to use several sources to solve a problem
F. Ability to judge the adequacy of one's information

V. Ability to adjust the method of reading to one's purpose and to the nature of the material

VI. Skill in using information

A. Skill in following directions
B. Skill in taking notes
C. Skill in classification
D. Skill in outlining
E. Skill in summarizing

VII. Ability to remember what is read

A. Ability to use the aids to retention
B. Ability to select facts to be remembered

The GINN BASIC READERS furnish systematic practice for developing the study skills listed above. Each skill is introduced in relation to the total reading ability a child is likely to have at a particular level. For example, a first-grade child may learn to use a very simple table of contents, to find the main idea of a group of related sentences, or to recognize the difference between a realistic and a fanciful story. Later, he will learn to use a more complex table of contents, find the sequence of ideas in a longer paragraph, and make use of a number of different reference books. As in the case of other strands, mastery of work-type reading skills is not attained at any one stage, and, consequently, instruction continues through various levels.

Creative Reading

On many occasions, boys and girls and men and women have to "read between the lines." They have to decide whether a statement is true, partly true, or false; whether or not the author is writing from a particular slant or for a particular purpose. They have to predict what may happen next. They have to achieve new insights by thinking while they read. All these diverse activities mean that they are doing creative reading. They are going beyond the specific facts of the selection to accept or reject, to interpret, and to judge. The reading act is not really complete until such thinking and interpretation are a part of it. The reading act is most valuable when it includes reflective thinking, such as seeing the implications of the material for oneself or others, evaluating statements in the light of one's own experiences, or interpreting an author's aim or purpose.

The lesson plans of this and other manuals contain literally hundreds of suggestions for interpreting materials read and for creating new ideas through analysis, association, organization, and use of these materials. They ask *why* questions or suggest *because* statements for students to complete. They suggest that rereading activities can be carefully guided by the teacher to stimulate thinking. Occasionally they suggest possibilities for discussion, dramatization, writing, and other creative activities. A number of the exercises at the end of each book for the middle and upper grades, under the section "Some Things to Do," are definitely planned to encourage creative reading of materials in the text.

Creative reading is possible at all grade levels. Thinking about one's reading is not an ability which appears suddenly at age eleven or fifteen, but one which develops slowly over the years. First-graders may learn to be critical of what they read if they are asked to cross out such statements as "Flip can fly" or erase statements which are true but not related to the story. After reading a simple family story the children may be asked, "How do you think Mother felt?" Of an airport story, "Could this have happened in our town?" In a story about older children the group may ask, "Why was Bob able to overcome his fear?" or "If we were to turn this story into a play, what kind of character would the uncle be?"

Creative reading is not a simple process, and the suggestions to encourage it do not follow a simple, repetitive pattern. In the manuals for the primary grades there are suggestions for such activities as discriminating between realistic and make-believe statements, making comparisons, drawing conclusions, and predicting outcomes. In the post-primary grades there are suggestions for seeing cause and effect, interpreting facts, making inferences, interpreting character, and pursuing other thought-provoking practices. Usually these suggestions are combined under the heading "Creative Reading" in the index of each manual. Tests of creative-reading abilities are included in many of the tests which accompany the GINN BASIC READERS for the first six grades, and these tests may be adapted for use in later grades. By consulting a number of such indexes and tests, the teacher or supervisor may see that a truly developmental program of creative reading is available for children as one of the vertically planned strands of the GINN BASIC READERS.

Reading Interests

Reading interests are among the permanent learnings resulting from the reading program. A love for reading, or for special types of books, developed in the early grades may last throughout a person's lifetime. Every teacher must know something of the preferences which a child brings to a reading group and accept some responsibility for the interests with which he ends a school year. The GINN BASIC PROGRAM is built on the assumption that there are few, if any, tasks more significant for a teacher to undertake than that of building permanent interests in the good things of literature.

Reading interests express themselves in children's habits and tastes. Even in the primary grades, children develop habits of turning to books in their spare time. A child's reading tastes refer to the levels of his likes and dislikes. In a world of comic books, movies, and television programs, the school can be one of the most important influences in raising standards of appreciation and promoting powers of discrimination. The school, and especially its reading program, can help children to choose reading materials that not only have beauty and charm but also possess permanent worth in the ideas and values expressed.

Story Material. The stories cover a wide range of interests. They include fairy stories, tall tales, and talking-beast stories, for these fanciful tales not only appeal to the child's interest but stimulate his imagination. Included are stories of rural and city life, of child life far away and long ago, of boys and girls and men and women at work and at play.

At all times effort has been made to show people living and working as they naturally do. The bizarre and the spectacular have been avoided. This does not mean loss of plot and suspense since the story characters are shown as they meet conflict, discouragement, and triumph in everyday life.

Humor, so characteristic of American life, has not been neglected. Stories are included throughout the series to invoke the chuckle as well as the

29

Interests developed during the school years are among the permanent learnings resulting from the reading program.

rollicking laugh and to make children sensitive to the many kinds of humorous situations which lie beyond the scope of the comic strip. Included are modern masterpieces of ridiculous nonsense; droll stories of the amusingly possible; feats of the Super-Duper glorified by the technological age; more subtle types of humor ranging from stories of personified machinery to the obscurity of the obvious.

Factual Material. Because the authors believe that factual material can have suspense, humor, movement, and other qualities which children are known to enjoy, the articles in the GINN BASIC SERIES are written from a child's point of view and in the style of the informal narrative. This material is designed to stimulate the child's interest beyond the limitations of his reader, leading him on to the great "republic of books" as well as to newspapers and magazines. When that happens, the best that any basic reader can achieve has been accomplished.

Character Training. The GINN BASIC READERS are not formally didactic. Yet, as is true of great literature, the stories are moral in their effects. Running through them is an emphasis upon those character values which, when present in an individual or a community, make for greater happiness and richer living. Without stressing morals as such, the stories demonstrate that such virtues as honesty, loyalty, sincerity, courage, and faith are as important today as they ever were, and that the kind of world children inherit will depend largely upon the degree to which those qualities are present in the affairs of men.

Correlation with General Reading. In the manuals and at the conclusion of the units in the readers from the fourth grade on, lists of books and stories are given which will greatly extend the range and variety of reading materials. Considerable care has been exercised in the selection of these titles both as to content and difficulty of material.

The classroom library and reading table, the school and home libraries, and the public library all play an important part in determining the degree and the types of interest the child has in books.

The goal of literary appreciation will not be attained unless children, through experiences with literature of high quality, learn to choose freely the genuine and the permanent. The GINN BASIC READERS are designed to develop and encourage such a choice.

Related Language Arts

Reading is one of the language arts which are concerned with the communication of ideas among children and adults. The wide range of the processes of listening, speaking, reading, and writing is evident from the content of all professional books published today in the area of the language arts. The authors of the GINN BASIC READERS also see letter writing, composition, handwriting, speaking, spelling, and reading, and such activities as grammar study, dramatization, and word study as different phases of the same process—the communication of ideas. Reading is an important part, but only one part, of the constellation of abilities needed to communicate.

The communication of ideas is a two-way process. To receive ideas, a child must be able to observe, to listen, and to read. In modern living, movies, TV, and the radio are often sources for the intake of ideas. To express ideas, a child must be able to speak with reasonable clarity and correctness, to read orally, to write, and to organize materials into some recognized form of social usage. He may express his ideas through pantomime, music, and the manual arts, but any such expression must of necessity follow thinking processes which involve the use of words.

Reading, then, is intimately bound up with the reception and expression of ideas. It contributes to the other activities and may be enriched by them.

31

In fact, research shows that the various language arts tend to reinforce one another. The child who speaks well tends to become a good reader. The good reader usually acquires an extensive vocabulary which enables him to write well. All these language abilities have a positive correlation. Accordingly, in this reading series, individual lessons suggest not only various forms of reading but also other phases of the related communicative arts. In the lesson plans there are suggestions for speech work, oral expression in various forms, written composition, handwriting, spelling, study of grammar and usage, dramatization, and word study.

Early and continuous attention is given to oral expression. From the pre-reading stage, conversing, enjoying rhythmic verses together, telling about personal experiences, and discussing pictures add to a feeling of

Speech-Analysis Chart

	Positive		Negative	
GENERAL	Direct	☐	Indirect	☐
SPEECH	Relaxed	☐	Tense	☐
	Easily erect	☐	Poor posture	☐
ATTITUDES	Converses easily	☐	Talks too much	☐
			Timid	☐
	Positive		**Negative**	
	Volume appropriate	☐	Speaks too softly	☐
VOICE			Speaks too loudly	☐
	Pitch quality pleasant	☐	Pitch too high	☐
			Monotonous pitch	☐
			Nasal voice	☐
AND			Denasal voice	☐
			Husky or hoarse	☐
	Speech rate good	☐	Speaks too fast	☐
			Speaks too slowly	☐
SPEECH	Easily understood	☐	Speaks indistinctly	☐
			Has a foreign accent	☐
			Omits sounds	☐
			Substitutes sounds	☐
CHARACTERISTICS			Transposes sounds	☐
			Lisps	☐
	Speech rhythm appropriate	☐	Hesitates	☐
			Stutters	☐

security in speaking and contribute to success in reading. Throughout the primary grades the reading program continues to promote the use of language to help the child maintain his individuality through the expression of creative ideas.

In the intermediate and upper grades, many speech activities are suggested, including storytelling, giving reports, debating two sides of a question, choral reading, and role-playing. In such activities, emphasis is given to the social setting in which the speech activity occurs. The children's speech difficulties, such as faulty articulation and inability to enunciate certain sounds, are given special consideration in appropriate situations.

Since the physical and personality factors affecting speech are largely individual matters, the teacher must consider the speech problems of each child separately. The preceding chart, reproduced for each group member having speech difficulties, will give the teacher a basis for individual diagnosis and corrective work.

In addition to the six phases of developmental reading planned from the point of view of the child, there are several phases of a continuous program which are primarily instructional problems. These include providing enrichment through varied reading and creative activities, evaluating growth, providing for differences, and relating reading activities to other areas of the curriculum.

Enrichment Activities

A reading lesson is not over when the children have read the selection silently and orally; it has only begun when the children have mastered the essential words, facts, and structure of the story or article. From this start, the child and the group can build in many directions. They can explore similar stories, sing related songs, and enjoy recordings, films, and filmstrips that are related to the material read. They can add to their own store of ideas through discussion, dramatic play, and doing something about the materials.

Because they are concerned about the effects of reading on children, teachers through the Enrichment Program ask the questions: "What is reading doing to Bill?" "How are the child's actions, ideas, and values being influenced by what he reads?" These changes in behavior and attitudes may result from the first quick reaction to a story plot as the child identifies closely with someone in the story. More often behavior patterns develop through worth-while activities growing out of the reading.

In many units of the GINN BASIC PROGRAM, a co-ordinating activity serves to connect the stories with the unit theme and often provides a basis for the culminating activity which is found at the end of each unit. These major activities are developed through excursions, construction activities, drawing, dramatization, bulletin-board activities, book clubs, story hours, and rhythmic interpretation of music.

The lesson plans presented in Chapter IV offer the teacher many helpful procedures in developing democratic participation. The enrichment activities help, not only to vitalize reading experiences, but also to develop good group living as the children are guided in the selecting, planning, and executing of classroom activities. Habits such as self-control, working together harmoniously, self-reliance, and responsibility are concomitant outcomes of an interrelated reading program.

The books suggested for independent reading have been carefully selected to provide variety in content and range in level of difficulty. Suggestions are included in the lesson plans for making these books available to the children for use during free or independent reading periods. Many opportunities are provided for the interchange of ideas gleaned from independent reading through discussions, conversations, reports, and graphic interpretations.

Songs which relate to the experiences of the children and the themes of the stories are suggested. Many songs appearing in the manuals have been written expressly to fit the theme and vocabulary of the stories to which they are related and can be used for dramatic play, speech improvement, and rhythmic interpretation. Recordings of most of these songs are available in the series of albums, SONGS ABOUT STORIES IN THE GINN BASIC READERS.

The ENRICHMENT READERS for the primary grades, such as *Open the Gate* and *Fun and Fancy*, extend the story themes of the basic books. The accompanying manuals offer a wealth of suggestions for creative activities. For the intermediate grades, book-length stories on themes related to the basic readers are offered for enrichment. These books provide for enjoyment of easy reading and help to satisfy the interest awakened by the stories in the GINN BASIC READERS.

No teacher can be sure that the enrichment activities are being "internalized" by the child, that they are becoming a part of his ideas and his personality. However, the titles of books, units, and stories in the GINN BASIC READERS suggest that the authors have consciously tried to influence the child's innermost thoughts and ideals. In the primary grades, his expanding world is reflected in such book titles as *Around the Corner* and *Friends Far and Near* and such unit titles as "People Who Work for Us," and "Children Everywhere." At all levels, the authors seek to introduce children to the broader aspects of the culture and to the world in which they live.

At the same time, the stories and selections in the readers often shed light on problems which normal boys and girls usually face. In one story, a child learns to share with others. In another, a boy overcomes his feelings of fear. In still others, the child is given insight into some of the peculiarities of adults which are to be enjoyed rather than scorned, and into the likenesses and differences of people scattered in time or place. Through such insights, it is possible for some children to understand themselves better, to discover "the self" as each mature person must do. The selections of the GINN BASIC READERS accordingly lead into varied activities through which the child adds to his store of ideas, broadens his horizons, understands himself and others better, and thus enriches his own life.

Relation of Reading Program to Other Areas of the Curriculum

Skills, habits, and attitudes developed as part of a basic reading program serve as important tools for the reading of materials in the various content areas. Word-study skills acquired through developmental reading lessons help the child cope with the meaning as well as the identification of words which he meets in a textbook. Techniques similar to those used in the readiness sections of lesson plans may be used to build meaning for the specialized words used in the various textbooks.

Because the basic reading program emphasizes the need for adjusting speed and method of reading to the material and to the specific purpose for which it is read, opportunities are provided for the practice of a variety of comprehension and study skills. Such abilities as noting specific details and checking the reasonableness of a statement or answer, developed in basic

The reading of readers prepares for reading in many subject-matter areas.

FOODS FOR ENERGY

MILK

BASIC READING PROGRAM

reading lessons, assume added significance in the reading of arithmetic problems.

Study sheets and workbook pages which call for different patterns of thinking on the part of the child contribute to an understanding of some of the types of organization used in various textbooks in the content areas.

The content of the readers, both fiction and factual material, serves as motivation to wide reading in such curricular areas as science, health, geography, and history. The reading of pictures, maps, diagrams, and graphs found in readers and workbooks provides learning experiences which contribute to ease in interpreting many of the specialized reading devices used in textbooks in the content areas.

Evaluation

The modern concept of evaluation places more emphasis on continuous appraisal of a student's development from day to day than on periodic testing. Not only his answers to factual questions but also his contributions to discussions, his written reactions, and the zest with which he approaches the reading period are indications of the degree of progress the child is making in reading. Appraisal will be made easier by the keeping of records of the child's behavior in such activities as well as responses on informal test items suggested in the manual under "All-Unit Activities" and under "Some Things to Do" at the back of the books for the middle and upper grades. Suggestions are included in various sections of the manuals for inventory charts which may be used to plot the strengths and weaknesses of individuals and small groups.

At all grade levels the children are constantly encouraged to evaluate their own reading performance. The questions, carefully devised for each lesson, help both child and teacher to determine whether full value is derived from the reading in terms of the degree of comprehension, interpretation, and application of the ideas which the child has met in his reading. Some evaluation of pupil progress in word meaning, comprehension, and use of word-study skills results from each related activity in the manual. These activities are followed by suggestions for additional practice at the end of each unit for the student who needs it.

For somewhat more formal evaluation of pupil progress the teacher may use the tests which accompany the GINN BASIC SERIES at all levels from the pre-primer through the sixth grade. Since these tests are designed to measure specific skills taught in the developmental reading lessons, they should be used as suggested in the accompanying manual of instructions.

Continuous Growth in Reading

Provisions for Individual Differences

Children differ widely in capacity, achievement, needs, and rate of development. Any group of six-year-olds or ten-year-olds differ in every way they can be measured, and a group of fourteen-year-olds differ even more widely. Because bright children learn faster than slow children, the variations within a group increase as the children advance through school. These conditions are normal. It is not the job of the teacher to reduce differences, to make all the children alike, or to bring them all up to a single standard. Some differences, such as differences in reading interests and in the specific skills involved in using a science text, give variety and strength to a group and should be cherished and encouraged by a school staff.

Teachers discover differences within a group by checking school records for comments by previous teachers, by keeping a behavior check list for individual children, and by using informal as well as composite reading tests. The readiness tests accompanying the Ginn Basic Readers at all levels

Good instructional planning cares for the needs of the least proficient, the average, and the superior reader.

from pre-reading level through the sixth grade help the teacher to discover differences and to identify specific needs of certain boys and girls.

At the *pre-reading level*, teachers invariably find that children differ in (1) ability to make a contribution to the discussion of a story; (2) background for the understanding of pictures or other printed materials; (3) speaking and listening vocabularies; (4) facility in the use of oral language; (5) auditory perception and visual discrimination; (6) interest in learning to read.

Careful observation, anecdotal records, or behavior check lists reveal differences. Considerable insight into children's abilities may be obtained by studying their reactions to reading-readiness tests such as those designed to accompany the GINN BASIC READERS.

At the *primary level*, teachers discover that children differ in (1) ability to move their eyes from left to right along a line and to make a correct return sweep to the following line; (2) ability to associate ideas with printed material; (3) ability to read for several purposes, such as getting the general idea, discovering details, and interpreting what is read; (4) ability to work independently in workbooks, language games, and worksheets; (5) ability to read whole stories independently.

The teacher may use various techniques to discover such differences, many of which are suggested in the teachers' manuals. Important instruments for this purpose are the batteries of tests which accompany the primary books of the series. The teacher may also check the children's responses as recorded in workbooks and on worksheets.

In the *intermediate* and *upper grades* children differ widely in (1) basic habits and skills contributing to ease and efficiency in reading; (2) knowledge of children's stories and their authors; (3) knowledge of sources of material valuable for different curricular activities; (4) ability to use a varied approach to reading material, depending upon the purpose for which the material is being read; (5) ability to interpret orally the mood and conversational text of the story; (6) ability to attack new words through phonetic and structural analysis and the use of the dictionary; (7) study and work-type skills associated with the use of books and libraries; (8) resources in the communicative arts which enrich reading experiences and are, in turn, enriched by them.

The readers, workbooks, and accompanying manuals suggest such ways of discovering differences among children in the intermediate and upper grades as observing pupils' reactions while reading; collecting evidence of existing competences through children's contributions to discussions, conversations, reports and dramatizations; using teacher-made tests of vocabulary,

39

speed, and various types of comprehension, and using the tests designed to accompany the GINN BASIC READERS.

Among the common provisions for individual differences are the grouping of pupils and the use of materials of different levels of difficulty. In the readers and workbooks, as well as in the lesson plans in this manual, suggestions are offered for making these two fundamental provisions. Grouping by grades and subgrouping within grades constitute an administrative arrangement whereby teaching procedures and activities approach more nearly to the needs of individuals. Materials of different degrees of difficulty provided in all grades through the diversified nature of readers, workbooks, and supplementary materials can be fitted to the needs of almost any child.

The authors of the GINN BASIC READERS offer a wealth of suggestions in the lesson plans of the manuals for meeting the needs of the least proficient reader, providing practice for the average reader, and giving additional reading experiences which are consistent with the needs and abilities of the gifted child or superior reader. Lesson plans include suggestions for such procedures as (1) rereading activities designed to give practice in specific skills needed by individuals and small groups; (2) a variety of exercises designed to build essential habits and skills; (3) language activities which can be adapted to fit needs of individuals and small groups; (4) independent reading activities planned around materials covering a wide range of interests and several levels of difficulty; (5) techniques and measures of evaluation leading to the discovery of individual needs; (6) all-unit activities designed to meet the needs of the superior as well as the least proficient readers.

More specifically, the procedures and materials listed below are among those suggested for meeting individual needs in the *primary grades*.

1. The use of the classroom or school library
2. Teacher-guided activities to correct special difficulties
3. Pupils' helping one another
4. Writing and reading of the class newspaper
5. The use of "invitations to read"
6. Games and jingles for vocabulary practice
7. The use of language charts as records of children's experiences
8. The use of prepared exercises duplicated for independent practice
9. Language activities to provide meaningful backgrounds for reading
10. Making of books, reading games, and notices by superior readers
11. Use of the materials made by gifted children

The specific procedures and materials listed below are suggested for meeting individual differences in the *intermediate* and *upper grades*.

1. The use of supplementary books and related materials
2. Teacher guidance to correct specific difficulties
3. Diagnosis and clinical study
4. Use of tests and worksheets based on specific selections
5. Compiling individual word lists
6. Reference materials for reading in other areas of the school program
7. Jokes, anecdotes, poems, etc., brought by individual children
8. Making use of individual records of free reading
9. Variation in assignments and reports
10. Using book reviews in ways which benefit the group
11. Workbook and how-to-study activities

The preceding suggestions are an indication of the variety of materials offered the teacher who uses this reading series. They will help in the solution of the number-one problem of the teaching of reading, namely, the wise adjustment of materials and methods to the individual differences among pupils.

41

III

Introduction to the Third-Year Program

For most children the third-grade level presents a change in the developmental reading program which has been approached gradually in the first and second grades. During the first two years children have worked under close teacher guidance in most of their reading activities. Now they are achieving greater independence. They have acquired a considerable sight vocabulary, and they are able to attack many new reading materials "on their own." The third grade, therefore, represents in many ways a period of transition from close teacher guidance to relatively independent reading in basic readers and in various other reading materials.

Whereas some children in third readers enter a period of rapid progress, others may fall into reading habits which will hamper and delay their ultimate reading development. These children must be helped to make a successful transition from the closely supervised reading to which they are accustomed, into a diversified, independent reading program. The third-grade program of the GINN BASIC READERS presents a scientifically planned and carefully organized group of activities designed to provide this transition.

This program takes into consideration not only the grade level of the skills that have so far been learned but also the physical, emotional, and social development of the children. Children of eight and nine tend to be physically vigorous and active. Because their muscles are now fairly well co-ordinated, they enjoy running and jumping games in which they can display their physical abilities. They are outgoing in nature and have begun to show concern for their peer group, forming and reforming in small groups to satisfy short-lived interests. Children of this age have started a definite interest in competitive team play. Most are able to follow set rules for games conscientiously, but their interest span is too short for long-continued activities. They can sit still for only a short time, and their plans and actions are concerned with immediate goals.

Developmental

Recreational

Emotionally, the eight-year-old is growing in independence and self-reliance. He is less dependent on home and on the help of the teacher and prefers to make many of his own decisions. He has left behind some of the egocentricity of childhood and is beginning to be interested in the problems of the people around him. He finds it easier to put himself in someone else's place and to understand how that person feels. Because he accepts differences among people, he can be guided in a constructive development of social and ethical attitudes. The GINN BASIC READERS attempt to provide such guidance in many different ways.

The ever-widening horizon of the third-grader's life, actions, and understanding causes him to react enthusiastically to his environment and everyday experiences. He likes to dramatize and exaggerate his feelings and to impersonate real and imaginary characters. Thus he finds self-expression through dramatic play and through his fast-increasing word power. He enjoys sharing his experiences with others and creating his own imaginary stories and tall tales. Throughout the year it is important to encourage and enrich the child's oral language in order that he may be able to read with understanding the varied new materials with which he now comes in contact.

Preferences in the reading matter of third-graders reflect the characteristics which have already been mentioned. The children are eager to find out about other people, other countries, and other times. Although some children at this age continue to enjoy reading factual material, many of them seem to be most interested in fairy tales and imaginary stories. All seem to enjoy stories with strong plot and surprise situations. Jokes, riddles,

Functional

Enrichment

and other types of humor are also much appreciated. As they develop the ability to read silently more rapidly than orally, and as they acquire the tools for independent word attack, third-grade children begin to read widely for enjoyment.

In addition to widening interests, the third-grade teacher must also be alert to possible reading disabilities which may accumulate at this time. A child's lack of background or inadequate oral vocabulary, as well as over-emphasis in earlier grades on oral reading, may serve to hinder full comprehension of material which is becoming more varied and complex. Failure to master a basic sight vocabulary or to develop skills of word attack blocks the development of other fundamental skills. A good teacher will diagnose the difficulties of individual children and provide instruction to help them overcome their deficiencies at the beginning of and throughout their third-year reading program.

A well-rounded reading program for the third grade then is made up of four distinct areas: first, *the developmental program*, which consists of systematic group instruction using the basal text and related materials, with the *Manual for Teaching the Third Reader—1* as a guide; second, *the recreational program*, through which children establish the habit of selecting and reading books for pleasure and information; third, *the functional program*, with its reading of daily plans, directions, announcements, reports, and other materials in everyday classroom situations; and fourth, *the enrichment program*, through which reading skills are used and extended to offer the related, stimulating experiences that cause reading to become personally meaningful.

45

Determining Readiness for Third-Grade Reading

Each GINN BASIC READER is an integral part of a reading program which is carefully graded throughout, both in content and in skills. The children who have successfully completed the preceding books in this series will be ready to begin *Finding New Neighbors*. In diagnosing the reading readiness of the children in her group the teacher should consider the maturity, specific abilities, and previous reading experiences of each child. Much of this information may be obtained from school records, former teachers, and both formal and informal tests. In a normal third grade the teacher will find that the group will vary considerably in reading speed, level of comprehension, and skill in attacking new material. After determining the reading readiness of the children the teacher may keep her findings in a notebook in order to help individual children and to note the progress they show during the year. The growth of each child may be considered in terms of such goals as the following:

1. The child enters enthusiastically into most types of reading activities.

2. He reads to satisfy his own desire for information and pleasure.

3. He reads a wide variety of material, such as supplementary readers, storybooks, and magazines.

4. He associates meaning with the 775 words presented in the first two grades.

5. He is able to recognize the main idea in a story or in a paragraph.

6. He has developed considerable skill in recalling story details, in reading to answer questions, and in following specific directions.

7. He can recall the sequential order of the events in a story.

8. He shows some ability to read critically and creatively, to generalize, and to make inferences from material read.

9. He is becoming independent in attacking unfamiliar words by analogy, by substituting consonants, and by structural clues; he is able to check his analysis by considering the meaning of a word in a sentence.

10. He recognizes variant forms of basic words: (1) the possessive and plural forms of nouns, (2) contractions in which one letter is omitted, (3) compounds of which each part is a known word, (4) verbs to which s, es, ed, or ing has been added, (5) words to which er (comparison), est, er (agent), y, or ly has been added, even if final e has been dropped, the final consonant doubled, or y changed to i before the endings.

11. He reads material at the lower third-grade level with ease, with an average of only two or three word difficulties per page.

Teaching *Finding New Neighbors*

12. He makes increasing use of the room, school, and public libraries.

13. He enjoys reading orally and listening to others.

14. He enjoys listening to poetry.

Children who seem to lack readiness for reading third-grade materials should be provided with textbooks of easier levels. As they read orally and silently, the teacher should observe them carefully and record the attitudes, habits, and skills of each child on an informal check list similar to the one below. She may then use the check list as a guide for determining the reading level of each child and as a help in the initial grouping within the class.

Informal Reading Check List

(Sample Items Only)

Directions: Under each heading mark *S* for satisfactory progress and *U* for unsatisfactory. Under "Level," mark the grade level of the child's oral and silent reading ability. Mark 1 for First Reader; 2^1 for Second Reader, Level I; 2^2 for Second Reader, Level II; 3^1 for Third Reader, Level I; 3^2 for Third Reader, Level II.

Name	Standardized Tests		Silent Reading						Oral Reading						Reading Activities (Workbook, etc.)				
	Reading Name of test	Intelligence Name of Test	Position of book	Lip movement	Rate	Recall of ideas	Habits of word attack	Level	Word recognition	Rhythm	Voice	Recall of ideas	Habits of word attack	Level	Interest	Prompt attack	Persistence	Corrects own errors	Independence
Peggy	3.2	115	S	S	U	S	S	3_1	S	U	S	S	S	3_1	S	S	S	S	S

The results of the *Second-Reader-II Achievement Test, Revised Edition,* if given at the end of the second grade, will help the teacher to discover the level of each child's reading achievement. Specific test items may reveal

47

both his strengths and his weaknesses in the basic skills necessary for success in reading *Finding New Neighbors*.

In addition to informal checks of each child's reading abilities and careful consideration of the results of his *Second-Reader-II Achievement Test, Revised Edition*, the teacher may administer the *Third-Grade Readiness Test, Revised Edition*, of the GINN BASIC READERS series. The results of these tests will be of the greatest help to the teacher in determining each child's needs and his present stage of development. Specific suggestions for the best application of the test results are given in the section "How to Use the Test Results," in *The Manual and Answer Key for Teachers*, which accompanies each test.

Objectives of the Third-Reader Program

The major objectives of the third-year program of the GINN BASIC READERS in terms of skills, habits, attitudes, and appreciations are stated on the following pages. Since child development is a continuous process, and growth in reading skills is a cumulative one, many of the desirable objectives stated at an earlier level are still applicable. Many of the goals of the previous levels, therefore, are carried over into the third-reader period, and the objectives of the third-reader levels are in turn continued at succeeding levels.

I. Skills

A. Comprehension

1. To promote the ability to read for the main idea (1) by selecting a title for a story, (2) by identifying the sentences that express the main idea in parts of a story or in a paragraph, (3) by locating the main parts of a story, and (4) by stating the main idea of a story simply and clearly.

2. To increase the ability to read for details, such as (1) recalling story facts for various purposes, (2) skimming to locate quickly specific information either in answer to a question or in support of a personal theory, (3) selecting details to support the main idea, (4) following specific directions, and (5) finding information to solve a problem.

3. To promote the ability to recognize the sequence of events in a story (1) by arranging sentences in the correct order, (2) by organizing information, and (3) by retelling or dramatizing story events in the right sequence.

4. To increase skill in critical reading in order (1) to select material relevant or pertinent to a certain idea, (2) to perceive cause and effect relationships, and (3) to judge whether material is true or false.

5. To increase the ability to read creatively in order to predict outcomes, draw conclusions, and use story content for further interpretation, dramatization, and construction.

The people could not find the peddler.

Where do you think he went next?

6. To develop skill in reading increasingly longer units of material with speed, accuracy, and comprehension.

7. To promote the ability to interpret orally the mood and conversational text of a story.

8. To increase the ability to read independently in related books to locate information, to give reports, to solve problems, and to satisfy personal reading interests.

B. Word-Study Skills

Word Meaning. 1. To enrich and extend word meanings through the use of (1) personal experience, (2) contrast and comparison, (3) context clues, (4) classification, (5) discussion and interpretation.

2. To promote the understanding of relationships in word meanings, such as words that have similar or opposite meanings, words that may be classified, or words that express shades of meaning.

3. To increase the understanding that some words have more than one meaning and to promote the ability to choose the correct meaning for the specific context.

4. To increase speaking and listening vocabularies through enriched language experiences.

Word Recognition. 1. To develop accurate recognition of the 335 sight words presented in the basic vocabulary of the Reader.

2. To establish the habit of using context clues along with other skills as an aid to word recognition.

3. To increase the ability to recognize the phonetic and structural properties of words as an aid to recognition.

Phonetic Analysis. (See "Index of Word-Study Skills," page 476 of this manual.)

1. To extend the auditory and visual recognition of all consonant sounds in initial, medial, and final position in words.

2. To develop auditory and visual recognition of the variant sounds of the consonants *c* and *g*, the silent letters in *kn*, *wr*, and *gh*.

3. To review two-letter consonant digraphs and blends previously taught, and to develop recognition of the three-letter blends *str*, *spr*, and *thr* as they appear in the text.

4. To extend the recognition and use of the variant sounds of the vowels.

5. To develop understanding of principles governing vowel differences such as (1) changes in vowels when followed by *r*, (2) vowels in one-syllable words lengthened by final *e*, (3) silent vowels in words.

6. To build skill in recognizing common vowel digraphs, diphthongs, and the principles governing the sound of the vowels in each combination, such as (1) the silent vowel in *ai*, *oa*, *ea*, etc., (2) the variant pronunciations of *ai*, *ea*, *oo*, *ow* and *ou*, (3) the pronunciation of *ew*, *oi*, and *oy*.

7. To increase skill in recognizing common phonograms in words.

8. To develop further skill in seeing differences in words commonly confused.

9. To strengthen power of independent word attack (1) by applying phonetic principles governing consonant and vowel sounds in words, (2) by using analogy and comparison with known or rhyming words, (3) by blending phonetic elements in words into meaningful wholes.

Structural Analysis. 1. To develop ability to recognize differences in word structure, such as variants of known words formed (1) by adding *s*, *es*, *ed*, *ing*, *er*, *est*, *y*, or *ly*, (2) by dropping final *e* before endings, (3) by doubling the consonant before endings, (4) by changing *y* to *i* before endings.

2. To develop the ability to recognize new compound and hyphenated words made up partly of known words.

3. To develop recognition and understanding of the meaning of the apostrophe when used to show (1) possession, (2) omissions in contractions.

4. To strengthen the power of independent word attack by recognizing changes in form and meaning of root words.

Syllabication and Alphabetizing. 1. To develop the ability to recognize syllables in a word, to see each syllable as a vowel unit, and to use the principles of syllabication in pronouncing new words as they appear in the text.

2. To develop the ability to arrange words in alphabetical order and to understand the meaning and uses of alphabetical order.

II. Good Reading Habits

1. To strengthen the habit of reading independently for pleasure and for the solution of problems.

2. To strengthen the habit of thinking critically about different types of material read.

3. To strengthen the habit of reading with concentration for increasingly longer periods of time.

4. To strengthen the habit of combining pertinent skills to attack unfamiliar vocabulary in independent reading.

5. To strengthen the habit of using the table of contents.

6. To strengthen good habits in the care of books and other materials.

7. To encourage the habit of using school and public libraries for information and enjoyment.

III. Attitudes and Appreciation

A. General

1. To foster the love of books.

2. To encourage the use of printed material to satisfy personal needs.

3. To increase the use of books in stimulating creative activities.

4. To foster an appreciation of rhythmic and sensory impressions from both prose and poetry through reading and listening.

5. To contribute to the child's total adjustment through the development of a sense of personal security gained from success in reading.

B. In Relation to Content

1. To develop attitudes of friendliness, co-operation, understanding, and appreciation of other people, especially those of diverse background.

2. To broaden interests in American life beyond the child's environment.

3. To broaden reading tastes through a variety of stories, realistic and fanciful, informative and amusing, modern and traditional.

Nature of the Third Reader

Meaningful Content. *Finding New Neighbors*, the Reader for the first level of Grade Three, offers the children an exciting variety of stories and many stimuli for creative thinking. The children's experiences in their neighborhood and school, the adventures with friends and pets, and their enjoyment and celebration of holidays during the year are treated in the realistic stories. New information is presented in the stories about Indian children and wild animals. Horizons are broadened by stories about life in different parts of the United States. Stories about children of varying backgrounds and customs are designed to deepen the children's understanding of the many different kinds of people who make up the American population. Eleven poems in the Reader, and many more in this manual, are included for listening and appreciation. Fanciful stories by modern authors provide an interesting contrast to traditional folk tales from all over the world. These tales inspire the children's appreciation of fantasy, stimulate their imagination, and spur them on to wider enjoyment of reading.

Each story in *Finding New Neighbors* has kept the particular literary style of its author. At the same time, each one of the stories is characterized by simplicity and logic in plot development so that the children can both enjoy the story's literary and stylistic qualities and easily follow the sequence of events. When the children have completed the Reader, therefore, they will have gained not only enjoyment from the material but also the feeling that new possibilities have opened for them to enrich their reading experiences.

Ease of Approach. *Finding New Neighbors* continues the easy and gradual approach to reading which characterized the previous Readers in this series. The total number of new words is 335. All the words taught at the first-grade and second-grade levels, with the exception of eleven proper nouns and two sound words, are maintained. No more than three new words appear on any one page, and each new word is repeated at least four times in the book to give practice through repetition. Pictures and context clues throughout the book provide valuable aids to independent word attack and recognition.

Unit Organization

The stories and poems in this book are organized into seven units, each of which is constructed around a major theme high in interest value for third-grade children.

A full-page picture introduces each unit and stimulates a discussion in which a child can join *the unit theme* to his own experience. The unit theme is further developed through reading the stories and participating in meaningful activities which assimilate new concepts, enrich language experiences, and provide opportunities for further pleasure and informational reading.

The first unit contains stories which mirror the children's own environment and experiences. The succeeding units gradually reach out to encompass new ideas, different kinds of people, and events of other times, all of which third-graders are beginning to understand.

The stories in the last two units of the book contain few new words so that the children may use the reading skills and vocabulary they have already learned and enjoy the confidence in independent reading which they have been acquiring. In this way they are able to concentrate on the meaning of the stories and to enjoy a feeling of accomplishment in their reading.

These seven units of related stories provide centers of interest around which activities in language, music, art, and literature can be planned. The many related experiences are an aid to emotional development, to rapid language development, to growth in appreciation and enjoyment of the environment, and to the use of reading as a functional tool.

Teaching Aids for the Third-Reader Program

Testing Program. The *Third-Grade Readiness Test, Revised Edition*, has been prepared in order to help the teacher to gauge whether individual children are ready to begin the third-grade reader. This test, combined with informal silent and oral tests, will aid the teacher in the initial group placement of the children.

A second test, the *Third-Reader-I Achievement Test, Revised Edition*, also prepared for use with the GINN BASIC READERS, may be administered when the children have finished reading *Finding New Neighbors*.

A *Third-Reader-II Achievement Test, Revised Edition*, is also available for use at the completion of *Friends Far and Near*. These tests are designed primarily for testing general achievement of the skills covered during the use of the individual Reader. The tests may also be used for diagnostic purposes and individual evaluation of reading skills.

My Do and Learn Book: Workbook. The Workbook which accompanies *Finding New Neighbors* makes an important contribution to a broad and well-balanced reading program. Exercises are carefully planned to give practice in all the comprehension skills, such as finding the main idea, reading for details, arranging sentences and story parts in the correct sequence, and also to give opportunities for critical and creative reading.

An important part of this workbook is the section devoted to the word-study skills needed for successful work in the third grade. Many of the activities required in many workbook pages give practice in and better understanding of the skills which are first presented in the pages of the Manual.

My Do and Learn Book is attractively illustrated and printed in full color. To give the children practice in following directions, as well as an opportunity to work independently, simple instructions are provided on each page. Thus the children may complete each exercise with a minimum of teacher direction.

The material in the Workbook reviews and gives practice in the use of the vocabulary taught in the Reader. Some of the pages in the Workbook test knowledge of story facts from *Finding New Neighbors*, whereas others use the new vocabulary in completely new and different context written expressly for the Workbook.

The Workbook contains some pages which are suggested as informal diagnostic checks of how much extra practice individual children may need. Vocabulary tests are provided for each unit in the Third Reader. These tests follow the exercises in the Workbook that accompany the unit, and can be

used to check the recognition of the basic words that have been taught. The same tests are included in the Manual and are placed with other material for the teacher's use at the end of the plans for each unit.

Method of Teaching the Third-Reader Program

Character of the Lesson Plans. Good teaching is based upon the needs of individual children and is adapted to meet these requirements. It is modified by varying environmental conditions and enriched by the ingenuity, creativeness, and interest of the teacher. The lesson plans in this manual are designed to satisfy the needs of widely different groups and individuals in each classroom. The primary purpose of these plans is to provide the teacher with an effective and flexible guide in methods of teaching reading.

The lesson plans are adaptable to many kinds of good teaching. The unified teaching steps suggested here have been tested and found to be most effective in achieving the objectives of the third-grade program, and can therefore be used with confidence by the busy teacher as a guide and time-saver. These steps ensure a gradual and thorough mastery of the reading process by emphasizing those attitudes, habits, and skills which are essential to child growth at each grade level. The GINN BASIC READERS offer a well-organized and clearly directed program which is easy to follow and which ensures the gradual and effective development of reading abilities.

At the beginning of each unit in the Manual, a two-page chart summarizes all the activities included in the unit. It shows all the steps in teaching each story, and also gives the workbook pages that are to be used at that time. At one glance the teacher can see the distribution of skills taught and the exercises and worksheets included.

Steps in the Lesson Plans. Each lesson plan consists of six steps. The amount of time spent on each step should be based on the needs and abilities of the particular group being taught. It is advisable that the teacher follow the first three steps in the order in which they are presented: "Developing Readiness for Reading," "Reading the Story," and "Building Essential Habits and Skills." The suggestions under steps 4 and 5, "Related Language Experiences" and "Enrichment Activities," may be used at any point in the daily or weekly program where they will prove most effective and constructive in providing a well-rounded program for each particular group.

A sixth step, consisting of "Evaluating Activities" and "Helping the Individual Child," is part of "All-Unit Activities" at the end of each unit in the Manual. The section "All-Unit Activities" includes a culminating activity which summarizes each unit, group tests to check pupil progress, and additional reading experiences for the slower, average, and superior readers.

Each lesson plan begins with a summary of highlights of the story taught in that lesson. The highlights call attention to story concepts which might otherwise be taken for granted or missed, and to qualities in the story which foster understanding and appreciation that may be of value to the children's emotional and social development.

The new words in the story are listed under "Vocabulary" after the highlights with the page number on which the word appears for the first time.

I. DEVELOPING READINESS FOR READING

The amount of preparation for reading a specific story should depend on whether or not the children already have enough maturity and background information to grasp fully the meaning of the story theme. Discussion, activities, and all kinds of visual aids may be used meaningfully to develop a rich conceptual background before the reading of each story. This readiness development, often done before the child opens his book, enables the child to read later with greater confidence and understanding. It should be brief, pertinent, and carefully co-ordinated with the story. *While stimulating the children's interest the teacher should be careful not to betray the plot of the story and thereby lessen the suspense and the children's subsequent enjoyment in reading.*

Meaningful Presentation of Vocabulary. The children should learn not only to recognize the new words but also to understand their use and meaning. The new words are presented in either written or oral context, sometimes in a combination of both. In this way word meaning, as well as word recognition is stressed.

Third-graders who have developed the skills necessary for independent word attack, such as use of context and word-analysis clues, should be encouraged to exercise the skills whenever possible. Suggestions for attacking the words which lend themselves to phonetic and structural analysis are frequently given in a separate paragraph in the readiness section of the lesson. This paragraph reviews the vocabulary just taught in such various ways as framing, defining, or using the words. These suggestions should, of course, be used according to the individual skills and difficulties of the children.

Setting Up Reading Purposes. Once the children's interest has been aroused by the discussion, the group will be able, with the help of the teacher, to define a general purpose for reading the story. Often a conversation involving concepts related to the story may end with questions that can be answered only through the reading of the story. For the long-term development of the realization in the children that they may read for a variety of purposes, the approach and the introductory questions should be as stimulating and varied as the stories.

II. READING THE STORY

Guided Reading. During the first reading of the story, which is always silent, the teacher has an opportunity to observe the children's abilities, their strengths and weaknesses. In the early lessons the questions and comments are detailed and numerous in order to help the children to interpret the pages correctly and critically and to recognize new ideas and vocabulary through carefully phrased context clues. Gradually less teacher guidance becomes necessary as the children grow in reading ability until, finally, many of them are able to read the entire story in response to the general purpose set up by the group. The reading units are relatively short at first. Beginning with one or two pages in a thought unit they are then increased to several pages, and later to whole stories.

The plans for the silent guided reading of each story provide the teacher with questions to aid the children in applying the new vocabulary that was presented earlier in the readiness section, or to attack new words independently. Usually further practice is provided at a later time to ensure the accurate recognition of words derived in this manner.

As in all good teaching, the needs and interests of the children should govern the amount and kind of instruction to be given. For this reason the instruction of individual groups will vary, of necessity, from that indicated in the plans. The resourceful teacher will always encourage and make use of the children's spontaneous reactions, questions, and comments. She will help each child to read at his capacity level through the adaptation, not adoption, of these plans to the individual children in her group. In this way she will keep enthusiasm and interest at a high pitch.

The lesson plans in this manual offer many different approaches, depending on the content, length, ease, and style of each story. Varied procedures not only stimulate interest but also allow children to read different materials in different ways. Examples are:

(1) The teacher may ask questions about a page or a series of pages. The children find and read the answers silently, then orally.

(2) Pages are read silently by the children to find answers to questions or problems the teacher has posed. A group discussion follows the reading.

(3) Questions may be written on the chalkboard or on mimeographed

sheets. They are read silently by the children and the answers located in the text.

(4) General or specific reading purposes are set up by the teacher and the children. The children read the entire story. Informal discussion follows.

(5) Questions based on the content of a story are listed on study-guide sheets which are distributed to the group. The children read the entire story silently first and then reread to find the answer to each question on

the guide sheet. In recording each answer, the children indicate the number of the question, the page on which the answer was found, the paragraph, the line, and the first and last words of the sentence or sentences which contain the answer. A discussion of the questions and answers follows the completion of the study guide. The answers on the individual sheets are checked, compared, and corrected by the children.

Rereading for Specific Purposes. Although the second reading of every story is not essential, suggestions for oral or silent rereading activities are given in every lesson plan. For an increased understanding of the many purposes that reading may serve, the purposes for rereading in this manual are varied according to the different types of stories.

Stories may be reread for the purpose of (1) preparing to read aloud to an audience, (2) planning a play, a pantomime, or a puppet show, (3) planning to retell a story at a story hour, (4) selecting favorite parts of a story, or (5) finding parts that verify an opinion.

Comprehension skills too are strengthened through rereading. Children reread to find the main idea, to recall or find specific details, to check sequence, to draw conclusions, to make inferences, or to compare styles of writing.

The new third-grade skill, skimming, is also practiced in rereading. The children skim to prove or disprove statements written on the chalkboard, to find specific information, to answer oral questions, to find word pictures, descriptions, or clues to solve a mystery.

The purposes for rereading will be numerous and the results valuable to the children's reading abilities. But no matter what the purpose, rereading should always result in pleasure and enjoyment for the children.

III. BUILDING ESSENTIAL HABITS AND SKILLS

The third step in each lesson plan consists of building the habits and skills essential to the growth of a child's reading power. The suggestions in this section include reading experiences to be carried on under teacher guidance, and many different exercises which may be duplicated and used for independent practice by the children.

Although children differ in reading abilities and in their rate of reading development, all need systematic practice in some reading skills. Children with unusual aptitude in reading may need to spend little time on the development of new vocabulary. However, they may still need some word-study skills presented during this developmental phase of the reading lesson to help them expand their ability to do independent reading.

Comprehension and Study Skills. Practice in reading for a wide variety of purposes is provided through the use of charts, chalkboard exercises, worksheets, and the text itself.

The list below includes major habits and skills emphasized at the third-reader level for the development of comprehension:

1. The habit of using the table of contents.
2. The habit of selecting suitable reading materials for different purposes.
3. The habit of reading for information.
4. Systematic habits of attacking unfamiliar words in independent reading.
5. The skills needed to follow directions, detect details, and answer questions.

6. The skills required to recognize and understand the main idea in a story and in other kinds of writing.

7. The skills needed to recognize and establish a correct sequence of events.

8. The skills needed to recognize relevance, to make judgments, to evaluate ideas, and to see relationships.

9. The skills required to draw conclusions, to generalize, and to make inferences.

10. The skills required to interpret material read in terms of personal and other reading experiences.

Word-Study Skills. An important section in each lesson plan is devoted to the many specific suggestions for developing accurate and quick recognition of basic sight vocabulary, for enriching and extending word meaning, and for further developing skill in the use of phonics as a tool in attacking unfamiliar words.

All the phonetic and structural skills of word attack taught in previous grades are carefully reviewed and maintained in this manual. At this level they are applied in different situations and practiced and developed to a point at which generalizations are possible. At the same time, skills that have been merely observed until now are taught, and new skills are introduced. These include extensive practice in the sounds of three-letter blends, new structural changes, alphabetization, and syllabication. The areas devoted to phonetic and structural analysis in the word-study section of each lesson plan are indicated by tinted blocks.

Known words are always used for an activity in which new phonetic elements and structural changes in words are introduced. When unfamilar words are used in a lesson they are taken whenever possible from the vocabularies of stories that are taught later in the Third Reader, Level I, or Level II. Practice and application of the word-study skills are provided in each lesson through exercises which are planned for duplication and independent work by the children.

The skills and abilities taught at the third-grade level include further strengthening and expansion of the skills taught previously, with the addition of syllabication as an aid to pronunciation and readiness for the use of the dictionary. A general list of these skills and abilities follows:

1. The ability to combine auditory and visual perception of consonants, vowels, digraphs, and diphthongs, in initial, medial, and final positions.

2. The ability to recognize, use, and arrange in order, all the letters of the alphabet, either isolated or at the beginning of words.

3. The ability to classify known words and phrases.

4. Skill in the use of contrast and comparison to understand word meanings.

5. Skill in choosing the right meaning of a word in a particular context.

6. Skill in attacking unfamiliar words through contrast and comparison with known words.

7. Skill in using phonetic and structural clues in attacking unfamiliar words.

8. Skill in auditory recognition of the number of vowel sounds or syllables in words.

Workbook. The exercises in *My Do and Learn Book* accompany each lesson plan. Since the pages in the Workbook are designed to parallel each lesson plan, the exercises will prove to be most helpful if they are used at the point indicated in the Manual.

The Workbook pages are planned so that the children may do them independently with a minimum of teacher guidance. The teacher should, of course, introduce the page if necessary and also devote some time to checking the completed exercises with the children. In this way she may discover the weaknesses of individuals in the group and plan additional practice for them.

IV. RELATED LANGUAGE EXPERIENCES

Language experiences which are closely related to the lesson constitute the fourth major step in the lesson plans. Relevant and interesting activities in both oral and written expression are carefully planned to provide a balanced language program.

This program offers definite instruction in listening for various specific purposes, such as plot development, humor, or descriptive words and phrases in a story. Other listening may be to gain specific information in an article, or to perceive sensory images or rhythmic patterns in poetry, to sense a mood, or to share a pleasurable experience.

Group planning of unit activities and conversation about subjects of interest serve an important purpose in drawing on the opinions and knowledge of all the children. In these group discussions the shy child should be encouraged to express himself, whereas the more aggressive child should be taught to contain his enthusiasm long enough to listen to others.

Reporting events and sharing personal experiences are still exciting to third-grade children. The lesson plans provide for many activities of this kind and stress accuracy and logical sequence in the child's report. The children are given frequent opportunities to tell both true and imaginary stories in an audience situation.

Original stories told by the children or stories from the Reader may be acted out in dramatic play, pantomime, creative rhythms, or a puppet show. All these activities allow the children to express their reactions to reading and listening creatively. Each of these activities will produce freer and fuller self-expression, increase the children's vocabulary, lead to a greater appreciation of language, and result in an increased interest in reading.

Specific language experiences are suggested also to help improve the child's speech habits. For effective oral expression and interpretation, his speech must be correct and clear. He should learn to adapt the tone and pitch of his voice to the individual mood and tempo of a particular situation. The speech-analysis chart on page 63 may be used for the diagnosis of the speech habits of individual children and will serve as a basis for speech instruction where it is necessary.

Children of the third grade possess a rich enough writing vocabulary and imagination to bring creative writing more and more into the foreground. Capitalization, punctuation, and the other tools needed for story-writing, written reports, and other writing should be taught as needed but never emphasized to such a degree that creativeness and self-expression are impaired.

V. ENRICHMENT ACTIVITIES

A wide variety of activities that will enrich and broaden the children's reading experiences is suggested in this fifth section of the lesson plans. The great number and variety of these activities will allow the teacher to select those which seem to her best suited to the interests and temperaments of the children in her group.

CONSONANTS

Directions: Show the child a picture representing a word below and ask him to name or tell about the picture. If a word cannot be pictured, ask the child to repeat a sentence containing the word. If the sound being checked is indistinct, draw a line through the word; if a substitution is made, write the substituted form above the word; if the sound is omitted, circle the word.

	Initial	Medial	Final		Initial	Medial	Final
b	boat	cabbage	tub	sh	ship	machine	dish
d	dog	puddle	hand	ch	chicken	teacher	match
f	father	muffin	knife	t	tie	mitten	gate
g	girl	wagon	frog	th	thumb	nothing	tooth
h	house	behind		~~th~~	them	mother	with
k	key	turkey	book	v	vine	river	stove
l	lamb	collar	ball	w	wood	twins	
m	mouse	hammer	farm	wh	white		
n	nose	pencil	barn	y	yellow	barnyard	
ng		singer	ring	z	zoo	magazine	rose
p	pig	apple	cap	zh		treasure	garage
r	rabbit	shirt	car	j	jacket	engine	page
s	sun	postman	horse				

VOWELS

Directions: Note words in which the child makes vowel substitutions, or nasalizes, or flattens vowel sounds. Typical examples are listed below.

Substitutes—<u>ji</u>st for just, <u>ki</u>n for can, <u>becuz</u> for because, etc.

Nasalizes—di̱nner, fe̱nce, fla̱me, ma̱n, li̱ght

Flattens—h<u>ou</u>se, r<u>ou</u>nd, t<u>ow</u>n

Suggestions for Improvement

Notes on Progress

Co-ordinating Activities. Each unit in the Reader is accompanied by a closely related suggested activity which is planned to be carried on for the duration of the unit. In this way the children are given a unifying and sustaining interest in the subject matter of each unit and have an incentive to use group work, research, discussion, writing, organization, speaking, drawing, field trips, and construction in a purposeful fashion. Making books, putting on a play and a puppet show, painting murals, and publishing a newspaper are a few of the co-ordinating activities suggested in the Manual. All-unit planning can give focus to varied activities.

Construction. Various activities are suggested in which projects related to the stories are constructed. Skills such as modeling, woodworking, sewing, and cutting, are practiced, and materials such as paper, cardboard, wood, cotton, and papier mâché are utilized.

Art. Opportunities are provided for drawing, sketching, illustrating, easel and finger painting, and paper design and composition, as the children interpret the stories they have read.

Stories in Other Readers. At the end of each lesson plan there is a suggested list of stories in other readers, all of which are closely related to the theme of the story in the basic reader. Stories are included from both second- and third-level readers, and the children should have no difficulty in reading any of them independently.

Stories to Enjoy. This section contains the titles of many books and stories closely related to the selections which they follow. The teacher should collect as many as possible of these books before the children begin each unit and display several on the library table. Many of the suggested books in this section are easy enough for the children to read by themselves. Others may be read to them for information and enjoyment.

Poems to Enjoy. In the body of the Manual are printed many poems with themes similar to those of the stories, so that it is easy for the teacher to use them with her group, either for reading aloud to the children, for choral reading, or for memorization. The titles of many other poems from poetry anthologies and books of verse are suggested for the use of both teacher and children.

Music to Enjoy. Four songs have been expressly written to fit the theme and mood of the stories which they accompany in *Finding New Neighbors*. Reference is also made to many other songs which may be used with the various stories.

Films and Filmstrips. The films and filmstrips suggested throughout the Manual were carefully selected to complement the stories in the Reader with which they will be used. Several of the films and filmstrips will also serve to enrich the science and social studies in the third grade.

Pictures to Enjoy. Sometimes there exists a painting which, if available in reproduction or in an art book, will have visual appeal for the children and enrich not only their appreciation of art but also their enjoyment of the stories in the Reader. References to such pictures and reproductions which may be obtained from a library have been included at intervals throughout the Manual.

VI. ALL-UNIT ACTIVITIES

Culminating Activities. At the end of the unit lesson plans in the Manual, suggestions are given for various kinds of activities which will summarize and organize the unit that has just been completed. The children have an opportunity to exhibit their finished projects, present their plays, invite their parents to see their programs, and generally pull together the ideas that have been developed throughout the unit.

Evaluating Activities. Tests of comprehension and of word-study skills that have been presented during the unit are included in this section, as well as facsimiles of the vocabulary tests from the Workbook.

Group Inventories. In the first part of the Manual there are different kinds of inventory charts for the teacher's use in checking the attitudes, the general abilities, and the strengths and weaknesses of the children in the group. These charts may also be used as guides for formulating other charts through which skills acquired later during the year may be checked.

Helping the Individual Child. In an average grade there is a usual range of some six grades in the children's reading abilities. For example, in many third grades a few advanced readers may be able to read at sixth-grade level whereas some of the slowest readers may be reading only at first-grade level. However, the reading abilities of most of the children will cluster around the third-reader level. The teacher may discover the particular reading level and ability of each child through observation of the child's daily work, periodic checks by the use of standardized tests, and by informal tests of the silent and oral reading of the basic text and of other materials.

65

The instructional program of the GINN BASIC READERS is designed to meet each child at his own level of reading development and to help him progress according to his own capabilities. At the end of the lesson plans for each unit, specific suggestions are given for additional reading experiences suitable for the individual children of slow or superior reading ability. Many of these activities may be carried on independently. Others are suitable for use by small groups led by the teacher or by a group leader. For the individual child who needs direct teacher guidance various reteaching exercises and games and devices for practice are also provided.

The specific suggestions made for small-group activities and for individual practice to strengthen all the reading skills are placed at the end of each unit. However, this material may be used at any point where it is needed to supplement the regular instruction and independent learning activities.

INVENTORY OF GROWTH IN ATTITUDES TOWARD READING	Barbara K.	Peggy H.	Julia W.	Ben L.	
1. Does he anticipate reading periods with pleasure?					
2. Does he use books frequently during free-time periods?					
3. Is he alert to opportunities for reading in his environment?					
4. Is he interested in reading a variety of books?					
5. Does he read for information?					
6. Does he make frequent use of the school or public library?					

Teaching *Finding New Neighbors*

The inventory of attitudes toward reading on page 66 is intended to help the teacher in evaluating the reading attitudes of individual children at the beginning of the year and again later in the year to see whether or not there has been any change. A similar check list for reading skills is reproduced on this page.

A chart like the one below may be helpful in checking the reading skills of individual children now, and again when they have finished *Finding New Neighbors*. It will show where progress has been made and where more special help is needed. Similar charts may be constructed throughout the year to check the children's skills in other fields, such as word attack, word recognition, language skill, or social and emotional adjustment.

INVENTORY OF GROWTH IN READING SKILLS	Nancy W.	Ray M.	Betsy G.	Jim B.	
1. Can he read silently with ease and concentration?					
2. Can he read orally with clearness and expression?					
3. Can he select the main idea from reading?					
4. Can he remember details when reading?					
5. Can he remember the sequence of ideas when reading?					
6. Does he read critically and generalize from material read?					
7. Can he draw conclusions and make inferences from material read?					
8. Does he react creatively to story plot and characterization?					
9. Does he use context, phonetic, and structural clues to identify words when reading?					

IV

Plans for Teaching
Finding New Neighbors

Introducing the New Book

Show the new book to the children and write its title, *Finding New Neighbors*, on the chalkboard. Have the title read aloud.

Ask the children what the word *neighbor* means to them and lead them to talk about the various ways in which neighbors might help one another. Ask: "How many of you have had a chance to meet new neighbors recently? Have some of them become your friends? This book has many stories about children whom you would like to have as neighbors." Presenting the new book

Distribute the books and encourage the children to discuss the picture on the front cover. Have the children recall briefly what they have learned about the proper care of books, such as holding a book at the bottom, turning the pages carefully from the upper right-hand corner, and keeping it clean.

Allow the children to browse through the book briefly, to look at the pictures, to satisfy their general curiosity, and to arouse their interest.

Discuss the title page with the children and help them read it aloud. Have the children turn to the table of contents and encourage comments about the pictures. Ask someone to read the title of the first group of stories. Ask, "What kinds of stories do you think you'll find in the first group?" Continue in the same way with the rest of the unit titles.

Story	Vocabulary	Developing Readiness	Reading the Story		Building Essential
Pages	New Words		Guided Reading	Rereading for Specific Purposes	Comprehension and Study Skills
Big Barby 7–16	Barby gentle Peggy Andrew brave sugar touches feel six	years wide arms clop afternoon carry slide presents colts			Reading specific parts to prepare for oral reading	Main Idea: discussing story subtitles; introducing the concept of skimming Details: skimming for specific details Main Idea and Details: classifying phrases (chalkboard exercise) Workbook: 1, seeing relationships between pictures and story incidents
Speckles and the New Boy 18–27	Speckles setting hatch cluck nest easy	pen straw feed chicken weeks twelve			Reading to prepare for dramatic audience reading Reading to illustrate a favorite part of the story	Main Idea: thinking of new subtitles Learning the meaning of paragraphs Story Details: answering riddles about story characters (worksheet) Sequence of Ideas: recalling order in new story material (worksheet) Workbook: 4, seeing cause and effect relationships
Cowboys Are Brave 28–35	thief Teddy Jane coyotes blankets woke scared howl alone				Reading specific parts to prove statements	Critical Reading: drawing conclusions (worksheet) Story Details: associating story characters with their lines (worksheet) Workbook: 6, sequence in new story material; 7, finding main ideas and drawing conclusions
Maggie the Magpie 36–41	Maggie magpie smart shoulder hello glasses cubes lemonade				Preparing to read the story aloud to another group Reviewing standards for oral reading	Story Details: associating characters with events (worksheet) Accurate Recall: discriminating between true and false statements (worksheet) Workbook: 8, following directions, using picture clues
A Dog of His Own 44–54	eyes Dad remember caught meadow toward whistled against leg fingers bites decided chewed				Reading to organize ideas	Skimming: locating paragraphs that give information (worksheet) Main Idea: selecting the main idea in illustrations (worksheet) Workbook: 11, finding the main idea in new story material; 13, drawing conclusions
All-Unit Activities Note: Poems are not included on the summary charts					Evaluation: recalling details in stories of the unit (worksheet) Sequence: recalling order of story facts in the unit Provisions for individual children: checking progress in oral reading Group inventory of word-attack skills

Developing Readiness (column, vertical text): Children are encouraged to identify new words through comparison with known words and the use of phonetic and context clues. New words are presented in context either written or oral. Through discussion and exchange of ideas, interest in the story is stimulated and background for understanding is developed. Purposes for reading are reached by the group with the teacher's guidance.

Guided Reading (column, vertical text): Silent and oral reading for comprehension and interpretation of story plot, mood, and characterization.

UNIT I, PETS AND PLAYTIME

Habits and Skills			Related Language Experiences	Enrichment Activities
Word-Study Skills				
Word Meaning	Phonetic Analysis	Structural Analysis		
Mastering words through meaning and phonetic clues Interpreting phrases (worksheet)	Reviewing consonant blends *bl, cl, fl, pl, sl, br, cr, dr, fr, gr, pr, tr, st, sn* Listening for consonant blends Workbook: 3, using initial consonant blends, phonograms, and context clues to make new words	Recalling one-letter contractions; meaning of apostrophe (worksheet) Recognizing compound words Workbook: 2, using compounds	Planning the unit activities (chart) Creative Writing: stories about pets Speech: analyzing speech difficulties Research: finding out about horses	Co-ordinating Activity: making a book, "Pets and Playtime" Bulletin Board: display of pictures and stories about pets Construction: building a papier mâché horse Stories in Other Readers Stories, poems, a filmstrip, and pictures
Seeing multiple meanings of words Word Recognition: mastering difficult words Workbook: 5, selecting words to express emotional responses	Recalling initial consonant blends *sp, spr, str, tw*	Reviewing compound words in the story	Discussion: learning more about chickens; learning to welcome newcomers Creative Writing: writing pet stories Listening: to the poem "Red Hen"	Co-ordinating Activity Bulletin Board: adding pet and chicken pictures Excursion: visiting a hatchery Stories in Other Readers Stories, poems, music, filmstrips, and a record
Recognizing words with opposite meanings (worksheet)	Reviewing names and sounds of vowels Discriminating between long and short sounds of vowels (worksheet) Recalling sounds of *y* when it is a vowel	Observing change in tense and structure of verbs ending in *y*	Conversation: about cowboys and their life Dramatization: adapting the story as a play	Co-ordinating Activity: writing and choosing stories for the class book Bulletin Board: displaying cowboy pictures A Story in Another Reader Stories and poems
Selecting descriptive words (chalkboard exercise) Using meaning to check word recognition	Recalling the principle of vowel lengthened by final *e* Checking meaning in sentences (worksheet) Seeing other sight words ending in *e* Workbook: 10, long and short vowels; vowels lengthened by *e*	Workbook: 9, recognizing words in which *y* is changed to *i* before *ed*	Conversation: about pet birds Creative Writing: writing stories about pet birds Speech: enunciating final *d* and *t* (chalkboard exercise)	Co-ordinating Activity Bulletin Board arranged and titled by children Library: finding and displaying pertinent books Story Chart: listing pet stories Stories in Other Readers Stories, a film, and a filmstrip
Reviewing opposites (chalkboard exercise) Word Recognition: using word cards to review vocabulary Workbook: 12, comparing words of similar and opposite meaning	Reviewing consonant digraphs *ch, sh, th, wh*		Research: learning about coyotes through books and a film Discussion: about pet care; setting up standards for short talks (chart) Listening: for lovable traits of pet in the poem "My Dog"	Co-ordinating Activity Construction: making book covers; modeling dogs Bulletin Board: mounting newspaper clippings about dogs Stories, poems, films, and filmstrips
Provision for less advanced readers: diagnosing individual needs; helps to improve word recognition and meaning Workbook: 14, Vocabulary Test I	Evaluation: word-analysis test of common phonograms (test) Provision for less advanced readers: discriminating between words of similar configuration (worksheet) Playing word-recognition games		Discussion: recalling the stories in the unit Sharing original stories and independent reading Provision for superior readers: preparing oral and written reports; planning dramatizations; consulting reference books for additional information	Culminating Activities: exhibit of pet books; oral summaries of stories in unit Provisions for superior readers: reading in supplementary books; collecting and illustrating poems and stories

Unit I · Pets and Playtime

Introducing the Unit

"Pets and Playtime" consists of five stories and two poems about real children and their everyday activities. The stories have the elements of unusual plot, surprising climax, and humor which will foster a lively interest in reading for pleasure. The material in this unit appeals to every child's desire to own a pet. It can help to deepen the children's understanding of the place which pets fill in the lives of people and of the responsibilities of proper pet care.

The stories emphasize also the development of personal qualities such as learning to make friends, overcoming fear, being thoughtful of others, and co-operating with one's playmates. The teacher may wish to develop these understandings as the material lends itself to such emphasis.

Set the stage for the unit by putting one or two pictures on the bulletin board. Encourage the children to supplement the exhibit later. Collect stories and poems suggested throughout the unit to read to the children. Arrange in the library corner a display of books suggested for independent reading.

To introduce the unit, guide a discussion of pictures pertaining to children's pets and play activities which have been posted on the bulletin board. The conversation should lead into the children's experiences which are related to the unit.

Pages 7–16

Big Barby

"Big Barby" is the story of a gentle horse which Father bought for his four children. The story relates how the children overcame their fear of their pet, how they helped her become used to the farm, and how they taught her to take them to school each day. Finally it tells how Barby presented twin colts on the twins' seventh birthday.

The story should be read for pleasure, but will suggest discussion of the children's feeling toward Barby, the care and training they gave her, and perhaps the training needed by the colts before they could be ridden.

Vocabulary

New Words: Page 7, ——; 8, *Barby, gentle;* 9, *Peggy, Andrew;* 10, *brave*, sugar, touches;* 11, *feel*;* 12, *six*, years*, wide*;* 13, *arms*, clop*;* 14, *afternoon*, carry, slide*;* 15, *presents;* 16, *colts*

NOTE. The starred words in this and all other vocabulary lists in the Manual may be attacked independently. Children of average or superior ability will have no difficulty in using picture, phonetic, or context clues to help them unlock these new words when they meet them in the story. For a slow-learning group, the teacher may find it advisable to present these words in phrases or sentences during the readiness development. Questions asked during the guided reading should reveal whether or not the children have been able to identify the words. Certain words which are phonetic are included in the readiness presentation for clarification of their meanings.

All words, phrases, and sentences that are printed in italics in these plans should be written on the chalkboard as they are suggested by the children or presented by the teacher. The combination of oral and written presentation strengthens word recognition and provides a meaningful background for the new words.

Developing Readiness for Reading

Meaningful Presentation of Vocabulary. Say: "The first stories in our book are all about children very much like you. Most of them go to school. Some of them have pets, and all of them have fun when they play together. As we read this unit we shall have a good time with them.

Interpreting story pictures

"Our first story is called 'Big Barby.' Find the story in the table of contents and turn to the page on which it begins. Look at the picture. Can you guess what *Barby* is? What words would you use to describe her?" Bring out in the discussion that Barby is a big farm horse; that she is a good horse for a farmer because she can *carry* heavy loads; that she is a good horse for farm children because she is *gentle*. List the names of the four children, *Andrew*, the oldest, then *Mary*, and the *six-year-old* twins, *Pat* and *Peggy*. Ask: "What do you think Peggy is doing? Why do you suppose she is hiding? Would you feel the same way?"

Have the children look at the picture on page 10. Ask, "What is Barby doing?" Explain, if necessary, that Barby is drinking at a watering trough.

Ask the children to look at the picture on page 11. Then have them read from the chalkboard and discuss the following questions:

Is Mary giving Barby a present?

Does Barby like sugar?

Will her mouth touch Mary's hand?

Is Barby a little colt?

Is she a gentle horse?

As the questions are read, clarify the word meanings. For example, be sure that the children understand the meaning of *gentle* and *colt*.

The words *brave, feel, six, years, wide, arms, clop, afternoon,* and *slide* should be readily recognized through phonetic and context clues during the guided reading. However, if the teacher wishes to include all the words in this presentation, each of these words may be analyzed thus: *brave, feel, slide,* blending consonants with long vowel phonograms; *clop, years,* and *arms* by analogy with *top, hears,* and *farms.*

NOTE. In every case where phonetic or structural analysis is used in attack on the new vocabulary, each word should be used in a meaningful sentence. Phonetic attack on words in isolation is not recommended. Each phonetic and structural clue suggested in these paragraphs may be only one of several good methods of attacking the particular words discussed. The teacher should use the clues most meaningful and helpful for each child.

After all the words have been taught, the slower readers may use the new words in sentences which the teacher will write on the chalkboard. Other children should then take turns reading the sentences and underlining the new words.

Setting Up Reading Purposes. Say, "Let's read the story to see how useful Barby is and what surprises she has in store for the children."

Reading the Story

Guided Reading

Ask: "How did the children feel about Barby when Father brought her home? Read the first page to find out." After discussion of this page, have the children read page 9 to find out what Father told Andrew to do.

As the children read silently, give help to individual children as needed. Jot down on a pad of paper any word difficulties that arise and plan to help the children master them later. After the silent reading, ask: "Why did Father buy Barby? Read aloud the part that tells how Father helped Barby get used to her new home." Remind the children to read dialogue as if they themselves were speaking.

"What brave thing did Andrew do? Read these two pages to find out." After the silent reading, ask: "How did Barby take the sugar from Andrew? Read that part aloud. How did you feel as you read that part? How did Andrew feel? Who else wanted to feed Barby? Why didn't Father want Pat or Peggy to feed Barby? Now read aloud the part that tells how Barby became a real pet.

Pages 10–11

"Look at the picture on pages 12 and 13. Do you think Barby looks strong enough to carry all four children? How did Barby's big feet sound when she walked along? Yes, clop, clop, clop. Now read those two pages to yourself."

Pages 12–13

75

Big Barby (7–16)

After the silent reading, ask the children to find and be ready to read aloud the part that tells how the children kept from falling off Barby. Ask about the road the children had to travel to school. "Who went with Barby and the children?

Page 14

"How do you think the children will get down from Barby's back?" (Slide down.) "Read this page to find out what Barby did every day. Do you think Barby was a smart horse? Why? What happened to Barby after school closed in the summer?

Pages 15–16

"One afternoon the twins had a birthday party. What do you imagine their friends brought them? Barby had a present for the twins too. Finish the story to find out what it was." After the silent reading, ask: "How did Barby let the children know she had a present for them? How do you think the children took care of the colts?"

Rereading for Specific Purposes

Preparing for oral reading

Write the directions for rereading on the chalkboard as shown below.

When the children have completed this activity, have individuals read aloud the pages that tell about the story parts. Be sure to praise good performance.

Read These Parts Again to Yourself

How Barby got used to the childr

The way to school

The birthday party

Building Essential Habits and Skills

Comprehension and Study Skills

Main Idea. 1. To help the children discriminate between main events and story details, ask them to find the subtitles in the story. Write them on the chalkboard: "Making Friends with Barby," and "Riding to School." Have the children re-read the first four pages of the story rapidly to recall the main events of the first section. Ask: "Is 'Making Friends with Barby' a good title for this part of the story? Why? Can you think of another subtitle that might be used?" ("A New Horse," "Getting Used to Barby.") Discuss with the group how the children learned to know Barby and what they did to help her to feel at home and to understand them. Lead them to the generalization that making friends is a two-way process, demanding give-and-take by all parties.

[margin: Discussing story subtitles]

2. At this time introduce the children to the concept of "skimming," by asking, "Did you read every word of the first story part or did you just look for the important ideas and pass over the unimportant ones quickly?" Explain to them that this kind of rapid reading is called *skimming.*

[margin: Skimming to judge a subtitle]

Have the children skim the next three pages to decide whether "Riding to School" is a good subtitle for the second part of the story. Why? Ask them to give their reasons and help them to suggest other subtitles.

Suggest that the children make a subtitle for the last two pages of the story which describe the twins' birthday party. "Presents from Barby" or "Barby's Surprise" are possible selections.

[margin: Making a subtitle]

Details. If there is time and if there are children who would benefit from more practice in skimming, have them skim for various different reasons, for instance to find details or descriptions of (1) the way to school, (2) how the children got on or off Barby, (3) the food at the party, (4) the children's reactions to the colts, and so on.

[margin: Skimming for other reasons]

Main Ideas and Details. To help the children develop skill in seeing the relationships between main ideas and details, write side by side on the chalkboard: *How Barby Looked— What Barby Did.* Have the children find in the text phrases

[margin: Classifying related ideas]

77   *Big Barby* (7–16)

which belong under these headings and read them aloud. Write the phrases they find under the proper headings. Guide the children in selecting such phrases as—

How Barby Looked	*What Barby Did*
big as an elephant	turned her big head
gentle	took sugar from Andrew
had a soft, wet mouth	carried the children

Word-Study Skills

Mastering difficult words

Word Meaning. 1. To strengthen the ability to attack words through the use of meaning clues, present on the chalkboard any words which children found difficult during the guided reading. Have them recall phonetic or structural clues that will aid recognition of these words. Review the words, using meaning clues, such as: "Find the word that tells how old the twins are." (*six*) "Which word describes Barby?" (*gentle*)

Interpreting the meaning of phrases

2. To strengthen the ability to interpret phrases meaningfully, discuss with the children the meaning of the words *where,*

when, and *why*. Write the phrases below on the chalkboard. Make certain that all the children can tell whether the phrases answer the questions *where*, *when*, or *why*.

down the hill (*where*)	*tomorrow* (*when*)
because she knew the way (*why*)	*into the shed* (*where*)

For independent practice, distribute copies of the following exercise.

NOTE. For the teacher's convenience, worksheet answers are indicated in color. Answers should not be duplicated.

Read the first phrase. Decide whether to write <u>when</u>, <u>where</u>, or <u>why</u> in the blank next to the phrase. Do the same with all the other phrases.

because she's so gentle why	in their pockets where
under the horse's nose where	the next morning when
on her wide back where	down the side road where
in the afternoon when	to carry the children why
through the spring when	to and from school where
because of the stones why	someday when
while they slept when	because she had colts why
on the far side of the yard where	to catch Peggy why

Phonetic Analysis. 1. To extend recognition of consonant blends, list on the chalkboard the groups of words below and have them pronounced. Have the children identify and underline the two letters or parts which are alike in each group of words. Lead the children to observe that the two letters make two speech sounds, thus applying the principle that *in a consonant blend each letter makes a sound which can be heard, but which is said very rapidly.*

Reviewing two-letter consonant blends

bl	*black, blew, blocks, blow, blue*
cl	*clean, click, climb, clop, clothes, clown*
fl	*flash, flat, flew, floor, flowers, fly, flip*
pl	*place, plant, play, please*
sl	*sled, sleep, slide*
br	*brave, bread, break, breakfast, bright, bring, brook, brought*

Big Barby (7–16)

cr	*crawl, cried, crow, cry*
dr	*dream, dress, drink, driver, drop, dry*
fr	*friend, frogs, from, front, fruit*
gr	*grandfather, grandmother, grass, gray, great, green, grew, ground*
pr	*presents, pretty, prize*
tr	*track, tractor, train, traveler, treasure, tree, tricks, tried, trip, truck*
st	*stairs, stand, start, station, stay, steam, steps, stick, still, stirred, stone, stop, store, storm, story, stove*
sn	*Snipp, Snapp, Snurr, snow*

Identifying similar consonant blends

2. To provide practice for those children who need more help in the auditory discrimination of consonant blends, proceed as follows: Say, "*Brave, brook, brown, block, bread.*" Ask the children to raise their hands when they hear the word that begins with a different consonant blend. (*block*) If necessary, have the children say the words after you. Continue in this manner to develop auditory recognition for the differences in any consonant blends which are confused.

Recalling one-letter contractions

Structural Analysis. 1. To review with the children the meaning and use of the apostrophe in one-letter contractions,

write on the chalkboard these sentences from page 8 of the text:

> *"She's big, but she's gentle," said Father.*
> *"I bought her because she is gentle."*

Have the sentences read; then underline the words *she's* and *she is*. Ask the children to look carefully at the underlined words. "Do they mean the same? How are they different?" Recall that a contraction is a shorter and quicker way of saying two words. Lead the children to observe how the contraction is written. Have them recall that the small mark is called an apostrophe and that it shows where a letter is left out. Ask, "What letter has been left out in the contraction *she's*?" Write *he's* and repeat the question.

Write on the chalkboard the following familiar contractions: *that's, didn't, isn't, wasn't, don't, I'm, it's, doesn't.* As shown on page 80, have individual children draw a line from a contraction to the two words the contraction stands for.

Ask the children to find contractions in sentences in their text on pages 10 and 12 and have them read each sentence, first with the contraction and then with the two words for which the contraction stands.

NOTE. The story contains two words in which an apostrophe indicates possession: *children's, horse's.* Some children may confuse this with the apostrophe in contractions. If so, explain the difference.

2. If more review is needed, distribute copies of the exercise on page 82 for independent work. Direct the children to insert the correct contractions in the blanks.

3. If children have experienced difficulty in recognizing any of the compound words in the story (*something, schoolhouse, afternoon, birthday, outdoors, someday*), help them recognize the two parts of each word, both of which they may know separately.

Reviewing compound words

NOTE. A compound word is a word the members of which are English words with meanings relatively unchanged in the compound. Compounds may be written as two words, as *ice cream*; hyphenated, as *good-by*; or solid, as *anything.* Present for practice in recognition only those words whose separate parts have meanings that are clear and easily defined.

Big Barby (7–16)

Afternoon Fun

One afternoon Bobby came to play with Andrew. Andrew took him to the barn to show him the new horse.

"(That is) —— Barby," said Andrew. "(Is not) —— she beautiful?"

"Yes," said Bobby. "(She is) —— big too. Can you ride her?"

"Not very well, but (I am) —— learning. Watch me!"

Andrew got on the horse. Clop, clop, clop, went Barby, round and round the yard. Andrew held on to her mane. "(Does not) —— she go fast?" he called to Bobby.

Andrew slid off Barby. He reached into his pocket and gave Bobby a piece of sugar. "Give Barby the sugar. (Do not) —— be afraid," he said. "(It is) —— all right."

Barby took the sugar. "(I am) —— not afraid of Barby now," said Bobby. "But (it is) —— time for me to go home. Will you let me ride Barby the next time I come?"

doesn't   that's   isn't   it's   I'm   she's   don't

Workbook

Pages 1, 2, and 3.

Related Language Experiences

Planning the unit activities

Discussion. Encourage the children to participate in making plans for the unit activities. Begin a pocket chart, as shown at the top of page 83, and encourage the children to add new group or individual activities as the unit is developed. When this unit is completed, the strips may be removed and new activities substituted.

Making a book about pets

Creative Writing. The children may suggest making a book about pets. Say, "What are some of the things we could put in a book about pets and playtime?" Lead the children to suggest riddles, original poems, songs, stories, pictures, dialogues, questions, puzzles, and descriptions.

Teaching *Finding New Neighbors*

Pets and Playtime

Things to Do

Find horse stories in the library.

Make up riddles.

Write stories about our pets.

Make a book.

Encourage individual children to write original stories about "Our Own Pets and Playtimes" (or a similar title). Let them suggest titles and select the most appropriate one. Have them write brief stories and draw pictures of their pets for illustrations, or write about and illustrate a play experience. Discuss what makes a good incident for a story, such as excitement, suspense, danger, fun, heroism, or a lesson learned. Each child may select his own best story for the class book.

Finding Information. Help the children consult the school encyclopedia or such references as *The First Book of Horses*, by Isabella McMeekin, to secure more information about horses, such as their food and care, colts and their training, and different breeds. Discuss this information with the children, drawing out what they know about horses, showing them the pictures in the books, and reading aloud or telling additional facts. Better readers may wish to report on additional information they have gathered from their own reading.

Finding out more about horses

Speech. Analyze each child's speech as soon as possible. Use the speech chart on page 32 of this manual as a guide to discover the needs of the individuals in the group. Listen

Discovering speech needs

carefully to each child and observe him as he speaks and reads. Help any children who have difficulties.

Enrichment Activities

Making a book about pets

Co-ordinating Activity. The children may already have decided to make a book of pets for the co-ordinating activity in this unit. Suggest that they keep all the material for the books together in a folder, so that later they may select their best stories to put in the book.

Using the bulletin board

Bulletin Board. Encourage the children to bring pictures of pets or vacation scenes and mount them on a classroom bulletin board. During the reading of the unit, late news about the children's pets or stories of pets from newspapers may be added to the display.

Let the children plan the arrangement of the bulletin board, which should be at the children's eye level and so placed that they themselves can post things upon it or change the display. A good movable, hanging bulletin board can be made from a large picture frame and heavy cardboard repainted attractively by the children.

Art and Construction. Either have the children model Barby and her colts in clay or show them how to construct a toy horse. For the skeleton, three rather loosely-rolled rolls of newspaper may be used. One roll will be bent to serve as the body and head, the other two rolls will be bent in half over the body and tied to it securely, as shown in the diagram

Making a toy horse

above. Have small groups of children who enjoy working together pad the animal into the desired shape with either papier mâché or alternating layers of newspaper strips and flour and water paste. The children may then paint it and make a mane and a tail of wool, and ears of felt. Later the horse could be nailed to a board with wheels, and, at the end of the unit, presented to the kindergarten as a pull-toy.

Stories in Other Readers. This section will consist of stories in other basic readers related in mood or subject matter to those in *Finding New Neighbors*. The readers mentioned are all on either the second- or third-grade level.

> *Friends and Fun,* by ARTHUR I. GATES and others
> "Billy and Blaze," pp. 68–80
>
> *Along the Way,* by GERTRUDE HILDRETH and others
> "The Fire in the Barn," pp. 101–116
>
> *Fun and Frolic,* by PAUL WITTY and BARBARA NOLEN
> Unit II, "They Wanted a Pet," pp. 44–98
>
> *The New More Friends and Neighbors,* by WILLIAM S. GRAY and others
> "Sleepy Sam," pp. 70–74

Secrets and Surprises, by PAUL WITTY and IRMENGARDE EBERLE
  "A Pet for the Roadside Stand," pp. 155–170
The New Friendly Village, by MABEL O'DONNELL
  "Friendly Village," pp. 6–44
Stories We Like, by GERALD YOAKAM and others
  "Little Star," pp. 165–174

Enjoying stories
and poems

Stories to Enjoy. The teacher should have on hand as many of the suggested books as possible. Good readers will be able to read a certain number of them independently and should be encouraged to do so. *Plug-Horse Derby*, by EMMA L. BROCK; *Blaze Finds the Trail*, by C. W. ANDERSON; *Kristie's Buttercup*, by EMMA L. BROCK; *Pony School* and *Sparkie and Puff Ball*, by PAUL BROWN; *World Full of Horses*, by DAHLOV IPCAR.

Poems to Enjoy. Children will enjoy hearing and learning these short poems.

RIDING HORSEBACK

When I rode horseback
behind Bud Brown
all the fence posts
jumped up and down!

AILEEN FISHER

COLTS[1]

A JAPANESE HOKKU
Arranged by Olive Beaupré Miller

Colts behind their mothers
Trot across the plain,
Rustling, zoro-zoro, like a lady's train.

Other poems the children will want to hear are "The Horse," by JAMES STEPHENS, in *200 Best Poems*, by MARJORIE BARROWS; "Little Horse," in *The Littlest House*, by ELIZABETH COATSWORTH; "Trot Along, Pony," from *Open the Door*, by MARION EDEY.

A Filmstrip to Enjoy. *Aubel and Leman* (CurriculumFlms), 25fr, color.

[1]From *Little Pictures of Japan*. Used by permission of the author, Olive Beaupré Miller, and the publishers, The Book House for Children, Lake Bluff, Illinois.

Pictures to Enjoy. "Red Horses," by Franz Marc; "Horse Fair," by Rosa Bonheur.

NOTE. Reproductions of some of the pictures mentioned in this manual appear in *Famous Paintings*, by Alice E. Chase, *Pictures to Grow Up With*, and *More Pictures to Grow Up With*, by Katharine Gibson. From time to time magazines carry colored reproductions, and the teacher will find it most helpful to build up a file of pictures on various subjects, not only for the bulletin board and background atmosphere for a story being read but also to awaken the children's interest in art forms, color, and design.

In Spring in Warm Weather Page 17

Developing Readiness for Listening

"Have you ever been on a farm in springtime? Many baby animals are born then. Can you tell us about some that you have seen? Have you ever seen how colts caper and prance around their mothers? Have you noticed how wobbly-kneed the colts are, and the calves too?" Point out during the discussion that on chilly days the animals look for a protected place where it is sheltered and warm.

Reading the Poem

"I'm going to read you a poem called 'In Spring in Warm Weather.' If you listen carefully, you will be able to see in your mind the young animals that you would find on a farm in springtime."

Read the poem to the group, and follow the reading with lively discussion. Ask: "What is the first thing animal babies know? What noises do some of them make?"

NOTE. The children's books should be closed while the poem is introduced and read by the teacher.

Rereading the Poem

Reread the poem as the children listen for words or expressions they particularly like or ones which make them visualize the baby animals.

Have the children open their books to page 17 and read along silently as they listen to the poem once more.

In some groups a child will now be ready to read the poem aloud while others listen. With less able groups encourage the children to read the poem together. Strive for natural, rhythmic expression, without sing-song.

NOTE. The teacher should read a poem to the children in its initial presentation. Give opportunity and encouragement for spontaneous comments by the group. If poems are presented interestingly, much memorization will be done voluntarily. Encourage, but do not force, memorization.

Related Activities

The children may enjoy discussing the baby animals mentioned in the poem: how soon after birth they are able to move about, how they are fed and kept clean, how they play. They may also be interested in collecting pictures of baby animals for their bulletin board.

Some children may wish to write poems about their pets. Do not require them to do so, but try to produce the relaxed, creative atmosphere necessary for free expression.

Copy some short poems on charts and hang them where the children can see them easily and memorize them if they wish. Some may be interested in starting an anthology of poems related to the unit themes in *Finding New Neighbors*. Continue reading poetry throughout the unit.

Poems to Enjoy. Read this poem to the children several times. They will want to chime in and say it themselves.

NEWNESS

This morning there is something
　That wasn't, yesterday.
A little calf is living
　All safely in the hay.

I offered her my cookie
　But she's not old enough
To know the use of cookies.
　She tried to eat my cuff!

MARCHETTE CHUTE

Other enjoyable poems follow: "The Pasture," by ROBERT
FROST, and "The New Baby Calf," by EDITH H. NEWLIN, in
Very Young Verses, by BARBARA GEISMER and ANTOINETTE
SUTER; "Familiar Friends," by JAMES TIPPETT, and "The
Wonderful Meadow," by OLIVE WADSWORTH, in *A Small
Child's Book of Verse*, by PELAGIE DOANE; "Tree on the
Hill," and "The Echoing Green," by WILLIAM BLAKE, in
1000 Poems for Children, compiled by ELIZABETH SECHRIST;
"Funniest," in *Up the Windy Hill*, by AILEEN FISHER.

A Film to Enjoy. *Seven Little Ducks* (Bailey), 1 reel,
b&w/color. Observation and care of a family of ducks.

Speckles and the New Boy

Pages
18-27

Jerry had trouble making friends at the new school until he took
his setting hen, Speckles, to hatch a dozen eggs in the classroom.
His knowledge of chickens earned the respect of his classmates who
no longer called him "the new boy."

Although the story will be read for pleasure, it will also stimulate
discussion of how a new child feels at school and of how the other
children might make him welcome. Children who have had no previous
experience with a setting hen will be interested in learning how the
chicks develop within the eggs, how they hatch, and are cared for.

Vocabulary

New Words: Page 18, *Speckles, setting, hatch**; 19, *cluck**,
nest*, *easy;* 20, ——; 21, *pen**, *straw**, *feed**; 22, *chicken,
weeks**; 23, ——; 24, ——; 25, ——; 26, *twelve;* 27, ——

Developing Readiness for Reading

Meaningful Presentation of Vocabulary. Say: "Did you
ever move to a new school where everyone was strange?
How did you feel? Perhaps it was not *easy* to make friends.

"Jerry, the boy in our story, has just started in a new school.
He wants to get better acquainted with the children so that

Discussing
related experiences

89

Speckles and the New Boy (18-27)

they will stop calling him 'the new boy.' Now Jerry also has an interesting pet. Turn to the table of contents and find the story 'Speckles and the New Boy.' From the picture on page 18 tell me what *Speckles* is. Speckles is a special kind of hen. She is a *setting hen*. Setting hens sit on their eggs to *hatch chickens*."

Using phonetic clues

The words *cluck, nest, pen, straw, feed, weeks, hatch,* may be written on the chalkboard and pronounced by application of phonetic skills: *cluck, nest, straw, weeks, hatch,* contain familiar phonograms; *pen* and *feed* may be compared with *hen* and *need*. The new word *twelve* will be taught during the guided reading.

Setting Up Reading Purposes. "What is the subtitle of this story?" ("Can Speckles Help?") "How do you suppose a hen could help a boy? Let's read the story to find out."

Reading the Story

Guided Reading

Page 18

Reading silently to answer questions

"Speckles is a setting hen. Read the first page of this story to find out what a setting hen is. What is Jerry going to do with Speckles? Read aloud what Jerry said to Speckles. Why was Jerry talking to Speckles?" After the oral reading, ask, "How do you think Jerry feels about Speckles?

Page 19

"Read the next page to find out how Jerry knew Speckles wanted to be set. Page 18 told us that Miss Baker needed a setting hen in school to hatch chickens. Read aloud the part that tells us Jerry's other reason for taking Speckles to school. Why was it easy to talk to Speckles?"

NOTE. Continue the practice of recording any words that cause difficulty and of helping children master them later. Make a habit of observing the children's reading habits, such as slow, laborious reading, pointing with the finger, or vocalizing during silent reading, and plan ways of helping the children improve.

After the reading, ask: "Did you find out how Jerry felt about Speckles? How did Jerry know that Speckles wanted to be set? How did he think that Speckles could help him at school?"

Pages 20–21

Discuss the pictures on these two pages. Let the children enjoy the scene of confusion when Speckles arrived at school.

Teaching *Finding New Neighbors*

90

Examine the picture of the pen, note its size and appearance, and discuss the nest, the straw and eggs in it. Ask: "Do you suppose the children will feed Speckles? Let's read these two pages to find how Speckles was settled at school." After the reading, discuss the humor of Speckles' introduction to the classroom and the provision of food, water, and straw for her.

Page 22

"Let's read this page to find out whether Speckles sat on the eggs." After the reading, ask: "Why didn't Speckles go to the nest immediately? How long would she have to sit on the eggs?" On a calendar, have a child show three weeks from the current date to see how long Speckles would have to wait.

Page 23

"What is the subtitle here? How do you suppose the children felt while they were watching and waiting? Speckles didn't always stay on her nest. Let's read to see why she left it." After the reading, discuss the hen's need for food, water, and exercise, and the danger to the eggs if she left them too long.

Pages 24–25

Examine the picture on page 25 with the children. Ask: "What do you suppose Jerry is listening for? Let's read these two pages to find out if the eggs really hatched." After the reading, ask: "Why did Speckles' feathers lose their shiny look? Which days of the week are week days? On which days of the week did Miss Baker and Jerry take care of Speckles? Why was Jerry happier at school now? How did Jerry know when the chicks were about to hatch?"

Pages 26–27

Discuss the pictures. Have the children count the chicks and present the word *twelve*. "Read these two pages to find out why Jerry looks so happy in the picture on page 27." After the reading, discuss the chicks, their soft down, and Speckles' care of them. Write *soft down* on the chalkboard and make certain that the children know what the words mean. Point out how gently Jerry handled the chicks. Then ask, "How did Speckles help Jerry make friends?"

Rereading for Specific Purposes

1. Have the children reread the story silently in preparation for interpretive oral reading. Plan with them how to read well to others, including such ideas as knowing all the words,

Reading orally for interpretation

91

Speckles and the New Boy (18–27)

reading as if they were talking, speaking clearly, and trying to make the audience enjoy the story.

During the oral reading, have all books closed except the one used by each child as he reads. Discuss standards for good oral reading and encourage the children themselves to set them down on a chart such as the following:

When We Read Aloud

We read a whole sentence.
We read clearly enough
for all to hear.
We make the story interesting
to our audience.

Plan for needed improvement but be sure to commend satisfactory performance.

NOTE. On a copy of the oral-reading checklist on page 193 record each child's oral-reading needs. Note his voice, facial expression, enunciation. Use this record in planning lessons for individual and group needs. Plan an individual conference with each child and help him to understand how to become a better oral reader.

Illustrating a favorite part of the story

2. Each child may select a favorite part of the story, reread it to refresh his memory, then *close his book* and draw or paint his own interpretation of the incident he has chosen.

Building Essential Habits and Skills

Comprehension and Study Skills

Discussing story subtitles

Main Idea. 1. To develop further the understanding of main ideas in story organization, call attention to the two subtitles and have the children recall the events under each. Encourage the children to think of other possible subtitles for the two parts of the story. If they need help, offer suggestions such as, "Speckles Comes to School" and "Hatching the Chicks."

2. To teach the meaning and recognition of paragraphs, have the children read both the title and the subtitle on page 18. Then say: "This page is divided into parts. Can you find the parts? How many do you see?" (Four.) Some children may know that these parts are called *paragraphs*. If they do not, tell them the word. Explain that a paragraph may have only one sentence, but that usually it is a group of sentences which belong together because they all tell about the same thing. Have the children turn to page 20. Ask, "How many paragraphs are there on this page?" Continue in the same manner with other pages in the story. Show the children how to recognize the paragraph indentions.

Learning about paragraphs

Story Details. To assist recall of important story details, make riddles about the characters in the story and duplicate them for independent work. For example:

Answering riddles about story characters

Riddles

Write the answer to each riddle on the line.

1. I work at the school.
   I asked the children for a setting hen.
   Who am I?   Miss Baker

2. I have soft yellow down.
   I crawl under my mother to keep warm.
   Who am I?   a chick

3. I am a boy.
   Bob and I helped pull Speckles home.
   Who am I?   Tony

4. I am black and white.
   I had a ride in a wagon.
   Who am I?   Speckles

Children who are able to write independently may make their own riddles to ask the class.

Sequence of Ideas. To aid children in independent recall of correct order of story events, distribute copies of the following exercise:

The Lost Chicken

One morning Peggy went to the barn to feed her chickens. Speckles ran over to her with a loud "cluck-cluck." The rooster and the white hen were there too, picking up the corn as fast as they could. But where was Frisky, the red hen?

Peggy looked in all the corners of the chicken house. At last she heard a gentle clucking sound. Way back, beside a pile of straw, the lost chicken sat on a nest.

"Here, chick, chick, chick," called Peggy. Frisky came to her and ate the corn. Peggy looked into the nest. She saw twelve brown eggs. Very soon Frisky went back to sit on the eggs.

"That's right, Frisky," said Peggy. "If you keep on setting, we'll soon have some baby chicks."

Read these sentences. Put 1 before the sentence that happened first, 2 before the one that happened next, etc.

　3　Frisky came to eat.

　2　Peggy couldn't find Frisky.

　1　Peggy went to the barn to feed the chickens.

　4　Peggy was glad that she would soon have some baby chicks.

Word-Study Skills

Word Meaning. To remind the children that some words have more than one meaning, write on the chalkboard the following phrases:

a _setting_ hen	_fly_ out the window
trip over the box	ate the chicken _feed_
a _pen_ for Speckles	chick's soft _down_

Ask the children to explain the meaning of the underlined word in each phrase, and to recall a different meaning of the same word.

Word Recognition. Continue to present on the chalkboard, after the guided reading and again, if necessary, any words which children found difficult as they read the story silently. To aid recognition, have them recall familiar phonetic or structural clues (such as rhyming words, consonant blends, vowel sounds, phonograms). Review these words from time to time, emphasizing meaning as well as word recognition.

Mastering difficult words

Phonetic Analysis. To maintain recognition of the consonant blends, *sp, spr, str*, write on the chalkboard *Speckles, spend*. Ask the children to pronounce the words, listening to the initial sounds. Then write the known words *sprinkler, spring*. Ask the children to pronounce these words and to underline the first three letters of each one. Have them tell how these words are alike and how they are different from *Speckles* and *spend*. Let the children both see and listen to the similarities between these two consonant blends. Explain that *sp* is a two-letter blend, that *spr* is a three-letter blend, and that we must look carefully at new words to make sure each sound is recognized and pronounced. Have them read other words which begin with these blends, as follows:

Recalling initial consonant blends "sp," "spr," "str," "tw"

> *Eat ice cream with a spoon.*
> *They watched Speckles spread her feathers.*

Write on the chalkboard the known words *straw, strange, street*. Have the children pronounce them, listening to the initial letter sounds. Ask them to give other words which begin with this blend. Better readers will be able to attack other words, such as *spraying, sparks, spread,* and *strike.*

To present the consonant blend *tw*, write on the chalkboard the known words *twelve, twins*. Call attention to the beginning sounds as the children pronounce them. Have the children suggest other words, such as *twice, twig, twenty,* and *twist,* which begin with these sounds.

Structural Analysis. To provide extra practice for children who have not mastered compound words, write on the chalkboard words such as *outside, henhouse, schoolroom, sunshine, afternoon, birthday,* and ask the children to divide them, tell the meaning of each word, and what two small words they can find in each one.

Pages 4 and 5.

Related Language Experiences

Learning about chickens

Presenting Additional Information. If the books are available, read the children *Egg to Chick*, by Millicent Selsam, *The Wonderful Egg*, by Warren G. Schloat, Jr., or *Chickens and How to Raise Them*, by Louis Darling.

Learning to welcome newcomers

Discussion. Initiate an exchange of ideas by asking, "If you were Jerry and had just started to attend a new school, what would you like the boys and girls to do to make you welcome?" List the children's suggestions on the chalkboard. Follow up this discussion by having the children carry out some of the suggestions when a new child enrolls in the class.

Writing original stories

Creative Writing. Allow time for the children to continue their original stories about pets. As stories are completed, plan a time to share them with the group. Comment favorably on good incidents for stories.

Listening to a poem

Listening. The poem "Red Hen" has a charm and realism which will appeal to the children. Read the poem aloud and encourage the children to express their feelings about it freely. Some children will wish to illustrate it, and superior readers may be interested in collecting, copying, and presenting other farm poems in available poetry anthologies.

RED HEN

She turned her head to this side,
  She turned her head to that,
Looking round for tidbits,
  Juicy ones and fat.

Scritchy-scratch went Red Hen's feet,
  Nib-nab went her bill.
She ate of juicy tidbits
  Until she ate her fill.

And then she flew into a nest
  And laid an egg, and then,
With a cut-cut-cut, ca-dah-cut,
  Flew off to eat again.

JAMES S. TIPPETT

Teaching *Finding New Neighbors*

Enrichment Activities

Bulletin Board. Encourage the children to collect pictures of chickens to add to their bulletin board about pets. Help them to arrange the pictures in an attractive way and to label the display. Collecting pictures

An Excursion. If possible, visit a hatchery or a home in the neighborhood where chickens are raised. Children will be interested in chickens and their care. Visiting a hatchery

Stories in Other Readers. The children will want to read these interesting stories about chickens. Reading in other books

Down Our Way, by GUY L. BOND and others
"Books and Pets," pp. 167–204

Friends and Fun, by ARTHUR I. GATES and others
"How the Hen Got Her Speckles," pp. 206–224

The New Friends and Neighbors, by WILLIAM S. GRAY and others
"Pet Can Do It Better," pp. 87–91

The New Streets and Roads, by WILLIAM S. GRAY and others
"Finding a Friend," pp. 86–92

Open Roads, by ULLIN W. LEAVELL and MARY L. FRIEBELE
"Susan's Chickens," pp. 18–25

Informational Books. *Fine Eggs and Fancy Chickens*, by MICKEY KLAR MARKS; *Animal Families*, by TRUDA WEIL.

Poems to Enjoy. "The Hens," from *Under the Tree*, by ELIZABETH M. ROBERTS; "The Chickens," Anonymous, and "The Call," by BJÖRNSTERNE BJÖRNSON in *Ring-A-Round*, compiled by MILDRED P. HARRINGTON; "Chicken," by WALTER DE LA MARE in *Time for Poetry*, by MAY HILL ARBUTHNOT. Enjoying literature and music

Music to Enjoy. "The Barnyard," "Dive, Ducks, Dive," "Go Tell Aunt Nancy," "My Black Hen," "Ku-Ku-Ri-Ku," "Little Baby Duckies," all in *Singing On Our Way*, by LILLA BELLE PITTS and others.

Film to Enjoy. *Let's Visit a Poultry Farm* (Coronet), 1 reel, sd, b&w/color. Enjoying a film, filmstrips, and a record

Filmstrips to Enjoy. *Gathering Eggs* (No. 2) and *Feeding the Animals* (No. 3) in LIFE ON THE FARM series (EBF), ea 45fr, color. *Chickens on the Farm*, in THE FARMER'S ANIMAL FRIENDS series (JamHandy), 24fr, color.

A Record to Enjoy. *Little Red Hen* (Decca).

Cowboys Are Brave

After playing cowboys all day and trying to catch an imaginary horse thief, the four children were permitted to sleep in the barn in order to catch the thief if he came again. The three older children were sure that Susan, the youngest, would be afraid to sleep in the barn, but as it turned out, Susan was the bravest of all.

Children will enjoy reading about everyday play activities, and will enjoy the humor of the night in the barn. The story lends itself to a discussion of the actual work of cowboys contrasted with the children's ideas expressed in their play.

Vocabulary

New Words: Page 28, *thief, Teddy*;* 29, *Jane*;* 30, *coyotes, blankets;* 31, *woke*;* 32, ——; 33, *scared*;* 34, *howl, alone*;* 35, ——

Developing Readiness for Reading

Talking about related concepts

Meaningful Presentation of Vocabulary. Introduce the theme of this story by asking, "Do you like to play cowboys?" Lead the children to discuss the qualities of a cowboy. Bring out that he must be honest, hardworking, and brave; that he must be especially brave when he is out *alone* guarding his cattle and horses against men who might try to steal them.

"What would you call a man who tried to steal a horse?" Write *horse thief* on the chalkboard.

"Do you know what a *coyote* is?" If the children are unfamiliar with coyotes, show them pictures and explain that a coyote is a kind of small wolf that lives on the prairie. "What kind of noise do coyotes make?" Point out that they yelp like dogs and *howl*, making long, loud cries at night which the cowboys can hear. Have the word *coyote* (kī′ōt) read and pronounced several times. Then ask: "Would you be *scared* if you *woke* up at night and heard a coyote howl? Would you cover your head with the *blankets?*"

Checking the presentation

For slower readers it may be wise to review the new words on the chalkboard, with directions such as the following: "Find the word that means 'someone who takes what isn't ·

his'; 'an animal that lives on the plains'; 'the noise a dog makes.' Find the words with long *o*, one meaning 'all by one-self,' the other meaning 'no longer asleep'; two words beginning with blends, one meaning 'covers,' one 'afraid.' "

Setting Up Reading Purposes. "In our story, 'Cowboys Are Brave,' we shall read about some children who played they were cowboys. Let's find out if they were brave. Find the story in the table of contents and turn to it quickly."

Reading the Story

Guided Reading

Encourage a spontaneous discussion of the double-page picture. Explain that the larger girl in this picture is named *Jane*. The little girl is *Susan*. *Peter* is the larger boy and *Teddy* is the smaller. Write the names of the children on the chalkboard and ask individuals to pronounce them.

Pages 28–29
Reading silently to answer questions

"Read pages 28 and 29 to find out what Peter wanted to do that night." After the reading, say: "Let's read aloud what the children shouted as they played cowboy. Make us know how excited they were." Allow two or three pupils to read this conversation. "Now, let's read aloud what they said as they made plans for the night. How will they talk now?

"Look at the picture on page 31. The children have brought their blankets to the barn. What else did the children bring with them?" (The two dogs.) "Why do you suppose they did that? Read these two pages to find out who woke up first." After the reading, ask: "Why didn't they want Susan to go? What kind of cowboy do you think Teddy was? What scared him?

Pages 30–31

"How does Jane look in this picture? Jane looks scared, doesn't she? Read the two pages to find out what happened to Jane and Peter." After the reading, ask: "What did Jane and Peter do? Would you be scared if you were Jane? If you were Peter?

Pages 32–33

"I wonder who will be the bravest cowboy of all. Finish the story and you will know." After the reading, ask, "How did Susan prove that sometimes make-believe cowboys are really brave?"

Pages 34–35

Rereading for Specific Purposes

Reading specific parts to prove statements

Have the children find and read aloud parts which prove the statements below. The statements may either be written on the chalkboard or read aloud by the teacher.

1. The children were noisy. (p. 28)
2. Teddy was not as brave as he thought he was. (p. 31)
3. Jane was afraid. (p. 32)
4. Susan wanted to do what the others did. (p. 30)
5. Teddy was afraid. (p. 31)
6. Peter was afraid. (p. 33)
7. Susan was afraid she would be scared. (pp. 34–35)
8. Susan knew that she had been brave. (p. 35)
9. Mother came to find Susan. (p. 35)

Building Essential Habits and Skills

Comprehension and Study Skills

Drawing conclusions

Critical Reading. To give practice in drawing conclusions from story ideas, distribute copies of the exercise below. Direct the children to underline the correct ending for each sentence.

1. The children made noise
   when they went to sleep.
   when they shouted "Bang! Bang!"
   when they wanted to be brave.

2. Peter ran home
   because he heard a coyote.
   because he liked the rain.
   because a door went bang, bang.

3. Cowboys are brave
   when they play.
   when they catch a thief.
   when they go for a ride.

4. Susan was brave
   because she was a real cowboy.
   because Mother was there.
   because she stayed alone in the barn.

5. A horse thief is bad
   when he eats dinner.
   when he takes horses.
   when he gets a coyote.

Story Details. To check the children's ability to recall story characters through their conversation, distribute copies of the exercise below.

NOTE. Most of the independent exercise sheets in this manual include directions to the children. Until the children become accustomed to these, the teacher should read the instructions aloud with the children to make certain that they understand such directional terms as *answers, question, sentence, phrase, paragraph, underline, person, space, blank, number,* and so on.

Who Said It?

Read each sentence. In the space write the name of the person in the story who probably said or thought that sentence.

1. "Do you know what we must do tonight?"   Peter
2. "Susan, you had better not sleep in the barn, because you are too little."   Peter
3. "I will not be afraid. I want to sleep in the barn, too."   Susan
4. "Oh, all right. But if you are afraid, you cannot be a cowboy. Cowboys have to be brave."   Peter
5. "Whoo-hoo-hoo!" he heard. "Maybe it's a coyote."   Teddy
6. "Maybe that noise is a mouse. It might be a coyote. I don't like it."   Jane
7. "I am glad to take off my wet clothes. I like my good dry bed."   Peter
8. "Teddy, is that a coyote? Teddy! Peter! Jane!"   Susan
9. "Good morning, Susan. Were you afraid?"   Mother
10. "No, I'm a cowboy. Cowboys are brave."   Susan

Mother   Teddy   Jane   Peter   Susan

Word-Study Skills

Word Meaning. To give practice in recognizing words with opposite meanings, distribute copies of the exercise on page 102. Direct the children to draw a line from each word in the first column to the word in the second column that has the opposite meaning.

Cowboys Are Brave (28–35)

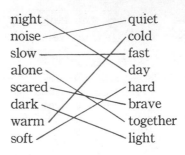

night — quiet
noise — cold
slow — fast
alone — day
scared — hard
dark — brave
warm — together
soft — light

For further practice, have the children find other words which have opposite meanings.

Phonetic Analysis. 1. To check what the children have learned about vowels, write on the chalkboard the letters of the alphabet in natural sequence and have the children read them aloud. Call for volunteers to name the letters called *vowels* and to circle each one. Recall some of the information about vowels learned in Grade Two: that (*a*) the vowels are *a, e, i, o, u,* and sometimes *y,* (*b*) no word can be made without a vowel, and (*c*) vowels have short and long sounds.

Reviewing the names of vowels

2. To test the children's ability to discriminate between short and long sounds of vowels, present a mixed list of familiar words and ask children to pronounce each word softly to themselves, to identify the vowels in each word, and to be ready to tell whether each vowel is short or long. The following list of words may be used: *colt, silk, feel, nest, use, hatch, cluck, pond, strange, wide.*

To review long and short vowel sounds, distribute copies of the exercise on page 103.

Reviewing short and long vowels in words

3. To recall the two sounds of *y* when it is a vowel, write the word *fly*. Ask, "Has the *y* a short or a long sound?" Write *funny*. Ask: "What sound has *y* in this word? Has the word one vowel or two?" Present for contrast and review the words *cry, dry, fly, my, by*. Let the children observe that in words where *y* is the only vowel it has the sound of long *i*.

Reviewing the sounds of "y"

Write on the chalkboard *Betty, bunny, cherry, city, every, lazy, shiny, bushy, hungry,* and lead the children to observe that the vowel *y* has its short sound at the end of these words. Tell them that at the end of words having more than one vowel, *y* usually has its short sound.

Read the list of words below. Say each word to yourself. Then follow the directions at the bottom of the page. Be sure that you make the right marks. Do one thing all the way through. Then begin on the next thing to do.

__hop	__sat	__get	__pan	__fell
__sail	__wake	__hat	__face	__high
__jump	__wife	__egg	__run	__feed
__use	__cup	__chick	__strange	__nose
__while	__colt	__name	__pond	__silk
__nest	__rope	__wide	__hatch	__weeks

1. Put a red **X** beside the words that have a short *a*.
2. Draw a red line under the words that have long *a*.
3. Put a green **X** beside the words that have short *o*.
4. Draw a green line under words that have long *o*.
5. Put a black **X** beside the words that have short *e*.
6. Draw a black line under words that have long *e*.
7. Put a yellow **X** next to the words that have short *i*.
8. Draw a yellow line under the words that have long *i*.
9. Write the words that have short *u* here.

_____

10. Write the word with long *u* here. _____

Structural Analysis. To show that the change of tense in words ending in *y* causes a structural change also, have on the chalkboard the following two sentences:

> Let us <u>hurry</u> outside now.
> The others <u>hurried</u> out to play long ago.

Ask the children to read the sentences aloud, to notice the underlined words, and to tell what the difference is between them. Then write on the chalkboard:

> Does your mother let you <u>dry</u> the dishes?
> Ted <u>dried</u> them yesterday.

Lead the children to understand that the form of *hurry* and *dry* was changed because the second sentence in each case told about something that happened before, or sometime ago. Write on the chalkboard the words *carry, carried, empty, emptied,* and *cry, cried,* and have the children supply sentences

103

that illustrate both the present and the past tense of each word. If the children need more practice in identifying the past tense of the words, give them more pairs of sentences, using the above known words.

Workbook

Pages 6 and 7.

Related Language Experiences

Talking together

Conversation and Research. Encourage the children to talk about cowboys and their activities, riding on the wide plains, tending horses and cattle, rounding up the herds, chasing horse thieves. Bring out the neighborly help which cowboys give one another. Some of the children may contribute their own experiences on a ranch or with cowboys, and bring snapshot pictures of them. Others may tell about playing cowboy.

Discussing pictures

Books and pictures of cowboys and cowboy activities should abound in the classroom and should be used as subjects for discussion and for reference to add to the children's own knowledge of television cowboys. Supply informational books such as *The Cowboy Encyclopedia*, by Bruce Grant. Lead the children to draw the conclusion that cowboys work hard in all kinds of weather.

Dramatizing the story

Dramatization. Allow the children to dramatize the story "Cowboys Are Brave." After a complete oral reading of the story they should plan and outline the dramatization, make simple costumes, play the story in short scenes with different casts, select actors for the final performance, and decide where and with what properties to act the scenes.

Enrichment Activities

Making a book

Co-ordinating Activity. Suggest that the children write and illustrate their stories of playing cowboy, their experiences with real cowboys, or an entirely imaginary experience with cowboys. Let them choose some of these stories to be added to the class book.

Having an exhibit

Bulletin Board. Plan with the children how best to display the cowboy pictures, their own painted pictures, and original drawings, and select the proper titles for them, as "Bucking

Horses," "Cowboy Snapshots," "How We Played Cowboy," "Cowgirl Pictures," etc.

A Story in Another Reader. Have the children read this easy story.

The New Friendly Village, by MABEL O'DONNELL
   "The Great Plains," pp. 122–148

Stories to Enjoy. *Big Book of Cowboys,* by SYDNEY FLETCHER; *The First Book of Cowboys,* by BENJAMIN BREWSTER; *Cowboy Sam and Freddy* and *Cowboy Sam and the Fair,* by EDNA WALKER CHANDLER; *Cowboy Small,* by LOIS LENSKI; *The True Book of Cowboys,* by TERI MARTINI.

Enjoying stories and poems

Poems to Enjoy. "The Haymow," by LUELLA MOCKETT, in *Bridled with Rainbows,* compiled by SARA and JOHN E. BREWTON; "The Wagon in the Barn," by JOHN DRINK-WATER, in *A Small Child's Book of Verse,* by PELAGIE DOANE, and in *The First Book of Poetry,* by ISABEL J. PETERSON.

Maggie the Magpie

Pages
36–41

Maggie was a pet magpie who had learned to talk. She had the run of the Woods' house and garden and was frequently caught collecting bright shiny objects which took her eye. When, on a hot summer day, Maggie collected the ice cubes from the lemonade glasses and hid them under a tree, the joke was on her.

Children will enjoy the humor of the story, as well as learn about an interesting pet with which they may not be familiar. They will like to hear other stories of Maggie's exploits from the book *Maggie: A Mischievous Magpie,* by Irma Simonton Black.

Vocabulary

New Words: Page 36, *Maggie, magpie;* 37, *smart, shoulder, hello*;* 38, *glasses*, cubes;* 39, *lemonade;* 40, ——; 41, ——

Developing Readiness for Reading

Meaningful Presentation of Vocabulary. Show the pictures on pages 36 and 37. Let the children discuss them

Talking about the pictures

spontaneously. "Have you ever seen a bird like this? It is called a *magpie*." If the children are unfamiliar with magpies, explain to them that a magpie is a little larger than a blue jay, and the only large black-and-white land bird with a long wedge-shaped tail in this country. Discuss other birds who talk.

"The magpie in our story is a pet and she is named *Maggie*. What can you tell about Maggie from the pictures? Do you think she is a *smart* bird?" Call attention to the trick she is playing and to the shiny bell in her cage. "Maggie did not stay in her cage all the time. Sometimes she rode on Mr. Wood's *shoulder*, and said '*hello*' to him."

Checking the presentation After the words have been presented and written on the chalkboard, ask the children to point out a name and say it (*Maggie*). Have them find a part of the body (*shoulder*); a kind of bird (*magpie*); a greeting (*hello*).

Setting Up Reading Purposes. "Maggie played many tricks. On one hot day Mrs. Wood was preparing some tall *glasses* with *ice cubes* and *lemonade*. Find the story in the table of contents and we'll read about a joke on Maggie."

Reading the Story

Guided Reading

Pages 36–37

Reading silently to answer questions

"Read pages 36 and 37 to find out what Maggie could do. Could she talk?" Give assistance with words if individual children need it. After the reading, ask: "Can you tell how Maggie looked? Read that part to us. What did she like to do?" (Play with shiny bells.) "Read aloud the sentences that tell what Maggie could do. What could Maggie say?" (Hello.)

Pages 38–39

Encourage further discussion of the pictures. "Let's read these pages to find out what Maggie will do with the ice cube she has in her beak. Mrs. Wood planned to pour lemonade in the glasses." After the reading, ask: "What did Betty and Timothy think of Maggie? Why do you think Mrs. Wood served cakes and lemonade? What trick did Maggie play with the cakes? with the ice cubes?

Pages 40–41

"Finish the story to find out what Maggie did next." After the reading, ask: "Why did Maggie play with the ice cubes?

How did Maggie get the ice cubes out of the glasses? What do you think will happen to the ice cubes?"

Rereading for Specific Purposes

Preparing to read the story aloud to another group

To prepare for interpretive oral reading, have the children reread the story silently. Plan with them how they will speak like Maggie and how they will bring out the humor in the story. Recall the standards for good oral reading.

Arrange for the group to read the story aloud to the entire class or to a younger class in the school. Point out that the listeners will not know the story, and that this will demand especially good performance by the readers.

Building Essential Habits and Skills

Comprehension and Study Skills

Story Details. To develop ability to recall story details, duplicate and distribute copies of the exercise below. Direct the children to write in each blank the name which makes the sentence true.

Associating story characters with story events

Maggie   Mrs. Wood   Mr. Wood   Betty   Timothy

1. _Mr. Wood_ and _Mrs. Wood_ had a pet magpie.
2. _Maggie_ could talk somewhat like Mrs. Wood.
3. _Betty_ and _Timothy_ were great friends of Maggie.
4. _Mr. Wood_ let Betty and Timothy help him in the garden.
5. _Mr. Wood_ carried Maggie on his shoulder in the garden.
6. _Mrs. Wood_ made lemonade and cakes.
7. _Maggie_ made a pile of ice cubes under a tree.
8. _Timothy_ said, "Maggie has something for us to see."
9. _Mrs. Wood_ told Maggie to go back to her cage.
10. _Mr. Wood_ wanted to watch Maggie as the ice cubes grew smaller.

Accurate Recall. To give practice in comprehending and recalling pertinent story facts, distribute to the children copies of the exercise at the top of the next page.

Recalling story details exactly

Read all these sentences.
Put **X** before the sentences that are true.

__X__1. Maggie was a pet magpie.

_____2. She was Betty's and Timothy's bird.

_____3. Maggie was a very small bird.

__X__4. Maggie was bigger than a robin.

__X__5. Her feathers were shiny black and snowy white.

__X__6. The sunlight made her feathers look green and blue and purple.

__X__7. Maggie had a long, beautiful tail.

_____8. She ate at the table with Mr. and Mrs. Wood.

_____9. She helped Mr. Wood in the garden.

__X__10. Maggie liked to play with bright shiny things.

__X__11. She could say, "Come here, come here. Hello! Hello!"

__X__12. She bobbed her head when she talked.

_____13. She carried cakes and lemonade to the garden.

__X__14. Every night she went to her cage to sleep.

__X__15. She made a pile of ice cubes under a tree.

Word-Study Skills

Selecting
descriptive words

Word Meaning. To foster the ability to use descriptive words, write on the chalkboard the list of words below. Explain that some of these words could be used to tell what kind of bird Maggie was. Let the children discuss the words, choose those that correctly describe Maggie, and give their reasons. Allow for differences of opinion on some of the words. After the exercise has been completed, have the children suggest other words which might describe Maggie.

smart	beautiful	brave	hungry	black	lazy
busy	different	noisy	scared	purple	kind
friendly	surprised	frisky	shiny	white	happy

Recalling the
principle of
vowel lengthened
by final "e"

Phonetic Analysis. 1. To recall and strengthen understanding of the phonetic principle that in a word containing two vowels, one of which is *e* at the end of the word, the first vowel is long, the *e* silent, proceed as follows:

Present the following word pairs, alike except for final *e*, and lead the children to observe their similarities and differences in form and meaning: *us, use; at, ate; not, note; tap, tape; cub, cube.* Ask, "What happens when I add *e* to these words?" Write *cub*; then write *cube.* (Do not add *e* to *cub,* as it is important that the children see both words for contrast.) "What is the difference between a *cub* and a *cube*? How many vowels do you see and how many do you hear in *cub*? How many in *cube*? Does the last vowel make any sound?" Lead the children to observe the principle stated at the beginning of this exercise.

2. To provide practice in using the correct word, distribute the exercise below. Ask, "How does thinking of the meaning of a word in the sentence help you to decide which word to use in these sentences?" If necessary, do the first two or three sentences orally with the children.

Applying the principle of the medial vowel lengthened by final "e"

SHORT OR LONG

Underline the word that gives the right meaning to each of the sentences.

1. Mary likes to $\frac{cut}{cute}$ pictures out of her coloring book.

2. She will $\frac{past}{\underline{paste}}$ them in a large book.

3. Maggie $\frac{\underline{hid}}{hide}$ the ice cubes under a tree.

4. He had a $\frac{\underline{hat}}{hate}$ on his head.

5. Andrew $\frac{rod}{\underline{rode}}$ the horse.

6. The children $\frac{mad}{\underline{made}}$ a pen for their pet.

7. Barby stood so high that the twins had to $\frac{slid}{\underline{slide}}$ down.

8. Mother put $\frac{tap}{\underline{tape}}$ around the box.

---

3. To show that the rule of final *e* applies to many words other than those which can be derived from short-vowel equivalents, list the following words from the vocabulary of the text: *side, cake, home, late, brave, wide, woke, Jane, strange, like, cage, face, fine, lake, nose, prize, rope.*

Have the children pronounce each word and tell how many vowels they see in it. Lead them to observe in each case that the first vowel is long and the *e* at the end is silent. Ask them how they know the vowel is long in these words. Call for a restatement of the principle that *in a word containing two vowels, one of which is* e *at the end of the word, the first vowel is long, the* e *silent.*

Workbook

Pages 8, 9, and 10.

Related Language Experiences

Conversation. Encourage the children to talk about other kinds of pet birds which they have owned or observed, such as canaries, parrots, parakeets. Discuss their appearance, habits, and the care they require.

Writing. Suggest that the children write and illustrate original stories about pet birds or about tricks that any pet has performed.

Speech Improvement. Observe the children's oral reading of the story, noting poor enunciation of final *d* or *t* sounds. If practice is needed, write the words from the story on the chalkboard and have the children take turns enunciating them.

bird	*pleased*	*pet*	*most*
touched	*carried*	*white*	*about*
looked	*lemonade*	*sunlight*	*basket*
sound	*joined*	*bright*	*front*
learned	*happened*	*smart*	*out*

Enrichment Activities

Co-ordinating Activity. Some of the children's original stories about pet birds or tricks performed by pets may be illustrated and selected by the group to add to the class book.

Teaching *Finding New Neighbors*

Bulletin Board. Let the children continue to choose stories and pictures for their bulletin board, arrange the displays, and change them often. Encourage them to title each display. Making displays

Library. A library committee might be responsible for helping to find and display books that are pertinent to the unit. In their spare time the children may help the teacher locate information and mark stories which they enjoyed and would recommend to others. Finding good books

For more detailed suggestions about a room library, see page 208 of this manual.

Chart of Favorite Stories. Make a simple chart with the title "Our Favorite Stories about Pets." List on the chart the children's favorite stories chosen from the reader, those read by the teacher, those read independently by the children, or those original stories written by the children. Include the name of the author of each story and a small sketch of the pet. Making a chart

Stories in Other Readers. Some children will be interested in reading stories about other clever birds. Reading stories

The New Friends and Neighbors, by WILLIAM S. GRAY and others
  "Black Tim," pp. 98–102
The Story Road, by GERTRUDE HILDRETH and others
  "Miss Crow's Shiny Stone," pp. 149–158

Stories to Enjoy. More about Maggie in *Maggie: A Mischievous Magpie*, by IRMA SIMONTON BLACK; *Parrakeets*, by HERBERT S. ZIM.

A Film to Enjoy. *Polly, the Parrot* (Coronet), 1 reel, b&w/color. Children will learn about the habits of parrots. Enjoying a film and filmstrip

A Filmstrip to Enjoy. *Peggy's Parakeet* (EBF), 46fr, color, in PET STORIES series.

The Animal Store

Pages 42–43

Developing Readiness for Listening

"If you were allowed to have a new pet, what kind would you choose?" Encourage the children to talk freely about their choices, and ask them to give reasons.

"Where would you get your pet?" The children will probably volunteer several sources, such as a friend, an animal
shelter or pound, a pet store.

Display the pictures on pages 42 and 43, pointing out "the
hound with the drooping ears," the "Cocker" and the "Cairn."
Let the children point out other animals that interest them.

Reading the Poem

"Suppose you had as much as a hundred dollars to spend
at an animal store. This poem tells what you might wish to
buy. Close your books and listen as I read it to see if you
agree with the author."

Read the poem aloud, and after the reading prompt the
children to relate their own experiences in a pet store. Ask:
"Do you think the author of this poem owned a pet? Why or
why not?" Encourage a lively discussion.

Rereading the Poem

Have the children open their books to the poem and discuss the pictures again if they wish. Reread the poem as
they listen for words or expressions that they particularly like.
Invite one or two pupils to read the poem while the others
listen with books closed. Finally, have all the children read
the poem together.

Related Activities

Pictures to Enjoy. *Playtime:* "The House of Cards," by
Jean Chardin; "The Bubble Blower," by Edouard Manet;
"The Calmady Children," by Sir Thomas Lawrence.

Pets and Animals: "The Blue Horse," by Franz Marc;
"The Hare," by Albrecht Dürer.

Children and Pets: "Daughter of Roberto Strozzi," by
Titian; "Boy with Rabbit," by Sir Henry Raeburn; "Don
Manuel Osorio," by Francisco Goya.

If children are interested in breeds of dogs, show them the
pictures in *What Dog Is It?* by Anna Pistorius.

Other Poems to Enjoy. "People Buy a Lot of Things," by
ANNETTE WYNNE, and "Shop Windows," by ROSE FYLE-

MAN, in *Under the Tent of the Sky*, compiled by JOHN E. BREWTON.

The children will appreciate the sentiments expressed in the following poem:

A DOG

If you DIDN'T have a dog
('cause everyone should)
and you knew they were fun
then, of course, you would.

If you couldn't have a Dane
('cause your house is small)
there are little, LITTLE dogs
with a wag and all.

I have a dog . . .
and he's black as night.
But you can have one,
if you want, that's WHITE.

Or you can have one
that is brown as wood:
but you OUGHT to have a dog
('cause everyone should).

AILEEN FISHER

A Dog of His Own

Pages 44–54

When Ben, a city boy, moved to the country, he was frightened at night by the dark, the quiet, and the howl of a coyote. His fear was increased the day that he observed the coyote watching him as he took the long, lonely walk to school. Ben's father promised to get a big dog to protect the chickens from coyotes. But the big dog turned out to be an appealing puppy given by a neighbor.

Ben was torn between his love for the puppy and his need for the protection which a big dog would afford. When he was aroused to protect the puppy from the coyote himself, he overcame his fear and gained a new appreciation of his own worth.

Children will readily identify themselves with the boy in the story and may profit from talking about some things that have frightened them and how they conquered their fears.

113

Vocabulary

New Words: Page 44, *eyes;* 45, *Dad*, remember, caught;* 46, *meadow, toward;* 47, *whistled, against, leg*;* 48, ——; 49, ——; 50, *fingers, bites*;* 51, *decided;* 52, *chewed*;* 53, ——; 54, ——

Developing Readiness for Reading

Talking about story concepts

Meaningful Presentation of Vocabulary. "Ben, the boy in our next story, had lived in a city all his life. Then his family moved to a farm. He found many things different in the country. What would he have to get used to in his new home?"

Lead the group to discuss such ideas as having no close neighbors in the country, enjoying fields and hills and *meadows*, walking a long distance through woods *toward* school. Explain that to a city boy it would seem very dark and quiet at night when the wind *whistled* and the tapping of the branches *against* the windows sounded like real *fingers*. Speak also of the domestic animals on the farm and wild animals the boys *caught* in the woods. In summary, say, "Yes, Ben kept his *eyes* open to see all the new things, but he could *remember* too the bright lights and the noise of the city. He may even have *decided* that he liked the city better than the country."

Better readers will recognize the new words *Dad, leg, bites,* and *chewed* through phonetic and context clues during the guided reading. Slower readers may need help in attacking them. One way of doing this would be to present them orally and write them on the chalkboard, pointing out the vowel sounds in *Dad, leg,* and *bites,* and the analogy between *chew* and *grew*.

Checking the vocabulary presentation through word meaning

To check the vocabulary presentation and to develop word meaning with a slower reading group write, or give orally, phrases or words which mean the same as the new words. The children should match the meaning with the new word, and use the new word in a sentence. The following are only examples: things with which to see (*eyes*), to recall (*remember*), trapped (*caught*), part of a hand (*fingers*), made up one's mind (*decided*), grassy place (*meadow*), Father (*Dad*), made a musical sound (*whistled*), etc.

Teaching *Finding New Neighbors*

114

Setting Up Reading Purposes. "In the table of contents find the story 'A Dog of His Own' and turn to it quickly. What does the title tell us? Does Ben already have a dog? What is the subtitle? How could a coyote have anything to do with Ben's getting a dog? Let's read the story to find out."

Guided Reading

"Ben's father made a suggestion as to how he might get a dog. You can find out what it was by reading these two pages." After the reading, ask: "Why was Ben frightened? Find the part of the story that tells." Ask a child to read the paragraphs aloud, emphasizing the quiet of the night and the coyote's howl.

Pages 44–45

Reading silently to answer questions

"We can learn several things about coyotes on page 45. Will you read the second, third, and fourth paragraphs again to see how many facts you can find." List on the chalkboard the details as the children suggest them. Include some of the new words, such as *caught* and *remember*, in the phrases or sentences which you write.

"Why do you think Ben wanted 'the biggest kind of dog there is'? Ben started to school the next day. In the picture you see that he had to go toward some woods. Read that page to see where else he had to go." After the silent reading, ask: "What did Ben see? How do you think he felt? How would you feel?

Pages 46–47

"What kinds of noises might Ben make to try to scare the coyote away? What would you do? Read that page to yourself to see what the coyote did." After the reading, ask: "What brave thing did Ben do? Why was it hard to be brave in the woods?

"When Ben reached school he found out where he might get a dog. Read two pages to find out what Ben thought of the offer." After the reading, ask: "Why do you think Ben didn't mention the coyote at school? Why didn't he tell May what kind of dog he wanted?"

Pages 48–49

NOTE. If the entire story cannot be read at one time, it may be broken here. Slower readers may need to review the new words before reading the next day. Write *bites*, *fingers*, and *chewed* on the chalkboard.

A Dog of His Own (44–54)

Pages 50–51

Encourage the children to discuss the picture. Ask: "Do you think these puppies tried *to bite Ben's fingers*? When Ben showed a puppy to his father, do you think he had decided to take it home? Hadn't he said he wanted a big dog? Let's read these two pages to check." After the reading, discuss the appeal of the puppies which Ben could not resist; his dilemma when the sight of the coyote made him remember his desire for a big dog.

Pages 52–54

"Ben loved that puppy. It ran to him and *chewed* at his shoes. It was soft and warm. But what should he do about the coyote? Finish the story to find out what Ben's decision was." After the reading, help the children understand that "Jet" has two meanings. Ask: "Why was 'Jet' a good name for the puppy? Why do you think Ben was brave enough to chase away the coyote? How do you think he felt after he found that he was no longer afraid of the animal?"

Rereading for Specific Purposes

Rereading the story to organize ideas

Have the children reread the story to recall ideas for short talks on their choice of these topics:

> *What Coyotes Are Like*
> *Why Ben Liked His Puppy*
> *How Ben Overcame His Fear*

Encourage the use of complete sentences, a clear voice, and thinking before speaking. Provide an atmosphere free from tension so that the children may talk freely. See the section "Related Language Experiences," for more suggestions.

Building Essential Habits and Skills

Comprehension and Study Skills

Skimming for paragraphs

Skimming. To develop skill in skimming to locate paragraphs in the text, first review with the children the meaning of *paragraph*, and if necessary, give some oral practice in identifying paragraphs in the text. Then say: "We shall see how quickly we can find certain paragraphs in the story. As you do the exercise, remember to skim the page until you locate the right paragraph, then to read it carefully to be sure you have the correct one."

After the exercise below has been distributed, instruct the children to write the number of the paragraph in the first blank and the first three words of the paragraph in the second. The teacher should use her judgment as to whether the group needs help with the first two or three items. She may ask the group: "How many paragraphs are on page 44? Which paragraph tells why Ben thought it was quiet at night?"

Find the paragraph that tells

Page 44: why Ben thought it was so quiet and dark at night.
    2   After living in

Page 45: what Ben knew about coyotes.
    4   Ben remembered that

Page 47: what Ben did to frighten the coyote.
    3   Ben made himself

Page 48: how Ben got through the woods.
    1   When Ben reached

Page 49: how Ben went home from school.
    3   When school was

Page 50: how one puppy made friends with Ben.
    2   One of them

Page 51: what Ben decided to do with the puppy.
    5   He decided that

Page 52: where the puppy stayed in the daytime.
    1   When Ben got

Page 53: how Ben named the puppy.
    2   "You're smart," said

Page 54: what Ben shouted at the coyote.
    2   You old coyote

Main Idea. To develop the ability to interpret the main idea of pictures, distribute copies of the following exercise:

Selecting sentences which express the main idea of the story pictures

Look carefully at the picture on page 44. Then read the two sentences beside that page number and decide which describes the picture best. Draw a line under that sentence. Choose the sentence that best describes each of the other pictures and underline it.

Page 44: Ben was asleep in his room.
    The coyote's howl scared Ben.

                    A Dog of His Own (44–54)

Page 46: Ben walked <u>across</u> a meadow toward the woods.
Ben wanted a big dog of his own.

Page 47: The coyote watched Ben with bright eyes.
<u>There were hills near Ben's farm home.</u>

Page 48: Miss Gray asked Ben to sing a song.
<u>Miss Gray asked about a dog for Ben.</u>

Page 50: Frisky wanted no one to play with her puppies.
<u>Ben played with the four puppies in the barn.</u>

Page 50: <u>Ben said, "Dad, this is the puppy for me."</u>
Ben's father wanted him to take two puppies.

Page 53: The puppy chewed at Ben's shoes.
<u>Ben was having fun with his puppy.</u>

Page 54: Ben never heard the coyote howl again.
<u>At night Jet stayed near Ben.</u>

Word-Study Skills

Recognizing words
with opposite
meanings

Word Meaning. To give practice in recognizing words opposite in meaning, write on the chalkboard the following words:

1.	*forget*	_4_	*ahead*
2.	*scared*	_5_	*slow*
3.	*toward*	_1_	*remember*
4.	*behind*	_2_	*brave*
5.	*quick*	_6_	*long*
6.	*short*	_3_	*from*

Ask the children to find in the second column a word which means the opposite of a word in the first column and place the same number in front of that word. Help the children attack *slow* if they have difficulty.

Give exercises of this kind in written form if the children need additional practice. Refer to the "Cumulative Vocabulary for the First and Second Grades and Third Reader, Level I" on page 480 of this manual as a source of words.

Using word cards
to review
vocabulary

Word Recognition. To provide added practice in recognizing the newly taught words, show the children cards on which the words have been printed. Ask them to read the word and to use it meaningfully in a sentence. At this time the teacher may also wish to review words taught in previous lessons.

Phonetic Analysis. To provide a review of consonant digraphs, write on the chalkboard the following words: *children, chewed, chatter, chickens, chair, cherry, chimney.* Have the children listen carefully to the sound of the first two letters as they pronounce the words. Ask, "What do you notice about *ch* in all these words?" (The letters *c* and *h* make one sound.)

Write on the chalkboard the words *shoulder, shiny, sheep, short, shoe, shout.* Have them pronounced and ask the children to generalize about the *sh* sound as for *ch* above.

Continue in the same way for *th* with the words *think, thought, thumb, thank* (voiceless *th*), *other, their, this* (voiced *th*), and for *wh* with the words *whistled, when, where, Wheeler.*

Reviewing consonant digraphs "ch," "sh," "th," "wh"

Workbook

Pages 11, 12, 13, and 14.

Related Language Experiences

Seeing Pictures and a Movie. Secure a copy of *Coyotes*, by Wilfrid S. Bronson, or the article on coyotes in the school

Learning more about coyotes through books and a movie

119   *A Dog of His Own (44–54)*

encyclopedia. Show pictures of the animal and discuss its appearance and habits. Emphasize its place in the balance of nature, even though the animal is a nuisance to farmers. If possible, show the children the movie *Shaggy, the Coyote* (Coronet, 1 reel, b&w/color), and note their comments and reactions.

Talking about the care of a puppy

Discussion. 1. Stimulate discussion about how the children care for the puppies they own: proper food, place to sleep, cleanliness, and training. If possible, consult *A Pet Book for Boys and Girls,* by Alfred Morgan, or any available book on the care of pets. Help the children recognize the obligation to take care of any pet.

Setting up standards for short talks

2. Let the children suggest standards for giving good short talks. You may wish to help them prepare a permanent chart which contains the standards. Allow the children to compose and illustrate the chart. Display it in the classroom in a convenient place so that it can be referred to frequently. Encourage the children to keep the standards in mind as they give their talks. Help each child to evaluate his own talks and to decide what he needs to do in order to improve them.

Giving a Good Talk

Know what you are going to say.

Use good sentences.

Speak clearly and correctly.

Look at the children.

Hearing a poem

Listening. Read to the children the poem "My Dog," by Marchette Chute, and ask them to listen for the qualities

that would make them love a puppy. Later have them recall
a particular trait their own pet possesses. Be sure that they
express themselves in coherent sentences.

MY DOG

His nose is short and scrubby;
   His ears hang rather low;
And he always brings the stick back,
   No matter how far you throw.

He gets spanked rather often
   For things he shouldn't do,
Like lying on beds, and barking,
   And eating up shoes when they're new.

He always wants to be going
   Where he isn't supposed to go.
He tracks up the house when it's snowing—
   Oh, puppy, I love you so!

MARCHETTE CHUTE

Enrichment Activities

Co-ordinating Activity. Allow time for the children to com- Assembling
plete and illustrate their original stories about pets for the the class book
class book. Ask each child to select the one story he considers
his best to place in the class book.

Art and Construction. Have the children make covers for Making book covers
their individual books of original stories and for the class
book. Let them decide whether to use finger paint, crayons, or
poster paint for these.

Children may model clay dogs, puppies, or coyotes. Modeling clay dogs

Bulletin Board. Ask the children to collect and exhibit on Preparing
their bulletin board pictures, stories, and newspaper clippings a dog exhibit
about dogs. Encourage them to make a title for their exhibit.

Stories in Other Readers. During their free time the children will enjoy these stories about dogs.

Down Our Way, by GUY L. BOND and others
  "Tim Wants a Pet," pp. 117–126

Friends and Fun, by ARTHUR I. GATES and CELESTE C. PEARDON
  "Where Is Christopher?" pp. 40–53
  "There Was Tammie," pp. 82–94
  "Smoky and the Red Fire Engine!" pp. 95–106

The New More Friends and Neighbors, by WILLIAM S. GRAY and others
"Wags," pp. 41–50

Beyond Treasure Valley, by EMMETT A. BETTS and CAROLYN M. WELCH
"No Room for a Dog," pp. 46–52

Enjoying
other literature

Stories to Enjoy. Put on the library table *Dog Stories,* by ELIZABETH COATSWORTH; *Madeline's Rescue,* by LUDWIG BEMELMANS; *Nothing at All,* by WANDA GÀG; *George,* by PHYLLIS ROWAND; *Henry and Ribsy,* by BEVERLY CLEARY.

Poems to Enjoy. "Puppy and I," in *When We Were Very Young,* by A. A. MILNE; "My Puppy" and "New House," in *Up the Windy Hill,* by AILEEN FISHER; "My Pets," by SARAH JANE S. HARRINGTON, in *Ring-A-Round,* by MILDRED P. HARRINGTON.

Enjoying films
and filmstrips

Films to Enjoy. *Peppy, the Puppy* (Coronet), 1 reel, b&w/color. *Five Little Pups* (Cornell), 1 reel, b&w/color.

Filmstrips to Enjoy. *The Adventures of Pete and His Dog* (JamHandy), 26fr, color. *Lost Dog* (PopScience), 40fr, color.

All-Unit Activities

Culminating Activities

Finishing
the books

Co-ordinating Activity. The children should complete their books on "Pets and Playtime," make attractive covers for them, and with the teacher's help bind them and exhibit them in the library corner. Children should have an opportunity to share some of the original stories and drawings in the books with children from other classes, parents, and visitors. Some of the children may wish to present their finished books to the library of a lower grade, to be used as independent reading, or they may prefer to take them home.

Recalling
the stories
in the unit

Discussion. To review the first unit, direct the children to turn back to the table of contents and to read the story titles. Each child may choose his favorite story from the list and report to the class why he liked it. Some children may wish to tell part of a story and have the group guess the name of it.

Presenting
original stories

Reading Original Stories. Have the children read aloud some of the original stories which they have prepared for the class book. Allow free discussion from the group and help the children analyze the things they liked most about the stories.

Sharing Independent Reading. Allow time for children to share the stories and poems from their supplementary reading. They may show the books and point out stories for others to read, or read aloud a few of their own favorite stories and poems.

Pointing out favorite stories and poems

Evaluating Activities

Vocabulary Test I (Workbook, p. 14). To check the children's ability to recognize the new words in Unit I, administer the test on page 124. Direct the children to draw a line under the word that you read in each group. Pronounce the underlined word in each group of three.

Comprehension Test: Story Recall. To check the children's ability to recall the stories in this unit, distribute copies of the exercise at the bottom of page 124.

Testing recall of story facts

All-Unit Activities

1. break, **brave**, brown	2. glasses, giant, <u>gentle</u>	3. pretty, <u>presents</u>, prize	4. apartment, afraid, <u>afternoon</u>	5. feel, <u>fell</u>, feed
6. dishes, different, <u>decided</u>	7. cannot, <u>carry</u>, candy	8. shiny, sugar, <u>shoulder</u>	9. twins, two, <u>twelve</u>	10. leg, <u>log</u>, left
11. howl, <u>hello</u>, hatch	12. <u>sugar</u>, supper, shouted	13. wolf, <u>woke</u>, work	14. <u>chewed</u>, showed, chicken	15. each, every, <u>easy</u>
16. hide, <u>wide</u>, <u>wife</u>	17. counted, coyote, caught	18. strange, straw, straight	19. tomorrow, told, <u>toward</u>	20. <u>weeks</u>, <u>wheat</u>, wheels
21. sled, <u>slide</u>, <u>sleep</u>	22. field, <u>fingers</u>, frogs	23. eyes, <u>ears</u>, eggs	24. <u>alone</u>, <u>across</u>, against	25. while, <u>whistled</u>, white
26. arms, <u>any</u>, are	27. through, <u>touches</u>, thief	28. <u>blankets</u>, black, blocks	29. sitting, selling, <u>setting</u>	30. yard, years, <u>your</u>
31. <u>cubes</u>, cup, colt	32. small, snow, <u>smart</u>	33. birds, <u>bites</u>, boats	34. <u>remember</u>, ready, reach	35. secret, six, <u>scared</u>

Choose and write the correct answer in each blank.

1. What did Andrew give Barby to eat? __sugar__
2. What was Barby's present for the twins? __colts__
3. What did Speckles want to do when she wouldn't get off her nest? __set__
4. How many chicks did Speckles hatch? __twelve__
5. Who was the bravest cowboy? __Susan__
6. Who said, "Come here! Hello! Hello!" __Maggie__
7. What animal scared Ben? __a coyote__
8. What animal made Ben forget he was afraid? __a puppy__

| twelve | sugar | a puppy | a coyote |
| Maggie | set | Susan | colts |

Comprehension Test: Sequence. To test the children's concept of correct sequence, distribute copies of the following exercise:

WHICH HAPPENED FIRST?

Read these sentences carefully. Put the number 1 before the sentence that happened first in the story, a 2 before the sentence that happened next, and a 3 before the sentence that happened last.

Big Barby

  3 Barby came to a birthday party.

  1 Andrew gave Barby some sugar.

  2 The children rode to school on Barby.

Speckles and the New Boy

  3 All the chicks ran to Speckles.

  2 Speckles flew all over the classroom.

  1 Miss Baker asked for a setting hen.

Cowboys Are Brave

  1 The children took their blankets to the barn.

  3 Susan picked up the little dogs and put them next to her.

  2 Teddy ran back to the house.

Maggie the Magpie

  1 Maggie was sitting on Timothy's shoulder, chattering to herself.

  2 Mrs. Wood carried some cakes, glasses, and a bowl of ice cubes into the yard.

  3 The ice cubes were gone and the bowl was tipped over.

A Dog of His Own

  1 Ben wanted a big dog.

  3 Ben threw a stone at the coyote.

  2 Ben's father took him to see the puppies.

Word-Analysis Test. Distribute copies of the test on page 126. Direct the children to read each sentence and think of the letter that has been left out. The ending of the word, corresponding to the phonogram at the beginning of the sentence, is given. The words at the bottom will help the children decide which consonant they should insert to complete the phonogram and the sentence.

NOTE. The purposes of the test on phonograms below are: (1) to review the phonograms frequently used in word-analysis activities of the first- and second-grade levels of this series and (2) to strengthen ability to use blending, analogy, and recognition of familiar parts in unlocking unfamiliar words. The exercise may be used as a basis for tests of a child's ability to make new words by prefixing or changing initial consonants and by using analogy with known words. The word analysis must always be checked in relation to the meaning of the word in a sentence.

Other phonograms which are used less frequently but which may be used in exercises similar to this one are: *air, ast, ail, ace, ape, ain, alk, ag, ash, ear, eg, ipe, ime, ilk, ife, ile, ike, on, og, out, oad, our, oke, ode, ot, ope.*

1.	an	The girl _c_ an walk to school.
2.	ap	Our baby has a _n_ ap every afternoon.
3.	ad	Tom likes to go fishing with _D_ ad.
4.	ake	It is time to _b_ ake the bread.
5.	en	We put the new chicks in a _p_ en.
6.	ed	Susan has a _r_ ed dress.
7.	it	The boy _b_ it the apple.
8.	ig	We like _b_ ig cookies.
9.	ight	The sunset was beautiful last _n_ ight.
10.	ite	John took a _b_ ite of meat.
11.	ock	Please bring me a _bl_ ock of wood.
12.	old	Mother _t_ old us a story.
13.	ust	We _m_ ust drink milk every day.

block	bit	bake	night	told	red	can
nap	bite	pen	must	big	Dad	

Helping the Individual Child

General Help. At the end of the unit the teacher will wish to check the children's progress in the following ways:

Checking progress of individual children

1. Check the notes made during each child's silent and oral reading for such difficulties as vocalization, pointing with the finger, word calling, lack of expression, and the like. Note any progress made and need for further emphasis on certain skills.

2. Check each child's workbook exercises and work sheets, noting persistent errors. Provide additional help in order that the errors may be corrected.

3. Diagnose the comprehension and vocabulary tests given at the end of the unit for any weaknesses that appear, and give help that is needed.

INVENTORY OF WORD-ATTACK SKILLS	Esther F.	David B.	Mark Y.	Carol H.
1. Does he try to attack unfamiliar words independently?				
2. Does he use context clues?				
3. Does he use phonetic analysis in unlocking words?				
4. Does he use structural analysis in pronouncing words?				
5. Does he check his phonetic and structural analysis of a word by using it in context?				
6. If one method of word attack fails, does he try another?				
7. Does he try to get the idea from a paragraph even though he does not know some of the words?				
8. Does he recognize a word quickly the second or third time he meets it?				

4. To check children's word-attack skills, duplicate a chart such as the one above and plan to give added help wherever it is needed. Check other skills of individual children by making use of the group-inventory charts on the following pages of this manual: to check attitudes toward reading, page 66; to check comprehension skills, page 67; for oral reading skills, page 193.

5. Note the amount and quality of supplementary reading done by each child. Determine the reading interests of different children and make available pertinent books and stories.

Plan to provide more supplementary stories for the next unit or particular stories that will interest those children who have read little. On page 66 of this manual there is an inventory chart with which children's attitudes toward reading may be checked.

Helping less
proficient readers

Specific Help. After identifying the children who require special help, group them according to their specific instructional needs and organize the work of the class in such a way that these needs can be met. It is essential that the slow-progress group feel the sympathetic understanding of the teacher. Every child deserves an opportunity to talk over his reading problems with a sympathetic counselor. Often a release of emotional tension in attacking the reading problem is the stimulus that the child needs. A frustrated and unhappy child must have any antagonistic emotional reactions toward school removed before he will succeed in reading.

The teacher's first instructional problem is to determine the level at which each of her in-need-of-help group is reading successfully and plan instruction to begin at that level. She should begin her instruction with the most immediate need of the children, using easy reading materials which will give them self-confidence and a feeling of success.

The GINN BASIC READING PROGRAM has stressed from the beginning carefully planned procedures in word perception through many activities involving visual and auditory discrimination. However, in any class at the third-grade level there may be children who have missed a well-directed initial program. It is therefore suggested that the third-grade teacher study the plans for developing word perception at lower levels, as given in the preceding manuals of this series, and incorporate these principles into the work planned for newly entered pupils or for children who may not have progressed as rapidly as the group as a whole.

Additional suggestions for helping the individual child and members of the slower-reading group follow:

Improving
word recognition

1. Write on the chalkboard an alphabetical list of the new words presented in Unit I. Group those children who need further practice in word recognition. Help them with leading directions or questions (see page 129) and have individuals read

and frame or underline the right word or words in the list. Use a variety of word-meaning techniques, such as:

a. Definition: "Find a word that means 'made up his mind.' " (*decided*)

b. Classification: "Find the words that are names of numbers." (*six, twelve*) "Find the words that are names of animals." (*colts, chicken*)

c. Relationship: "Find a word that goes with *hard.*" (*easy*) "Find a word that goes with *morning.*" (*afternoon*)

d. Descriptive Words: "Find a word that tells about Maggie." (*smart*) "Find a word that tells about Barby." (*gentle*)

e. Action Words: "Find a word that tells what will happen to Speckles' eggs." (*hatch*) "Find a word that tells what Susan did when Mother came to the barn." (*woke*)

Word List I (from "Big Barby" and "Speckles and the New Boy")

afternoon	chicken	feel	presents	sugar
Andrew	clop	gentle	setting	touches
arms	cluck	hatch	six	twelve
Barby	colts	nest	slide	weeks
brave	easy	Peggy	Speckles	wide
carry	feed	pen	straw	years

Word List II (from the rest of Unit I)

against	coyotes	glasses	Maggie	smart
alone	cubes	hello	magpie	Teddy
bites	Dad	howl	meadow	thief
blankets	decided	Jane	remember	toward
caught	eyes	leg	scared	whistled
chewed	fingers	lemonade	shoulder	woke

2. Provide exercises using the vocabulary of the unit in new context to develop recognition and understanding. Organize the practice to include any technique in the Manual or Workbook which may have given difficulty.

Seeing vocabulary in new context

3. Let the group arrange a colorful bulletin-board display of magazine pictures which illustrate the words or phrases of the unit on which they need practice, such as *shoulder, caught the ball, sugar.* Let individuals place the correct label under each picture as shown on page 130.

Enriching word meaning

4. With some slow-learning children the simple techniques for developing skill in word recognition which were used in earlier grades should be repeated. Several that may prove helpful are given below:

a. Try to determine how many words a child can master in one day and pace the introduction of new words in accordance with his ability to learn them. If a child can learn only about eight new words, do not provide reading material that requires him to do more. Often stories are divided into two or more parts for readers who must proceed at a slow pace.

b. Have an informal discussion about what to do when you meet a word that you do not know. Emphasize the fact that effective readers learn to recognize words independently. Some points to be brought out in the discussion will include the following:

(1) Read the rest of the sentence and decide from its meaning what the difficult word is.

(2) Look at the pictures.

(3) Find a part of the word that you know.

(4) Blend the parts of the word.

(5) Write the word and underline the parts.

(6) Make a try! Read the sentence as you think it should be and see if its meaning is clear.

c. Provide frequent opportunities for word comparisons. A child must be able to perceive likenesses and differences in very similar words. For example, if he confuses the words *come* and *came*, place the two words on the chalkboard. When he has completed his oral reading, discuss the pronunciation of both words and point out the difference in the words on the chalkboard as you use the words orally in sentences, such as: "He came to school." "I will come to school tomorrow." Ask the child to find again in his book the sentence which contains the word *come* and to reread it.

Because of faulty vision or careless habits of word inspection, some children have difficulty in developing skill in visual discrimination. Encourage them always to check their tentative pronunciation of a word with the sense it makes in the context.

To provide extra practice for children who have trouble discriminating between words of similar configuration, distribute copies of the following exercise:

> Discriminating between words of similar configuration

Write the correct word from the side in each blank. Read each sentence to yourself and be sure that it makes sense.

1. A _real_ cowboy can ride a horse. We shall _read_ about his work.	read real
2. A _tall_ man gave a good _talk_ about pets.	tall talk
3. We saw _some_ girls with hats the _same_ color.	some same
4. We heard our _new_ kitten _mew_ because it was hungry.	mew new
5. The farmer threw a _pan_ of food to the pigs in the _pen_ .	pan pen
6. Try to _feed_ the puppy at six. He will _feel_ hungry then.	feed feel

---

d. Children will be helped in learning new words by keeping word lists, individual study cards, and word booklets or charts. The words should be illustrated by the child when they are concrete and used in a sentence when they are not.

e. If necessary, review the basic sight words previously presented in this series. Word cards containing these words may be used in group games or by two children who want to "say the cards to each other."

In presenting the word cards, expose each one briefly by using a cover card over the pack. Lift and lower the cover card rapidly so as to give the child a quick look. Basic words should be "one-look words."

Playing word games

Two word-card games that promote keener visual and auditory perception are described below:

Stop and Go

Prepare several red and green cards and place them in the pack of cards to be reviewed. Allow one child to say the words on the cards as they are exposed until he meets a red, or Stop, card. Then another child will take his place. If a child meets a green, or Go, card, he may continue.

Look and Find

Show and discuss a particularly difficult word card. Then place it in the pack. Expose the cards rapidly. The watching children may quietly clap their hands when the hidden card is exposed.

Using a tachistoscope

For children who have trouble remembering new words, cut a tachistoscope, as follows: cut the front piece from tag-

board. Cut a slit in the middle. Tack to the back a card, fastening it only to the sides of the front piece. Leave the center, top, and bottom free. On a strip of stiff paper type or print the words, phrases, or sentences the children need to review. Show one line at a time. Some children may want to make their own tachistoscopes.

f. Many teachers find that a window card is helpful in encouraging the child to isolate and look carefully at a troublesome word as it appears on a page in the text. As the children hold their window cards over a page, direct them to—

(1) Find a word that begins like *Mary.*

(2) Find a word that ends like *sing.*

(3) Find a word that means "fast."

(4) Find a compound word.

(5) Find a word that you do not know. Look at it carefully. Then reread the sentence and try to tell what it is.

Provision for Superior Readers. As the stories in this unit are read by the class, the superior readers may be challenged by additional activities, such as:

Challenging the better readers

1. Reading widely in the books suggested for supplementary reading and in the more difficult storybooks suggested for the teacher to read aloud; preparing to read some of these orally to the class.

2. Consulting any reference books available in the school to learn more about pets and their care.

3. Preparing written or oral reports on related topics, presenting the findings to the class, and leading discussion groups on these subjects. Often the enthusiasm and intellectual curiosity of these children arouses interest in the rest of the group.

4. Collecting and illustrating additional poems about pets and children's play activities.

5. Planning a dramatization or a simple puppet play based on one of the stories read independently.

6. Making dioramas to illustrate favorite stories.

7. Writing original verses about pets.

All-Unit Activities

Monkeys like to jump and climb.
They swing by their tails.

Unit II · At the Zoo

Introducing the Unit

The five stories and two poems in "At the Zoo" will add to the child's knowledge of the lives of wild animals both in the zoo and in their native habitat. The unit is designed to promote a desire to read independently for interesting factual information.

Every third-grade child has at least heard about the animals in a zoo. In this unit he will read about many things which go on behind the scenes at a zoo. The stories are written in such a way that every child will feel as if he were really taking part in the experiences which are described. He will discover that in many ways animals are much like people.

Before beginning this unit, the teacher may find it helpful to follow these suggestions:

1. Read through the plans for the entire unit in order to know which skills are presented and to become familiar with the activities which are suggested.

2. Collect informational books, pictures, and filmstrips about wild animals.

3. Find out about a zoo in the community which the class may visit.

To arouse further interest in the unit, the teacher may wish to show one of the suggested filmstrips, such as *Ann Visits the Zoo* (CurriculumFlms) or read to the children a zoo story, such as *When You Go to the Zoo*, by Glenn O. Blough.

| Story | Vocabulary | Developing Readiness | Reading the Story | | Building Essenti |
Pages	New Words		Guided Reading	Rereading for Specific Purposes	Comprehension and Study Skills
Teeny and the Tall Man 55–63	zoo jungles spider trunk end body giraffe almost neck vegetables	New words are presented in context either written or oral. Children are encouraged to identify new words through comparison with known words and the use of phonetic and context clues.	Silent and oral reading for comprehension and interpretation of story plot, mood, and characterization.	Reading to organize information (chart)	Story Details: using cont clues to recall story facts (worksheet) Creative Reading: form judgments and making inf ences Workbook: 15, detecting cause-and-effect relationsh
The Chimpanzee That Mopped the Floor 64–69	chimpanzee mopped Josephine bucket swish cloth licked spot			Reading to prepare for interpretive audience reading	Skimming: finding answe to questions (worksheet) Creative Reading: makin inferences and forming ju ments Workbook: 17, solving riddles; improving paragra comprehension
Strange Friends 70–75	pieces meat less sick thinner wild stood tiger seemed sniffed			Reading to verify information; reading aloud parts that prove statements	Main Ideas and Details: classifying related ideas (worksheet) Sequence of Ideas: arran ing story facts in order (wo sheet) Workbook: 18, distinguish between relevant and irre vant answers; forming ju ments
The Doctor at the Zoo 77–83	doctor hospital medicine potatoes hurt cockatoo wing Doc swallow sure bananas			Reading silently to choose the main idea in story parts (chalkboard exercise)	Specific Details: making sociations based on story fa (worksheet) Critical Reading: evaluati statements (chalkboard ex cise) Workbook: 20, finding t main idea by selecting titl 21, making inferences
The Little Cat That Could Not Sleep 84–89	awake really breathing swaying purr rocking	Through discussion and exchange of ideas, interest in the story is stimulated and background for understanding is developed. Purposes for reading are reached by the group with the teacher's guidance.		Reading to sense the mood of the story	Creative Reading: makin inferences from paragraphs (worksheet) Workbook: 22, drawing c clusions
All-Unit Activities					Evaluation: testing comp hension of main ideas and tails (group activity and wc sheet) Group Inventory for Oral Reading Provisions for less profi cient readers; suggestions for better silent and oral reading; practice in senten reading, in chorus

Habits and Skills			Related Language Experiences	Enrichment Activities
Word-Study Skills				
Word Meaning	Phonetic Analysis	Structural Analysis		
Associating related ideas; recalling descriptive phrases (worksheet)	Recalling the two sounds of *oo* Recognizing the digraph *ui* Workbook: 16, reviewing long and short vowel sounds; attacking words ending in silent *e*	Seeing the meaning and structure of words ending in *ly*	Discussion: making plans for the unit (chart) Excursion: to the zoo (chart) Reporting: taking notes on appearance of animals	Co-ordinating Activity: making a zoo exhibit; painting animal charts Construction: making habitat murals Stories in Other Readers Stories, poems, films, filmstrips, and pictures
Classifying words according to types of stories (chalkboard exercise)	Using initial consonant blends to attack unfamiliar words (worksheet)	Perceiving the comparative ending *er* Perceiving *est* as an adjective ending Using the comparative and superlative forms (worksheet)	Program: having a zoo animal quiz program	Co-ordinating Activity: habitat murals Construction: making a mobile Stories
Matching words with definitions (chalkboard exercise)	Recalling sounds of *ea* Reviewing the principle governing vowel digraphs *ai, oa, ee* Observing exceptions to the digraph principle Attacking new words Classifying words according to vowel digraphs (worksheet)	Recognizing *er* of agent Workbook: 19, recognizing comparative and superlative forms of adjectives	Storytelling: thinking of different story endings Creative Writing: writing original riddles, stories, reports; writing a letter to invite a zoo worker	Co-ordinating Activity: adding lions to habitat murals making lion charts Construction: making animal puzzles Stories, poems, and a film
Extending word meanings Defining words in the story (worksheet)	Recalling variant sounds of *a* Attacking new words containing sounds of *a* Using phonetic analysis in pronouncing the new words of the lesson	Generalizing about *ly* Perceiving how *y* changes to *i* before *ly* Adding *ly* to words (worksheet) Alphabetizing: learning and arranging the letters of the alphabet in order Workbook: 21, recognizing the suffix *ly*	Listening: to a record and pantomiming animals to the music Choral speaking: collecting favorite poems to present them in chorus	Co-ordinating Activity: adding animals to habitat murals Stories and a poem
	Recognizing variant sounds of *o* Perceiving sounds of *o* before *r* Attacking unfamiliar words through phonetic clues (worksheet)	Recognizing plurals in which *y* changes to *i* before *es* (exercise) Recalling verbs made variant by the change of *y* to *i* Changing *y* to *i* (worksheet) Alphabetizing: seeing words in relation to their place in the alphabet (exercise) Workbook: 23, alphabetizing	Speech: using expressive speech; enunciating words ending in *ing* Listening: learning to listen through games Listening to the poem "Wind is a Cat" to capture the mood	Co-ordinating Activity Library: questions for research Study chart for better readers Song: Little Cat's Lullaby A story, poems, and music
General help: using descriptive words Vocabulary review for less advanced readers Workbook: 24, Vocabulary Test II	Provisions for specific help: less proficient readers; phrases, sentence cards, games	Provisions for less proficient readers; window cards for adjective endings; word wheel for verb endings	Provisions for superior readers: suggestions for assuming extra responsibilities, research, finding poems, writing stories, plays; helping slower readers; reading aloud zoo animal stories and poems to the group	Culminating Activity: having a zoo party Provisions for superior readers: planning trips, reading comments, conducting programs

Teeny and the Tall Man

Teeny was invited to visit the zoo with her neighbor, the Tall Man, whose real name was Mr. Bush. They spent a long time looking at the monkeys, who reminded Mr. Bush of some children he knew. The giraffe proved equally interesting for he reminded Teeny of her tall friend. She decided that if Mr. Bush looked like a giraffe, she wanted to look like a white-nose monkey because "he's such a friendly animal."

The story introduces children to several animals which can be seen in a zoo, points out their characteristics, and tells the kind of country from which they come. Children will enjoy the humor of the story and will wish to find out more about other animals in a zoo.

Vocabulary

New Words: Page 55, *zoo;* 56, *jungles;* 57, ———; 58, *spider;* 59, *trunk*, end*, body*;* 60, *giraffe, almost*, neck*;* 61, *vegetables;* 62, ———; 63, ———

Developing Readiness for Reading

Discussing experiences related to the background of the story

Meaningful Presentation of Vocabulary. One way to introduce the story is to show the children a picture which clearly shows the density of jungle vegetation. Ask, "What kind of place do you think this is?" If the right answer is not volunteered, tell them that it is a *jungle.* Explain, if necessary, that a jungle is a dense growth of trees and plants, and that jungles are found in parts of the world that are hot and have heavy rainfall. If a globe is easily available, show the children the locations of these areas.

Ask, "Do you know what wild animals you would find in a jungle?" Write on the chalkboard the names of animals as children mention them. In the list include *spider monkeys, lions, elephants.* To clear up any misconceptions for the children, show pictures of the animals. Say: "We don't live close enough to the jungle to see any of these animals. Where can we see them? Yes, we find them in a *zoo.* What other animals might we see in the zoo?" (*Bears, giraffes, snakes,* etc.)

The words *trunk, end, almost, neck,* should be easily recognized by phonetic and context clues. The words *body* and *vegetables* are presented as they are met in guided reading.

Using phonetic clues to attack new words

Setting Up Reading Purposes. "Now open your books to the table of contents and find the unit called 'At the Zoo.' What is the name of the first story? Turn to it quickly." Have one child read the title of the story aloud. "Look at the picture across the top of the two pages. Where do you think Teeny and her tall friend are? Yes, at the zoo.

"Do you think that Teeny and her friend are enjoying the monkeys? Let's read this story to find out about all the animals they saw."

Reading the Story

Guided Reading

Ask: "Can anyone find the name of Teeny's tall friend on page 56? Yes, Mr. Bush. Do you think Mr. Bush has a good nickname? Read these two pages to find out what the monkeys were doing." After the reading, ask: "Why do you think the Tall Man took Teeny to the zoo? What did Teeny think one monkey wanted to do?

Pages 56–57

Reading silently to answer questions

"Read the next page silently to find out what else Teeny saw at the zoo." After the reading, ask: "In what way is a white-nose monkey like a clown?

Page 58

"What animal has a large gray *body*? Do you know what an elephant has that no other animal has? For what does he use his trunk? Read page 59 to find out why spider monkeys make good pets." After the reading, ask: "What animal sleeps in his stone house all winter? Which one roared loudly? How did the elephant look?

Page 59

"The next two pages tell us about a very tall animal with a long neck. Do you know who he is? Yes, a giraffe. Did you know that he eats leaves and hay and *vegetables*? Read these pages to find out why Mr. Bush thought the giraffe was polite at dinner." After the reading, ask: "Why did Teeny think that Mr. Bush looked like one of the animals in the zoo?

Pages 60–61

"Finish the story to find out what animal Teeny thought she was like." After the reading, ask: "How do you think

Pages 62–63

Teeny and the Tall Man (55–63)

the lady felt when the giraffe played a trick on her? How would you feel? Why do you think Teeny said she looked like a white-nose monkey? Why didn't she mind? Why was Mr. Bush a good friend?"

Rereading for Specific Purposes

Organizing information on a chart

Help the children recall what they read about zoo animals by looking for sentences that tell about the appearance, habits, and food of each one. On the chalkboard or on a chart list the four headings shown below. Ask the children to look in the story for information which belongs under each heading, for example:

This information should be transferred to a permanent chart and kept for later reference and additions.

Building Essential Habits and Skills

Comprehension and Study Skills

Using context clues in recalling story facts

Story Details. To help the children recall important details, distribute copies of the exercise on page 141. When the children have finished, call on individuals to explain their reason for each word selected.

Read the first sentence. One of the words at the bottom of the page will complete the sentence. Write that word in the blank. Complete each sentence the same way.

1. Mr. Bush was Teeny's neighbor and friend.

2. Some of the monkeys came from a jungle far away.

3. The spider monkeys can reach for things with their tails.

4. The bear sleeps all winter in a stone house.

5. The elephant looked as if he had a tail at each end of his body .

6. The giraffe was almost three times as tall as Mr. Bush.

7. Teeny decided that she looked like a white-nose monkey.

| jungle | spider | body |
| white-nose | neighbor | giraffe | bear |

Creative Reading. To help the children develop some insight into human behavior, ask the questions below. Caution the children to think before they offer their opinions and allow for differences.

Page 57. "Although Teeny had seen the monkeys many times, why do you think she was glad to see them again?"

Page 59. "Why did the animals look different to Teeny when she was with the Tall Man?"

Page 60. "After admitting to Mr. Bush that he did look a little like the giraffe, why did Teeny say about the animal, 'But I think he's a very fine giraffe'? "

Page 60. "Why do you think Mr. Bush would rather look like a giraffe than an elephant?"

Page 63. "Do you agree with Teeny that talking is fun? Why?"

Word-Study Skills

Associating
related ideas

Phrase Meaning. To foster the ability to recall descriptive phrases and story details, distribute the following exercise:

Read the first phrase. At the bottom of the page find the name of the animal the phrase tells about. Write it in the space next to the phrase. Do the same with the other phrases. Skim the story for help.

Phrase	Animal
eating the candy	white-nose monkey
always showing off	white-nose monkey
a very long neck	giraffe
looks like Teeny	white-nose monkey
vegetables and hay	giraffe
a white nose	white-nose monkey
very long tail and legs	spider monkey
never talks	giraffe
looks like the Tall Man	giraffe
a long trunk	elephant
roaring loudly	lion
sleeping all winter	bear
ate a lady's hat	giraffe
looks like a spider	spider monkey
a new spring hat	giraffe
a tail at each end	elephant

white-nose monkey   elephant   giraffe
spider monkey   bear   lion

Recognizing the
long sound of "oo"

Phonetic Analysis. 1. To recall the long sound of *oo*, proceed as follows: Write *zoo* on the chalkboard and have it pronounced. Ask the children to listen to the sound of *oo*. List on the chalkboard the following known words: *school, too, zoom, afternoon, soon.* Have the children supply other known *oo* words. Have individual children underline the *oo* in the familiar words *balloon, caboose, food, goose, root, rooster.*

Recognizing the
short sound
of "oo"

2. To call attention to the short sound of *oo* in words, write on the chalkboard *look, foot.* Have them pronounced.

Teaching *Finding New Neighbors*

Ask, "Does the *oo* sound the same in *look* as it did in *school*, *too*, and *food*?" Write on the chalkboard the following words: *book, good, took, brook*. Have them pronounced. When the auditory difference in the two groups of words seems well understood, say: "Now we know two sounds of *oo* which we can use in recognizing new words. The *oo* in *soon* is long; the *oo* in *look* is short."

Present for phonetic word attack the following third-grade words, still unfamiliar to the children: *stood, shook, hook, wool; shoot, booming, choose, cool, tools, stool.* Have the words used orally in sentences.

3. To recall the digraph *ui*, write on the chalkboard the two words *fruit* and *suit*, and have them pronounced. Point out the digraph *ui* to the children and have them note that in these words *ui* sounds much like *oo*. Explain that the *u* in *ui* gives the word its sound, and that *u* often has the sound of *oo* in words.

Recognizing the digraph "ui"

Structural Analysis. To introduce the children to the use and meaning of *ly* at the end of words, write on the chalkboard:

Observing "ly" at the end of words

> *He's a friendly animal.*
> *The lion roared loudly.*

Teeny and the Tall Man (55–63)

Call attention to the words *friendly* and *loudly*, pointing out that *ly* has been added to words which the children know. Explain that *ly* means "in a way that is," and that *loudly* means "in a way that is loud"; *friendly* "in a way that is like a friend."

As shown on page 143, have the children build other words by adding *ly* to the root words *brave, bright, glad, light, dark, quick, quiet, sad*. Have them use the words in sentences, with and without the suffix *ly*.

Workbook

Pages 15 and 16.

Related Language Experiences

Planning the
unit activities **Discussion.** Have the children suggest some of the things they would like to do while they are reading about the zoo. Help them to divide into groups according to their interests and plan a zoo activity. Record the following (or other) activities on a chart:

Our Plans

Take a trip to the zoo.

Make a wild animal exhibit.

Write true and make-believe animal stories.

Make the classroom look like a zoo.

Make a list of animal books.

Planning an
excursion **Excursion.** If there is a zoo in the vicinity, a class excursion would add to the children's enjoyment of this unit. Help a planning committee to find out how to go to a zoo, figure the cost of the trip, and list the safety precautions necessary. It

Trip Manners

On the Way

Stay together.
Talk softly.
Pay attention.

At the Zoo

See everything.
Listen politely.
Never interrupt.
Ask questions one at a time.

may help to write plans on the chart or on the chalkboard so that the children will better remember them. Have the children decide on definite things to do during the visit.

Children who like to draw may plan to make a quick pencil sketch of an animal from life. Some children may plan to write brief notes on the appearance, color, and eating habits of certain animals. Other children may plan an interview (two or three well-constructed questions) with a keeper and report on it later.

Enjoying the zoo

Enrichment Activities

Co-ordinating Activity. The children may plan a zoo exhibit to be shown to another group or to their parents after all the stories in the unit have been read. They may carry out the plan in any of several ways, depending upon their

Making a zoo exhibit

interests and upon materials available in their classroom and neighborhood.

Making zoo charts

Charts. The children may plan a special zoo display consisting of attractive charts of original wild-animal pictures, together with their own interesting or amusing captions. Each chart may be about one animal or species. Charts for giraffes or monkeys, such as the one below, may be made after the reading of the first story.

Giraffes live on the plains.

They have long necks.

They eat leaves from trees.

They cannot make a sound.

Making murals

Art and Construction. As the children learn in their outside reading about the natural habitats of various animals they may decide to make murals. One group may enjoy painting background murals denoting a jungle, plains, a desert, mountains, and ice and snow. During the next stories the children may draw or paint animals, cut them out, and paste them on the appropriate background. If the teacher prefers to have the animals painted on the mural directly, the children may divide into small groups, each group having the responsibility for one mural.

Stories in Other Readers. Throughout this unit the children may read zoo stories such as the following in other readers: Reading other animal stories

Friends and Fun, by ARTHUR I. GATES and others
"Humpy the Baby Camel," pp. 192–205

Down Singing River, by EMMETT A. BETTS and CAROLYN R. WELCH
"The Boxing Monkey," pp. 124–129

Stories from Everywhere, by GUY L. BOND and others
"At the Zoo" (a whole unit), pp. 1–60

The Story Road, by GERTRUDE HILDRETH and others
"Three Little Monkeys," pp. 43–52

Children Everywhere, by GERALD YOAKAM and others
"Elephants of the Jungle," pp. 193–207

Stories We Like, by GERALD YOAKAM and others
"Mickey Longtail," pp. 37–51
"Bears in Winter," pp. 178–183

Come Along, by PAUL McKEE and others
"Katy-No-Pocket," pp. 39–59
"Curious George," pp. 108–130

On We Go, by PAUL McKEE and others
"Bob's Elephant," pp. 165–186

Skipping Along, by BERNICE E. LEARY and others
"The Big Baby," pp. 69–78
"The Monkey and the Crocodile," pp. 79–84

Down Our Way, by GUY L. BOND and others
"Five Little Red Caps," pp. 222–230

Just for Fun, by GUY L. BOND and others
"Niki the Monkey," pp. 101–110

Good Times Today and Tomorrow, by ARTHUR I. GATES and CELESTE C. PEARDON
"Adventures in the Jungle," pp. 80–88

Treat Shop, by ELEANOR M. JOHNSON and LELAND B. JACOBS
"The Old Man and the Monkeys, pp. 114–118

Fun and Frolic, by PAUL WITTY and BARBARA NOLEN
"Granny's Blackie," pp. 268–272

Stories to Enjoy. *Lost in the Zoo*, by BERTA and ELMER HADER; *Five Little Monkeys*, by JULIET KEPES; *Here Come the Bears!* by ALICE GOUDEY; *When You Go to the Zoo*, by GLENN O. BLOUGH. Some books that are easy to read are *Zoo Babies* and *Zoo Pets*, by WILLIAM BRIDGES. Enjoying stories and poems

Poems to Enjoy. Read to the children the poem on page 148 and other poems by James Whitcomb Riley. Try to communicate the colloquial tone of the poem.

Teeny and the Tall Man (55–63)

THE FUNNIEST THING

The funniest thing in the world I know,
Is watchin' the monkeys in the show!
Jumpin' and runnin' and racin' roun',
Way up to the top o' the pole, then down!
First they're here, an' then they're there,
An' just almost any an' everywhere!
Screechin' and scratchin' wherever they go,
They're the funniest things in the world, I know!

JAMES WHITCOMB RILEY

"Furry Bear," in *Now We Are Six*, by A. A. MILNE; "When You Talk to a Monkey," "Tails," "Pockets," "Sea Lions," "Noses," "Necks," and "On the Way to the Zoo," in *Story-Teller Poems*, by ROWENA BENNETT; "The Elephant," by HERBERT ASQUITH in *Very Young Verses*, compiled by BARBARA GEISMER and ANTOINETTE SUTER; "The Four Friends," "At the Zoo," and "In the Fashion," in *When We Were Very Young*, by A. A. MILNE; "The Ostrich Is a Silly Bird," by MARY E. WILKINS FREEMAN in *Favorite Poems, Old and New*, by HELEN FERRIS.

Enjoying films and filmstrips

Films to Enjoy (suitable for entire unit). *Rikki, the Baby Monkey, Elephants,* and *The Zoo* (EBF), ea 1 reel, b&w/color. *Flipper, The Seal* (Coronet), 1 reel, b&w/color. A group of children watch Flipper go through his antics. *Zoo Animals of Our Storybooks* (Coronet), 1 reel, b&w/color. Shows our zoo animals in action at close and at long range.

Filmstrips to Enjoy. THE AFRICAN LION series: *Elephants in Africa, King of Beasts,* and *Larger Animals of Africa* (EBF). ALL AROUND THE ZOO series: *The Animal Kingdom Is Big, Arriving at the Zoo, Mealtime at the Zoo, Animal Habits, Fun for Everybody* (ClassroomFilms), ea b&w. *Let's Go to the Zoo* (JamHandy), 12 fr, color.

Seeing pictures

Pictures to Enjoy. "Monkeys in Forest," by Henri Rousseau (Prints available from Artext.) "Monkeys"—Japanese screen by Sesshu (original in the Museum of Fine Arts, Boston, Mass.) and detail from "Chin Pao and the Giant Pandas," by Chiang Yu, both in *More Pictures to Grow Up With*, by KATHARINE GIBSON.

The Chimpanzee
That Mopped the Floor

This true story of a baby chimpanzee will delight children. Josephine was found alone in the jungle and for some time was kept by a man and wife in their home. Later she was given to a zoo where she "helped" the keeper mop the floor.

The story will be read for pleasure, but will also provide information about an interesting animal.

Vocabulary

New Words: Page 64, *chimpanzee, mopped*, Josephine;* 65, ——; 66, *bucket*, swish*;* 67, *cloth*;* 68, *licked*, spot*;* 69, ——

Developing Readiness for Reading

Meaningful Presentation of Vocabulary. Show the children the picture on page 64. Say: "This man has found an animal. Do you know what it is?" The children will probably say that it is a monkey. "Yes, it is something like a monkey. It is a chimpanzee (chǐm′ păn zē′)." Have the word repeated several times if it is unfamiliar to the children. "What do you think the man will do with the chimpanzee? Why doesn't he let her go? What would you do?" Discuss what might happen to a baby animal alone in the jungle.

"The man took the baby chimpanzee home. He named her *Josephine*. Our story is about some of her adventures. The title will surprise you. I shall write it on the chalkboard." Write, *The Chimpanzee That Mopped the Floor*. Ask a child to read the title aloud. Then ask, "What would a chimpanzee need to wash a floor?" As the children answer, write these phrases on the chalkboard:

> a *bucket* of water
>
> a *mop* or a *cloth* to *swish* around

The words *licked* and *spot* should be readily recognized by the children during the guided reading. If any help is needed call attention to the short-vowel phonograms in each word and encourage the children to blend the familiar phonetic and structural parts.

Setting Up Reading Purposes. Say: "How could a chimpanzee mop the floor? Let's read the story to see what happens to Josephine."

Reading the Story

Guided Reading

Pages 64–65

Reading silently to answer questions

"Read these two pages to find out if Josephine really mopped the floor in the man's house." After the reading, ask: "How did Josephine feel when the man found her in the jungle? How did the man's wife take care of her in their house? Do you think that Josephine was sometimes a nuisance? Why?"

Pages 66–67

Call attention to the picture on page 67. "Read these two pages to find out who is giving Josephine a mop and a pan of water. After the reading, say: "Tell us some other things that happened to Josephine in the zoo. How do you think she liked the zoo? Tell us what the keeper told Josephine."

Pages 68–69

Allow the children to look at the pictures. Have them read page 68 silently to find out how Josephine helped the keeper that day. Ask: "Why do you think Josephine licked the pan and the mop? Have you seen other animals get acquainted with new things in that way? Why did the keeper decide that Josephine had done enough mopping?"

Rereading for Specific Purposes

Reading orally for interpretation

Have the children reread the story silently in preparation for interpretive oral reading. Recall the standards for good oral reading which were developed previously. Plan to have the story read to another group in the room or to a younger class.

During the oral reading, use only one book which one child reads and passes to the next child. Other members of the reading group should listen in an audience situation. They may participate afterward in a discussion of the story and of the quality of the oral reading.

Comprehension and Study Skills

Skimming. To maintain the skill of skimming to locate answers, distribute copies of the following exercise:

Skim the page to find the answer to the question. In the space write the number of the paragraph where you found your answer. Be ready to give your answer orally.

Page 64. Where did Josephine live before the man found her?   1

Page 64. Where did Josephine sleep at the man's house?
   2

Page 65. What did Josephine do when someone mopped the floor?   3

Page 66. Why did Josephine go to live in the zoo?
   1

Page 66. What did Josephine do when the keeper got a bucket of water?   4

Page 67. How did the keeper make a mop for Josephine?
   2

Page 68. What part of the floor did Josephine mop?
   3

Page 69. What did Josephine do with the water in her pan?   1

Page 69. Why did Josephine never mop the floor again?
   4

Creative Reading. To foster the ability to make inferences from reading a story, ask the children questions like those below. Tell them to think before answering and then to answer in a complete statement. This exercise may also be done independently and the varying answers to the questions discussed afterwards.

"Why do you think Josephine was afraid in the jungle?"

"Why do you think the man took Josephine home?"

"Why do you think people were always saying, 'No, no,' to Josephine?"

The Chimpanzee That Mopped the Floor (64–69)

"Why do you think the keeper let Josephine go into the hall?"

"Why did Josephine lick the pan and the cloth?"

"What would you do if Josephine were your pet? Why?"

Word-Study Skills

Relating words to story theme

Word Meaning. To help the children classify words according to the different types of stories in which they might appear, write on the chalkboard the list of words below. Ask the children to arrange the words under the two headings, "Farm Stories" and "Zoo Stories." Some children may decide that a few of the words belong under both headings.

cluck	*trunk*	*bird*	*eggs*	*pets*
nest	*colts*	*cubs*	*field*	*pond*
giraffe	*corn*	*elephant*	*horse*	*turkey*
cage	*meadow*	*monkey*	*lions*	*chimpanzee*
barn	*chicken*	*pigs*	*bear*	*lambs*

Using familiar blends to attack new words

Phonetic Analysis. To give practice in using known consonant blends in independent word attack, distribute copies of the exercise below. Give help to individual children if they need it.

The underlined words on this paper are new. They start like words you know. Write one of the two words from the right in each blank. Be sure that each sentence makes good sense.

<u>close</u>, <u>cliff</u>, <u>clear</u>, and <u>clever</u>, all start like <u>cloth</u>.

1. The sun was shining. It was a <u>clear</u> day.

    cliff
    clear

2. Josephine could open and <u>close</u> doors.

    clever
    close

<u>swift</u>, <u>swing</u>, <u>sway</u>, <u>sweet</u>, and <u>swallow</u>, all start like <u>swish</u>.

3. Josephine liked to <u>swing</u> on the open door.

    sweet
    swing

4. She would <u>swallow</u> all her food in one big bite.

    sway
    swallow

5. She liked <u>sweet</u> things like candy.

    sweet
    swift

Structural Analysis. 1. To teach children to recognize changes in form and meaning of adjectives which add *er* to denote comparison, write on the chalkboard the sentence:

Perceiving adjectives ending in "er"

Josephine grew smarter and smarter.

Underline the word *smarter* and ask the children to pronounce it and give its meaning. Then write:

Josephine was smart.
As she grew up, she grew smarter and smarter.

"What happened to the word *smart* when we wanted to say 'more smart'?" Underline the *er*. Have this familiar phonogram pronounced.

"What happens to these words when I add *er* to them?" Write *louder, faster, wider, bigger, cleaner, nearer, darker.* As you add *er* to each word, have the new form pronounced and used in an original sentence. At this point do not call attention to the variant spellings of the inflectional forms.

2. To extend the concept of degree in familiar adjectives and to present the ending *est*, write the following words on the chalkboard:

Perceiving adjectives ending in "est"

hard	*harder*	*big*	*bigger*
loud	*louder*	*dark*	*darker*
near	*nearer*	*green*	*greener*

Then write on the chalkboard:

The zoo keeper mopped the floor <u>clean</u>.
He tried to get it even <u>cleaner</u>.
Josephine got it <u>cleanest</u> of all.

Ask the children which word means "most clean." Refer again to the list of words on the chalkboard. Call on individual children to supply the word that means the "most" of these words and write the word on the chalkboard. Ask volunteers to underline the part in these words that makes them mean "most." Have the children make sentences with each word.

Call two children to the front. Ask the group which is the taller of the two. Call another child to stand beside them. Ask, "Which of the children is the tallest?" Proceed in the

Using the "er"
and "est" forms
of adjectives

same way with objects until the children understand that *est* is used only when more than two things are compared.

3. To provide practice in the use of words ending in *er* and *est*, distribute large sheets of blank paper, with instructions such as the following:

Fold your paper into six parts. Number them. In each box draw just what the directions tell you.

1. Draw a *tall* boy. Next to him draw a *taller* one.
2. Make two trees, one *smaller* than the other.
3. Draw three mops. Color the *biggest* one blue.
4. Make three baskets. Draw a circle around the *lightest* basket.
5. Draw a chair. Make another one that is *lower*.
6. Draw four balloons, all different sizes. Color the *smallest* one green. Color the *biggest* one yellow.

Workbook

Page 17.

Related Language Experiences

Quiz Program. Suggest having a quiz program about zoo animals. Have the children talk about quiz programs and how they are carried out. Let them arrange for a master of ceremonies, two teams for answering questions before a make-believe microphone, and an audience. Have the children compose questions and write them on slips of paper. The master of ceremonies will pull the questions out of a box and read them. Volunteers will answer them. If additional reading is desirable, have the children find the answers to the questions in the Reader and read the sentences which prove their answers. Encourage the children to speak clearly and to use complete sentences. Have them outline the procedure to be followed and write it on the chalkboard so that they may refer to it. For example:

1. *The master of ceremonies reads a question.*

2. *The players from each of the two teams raise their hands if they know the answer.*

3. *The master of ceremonies picks a child from one team to answer.*

4. *That child comes to the microphone and gives his answer.*
5. *Then a child from the other team is chosen.*
6. *The team that has given the most right answers is the winner.*

Enrichment Activities

Co-ordinating Activity. Have the children construct a chart for the chimpanzee, illustrated by their own drawings and with original stories or rhymes. (See example on page 156.)

Making a chimpanzee chart

Art. The children who are studying the different habitats of animals might continue to paint animals and add them to appropriate murals. Superior readers may wish to write explanatory captions telling about the animals they have studied.

Making murals

Art and Construction. In their spare time the children may construct monkeys and chimpanzees that move. Have the children draw the body parts freehand. Cut out separate arms and legs. Fasten them to the bodies with brass fasteners so that they can be manipulated. If desired, these monkeys,

Making a mobile

Chimps in a Zoo

This is a happy chimp.
He lives in the zoo.
He climbs trees all day long.
Wouldn't you like that, too?

birds, or chimpanzees may be attached to a mobile and suspended from the ceiling.

Reading stories about monkeys

Stories to Enjoy. *Monkeys*, by HERBERT ZIM; *Curious George*, and *Curious George Takes a Job*, by H. A. REY.

Pages 70–75

Strange Friends

Because her two cubs had been sent to another zoo, the lioness was disconsolate. She refused food, slept little, and paced back and forth in her cage searching for the cubs. The keeper was worried about her. One day a stray dog wandered into the zoo and discovered the cage of the sad lioness. No matter how often he was put outside the gate, the dog returned and eventually crawled into the lioness's cage. She sniffed at him, licked him, shared her food with him, and slept beside him. The two became fast friends, and the dog was permitted to remain in the zoo.

Children will respond emotionally to the story and can be led to understand the need for companionship among animals as well as among human beings.

Teaching *Finding New Neighbors*

Vocabulary

New Words: Page 70, *pieces, meat*, less*;* 71, *sick*, thinner*, wild*;* 72, *stood*;* 73, *tiger;* 74, *seemed*, sniffed*;* 75, ——

Developing Readiness for Reading

Meaningful Presentation of Vocabulary. Write the story below on the chalkboard before the lesson:

Using context and phonetic clues

> The <u>wild</u> animals in the zoo must have food.
> Giraffes eat hay and vegetables.
> Lions and <u>tigers</u> eat big <u>pieces</u> of <u>meat</u>.
> Small animals eat <u>less</u> than big animals.
> Sometimes an animal will not eat.
> It will get <u>thin</u> and <u>sick</u>.
> The keeper must find a way to help it.

Call attention to the story and explain that it tells about some animals in a zoo. Ask the children to read the story silently. Encourage them to attack the underlined words independently if they can. Give individual help if necessary by asking one child to read the entire sentence, then to look carefully at the unfamiliar word to find phonetic clues. Have the story read aloud, and point out the new words *wild, tigers, pieces, meat, less, thin, sick.* Ask: "If an animal became more thin, what word would we use? Yes, *thinner.*"

The words *stood, seemed,* and *sniffed* will be readily recognized through context clues during the guided reading. For slower readers call attention to the consonant blends in *stood* and *sniffed* and to the vowel digraphs in *stood, seemed,* and *meat.* Point out the *nn* in *thinner* and the *ff* in *sniffed.*

Setting Up Reading Purposes. "Sometimes wild animals are lonely in a zoo. Why? How would a keeper know that something was wrong with the animal? What could he do to help?

Talking about related concepts

"The next story is about just such a lonely animal in a zoo. A surprising thing happened to make the animal contented again. The story is 'Strange Friends.' Find it in the table of contents and turn to the correct page."

157

Reading the Story

Guided Reading

Pages 70-71

Reading silently to answer questions

"Let's find out what is wrong with this lion. What do you think might help her? You will find a clue by the time you finish page 71." After the reading, discuss the fact that the lion cubs were probably half-grown and no longer in need of their mother, or they would not have been sold to another zoo. Point out that people too may show signs of illness if they are sad or unhappy. "Why couldn't the little dog stay in the zoo?"

Page 72

"Read page 72 to find out how the lion seemed to feel when the little dog stood in front of her cage." After the reading, ask: "Do you think lions usually act this way when they see a dog? Read that page aloud and make your voice tell that something strange is happening.

Pages 73-75

"How might dogs frighten the wild animals? Read page 73 to yourself to find out what went on in the zoo that day and what the keeper heard." After the reading and discussion, ask: "What were the children watching? Look at the picture on page 74. What did the lioness do? Yes, she *sniffed* at the dog. In the last picture do the lion and the dog *seem* happy? Finish the story to find out what happened between the mother lion and the little dog." After the reading let the children discuss the happy ending.

Rereading for Specific Purposes

Verifying statements

Have the children find and read aloud parts of the story which prove that—

The mother lion was sad.
The keeper was worried about the lion.
The little dog was not in good condition.
The lion and the dog needed each other.
The lion and the dog could live together.

Building Essential Habits and Skills

Comprehension and Study Skills

Classifying related ideas

Main Ideas and Details. To help the children recall story details as they relate to story characters, distribute copies of the exercise at the top of page 159.

Read each phrase carefully. Draw a blue line under each one that tells about the lion and draw a red line under each one that tells about the dog.

came again and again	stood outside the cage
would get thinner	ate less and less
had big soft paws	crawled through the fence
might scare the animals	walked up and down
tried to make friends	ate some of her meat
did not sleep long	sniffed the strange animal
stopped walking	had a home in the zoo
was thin and little	began to lick him

Sequence of Ideas. To give practice in recalling story events in the order in which they happened, distribute copies of the exercise below. Have the children read all the sentences silently and then decide in what order they should be arranged to make a sensible story. Show them how to number the first sentence 1, the second 2, and so on.

Arranging story events in correct sequence

_1_ The mother lion was sad.

_2_ The keeper saw a little dog near the lion's cage.

_5_ Inside the cage were the little dog and the mother lion.

_4_ The keeper heard the children give a shout.

_3_ He put the dog out of the zoo.

Word-Study Skills

Word Meaning. To enrich word meaning, write on the chalkboard the exercise given on page 160. Have children read the first word and find its definition in the second column. Then have them put the number of the word in the space beside its definition. Continue in the same way with the other words.

Finding word definitions

1. *vegetables*	3	*not so much*
2. *sniffed*	1	*plants used for food*
3. *less*	5	*not fat*
4. *seem*	8	*in a gentle way*
5. *thin*	4	*look as if*
6. *sick*	2	*smelled*
7. *piece*	9	*not seen before*
8. *gently*	6	*not feeling well*
9. *strange*	7	*a part of something*

Phonetic Analysis. 1. To recall with the children the vowel digraph *ea*, list on the chalkboard these words: *meat, clean, easy, beans, leak, sea, reach.* Have the children pronounce the words and underline the vowels *ea*. Lead them to recall that although there are two vowels in these words, only one is pronounced. Elicit the generalization that in most words containing two vowels together, such as *ea* in *meat*, the first vowel is pronounced and the second vowel is silent. Ask, "What sound of *e* do you hear in these words?" (Long.)

2. Write on the chalkboard the lists of words below and ask the children to pronounce them, find the digraphs, and discuss the sound of each. Help them to apply the principle governing the sound of double vowels in each group.

> ai: *paint, train, straight*
> oa: *coat, road, load, boat*
> ee: *keeper, seem, needs, peep, wheels, feel, street, weeks*

3. If the children are ready to note exceptions to the above principle, present the known words *spread* and *head*. Lead them to observe that the *ea* has a short sound in these words.

4. To give practice in recognizing words containing double vowels, distribute the exercise at the top of page 161.

5. To check the children's ability to attack new words through the phonetic principle just taught, present on the chalkboard the following unfamiliar words: *chain, trail, team, teacher, speak, leader, meal, feast, feet, sweet.* Have the words used in meaningful, original sentences.

Structural Analysis. To maintain the ability to recognize words ending in *er* as agent, write on the chalkboard the following words: *driver, traveler, keeper, farmer, shoemaker, baker,* and

Reviewing the principle governing vowel digraphs through "ea"

Reviewing the vowel digraphs "ai," "ee," "oa" in words

Observing exceptions to this principle

Attacking new words

Recognizing words with "er" of agent

Put the words in the right boxes.

tail	meat	road	week
street	feel	train	seem
clean	mail	load	easy
paint	coat	leak	boat
beaver	straight	keeper	goat

ea	ai	ee	oa
clean	tail	street	coat
beaver	paint	keeper	road
meat	mail	week	load
leak	straight	seem	boat
easy	train	feel	goat

Think of more words with ea, ai, ee, oa. Write them in the blanks.

have them pronounced. "What part of these words is the same?" (*er*) "Yes, *er* is a very useful ending. It makes these words mean 'one who drives,' 'one who travels,' 'one who bakes,' etc." Have individual children make more words by adding the ending *er* to *paint, work, play, follow, jump, talk.*

Workbook

Pages 18 and 19.

Related Language Experiences

Storytelling. "Is the story we have just read a sad or a happy story?" Bring out that, although it seemed sad at the beginning, it ended happily. Suggest that the children think of and tell another happy ending for this story. Explain that as they plan their new ending they should think of ways to make it particularly interesting. They may suggest that the lion cubs were returned to their mother or that the mother was sent to the zoo where the cubs were.

Making up different endings

161   *Strange Friends* (70–75)

Creative Writing. 1. The children will enjoy composing riddles about wild animals. These may be placed in a booklet. If the bottom of each page in the booklet is folded up to form a pocket that is held in place by a paper brad, a picture of the animal whose name answers the riddle may be slipped into the pocket on each page.

2. Following their excursion to a zoo, the children will enjoy writing brief reports on one thing that interested them most, or writing original stories (imaginative or real) about one of the animals they saw there. If an excursion to the zoo is not possible, the teacher may have the children write individual letters to invite a worker from the zoo to visit their classroom to tell about his job. This will stimulate questions, discussion, reports, and, later on, thank-you notes.

Enrichment Activities

Co-ordinating Activity. Have the children construct a chart about the lion and her cubs or about lions in general to add to their chart exhibit. They may use their own illustrations with their own original stories of lions on such subjects as "The Lions in Our Zoo," "The Lion, Its Appearance and Habits," "Where the Two Cubs Went," "If I Had a Pet Lion Cub," or on their own ideas.

Art and Construction. Add lions and cubs to the habitat murals or make a mural depicting lions and cubs in their native habitat.

Making Puzzles. If large pictures of animals are available, they may be pasted to chip board and cut into puzzles. After the children have enjoyed using the puzzles for a time, they may give them to a primary class in the school.

Stories to Enjoy. *Andy and the Lion,* by JAMES H. DAUGH-ERTY; *Big Cats,* by HERBERT S. ZIM; *Here Come the Lions!* by ALICE E. GOUDEY.

Enjoying literature and a film

Poems to Enjoy. Dorothy Aldis knows what goes on in the minds of children. The following poem is a good example.

SUPPER FOR A LION

Savage lion in the zoo,
Walking by on padded feet,
To and fro and fro and to,
You seem to think it's time to eat.

Then how about a bowl of stew
With jello for dessert? Or would
A juicy bone be best for you?

Oh, please don't stare as though you knew
That I'd taste good!

DOROTHY ALDIS

Read to the children "Radiator Lions," also by Dorothy Aldis, in *Under the Tent of the Sky*, by John E. Brewton. **A Film to Enjoy.** *Tommy the Lion* (YoungAmerica), 1 reel.

Page 76 # Wonderful Day

Developing Readiness for Listening

"When boys and girls go to a zoo, they usually have a wonderful time. If you were planning to spend the day at a zoo, what would make it a wonderful day? David H. Russell has written a poem called 'Wonderful Day.' As I read it, listen to find out whether or not the boys and girls had any of the experiences you think that you would like to have."

Reading the Poem

Read the poem to the children, whose books are closed. After reading it through, ask: "Did the children in the poem see anything you would like to see? Did they do anything you would like to do?"

Let the children recall pleasing words and phrases and encourage them to ask freely for rereadings of certain lines.

Rereading the Poem

"Listen as I read the poem again. Be ready to tell us some of the words which helped you to see the animals."

Have the children open their books to the poem and look at the pictures. Call on several children to read the poem together. Select children who read well. Keep in mind that poetry is to be enjoyed, not drilled upon, and that a light, rapid presentation will keep alive the children's interest in poetry.

Related Activities

The children may wish to show their enjoyment of the zoo and zoo animals in one of the following ways:

Teaching *Finding New Neighbors*

Write a poem about our day at the zoo.

Use colored chalk to make a large picture showing "a wonderful day."

Try to make up a tune so that the poem can be sung.

Pantomime zoo animals. Music for dramatic interpretation and suggestions for animal stunts may be found in *Come and Caper*, by VIRGINIA B. WHITLOCK, pp. 40–60.

Another Poem to Enjoy. "Under the Tent of the Sky," by ROWENA BENNETT, in *Under the Tent of the Sky*, compiled by JOHN E. BREWTON.

A Film to Enjoy. *Fluffy, the Ostrich* (Coronet), 1 reel, b&w/color.

The Doctor at the Zoo

Pages
77–83

"The Doctor at the Zoo" introduces children to a feature of a zoo with which they are probably unfamiliar. The story relates how the doctor cares for sick animals and emphasizes the extreme care with which the doctor approaches and handles wild animals. It will lead to a discussion of the safety regulations which children should observe at a zoo.

Vocabulary

New Words: Page 77, *doctor, hospital, medicine;* 78, *potatoes, hurt*;* 79, *cockatoo, wing*, Doc*;* 80, *swallow, sure;* 81, ——; 82, *bananas;* 83, ——

Developing Readiness for Reading

Meaningful Presentation of Vocabulary. "Do you remember that we read and talked about taking good care of pets? Who takes care of the animals in the zoo?" (The keepers.) "Do you know who helps the keeper if an animal is hurt or sick?" Have the children offer opinions as to how the animal might be cared for. In the discussion tell the group about the animal doctor and the zoo hospital.

Talking about
related concepts

"How could the zoo keeper help when the doctor made his visits? Yes, in order to give it confidence he might talk quietly to an animal, hold it, pet it, or feed it.

Reading a chalkboard story

"Let's read this chalkboard story. It tells us about the zoo doctor. Read it to yourselves first."

The zoo doctor has a strange job.
He works at the animal hospital.
He takes care of the animals who are hurt or sick.
Sometimes he gives them medicine to swallow.

Checking the new words

After the silent and oral reading, have the children frame, look at, and say the new words *doctor, hospital, hurt, medicine, swallow*. The new words *potatoes, cockatoo, wing, Doc, sure, bananas,* may be attacked during guided reading through phonetic and context clues.

Setting Up Reading Purposes. "What kind of man do you think an animal doctor would have to be? How would he take care of the dangerous animals? Let's read the story to find out just how patient and clever the doctor was. Find the title, 'The Doctor at the Zoo,' in the table of contents and turn to the correct page in your books."

Reading the Story

Guided Reading

Pages
77-78
Reading silently
to answer questions

"Read the subtitle. In what way does the picture on page 77 give you an idea of the doctor's strange job? Read two pages to find out how the doctor took care of a sick elephant." After the reading, ask: "Why do most people never see the zoo hospital? Why did the doctor give the elephant a bucket of *potatoes* while he put medicine into her leg? What tells you that the elephant scarcely felt the doctor's needle? How did the keeper help the doctor? Why was it a good idea to have the keeper present?" (He took daily care of the elephant and she knew him.)

Page 79

"Look at the picture on page 79. Do you know what kind of bird the doctor is caring for? It is a *cockatoo*." Have the word spoken orally until the children are familiar with it. "Is the cockatoo like any other bird you know? Yes, it is a kind of parrot. Read this page to find out what part of the bird was injured." (Its wing.) "What did the cockatoo do that most animals cannot do?"

NOTE. The story may be broken here and continued the next day. Whether or not this is done will depend upon the maturity and ability of the group. If the entire story is read in one day, be sure to provide adequate time for discussion of its content and for helping individual children as needed.

"Turn to page 80. Read the subtitle. If you had to give medicine to a mountain lion, how would you make *sure* that he swallowed it? Do you think the doctor has a hard job?

Pages 80–81

"Let's read this part of the story to find out what a clever idea the doctor had." After the reading, ask: "Why didn't the doctor want the lion to chew the meat? In what two ways did he keep the lion from chewing it?

"Read the subtitle. Look at the picture on page 83. What is the doctor doing? Does the monkey look as though he is going to eat the *banana*? Finish the story to find out how the doctor helped the monkey. Why wouldn't the monkey try to eat?

Pages 82–83

"How did the doctor prove that he understands animals? What qualities should an animal doctor have?" Have the children discuss his love of wild animals and birds, his great patience, his slow, careful manner (no quick movements), his low, gentle voice, his firm touch, his special knowledge of animals and animal medicines. "Should you like to be an animal doctor? Why (or why not)?"

Making inferences

Rereading for Specific Purposes

Write on the chalkboard the exercise below to help the children recognize the main idea of each story part. Have the children reread each part of the story silently and choose the statement which tells most about that part. Ask the children to explain their choices.

Reading silently; choosing the main idea of each story part

A Strange Job

1. *A zoo has an animal hospital.*
2. *The doctor feeds the elephant potatoes.*

The Doctor at the Zoo (77–83)

Medicine for a Mountain Lion

1. *The doctor was smart when he gave the lion his medicine.*
2. *The mountain lion was sick.*

A Sick Monkey

1. *The monkey was sick and thin.*
2. *The doctor understands the ways of animals.*

Building Essential Habits and Skills

Comprehension and Study Skills

Making associations
based on
story facts

Specific Details. To provide independent practice in associating details with animals in the story, distribute copies of the following exercise:

Read the names of the four animals. Each animal has a number. Read the first sentence, decide which animal it tells about, and put the number of that animal beside the sentence. Do the same for every other sentence. If a sentence tells about more than one animal, put both numbers before the sentence. If you cannot remember, use your book to help you.

1. elephant   2. mountain lion   3. monkey   4. cockatoo

  3   He likes to keep very clean.

  2   The doctor touched his meat with a stick.

  4   His wing had been hurt.

  2   He must not bite into the meat.

  1   She had medicine put into her leg.

  4   The keeper liked him best.

  1   She did not pull away from the doctor.

  3   He licked the banana from his paws.

  4   He talked to the doctor.

  2   He swallowed each piece of meat quickly.

  1   The keeper gave her a bucket of potatoes.

  3   He came on a boat from a far country.

Critical Reading. To maintain the ability to evaluate what has been read, write on the chalkboard the exercise below. Have the children write their answers on paper. Discuss them later in a group.

Read each sentence and decide whether it is true or false, or whether the story gives you enough information to answer.

1. *A mountain lion can be a very gentle animal.* (Not enough told.)
2. *All the elephants like the doctor's visit.* (Not enough told.)
3. *The cockatoo understood what the doctor said.* (True.)
4. *The new monkey ate so much that he got sick.* (False.)
5. *Most people never see the zoo hospital.* (True.)
6. *Elephants like potatoes.* (True.)

Word-Study Skills

Word Meaning. 1. Discuss with the group the meanings of the new words in this story. For example, "What is a doctor? a hospital? a banana?" Help the children to give simple, concrete definitions and write one or two on the chalkboard. For example:

doctor: a man who helps us when we are hurt or sick

2. To review meanings of newly taught vocabulary, distribute copies of the following exercise:

Draw a line connecting each word with its definition.

zoo — a beautiful bird that can talk
medicine — a place where wild animals are kept
potato — to make afraid
cockatoo — something to make sick animals well
scare — a kind of vegetable
monkey — a large animal with a trunk
giraffe — a friendly animal with a long tail
elephant — an animal with a long neck and long legs

24

The Doctor at the Zoo (77–83)

Phonetic Analysis. 1. To recall the variant sounds of *a*, write in a list on the chalkboard the words below from the basic sight vocabulary. Have the children underline the letter *a* in each one and tell what sound it has—long, short, *a* followed by *w* as in *saw*, *a* followed by *r* as in *farm*, *a* followed by *l*: *sand, arms, mane, dark, crawl, giraffe, blanket, always, straw, lemonade, fall, candy.*

Help the children attack words with variant sounds of *a*: *bad, magic, tap, rat; hard, jar; trade, plate; shawl; almost.* Have each word pronounced, the sound of *a* identified, and the word used in a meaningful sentence.

NOTE. For purposes of review, the children may find it helpful to make a large vowel chart similar to one of those suggested in Grade Two level of this series. Each variant sound of the letter *a* may be developed with its key word and referred to as a guide to pronunciation in unlocking new words.

Using word analysis
in pronouncing
the new words
of the lesson

2. To encourage independent word analysis in reading, write on the chalkboard the new word *cockatoo* and ask the children to tell what sound each vowel makes in the word. Ask them how knowing the sounds of the vowels helps them to say the word.

Write *hospital* on the chalkboard and show how thinking about a new word in several ways will help in pronouncing the word, for example, noticing short *o*, short *i*, and *a* before *l*. Have the children find the sentence in the text which makes the meaning of the word clear and have them show how context clues help them to know a new word.

Structural Analysis. 1. To improve skill in structural analysis, have the children find the root words in *hurting* and *eating*. Have both forms of the word used in sentences. Continue this practice with other words from the story.

Generalizing
about "ly" at
the end of words

2. To recall the meaning of *ly*, write the following words on the chalkboard: *friendly, loudly, surely, quickly, brightly, sadly.* Help children to state the generalization that *ly* can be added to words and that it means "in a way that is."

Perceiving how
"y" changes to
"i" before "ly"

3. Write *happy* on the chalkboard. Say, "We can add *ly* to this word too but we must change the spelling of the word when we do so. Look on page 78 in your books to find a word that shows how to add *ly* to *happy*." Have a child write *happily* on the chalkboard and note that the *y* is changed to *i*.

Write on the chalkboard other words ending in *y*, such as *busy*, *lazy*, *merry*, *pretty*, *noisy*. Ask individual children to change *y* to *i* and add *ly* to the words.

4. To provide practice in the addition of *ly* to words, distribute copies of the following exercise:

Read this story. Then write the right word ending in ly in the blanks.

There once was a friendly lion who lived in a zoo. This lion used to walk up and down in his (in a bright way) _____ lighted cage. He could see the monkeys (in a light way) _____ climbing in and out of their tree.

Every morning the lion would roar at them (in a loud way) _____ to say "Good Morning." Then the monkeys would chatter just as (in a loud way) _____ because they were afraid.

The lion would roar (in a happy way) _____ at the giraffe. But the giraffe would (in a quiet way) _____ go to the other side of its yard because it was afraid too.

(In a way that is sad) _____ the lion now had no one to roar at, until one day a tiger was put into the next cage. And now every morning the lion roars (in a happy way) _____ at the tiger and the tiger roars back just as (in a loud way) _____.

What a noisy zoo!

Alphabetizing. To develop readiness for alphabetizing, make sure that the children know the meaning of alphabetical order and can say and write the letters in correct sequence. Use one of the following procedures:

1. Write on the chalkboard the letters of the alphabet in order, have the children say them aloud, and then copy them in a column on their papers.

2. If the children have previously learned to recognize the letters by making letter charts and dictionaries as suggested in the Manuals for Grades One and Two of this series, dictate these letters in order and have the children write them in a column on their papers.

3. Write the following words on word cards and help several children to arrange them in alphabetical order: *chimpanzee*,

giraffe, elephant, animal, hay, fox, beaver, deer, lion, owl, Jose-phine, noise, quiet, people, ice cream, monkey, keeper, uncle, raccoon, yard, tiger, vegetables, squirrel, wolf, zoo.

Workbook

Pages 20 and 21.

Related Language Experiences

Listening and
pantomiming

Listening. To develop more fully the skill of listening appreciatively, try to obtain a recording of "The Carnival of Animals," by Camille Saint-Saens. Play all of it to the children for their enjoyment. Play it through a second time and encourage the children to listen for the sounds of certain animals. Then, when the children have become familiar with the music, have them organize into small groups and, as the music is playing, pantomime the animals. Provide time for the children to share their pantomimes with another group, and allow the observers to guess what animal is being portrayed. Encourage the shy children particularly to participate in this activity.

Teaching *Finding New Neighbors*

Choral Speaking. Collect favorite poems about zoo animals, To provide a copy for each child, duplicate a few of these, such as "The Monkey's Baby" on page 174. Help the children plan how to interpret each poem in choral reading. Encourage them to memorize a few of the poems.

Collecting favorite poems

Enrichment Activities

Co-ordinating Activity. The children may construct for their zoo exhibit a unique chart about the zoo doctor and his job. It will be particularly valuable if the subject matter of the stories has been obtained through interviews with the doctor or the keepers during a visit by the children to a zoo.

Making a chart

Art and Construction. Continue the murals and exhibit them along the wall.

Stories to Enjoy. Good books are *Elephant Herd*, by MIRIAM SCHLEIN; *Elephants*, by HERBERT S. ZIM; *Here Come the Elephants!* by ALICE GOUDEY; *Zoo Doctor*, by WILLIAM BRIDGES.

Enjoying literature

A Poem to Enjoy. Children will appreciate the scene depicted in the following poem and may wish to illustrate it at the second reading. Ask them to listen for descriptive words.

THE MONKEY'S BABY

We saw the monkeys at the zoo,
The monkey's baby too.

She perched the baby on her knee
For all of us to see.

He looked so soft, so gray and small,
And made no sound at all.

But when she leaped to a higher swing,
He made a sudden spring

And with his claw, so thin and frail,
He swung on the end of her tail!

MARION EDEY

Pages
84–89

The Little Cat
That Could Not Sleep

A little cat once wanted to stay awake all night. As she walked around the farm she found all the animals quietly sleeping. This was no fun so she set out for the zoo to find some other animal who wanted to stay awake all night. Even there the lion and the deer were sleeping. The little cat sat watching the elephants as they slept standing up, swaying from side to side, one foot, another foot. . . . Before she knew it, the little cat herself was sound asleep.

The story has delightful rhythm and lends itself to oral reading to evoke feelings of relaxation and sleepiness.

Vocabulary

New Words: Page 84, *awake**; 85, *really**; 86, *breathing**; 87, ——; 88, *swaying**, *purr**; 89, *rocking**

Teaching *Finding New Neighbors*

174

Developing Readiness for Reading

Meaningful Presentation of Vocabulary. "Have you ever watched animals sleeping? Today.we're going to read a sleepy animal story just for fun.

Playing a guessing game

"Can you guess what animals might be doing these things?"

> *breathing up, breathing down*　　*purring happily*
> *swaying and rocking*　　*really sleeping*

Have the children read the phrases and make suggestions. Write the names of animals as the children volunteer them. After the story has been read, have the children check their guesses about which animal actually did each thing.

Checking the vocabulary presentation

Setting Up Reading Purposes. Ask: "Have you ever not wanted to go to sleep at night? How did you stay *awake*? Find the story, 'The Little Cat That Could Not Sleep.' Let's see what one little cat did who did not want to fall asleep."

Reading the Story

Guided Reading

"This story is so much fun you will enjoy reading it by yourselves. If you come to any words you cannot read, what should you do? Yes, read ahead to look for a clue; look at the pictures for a clue; and look carefully at the word itself for a clue. If you still can't read the word, ask for help."

Pages 84–89

Reading the entire story silently

Following the silent reading, encourage the children to discuss the story spontaneously. Then ask: "Why do you think the little cat went to sleep? What new thing did you find out about the way animals sleep? Who will tell us about a time he decided to stay awake all night and just could not do it?"

Rereading for Specific Purposes

Have the children divide into smaller groups and have each group select one child to read the story aloud as rhythmically as possible. Tell the children to listen with their books closed and to notice whether or not anything happens to them as they listen. For discussion, ask: "Did your feelings change as you listened? How did the story make you feel?"

Reading and listening to sense the mood of the story

175　　*The Little Cat That Could Not Sleep (84–89)*

Building Essential Habits and Skills

Comprehension and Study Skills

Making inferences

Creative Reading. To develop skill in drawing conclusions and making inferences, distribute copies of this exercise:

Read each question and the paragraph under it. Then look at the answers under each paragraph. Underline the one that answers the question best.

What time of day was it?

It was getting dark. The stars came out one by one. The animals went to sleep. No one was awake.

morning   <u>nighttime</u>   noontime   afternoon

Where do you think these animals live?

Horses, cows, and sheep stay in the barn at night. The farmer takes care of them. He gives them food to eat and water to drink. When they are sick, he calls the animal doctor.

in the zoo   in the hospital   <u>in the country</u>

What time of year do you think it is?

The trees are black against the gray sky. The ground is white. Cats, rabbits, and foxes have their thick fur.

spring   summer   fall   <u>winter</u>

Where is this?

There are no houses, no trees. The wind blows cold. The men had to climb a long way to get here. Now they have stopped and are looking down.

<u>top of a mountain</u>   across the meadow   down the hill

Word-Study Skills

Recognizing variant sounds of "o" in words

Phonetic Analysis. 1. To recall the different sounds *o* has in words, write the words *no, rode, old, toe,* on the chalkboard. Ask the children to tell what the sound of the vowel is (long *o*) and to name other words that contain this sound. In the same way check recognition of short *o* in *clock, clop, body, rocking.* Then have the two lists read once more for comparison.

2. Write the words *or, for, morning, storm, horse,* and discuss the special sound which *o* has in these words. Help the children understand that the *o* in *or* is neither long nor short and that the *r* which follows it gives it a special sound.

Perceiving the sound of "o" before "r"

3. To develop the ability to attack unfamiliar words through phonetic clues, distribute copies of this exercise.

Attacking new words

The new words below have different sounds of "o." Read each word. Write it in the right blank.

Short o

fog   lot   rock   bottle   dock

1. A little cat got lost in a strange town near the sea. She could not find her way in the gray ___fog___ that covered the town.
2. She could not see the ___dock___ where the boats were tied.
3. She could not see the high ___rock___ where the lighthouse was.

Long o

only   lonely   those   ghosts   drove

4. There was no one on the streets and the cat felt very ___lonely___ .
5. The ___only___ colors she could see were gray and white.
6. Some of the white things looked like ___ghosts___ and the cat was afraid.

or

seaport   torch   north   fort   torn

7. A cold ___north___ wind began to blow the fog away.
8. The cat could see that she was in a town that was a ___seaport___.
9. The white things she had seen were not ghosts but ___torn___ sails of boats.

---

177   *The Little Cat That Could Not Sleep* (84–89)

Recognizing plurals formed by changing "y" to "i" before adding "es"

Structural Analysis. 1. To review plural nouns formed by changing *y* to *i* before *es*, write on the chalkboard the following known words: *cherry, bunny, city*. Have the pupils tell the form of the word that means more than one and write it beside the singular form on the chalkboard.

Give pupils who need such practice exercises in which they match the variant forms, or in which they write the correct endings, as shown below.

cherry   cherries
bunny   bunnies
city   cities

Changing "y" to "i" and adding "es"

2. After reviewing the plural forms of nouns ending in *y*, offer extra work for the more advanced readers. Recall how *hurry, carry, try, cry*, change to *hurries, carries, tries, cries*. Check the children's ability to recognize this variant by having them read the sentence: *The airplane flies high in the sky*.

Recognizing verb variants formed by changing "y" to "i" and adding "ed"

3. To maintain the ability to recognize verbs formed by changing *y* to *i* and adding *ed*, direct the children to find the sentences in their textbook which have the words *hurried* and *carried* (p. 52) and to read them aloud. Write opposite each word the basic form, thus:

hurried	*hurry*
carried	*carry*

Show the children what has happened in these words—that the *y* is changed to *i* and *ed* is added. Ask them to change the words *try*, *cry* in this way. Present sentences in which both forms are used correctly and discuss the difference in meanings and spellings.

4. To give practice in changing *y* to *i* before adding endings, distribute copies of the exercise below. Let children attack *twenty* and *cookies* independently.

A Rabbit Story

Put the right ending on each word in the story.

A mother bunn___ lived in the countr___ with her twent___ little bunn___. One day the mother bunn___ brought home a bag of cherr___ and cook___ from the cit___.

One of the little bunn___, Peter, hurr___ and ate his cook___ too quickly. He started to cr___. He cr___ for a little while. Then his mother dr___ his eyes, carr___ him to bed, and began to read him a stor___. She started to read him a second stor___. After three stor___, she looked up, and Peter was fast asleep.

Alphabetizing. To maintain the skill of alphabetizing, assign the chalkboard exercise below. Have the letters of the alphabet on the chalkboard and help slower readers do the exercise orally. Tell the children to read each group of 3 words. Before the word that comes before the other two in the alphabet, tell them to write 1; before the one that comes next, to write 2; and before the one that comes after the other two in the alphabet, write 3. Help the children with the first group.

Seeing words in relation to their place in the alphabet

2 *end*	(2) *elephant*	(2) *horse*	(3) *wind*	(1) *jungle*
1 *breathing*	(3) *tiger*	(3) *squirrel*	(2) *light*	(2) *spider*
3 *purr*	(1) *awake*	(1) *feed*	(1) *dog*	(3) *trunk*

Workbook

Pages 22 and 23.

The Little Cat That Could Not Sleep (84–89)

Related Language Experiences

Using expressive speech

Speech. Discuss with the children how words of stories and poems often help readers to feel different moods. Have them pick out phrases from this story which give them a sleepy feeling. Explain that they can often express the mood of a selection by changing the speed of reading or speaking or by the pitch of their voices.

To emphasize the importance of variety in rate and pitch of reading, have the children practice the following sentence from this story: "*Not I! I shall stay awake all night.*" Let each child in the group say the sentence, using the same words but expressing a different mood. If the children enjoy this activity, try it with other sentences.

Enunciating clearly words ending in "ing"

Group those children who need help in enunciating the *ing* endings clearly. Have them locate and read orally sentences containing *ing* words. List phrases from the story on the chalkboard and have the children read them. Whisper phrases from the list and have the children "play parrot" and repeat them after you.

Playing making the "ing" ring

breathing up, breathing down	*waving her tail*
sleeping, sleeping, sleeping	*sleeping standing up*
moving and swaying	*purring happily*
purring and purring	*reaching to the ground*
swaying, rocking, swaying	*sleeping soundly*
getting dark	*watching them*
staying awake	*sleeping on the step*

Playing listening games

Listening. 1. If there are children in the class who are unable to listen with full attention, the teacher should read aloud interesting stories and poems and test comprehension and recall through meaningful questions.

For practice in listening and in sentence reading, prepare cards with short directions as, "Tell your favorite sport"; "Write a word with *or*"; etc. Have children take turns reading the directions aloud and calling on individuals to follow them.

A game to develop listening ability and attention span is "Going on a Trip," or "I Packed My Suitcase and Took—." The first child names one article, and each child from then on

must repeat all the articles already mentioned, and must add one of his own. A child is "out" if he misses one of the articles.

In another listening game the teacher whispers a sentence in the ear of the child next to her. That child whispers what he hears to his neighbor, and so on around the circle. The last child says aloud what he has understood.

A variation of this game might include a set of directions whispered around the circle, to be executed by the last child, then repeated aloud.

2. Introduce the poem, "Wind Is a Cat," on page 182, by asking the children to tell a few things that cats might do. Then say: "Can you think of some things that sound or seem like cats? Ethel Romig Fuller has written a poem, called, 'Wind Is a Cat.' As I read it to you, listen to see whether you agree with her that wind can be like a cat." After the reading, some children may wish to illustrate a stanza of the poem. The changing mood of this poem also suggests choral reading.

181   *The Little Cat That Could Not Sleep* (84–89)

WIND IS A CAT

Wind is a cat
　That prowls at night,
Now in a valley,
　Now on a height,

Pouncing on houses
　Till folks in their beds
Draw all the covers
　Over their heads.

It sings to the moon,
　It scratches at doors;
It lashes its tail
　Around chimneys and roars.

It claws at the clouds
　Till it fringes their silk,
It laps up the dawn
　Like a saucer of milk;

Then, chasing the stars
　To the tops of the firs,
Curls down for a nap
　And purrs and purrs.

ETHEL ROMIG FULLER

Enrichment Activities

Finishing the
habitat murals

Co-ordinating Activity. The children may draw or paint such story characters as will complete the zoo and habitat displays they have been making. Figures of sleeping animals will add pleasing variety to the displays.

Using a study chart

Library Activity. Post on the bulletin board or chalkboard a list of questions about wild animals. Leave a space after each question. Encourage the children to read widely in library books to locate the answers to the questions and have them sign their names in the blank space after each question which they can answer.

Better readers may be able to extend this library activity by developing further the study-chart introduced on page 140. The study chart might be either in the form of a large wall chart or in individual sheets for each child to work on at his own convenience.

Teaching *Finding New Neighbors*

A Story to Enjoy. *Lost in the Zoo*, by BERTA and ELMER HADER.

Poems to Enjoy. "The Sleepy Song," by JOSEPHINE DASKAM BACON, in *Silver Pennies*, compiled by BLANCHE J. THOMPSON; "Sleepy Barn," in *Summer Green*, by ELIZA- BETH COATSWORTH; "Somersaults" in *Up the Windy Hill*, by AILEEN FISHER; "Check," by JAMES STEPHENS, in *Ring- A-Round*, by MILDRED P. HARRINGTON.

When the children hear the poem "Cat," they will want to act it out themselves. It is a good selection for "stretching time" or times when the children are restless.

CAT

The black cat yawns,
Opens her jaws,
Stretches her legs,
And shows her claws.

Then she gets up
And stands on four
Long stiff legs
And yawns some more.

She shows her sharp teeth,
She stretches her lip,
Her slice of a tongue
Turns up at the tip.

Lifting herself
On her delicate toes,
She arches her back
As high as it goes.

She lets herself down
With particular care,
And pads away
With her tail in the air.

MARY BRITTON MILLER

Music to Enjoy. The children will enjoy the gentle, sleepy rhythm of the song about the little cat on page 184.

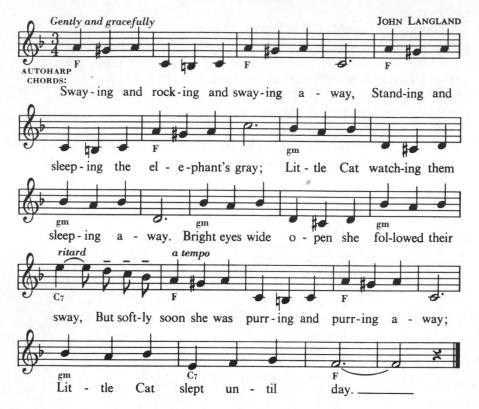

Gently and gracefully   JOHN LANGLAND

AUTOHARP CHORDS:

Sway-ing and rock-ing and sway-ing a - way, Stand-ing and

sleep-ing the el - e -phant's gray; Lit - tle Cat watch-ing them

sleep-ing a - way. Bright eyes wide o - pen she fol-lowed their

sway, But soft-ly soon she was purr-ing and purr-ing a - way;

Lit - tle Cat slept un - til day. _____

Page 90

Tiger

Developing Readiness for Listening

"Have you ever watched a tiger in a zoo? He walks back and forth, back and forth, in his cage. Listen as I read a poem called 'Tiger,' by Rhoda Bacmeister. See if it helps you to see a big tiger walking back and forth."

Reading the Poem

Read the poem in such a way that the children develop a feeling for the mood and get the swing of it. Make them hear the tiger roar when you read that line. Show by your voice the contrast in the way the tiger feels after he has eaten.

Rereading the Poem

Read the poem again. Have the children listen to decide whether or not it would be a good poem to use for choral speaking. Call on the children for their suggestions. Ask, "What parts shall we have to say particularly well?" Call attention to: *in the zoo! hears him roar, meat to eat, grin on his chin, whiffles with his nose, goes to sleep.*

Related Activities

Encourage the children to write original poems or rhymes about zoo animals. If the opportunity presents itself, help them to write a group poem.

All-Unit Activities

Culminating Activities

Zoo Party. The children may invite their parents or another group of children to their exhibit (the zoo charts, the zoo habitat murals). For entertainment they might plan a quiz program on the entire unit. Some of the visitors may be invited to answer questions. Have the children plan the program, make and send the invitations, arrange the exhibit, discuss and select the quiz questions to be used (and their correct answers), receive the visitors, and conduct the program.

Having a Zoo Party

If pupils from other rooms in the school are to be the guests at the Zoo Party, the children may prepare the invitations by printing a colored card for each word in the following sentence:

Please come to our Zoo Party on Thursday. Third Grade.

On the reverse side of each card the children may draw a zoo animal. Choose a different child to carry and display each card in its correct place in the sentence. When the children stand in front of another grade they first show the pictures. Then, at a signal, they reverse the cards so that the message can be read.

185

Evaluating Activities

Vocabulary Test II (Workbook, p. 24). *Word Meaning.* Direct the pupils to read each definition, to find at the bottom of the page the word that matches the definition, and to write it on the line.

1. A place for sick animals.	hospital
2. An animal who likes to do what people do.	chimpanzee
3. A place where wild animals live in cages.	zoo
4. A vegetable that is good for dinner.	potato
5. An animal who is one of the cat family.	tiger
6. This makes an elephant look very different from other animals.	trunk
7. What animals and people do after they have chewed their food.	swallow
8. It helps a giraffe reach high places.	neck
9. A big white bird that talks.	cockatoo
10. A kind of fruit that monkeys like.	banana
11. Something the doctor gives to sick animals.	medicine
12. Where some animals in the zoo once lived.	jungle
13. A monkey with long legs and a long tail.	spider
14. A man who cares for sick people or animals.	doctor
15. An animal with a very long neck.	giraffe
16. The part of a bird that helps it fly.	wing
17. The kind of food that lions and tigers eat.	meat
18. Moving from side to side.	swaying
19. A sound made by a cat.	purr
20. The sound of a wet mop on the floor.	swish

banana	wing	medicine	tiger
potato	jungle	giraffe	zoo
spider	doctor	swaying	hospital
meat	purr	swish	trunk
chimpanzee	swallow	neck	cockatoo

Comprehension Test. To test comprehension of the main idea and details, proceed as follows: On four cards duplicate the story below, each section on a card. Let the children in groups of four read the story aloud, each child reading one section. Then distribute copies of the exercise on page 188.

Mr. Bush was visiting the zoo. He walked by the cage of strange-looking birds, but he did not say "hello" to the cockatoo. He walked by the friendly monkeys. He walked by the wild tigers and lions. He was looking for the long-necked giraffe.

Soon he met Mr. Gray, the zoo keeper. "What has happened to High-Up?" he asked.

"Oh, High-Up is sick," said Mr. Gray. "The doctor thinks he ate something that was not good for him. He does not swallow any food, and he does not drink. He will not take medicine from the doctor. We have had him in the hospital, but he does not seem any better."

All at once they saw High-Up. He did not look as if he were awake. They could see him breathing gently. Mr. Bush called softly, "Here, High-Up! Here, High-Up! Don't you know me?"

High-Up opened his eyes. He looked all around. He walked very slowly, oh, so slowly over to the fence. He stretched his long neck down so that his head was near Mr. Bush. He sniffed and sniffed. He seemed to understand that Mr. Bush was his old friend.

Mr. Bush patted High-Up's thin neck and legs, talking to him all the time. Then Mr. Bush gave him some green vegetables to eat, one at a time. High-Up ate each one slowly.

How pleased Mr. Gray was! He said, "Will you come again to help feed High-Up?" Mr. Bush laughed and said, "I'll come tomorrow. I want to make sure that High-Up is well."

Mr. Bush came back to the zoo day after day to feed High-Up. High-Up was glad to see Mr. Bush. Soon he gobbled his vegetables. He was well again.

All-Unit Activities

To test recall of the story just read, distribute the exercise below. Tell the children that sometimes there is more than one right answer. After the children have completed the exercise, have them compare and discuss their responses.

Later, during the discussion, let the children talk about

Draw a line under the right answer or answers.

1. What is the best name for this story?

   Mr. Bush, Mr. Smith, Mr. Doctor
   <u>High-Up Finds a Friend</u>
   A Queer Giraffe

2. What is this story about?

   a giraffe, a tiger, and a lion
   a giraffe that could not chew or swallow
   <u>a giraffe that was sick</u>

3. How did High-Up feel at first?

   <u>sad, sick, and sleepy</u>
   proud, gentle, and brave
   wonderful and well

4. What animals did Mr. Bush see at the zoo?

   coyotes and spiders
   <u>monkeys, tigers, lions</u>
   elephants, beavers, and ponies

5. Who tried to help High-Up first?

   the zoo keeper
   the cockatoo in his cage
   <u>the animal doctor</u>

6. What did High-Up need to help him get well?

   <u>a kind friend to feed him vegetables</u>
   children to give him sweet food
   somebody to take him to the hospital

7. What do you suppose happened after Mr. Bush took care of High-Up?

   <u>High-Up was soon well and strong.</u>
   High-Up went back to live with the other giraffes.
   High-Up scared Mr. Bush away.

---

other details in the story and lead them to make inferences based on the story facts. Observe the individuals in the group, noting those who need additional help.

Helping the Individual Child

General Help. To develop a broader speaking and writing vocabulary, write on the chalkboard a paragraph about some person or thing. Below it write a list of descriptive adjectives, some of which are applicable to the names used in the paragraph. Have the child read the paragraph silently and choose the adjectives that might be used with various words in the paragraph. Show him how adding descriptive words may make a paragraph more interesting and meaningful. For example:

Using descriptive adjectives

Some ———— bunnies were hopping around a ———— garden. They sniffed at the flowers and every once in a while they stopped to eat some vegetables. Suddenly a ———— cat that was curled up by the gate heard the ———— bunnies. She ran down the walk and into the garden. The ———— bunnies did not stop to chew another bite. They seemed to understand that they were in ———— danger. Off they ran back to their mother!

scared	proud	beautiful
hungry	sick	sleepy
bad	wild	great

Helps for Less Advanced Readers. Children who have difficulty with word recognition may benefit from the games and devices below.

Devices for slower readers

Phrase cards: to be used orally for following directions, making sentences, "finding the phrase that tells."
Sentence cards: to be used both in a group and for independent work for story-sequence exercises.

Beanbag Toss—Vocabulary Review Game. To help children remember new words in the unit, print the words, phrases, or sentences on 4" by 6" cards. On the back of each card write a number. Arrange the cards on the floor so that the numbers are showing. The children take turns tossing a beanbag and reading the reverse side of the card, the beanbag

Playing a game

lands on. Their score is the number on the reverse side of the card.

Structural Analysis. To help children who have difficulty with the *er* and *est* endings for adjectives taught in this unit, make a window card for independent practice. In the top piece of tagboard cut two windows, one next to the other. To the right of one window, write *er*; to the right of the other, *est*. On the strip of tagboard which will be pulled through, write each adjective twice so that both words will show at the same time. Construct this card like that shown on page 132.

List of Adjectives for Tachistoscope

black	fresh	long
brown	full	low
clean	green	new
cold	gruff	sick
dark	kind	wild
fast	light	young

Verb Endings. To help children review structural changes in the endings of regular verbs, make a word wheel for independent practice. Cut two circles the same size and one larger. Circle 1 has the endings *s, ed, ing* along the side. Circle 2 has a list of known regular verbs. Circle 3 has a window to allow the verbs to show one at a time. Circle 1 and Circle 3 need tabs so that they can be turned, 3 to change the verb, 1 to change the endings of that verb.

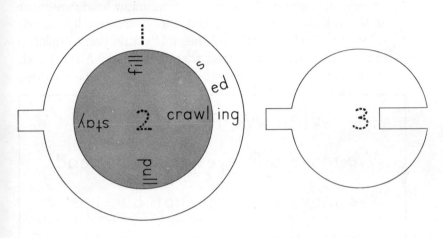

List of Verbs for Word Wheel

bring	chatter	crawl	find	sniff
bump	clean	fall	pull	stay
burn	climb	fill	shout	

Library. Place on the library table a number of easy textbooks and storybooks. Select those that contain a high percentage of recreational reading and those that meet the children's interests. The following discussion questions may bring out a child's current interests and help the teacher select the books:

Making an interest inventory

If you could have three wishes, what should you ask for?

What do you sometimes think about when you are alone?

What would you buy if you had five dollars? one hundred dollars?

If you could meet three people, whom would you want to meet?

All-Unit Activities

If you could go anywhere that you want, where would you go?

Suggest to the children that they browse awhile in the books on the library table and then select interesting stories to read to the group. Observe the methods employed by each child in selecting and preparing for his audience reading.

Improving
silent reading
Specific Help. Some children may still be having difficulty in their silent reading. Reading speed and enjoyment of the material are hampered by such habits as undue head movement and vocalizing. Since such difficulties are usually unconscious, the teacher should call the child's attention to them so that he may be able to correct them gradually. A chart such as the one below may serve as a reminder for the children.

When We Read Silently

We move our eyes, not our heads.

We move our eyes, not our lips.

We think about what we read.

Checking oral
reading
Oral Reading. It may be that some of the children in the group are having difficulty in developing effective oral reading abilities. The check list of characteristics related to oral reading on page 193 may be used to make an inventory of the specific needs of individuals within the group.

Reading aloud
Enlist each child's co-operation in making a real effort to improve oral-reading abilities. This may be done by providing opportunities for the members of the group to prepare

Teaching *Finding New Neighbors*

192

stories or some other reading material for another group. Each child may be allowed to choose a partner to help him prepare his selection. In group discussion ask the children to tell what constitutes good oral reading. A chart of suggested standards may be prepared after the discussion.

CHECK LIST FOR ORAL READING	Mary	Tom	Jim	Betty
1. Points with finger				
2. Loses place frequently				
3. Has frequent repetitions				
4. Adds words to context				
5. Ignores punctuation				
6. Pitches voice too low				
7. Has a high, strained voice				
8. Uses poor phrasing				
9. Is a word-by-word reader				
10. Enunciates poorly				
11. Holds book too close				
12. Holds book too far away				
13. Seems nervous and tense				
14. Has poor breath control				
15. Shows lack of interest				
16. Moves head				
17. Gives up on hard words				
18. Reads slowly and laboriously				

Some points that the teacher should keep in mind in trying to improve oral-reading abilities are listed here:

Improving oral reading

1. Silent reading should precede oral reading. A child cannot read orally in an effective manner unless he comprehends fully what he is reading. If help with words is needed, it should be given during the time allotted to preparation.

2. If a child is reading orally before an audience of his classmates and is blocked by a word that he does not know, the teacher should tell him the word at once in an informal

Reading aloud

way. The teacher may keep a list of such words for meaningful drill at a future time.

3. If a child persists in reading in a high-pitched, unnatural voice the teacher should, before the child begins to read aloud, direct some item of conversation toward him, speaking in a low, well-modulated conversational tone. She should encourage the child to match her tone in his reading.

Sentence reading
4. A word-by-word reader may be asked to read a sentence with his eyes and then to look up from the book and tell what he has read. He is often able to retell the sentence in a conversational tone with adequate attention to phrasing. The word-by-word reader should be given special help in increasing his eye-voice span. Encourage him to look ahead as he reads, to read a "big span" at one time, and to swing along the line. He is often helped by being permitted to read aloud with the teacher. At times the teacher will read one sentence and suggest that the child read the next with her help. If material is placed on the chalkboard for the child to read, the teacher should allow her hand to progress across the board in long rhythmic sweeps as the child reads aloud.

Reading in chorus
5. Every effort should be made to create an interest in good oral reading and to see that a child derives pleasure from participating in the activity. Providing an opportunity for the child to take part in the simple choral reading of a well-liked poem will often develop pleasant associations and will produce good results. Through such an activity the child learns to appreciate the rhythmic pattern of words and phrases.

6. If the child holds his book too close or too far away or moves his head unnecessarily, the teacher should consult with parents and perhaps suggest a further check on vision.

7. It is important to avoid giving the child material to read aloud that is too difficult for him. Nervous tension can be allayed only when the child is reading a book that is easy enough to permit his giving a successful oral interpretation. Satisfactory results cannot be attained if the child is reading at frustration level.

Audience reading
8. Oral reading may be evaluated by the kind of attention the reader receives from his audience. Its effect on the

Teaching *Finding New Neighbors*

reader may be estimated in his personality development. Good oral reading is a social qualification that brings pleasure to the listener and joy and self-confidence to the reader.

9. Reading clubs and library story hours are excellent activities to develop interest and ability in oral reading. Programs for holidays and special days also provide excellent motivating opportunities.

Provision for Superior Readers. Superior readers may be Challenging better readers challenged during the reading of this unit by some of the following activities:

1. Assuming extra responsibility for planning a trip to the zoo, such as writing a letter to the zoo to make an appointment for the excursion, computing cost of transportation, listing the questions the children wish to ask, listing materials needed on the trip, planning the time schedule for the trip, and writing thank-you letters afterward.

2. Preparing to read the comments which accompany a filmstrip about zoo animals.

3. Consulting various sources to learn more about the zoo animals described in the stories, organizing the information and presenting it to the class.

4. Looking through poetry books to find poems about zoo animals which lend themselves to choral speaking.

5. Reading stories about zoo animals in their native habitats, locating these places on the globe, and reading some of the stories to the class.

6. Children who have lively imaginations might enjoy creating fantastic animals for a strange zoo, inspired possibly by those in *If I Ran the Zoo*, by Dr. Seuss. Descriptions of these animals as to habits, food, etc. can be just as fantastic. The children might also write original stories, make masks, write a play and present it.

7. The study chart mentioned in the last story may serve as a spare-time activity for the superior readers, and may be adapted to any subject in which the children show interest.

8. Occasionally children who finish their assignments early may play drill games with those children who need help.

All-Unit Activities

Unit III · Just for Fun

Introducing the Unit

This unit includes five stories and one poem, all of which are designed to be read for pleasure. Included are humorous, imaginative stories of a girl who "helped" her aunt make gingerbread, a peddler's magical shoes, two mischievous baby bears, a hunter's trick to catch a tiger for the circus, a boy to whom animals talked, and a nonsense poem about two boys who went fishing for "pollothywogs."

As in previous units the teacher should study the summary chart and read through the plans for the entire unit to know which skills are presented and to become familiar with the activities which are suggested. She may wish to collect the suggested stories and poems to read to the children or to begin an interesting display of books for independent reading in the library corner.

The teacher may then set the mood for the unit by reading to the children a fanciful poem, such as "Topsy-Turvy World," on page 211.

After the reading, say, "Do you know why I read this poem to you? This will tell you." Write *Just for Fun* on the chalkboard. Tell the children that this is the name of the new unit. Ask, "What kinds of stories do you think you'll find in this unit?" (Humorous, funny.) Have them find Unit III in the table of contents and read the names of the stories. "Which title looks most interesting to you? Why? Do you think these are true stories?" Explain that most of the stories in this unit are fanciful or make-believe.

Story	Vocabulary	Developing Readiness	Reading the Story		Building Essent...	
Pages	New Words		Guided Reading	Rereading for Specific Purposes	Comprehension and Study Skills	Word Meaning...
Helping Hilda 91–102	*Hilda* *shell* *only* *spoon* *Selma* *slowly* *village* *slid* *market* *scrub* *mind* *bottle* *important* *Nils* *molasses* *feet* *apron* *curtains* *sneeze* *stool* *shook* *which*	New words are presented in context either written or oral. Children are encouraged to identify new words through comparison with known words and the use of phonetic and context clues.		Skimming to re-call sequence Illustrating story events Reading to find humorous parts	Creative Reading: drawing conclusions from new story material (worksheet) Workbook: 25, seeing sequence in a new story; 27, skimming	Playing a wor... game: "Building New Words"
New Shoes 103–109	*peddler* *stuck* *forest* *angry* *business* *lift* *Gruff* *squeak* *silly* *hard* *kick* *words* *promise* *chocolate* *Tumble*			Reading the story orally Reading parts that justify names of story characters	Sequence: placing story facts in the right order (worksheet) Main Idea: finding the main idea in story pictures (worksheet) Workbook: 29, detecting cause-and-effect relationships	Enriching wo... meaning throug... synonyms (wo... sheet)
Baby Bears 110–117	*Iva* *pillows* *hunter* *brick*			Reading to make inferences (chalk-board exercise)	Creative Reading: predicting outcomes Creative Reading: illustrating story parts Workbook: 32, judging feelings of story characters	
How Percival Caught the Tiger 118–121	*Percival* *trap* *danger* *sweet* *sent* *closed* *whole* *hang* *full* *branch*			Reading aloud favorite parts	Critical Reading: Choosing sentence endings to change a story (worksheet) Main Idea: Choosing titles for paragraphs (worksheet) Workbook: 34, discriminating between fanciful and realistic material	Seeing oppos... meanings of w... Recognizing ... tion words
Azor 122–131	*Azor* *Larry* *believed* *Pringle* *half* *sense* *Woodfin* *Ambrose* *Frost* *snowplow* *Chrissie Orne* *finished* *valentine* *Ella Snook* *send*			Reading orally to take the parts of the characters	Specific Details: finding answers to questions (worksheet) Creative Reading: illustrating story characters and situations (worksheet) Workbook: 36, skimming for details	
All-Unit Activities					Provision for superior readers: writing classification exercises Workbook: 39, recalling content of stories in Unit III	Evaluation: checking word recognition thr... context clues; word meaning... for making ass... ciations Provisions f... individual hel... picture diction...

Developing Readiness column (full text, spanning all story rows): Through discussion and exchange of ideas, interest in the story is stimulated and background for understanding is developed. Purposes for reading are reached by the group with the teacher's guidance.

Guided Reading column (full text, spanning all story rows): Silent and oral reading for comprehension and interpretation of story plot, mood, and characterization.

bits and Skills

Word-Study Skills			Related Language Experiences	Enrichment Activities
Phonetic Analysis	**Structural Analysis**	**Syllabication**		
calling initial consonant ds *sl, st, sp, sm, sn* viewing *scr, spl, str, thr*	Reviewing the addition of *ed* and *ing* to verbs Adding endings to verbs that double the final consonant Adding endings to verbs that drop silent *e* Workbook: 26, recognizing the doubled consonant before *ed* and *ing*; 28, using comparative form of adjectives, *er* of agent	Listening and clapping to vowel units in words Learning the meaning of "syllable"	Storytelling: retelling the story in sequence; making a "movie" with the drawings Organization of Ideas: learning to give clear directions Planning the unit activities (chart)	Co-ordinating Activity: conducting the library Story Hour: sharing stories read Excursion: visiting the public library Cooking: making gingerbread at school Stories in Other Readers Stories, poems, songs, a filmstrip, and pictures
cognizing variant sounds calling *ar, er, ir* phono- s rkbook: 30, checking gnition of *spl, scr, spr, thr*; 31, recognizing the and short sounds of *oo*		Perceiving syllables in words through listening	Discussion: forming judgments about the story Puppet Show: dramatizing the story through puppets Speech: recognizing differences in voice quality	Co-ordinating Activity Construction: making hand puppets; puppet theater Program: presenting the puppet show Stories in Other Readers Stories, poems, and music
viewing the sounds of *i* kboard exercise) rceiving vowel principles cognizing hard and soft *c*		Playing "Listening for Vowel Sounds" Workbook: 33, hearing the number of vowel sounds in words	Storytelling: telling and dramatizing stories	Co-ordinating Activity: suggestions for operating the library Puppet theater Construction: making background scenery, book covers Stories and poems
rceiving the principle of ls influenced by *r*		Learning the meaning of vowel sounds for determining syllables Workbook: 35, learning that the number of syllables in a word depends on the number of vowel sounds	Discussion: about kinds of stories Creative Writing: original tall tales Making up different story endings (worksheet) Listening: to see opposites in the poem "First and Last" Choral Speaking: learning, reciting, and pantomiming poems	Co-ordinating Activity Construction: making an independent reading chart Drawing: illustrating "tall tales" Stories and a poem
tacking words through us word-analysis tech- es viewing *sh, ch, ck* rkbook: 37, recognizing igraphs *ch, ck,* and *sh*	Recalling pronouns ending in *self* Reviewing the two uses of the apostrophe Recognizing compound words Recalling the use of hyphenated words as adjectives Workbook: 38, recognizing contractions		Puppet Show: writing a fanciful tale to present with puppets Creative Writing: writing more tall tales; writing invitations	Co-ordinating Activity: a committee planning refreshments for the book party Stories and poems
ovision for less advanced ers: recognizing variant ds of vowels (worksheet)	Evaluation: alphabetizing test on names and words in the unit	Evaluation: syllabication (test)	Culminating Activities: discussion about relationships between characters in different stories, writing riddles Provision for superior readers: library activities	Culminating Activities: book party with puppet show, choral reading, refreshments

Helping Hilda

"Helping Hilda" is the story of Hilda's efforts to make ginger-bread. She is visiting her Aunt Selma and decides to make ginger-bread while Aunt Selma is at the market. She drops the eggs, spills the molasses, and with the help of Nils, the cat, creates general disorder in the kitchen.

Although the story will be read primarily for its humor, it will stimulate a discussion of how much children should attempt alone.

Vocabulary

New Words: Page 91, ——; 92, *Hilda, only, Selma;* 93, *village, market*, mind;* 94, *important, molasses;* 95, *apron, sneeze*;* 96, *shook*, shell*, spoon*;* 97, *slowly*, slid*, scrub*;* 98, *bottle, Nils;* 99, *feet*, curtains;* 100, *stool*, which;* 101, ——; 102, ——

Developing Readiness for Reading

Using context
clues to attack
new words

Meaningful Presentation of Vocabulary. "Do you ever help your mother at home? What do you do? Do you ever go to *market?* Do you sometimes *mind* the baby? Are you sometimes the *only* one at home? Does it make you feel *important?*"

Encourage the children to talk about experiences in helping at home. In order to establish the mood of the story, try to direct the discussion to humorous happenings.

"Have you ever made *gingerbread?* What would you put on if you were going to cook?" (*an apron*) "What things do you think you would use to make gingerbread?" As the children suggest the ingredients, write on the chalkboard *eggs, flour, sugar, milk, ginger,* and *molasses.* Be sure children know what ginger and molasses are. Leave this list to be checked for accuracy as the story is read.

Attacking
new words
through use of
phonetic analysis

Help the children to attack phonetically the words *shook, shell, spoon, sneeze, slid,* and *scrub* by calling attention to the consonant digraphs and blends with which each word begins and the familiar phonograms with which each ends. The words *sticky* and *slowly* offer opportunity to apply structural attack when *y* and *ly* are added to known words.

NOTE. The words *bottle, Nils, feet, curtains, stool, which,* should be developed before page 98 is read. Because this story is longer than most, some groups will read it at two sittings.

Setting Up Reading Purposes. "In this story *Hilda* was visiting her *Aunt Selma.* She enjoyed helping, and one day when Aunt Selma had gone to the *village,* Hilda thought she would help by making gingerbread. Hilda got into great trouble before her aunt came back." Let's read the story to find out what it was and what Hilda did about it.

Reading the Story

Guided Reading

"Read this page to find out why Aunt Selma might be glad to have Hilda visit her." After the reading, have the children read aloud the sentences which tell what Hilda was doing. **Page 92**

"This page tells some of the things Hilda could do to help. Read it and tell us what Hilda was going to do. Why was her aunt surprised? Read aloud the sentence that tells. **Page 93**

"Finish the rest of this section to find out what happened when Hilda started to make the gingerbread." After the reading, ask, "What did Hilda do first, then next, then next?" **Pages 94-97**

Have the children check the list of ingredients they thought would be needed to make gingerbread to see if the list agrees with the facts of the story. *Checking ideas with facts*

Ask the children to describe what happened to the egg. Have them read aloud the funny parts of the story.

NOTE. The story may be broken here if the pupils are unable to read it in one period.

Before reading this part of the story, introduce the words *feet, stool, which,* by phonetic analysis or context clues. For example, write the word *feet.* Say: "This word means more than one foot. What is it?" Help children blend *which* through its consonant digraphs. *Stool* may be compared with *school. Nils, bottle, curtains* will be more easily recognized in context during the guided reading. If the variant forms *scrubbed* and

Helping Hilda (91–102)

scrubbing on page 100 seem to give trouble, write them on the chalkboard under *scrub* and have them pronounced.

Page 98   Have the children read the subtitle, "Molasses for Gingerbread." Ask, "What do you know about molasses?" Write on the chalkboard: *Molasses comes in a bottle. Molasses is sticky. Molasses is brown.* Have the sentences read aloud.

"You know from the story about Josephine that animals can sometimes be a nuisance in the kitchen. Read page 98 to find out what trouble *Nils*, the cat, made for Hilda. Read aloud what happened to the bottle of molasses.

Page 99   "Look at the picture on page 99. What is Nils doing? He is climbing up the kitchen *curtain*. Now read this page to see what happened to the kitchen." After the reading, say, "Tell in your own words what Nils did.

Pages 100–101   "What will Hilda do now? Read the next two pages to find out." After the reading, ask: "What did Hilda do? What did Aunt Selma say when she returned? Do you think she was really happy about Hilda's help?

Page 102   "Find out what Hilda told Aunt Selma." After the reading, ask: "Why did Aunt Selma laugh? How do you think Hilda felt? Why? Why do you think she was called 'Helping Hilda'? Do you know any people like Hilda? Is 'Helping Hilda' a good title for the story?"

Rereading for Specific Purposes

Reading for sequence of events

1. Ask the children to skim the story in order to recall the sequence of things Hilda did to help Aunt Selma make gingerbread. Have the children dictate the events and write them in phrases on the chalkboard.

Illustrating the events of the story

2. Help the children plan to illustrate the events of the story. Using the sequence written on the chalkboard, decide which of the events will make good pictures. Let each child choose one event he wishes to illustrate; then have the children close their books as they draw or paint their pictures. See the "Enrichment" section for further suggestions.

Reading to find humorous parts

3. Some children will want to reread the story to find parts that to them seem particularly humorous. Allow the children to share these parts with the rest of the group by reading them aloud.

Comprehension and Study Skills

Creative Reading. To give practice in using significant details to draw conclusions, distribute the following exercise:

Forming judgments

How Could They Have Helped More?

In the spaces write sentences that tell how these children could have helped more than they did.

---

1. Billy's mother called him. He laid his baseball glove on the front steps and went right in.

<u>He might have put away his glove.</u>

---

2. It was a cold day. The children went outside and ran down the street. The front door stood open.

<u>They might have closed the door.</u>

---

3. Tom and Betty ran through the snow. They went through the kitchen in all their outdoor clothes, hats, coats, rubbers.

<u>They should have taken off their rubbers.</u>

---

4. Ann baked a cake. She stirred the batter and splashed some on her new dress.

<u>She might have worn an apron or an old dress.</u>

After the children have completed the exercise, have the answers read aloud and discussed. Allow for differing answers if they are reasonable.

Word-Study Skills

Word Meaning. To encourage interest in words and word meaning, play the following game with the children:

Playing a word game

On the chalkboard write words like *arm, all, net, men, old.* Have the words pronounced and say, "Can you add a letter to *arm* to make a word that means a place where corn grows?" (*farm*) Use the other words in the list in a similar way. Ask the children to add a letter to *all* to make a word that means

Helping Hilda (91–102)

"high" (*tall*); to *net* to make a word that means "a bird's home" (*nest*); to *men* to make a word that means "repair" (*mend*).

Have the children take turns in thinking of words to which letters may be added. Have better readers write lists of words and definitions independently. The teacher may help them write clear, correct definitions for the words. After a little practice they may present their words and definitions to other children. An advantage of this procedure is that the difficulty of words used will be controlled by the ability of the children.

Reviewing initial consonant blends "sl," "st," "sp," "sm," "sn"

Phonetic Analysis. 1. If, in attacking the new words of the lesson, children had trouble in the use and recognition of initial consonant blends beginning with *s*, have them read an additional list of known words, such as *sled, sleep, small, smell, slide, snow, spend, smart, smoke, sniff, spot, spider, stood, stand, star, start.* Check their ability to use these blends to attack new words in sentences such as the following:

Hilda's feet <u>stuck</u> to the sticky floor.

What would Nils say if he could <u>speak</u>?

Reviewing consonant blends "spr," "scr," "spl," "str," "thr"

2. To recall three-letter consonant blends and to develop greater skill in using them in word attack, write the following words on the chalkboard: *spring, scrub, splashing, sprinkler, straight, straw, threw, strange, throw.* Have one child pronounce all the words that begin with *spr*, another child the one that begins with *scr*, and so on with the blends *spl, str*, and *thr*. If it seems desirable, have children rearrange the words on the chalkboard according to the beginning blends.

Have the children use the blends to attack new words in sentences such as the following:

Are you <u>strong</u> enough to carry this big bag?

A king sits on a <u>throne</u>.

Reviewing changes in verb forms and meaning by adding "ing" and "ed"

Structural Analysis. 1. To review the change in form and meaning of verbs when the endings *ed* and *ing* are added to the root word, write on the chalkboard *help, helping, helped.* Ask a child to use each word in a sentence. Write these sentences on the board. Make sure that the children have a solid grasp of the concept that the addition of *ing* usually indicates that something is still going on, and that the addition of *ed* to a verb indicates that something has happened or is finished. The teacher should use her judgment as to whether her group will need more examples of the *ing* and *ed* endings of regular verbs before going on to those that double the consonant before adding *ing* or *ed*. Verbs from the story which may be used for extra practice are *climb, walk, open, work, want.*

2. To recall the doubling of the final consonant before adding *ed* and *ing*, write on the chalkboard this list of words:

Doubling the final consonant and adding "ed" and "ing"

rub	*rubbed*	*rubbing*
drop	*dropped*	*dropping*
scrub	*scrubbed*	*scrubbing*
hop	*hopped*	*hopping*

Ask a child to come to the chalkboard and circle the endings of the words in the first line. Ask another child to box the root word in *rubbed* and *rubbing*. Note that an extra *b* has been added to each root word. Continue through the list. Call attention to the sound of the vowel in each root word. Lead the children to understand that these and some other words that have a short medial vowel double the final consonant before

adding *ed* and *ing*. Give as many examples as necessary. Other familiar words are *chip, drum, shop, tip, trip,* and *trot.*

NOTE. For children who need extra practice in verb endings, see the section "Helping the Individual Child" in the All-Unit Activities in Unit II.

3. To review the dropping of silent *e* before adding the ending *ing*, proceed as follows: Write on the chalkboard *sneeze* and *sneezing*. Ask the children how the word was changed when *ing* was added. Then write *slide* and *sliding*. Ask, "What was changed in *slide* when *ing* was added?" Continue in the same way with words like the following: *move, moving; make, making; take, taking*. Other familiar words are *have, live, bounce, come, care, dance, decide, face, rise, scare, strike, tape, time, tire*, and *trade*.

Write *sneeze, sneezed; decide, decided; trade, traded;* and so on. Lead the children to see that these words also drop the final *e* before adding *ed*.

Help the children draw the conclusion that words like those above drop their final silent *e* when *ing* or *ed* is added to them.

Syllabication. To develop auditory perception for vowel units (syllables) in words, write the following words on the chalkboard: *Selma, village, market, apron, curtain, bottle, slowly, sticky*. Ask the children to say these words one at a

time, to listen for each different vowel sound in the word, and to clap for each one. Illustrate by clapping with the children for the first word given. Explain that each vowel sound makes one word part. Continue having the children clap for each word part they hear as they say the words. Ask: "How many claps are there for each word? How many word parts for each?"

Have the children say the following words as you write them on the chalkboard: *shook, shell, spoon, scrub, feel, stool, sneeze, mind.* Ask the children to clap the word parts they hear in these words. "How many claps? How many word parts?"

Write the words *molasses* and *important* on the chalkboard. Repeat the activity of saying, listening, and clapping. Ask: "How many claps? How many word parts?"

Lead the children to state the generalization that some words have one part, some two, and some three parts. Tell the children that these word parts are called syllables.

Learning the meaning of syllables

Workbook

Pages 25, 26, 27, and 28.

Related Language Experiences

Storytelling. Help the children to arrange their drawings about the story in sequence and have the story told briefly. Children who have trouble remembering story facts and sequence will be guided by the drawings.

Telling the story

Movie. The children may enjoy printing captions for the pictures in their own words, and pasting the sequence together to make a movie as shown in the illustration on page 208.

Making a movie

Organization of Ideas. If there is time, the teacher may encourage a discussion about some gingerbread recipes. The advantages of clear organization of ideas and simple, direct instructions should be brought out. In a mature group the children may practice giving oral instructions to the class on such topics as how to get to a certain street; how to set a table; how to play a game.

Learning to give clear directions

Superior readers may want to do additional research on simple games for which they may, with the teacher's help, write down the directions. These might be presented to the group or be bound into a book for the library.

Planning the unit activities

Group Discussion. Throughout the unit let the group suggest activities in which they would like to participate while they are reading the stories. Remember that it is very important that the children understand the purpose of what they are doing. Record their plans on a chart as the plans are suggested and help committees to organize. Use the chart frequently to check progress and to modify or supplement activities. A chart such as the one at the bottom of the next page may be made.

Enrichment Activities

Constructing a library

Co-ordinating Activity. During this unit the children may center their interest on library activities, such as reading and telling fanciful tales and building up their classroom library.

If the library has not already been built, wooden boxes may be made into bookshelves and chairs by the children themselves. An old table donated from some home may be cut down, repaired, and finished for a reading table. The children should use the library freely, but should also take the responsibility for its care and appearance. A bulletin board with mounted pictures of storybook characters and scenes will add greatly to the general interest during the reading of the unit.

Encourage the children to bring books and magazines and supply others from a larger library. Be sure to include a few easy books for slower readers, a few materials to challenge good readers to extend their reading, and some materials relating to the themes which interest the children at the time. Collections of simple poems should also be included.

The easily read books should be clearly indicated, and the slow-reading child, in particular, should be guided in selecting library reading matter. Short, well-illustrated stories may be brought to his attention and every encouragement given him to browse through all the books. Easy books for slower readers are marked with a single asterisk in the bibliography at the end of this book.

Things We Shall Do	Things We Have Done
Read more stories.	Fix up the library.
Fix up the library.	Bring in books.
Draw storybook people.	
Have story hours.	
Bring in books.	
Make puppets.	
Make a puppet theater.	
Give puppet shows.	

209   *Helping Hilda* (91–102)

Encourage the children to use the library when other activities have been completed. Set aside a regular period, at least once a week, for each child to do individual reading.

Sharing stories

Story Hour. Let the children tell about stories they have read. The children's reports on their readings should be brief and informal. Encourage them to tell only what is important and to speak clearly and in complete sentences. A child may interest others in a story by reading aloud from it a short, interesting selection.

Visiting a library

Excursion. The children should visit the school library frequently. Help the group plan an excursion to the children's room in the public library. Ask a committee to talk with the librarian so that she will have ready for their visit some simple exhibits related to the children's interests and some books suited to their different reading levels. Public-library visits should take place a number of times during the school year.

Cooking. If possible, make gingerbread at school. Discuss the precautions that Hilda should have taken to save herself much work. Then have the children themselves plan how to prepare the gingerbread. If time or cooking facilities are limited, good packaged gingerbread mix is available.

Reading funny stories

Stories in Other Readers. The stories below are all humorous and closely connected with this unit.

Friends and Fun, by ARTHUR I. GATES and others
"The Tinker and His Wife," pp. 225–253

Fun and Frolic, by PAUL WITTY and BARBARA NOLEN
"The Little Scarecrow Boy," pp. 11–17

Good Times Today and Tomorrow, by ARTHUR I. GATES and others
"The Hole in the Wall," pp. 135–140
"Mrs. Goose's Rubbers," pp. 141–147
"Nothing at All," pp. 148–151
"The Waggable Pig," pp. 152–160

I Know a Story, by MIRIAM BLANTON HUBER and others
"The Gingerbread Boy," pp. 6–24

Making Story-book Friends, by GERALD YOAKAM and others
"The Gingerbread Man," pp. 92–98

Meet Our Friends, by WILLIAM H. BURTON and others
"The Surprised Peddler," pp. 197–202

The New Streets and Roads, by WILLIAM S. GRAY and others
"Sojo," pp. 140–147
"The Story of White Satin," pp. 155–164

Cookbook. *The Step-by-Step Cook Book for Girls and Boys,* by JULIA KIENE.

Stories to Enjoy. *Tiny Toosey's Birthday,* by MABEL G. LARUE; *And to Think That I Saw It on Mulberry Street,* by THEODORE GEISEL (DR. SEUSS, pseudonym).

Poems to Enjoy. Unit III may be introduced with "Topsy-Turvy World."

TOPSY-TURVY WORLD

If the butterfly courted the bee,
   And the owl the porcupine;
If the churches were built in the sea,
   And three times one was nine;
If the pony rode his master,
   If the buttercups ate the cows,
If the cats had the dire disaster
   To be worried, sir, by the mouse;
If Mamma, sir, sold the baby
   To a gypsy for half a crown;
If a gentleman, sir, was a lady, —
   The world would be Upside-down!
If any or all of these wonders
   Should ever come about,
I should not consider them blunders,
   For I should be Inside-out:

Chorus

Ba-ba, black wool
   Have you any sheep?
Yes, sir, a packful,
   Creep, mouse, creep!
Four-and-twenty little maids
   Hanging out the pie,
Out jumped the honey-pot,
   Guy Fawkes, Guy!
Cross latch, cross patch,
   Sit and spin the fire;
When the pie was opened,
   The bird was on the brier!

WILLIAM BRIGHTY RANDS

Other poems which might be suitable here are: "Jorridge and Porridge," by LOUISE AYRES GARNETT; "Buzzy Brown"

211   *Helping Hilda* (91–102)

or "Off to Yakima," by LEROY F. JACKSON, all found in *Gaily We Parade,* compiled by JOHN E. BREWTON.

Read the children other humorous poems such as "Sneezing" and those listed below.

SNEEZING

Air comes in tickly
Through my nose,
Then very quickly—
Out it goes:
Ahhh—CHOO!

With every sneeze
I have to do,
I make a breeze—
Ahh—CHOO!—Ahh—CHOO!

MARIE LOUISE ALLEN

"The Gingerbread Man," in *Story-Teller Poems,* by ROWENA BENNET; "Tea Party," in *Up the Windy Hill,* by AILEEN FISHER; "Calico Pie," by EDWARD LEAR, "Song of the Pop-Bottlers," by MORRIS BISHOP, "After the Party," by WILLIAM WISE, "Strawberry Jam," by MAY JUSTUS, "Goody O'Grumpity," by CAROL RYRIE BRINK, all in *Favorite Poems Old and New,* by HELEN FERRIS.

Enjoying music

Music to Enjoy. "The Gingerbread Boy," a song-play by FRANK LUTHER, in *The First Grade Book;* "Helping Mother Bake a Cake," in *Singing and Rhyming,* and "Bake a Cake," in *Singing on Our Way.* The three books are by LILLA BELLE PITTS and others.

Seeing a filmstrip
and pictures

A Filmstrip to Enjoy. *Gingerbread Boy* (CurriculumFlms), 38fr, color.

Pictures to Enjoy. "The Bread-winner," by Erskine Nicol; "The Buttery Door," by Pieter de Hooch; "Young Girl Paring Apples," by Nicolaas Maes; "A Shepherdess," by Jean François Millet. Each of these paintings shows a child engaged in some kind of work. The group will enjoy seeing prints of some of the paintings, and discussing not only the work being done but the details and color in the pictures.

New Shoes

"New shoes for old!" cried the peddler in the market place. The people were delighted with their gifts until Farmer Gruff discovered that the new shoes would not let him kick the dog. Tommy Tumble's new shoes would not let him walk in puddles or stay away from school!

Children will enjoy this kind of humor and may be able to relate this story to other fanciful tales which raise the question—could this really happen?

Vocabulary

New Words: Page 103, *peddler, Forest, business;* 104, *Gruff*, silly*, kick*;* 105, *promise, Tumble;* 106, *stuck*;* 107, *angry, lift*;* 108, *squeak*, hard*;* 109, *words, chocolate*

Developing Readiness for Reading

Meaningful Presentation of Vocabulary. The story may be introduced by reading this stanza of "Choosing Shoes" by FFRIDA WOLFE: Discussing related concepts

> New shoes, new shoes,
>> Red and pink and blue shoes.
> Tell me, what would *you* choose,
>> If they'd let us buy?

"Isn't it fun to get new shoes? Do you *promise* your mother that you will take care of your new shoes when you get them? Why? I've seen children with mud *stuck* all over their new shoes. Do you think that would be very good for them? We usually get our new shoes from a store, but in the story "New Shoes," *Farmer Gruff, Tommy Tumble,* and others got them from a *peddler.* What is a peddler? How do peddlers travel? Do you think there may be fewer peddlers now than long ago? Why?

"The peddler in the story came to *Forest Hill* to do *business.* After he went away some of his customers were *angry.* We shall find out why when we read the story."

213   *New Shoes* (103–109)

Using phonetic
clues to attack
the new vocabulary
The phonetic words *silly, kick, lift,* may be attacked independently through the sound of short *i* and familiar phonograms; *Gruff, promise, stuck,* begin with consonant blends; in *squeak* the sound of *squ* should be pointed out to the children to help them blend the word. Help children attack *chocolate* through both meaning and phonetic clues.

Setting Up Reading Purposes. Say, "Let's read to find out the strange things that happened when people got shoes from the peddler and why some of his customers were angry."

Reading the Story

Guided Reading

**Pages
103–105**

"Read the first three pages of this story to find out what the peddler was like and about the strange promise he made. After the reading, ask: "What do you think of such a promise? Would you be suspicious? Who got new shoes from the peddler? What is meant by 'kicked through'? What happened to Farmer Gruff?

**Pages
106–109**

Reading silently
to answer
questions

"Look at the picture on page 106. Farmer Gruff had strange trouble with his new shoes. How do you imagine Farmer Gruff felt?" (Angry.) "Finish the story to find out what happened to Farmer Gruff and all the other people who had new shoes. After the reading, ask: "Why didn't the farmer's wife agree with what her husband said about the peddler? How did he free his foot? What happened to Tommy Tumble? Was Tommy a thoughtful, good boy? What happened to Miss Painter?

"Why did Mrs. Friendly's shoes behave differently from the others? How were the people going to tell the peddler what they thought of him? Which one of the people in the story would you like to have as your neighbor? Why?"

Rereading for Specific Purposes

Reading parts that
describe story
characters

Have the children listen with books closed as seven individuals volunteer to read the story, one page each. Listen for parts which justify Farmer Gruff's name, Tommy Tumble's name, Patsy Painter's name, and Mrs. Friendly's name.

Building Essential Habits and Skills

Comprehension and Study Skills

Sequence. To give practice in recalling the order of story events, distribute copies of the following exercise: Recalling story events in sequence

---

When Did These Things Happen?

Read the three sentences in each group. Then number them 1, 2, 3, to show the order in which things happened.

The Peddler

3   The people in town couldn't find him.
1   A strange peddler came to Forest Hill.
2   The peddler promised to give new shoes for old.

Farmer Gruff

1   He got shoes that were not kicked-through.
3   His wife was glad that he could not kick the dog.
2   He wanted to use his shoes for something not right.

Tommy Tumble

1   He had to go straight to school.
2   The new shoes squeaked as if they were laughing at him.
3   He wanted his old shoes back.

Patsy Painter

1   She used to stand in front of the looking glass all day.
3   She was angry at the peddler.
2   She sat on the stool to get new shoes.

To check further the comprehension of story events, let individual children take turns retelling orally the story as it affects each story character.

Main Idea. To develop skill in recognizing main ideas have the children choose the best titles for pictures in the story. Help them recall that a good title tells exactly what is happening in the picture. Then distribute copies of the exercise at the top of page 216. Finding main ideas in pictures

Turn to the picture on page 103. Read the three titles below. Underline the one that tells most about the picture. Do the same with the other picture titles.

p. 103   <u>The Peddler</u>
Forest Hill
A Stool

p. 104   The Peddler Opens His Bag
Farmer Gruff Kicks His Way to the Train
<u>Farmer Gruff Will Get New Shoes</u>

p. 106   <u>Farmer Gruff's Feet Are Stuck</u>
Farmer Gruff Kicks a Dog
Mrs. Gruff is Running In from the Kitchen

p. 108   Tommy Tumble Goes Swimming
<u>Tommy Tumble Goes to School</u>
Tommy Tumble Steps into Puddles

p. 109   Mrs. Friendly Is Happy
<u>Most People of Forest Hill Want to Give Back Their Shoes</u>
Farmer Gruff Kicked the Peddler

Word-Study Skills

Enriching word meanings by use of synonyms

Word Meaning. To extend the ability to recognize synonyms, distribute copies of the exercise at the top of page 217. Have the children do it independently and then have it read orally for correction. At that time comment upon the two uses of *stuck*.

Recognizing variant sounds of "i" in words

Phonetic Analysis. 1. To maintain recognition of the sounds of *i*, write on the chalkboard the following words containing short *i*. Direct the children to tell which sound of *i* they hear: *silly, kick, lift, Hilda, village, slid, Nils, which.*

In another list on the chalkboard write words containing long *i: slide, mind, wide, bite, wild, spider, tiger.* Have these words pronounced and ask the children which sound of *i* they hear in each one.

Farmer Gruff's Shoes

Read the story about Farmer Gruff's shoes. Then find a word in the list that might be used instead of each underlined word or phrase. Write the word in the right blank.

A man who was selling things ___peddler___ came to Forest Hill. No one knew what his work ___business___ was. He said he would give new shoes for old ones. Farmer Gruff thought that was very funny ___silly___ . He put ___stuck___ out his foot and said, "Give me some new shoes for my old ones. That is what you said ___promised___."

When Farmer Gruff got home he tried to hit ___kick___ his dog with his foot. He could not do it. His foot would not move ___was stuck___ . He tried with all his might ___hard___ to move it. He could not move ___lift___ his foot.

was stuck	silly	kick	promised	stuck
lift	peddler	hard	business	angry

Present the words *girl, first, circus, bird*, and have them pronounced. Call attention to the sound of *i* when followed by *r* in each of these words. Lead the children to observe that when *i* is followed by *r*, it is neither long nor short, but has a special sound as *ir* in *bird*.

Across the chalkboard write as headings *long i, short i*, and *ir*. Ask individual children to think of other words that contain sounds of *i*. Have them identify the sound of *i* in each word and write the word under the correct heading.

2. (*a*) To note the special sounds of vowels followed by *r*, present the following pairs of words on the chalkboard:

Hearing "ar, er, ir, or, ur" in words

hard	*tiger*	*bird*	*lord*	*purr*
arms	*peddler*	*stir*	*horse*	*hurt*

Have each pair of words pronounced. Ask the children what two letters come together in each to give the words their special sound. Draw a line around *ar* in the first pair. Repeat the procedure for each pair given, isolating the familiar parts previously presented as phonograms: *ar, er, ir, or, ur*.

NOTE. At this point avoid bringing in the many exceptions to these phonetic sounds, as in *care, word*, etc. These will be presented later.

(b) To offer practice in identifying these special sounds, have the children pronounce the words below, met recently in their Reader, and isolate the r phonogram in each word by drawing a line around it. The following words may be used: *peddler, curtains, market, important, stranger, circus.*

3. To review the two sounds of *oo*, write on the chalkboard the following words from the story: *good, looking, stool, too, school, soon.* Have them pronounced. Ask the children to tell which words have the long sound of *oo*, and which words have the short sound of *oo*. Continue with other known words like *stood, shook, brook, took, spoon, stool, food.* Help the children to attack the new words through simple rhymes, such as the ones that follow:

John took a look   *Take your coat to school*
At his coat on the <u>hook</u>.   *When the air is <u>cool</u>.*

Syllabication. To strengthen auditory perception for syllables (vowel units) in new words of the unit, prepare word cards for each of the following words: *peddler, promise, angry, Tommy, Tumble, silly, Gruff, stuck, hard, word, lift, chocolate, important, molasses.* Tell the children that as each card is shown and pronounced, they are to clap the number of word parts or *syllables* that they hear in the word. The one-syllable words will go in one pile; two-syllable words in another pile; three-syllable words in a third pile.

If word cards are not available, repeat the activity of identifying word parts by saying, listening, and clapping that was used on pages 206 and 207.

Workbook

Pages 29, 30, and 31.

Related Language Experiences

Discussion. Help the children to form judgments by asking: "Could this story really have happened? Why or why not?"

Let the children extend the story by thinking of other persons who might have been given shoes by the peddler. What might have happened in each case?

Puppet Show. Have the group dramatize the story or plan a puppet show. In either case, let the children themselves plan, arrange, and carry out as much of the construction and as many of the activities as possible. Invite original ideas and give encouragement to workable plans. Suggestions for constructing a puppet theater and puppets are in the "Enrichment" section for this story.

Planning a dramatization

Speech. To aid in the dramatization of this story, have the children discuss the differences among the voices of the story characters. The children may reread parts orally in the kind of voice which the group has decided each character would have, for example: the peddler, happy; the farmer, gruff; Patsy Painter, silly; Tommy Tumble, whiny; Mrs. Friendly, friendly.

Recognizing differences in voice qualities

Enrichment Activities

Co-ordinating Activity. Specific suggestions for the management of the library throughout the year, and suggestions for carrying out a story hour are described at length on pages 227 and 228 of this manual.

Managing the library

Construction. Since the characters in fanciful stories need not look real, selections in this unit lend themselves to dramatization with puppets. Any one of several different kinds of puppets can be constructed in a relatively short time from easily available materials.

Making hand puppets

Very satisfactory hand puppets can be made from bits of cloth, felt, and papier mâché. Have the children bring in old darning eggs. If none of these are available, mold head shapes for the puppets from clay. For the actual puppet heads, cover the darning eggs or clay balls with papier mâché made from facial tissues, and mold the features. Mold the neck as part of the head, leaving an opening for the forefinger. Allow the heads to dry thoroughly. Cut across the top and around the sides of the head to take it off the darning egg as shown on page 220. Glue the two pieces together and paint the head a flesh color. Help the children to ink in the eyes. Help the girls design, cut out, and sew appropriate clothing to dress the puppets.

219 New Shoes (103–109)

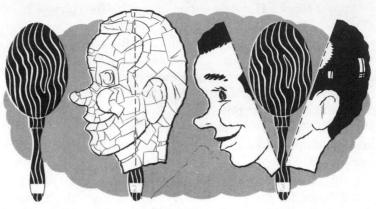

Building a puppet theater

A temporary puppet theater can be cut from a large cardboard carton or put together from an orange crate. A more permanent theater may be fashioned from an old screen or from sheets of plywood. The stage should be high enough so that the children are comfortable as they manipulate the puppets. An effective and simple curtain may be made from a window shade cut to size and attached to the inside of the theater.

Fuller, more detailed instructions for both puppets and theater may be found in *Easy Puppets*, by GERTRUDE PELS, in *The First Book of Puppets*, by MORITZ JAGENDORF, or in *The Puppet Book*, by HELEN J. FLETCHER and JACK DECKTER.

Putting on the puppet show

Dramatization. After rereading the story, the children will enjoy making up their own lines. The characters of Farmer Gruff and Tommy Tumble, for instance, present numerous possibilities for original interpretation. The activity will be more challenging and enjoyable if the teacher allows the children to interpret the story freely. Each child should be permitted to change his lines during the first few times a scene is played while the group decides (with some guidance) the best way to play the part. After this the lines may be memorized if the show is going to be presented to a critical audience.

Reading stories about peddlers

Stories in Other Readers. Let children read the materials listed for the first story in the unit and call attention to the stories about peddlers mentioned here.

Story Caravan, by WILLIAM D. SHELDON and others
"The Peddler's Clock," pp. 6–24

Stories to Enjoy. "The Cobbler's Tale," by ELIZABETH O.   Enjoying literature
and music
JONES, in *Told under the Magic Umbrella,* by The Association
for Childhood Education International; "The Elves and the
Shoemaker," in *Story and Verse for Children,* compiled by
MIRIAM B. HUBER; *Pitschi,* by HANS FISCHER. Mature
readers may be able to read *The Peddler's Cart,* by ELIZA-
BETH COATSWORTH. All children will enjoy listening to it.

Poems to Enjoy. The children will sympathize with the
sentiments expressed in this poem.

CHOOSING SHOES

New shoes, new shoes,
  Red and pink and blue shoes.
Tell me, what would *you* choose,
  If they'd let us buy?

Buckle shoes, bow shoes,
  Pretty pointy-toe shoes;
Strappy, cappy low shoes;
  Let's have some to try.

Bright shoes, white shoes,
  Dandy-dance-by-night shoes,
Perhaps-a-little-tight shoes,
  Like some? So would I.

But

Flat shoes, fat shoes,
  Stump-along-like-that shoes,
Wipe-them-on-the-mat shoes,
  That's the sort they'll buy.

FFRIDA WOLFE

Some other poems about shoes are "The Cobbler's," in
Taxis and Toadstools, by RACHEL FIELD; "New Shoes,"
in *Up the Windy Hill,* by AILEEN FISHER; "New Shoes,"
by ALICE WILKINS, in *The Golden Flute,* by ALICE HUBBARD
and ADELINE BABBITT.

221   *New Shoes* (103–109)

Music to Enjoy. "The Shoemaker and the Elves," a song-play by FRANK LUTHER, in *Singing on Our Way,* and "Shoemaker Dance" in *Singing and Rhyming,* both books by LILLA BELLE PITTS and others.

The children will like the spirited tempo of the song that fits the mood of this story.

**Pages
110–117**

Baby Bears

A man once found two baby bears in the forest and brought them home in his hat. He and his wife gave them a home in their cottage. As the bears grew up they became a problem, playing tricks on the entire neighborhood. A hunter was finally persuaded to take them to the city where he sold them to the circus. There the bears enjoyed doing their tricks for the children.

Children will enjoy the humor of this story.

Teaching Finding New Neighbors

Vocabulary

New Words: Page 110, *Iva;* 111, *pillows*;* 112, ————;
113, *hunter*;* 114, *brick*;* 115, ————; 116, ————;;
117, ————

Developing Readiness for Reading

Meaningful Presentation of Vocabulary. "Today we are
going to read a good story from another country. The woman
in the story, *Iva*, lived in a forest. One day her husband
brought her two pets who caused a great deal of mischief.
What do you suppose the pets might be?"

Talking about
related concepts

Let the children speculate about the pets. Then ask: "Do
you have a pet at home? Does it live in the house? Does it
ever get into mischief? How does your mother feel about that?"

Allow the children to attack the new words independently
in context but give individual help if it is needed. The words
brick and *pillows* both have familiar phonograms; *hunter* has
the *er* of agent.

Setting Up Reading Purposes. "The pets that came to
live with Iva and her husband were baby bears. Would you
like to have two baby bears live with you? What might happen if you did have them at your house? Things happened at
Iva's house too. Let us read to find out what they were. On
what page will we find the story?"

Reading the Story

Guided Reading

"Read the first page to find out how Iva and her husband
got the bears." After the reading, ask: "How big were the
bears? How do you know?

Page 110

"Read the first paragraph on this page silently." Ask one
child to read the paragraph aloud. "What tricks do you think
the bears played? Read the rest of the page to find out. What
did Iva say at last? Why   What happened to the bears?

Page 111

"Find out what the bears did when they started to live out
of doors." After the reading, ask: "Why do you think they

Page 112

223

Baby Bears (110–117)

ran home? What does the expression 'as gentle as a lamb' mean?

Pages 113-114
"Iva wanted to get rid of the bears. Read two pages to find out why she couldn't sell them and what happened when the *hunter* came.

Page 115
"Read this page to see what the bears did. Why do you think the bears obeyed Iva? Why did Iva begin to cry?" Ask a volunteer to read the last paragraph on page 115. "What did Iva mean?

Pages 116-117
"What happened to the bears? Why was Iva happy now? Why was the circus owner happy? Why were the bears happy? Did you like this story? Why? Do you think this could really have happened? Why or why not?"

Rereading for Specific Purposes

Making inferences

To give practice in focusing on concepts not expressly stated in the text, put the questions below on the chalkboard. Instruct the children to read each page and find the answers to the questions in order to discuss them with the group later. Good readers may wish to write their answers in sentences.

Read page 110. What kind of man found the bears? How do you know? What kind of person was Iva?

Read page 111. About how many inches tall were the bears by summer? Then how large did they get?

Read page 112. How did the bears feel when they had played a trick?

Read page 113. What do you know about the place they lived?

Read pages 114 and 115. How did the bears feel about Iva?

Read pages 116 and 117. How did the bears feel about the hunter? Why could the circus man sell more tickets?

Building Essential Habits and Skills

Comprehension and Study Skills

Drawing conclusions and predicting outcomes

Creative Reading. 1. To give the children more experience in drawing conclusions, distribute copies of the exercise at the top of page 225. When the children have finished, ask individual children to read aloud each story and answer. Expect varying answers and decide which are the most sensible.

Read each of the stories. Think about the question. Then write your answer on the line. Be sure that you answer in a sentence. When you have finished the exercise write a good title for each story.

Peter went into the back yard with a toy. He wanted to hunt bears. All afternoon he waited for a bear. It was almost dark now. What might happen next?

One summer morning Iva put her feather pillows on the grass to air them. The bear cubs were playing nearby. When Iva looked out the window, it looked as if it were snowing. The bears could not be seen. Then Iva saw the pillows start to move. What was going on?

In the forest the bear cubs found a honey tree. They climbed up. One reached in the hole to get the honey. All at once he cried and ran away quickly. What had happened to him?

2. To give practice in the recall of story events, write on the chalkboard the following topics:

Illustrating a part of the story

> *The Man Brings the Bears Home to Iva*
> *The Bears Are Trouble in the House*
> *The Hunter Sees the Bears on the Roof*
> *The Bears Are in the Circus*

Distribute sheets of drawing paper to the group and ask them, without using their books, to illustrate one of the topics above. Caution the children to try to remember the information in the story, for instance, the size of the bears, Iva's clothes, and what was going on.

Word-Study Skills

Phonetic Analysis. 1. To strengthen the ability to distinguish between the long and short sounds of *i*, direct the children in

Reviewing sounds of "i"

the activity below. Write the list of words below on the chalk-board or duplicate them. Have the children write all the long-*i* words in one column and all the short-*i* words in another.

> *wife, in, Iva, drink, lived, drive, tip, think, hide, winter, fine, brick, slide, pillow, city, tricks, bigger, white, miss, pile, digging, village, slid, slide, bite, chimneys, while, tickets, children*

Deriving vowel principles in one-syllable words

2. After the above exercise write in one list on the chalk-board the following words: *drink, tip, brick, slip, bit.* Ask: What sound has the vowel *i* in these words? How many syllables has each word? How many vowels? Help the children to derive the principle that *in most one-syllable words with only one vowel, that vowel is short.*

Write the following words on the chalkboard and ask what sound *i* has in each one: *white, bite, slide, wife, while.* Ask: "How many vowels do you see? How many do you hear? How many syllables has each word?" Lead the children to generalize that the final *e* in each of these words is silent. Help them to arrive at the principle that *when a word contains two vowels, one of which is final e, the first vowel is long, the e is silent.*

Recognizing hard and soft "c"

3. To review the variant sounds of *c*, call attention to the sound of *c* in *city* and *cellar.* For contrast, compare the *c* in *cat* and *can.* Tell the children that *c* has the hard sound like *k* in *cat* and *can*, the soft sound like *s* in *city, cellar,* and *decide.*

Help the children observe that when *c* is followed by *e* or *i*, as in *city* and *cellar*, it is usually soft. When *c* is followed by *a, o,* or *u,* as in *cat, came, come,* and *cut,* it is usually hard.

Lead the children to observe and identify soft and hard *c* in the following words: *cent, mice, face; coat, cover, cart, curtains.* Ask them to state in their own words the generalization about the pronunciation of *c* when it is followed by *e* or *i.* Let them demonstrate the application of this principle by attacking the new words in the following sentences:

> *Have you ever seen a <u>princess</u>?*
> *May I use your <u>pencil</u>?*
> *Rabbits like to eat <u>carrots</u>.*

Syllabication. To give practice in recognizing the number of vowel sounds in words, play the following game with the children: Playing "Listening for Vowel Sounds"

Pronounce a word. If the children hear one vowel sound, they raise one finger; if they hear two, they raise two fingers; if three, three fingers. Use a list, such as the following: *village, climb, brave, meadow, against, chimpanzee, bucket, hospital, swallow, important, curtains, hunter, brick, molasses, mind, stock, bananas.*

Workbook
Pages 32 and 33.

Related Language Experiences

Storytelling. Throughout this unit encourage small groups or individual children to make up original stories. Allow time for the stories to be told orally. Guide the children in dramatic presentation, such as how to use their voices, hands, and facial expressions to convey a variety of emotions. Then have the best stories retold during the regular story hour, dramatized by the children themselves, or acted out with puppets. Telling stories

Enrichment Activities

Co-ordinating Library Activities. The suggestions below will be useful for the entire unit, and even for the entire year. Operating the library

1. *Participation.* The class may elect a library committee of one, two, or even three children each week so as to give every child an opportunity to plan the various library activities and to take responsibility for them.

2. *Sharing Books.* To increase the size of the library and the reading interest of individual children, ask the group whether they would like to lend some of their own books to the room library. Discuss with them their obligation to care for other people's property. These particular books might be kept on reserve to be read only in the classroom. Bringing books from home

For a colorful library table and for safer handling of the books borrowed from individual children, help the group make attractive book covers with finger paints.

Baby Bears (110–117)

3. *Keeping Order in the Library.* Set aside other books which the children may borrow and take home to read for enjoyment. It would then be the library committee's job to keep a record of the book's name, the author, the borrower, and the date due. A mature group will be able to keep the books in order either by classifying them by subject matter or by arranging them in alphabetical order by author.

4. *Story Hour.* The library committee might choose a favorite story to read or tell to an audience. The class may set a convenient time, once or twice a week, to have a story hour. They might invite other classes to hear the story, or the committee might design posters telling the time and place of the story hour and post them throughout the school.

Puppet Theater. In their spare time children will want to keep adding to the room's collection of puppets of favorite characters. They may put on puppet shows either for their own amusement or for an audience. A large sheet of drawing paper may be used to design background scenery to be tacked to the back of the puppet theater.

Stories to Enjoy. *Major,* by ROBERT M. McCLUNG; *Lambert's Bargain,* by CLARE NEWBERRY; *Two Little Bears,* by

YLLA; *Bear's Land*, by NICHOLAS MORDVINOFF; *A Bear Named Grumms*, by BESSIE E. WHITE; *My Father's Dragon*, by RUTH GANNETT; *The Backward Day*, by RUTH KRAUSS.

Poems to Enjoy. "Riddles," pp. 211–222, in *The Golden Flute*, compiled by ALICE HUBBARD and ADELINE BABBITT; "Furry Bear," "Disobedience," and "Rice Pudding," in *When We Were Very Young*, by A. A. MILNE.

A Record to Enjoy. "Of a Tailor and a Bear," by EDWARD MACDOWELL, in *Listening Program*, Volume III. (RCA Victor.)

How Percival Caught the Tiger

Pages 118–121

Percival, a boy with a great imagination, tells a tall tale about capturing a tiger by feeding him sweet potatoes.

The story introduces children to the "tall tale," and may be supplemented with other similar tales. Children will be able to read the entire story silently to enjoy its humor.

Vocabulary

New Words: Page 118, *Percival, trap*, danger;* 119 *sweet*, sent*, closed*;* 120, *whole;* 121, *hang*, full, branch**

Developing Readiness for Reading

Meaningful Presentation of Vocabulary. "Have you ever thought what it would be like to *trap* a tiger? Today's *whole* story is about a boy who traps a tiger in a very strange way. The boy's name is *Percival*. Let us tap out the parts in his name. How many syllables are there? How many vowels? What are they?

"Now look at the sentences. The new words are underlined. Read the sentences and be able to tell us how you know the new words."

He was no longer afraid. He was out of <u>danger</u> *now.*
He <u>sent</u> *the boys to get a rope.*

Introducing the story

Using context clues to attack new words

229

He threw the rope over a branch of a tree.

He wanted to hang up a bag full of meat. If a wild animal tried to eat the meat the open trap would spring closed.

Take time to discuss with the children how they unlocked the new words.

Setting Up Reading Purposes. "Find the story called 'How Percival Caught the Tiger' in the table of contents and turn to it. If you think that Percival caught the tiger by shooting it, you're in for a surprise."

Reading the Story

Guided Reading

Pages 118–121

Reading for enjoyment

"Read the entire story silently to find out if you had the right idea about how Percival caught the tiger." After the silent reading, ask: "Why did Percival become frightened? Why did Percival and the boys run? How did they trick the tiger? Why did they throw the rope over the branch of a tree? How do you know that Percival's plan was a good one?"

Have the children ask and answer one another's questions about the story. Then ask: "Do you think this is a true story? Why not?" Expect such responses as: "A tiger would not be silly enough to swallow big stones"; "A wild tiger could be trapped best with meat." "Who do you suppose made up this story?" (Percival Summers himself.)

Rereading for Specific Purposes

Reading aloud favorite parts

Have the children find their favorite parts of the story and prepare to read them aloud. Ask the children to give reasons as to why these parts appealed to them.

Building Essential Habits and Skills

Comprehension and Study Skills

Choosing sentence endings to make a silly story a sensible story

Critical Reading. Distribute copies of the exercise on page 231, and say to the children: "Here is a new story about Percival. Read the title aloud. How is it different from the title in your book? After you read each sentence, underline the endings that are the most foolish, and you will have a very

Teaching *Finding New Neighbors*

230

silly story. Then circle the sentence endings that are the most sensible and you will have a more sensible story." Later have both stories read aloud and ask: "Which do you like better? Why?" Many children will feel that Percival is a silly hunter, and that the silly story is more fitting.

How the Tiger Caught Percival

1. The tiger saw Percival Summers in the ————.

    branches   jungle   sweet potatoes

2. The tiger heard Percival ————.

    breathing hard   roaring   calling

3. Percival covered himself with ————.

brown sugar and butter   branches   little stones

4. The tiger said, "I shall swallow you ————."

    with a few branches   whole   tied together

5. But Percival crawled ————.

under the tiger   under a little stone   into a strong cage

6. The tiger sent him away ————.

to eat potatoes   to the circus   with his legs tied together

---

Main Idea. To develop the skill of finding the main idea in a paragraph, distribute copies of the exercise on page 232. After the children have done the exercise independently, have the answers discussed in a group.

Finding titles for paragraphs

Word-Study Skills

Word Meaning. 1. To show how verbs carry along story action, have the children tell what each of the following words recalls to them about the story: *jumped, baked, covered, kicked, ran, swallowed, sent, cut, fell.* Call attention to the fact that each word tells about something that happened. Ask the children to think of other action words and to use each in a sentence.

Recognizing action words

Read each paragraph. Underline the best title for it.

On his trip to the jungle Mr. Summers took pictures of a big yellow tiger. The tiger was very near, and his teeth were showing. Mr. Summers' friends were all surprised that he had been brave enough to get such clear pictures.

Mr. Summers' Trip   Mr. Summers' Friends

Pictures of a Bear   <u>Mr. Summers and the Tiger</u>

_____

Mother went to the kitchen to get supper. First she made a cake. Then she baked the potatoes and a chicken.

A Good Cake   <u>Mother Gets Supper</u>

A Pretty Kitchen   A Good Chicken

_____

Once there was a strange jungle. The trees were all blue and yellow. The birds' nests were as big as easy chairs. The lions were as big as elephants, and the tigers were pink with green spots.

A True Story   <u>A Tall Story</u>

A Bird Story   A Chair Story

Perceiving opposite meaning in words

2. Copy the words below in two columns. Have the children draw a line from each word in the first column to a word in the second column which expresses an opposite meaning.

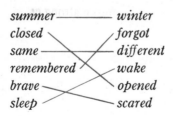
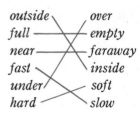

Reviewing the principle of vowels influenced by "r"

Phonetic Analysis. To recall the principle of vowels influenced by _r_, write in a row on the chalkboard the words _car, her, stir, for, fur._ Point to the word _car_ and say: "What sound has _a_ in this word? Name some other words that have this

Teaching _Finding New Neighbors_   232 sound." Elicit a few words, such as *barn* and *farm*, and write them under *car* on the blackboard.

Point to *her* and have it pronounced. "What vowel do you see in this word? Do you hear the *r* in the word? It gives the *e* a special sound of its own. We know that when we see *er* in words it will usually have this special sound. Who can name some more words with this sound?" List several *er* words under *her* as they are given by the pupils.

Continue in the same way to call attention to the special sounds of the vowels in *stir, for, fur* and to elicit other words containing these sounds.

When the lists have been completed, lead the children to observe the similarity in sound of the vowel in *her, stir, fur,* and emphasize the need for observing closely in sentences the spelling and meaning of the words for their correct recognition.

Syllabication. To teach the relation between the number of vowel sounds in a word and the number of syllables, write on the chalkboard the following words: *full, hang, trap, sent, mud, cage, rope, sweet, roar, wait.* Have the children pronounce the words and tell how many vowel sounds they hear in each one. Write over the words *One-Vowel Sound.* Bring out that it is necessary to listen carefully to a word to find out how many vowel sounds it contains. Recall that words sometimes contain vowels which are not sounded.

Explain that there is another way of describing a one-vowel word. Tell the children that *a word or a part of a word that contains a vowel sound is called a syllable.* Have the children see that the words above are one-syllable words. Write the new heading *One Syllable* over the heading "One-Vowel Sound."

Say: "Some words contain more than one vowel sound or syllable. Listen to these words and tell me how many vowel sounds you can hear." Pronounce clearly *frighten, kicking, danger, plenty.* Have the children tell how many vowel sounds or syllables they hear. Write above the words the headings *Two-Vowel Sounds* and *Two Syllables.*

"Let's see what sharp ears you have. Listen to these words and tell me whether they are one-syllable words or two-syllable words." Pronounce, one at a time, *jungle, sharp,*

> Learning the meaning of vowel sounds for determining syllables

233   *How Percival Caught the Tiger* (118–121)

peddler, *pads*, *swaying*, *swallow*, *visit*, *free*, *glass*. Continue this practice until the children give evidence of understanding that *a syllable contains one vowel sound* and that *a word contains as many syllables as there are vowel sounds*.

For additional auditory practice pronounce words clearly and have the children clap when they hear each vowel sound.

Workbook

Pages 34 and 35.

Related Language Experiences

Talking together

Discussion. Discuss different kinds of stories—true, fairy, funny, sad, animal. Let the children tell which kind they like best. Discuss with the children what makes the story of Percival humorous. Ask the children if they think the author of this story expected them to believe it.

Writing
original stories

Creative Writing. 1. Encourage the children to write and illustrate their own stories of "How _____ Caught the _____." Encourage humorous, highly imaginative stories. Have children write their own tall tales of all kinds.

Making up different
story endings

2. To encourage finding imaginative solutions for tall stories, distribute copies of the exercise on page 235.

Hearing a poem

Listening. Read the children "First and Last," by Ilo Orleans. Ask them to listen for the opposites and the contrasting pictures the poem portrays.

FIRST AND LAST

Dwarfs are short,
Pines are tall,
Mountains are great,
Kittens are small,
Ponds are shallow,
Oceans are deep.
Daddy's awake
While I'm asleep.
Skates are slow,
Planes are fast.
"A" comes first,
And "Z" comes last.

ILO ORLEANS

TALL TALES

These are all silly stories that cannot be true. Read each story. Think about it. In the space write a funny ending.

1. Down the street lived a girl who had green hair. Her friends thought that she should color it brown, but she liked looking so different. She _

_ _

2. Once there was a giraffe who liked to play jump-rope. His monkey friends turned the rope for him, but at least one of his four legs always got caught. He knew he had to do something about that because he always got hurt.

_ _

_ _

3. A tiger who liked to eat sweet potatoes could find no one to cook for him. _

_ _

4. A funny lion was born without a tail. He thought and thought about what he could do to get one. _ _ _ _ _ _ _ _ _ _ _

_ _

5. If there is time, make up a tall tale of your own.

Choral Speaking. Collect several narrative poems to read to the children. Good choices are poems such as: "Market Place," and "The King's Breakfast," in *When We Were Very Young*, by A. A. MILNE; "The Owl and the Pussy-Cat," by EDWARD LEAR; "The Pirate Don Durk of Dowdee," by MILDRED PLEW MEIGS, and "The Foolish Animals," in *Merry-Go-Round of Verse*, by ELSIE M. FOWLER. A particularly good poem for both listening and choral speaking is "The Tale of Custard, the Dragon," by OGDEN NASH, in *The Face Is Familiar*, in *The Golden Book of Poetry*, by JANE WERNER, and in *Read-Aloud Poems*, by MARJORIE BARROWS.

During this unit read aloud several of these narrative poems and let the children choose a favorite. Read this poem several

How Percival Caught the Tiger (118–121)

times, once for the story and again for appreciation of humor, rhythm, or dramatic expression. Encourage the children to learn the poem and to prepare it for choral speaking. One group may read or recite the poem in chorus while individual children act it out in pantomime. Each child should have an opportunity to play several different parts. The pantomimes may be rehearsed and presented for parents or for another group.

Enrichment Activities

Printing a "Free Time" chart

Co-ordinating Activity. In planning the decoration of the library corner, the library committee might take a poll of favorite free-time activities in the classroom. The interests may be organized and transferred to a chart. Children who need suggestions about using their spare time to best advan-

What Shall I Do Now?

Read a book.

Paint a picture.

Illustrate a story.

Do a puzzle.

Play a game.

Write a story.

Study spelling words.

Work with a friend.

tage will find out what books, games, or tools are available. The chart could be changed from time to time as the room's available activities change.

Story Hour. The children should continue to make new puppets as they come upon an interesting character in their reading. From this story, the tiger could fit into most original puppet plays. The teacher might encourage the children to present their original plays during a regular story hour.

Giving original puppet shows

Art and Construction. As the children read more and more independently, they will probably want to show their accomplishments to parents, friends, and other classroom visitors.

In order to recall quickly the titles of stories that have been read, the children might construct a chart. Help them record the title of the story and its author. The children themselves will probably have an original idea for the shape of the chart.

Making an "Independent Reading" chart

Drawing. Have the children originate and draw or paint funny pictures of hunters and their "tall tales." Let the children write their own original titles for their scenes, as "How Percival Rode a Lion," "My Pocket-Size Hippo," etc.

Illustrating "tall tales"

Stories to Enjoy. *Bears on Hemlock Mountain*, by ALICE DALGLIESH; *The Happy Lion* and *The Happy Lion Roars*, by LOUISE FATIO; "The Lion-Hearted Kitten," by PEGGY BACON, in *Story and Verse for Children*, compiled by MIRIAM B. HUBER.

Enjoying stories and a limerick

Poems to Enjoy. The nonsense poem that follows will delight the children:

> There was a young lady of Niger
> Who smiled as she rode on a tiger;
>   They returned from the ride
>   With the lady inside,
> And the smile on the face of the tiger.

COSMO MONKHOUSE

Read the children other nonsense poems and limericks, such as the following: "The Centipede," "The Panther," "The Fly," and "The Eel," by OGDEN NASH; "The Rhinoceros," by HILAIRE BELLOC; and the limericks of EDWARD LEAR; all in *Favorite Poems Old and New*, by HELEN FERRIS.

Azor

There was something strange about Azor. Animals talked to him. Larry, the big black-and-white cat, told him where Mrs. Woodfin had lost her earring. Ambrose, Mr. Frost's horse, told him who sent the valentine. All the children laughed at him, and in the end he learned a lesson.

Children will enjoy this story. It lends itself well to oral reading for interpretation and to reading for detail.

Vocabulary

New Words: Page 122, *Azor, Larry;* 123, *believed, Pringle, half;* 124, *sense*, Woodfin;* 125, ———; 126, *Ambrose, Frost, snowplow*;* 127, *Chrissie Orne, finished*;* 128, *valentine;* 129, *Ella Snook;* 130, *send*;* 131, ———

Developing Readiness for Reading

Understanding
related concepts
through a poem

Meaningful Presentation of Vocabulary. Read the children the poem "Boys' Names," by ELEANOR FARJEON.

BOYS' NAMES[1]

What splendid names for boys there are!
There's Carol like a rolling car,
And Martin like a flying bird,
And Adam like the Lord's First Word,
And Raymond like the Harvest Moon,
And Peter like a piper's tune,
And Alan like the flowing on
Of water. And there's John, like John.

Let the children talk about boys' names and mention some that they like especially well. Then, as you write *Azor* on the chalkboard, ask them whether this is a name that they have ever heard before. Say: "The story we are going to read today has several names and some of them may seem strange to you. *Azor* has a friend whose name is *Abel*. Two other names in the story are *Larry* and *Ambrose*.

[1]From *Over the Garden Wall*, by ELEANOR FARJEON. Copyright, 1933, by Eleanor Farjeon. Published by J. B. Lippincott Company. Reprinted by courtesy of J. B. Lippincott Company and Pearn, Pollinger & Higham, Ltd.

"Azor had many friends and neighbors. See if you can read some of their names." Write *Chrissie, Pringle, Mrs. Woodfin* on the chalkboard and tell the children that the vowel sounds may help them to recognize the words. Help the children with these words if they have difficulty.

"Chrissie's last name was *Orne*. Azor's teacher was *Miss Burns*. *Ella Snook* was a classmate of Azor's."

Ask one child to read aloud all the names that he thinks are unusual. Ask another child to find the names that are last names. Ask someone to point out two names that are nicknames. Discuss the meaning of nicknames and the advantage of "different" names.

Checking presentation of vocabulary

The other new words in the story may be attacked phonetically. *Send* and *sense* begin with the same three letters; *snowplow* is a compound; *finished* and *Valentine* may be blended through known phonograms; *half* will be taught during the guided reading.

Attacking words phonetically

Setting Up Reading Purposes. "Azor was like other boys but there was one strange thing about him which you could never guess. You'll want to read the story to find out what it is. Find the story in the table of contents, turn to the correct page, and we'll discuss what was strange about this boy. As you read the story decide whether any part of it could really have happened."

Reading the Story

Guided Reading

"Azor was different from other boys. No one believed what he said but little Pringle. Read the first page to find out what was strange about Azor." After the reading, ask: "What could Azor do that other boys do? Would you have believed that animals talked to him?

Page 122

Reading silently to answer questions

"Look at the picture on page 123. This is Azor's friend Larry, whose eyes were usually *half-closed*. Read this page to find out what Larry did most of the time. Was he a friendly cat? Do you think Larry had good sense? Why?

Page 123

"Read two pages to see what Larry did for Azor and what happened as a result." After the reading, ask: "Why did Larry like Azor? Why did Mrs. Woodfin give Azor money?

Pages 124–125

Should Azor keep the dollar? Why? What did Azor's mother say to him? his father? his big brother? How did Azor speak when he answered his family? Read the sentence aloud as you think he said it.

Page 126 "Who can read the subtitle aloud? On this page we'll learn about another friend who tells Azor things. Read this page to find out more about him." After the reading, ask: "Who was Ambrose? What did he do? What else do you know about Ambrose?

Pages 127–129 "Let us read until we find out how Ambrose helped Azor." After the reading, ask: "What did Ambrose say to Azor? Do you think Pringle believed him? Why or why not?

Page 130 "The next day at school Azor saw Ella Snook. Read to find out what he said to her and what her answer was." After the reading, ask: "What kind of boy do you think Azor was?" (Polite.) "Why? Read aloud the part that proves he was polite. Why did Ella say, 'I didn't send you any'? Was that truthful? Why didn't she put her name on the valentine?

Page 131 "Finish the story to see what happened in school when Azor told how Ambrose had helped him. Read aloud what Ambrose said as Azor went past him. What does it mean?"

Rereading for Specific Purposes

Reading orally to take parts of the characters

This is an excellent story for oral reading with children taking the parts of the characters. Have the children reread the story silently to find out how many speakers will be needed. Have one pupil be the reader and others take the character parts. Discuss how the characters would read their parts. Practice oral expression on such sentences as—

"You are a good boy, Azor, . . ." (page 124)
"He really did, . . ." (page 125)
"Yes, you did—Ambrose told me." (page 130)
"A HORSE!" (page 131)
"He says he TALKED to him!" (page 131)

Building Essential Habits and Skills

Comprehension and Study Skills

Finding answers to questions

Specific Details. To develop the ability to select information to answer questions, distribute copies of the exercise below. Have the children use their books to find the answers to the questions.

Read each question. On another sheet of paper write the answer and the page on which you found it in your book. Be sure you answer in a complete sentence.

1. What three things could Azor do pretty well? p. 122
2. Who thought it strange that the animals talked to Azor? p. 122
3. Tell three things that the story tells about Larry. p. 122
4. Tell why Larry thought Azor had sense. p. 124
5. Why did Mrs. Woodfin give Azor a dollar? p. 124
6. What was on the valentine that Azor got? p. 128
7. How did it happen that Ambrose stopped at Azor's house? p. 129
8. How did Pringle think Ambrose knew who sent Azor's valentine? p. 129

Creative Reading. To give practice in understanding and following instructions and in drawing conclusions, distribute the following exercise to the children:

Illustrating story characters

Drawing Some Pictures

1. Fold a large piece of drawing paper into four parts.
2. Read this exercise all the way through and find the directions for drawing four pictures.
3. Write the name of one picture in each of the four spaces of your drawing paper.
4. Read the directions for each picture again and make your drawings.

LARRY

Make Larry sitting on a chair, almost asleep. His eyes are half-closed. He is watching Mrs. Woodfin mopping the floor. She is dressed in old clothes and she would like Larry to get out of her way.

AZOR

Draw Azor ready to go outside to shovel the walk. Put in his hand what he needs to do a good job.

AMBROSE

Ambrose is cleaning the street too. Draw him with all he needs to do a good job. Draw someone to drive Ambrose. Remember to dress the man warmly.

VALENTINE

Make the valentine that Ella Snook sent Azor. Look in your book to find out what it was like. Beside it draw a valentine that you would like to get.

Word-Study Skills

Applying word-attack skills

Phonetic and Structural Analysis. 1. To maintain the ability to apply word-analysis skills to new words met in the lesson, list on the chalkboard *sense, send, valentine, finished, snowplow.* Ask the children to identify phonetic parts in each word that help them to pronounce it. Lead them to point out the special structure of the last two and discuss the *ed* ending of *finished* and the parts of the compound *snowplow.*

Reviewing "sh," "ch," "ck"

2. To recall the digraphs *sh, ch, ck,* when used at the end of words, write the following words on the chalkboard: *finish, swish; which, branch; kick, stuck.* Have each pair of words pronounced and point out the final digraphs in each, especially the sound of final *ch* in *which* and *branch.* Have the children attack new words through blending word parts, paying particular attention to the final digraph in each case:

> *Lions like to eat fresh meat.*
> *The church bells were ringing.*
> *A ship was tied to a dock.*
> *We wished the boys good luck.*

Recalling pronouns ending in "self"

Structural Analysis. 1. To call attention to the structure and meaning of words ending in *self,* write on the chalkboard the following sentence from the text:

> *Azor promised himself to mind his own business.*

Call attention to the word *himself.* Discuss what it means. Write also the words *itself* and *myself,* and have the children tell which part of these words is the same. Have them read

Teaching *Finding New Neighbors*

242

the two new *self* words in the following sentences and tell what they mean.

> *Mary made a new dress all by <u>herself</u>.*
> *Can you make your bed by <u>yourself</u>?*

NOTE. The meaning of the pronouns ending in *self* is confined to "only or alone," that being the meaning which they have in this text. If the group suggests sentences in which the word is used for emphasis, as "You, yourself, told me to do it," develop this meaning also.

2. To recall the significance of contractions, ask a child to find *wasn't* on page 122. Have the child read the sentence. Then ask him to read it with the words *was not*. Have the child go to the chalkboard and write *was not* and *wasn't*. Do the same with *didn't* on page 123, *didn't* on page 125, *wasn't* on page 126, *who's* and *don't* on page 128, *it's* on page 129, *didn't* on page 130, *he's* on page 131.

Reviewing contractions

3. Have the children skim to find the following phrases: *Mrs. Snow's house, Mrs. Woodfin's house, Orne's walk, Azor's yard, Azor's house, Mr. Frost's Ambrose, grandfather's horse.* Have them identify each possessive form and help them understand that in these words the apostrophe denotes ownership.

Reviewing the possessive form of nouns

4. To lead into a development of hyphenated words, discuss with the children the compound words that appear in this story: *sidewalk, snowplow, postman, snowman.* Have them tell the two words which comprise each compound.

Recognizing compound words

Then tell the children that there are other words which are used together, but that these are joined differently. List on the chalkboard the following phrases: *black-and-white cat, half-closed eyes, right-hand fence picket, said good-by.* Explain to the children that the small mark between two words is called a hyphen, and that a hyphen often joins two words which are usually written separately. Have the children read the phrases orally and frame the hyphenated words.

Reviewing hyphenated words as adjectives

For further practice, list *strange-looking animal, cock-a-doodle-doo, hoppity-hop, rain-maker,* and *front-yard gate.* Lead the children to observe that the hyphen helps them to pronounce words and to understand their meaning.

Workbook

Pages 36, 37, 38, and 39.

243

Related Language Experiences

Planning
a puppet show

Puppet Show. If the group has not already worked a story into a puppet show for the book party suggested in the "All-Unit Activities," they may want to begin by writing an original fanciful or tall tale. The teacher may open the discussion by reading a fanciful tale to the children. Several good ones are contained in *Time for Fairy Tales*, by May Hill Arbuthnot, and in *Children's Literature by Grades and Types*, by Ollie Depew.

The children themselves will probably offer ideas for a play which may be put down in outline form. The teacher may help in organizing the play by scenes. As the children enter into the mood of each scene, they should be allowed to make up their own lines. Later the teacher may write the lines down to be memorized.

As the puppets are constructed and the play is being rehearsed, the teacher may guide the group in offering constructive criticisms to those speaking the lines and manipulating the puppets. Such criticisms should, of course, be preceded by a discussion of the tact, kindness, and co-operation which are needed for successful group projects. A free give-and-take of ideas and criticisms on a constructive level will help raise the standards of performance and develop the children's ability to take criticism.

Writing tall tales

Writing Stories. Continue to have children create fanciful and tall tales. If they enjoyed "Azor," they may want to write about talking animals.

Writing letters

Writing Invitations. Have each child write a letter inviting his parents or friends to the class book party. Be sure to check the children's letters for correct form and spelling.

Enrichment Activities

Preparing
for a book party

Co-ordinating Activity. If the teacher has followed the suggested co-ordinating activity, she may also wish to carry out the suggested culminating activity, a book party. To prepare for it, the library committee should check the library corner to see that it is well arranged and displayed. Books of original stories should be attractively bound and displayed.

Stories to Enjoy. Read more about Azor in *Azor, Tor and Azor, Azor and the Blue-Eyed Cow*, and *Azor and the Haddock*, all by MAUDE CROWLEY; *Babar's Fair Will Be Opened Next Sunday*, by JEAN DE BRUNHOFF; *The Song of Lambert*, by MAZO DE LA ROCHE.

A Poem to Enjoy. "Girls' Names," by ELEANOR FARJEON, in *Sung under the Silver Umbrella*, compiled by the Association for Childhood Education International.

Some Fishy Nonsense

Page 132

Developing Readiness for Listening

"Have you ever gone out looking for polliwogs in the spring? Where do you look for them?" Point out that frogs usually lay their eggs in quiet water, sometimes in swampy places, or *bogs*. Have the children recall the fact that polliwogs have no legs but that they will develop them before they become frogs.

Reading the Poem

"Today I am going to read a poem called 'Some Fishy Nonsense.' The author, Laura E. Richards, tells about two boys who went fishing for polliwogs. As I read it to you, see if you can decide what makes it funny."

Read the poem with strong, rollicking rhythm, being sure to emphasize the words *pollothywogs* and *bogothybogs*. The children's books should be closed.

"What did you like about the poem?" The children will probably mention the rhythm, the humor, and the unusual words. After brief discussion read the poem again.

Rereading the Poem

Have the children open their books to page 132 and discuss the picture. Read the poem once more as the children follow the text. Have them practice the words *pollothywogs* and *bogothybogs* orally, then read the poem in unison.

Related Activities

Poems such as this are greatly enjoyed by children because of their strong rhythm, their use of unusual words, and their humor. The children will enjoy hearing more humorous poems read by the teacher. They may wish to memorize one or two of the poems for choral speaking as part of the culminating activities at the end of the unit.

Poems to Enjoy. Humorous poems by the following authors, selected from poetry collections or from their own books of verse: *Book of Nonsense,* by EDWARD LEAR; *Picture Rhymes from Foreign Lands,* translated by ROSE FYLEMAN; *Tirra Lirra,* by LAURA E. RICHARDS; poems by LEWIS CARROLL; the sections "Just for Fun," in *Very Young Verses,* by BARBARA GEISMER and ANTOINETTE SUTER, and in *The First Book of Poetry,* by ISABEL J. PETERSON.

All-Unit Activities

Culminating Activities

Giving a party

Book Party. Help the class execute some of their plans for a book party. The classroom should be attractively decorated with library posters, and original stories, book reviews, book-cover designs, and interesting books should be displayed.

The program might consist of any or all of the following items: the puppet show, original or adapted from a story; oral book reviews; the telling of original stories or the retelling of an old tale; a choral reading of poetry; pantomime or recitation of a dramatic poem or poems about the care of books; recitations of short, favorite nonsense poems.

Refreshments of decorated gingerbread cookies and punch or cocoa might be served to the guests after the program has been presented.

Discussing the
stories in the unit

Review and Discussion. Discuss the stories in this unit to help children see relationships among them. In what way are the stories alike? Elicit the fact that all are humorous stories.

Help children compare the story characters and the situations by such questions as the following:

> In what way was Iva like Aunt Selma? (Good disposition.)
>
> In what way might Percival be like or unlike Azor? (Relations with animals.)
>
> What did the hunter have to do that was somewhat like what Percival had to do? (Trap the animals.)
>
> In what way was the tiger like the baby bears? (Both ended in the circus.)

Riddles. Ask children to write riddles about the characters in these stories, for example: Writing riddles

> I am an animal.
> I lived in a jungle.
> I liked sweet potatoes.
> Because I ate so much, I was caught.
> Now I am in the circus.
> Who am I?

Evaluating Activities

Testing skill in alphabetizing

Test for Alphabetizing. To test the skill of alphabetizing, distribute copies of the following words to be arranged alphabetically. Tell the children that they will not find a word for every letter.

1. People and Animals in the Stories

Nils	Chrissie	Ambrose	Joe
Percival	Iva	Larry	Frost
Tommy	Selma	David	Ella

After they have completed the exercise, have children identify and discuss each story character.

2. Words Appearing in the Stories

danger	branch	molasses	only
promise	finished	curtains	half
apron	important	gruff	just
laughing	kick	right	trap
everybody	neighbors	village	until
which	sense	quickly	yard

Checking word recognition through context clues

Vocabulary Recognition Test. To test the ability to use context clues as an aid to recognizing words, distribute copies of the following exercise:

Read each sentence. Put in the missing word.

1. The __curtains__ were hanging at the windows.
2. The sticky, brown __molasses__ went into the gingerbread.
3. She __promised__ him she would do what he asked.
4. The __peddler__ was giving new shoes for old.
5. He shook all over when he gave a big __sneeze__.
6. Now she was all through. The gingerbread was __finished__.
7. He thought the cake was chocolate. She __believed__ so too.

Teaching Finding New Neighbors

8. He put his head down on the ___pillow___ .
9. He must do the work because it is very ___important___ .
10. Ella sent a pretty ___valentine___ to Azor.

valentine	important	curtains
peddler	molasses	believed
promised	sneeze	pillow
	finished	

Word-Meaning Test. To check the ability to make associations between words and their meanings, distribute copies of the following exercise:

Testing the ability to classify

Find the words which make you think of a jungle. Draw a line under them.

branches of trees	peddlers
animal trap	forest
danger	snowplows
pillows	hunters

Underline the words which make you think of making gingerbread.

valentines	danger
sticky spoons	chocolate
going to market	sea shell
scrub	molasses
ginger	angry words

Underline the words which make you think of animals.

kick	forest
hunter	ropes around necks
half-finished	circus
important promises	tricks
tiger	peddler

Test of Vowel Sounds in Syllables. To check auditory discrimination of syllables, distribute copies of the exercise on page 250. Direct the children to say the words softly to themselves; then to write the number of vowel sounds and the number of syllables that they hear.

Noticing the number of syllables in a word

249   All-Unit Activities

	Vowel Sounds	Syllables		Vowel Sounds	Syllables
hunter	2	2	market	2	2
apron	2	2	Hilda	2	2
full	1	1	peddler	2	2
danger	2	2	pillow	2	2
molasses	3	3	important	3	3
forest	2	2	Percival	3	3
kick	1	1	hard	1	1
trap	1	1	stuck	1	1

Helping the Individual Child

Evaluating individual needs

General Help. The teacher should observe each child's reading habits constantly. Such questions as the following will help to evaluate both progress and difficulties:

1. Does each child seem to be enjoying the stories?

2. Is each child reading some stories or entire books independently with enjoyment?

3. Do the reading activities seem too difficult for certain children? too easy? Regrouping may be indicated.

4. Is each child making use of a variety of methods to attack new words? Does he use context clues? phonetic analysis? structural analysis? Does he apply known principles of word attack and identify words by analogy?

5. Has the child formed the habit of checking his recognition of a new word by reading it in the sentence and asking himself, "Does this make sense?"

6. Is each child aware of errors he makes in the workbook or in written exercises, and is he learning to overcome those errors?

Word Meaning. To help individual children enrich and extend their reading and speaking vocabularies, give them extra practice in classifying, in recognizing multiple meanings, and in defining words.

Making picture dictionaries

Some children may benefit from making their own picture dictionaries. These might include words, their definitions, and simple illustrations.

Phonetic Analysis. To give extra help in recognizing the variant sounds of vowels, distribute copies of the following exercise:

Say each word to yourself. If the vowel is long, write L; if it is short, write S; if it is followed by r, write R.

S	brick	S	sent	L	closed	S	sense	S	hunt
S	trap	L	use	R	hard	S	hang	R	horse
L	feel	L	bite	R	burn	L	cake	R	hurt
S	which	L	sneeze	L	wake	S	scrub	L	nose
R	bird	R	harp	R	horn	L	no	L	these
L	old	L	ride	L	rode	L	shine	S	bugs

Structural Analysis. If certain children need additional practice in recognizing compound words, write on the chalkboard the following words and help these children frame the two parts of each word:

anything	*nobody*	*anyone*	*everything*
earring	*suppertime*	*everybody*	*outside*
sidewalk	*snowplow*	*snowman*	*snowstorm*
postman	*anyway*	*nearby*	*schoolyard*

Specific Help. The teacher must ask herself *why* an individual child is having difficulty. Is he trying to read at a frustration level? If there are specific areas in which he needs help, find those trouble spots. Go over the evaluating activities orally with the child. Recheck his test scores on the Ginn *Third-Grade Readiness Test, Revised Edition.*

After the child's difficulty is diagnosed, use some of the following suggestions if they meet his particular needs:

1. Have the pupil write some of the new words.

2. Have him choose a reading helper to whom he may read orally or to whom he may go for help when the teacher is busy.

3. Give the child experiences in *hearing* sounds and word parts. Have him *listen* as the teacher carefully pronounces words. Have him *watch* as she writes words.

251

4. Plan a few minutes alone with the child who is having difficulty. Praise him for his attempts, help him relax, and help him make a new attack on reading skills.

5. Try to help each child to see that reading can be fun. Make available books that are both easy to read and at the child's own interest level. Most third-grade children enjoy easy stories by the following authors: Hetty Beatty, Jerrold Beim, Margaret Wise Brown, Clyde R. Bulla, Virginia Lee Burton, Lois Lenski, Robert McCloskey, H. A. Rey, and Miriam Schlein.

Library activities for better readers

Provision for Superior Readers. Have the superior readers go to the card catalogue in the library and find other humorous stories in the subject index.

These children may arrange the library table and a bulletin board for related stories. Encourage them to take turns expressing their own ideas in changing the display. Some of the superior readers may annotate their list of stories. Help them make notes from which they can report about their extra reading.

Refer to the word-meaning test, on page 249, of words that make one think of the jungle, animals, etc. Have the children build similar exercises for the rest of the class.

Children who enjoy writing will want to write their own

stories and poems. Help these children select their best stories and bind them in a book for the library.

Encourage the better readers to read poetry in the available children's collections. Help individual children interpret their favorite poems to be read aloud during a story hour.

The teacher will want to stimulate these children to further reading. Their supplementary reading may be on a level higher than that of their basal reader. She will wish to broaden their interests in reading; however, she will not give so much attention to their special abilities that the less able feel discouraged.

All-Unit Activities

Unit IV · Indian Children

Introducing the Unit

Through the reading of this unit the children will gain a deeper insight into the Indian ways of life. These exciting stories about boys and girls of different cultures will help children to realize that Indian children are much like themselves. The children will learn to admire the courage and resourcefulness of the Indians in meeting their needs for shelter, clothes, food, transportation, and recreation. They will also become acquainted with Indian children of different tribes, their life, their work, their play, and their dress, both in the past and in the present.

An inventory of what children already know about Indians would be useful before completing plans for developing this unit. If the children have little knowledge of Indian life, prepare to build up conceptual background through pictures, stories, and other materials containing accurate information. The amount of time available for studying the Indians should determine the types of activities.

This unit might be introduced by a display of Indian clay bowls, baskets, or jewelry, as well as several colorful pictures portraying different Indian tribes and customs. Some of these pictures might be historical, others contemporary. The children themselves will probably initiate a lively discussion.

With the help of an Indian map, such as the one in *The First Book of Indians* by Benjamin Brewster, give the children some idea of the great number and variety of Indian tribes. Explain briefly how very well Indians adapted to their environment and how the life of Woodland, Plains, Desert, and Everglades Indians differed.

Say: "What kinds of stories did you find in the last unit? (Humorous, make-believe.) Now we are going to read some stories that might really have happened. The information in these stories is true. Our new unit is called *Indian Children.* Some of the stories in this unit tell about Indians of long ago. Others tell about Indians who are living today."

Talking about the unit theme

Story	Vocabulary	Developing Readiness	Reading the Story		Building Es	
Pages	**New Words**		**Guided Reading**	**Rereading for Specific Purposes**	**Comprehension and Study Skills**	**Word M**
Little Fox of the Forest 133–143	Indian bow arrows stew moccasins knife skin beads — bad magic tired hit should young fresh feast	New words are presented in context either written or oral. Children are encouraged to identify new words through comparison with known words and the use of phonetic and context clues.		Reading to identify oneself with a story character	Locating and Organizing Information: summarizing information about Woodland Indians on a chart Critical Thinking: judging the pertinence of answers (worksheet) Workbook: 40, making comparisons; 41, choosing titles	Workboo using cont as an aid meaning
Blue Cornflower 144–151	Strong mud belts boots shawl moon eagle — understand prayer those above teachers sorry pencil			Reading for the main idea: making subtitles	Organizing Information: adding to the Indian chart Creative Reading: drawing conclusions (chalkboard exercise) Details: comparing stories (worksheet) Workbook: 43, classifying ideas	Context emphasiz text clues tacking ne Workboo enriching of Indian and custo
The Eagle Hunt 156–164	cliff cloud swift below frightened edge partly trail cave — jar Dawn filled turquoise speak circles buckles even		Silent and oral reading for comprehension and interpretation of story plot, mood, and characterization.	Reading orally to prove statements and to find answers to specific questions	Sequence of Ideas: recalling order of new story material (worksheet) Organizing Information: Indian chart Workbook: 46, recalling story details; 47, using context clues; comprehending new story material	Sentenc ing: build tences fro of words
He-Who-Thinks-Well-and-Runs-Quickly 165–179	prairie buffaloes herds rumbling thud east west pound leaders signal lines — suddenly pushed save women dust shooting shot minute messenger proudly	Through discussion and exchange of ideas, interest in the story is stimulated and background for understanding is developed. Purposes for reading are reached by the group with the teacher's guidance.		Reading to show varying emotions and moods	Main Idea: associating story facts with correct subtitles (worksheet) Story Sequence: rearranging sentences in sequence Organizing Information: Indian chart Workbook: 48, following directions; recalling story details; 49, determining sequence in new story material	Associa ferent mea with word Unlocki pound wo through of the wo
Billy Tigertail 180–188	alligator camp sofkee pot meal swings wears			Reading silently to draw conclusions	Details: Checking the ability to use context clues in recalling story details (worksheet) Organizing Information: completing the Indian chart Workbook: 52, recalling details; using context clues; 54, organizing information	Observi different and uses nyms (wo
All-Unit Activities					Evaluation: checking concepts about Indians (test) Provision for less proficient readers: improving phrase reading	Word-St Test: che word mea Provisio proficient word gam context cl Workbo pages 55 Vocabula III, parts

its and Skills			Related Language Experiences	Enrichment Activities
Word-Study Skills				
Phonetic Analysis	Structural Analysis	Syllabication		
rning to attack new through phonetic and ural clues	Reviewing comparative and superlative forms of adjectives Alphabetizing: reviewing the alphabet; making an Indian picture dictionary		Discussion: talking about Indians; making plans for the unit (chart)	Co-ordinating Activity: planning and presenting an Indian play Indian booklet: collecting information about local Indians Construction: making Indian objects Informational Books Stories in Other Readers Stories, music, filmstrips
		Recognizing syllables in words Observing vowel digraphs in syllables Identifying one- and two-syllable words Seeing a and be at the beginning of words as syllables Dividing words into syllables (worksheet) Workbook: 44, recognizing syllables	Listening: to the poem "Home Song" to capture the mood and notice the lack of rhyme Organizing ideas: giving short talks	Art: painting a mural; making properties for the play; making Indian dolls Cooking: making Zuñi succotash Story Hour: reading and dramatizing a story Stories in Other Readers Informational Book Stories, a record, poems, films, and filmstrips
rning diphthongs oi, oy iewing ou, ow ognizing hard and soft s of c			Discussion: about symbolism; conservation of eagles Creative Writing: writing stories about different groups of Indians Speech: observing speech habits	Construction: making costumes, a picture map Collections: setting up a class museum Chartmaking: word and picture chart Library: finding Navajo stories and legends Dancing: preparing an Indian dance Stories in Other Readers Stories, folk tales, films, and filmstrips
alling short u and short u grams rkbook: 50, recognizing ar phonetic elements; calling oi, oy, attacking words	Reading a new story and recalling the suffix ly (worksheet) Reviewing contractions		Oral Expression: retelling the story Research: learning how Indians communicated Dramatization: of the story Letter Writing: writing invitations	Co-ordinating Activity: learning the steps of the Buffalo Dance Construction: making properties A Story in Another Reader Informational Books Stories, rhythms, and filmstrips
viewing the variant ds of ea alling sounds of ou and acking new words con- g ou and ow rkbook: 53, discriminatetween long and short ds of vowels	Recognizing the possessive form of nouns Recalling contractions Discriminating between possessive forms and contractions (worksheet)		Discussion: finding out about alligators; learning how to treat burns; discussing care of younger children Story telling: telling folktales	Construction: making a peace pipe; painting a mural A Story in Another Reader Informational Book A story and a film
aluation: testing long and vowel sounds; testing and soft c	Evaluation: testing er and est endings; checking the ability to drop ly (test)	Evaluation: checking the number of vowel sounds and syllables (test)	Provision for superior readers: reporting on Indians; writing original stories and verse; reading aloud favorite Indian stories	Culminating Activities: presenting the Indian play; exhibiting Indian articles; explaining the Indian chart Provisions for superior readers: reading informational book; making a scrapbook; doing research on local Indians; dramatizing folktales; building Indian villages; learning sign language

Little Fox of the Forest

This story of an eastern Woodland Indian boy depicts the home life and some of the beliefs of these Indians. Little Fox and his mother were left alone during the winter while the father and other men of the village were away on a long hunt. On the return of the hunters with a plentiful supply of fresh meat and skins, there was a great feast for all the village.

Children will enjoy the story because of the different way of life it depicts. They will learn something of the life of Indian people who lived in our country long ago and will appreciate ways in which Indian children were like themselves.

Vocabulary

New Words: Page 133, *Indian;* 134, *bow*, arrows*;* 135, *stew*;* 136, *moccasins, knife*, skin*;* 137, ——; 138, *beads*, bad*, magic;* 139, *tired*, hit*;* 140, *should*, young;* 141, ——; 142, *fresh*, feast*;* 143, ——

Developing Readiness for Reading

Talking about
a picture

Meaningful Presentation of Vocabulary. "Our first story tells us about an Indian boy who belonged to a tribe of Indians that lived in the eastern part of our country a long time ago. Find the story in your table of contents. What does the title tell you about Little Fox? Try to think of some of the equipment a *young* Woodland Indian would probably need. Yes, Little Fox hunted with a *bow* and *arrow.*

"Open your books to page 134. What can you find out from the picture? Little Fox is bringing home a turkey so that his mother can have *fresh* meat to make some *stew* for him. Do you suppose Little Fox is *tired* after his day? What is Little Fox wearing on his feet? Why would *moccasins* be especially good to wear on a hunting trip?"

Attacking new
words through
phonetic clues

The children may be able to attack the phonetic words below through the word-analysis skills which they have already learned and which include blending, analogy, and recognition of familiar phonetic parts: *stew, fresh, knife, skin, should* (consonant blends and digraphs); *feast, beads* (vowel digraphs);

bad, hit (vowel sounds and phonograms). The new word *magic* will be introduced in the guided reading.

NOTE. If necessary, this story may be broken at the subdivision. The amount of material to be read at one sitting should be determined by the maturity and the ability of the group.

Setting Up Reading Purposes. "What kind of clothes is Little Fox wearing? What kind of house would you expect him to live in? What kind of work might Little Fox's mother, *Singing Water*, do? Let us read the story to find out how Little Fox and his people lived a long time ago."

Reading the Story

Guided Reading

"What is the first subtitle of our story?" ("One Winter Night.") "Let's read the first two pages to find out why Little Fox was hunting." After the reading, ask: "How did Little Fox let his mother know he was coming? Do you ever signal to your mother in any way? Why do you imagine Singing Water felt proud of her son? What do you think her surprise for Little Fox can be?

Pages 134–135
Reading silently to answer questions

"Look at the pictures on the next two pages. In what is Singing Water cooking the stew? Where do you imagine she got the cooking jar? What do you think Little Fox will do with some of the stew he doesn't eat?

Pages 136–137

"Read two pages to find out whether you would like to spend a winter evening as Little Fox did." After the reading, ask: "Why do you think they were all warm and happy? What do you think Little Fox meant by the 'Little People'?

"Read page 138 to find out about the Little People and the *magic* that Singing Water believed in." After the reading, ask: "Why did Singing Water touch the bag that was hanging around her neck? Who was the medicine man? How had the Little People once helped a woman?"

Page 138

Have the children discuss the picture on page 139 and describe what they think is happening. "Read page 139 quickly to find out what woke Little Fox. What kind of blanket did Little Fox have? Do we use beaver skins today?"

Page 139

Have the children examine and discuss the pictures on pages 140 and 141. Say: "Read the subtitle on page 140. What do you suppose is going to happen? Do you think Little Fox will go to meet his father? When the men came home with fresh meat, there usually was a feast. What might happen at such a feast? Finish the story to find out what happened when Little Fox's father came home." After the reading, ask: "Why did Singing Water go to the wise old men? Why did the Indians have a feast? What did they do after the feast? Could this story happen to Woodland Indians today?"

Rereading for Specific Purposes

Reading silently
to identify oneself
with a character
in the story

Have the children reread the story silently to find ways in which they are like Little Fox. A child may read aloud a part which he thinks tells something about Little Fox that reminds him of himself. Have the other children tell whether or not they agree. Guide the children in selecting parts which show that Little Fox helped his mother, liked to hear stories, fed his dog, thought about growing up, and so on.

Building Essential Habits and Skills

Comprehension and Study Skills

Locating and
organizing
pertinent
information

Organizing Information. To develop skill in comprehending and organizing information, guide the children in making a chart about the Indians in the stories of this unit. Help them to suggest headings and to locate details in the story that belong under the headings. Continue this guided chart development as each story in this unit is read. The chart below is suggestive of one which may be developed.

INDIANS	HOME	FOOD	TRAVEL	WEAPONS	CLOTHES	FUN
Woodland	in the forest bark house skin door- way smoke hole in roof grass mats	turkey birds small ani- mals stew corn cakes fresh meat	by boat on foot	bow and arrows stone knife	moccasins skins	feasts stories games

Encourage the children to hunt for additional information about Indians in library books and magazines. Help them to organize the information and to add it to the chart.

Using other sources of information

Critical Thinking. To check the children's recognition of relevant details, distribute copies of the exercise below. Have the children draw a line under the sentence that answers each question. Let them discuss the reasons for their choices.

Judging the pertinence of answers

PART I

1. Why did Little Fox see no frogs at the pond?

    The frogs were hiding behind the trees.
    The frogs were sleeping in the pond under the ice.
    The frogs had gone to a warmer country.

2. Why was Little Fox pleased with his mother's surprise?

    He needed some new moccasins.
    He liked stew for his supper.
    Now he could carry his stone knife.

3. Why could the Indians talk about the Little People in winter?

    The Little People were covered up in ice and snow.
    The Little People were afraid of the Indians.
    The Little People were busy getting firewood.

4. Why did Singing Water believe in the bag hanging from shell beads around her neck?

    She could keep a stone knife in it.
    The bag would keep her warm.
    The medicine man gave it magic to keep her safe.

5. Why did the basket of nuts fall on Little Fox?

    Little Fox liked nuts to eat.
    The wind shook the walls of the bark house.
    The Little People made it fall.

PART II

6. Why did the older men of the village talk together?

    They thought they might have to send help to the hunters.
    They had nothing else to do.
    They were angry with Singing Water.

261   *Little Fox of the Forest* (133–143)

7. Why did the young men go out in a boat?

>They wanted to go fishing.
>They were taking Little Fox for a ride.
>They went to pilot the tired hunters home.

8. Why did the hunters bring home piles of skins?

>They thought the skins were pretty to look at.
>They would sell the skins to white men.
>The people needed skins to make moccasins and clothes.

9. Why had the hunters dried some of the meat in the sun?

>Drying the meat kept the men busy.
>The dogs liked dried meat better than fresh meat.
>They had no other way of keeping meat a long time.

10. Why did the Indian mothers build fires as soon as they saw the men coming?

>It was a very cold day.
>They knew the hunters would bring meat for a feast.
>It was night time and they needed fires to give light.

Word-Study Skills

Applying word-analysis skills to words of the lesson

Phonetic and Structural Analysis. To strengthen the skill of attacking words independently through word-analysis, list on the chalkboard all the new words in this story. Add to this list the words *deerskins, highest, cubs, firewood, falling, smaller, doorway, hunter, part, send, treetop, dark, nuts.*

Discuss with the children how close examination of the parts and characteristics of a word can help them in unlocking it. In the words mentioned above help them to look for familiar characteristics and group the words in such ways as the following:

>short *u* and short-*u* phonograms (*cubs, nuts, hunter*)
>digraph *ea* (*beads, feast*)
>*a* as in *all* (*smaller, falling*)
>*a* followed by *r* as in *far* (*dark, part*)
>compound words (*deerskins, firewood, doorway, treetop*)

During this vocabulary practice, note any confusions or hesitancies on the part of individual children and follow this word study with exercises for extra practice. It is largely through the teacher's observation of individual attack on the new words of each lesson that word-analysis techniques can be made to fit the needs of the group and of individuals within the group. The words in this lesson provide a good opportunity to review vowel sounds and consonants:

short vowel—*skin, bad, hit, fresh*
long vowel—*knife, tired, feast, beads, bow, home, hole*
consonants and blends—*y* as in *young,* medial soft *g* in *magic,* silent consonant in *knife,* blends in *stew* and *feast.*

Have frequent reviews of common phonograms and vowel differences in words. Help the children apply this knowledge in attacking unfamiliar words.

Structural Analysis. To review the comparative and superlative forms of adjectives, write on the chalkboard the sentences below. Have them read orally and ask the pupils to explain the meaning of the words *older* and *highest.*

Reviewing words ending in "er" and "est"

> *The older men talked about what should be done.*
> *Little Fox climbed the highest tree on the highest hill.*

Write the sentences below on the chalkboard; then have them read and the underlined words explained.

> *Jim climbed to a high branch of the tree.*
> *Tom climbed up higher than Jim.*
> *Jerry climbed up to the highest place of all.*

Have the pupils read the following word groups and then use each word in a sentence: *great, greater, greatest; loud, louder, loudest; near, nearer, nearest; small, smaller, smallest.*

Explain why it is always a good idea to look at the ending of a word, as well as at the beginning, for help in pronunciation and meaning.

Alphabetizing. To develop auditory and visual recognition for letter sequence in the alphabet, ask such questions as: What letter comes after *c*? before *l*? first? last? Then direct the pupils to write the numbers 1, 2, 3 before the letters—1a, 2b, 3c—and ask such questions as: How many letters are there in the alphabet? Which is the ninth letter? letter number 20? and so on.

Reviewing the alphabet

Then say: "Now let us find some words that begin with each of these letters. Who knows a word beginning with *a* that means something an Indian uses for shooting game?" Write *arrow* after the letter *a*. In the same way have the children suggest picturable words, such as *bow, chipmunk, dog, feast, hunter, Indian, knife, Little Fox, moccasins, nuts, owl, pond, rabbit, skins, turkey, village*; or write the words above in mixed order on the chalkboard and have the pupils write them after the proper letters on their paper.

After these words have been arranged in order, show the pupils how to make a dictionary, one page to a letter. The words may be illustrated to serve as a guide and new words added to the individual dictionaries from time to time.

Have children see other picture dictionaries. Let them decide whether they wish to make individual dictionaries or a large illustrated alphabet book for the library table.

If a few children are gifted in making rhymes, they may be encouraged to make a rhyming alphabet book which others may help to illustrate.

Workbook

Pages 40, 41, and 42.

Related Language Experiences

Discussion. 1. Let the children discuss freely what they know about Indians. Distinguish between what they *know* and what they *think*. Write on the chalkboard any special words that are needed in talking about Indians and refer to them during the discussion. Emphasize that the pupils will obtain accurate information about Indians. Have on the library table as many books about different Indians as are available. Make it clear to the children that, because Indians depended upon their local environment for the things they needed, different environments (Woodland, Plains, Desert, Everglades) supplied different materials for meeting life needs.

2. During the unit let the children plan, organize, and carry out activities which they suggest. They may make a planning chart such as the one on page 265.

Teaching *Finding New Neighbors*

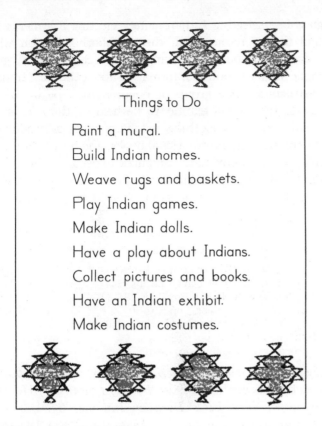

Things to Do

Paint a mural.

Build Indian homes.

Weave rugs and baskets.

Play Indian games.

Make Indian dolls.

Have a play about Indians.

Collect pictures and books.

Have an Indian exhibit.

Make Indian costumes.

Enrichment Activities

Co-ordinating Activity. Encourage the children to plan and produce an Indian play. Allow them to discuss whether they wish to dramatize one of the stories in the Reader, or whether they would prefer creating their own story. In either case the children should use their own words and make up their own lines. Committees may be appointed to make the scenery and costumes, to learn dances and songs, and to plan the scenes. The class may be divided into groups with pupil leaders to work on the suggested activities which will contribute to the play.

Planning an Indian play

Indian Booklet. If the children live in a community in which Indians live now or have lived, they may wish to write a class booklet called "Indians in Our Community." The children may be interested in pretending that they are an

Composing an Indian booklet

Little Fox of the Forest (133–143)

Indian tribe—selecting Indian names, electing a leader, going out and finding resources in the neighborhood upon which the Indians depended for a living. Other children may go to the public library to obtain information about the local Indians.

Making Indian objects **Construction.** One group of children may begin making objects for the Indian exhibit to be held at the end of this unit. Such articles of clothing as food pouches or headdresses may be copied from informational books, and authentic Indian designs may be approximated and used to decorate the objects. Girls may sew little bags like Little Fox's to wear around the neck, or they may color macaroni shells and string them for bead necklaces.

Reading Indian stories **Stories in Other Readers.** Show the children these interesting Indian stories in other readers.

> *Our Good Neighbors*, by WILLIAM H. BURTON
> "Our Country in Other Days," pp. 103–144
> "Augustus and the Indian Boy," pp. 194–201
> "Paddyfoot and the Bear," pp. 202–209
> *Stories from Everywhere*, by GUY L. BOND and others
> "Naki and Bluebird," pp. 62–72
> "Ousta and His Family," pp. 73–84

Informational Books. *American Indian* and *Big Book of Indians*, by SYDNEY FLETCHER; *Book of Indians*, by HOLLING C. HOLLING; *The First Book of Indians*, by BENJAMIN BREWSTER; *Indians of the Longhouse*, by SONIA BLEEKER; *The True Book of Indians*, by TERI MARTINI; *How the Indians Lived*, by FRANCES R. DEARBORN.

Enjoying literature, music, and filmstrips **Stories to Enjoy.** *Dicky and the Indians*, by MABEL G. LA RUE; "Young Indian Hunter," in *Do and Dare*, by BARBARA NOLEN, pp. 222–231; *Our Country*, by LUCY SPRAGUE MITCHELL and DOROTHY STALL, pp. 146–189.

Music to Enjoy. "Indian Cradle Song," in *The American Singer*, Book Three, by JOHN W. BEATTIE and others; "Smoking the Peace Pipe," in *Our Songs*, by THERESA ARMITAGE and others.

Filmstrips to Enjoy. *Woodland Indians* (JamHandy), 42fr, color, in HOW THE INDIANS LIVED series. *Indians of the Northeastern Woodlands—Hunter from the Longhouse* (SVE), 32fr, color, in ADVENTURES WITH EARLY AMERICAN INDIANS series.

Blue Cornflower

Blue Cornflower, a Pueblo Indian girl, was leaving her village home to attend the Big Rock Indian School where she would live twenty-four hours a day. Her family made presents for her, and her grandfather, a medicine man, admonished her never to forget the ways of her people.

At the new school Blue Cornflower was homesick, and particularly so at feather-planting time. With the help of her teacher's feather and a blue pencil she was able to send her prayer wish to Those Above and to prove that she had not forgotten the ways of her people.

In reading the story, children will sympathize with the Indian child who was plunged into a new and strange environment. They will learn something of the life of the Pueblo Indians and be able to contrast it with that of the Eastern Woodland Indians.

Vocabulary

New Words: Page 144, *Strong*, mud*;* 145, *belt*, boots*;* 146, *shawl, moon*;* 147, *eagle*, understand*;* 148, *prayer, those*, above;* 149, *teachers*, sorry;* 150, *pencil*;* 151, ———

Developing Readiness for Reading

Meaningful Presentation of Vocabulary. "Our next story is about Indians of the Pueblo tribe. Do you know what *tribe* means? In some ways a tribe is like a big family with one leader. Different tribes lived in different places; so they lived in different ways. The Pueblo Indians still live in the southwestern part of our country where trees are scarce. They make their homes of sun-dried *mud* bricks." If possible, show the children pictures of adobe houses and of pueblos.

Discussing related concepts

"Turn to page 144 and compare the picture with the one on page 133. This little girl is *Blue Cornflower*. How is Blue Cornflower's home different from Little Fox's home? What do you suppose the ladders are used for? Why do you think the Pueblo Indians built their homes in this way?" (To protect themselves from wild animals and other Indians.) "Blue Cornflower's little brother is named *Strong Boy*. What does that name tell you his parents wanted him to be one day?

Talking about a picture

267   *Blue Cornflower (144–151)*

"Now look at the picture on page 145. What do you think Blue Cornflower's father is making?" (*boots*) "What animal's skin might he use?" (*deerskin*) "All the women in this tribe wore *boots* like *those*. They wore *shawls* over their shoulders and *belts* around their waists."

Using phonetic clues for word attack

Many new words may be attacked through familiar methods of word analysis, for instance, *boots, moon, eagle, teacher* (double vowels and vowel digraphs); *strong, mud, belt, those* (blending and familiar phonograms); *pencil* (medial soft *c*).

The words *above, sorry,* and *understand* will be introduced during the guided reading.

Setting Up Reading Purposes. "What would you like to know about a Pueblo Indian girl and her family? What do you think our story will tell? How do you suppose her life compares with that of Little Fox?" Write the children's questions and suggestions on the chalkboard. Then say, "Let's read the story to see how many of your questions it will answer."

Reading the Story

Guided Reading

Pages 144–145

Reading silently to answer questions

"These two pages will tell why Blue Cornflower's father made a present for her. Read them to find out." After the reading, ask: "Why was Blue Cornflower's home not made of bark as Little Fox's home was? Why were her parents sad because she was going to school? Were they *sorry* to see her go away? Was the school like the one you attend?

Pages 146–147

"Look at the picture on page 146. What presents is Blue Cornflower receiving?" (A new dress with a red belt, white deerskin boots, earrings of silver with blue beads, paper bread, a red shawl, Strong Boy's lamb.) "Who are the older people? Blue Cornflower's grandfather, you will discover, was a special person.

"Now read pages 146 and 147 to find out what Grandfather told Blue Cornflower and what her new school was like." After the reading, ask: "What did Grandfather mean when he talked to Blue Cornflower? How did Blue Cornflower get to school? How did she feel when she rode in the car? In what ways was the school different from Blue Cornflower's home? Why was she homesick? How would you feel if you were in her place?

"What is Blue Cornflower looking at in this picture?" **Page 148** Encourage free discussion. "The Indian people had certain customs which they followed when the moon was new. This was the time of year to send a *prayer wish* to *Those Above*. Read this page to find out how a prayer wish was sent." After the reading, discuss the meaning of the page.

"Do you think the people in the school would *understand* **Pages 149–151** Blue Cornflower's problem? Why or why not? Finish the story to find out how Blue Cornflower's teacher found a way to help her." After the reading, ask: "Why was Blue Cornflower so sad? Why wasn't her teacher cross when Blue Cornflower pulled the feather from her hat? What was Blue Cornflower's prayer wish? Do we sometimes make prayer wishes, too, even though we don't do it as Blue Cornflower did? In what ways was Blue Cornflower's life different from Little Fox's life? Which of your questions about Blue Cornflower were answered?"

Rereading for Specific Purposes

The story divides easily into three parts: Blue Cornflower's departure from home, the Big Rock Indian School, and feather-planting time. Have the children reread the story silently under the teacher's direction, decide where they would divide the story, and make a subtitle for each part.

Making subtitles for the story

Building Essential Habits and Skills

Comprehension and Study Skills

Organizing Information. Help the pupils add information about the Pueblo Indians to their Indian chart.

Locating pertinent information

Creative Reading. To encourage a closer examination of reasons and motives, write on the chalkboard the questions at the top of page 270. For an average group it may be well to discuss the questions orally. A superior group will be able to answer them independently on paper, to be discussed later. Allow for varying answers if they show logic and insight.

Thinking of answers not given in the book

269   *Blue Cornflower* (144–151)

Why did Desert Indians live in pueblos?

Why couldn't Blue Cornflower live at home and go to school?

Why was the brick school so very different from Blue Cornflower's pueblo?

Why did Blue Cornflower make a prayer wish?

Recalling
story details;
comparing stories

Story Details. To provide practice in recalling story details, distribute copies of the following exercise:

Next to each question write the answer.

	Blue Cornflower	Little Fox
1. Which one had moccasins?		Little Fox
2. Which one ate paper bread?		Blue Cornflower
3. Which one used a bow and arrow?		Little Fox
4. Which one lived in a bark house?		Little Fox
5. Which one made a prayer wish?		Blue Cornflower
6. Which one hunted wild turkeys?		Little Fox
7. Which one lived in a mud-brick house?		Blue Cornflower
8. Which one had white deerskin boots?		Blue Cornflower
9. Which one had a stone knife?		Little Fox
10. Which one believed in the Little People?		Little Fox
11. Which one had trees to climb?		Little Fox
12. Which one believed in Those Above?		Blue Cornflower
13. Which one had ladders to climb?		Blue Cornflower
14. Which one went to school?		Blue Cornflower
15. Which one had a new red shawl?		Blue Cornflower

Word-Study Skills

Finding
context clues

Word Meaning. To give practice in the use of context clues, say: "Find a sentence on page 145 in which the word *boots* is used. How did the sentence help you to get the meaning of the new word?" Proceed in the same manner with the new words below. Evolve a definition for each word as it is discussed. Help the children to understand how reading to the end of a sentence or paragraph often helps in discovering the meaning of an unfamiliar word.

belt	*understand*	*moon*	*mud*	*teachers*
eagle	*prayer wish*	*sorry*	*pencil*	*shawl*

Syllabication. 1. To strengthen recognition of the number of syllables in a word, write on the chalkboard a group of one-syllable words, such as the following: *bow, belt, shawl, which, mud, bricks.* Have the children pronounce the words and tell how many vowel sounds they see and hear in each word. Recall the principle that when a word contains only one vowel sound it is called a word of one syllable. Write *one syllable* on the chalkboard, as this phrase will be used frequently in giving directions for activities.

Recognizing syllables in words

Write the words *brother, below, eagle, sorry, teacher, pencil, magic.* Have the children pronounce each word and tell how many vowel sounds they hear. Tell them that when a word contains two vowel sounds, each of which can be heard and pronounced, it is called a word of *two syllables.* Emphasize the importance of listening carefully.

2. To teach the recognition of a syllable with a vowel digraph, call attention to the word *beads* and explain that although two vowels are seen in the word they make only one sound; therefore it is a one-syllable word. List *rain, week, boots,* as further examples and let the children suggest others.

Observing vowel digraphs in syllables

3. To give practice in recognizing syllables, write on the chalkboard the words below. Have the children pronounce each word in turn and tell if it has one syllable or two syllables.

Identifying one- and two-syllable words

moon	*hear*	*peep*
arrow	*strong*	*doctor*
stew	*plenty*	*rocking*
homesick	*feast*	*thin*

4. To teach recognition of the syllables *be* and *a*, proceed in the following way: As the children watch, write the word *sleep* on the chalkboard and have it pronounced. Ask how many syllables it has. Then write *asleep*, pronounce it, and ask the children how many syllables they hear now. Suggest to the children that the word has been changed both in meaning and form by the addition of *a*. Write the following one-syllable words on the chalkboard: *long, way, lone, head, cross, wake, part, round.* Ask the children to put *a* before each word in the list, read the word aloud, tell how many syllables they hear, explain its meaning, and use it in a sentence.

Learning that "a" and "be" at the beginning of a word are syllables

271

If the children are ready, show them that the words *believe,* *behind, began, below, because,* and *become* begin with the syllable *be.* Have the children underline *be* in each of the words.

Conclude by telling the children that both *a* and *be* are syllables. Have the children divide words with *a* and *be* into syllables. Show them how to divide a word into syllables by writing the word *below* with a space between the syllables— *be low*—or by drawing a vertical line between the syllables —*be|low.* Then distribute copies of the following exercise:

Write the words below in syllables. The first one is done for you.

away	a|way	because	be|cause	before	be|fore
afraid	a|fraid	began	be|gan	above	a|bove
awake	a|wake	behind	be|hind	ahead	a|head
again	a|gain	alone	a|lone	against	a|gainst

Write the correct word in each sentence.

The rain came down from the clouds __above__ .

above   below   around

Blue Cornflower's grandfather told stories __about__ strange animals.

awake   about   again

In the stories bears would fight __against__ foxes.

afraid   ahead   against

The white boots __belong__ to Blue Cornflower.

behind   belong   before

Read the sentences with the underlined words. Underline the meaning of each new word.

Blue Cornflower did not __believe__ all the strange stories.

__think to be true__   stop   think about

Did Blue Cornflower's mother put her __aboard__ a train to go away?

next to   under   __on__

Blue Cornflower __became__ tired as she rode along.

__grew to be__   below   had to be

Pages 43, 44, and 45.

Related Language Experiences

Listening. Read the children the poem "Home Song." Ask them to listen for the gentle rhythm and for the pictures the poem brings to mind. Point out that the lack of rhyme in this poem does not make it any less beautiful or musical. Ask the children to tell some of the things they have learned about Pueblo Indians from the poem. Discuss with them the importance of corn in the Pueblo way of life and the love of nature that the poem expresses. Ask: "Is this a happy poem? What does 'rich in blessings' mean?"

When the children have expressed their reactions, reread the poem and have them listen for elements to illustrate.

Listening to an Indian poem

HOME SONG[1]

My mother's house
My father's fields
Are all around me.
The ways of my people
From the oldest times
They are around me, too.
The sun is over us.
The moon is over us.
The stars shine on us.
The earth is beneath us.
They bless us all.
Corn grows in our fields,
Deer run on the mountains,
The snow melts into the rivers,
And the clouds gather to bring us rain.
All these things bless us.
We are rich in blessings.
We hold our blessings close
And open our arms
To share our blessings with all people.

ALICE MARRIOTT

[1]From *Indians of the Four Corners*, by ALICE MARRIOTT. Copyright, 1952, by Alice Marriott. Reprinted by permission of the publishers, Thomas Y. Crowell Company, New York.

Giving Talks. After a rereading of both "Blue Cornflower" and "Little Fox," the children may enjoy talking to the group about likenesses and differences between the lives of the two children. For instance, some may choose to talk on such subjects as the houses in which Blue Cornflower and Little Fox lived, the kind of food they ate, or the occupation of their parents. Help the children to construct a simple outline to organize their talks. Encourage them to speak clearly and distinctly so that all can hear. Show how a plan helps to make a speech move along smoothly. Help the children evaluate their own talks.

Enrichment Activities

Art and Construction. Some children may wish to make a mural of an Indian village. The pictures should show the type of dwelling and the occupations of the people. Before the children begin this project, encourage them to make use of informational books both in the school library and in the public library so that the mural will be authentic in details of clothing, dwellings, tools, and activities. Provide an opportunity for the children to explain their mural to the rest of the group.

Have the children model clay bowls and jars to be used as properties in their Indian play. The bowls and jars may be dried in the sun and painted with Indian designs.

Indian Dolls. Suggest that some children make dolls of simple materials, such as paper bags stuffed with crushed newspaper, pipe cleaners, or lumber scraps, and dress them as accurately as the available materials and skill will permit. Simple directions for making a Hopi Kachina Doll are in *McCall's Giant Golden Make-It Book*, by John Peter.

Cooking. If the children are interested in finding out about food eaten by Blue Cornflower's people, they might try the recipe given below and serve the dish at lunch-time.

> *Zuni Succotash:* Cook some small cubes of beef until tender. Add green corn and string beans. Use sunflower seeds to thicken the stew and add salt. Cook until quite thick.

Story Hour. Plan a special meeting of the class for the audience reading or dramatization of Indian stories and poems that have been enjoyed by the group.

Reading or telling Indian stories

Stories in Other Readers. The three stories mentioned below give much information about Pueblo customs.

Stories from Everywhere, by GUY L. BOND and others
  "Cliff Homes," pp. 95–103

Beyond Treasure Valley, by EMMETT A. BETTS and others
  "Happy Days," pp. 226–233

Along the Way, by GERTRUDE HILDRETH and others
  "Indians" (a whole unit), pp. 48–74

Informational Book. *Pueblo Indians,* by SONIA BLEEKER.

Stories to Enjoy. *Chi-Wee,* by GRACE MOON; *One Little Indian,* by GRACE and CARL MOON; *Our Country,* by LUCY SPRAGUE MITCHELL and DOROTHY STALL, pp. 253–264; *Little Wolf the Rain Dancer,* by TERRY SHANNON; *Hah-Nee of the Cliff Dwellers,* by CLYDE R. BULLA.

Enjoying literature and music

A Record to Enjoy. *The Pueblo Indians in Story, Song, and Dance,* Soundbook (Book-Records Inc.—4095). An Indian medicine man presents Pueblo legends, chants, and dances.

Poems to Enjoy. Read the poem below to the children. Discuss the meaning of the rainbow, the swallow, and the cloud. Bring out that the corn, which is the Indians' food, needs rain to grow, and that these Indians are thankful for rain, because in their part of the country it rains very little.

CORN–GRINDING SONG

Zuñi Indians

Yonder, yonder see the fair rainbow,
See the rainbow brightly decked and painted!
Now the swallow bringeth glad news to your corn,
Singing, "Hitherward, hitherward, hitherward, rain,
     "Hither, come!"
Singing, "Hitherward, hitherward, hitherward, white cloud,
     "Hither come!"
Now hear the corn-plants murmur,
"We are growing everywhere!"
Hi, yai! The world, how fair.

Translated by NATALIE CURTIS

Also read "Lullaby" and "Wind-Song," translated by NATALIE CURTIS, and "The Locust," translated by FRANK CUSHING, all in *Sung under the Silver Umbrella*, compiled by the Association for Childhood Education International; "Rain Chant" and "Prayer to the Sun God," by LOUIS MERTINS, in *Story and Verse for Children*, by MIRIAM BLANTON HUBER.

Films to Enjoy. *The Hopi Indians* (Coronet), 1 reel, b&w/color. *Hopi Indian Village Life* (Coronet), 1 reel, b&w/color.

Filmstrips to Enjoy. *Southwest Indians (Hopi)* (Jam-Handy), 35 fr, color, in HOW THE INDIANS LIVED series. *Indians of the Southwest—Pueblo Dwellers and an Apache Raid* (SVE), color, in ADVENTURES WITH EARLY AMERICAN INDIANS series.

Home

Developing Readiness for Listening

"How do you imagine Little Fox and Blue Cornflower felt about their homes? What are some of the things about your home which make you like it very much? Look at the picture on page 152. It shows an Indian home, and in the poem called 'Home,' by Ann Nolan Clark, we shall find out how an Indian child feels about his home. Close your books and listen as I read it to see if you agree. Try to remember some of the things this child likes about his home."

Reading the Poem

Have the children listen as you read the entire poem clearly and with expression. Then encourage free discussion about the children's reactions to the poem and about the things which made the little Indian like his home.

Rereading the Poem

Encourage the children to reread the poem with you. Have them wave hands gently to the melody of the poem as you read it again. Then have some good readers each read a stanza. The whole group may enjoy choral reading of the poem.

Related Activities

Creative Writing. Guide the children in writing a group poem. As they suggest ideas which they would like to put into their poem, write them on the chalkboard. Guide the children in classifying what has been recorded—outside, inside, the family, activities in the home. Discuss words which make them see a picture, words which make them feel. Record these on the chalkboard. Guide the children in expressing their ideas in a simple, effective way. Help them to understand that poems need not rhyme.

Art. Suggest that each child draw a picture to illustrate his favorite stanza of the poem. Exhibit the pictures on the bulletin board. Show the group the illustrations in the book *In My Mother's House,* by Ann Nolan Clark. Explain that this poem was made by Indian children with their teacher's help.

The last stanza of "Home" has been set to music that captures the mood of the poem. Help the children learn it and have one child accompany its rhythm with a soft drumbeat.

HOME

ANN NOLAN CLARK

Quietly

PAUL FORDE

In my moth-er's house all day I play and work; All night I sleep. The walls come close a-round me in a good — way. I can see them; I can feel them; I live with them. This house is good to me, It keeps me; I like it, My moth-er's house.

The children will enjoy learning some Indian games and dances. See "Indian Melodies," pp. 181–184, and "Indian Games with the Tom-Tom and Indian Rattles," pp. 68–71, in *Rhythmic Games and Dances,* by DOROTHY HUGHES.

Poems to Enjoy. "Hiawatha's Childhood," by HENRY WADSWORTH LONGFELLOW, in *Story and Verse for Children,* compiled by MIRIAM B. HUBER; "Little Papoose," by HILDA CONKLING, "Indian Children," by ANNETTE WYNNE, and "Foreign Children," by ROBERT LOUIS STEVENSON, all in *Gaily We Parade,* compiled by JOHN E. BREWTON.

The Eagle Hunt

On their way to get eagle feathers for the feather dance, two Navajo boys found a hidden cave in which was stored an ancient jar filled with turquoise. Although the boys feared the presence of Dawn People in the cave, they nevertheless decided to take the stones home. Dancing Cloud's father assured the boys that the Dawn People would not be angry unless one spoke badly of them. The village silversmith then helped the boys make silver belts set with turquoise.

The story introduces children to another tribe of Indians, their desert country, and their customs and beliefs. It will stimulate comparison with the life of the other Indians about whom the children have already read.

Vocabulary

New Words: Page 156, *cliff**, *cloud**, *swift**; 157, *below**, *frightened*, *edge*; 158, *partly**; 159, *trail**, *cave**; 160, *jar**, *Dawn*; 161, *filled**, *turquoise*; 162, ——; 163, *speak**, *circles*, *buckles*; 164, *even*

Developing Readiness for Reading

Meaningful Presentation of Vocabulary. Before beginning this story it may be a good idea to have on hand some turquoise or Navajo jewelry to show the children, as well as several pictures of the desert, a butte, hogans, and Navajo activities.

Giving story background

Say: "This is a story about two Navajo boys, *Dancing Cloud* and *Swift Boy*. Do you know in what part of the country the Navajo Indians live? Like the Pueblos they live in the desert. In this story we shall learn about some Navajo customs, like the feather dance, about their belief in the *Dawn People*, and about the kind of clothes and jewelry that they wear." Show the children a piece of Navajo jewelry and allow them to tell about Navajo ornaments their friends or relatives may own. "Does anyone know what this jewelry is made of? Yes, silver and *turquoise*. Often belts are made of turquoise *circles* and silver *buckles*."

Talking about related concepts

If more background is needed, discuss Navajo customs and crafts, but be careful not to give away this story.

The Eagle Hunt (156–164)

NOTE. There are various opinions about the identity of the Dawn People mentioned in the story. It is thought that they were an early people who lived on top of the buttes. The echoes of the voices were probably so magnified by the canyon walls that the people who lived in the canyon thought them to be of supernatural origin. The Navajos also have a mythology based on the personification of natural phenomena.

Attacking vocabulary independently

To encourage children to attack vocabulary independently through analogy, write the following words on the chalkboard:

LIST I		LIST II	
brave	car	cliff	cave
loud	will	below	fill
slow	sniff	trail	speak
mail	smartly	cloud	jar
leak		partly	

Ask a child to read the familiar words in List I. Have the children take turns finding the new word in List II that rhymes with the familiar word in List I. Help children with meanings of the new words.

Talking about pictures

Have the children look at the picture on page 156 and comment freely. They will probably note that these boys are dressed differently from the Pueblo Indians and that they have horses.

"Look at the picture on page 158. Can you tell how Dancing Cloud got up the *edge* of the cliff?" Draw from the children the idea that there was a *trail*.

Setting Up Reading Purposes. "These boys are not at all afraid of steep cliffs and narrow trails, but there are things that do *frighten* them. Let's read this story to find out what they are and what adventures the boys have."

Reading the Story

Guided Reading

Pages 156–164

This lesson provides an excellent opportunity for the initiation of the study-guide procedure indicated below. Distribute copies of the study guide, using a form such as the one shown at the top of page 281.

Using the study guide

Before the children begin to read, discuss the study guide with them. Then say: "Today you are going to read a story

---

THE EAGLE HUNT

1. What are the names of the Indian boys in this story?
2. Why did Dancing Cloud climb the high cliff?
3. Where do eagles build their nests?
4. What did Dancing Cloud let down over the edge of the cliff?
5. Why couldn't the Indian boys catch the young eagle?
6. What did they find at the end of the trail?
7. Where did the Dawn People live?
8. With what was the jar half filled?
9. What is a turquoise?
10. Why did Wildhorse tell his son not to speak badly of the Dawn People?
11. What did the Indian boys want to put in the silver circles on their belts?

Question	Page	Paragraph	Key Words
1	156	1	Dancing Cloud—friend
2	156	2	Let—Black Cliff
3	156	2	Let—Black Cliff
4	157	3	Dancing Cloud—anything
5	158	2	But—more
6	159	5	Look—frightening
7	160	7	Oh—it
8	161	3	The—stones
9	161	4	The—stones
10	163	2	Quiet—them
11	164	2	Swift Boy—stones

---

silently by yourselves. On the paper you will find some questions about the story. Let's answer the first question together. Under the heading 'Question' write the number of the question you are answering. Yes, number 1. Now look in your Reader for the answer. Under the heading 'Page,' write the number of the page in the story where you found the answer. Under 'Paragraph' write the number of the paragraph on that page. The first and last words of that paragraph are the 'Key Words.' What key words will you write for question 1?"

When you are sure that the children understand the procedure, say: "Let's see how many of the questions you can answer without help. As soon as you have finished, we shall discuss the answers together."

The children work individually on the study guides while the teacher observes them and assists those who need help in mastering the technique.

During the group discussion of the questions and answers on the study guides, call upon various children to give the information they have found in connection with each question. At this time show children how to correct their own errors.

NOTE. Care should be taken that the study-guide procedure is well understood. Samples of certain pupils' completed study guides may be shown to illustrate such qualities as neatness, accuracy, and completeness.

Rereading for Specific Purposes

Reading orally to find answers

Some children may have encountered difficulty in filling out the study guide because they were unable to distinguish paragraphs or because they could not locate the key words. Practice in these skills can be provided by asking simple questions, such as those below, on the content of each page in the story. Have children locate the paragraph containing the answer and read it aloud.

Look on page 157.
What did Dancing Cloud do with the can?
What did the baby eagle do?

Look on page 158.
How did Dancing Cloud scare the second eagle?
Why didn't the boys get that eagle?

Look on page 159.
When did the boys find a trail?
Why was Swift Boy afraid?

Look on page 160.
What else was at the back of the cave?
Why did Swift Boy not want to take the jar?

Look on page 161.
Where did the Dawn People live?

Look on page 163.
When would the Dawn People be angry?

Building Essential Habits and Skills

Comprehension and Study Skills

Sequence of Ideas. To give practice in recalling the order in which story events took place, distribute copies of the exercise below.

Recalling order of ideas in new story material

NOTE. The children should be able to attack through phonetic clues the unfamiliar words in this exercise (*spinning, woolen, loom, dipping, soap*). If not, tell them the words.

Read the story. Number the sentences at the bottom of the page in the order that they happened in the story.

The mother of Turquoise Horse made woolen blankets to sell to the trader. Every spring Turquoise Horse rounded up his mother's sheep. The whole family helped in cutting the wool from the sheep. The wool was then put in two piles, one to be put in bags for selling, the other to be used for making blankets. Soap from a plant was used to wash the wool so that it would be soft and clean.

All the next day the mother was busy spinning and dipping the wool into color she had made from plants. After putting white wool up and down on the loom she put red, black, and gray colored wool across. In and out went her quick hands.

After a week the finished blanket was bright with gay, red and white blocks and black and gray lines.

When Turquoise Horse took the blanket to sell, the trader gave him money for groceries.

5	The trader bought the blanket.
1	The wool was cut from the sheep.
2	The children washed the wool.
4	The mother made a beautiful red, white, gray, and black blanket.
3	The mother colored the wool.
6	Turquoise Horse could buy groceries.

Organizing Information. Help the children add information about the Navajo Indians to the Indian chart discussed on page 260 of this manual.

Adding to the chart about Indians

The Eagle Hunt (156–164)

Word-Study Skills

Building
sentences

Sentence Meaning. To give practice in recognizing new words and in composing sentences, write on the chalkboard the groups of words below. Direct the children to make a sentence of each group.

their nests	*turquoise*	*the trail*
eagles	*Big Arm*	*The boys*
high cliff	*in the*	*to the cave*
build	*put*	*walked along*
on a	*silver belts*	*in the woods*
Wildhorse	*around it*	*Swift Boy*
Dancing Cloud	*made*	*the jar*
to speak badly	*The children*	*of water*
did not want	*and danced*	*filled*
of the Dawn People	*a circle*	*half full*

Learning to
recognize
the diphthongs
"oi" and "oy"

Phonetic Analysis. 1. To develop understanding of the sounds of the diphthongs *oi* and *oy*, write on the chalkboard the words *toys* and *noise* and have them pronounced. Lead the children to observe the similarity of the two sounds and the difference in their spelling. Explain that in *oi* and *oy* two letters combine two sounds to make one speech sound. Have the children listen as they pronounce other known words containing *oi* and *oy: join, boy, oil.* Ask them how the sound of these vowels helps them to pronounce the new word *turquoise* and have them underline the diphthong *oi* in the word.

Present the sentences below containing unfamiliar *oi* and *oy* words and have them read. Later present other words such as *voice, boil, enjoy,* and have them used in sentences.

The rain came to <u>spoil</u> our sand house.
The birds were singing for <u>joy</u> in the beautiful morning.
Will you <u>point</u> to the word you know?
Do you like <u>soy</u>-bean soup?

Reviewing
"ou" and "ow"

2. To review other diphthongs—*ou* as in *mouth* and *ow* as in *cow*—have volunteers give words containing each sound. Lead the children to observe the different spellings of the sound.

3. To review hard and soft sounds of *c*, write on the chalk-board in one column the words *cave, curtain, canyon, caught, colt, coyotes*; in another column write *city, place, once, piece, cellar*. Have the children observe the difference in the sounds made by *c* in these words. Write over the first column the word *Hard;* over the second, *Soft.* Maintaining hard and soft sounds of "c"

Say, "In these words what sounds of *c* do you hear?" Write *dancing, country, circle, pencil, doctor, circus*. Write the words again, divided into syllables, and ask: "In which syllable is *c* soft? In which is it hard?" Call attention to the two sounds of *c* in both *circle* and *circus*.

At the end of the discussion bring out that when *c* is followed by *e, i,* or *y* in a word, it usually has a soft sound; when *c* is followed by *a, o,* or *u,* it is hard. Then have children attack the unfamiliar words *cap* and *princess* and ask to have these words used in sentences.

Workbook

Pages 46 and 47.

Related Language Experiences

Discussion. 1. Better readers may be interested in doing either independent or group research on the origins and meanings of some typical designs used by the Navajos, such as the thunderbird, teardrop, lightning, and sun designs. With the help of the teacher they may organize the material and tell their discoveries to the rest of the group. The information might then be utilized for the program or play described at the end of the unit. Finding and discussing symbolism

2. Discuss with the children the ancient Indian custom of destroying or capturing birds in order to use their feathers for decoration. Point out the relatively small danger of exterminating eagles and other birds in the days when the population was small and when the Indians took only the birds they had use for, compared with the problem created by the large population now. Bring out the fact that we have made laws to protect birds today. Talk about the usefulness and attractiveness of birds in the community. Talking about conservation of eagles

Writing Stories. Post on the bulletin board a pocket chart made by folding up the bottom of a piece of tagboard. Encourage the children to write stories or to draw pictures that tell about each group of Indians and to place the stories or pictures in the correct pockets.

Speech. Pay special attention to each child's choice of words as he speaks. Does he connect sentences with *and*? Does he use words correctly and speak in complete sentences? Watch for wrong expressions, such as the use of *learned* for *taught; leave* for *let; them* for *those;* and *don't* for *doesn't.* Help should be provided later for those children who need it. Do not, however, interrupt an interesting discussion for corrections.

Enrichment Activities

Construction. Have the children make Indian costumes from brown wrapping paper; headbands and headdresses for Indian chiefs, and strings of beads from rolled paper and shellac. These costumes may be worn by the actors in the Indian play described at the end of the unit.

Collecting. Suggest that the children bring to school Indian novelties and set up a little museum in the classroom.

Encourage each child to write a card that tells briefly some interesting facts about his contribution.

Art. The children may wish to make a picture map that shows where Indians of various tribes lived. Furnish an outline map of the United States and guide the work carefully. Making a picture map

Chart-making. The children will enjoy making a word-and-picture chart. They may list and illustrate the new Indian vocabulary met in the stories. Illustrating new vocabulary

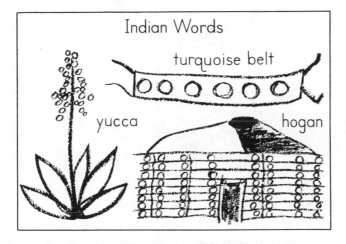

Indian Words

turquoise belt

yucca   hogan

Library Activity. The library committee may locate and arrange in groups the books and stories about Indians of the four regions stressed in this unit. Paper markers of different colors may be placed in books to indicate stories about (1) Indians of the Woodlands, (2) Indians of the Plains, (3) Indians of the Desert, (4) Indians of the Everglades. Have children collect Navajo legends and folk tales and illustrate them to decorate the library corner. Collecting Navajo stories and legends

Picture Dictionary. The picture dictionary begun earlier in this unit should be continued and enlarged. Some children may carry on this activity independently. Enlarging the picture dictionary

Dancing. One group of children may wish to prepare some form of the Eagle Dance to be performed at the time of the Indian play. One easy dance step is illustrated on page 288. The shaded footprint represents the foot on which the weight of the body rests at that moment. Working out an Indian dance

Indian dance steps are well described both in *The Book of*

Indian Crafts and Indian Lore, by JULIAN H. SALOMON, and in *The Golden Book of Indian Crafts and Lore,* by W. BEN HUNT. Instructions for making the Eagle Dance costume are also in these books, as well as various dance songs.

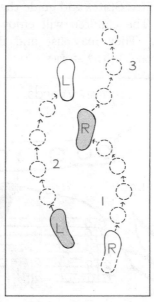

Reading about
Navajos
Stories in Other Readers. The following books contain other Navajo stories:

> *The New Friends and Neighbors,* by WILLIAM S. GRAY and others
> "The First Woodpecker," pp. 223–227
>
> *Our Good Neighbors,* by WILLIAM H. BURTON and others
> "The Great Cloudburst," pp. 218–223
> "Spring Shearing," pp. 224–228

Enjoying
literature
Folk Tales to Enjoy. *A Ball for Little Bear, An Ojibway Legend,* by EMMA G. STERNE (Emily Broun, pseud.); *Don Coyote,* by LEIGH PECK; *Feather Mountain,* by ELIZABETH OLDS.

Stories to Enjoy. More about Dancing Cloud in *Dancing Cloud, the Navajo Boy,* by MARY and CONRAD BUFF; *Kee and Bah, Navajo Children,* by ELIZABETH PACK; *Little Navajo Bluebird,* by ANN NOLAN CLARK; *Blue Canyon Horse,* by ANN NOLAN CLARK; *Little Boy Navajo,* by VIRGINIA K. SMILEY. An easy book for slower readers is *Eagle Feather,* by CLYDE ROBERT BULLA.

Films to Enjoy. *Boy of the Navajos* (Coronet), 1 reel b&w/ color. Life of a present day Navajo boy.

Filmstrips to Enjoy. *Navajo Children* (EBF), color. *Southwest Indians—Navajo* (JamHandy), 35fr, color, in HOW THE INDIANS LIVED series. *Indians of the Southwest* (SVE), color, in ADVENTURES WITH EARLY AMERICAN INDIANS series.

He-Who-Thinks-Well-and-Runs-Quickly

This exciting story of a Plains Indian boy who participated in a buffalo hunt will have particular interest for the children. Crying Coyote was known as a swift runner, but he was afraid, and the older boys laughed at him. During the hunt he was able to overcome his fear and to save the hunt for his people. His reward was a new name which signified his worth among his people.

The story will be read for pleasure and for the information it contains about the Indians of the plains. It will also help the children become more aware of how fear may be overcome.

Vocabulary

New Words: Page 165, *prairie, buffaloes, herds*;* 166, *rumbling*, thud*, east*;* 167, *west*;* 168, *pound*, leaders*;* 169, *signal, lines*;* 170, *suddenly*;* 171, *pushed, save*;* 172, *women, dust*;* 173, *shooting*, shot*;* 174, ————; 175, ————; 176, *minute;* 177, *messenger;* 178, *proudly*;* 179,

————

Developing Readiness for Reading

Meaningful Presentation of Vocabulary. "The Indian boy in our story today has two names, one at the beginning of the story and a different one at the end. What do you think might have happened to change his name?

"This Indian boy lived where there were few trees; only grass grew as far as you could see. Do you know what this flat grassland is called?" (*prairie*) "What animals lived on the prairie?" (*buffaloes*) "They used to travel across it in great *herds*. First came the *leader*, and the others followed. The *thud, thud* of their hoofs made a *rumbling* noise.

"The Indians could not have lived on the prairie without the herds of buffaloes. Indian men went out *shooting* buffaloes. Did they shoot for fun? No, they *shot* only what they needed for food and clothing and tents. The buffaloes traveled in such large herds that the men had to get them into a place which was fenced in before they could shoot them. This place was called a *pound*. The men would go far to the *east*. *Suddenly*, at a *signal*, they would drive the herd *west* toward the pound. Which direction is east? Which direction is west? The *minute* the hunt was over, the men sent a *messenger* to tell the *women*. What is a messenger? Why do you suppose they wanted the women to know that the hunt was over?"

Attacking new words through phonetic clues

Some of the children may benefit from phonetic help with some of the new words. Several methods of phonetic attack are given here: *buffaloes, dust, thud, rumbling, suddenly* (short *u*); *proudly, pound* (*ou*); *prairie, leaders, east* (vowel digraphs); *herds, messenger* (*e* followed by *r*); *shooting, shot, pushed* (*sh* in initial and medial positions).

Reviewing the new words

Review the new words by having the children find, frame, and say them in answer to a question or a definition from the teacher. Have the words used in meaningful sentences.

Setting Up Reading Purposes. "Find the next story in this unit. Who can read its title? What do you think it means? Read the subtitle. Do you remember what a coyote is? Let's read the story to find out what the title means and how the Indian boy got a new name."

Reading the Story

Guided Reading

Pages 165–179

Reading silently to answer questions

The silent reading of the story may be directed through the use of questions written on the chalkboard or duplicated on sheets of paper. By using this procedure occasionally, the teacher has a better opportunity to observe each child's work habits, to answer his individual questions, and to note his specific needs. Questions such as those on page 291 may be used.

Say: "Read the story silently. Then read each question. Next to each question write the number of the paragraph or paragraphs where you found the answer. Be ready to give your answer orally without looking at your book."

Page 165: How did the prairie look? ___1___
How did the buffaloes travel? ___2___
Why did the Indians hunt buffaloes in summer? ___2___

Page 166: What was Crying Coyote's part in the hunt? ___1___
Why was the boy called Crying Coyote? ___3___
How could Crying Coyote tell when the buffaloes were near? ___4___

Page 167: How did the hunters drive the herd of buffaloes? ___1___

Page 168: What kind of trap did the men build? ___2___

Page 169: What signal did Crying Coyote give to the men at the pound? ___1___
Why was Crying Coyote frightened? ___3___

Page 170: How did the men drive the buffaloes toward the pound? ___5___

Page 171: How did Black Eagle help Crying Coyote? ___3___

Page 172: Why was Crying Coyote sad? ___3___
How did the men close the pound? ___6___

Page 174: What danger did Crying Coyote see? ___4 or 6___

Page 176: How was the hunt saved? ___5___

Page 177: How did Black Eagle show that he was Crying Coyote's friend? ___1 and 5___

Page 178: How did Great Bear show that he was proud of his son? ___4 or 6___

After the children have completed the exercise, have them take turns in reading aloud both the question and the paragraph that answers it. If the children cannot read the whole story in one period, the end of page 172 would be a good breaking point. New words that appear after page 172 are *women, dust, shooting, shot, minute, messenger, proudly.*

Follow the checking of the questions and answers with a discussion of the change in Crying Coyote that took place during the story.

Rereading for Specific Purposes

Reading orally
to find
specific moods
of the story

Have the children find and read aloud parts which they think show fear, shame, anger, sadness, excitement, courage, pride, happiness. For example: Black Eagle's anger is shown as he says, "You're no hunter! You're just a crying baby!" (p. 172); Black Eagle's pride is shown as he says, "The arrows are Crying Coyote's" (p. 178).

Building Essential Habits and Skills

Comprehension and Study Skills

Classifying
events under the
correct heading

Main Idea. To develop the skill of recalling story ideas and associating them with the correct subtitle, review with the children the three subtitles in the story—"Crying Coyote," "Saving the Hunt," and "Great Bear's Messenger." Then distribute copies of the following exercise:

Read the first sentence. Decide in which section of the story it happened. If it happened in the first part of the story, write the subtitle "Crying Coyote" in the blank. If it happened in the second part, write "Saving the Hunt"; and if it happened in the last part, write "Great Bear's Messenger." Do the same with the other sentences.

Great Bear made his son messenger. Great Bear's Messenger

Crying Coyote wished for another name. Crying Coyote

The body of the dead buffalo blocked the opening in the fence. Saving the Hunt

Black Eagle told Crying Coyote he was no hunter and should stay with the women. Crying Coyote

Swiftly and proudly Crying Coyote ran along the trail. Great Bear's Messenger

A tree fell across Crying Coyote's leg. Saving the Hunt

Great Bear was proud of his son. Great Bear's Messenger

Crying Coyote shot three arrows into the buffalo. Saving the Hunt

Crying Coyote gave the signal that all was well. Crying Coyote

---

Story Sequence. When the children have completed the exercise on page 292, discuss it with them, and help them to write the events under each subtitle in the correct sequence.

Organizing Information. Help the children add information about the Plains Indians to the Indian chart (see page 260 of this manual).

Adding to the chart about Indians

Word-Study Skills

Word Meaning. To extend word meaning, write on the chalkboard the words below. Have the children think of at least two different meanings of each word and ask them to illustrate the meanings in sentences. Call on individuals to give their sentences.

Associating different meanings with words

block	*hunt*	*rolling*	*signal*	*rock*	*bark*	*shot*
trail	*trip*	*dress*	*pound*	*hard*	*circle*	*dust*

Word Meaning and Attack. To strengthen the ability to use meanings in word attack, write on the chalkboard some of the compound words in the Indian unit:

Using knowledge of word parts to unlock compound words

firewood, p. 135	*sheepskins*, p. 147	*suppertime*, p. 162
deerskin, p. 138	*homesick*, p. 147	*faraway*, p. 166
doorway, p. 138	*bedtime*, p. 148	*hilltop*, p. 166
treetop, p. 141	*halfway*, p. 156	*daylight*, p. 179

Show the children how the meaning of each part of a compound helps them to interpret the word and to derive definitions as follows:

homesick: wanting to return home
sheepskins: rugs made out of the skins of sheep
deerskin: skin of deer

Recall the meaning of a compound word as one made of two other words. Point out the difference between parts of a compound word and the syllables in words. For example, show that there are two parts of the compound *faraway*, but three syllables.

Phonetic Analysis. For children who had difficulty in attacking the words of this lesson, write on the chalkboard the following words from the story: *thud, dust, summer, hunt, jump, upon, much, trunk, runs.* Have them pronounced, and the short *u* in each one pointed-out or underlined.

Recalling the sound of short "u"

On the chalkboard write also the short-*u* phonograms, *um*, *un*, *ung*, *up*, and ask the children to supply the consonants and the consonant blends to construct words.

Recalling how the suffix "ly" changes the meanings of words

Structural Analysis. 1. To recall how variants are formed by adding *ly*, write on the chalkboard the new words *suddenly* and *proudly* and the known word *quickly*. Discuss their meanings. Lead the pupils to observe the *ly* ending of each. Tell them that it makes the word mean "in that manner," as:

He went out the door quickly.   *The boats went slowly by.*

Ask the children to find words ending in *ly* on pages 172, 173, 177, and 179 of their Reader and to read aloud the sentences containing each word. Help them see how the ending *ly* gives new meaning to a word. Have the children pronounce each word, divide it into parts, and tell what each part means.

Using the "ly" ending

2. To give practice in the use of words ending in *ly*, distribute copies of the exercise below. Help the children attack *roast, tan, loose, snorting,* and *galloped* before they begin.

Read the story. Then read the words above the story. Choose a word that means the same thing as each phrase in parentheses and write it in the blank beside the phrase. Reread the story to yourself to see if it makes sense.

Try to finish the story in your own way on the back of this paper.

| nearly | bravely | softly | quickly | easily |
| swiftly | proudly | suddenly | lightly | gently |

The Indians had made camp near the buffaloes so that the women could roast and dry the buffalo meat and tan the hides. The sun was (almost) _nearly_ at its highest in the sky. The wind was blowing (in a gentle way) _gently_ . (In a sudden way) Suddenly one of the horses broke loose. Messenger Boy looked up and saw that it was a young colt who carried his head (in a proud way) proudly . (In a swift and light way) Swiftly and lightly he galloped across the prairie, snorting (in a soft way) _softly_ .

Messenger Boy did not wait long however. (In a quick way) Quickly he jumped on his horse and followed. In a cloud of dust he came up beside the runaway colt. Working (in a quick and brave way) quickly and bravely he jumped (in an easy way) _easily_ onto the back of the runaway.

---

3. To review one-letter contractions, write on the chalk-board the following sentence from the text:

Recalling the contraction "you're"

"*You're no hunter! You're just a crying baby!*"

Have the pupils tell what words the contraction *you're* stands for. Write the pronoun *we* and the verb *are* and have the children write these words in a short form in the sentence:

_____ *proud of Crying Coyote now.*

Recall other contractions with one-letter omissions, as *he's*, *it's*, and *let's.*

Workbook

Pages 48, 49, 50, and 51.

Related Language Experiences

Oral Expression. Have the children retell the story of the buffalo hunt in several ways. Some may tell it as if they had been Indians taking part in the hunt; some, as if they were old men telling an old Indian tale; still others may tell the story as it is in the text. Before each child tells a part of the story, discuss what tone of voice he will use most frequently—sad, mysterious, angry, excited, happy, or funny.

Retelling the story

Dramatization. Have the children choose one of the Indian stories to dramatize. Allow different children to play the parts in each scene, and finally for the whole play. Then let the children choose a final cast and have one dress rehearsal. Help children make simple properties. Present the play as part of the Indian program at the end of the unit.

Dramatizing the Indian story

Letter Writing. Suggest that the children write letters to parents inviting them to come to the Indian play. These may be informal notes decorated with Indian symbols. Invitations to another group of children may be written in Indian picture writing.

Writing invitations

Research. The story describes three ways in which the Plains Indians sent messages: by signaling with a wolf skin from a hilltop, by sending an arrow straight into the air as a signal to begin shooting buffalo, by sending a runner to the Indian village. Discuss these incidents in the story, drawing comparisons with modern ways of communication.

Learning how the Indians sent messages

Encourage children to consult some of the available informational books to learn other ways in which Indians communicated, by smoke signals, picture writing, and sign language.

Let the children try writing a simple story in picture writing or speaking to one another in sign language.

Enrichment Activities

Preparing for
the Indian play
Co-ordinating Activity. *Indian Program.* Since this is a story about the Plains Indians, one group of children may be interested in creating and presenting a Buffalo Dance as part of the play. Instructions for both the dance and costumes are in *The Book of Indian Crafts and Indian Lore*, by JULIAN H. SALOMON and in *The Golden Book of Indian Craft and Lore*, by W. BEN HUNT.

Enjoying books
and music
A Story in Another Reader. For more information about Plains Indians have the children read the following story:

Stories from Everywhere, by GUY L. BOND and others
"Buffalo Hunters," pp. 85–94

Informational Books. *Indian Sign Language*, by ROBERT HOFSINDE; *Indians on Horseback*, by ALICE MARRIOTT.

Stories to Enjoy. *Buffalo Harvest*, by GLEN ROUNDS; *Indians of the Plains*, by SANFORD TOUSEY: *Little Owl Indian*, by HETTY BEATTY; *Our Country*, by LUCY SPRAGUE MITCHELL and DOROTHY STALL, pp. 66–91; *War Paint, an Indian Pony*, by PAUL BROWN; *The Mighty Hunter*, by BERTA and ELMER HADER.

Rhythms to Enjoy. "Indians," pp. 1–3 in *Come and Caper*, by VIRGINIA WHITLOCK.

Filmstrips to Enjoy. *Plains Indians (Dakota)* (JamHandy), 35fr, color, in HOW THE INDIANS LIVED series. *Indians of the Plains—Buffalo Hunters on Horseback* (SVE), color, in ADVENTURES WITH EARLY AMERICAN INDIANS series.

Enjoying filmstrips

Billy Tigertail

Pages
180–188

Billy Tigertail, a present-day Seminole Indian boy, lived in the Everglades of Florida. One day when his father and his older brother had gone hunting alligators and his mother had taken the bus to town on an errand, Billy was left in charge of his two younger sisters. When Patsy burned her hand on the *sofkee* pot, Billy had the presence of mind to put the juice of a wild plant on her burn. His parents were pleased with Billy's resourcefulness and granted his dearest wish—to go along on the next alligator hunt.

The story should be read for enjoyment and for identification with the boy who took care of his little sisters. It introduces children to still another Indian culture, and because it is laid in modern times, helps them know that Indians are part of American life today.

Vocabulary

New Words: Page 180, *alligator, camp*;* 181, *sofkee, pot*;* 182, *meal*, swings*;* 183, ————; 184, ————; 185, ————; 186, ————; 187, *wears*;* 188, ————

Developing Readiness for Reading

Meaningful Presentation of Vocabulary. To introduce this Seminole Indian story, lead the children to comment freely on

Discussing related concepts

the different parts of the country with which the other Indian stories have dealt. Let them suggest other regions where Indians live. Discuss the Indian chart or an Indian map and mention Indians not yet studied.

Tell the children that the next story is about Indians in Florida. Ask them about the climate of Florida and talk about how this would affect the lives of the Indians. Tell them that these Indians live near swamps. Ask, "What kinds of animals live in swamps and warm rivers?" (*alligators*)

Show the children the pictures on page 180 and 181 and ask: "What in the picture tells you that the weather is warm? What tells you that these are modern Indians?" (The sewing machine.) "What is Billy's mother doing? She is cooking a stew called *sofkee* in a *pot* over an open fire."

Setting Up Reading Purposes. "One day when his parents were away, Billy was given a very responsible job. What do you suppose it was? Let's read the story to find out about Billy's job and about the unexpected thing that happened."

Reading the Story

Guided Reading

**Pages
180–188**

Using the
study guide

Provide each child with a copy of the study guide, using a form such as the one at the top of page 299. Be sure that the children remember how to use the study guide.

When the children have finished the study guide, ask individuals to read aloud a question, tell the page on which they found the answer, and read the answer itself.

Allow time for a discussion of similarities between the life of Billy Tigertail and the lives of children in the class, for example, the desire to help with important tasks, the need to help one's parents, or how to act in an emergency.

Rereading for Specific Purposes

Reading silently
to draw conclusions

Have the children reread the story silently and study the illustrations to find statements or picture details that tell whether the Tigertail family lived long ago or in the present. Ask them to jot down ideas and the pages on which they find them as shown on pages 299–300.

BILLY TIGERTAIL

1. Why was it so quiet when Billy woke?
2. Why would Buffalo Tigertail not take Billy hunting the alligator?
3. How could Billy's family get to town?
4. Why did his mother leave Billy alone with the two little girls?
5. What did Billy and Patsy do after their mother left?
6. What did Billy do first when Nancy cried?
7. How did Patsy happen to hurt her hand?
8. What did Billy do for Patsy's hand?
9. What did Billy tell his mother as soon as she came home?
10. What present did his mother bring to Billy?
11. What would the Tigertails do with the alligator?
12. What did Buffalo Tigertail promise Billy?

Question	Page	Paragraph	Key Words
1	180	2	Then—camp
2	181	1	You—alligator
3	182	2	Billy—lived
4	182	5	Mother—alone
5	183	3	After—pies
6	184	1	Suddenly—milk
7	184	6	I—Ow-eee!
8	185	1	Billy—hand
9	186	2	When—pot
10	187	2	A—you
11	188	2	What—sofkee
12	188	5	It—trip

Page 180. Illustration of sewing machine.
Page 182. "Nearby was the highway leading into town."
Page 182. ". . . while I go to town to get cloth. I need it to make aprons to sell."
Page 183. "Then she walked to the highway to take the bus into town."
Page 183. ". . . he worked in his vegetable garden."
Page 184. ". . . gave her some milk."
Page 186. Illustration—The children are playing with puzzles.
Page 187. "Mother handed Billy a brown-paper bag . . ."

299   *Billy Tigertail* (180–188)

Page 188. "We will sell the alligator hide, . . ."
Page 188. ". . . sat down to a supper of chicken . . ."

Have a discussion of the children's findings, and help them conclude that these Indians are living in our country today.

Building Essential Habits and Skills

Comprehension and Study Skills

Using context clues

Details. To check comprehension of story details, distribute copies of the following exercise:

type

Complete each sentence by writing on the line the correct word from the list at the top of the page.

danger	dark waters	proud	Alligators
Nan	corn meal	Patsy	swinging bed
piles	Dick	promised	wear

Billy Tigertail was an Indian boy who lived near some dark waters . His house stood on piles above the ground because there was so much water all around.

 Alligators lived in the dark still waters. There is great danger in hunting these animals. "Someday you will be man enough to wear the wide belt and go hunting with Dick and me," his father told him.

Billy's mother left him to take care of Patsy and Nan while she went to town. Billy gave milk to the baby and rocked her swinging bed .

When Patsy hurt her hand in the *sofkee* pot, Billy cleaned off the hot corn meal . Then he put the yellow part from a leaf on her hand.

His mother was proud of Billy when she heard what he had done. His father promised to take him on the next hunting trip.

Completing the
Indian chart

Organizing Information. To give practice in classifying, complete the chart about Indians (see page 260 in this manual) by adding facts about the Seminoles found in this story.

Discuss the information on the chart, pointing out the differences among the Indian tribes. Try to find out which customs and ways depended upon the environment in which the Indians lived, which depended upon their tribal customs, and which depended upon their contacts with the white man.

Word-Study Skills

Word Meaning. To give practice in discriminating between the meanings of homonyms, duplicate copies of the exercise below or write it on the chalkboard. Explain to the children that some words sound the same but are spelled differently and mean different things. Give some examples, such as *write, right; threw, through; to, too, two;* and ask the children to use them in sentences.

Observing the different meanings of homonyms

have run off

Read each sentence. Underline the word that makes the sentence correct.

Billy Tigertail wanted to (<u>write</u>, right) a letter. He picked up a pencil in his (write, <u>right</u>) hand. The pencil was made of (would, <u>wood</u>) and painted (<u>red</u>, read). When Billy was (threw, <u>through</u>) with the letter, he (red, <u>read</u>) it to his sister. Then he (<u>threw</u>, through) the pencil over to her so that she could write a letter to (there, <u>their</u>) father (two, <u>too</u>).

Phonetic Analysis. 1. To recall the variant sounds of *ea*, have the children skim through the story to find words containing *ea*. List these on the chalkboard, placing in one column the words in which *ea* has the sound of long *e*, as in *eat, steaming, meal, eating, cleaned, beads, speak,* in a second column the words in which *ea* has the sound of short *e*, as in *bread, breakfast, ready.*

Reviewing sounds of "ea"

Let the children suggest other words for each column. If such words as *wear, heard,* or *near* are mentioned, explain that *ea* sometimes has other sounds than long and short *e*, especially when the digraph is followed by *r*.

2. To make the children aware of various sounds of the diphthong *ou*, first write on the chalkboard the words in the story having the sound of *ou* as in *house*. For example: *houses, sound, ground, shouts, found, proud, about.*

Recalling sounds of "ou"

Ask the children to think of other words with *ou*. Call attention to such words as *four* and *pour*. Derive the generalization that in some words *r* gives *ou* a special sound, just as it gives a special sound to other digraphs and vowels.

Write on the chalkboard the following list of words from the story: *would, young, touch, through, enough*. Point out the sound that *ou* has in each of these words. Caution the children to watch for exceptions, both in sound and use of vowel digraphs and diphthongs.

For a mature group write on the chalkboard a few sentences containing unfamiliar words with *ou* and help the children attack them through phonetic and meaning clues.

> *To the <u>south</u> of the camp was a swamp, to the east a highway.*
> *<u>Thousands</u> of cars went by on the road every day.*
> *The book had <u>fourteen</u> stories.*

Structural Analysis. 1. To check understanding of the possessive form of nouns, write on the chalkboard—*Patsy's hand* and *the plant's leaf*. Ask the children to recall the use of the apostrophe here. Have individual children tell the meaning of the phrases. Review that an apostrophe followed by *s* and used after a noun denotes possession.

2. At this time remind the children also of the other use of the apostrophe, a shorter way of saying two words. Write the following phrases in a column on the chalkboard: *let us, do not, are not, can not, does not, is not,* and *were not*. Ask individual children to come to the chalkboard, write the contractions for the phrases, and give a sentence using first the long form, then the contraction.

3. For children who need more practice, provide an exercise such as the following;

have run off

Read each phrase. If the apostrophe in that phrase shows possession, write P in the blank. If the phrase has a contraction, write C.

P	Patsy's hand	C	weren't there	P	mother's skirt
C	don't touch	C	can't go	P	father's belt
C	doesn't cry	C	I'll go	C	she'll stay
P	Dick's boat	P	alligator's hide	C	let's play
C	isn't a baby	P	the plant's leaf	C	he'll promise

Workbook

Pages 52, 53, 54, and 55.

Related Language Activities

Conversation. 1. Children may consult the school encyclopedia, or such references as *Alligators and Crocodiles,* by Herbert Zim, for information about alligators. They will want to discuss the alligators' strength and their powerful jaws which make hunting them dangerous. Raise the question, "Would Billy Tigertail be likely to swim in water where alligators lived?"

Finding out
about alligators

2. Ask advice from the school nurse or physician or have the children read in their health books about the treatment of burns. Discuss with them the safety rules one should observe when near an open fire or pots of steaming hot food.

Learning how
to treat burns

3. Have a discussion about caring for younger children in the family: the routines to be observed, suitable games to play with them, and the safety of the young child.

Talking about care
of younger children

Storytelling. Offer practice in reading or telling folk tales from different tribes. Encourage the children to tell several in the program for the parents. Help them capture a storytelling style which will put the audience in a listening mood.

Telling folk tales

Giving Directions. Teach the children a few Indian games from a book such as *Indian Games and Crafts* by Robert Hofsinde. Have them take notes and plan to explain and demonstrate the games to the audience at the Indian program.

Learning to
give directions

Enrichment Activities

Art and Construction. Help a group make a calumet or peace pipe for the play. Others might make a mural of a Seminole dwelling. Remind them to include some alligators.

Making a peace
pipe and a mural

A Story in Another Reader. The following story is about two Seminole children and how they find a bee tree:

Stories and
a film

Our Good Neighbors, by WILLIAM H. BURTON
"Little Horse," pp. 210–217

Informational Book. *The Seminole Indians,* by SONIA BLEEKER.

A Story to Enjoy. *When the Moon Is New,* by LAURA BANNON.

Film to Enjoy. *Boy of the Seminoles—Indians of the Everglades* (Coronet), 1 reel b&w/color.

Culminating Activities

Indian Exhibit. Help the children complete their Indian chart and mount the murals, each with a descriptive paragraph. Make certain that all the articles in the classroom's Indian museum are clearly labeled and that every child in the group is able to read the label and is prepared to tell something about the objects. The booklets about local Indians should also be bound and exhibited. The children who are responsible for these booklets may wish to tell at the program how they obtained their information.

Presenting a program

Indian Play. Let the group give the Indian program for their parents or for another group of children. All the children should take part in some way. Some of the children may perform an Indian dance. Others may pretend to be Indian storytellers and tell some of the old tales that have been collected.

Several children may demonstrate Indian sign language or an Indian craft. Some may be actors in the play, some scene-shifters, two may have charge of the curtain, others may be ushers. Help the children to understand the importance of each person who works on the production and lead them to see how each contributes to the success of the play.

An Indian dish, such as corn bread, might be served to the guests after the program. The children should also explain to the guests the information on their chart about different Indian tribes and show their exhibit of Indian articles.

Evaluating Activities

Vocabulary Test III. (Workbook, pp. 55 and 56). To check the pupils' ability to recognize the new words in Unit IV, administer both parts of the test below. Direct the children to underline the word that you read in each row. Pronounce only the underlined word in each row.

PART I

1. even	easy	else	eyes	end
2. brave	save	came	cave	cage
3. morning	messenger	moccasin	never	vegetable
4. cliff	rings	circles	coyote	chocolate
5. branch	bricks	brother	buffaloes	potatoes
6. half	hang	herd	save	belt
7. peddlers	leaders	letters	kicking	left
8. engine	cage	edge	feet	legs
9. promise	trail	presents	prayer	prairie
10. west	each	east	nuts	earn
11. swiftly	squeak	slowly	sweetly	silly
12. pot	pencil	beads	danger	glass
13. tumble	telling	leader	teachers	toward
14. those	noise	turtle	turkey	turquoise
15. thud	trap	full	mud	three
16. wheels	which	west	whole	hit
17. every	enough	speak	eagle	east
18. crawl	shovel	stew	shot	shawl
19. tumbling	rattle	rolling	rumbling	licking
20. sorry	stuck	son	merry	circles
21. filled	frightened	frisky	friendly	fresh
22. swaying	hanging	ringing	pushing	filling
23. Indian	feast	boats	bow	beads
24. happened	happy	half	hard	hammer

1. below	brother	behind	because	before
2. along	always	above	awake	alligator
3. shell	shot	should	sofkee	stool
4. forest	feast	field	filled	feather
5. west	women	woman	world	winning
6. moccasins	remember	moon	wonderful	mountains
7. around	windows	arrows	fellow	angry
8. meal	mud	mill	little	meat
9. just	jar	join	jumped	jingle
10. pretty	puppy	purple	proudly	promise
11. woke	sent	were	words	wears
12. signal	saved	sugar	sign	circle
13. fast	fresh	feast	best	first
14. moved	milk	moon	minute	merry
15. ahead	again	afraid	dust	above
16. supper	suddenly	shooting	slowly	nearly
17. magic	matter	meal	lines	maybe
18. your	yard	young	yellow	understand
19. bus	button	buckles	bucket	busy
20. cloud	clown	color	could	crawl
21. son	soon	skin	so	song
22. jar	hit	bow	hide	pot
23. know	king	kind	knife	knew
24. partly	dance	dawn	danger	tired

Comprehension Test. To check the children's understanding of concepts about Indians, provide the pupils with copies of the following test:

Write Yes at the end of each sentence that is right, <u>No</u> at the end of each one that is wrong.

type

1. There are still Indians in this country. Yes
2. All Indians lived in the same part of our country.   No
3. Indian people believed strange stories. Yes
4. Indian hunters caught animals for food and clothes. Yes
5. Some Indians lived in bark houses, some lived in mud-brick houses, and some lived in tents made of skins. Yes
6. Some Indians today have cars of their own. Yes
7. A medicine man was a hunter who climbed up old trails. No
8. Some Indians can make pretty things from turquoise stones and silver. Yes
9. Indian boys are sometimes named for great things they have done. Yes

10. Indians never played or danced.   No
11. Some Indian stories tell about Indians who lived in our country long ago.   Yes
12. Most Indian children today dress somewhat as you do. Yes
13. Indian mothers ground corn into flour.   Yes
14. Indian girls like beads just as the girls in our room do. Yes
15. All Indians keep feathers in their hair.   No
16. Indians who lived in prairie lands hunted for buffaloes. Yes
17. The Indians who lived in the forest used the trees in many ways.   Yes
18. Indians who live near water sometimes travel by boat.   Yes

Word-Study Test. To provide a general check of skills taught in this unit, distribute copies of the exercises below. Have the children follow the directions as given. Check the exercises orally with the children.

1. Put one line under each hard *c*. Put two lines under each soft *c*.

magic	camp	circles	policeman
pencil	moccasins	could	cared
country	cellar	cave	circus
dance	colt	furnace	city
coyotes	cubes	decided	

Testing hard and soft "c"

have master type (handwritten)

2. Write *L* beside the word if the vowel has the long sound. Write *S* beside the word if the vowel has the short sound.

S	dust	S	fill	L	time	L	beads
L	knife	L	save	S	fresh	S	hit
L	east	S	bad	L	trail	S	thud
S	swift	L	speak	S	mud	L	feast
S	belt	S	shot	L	meal	S	pot

Testing long and short sounds of vowels

3. How many syllables do you hear in each word? Write the number beside the word.

1	shawl	2	buckle	1	jar	1	boots
2	turquoise	1	young	2	leader	2	even
1	west	2	above	3	buffalo	1	skin
1	dawn	1	moon	1	pot	1	strong
3	understand	2	signal	2	rumbling	2	frighten
2	signal	3	suddenly	2	pushing	3	messenger

Reviewing syllables

All-Unit Activities

4. Make a line from the word to its meaning.

eagle — rolling land covered with grass
alligator — many animals together
prairie — a large, strong bird
suddenly — something shot from a bow
herd — a large animal that lives near water
arrow — quickly, in a hurry
messenger —— someone sent to carry news

Structural-Analysis Test 1. To evaluate the children's ability to recognize the comparative and superlative forms of adjectives, distribute copies of the following test:

Read each sentence. Put the right word in each space.

1. Little Eagle and his two brothers lived in a village in the forest. They lived in the __biggest__ of all the bark houses.

big   bigger   biggest

2. Little Eagle was __shorter__ than his big brother, but __taller__ than his little brother.

shorter   shortest   taller   tallest

3. His mother needed a very __deep__ pot to cook a fish stew for the family.

deep   deeper   deepest

4. It seemed that the __youngest__ of the three boys always ate the __greatest__ helping.

young   younger   youngest   great   greater   greatest

Checking
the ability
to drop "ly"
as an ending

Structural-Analysis Test 2. To test recognition of the root word in words ending in *ly*, distribute copies of the exercise at the top of page 309.

Helping the Individual Child

General Help. Motivate word practice by letting the children match words with definitions. Write each word and each definition on a separate slip of paper. Give each child a word slip, or several word slips, and place the definitions in a box. Have a child pull a definition from the box and read it

Teaching *Finding New Neighbors*

Find the root word in each of these words. Write it on the line. Remember that in some of the words *y* was changed to *i* before the ending *ly* was added. The first one is done for you.

happily	happy	drily	_____
merrily	_____	easily	_____
friendly	_____	evenly	_____
kindly	_____	freshly	_____
brightly	_____	proudly	_____
closely	_____	yearly	_____

type

aloud. The child who holds the word defined will say: "I have it. It is —————————." Let the children take turns pulling definition slips from the box. Collect and redistribute the word slips several times.

In a variation of this game, the one who holds the word is then given the definition. The child with the most words and matching definitions at the end wins the game. Better readers may attack new words in this way.

Using context clues

To strengthen skill in using context clues, compose a story about Indians. Tell it to the children, pausing occasionally to allow them to supply the next word from a list of words written on the chalkboard.

Improving phrase reading

Specific Help. Faster, smoother, and more fluent reading is usually accompanied by improved ability to see words in phrase relationship. Some of the following suggestions may be helpful in increasing a child's eye-span and in improving his ability to recognize longer thought units:

1. Brief word-card exercises are often helpful. If phrases are written on cards, be sure that the child is given a quick look. If on his first trial with the cards he requires a more detailed look, repeat the opportunities for practice until he is able to see a phrase at a glance.

2. Typewritten practice exercises or hectographed sheets are often more helpful than work with cards because the type is nearer in size to the type in the book. In providing practice to develop eye span, this factor· is important. Phrases, such as those on page 310, may be typed and duplicated. Provide each pupil with a cover card which he may slide over

the page as he uncovers a phrase and then quickly re-covers it so as to allow a quick look at each phrase.

bow and arrow	her little son
soft moccasins	good hot stew
fresh meat	a turquoise ring
in the forest	silver circles
beautiful belt	on the plain
the great herds	a rumbling noise

3. A piece of cardboard with a "phrase window" may be given to a child. Direct him to find with his window a certain phrase on a page in his text. Say, "Frame with your window the phrase *in the forest.*"

4. To help children recognize the rhythmic pattern of words, the teacher may read aloud a section of the text while the children follow her in their own text. The teacher may give slight emphasis to the phrases she reads.

5. Provide practice for a child to "think in phrases" by asking questions after the guided silent reading that may be answered in phrases. Say, "What did he cut with?" The child will answer *with a stone knife.*

6. Give practice in speaking a phrase fluently. Demonstrate the difference in sound between a phrase read word for word, as *in | the | forest,* and the same phrase read as a unit, *in the forest.* Play the game "Where Is It?" The teacher will say, "Where is the plant?" And a child will answer *in the window.* The child who answers correctly may ask the next question, as "Where is the red book?" and receive the answer *on the table.*

7. Give practice in recognizing prepositions, as *on, in, for,* and *of,* in their relationship to the phrase. Direct the child to look forward in his text when he meets such words and to read the phrase after he has seen the words that follow the introductory words.

8. Children will gain ability in phrasing if word recognition and meaning difficulties are eliminated before silent reading. This preliminary practice on words builds readiness and enables the child to read more fluently.

9. The teacher should provide many opportunities for re-reading and reading in an audience situation. Show that smooth rhythmic reading wins an appreciative audience.

10. Appreciation of the importance of good phrasing is emphasized in choral reading. Provide opportunity for easy exercises.

11. Emphasis should always be placed on the thought of the context. A child reading for thought is more likely to read in natural thought-units. When a child is reading aloud, pronounce for him the word on which he hesitates. This helps him to read ahead for the thought. Provide short comprehension questions to follow both oral and silent reading.

12. If phrase practice is provided on the chalkboard for children who need special help, the teacher should use her hand or a pointer to demonstrate with a quick left to right movement the direction for the eyes to follow. Her hand or the pointer should not stop until the end of the phrase.

Provision for Superior Readers. Activities for superior readers during the reading of this unit may include:

1. Reading some of the informational books about Indians, which are listed under each story, and reporting on them to the rest of the group.

2. Making a scrapbook about different tribes of Indians and their way of life.

3. Assuming responsibility for making the dictionary of Indian words and illustrating it.

4. Finding out from local sources about Indians who live now or have lived in the local community and planning interesting ways of reporting the information to the class.

5. Planning and carrying out pantomimes or dramatizations of Indian myths.

6. Organizing and labeling objects brought to school for the Indian exhibit.

7. Making a picture-map of the United States showing the location of the Indian tribes represented in the stories.

8. Leading a group in constructing models of Indian dwellings.

9. Making background and properties for the play.

10. Writing original stories and verses about Indians.

11. Learning some of the Indian sign language.

12. Reading independently many stories about Indians.

13. Reading favorite Indian stories aloud to the class.

311

Unit V · Americans All

Introducing the Unit

The unit just completed gave a picture of American Indian life of both earlier and present times. This unit deals with the lives of other Americans in various parts of the country. Each one of these stories has a different background, and each one shows how the people in different walks of life fit into our American way of life and contribute to it.

"The Rodeo" is about western ranch life. "The Horse Who Lived Upstairs" contrasts life in the city with life in the country. "Bob Learns to Pitch" tells how a boy in a small town achieves an ambition through hard work. "El Burrito" is a story about a Mexican-American boy who lives in the Southwest. The last story, "New Moon and the Dragon," tells of the New Year's celebration of a Chinese-American girl. Finally, the concept "Americans All" is rounded out by two poems, "The Harpers' Farm" and "The Ice-Cream Man."

For this unit, as for the others, the teacher will probably want to have on hand many interesting pictures, stories, poems, and books pertaining to the theme "Americans All." She will wish to plan some all-unit activities which will help this particular group of children learn more about other children of America, and understand and appreciate them.

During the introductory discussion, find out what the children know about life in different regions of America. Have them recall that at one time only the Indians lived in America. Help the children locate the United States on a world map or on a globe. Point out that all other people came here from other countries. If the children know or can find out from what part of the Old World their parents or grandparents came, help them locate these places on the map or globe. Emphasize the fact that no matter where we or our parents came from or in what part of the country we live, we are now "Americans All." Suggest that each group has brought to this country good ideas and customs that have made America a better place in which to live.

Story	Vocabulary	Developing Readiness	Reading the Story		Building Essen	
Pages	**New Words**		**Guided Reading**	**Rereading for Specific Purposes**	**Comprehension and Study Skills**	**Word Mean**
The Rodeo 189–197	*Americans* *rodeo* *Danny* *Judy* *grandstand* *Pepper* *pasture* *tapped*	New words are presented in context, either written or oral. Children are encouraged to identify new words through comparison with known words and the use of phonetic and context clues.		Skimming to recall main events	Story Details: using story details to build mental pictures (chalkboard exercise) Creative Reading: drawing conclusions and making inferences Workbook: 57, distinguishing between relevant and irrelevant ideas	Observing t effect of dra and descriptiv words (works
The Horse Who Lived Upstairs 200–207	*discontented* *Polaski* *stall* *interesting* *ladies* *carrots* *poor*		Silent and oral reading for comprehension and interpretation of story plot, mood, and characterization.	Reading to check the realistic parts of the story Reading orally for expressive interpretation	Main Idea: illustrating main parts of the story Details: recognizing pertinent story facts (worksheet) Workbook: 59, using judgment	Matching w with their d tions (worksh
Bob Learns to Pitch 208–216	*pitch* *team* *strike* *read* (past) *plate* *batter* *thrown* *felt*			Reading to find main events and to arrange them in sequence	Critical Reading: evaluating information (worksheet) Creative Reading: making inferences in new material (worksheet) Workbook: 61, finding specific information; predicting outcomes	Matching b ball words wit their definitio (chalkboard e cise) Workbook: enriching wor meaning; cla ing; forming ments
El Burrito 217–223	*El Burrito* *Miguel* *burro* *newspapers*	Through discussion and exchange of ideas, interest in the story is stimulated and background for understanding is developed. Purposes for reading are reached by the group with the teacher's guidance.		Skimming to locate ideas about personal qualities of story characters Reading to give specific information	Specific Details: recalling story facts (worksheet) Creative Reading: translating new story material into another medium; following directions Workbook: 64, skimming; locating information; recalling story details	Attacking a discussing hy ated words
New Moon and the Dragon 224–233	*dragon* *luck* *Chinese* *slippers* *firecrackers* *balcony* *flag*			Reading orally to present word pictures	Critical Reading: associating related ideas (worksheet) Sequence: testing recall of order of events (worksheet) Workbook: 68, finding the main idea; drawing conclusions	Observing t words change Workbook: developing wo meaning
All-Unit Activities					Evaluation: tests on story characters; story events; and making inferences Individual Help: specific help understanding the main idea Provision for superior readers: suggestions for better reading skills, poetry references	Individual suggestions fc help in word r ing; word bo action picture Word recog of endings; g ing riddles Rhyming w game "Quick Look" Workbook: word-meanin

its and Skills

Word-Study Skills			Related Language Experiences	Enrichment Activities
Phonetic Analysis	Structural Analysis	Syllabication		
	Recalling root words and endings Reviewing addition of *ing* and *ed* to words that double final consonant Reviewing addition of *ing* and *ed* to words that drop final silent *e*; adding endings to root words in sentences (worksheet) Workbook: 58, adding *ing* and *ed* to verbs; using context clues		Discussion: talking about competition Making plans for the unit (chart) Listening: to the poem "Young Cowboy" for enjoyment Letter Writing: corresponding with third-grade children who live on a ranch	Singing: learning western songs Art and Construction: making things out of leather Making a picture-story map Stories in Other Readers Stories, poems, music, records, films, and filmstrips
	Recalling the plural form of nouns ending in *y*	Perceiving double consonants in words; dividing words with double medial consonants Workbook: 60, auditory recognition of syllables; skimming	Listening: to other stories of people and animals who were dissatisfied Writing: corresponding with third-grade children who live in the country	Drawing: adding to the picture-story map of the United States; painting a mural A Story in Another Reader Stories, poems, and songs
...lling the difference between long and short *ea* ...g context clues to attack ...ords with *ea* ...criminating between ...t sounds of *o*	Reviewing *er* of agent (worksheet) Workbook; 63, answering questions; recognizing *er* of agent		Discussion and Research: talking about baseball; making a fair-play chart; finding out about baseball players	Playing Games: learning a new game Stories and music
...ewing variant sounds ...lling variant sounds of *e* ...kbook: 65, attacking ...ords through familiar ...arts; 66, recognizing ... digraphs *ai, ay, ea, ee* ...ent vowels	Alphabetizing: listing children's names alphabetically		Discussion: comparing individual interpretations of the creative reading exercise Discussing origins of Americans	Co-ordinating Activity: comparing the life on a ranch, in a small town, and in a big city A Story in Another Reader Stories, a poem, a song, and a record
...ewing vowel digraphs ... serving exceptions ...ewing the sounds of *ow* ...kbook: 69, recognizing ... sounds of the diph-...ow; attacking new ...with *ow*	Unlocking new words by recognizing structural changes (*er* agent, change of *y* to *i* before endings)	Reviewing syllables and vowel sounds	Making a background chart Dramatization: dramatizing the story Research: finding and reporting information on Chinese customs	Co-ordinating Activity Construction: adding to the picture-story map; making dragon-heads Stories and music
...ing the individual ... recalling the sounds of ...ow (worksheet)	Evaluation: adding *es* to words ending in *y* (test) Specific Help: classifying in alphabetical order Provision for superior readers: cataloguing poems alphabetically	Evaluation: dividing words into syllables (test)	Provision for superior readers: research on people who came from other countries; sharing outside reading with the group	Culminating Activities: exhibiting objects from other countries, presenting an international program Provision for superior readers: writing Chinese characters; museum visit to see Chinese objects; collecting poetry

The Rodeo

Danny and Judy had trained their ponies to do tricks in order to participate with other children in the rodeo. At the last moment Judy was unable to attend because her grandfather, with whom she lived, was ill. Danny watched the rodeo events, feeling sad at being on the side lines. He had a pleasant surprise when Judy arrived on her pony in time for the children's events. After a quick practice outside the grandstand, Judy and Danny put their ponies through their tricks and won first prize for trick riding.

The story lends itself to a discussion of good sportsmanship in contests of all kinds, of winning and losing, and of the feelings of the contestants.

Vocabulary

New Words: Page 189, *Americans;* 190, *rodeo, Danny*, Judy;* 191, *grandstand*;* 192, *Pepper*;* 193, ————; 194, *pasture;* 195, ————; 196, *tapped*;* 197, ————

Developing Readiness for Reading

Talking about
story concepts

Meaningful Presentation of Vocabulary. The title of the first story in this unit is "The Rodeo." Write *rodeo* on the chalkboard while the children watch. Help them pronounce the word, taking into consideration both common pronunciations (rō′dē-ō and rŏ-dā′ō). Ask: "Do you know what a rodeo is? Have you seen a rodeo?" Then allow a free discussion of rodeo events that the children may have seen. Ask: "Where in our country would you be most likely to see a rodeo? What animals would you see?" Show the cattle-raising areas on a map of the United States and let the children talk briefly about ranch life. Lead into a conversation about cowboys, ponies, and other "western" lore that children enjoy. Then ask: "Where are rodeos usually held? Where do you sit when you watch a rodeo? (*grandstand*)

"Our story is about two children named *Danny* and *Judy*. Danny has a pony named *Ginger*. Judy owns one called *Pepper*. Why might the children have given their horses these names, Ginger and Pepper?"

"Do city children usually have ponies? Why, or why not? If you had a pony, where would you keep it? Where do the ponies on a farm stay in the summer?" (In a *pasture*.) Discuss what a pasture is and, if possible, show a picture.

The new word *tapped* may be attacked through phonetic, structural, and context clues in the guided reading, or presented at this time in meaningful context, such as, "Danny *tapped* Judy on the shoulder." Have a child find and frame the small word *tap* in the variant form and compare the word *tap* with *cap*. Most children will see the short *a* in *Danny* and *tapped* and whole word parts in *grandstand*.

Using phonetic clues to unlock new words

Setting Up Reading Purposes. "Danny was disappointed. Without his partner, Judy, he could only watch the rodeo, although what he wanted most was to ride in it himself. Let's read the story to find out whether he got his wish."

Reading the Story

Guided Reading

Have the children read the first paragraph silently to find out what Danny was doing. Ask one child to read it orally. Ask: "Why do you suppose Judy was not there to ride with Danny? Read these two pages silently to find out." After the reading, ask: "Why did Danny want Judy at the rodeo? What was in the parade? Does the picture tell more than the story? Where was Danny going to sit?

Pages 190–191

"What does it mean 'to sit on the side lines'? Read this page to see whether Danny was having fun sitting on the side lines." After the reading, ask: "What happened to surprise Danny?

Page 192

"Was it too late for Danny and Judy to enter the trick riding? Read this page to find out." When the children have read the page, ask, "Why was Judy able to come after all?"

Page 193

Say: "Remember that Judy and Danny had had no chance to practice the week before the rodeo. What do you think they will do now? Read page 194 to find out what Judy and Danny did as the trick riding started." After the reading, ask: "What tricks did some of the other children do? Where did

Page 194

The Rodeo (189–197)

the children go to practice their tricks?" (A pasture.) "Why would a pasture be a good place to practice?

Page 195

"Do Danny and Judy look worried in the picture? How would you feel if you were in their place? Read this page to see what tricks Judy and Danny did.

Page 196

"When Judy and Danny tapped their ponies on the neck, what happened?" When the children have read, ask: "What was the noise the children heard? Judy and Danny did one more trick. What was it?

Page 197

"What prize did Danny and Judy win?" When the children have read the page, ask one child to describe the prize. Ask: "Do you think Danny and Judy deserved to win first prize? Why? What were the tricks the other children did?" Have the children read aloud the sections telling all the tricks the story children performed.

Rereading for Specific Purposes

Skimming to recall main events

Have the children skim the story to recall all the events of the rodeo (the opening parade, roping and riding wild horses, the children's events, the awarding of prizes). List these on the chalkboard. Enlarge on the discussion of rodeos which children have seen, and have them describe events other than those in the story. Point out that a rodeo provides an opportunity for ranch people to show the skills needed in their work and that people in other kinds of work sometimes have similar contests.

Building Essential Habits and Skills

Comprehension and Study Skills

Utilizing details about the story from the text and pictures

Story Details. To give the children practice in utilizing details from the text and pictures, write the phrases below on the chalkboard. Ask the children to think about the meaning of each phrase and to use it in a sentence.

1. *a ranch over the mountain*
2. *an Indian in the parade*
3. *riding wild horses*
4. *in front of the grandstand*
5. *a belt with a gold buckle*

Creative Reading. To strengthen the ability to draw conclusions, distribute copies of the exercise below or write the questions on the chalkboard. Ask the children to reread the story and be able to discuss these "why" questions.

Reading between the lines

---

1. Why did Danny think it would be great fun to have Judy there to ride with him? Why would it matter?

2. Why could Judy not ride with Danny before the rodeo? What might she have had to do?

3. Why was it hard for Danny to sit on the side lines?

4. Why did the wild horse try to throw the cowboy?

5. Why did Mr. Hill say, "You will have to be at the end?" Was that right?

6. Why did Judy and Danny tap their ponies on the neck?

7. Why did Mr. Hill look at the paper in his hand?

---

type

Word-Study Skills

Word Meaning. To develop the children's sensitivity for shades of word meaning, write on the chalkboard the following sentences:

Using descriptive words

> *Judy turned her pony.*
> *July wheeled her pony.*

Have the sentences read aloud and ask several children to tell which of the two sentences sounds more dramatic or interesting to them. Lead them to see that using the word *wheeled* gives the reader or listener a clearer picture than *turned* because it tells how Judy turned her pony (quickly and in one motion). Continue with similar examples, using other action verbs from the story, such as the following: *trotted, tapped, backed, danced, bowed.*

To strengthen the ability to recognize and use dramatic and descriptive verbs, distribute an exercise such as the one at the top of page 320.

319   *The Rodeo* (189–197)

Read each sentence. Decide which word at the right sounds more exciting. Write the word in the blank.

1. The plane _zoomed_ right over the children's heads.

went
zoomed

2. Big bells _boom_ out.

ring
boom

3. Little bells _jingle_ .

jingle
ring

4. The giant _gobbled_ a whole sheep.

ate
gobbled

5. The water in the brook _shines_ like silver.

is
shines

6. A cowboy _roped_ a wild horse.

caught
roped

Recalling root words and endings

Structural Analysis. 1. To review the rules for adding the ending *ed* and *ing,* write on the chalkboard the following list and ask the children to underline the root words: *ended, joined, watched, wanted, turned, asked, reached, walked, started, jumped, played, wheeled, backed.* Note that these words are not changed when *ed* and *ing* are added. Then have individual children copy the root words and add *ing* to each of them.

2. Then ask the children to go to the chalkboard and underline the root words in the following: *trotted, tapped, dropped, stopped, shopped.* Discuss the doubling of the final consonant when it is preceded by a short vowel. If necessary, give the children additional help with familiar words like *mopped, scrubbed, slipped, trapped,* and *hopped.* Superior readers will be able to attack *begged, flapped, fitted, clapped.*

Write several of the above root words, such as *slip, trap,* or *hop,* on the chalkboard. Help the children come to the conclusion that these words double the final consonant before *ing* is added. Have one of the children restate the generalization that *words ending in a consonant which comes after a single short vowel double that consonant before* ed *or* ing *is added.*

3. Discuss the words *riding, roping,* and *taking* by asking, "Who can tell the root word in each of these words?" Ask a child to come to the chalkboard and write the root word be-

side its variant form. "What is the same in the words *ride*, *rope*, and *take?*" Elicit from the children that in these words the final *e* is dropped before *ing*. Continue by writing on the chalkboard words like *decide, close, dance, live, move, paste, promise, race,* and *wave*. Next to each word write the past tense (*decided, closed,* and so on). Ask the children what happened to these words before *ed* could be added. Lead them to observe that the final silent *e* was dropped before the ending *ed* was added. Help them make the generalization that *words ending in silent* e *drop the final* e *before* ed *or* ing *is added.* Write *smiled* and *raked* on the chalkboard and let the children attack them.

4. To check the understanding of structural changes in words when *ed* and *ing* are added, distribute this exercise:

Adding "ed" and "ing" to root words in sentences

Complete the sentences by adding <u>ed</u> or <u>ing</u> to the root word given. Look at each word closely to see whether you need to double or drop any letter.

Make the words end in <u>ed</u> in these sentences.

1. Danny ———— a wild horse. rope
2. Betty ———— on one foot. hop
3. The dog ————. bark
4. The man ———— his hat to the lady. tip
5. She ———— over a rock and fell down. trip
6. Father ———— the car into the street. back
7. The baby ———— on the floor. crawl
8. The clown ———— to the grandstand. bow

Make the words end in <u>ing</u> in these sentences.

1. We saw Bill ———— up the street. come
2. The wind was ———— hard. blow
3. The girls were ———— for the baby. care
4. We are ———— the house painted. have
5. Two boys were ———— the stairs. climb
6. A hunter was ———— along the ground. crawl
7. A rabbit was ———— down the trail. hop
8. Judy and Danny were ———— their ponies. ride

Workbook

Pages 57 and 58.

The Rodeo (189–197)

Related Language Experiences

Talking about competing

Discussion. 1. Encourage a discussion of contests and competition by asking questions such as the following: "Why do you think Danny and Judy won a prize? Would you have voted for them? How did the other children feel? How would you have felt if you had won? if you had lost? Have you ever tried hard and not won? Is it worth while to take part in games and contests whether you win or lose? Why?"

Making plans for the unit

2. Initiate the discussion of plans for this unit by asking individual children to tell about different parts of the country in which they have lived or which they have visited. Let the group suggest activities in which they would like to participate while they are reading the stories of this unit. The interest might be centered on finding out about people who live in different parts of the United States. Record such plans as the following:

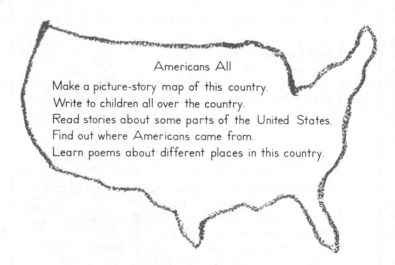

Americans All

Make a picture-story map of this country.
Write to children all over the country.
Read stories about some parts of the United States.
Find out where Americans came from.
Learn poems about different places in this country.

Starting a correspondence

Letter Writing. Help the children to plan and write letters to third-grade children who live in the ranch country. Suggest that they ask for information on things they do for fun, the food they eat, etc. Try to establish a correspondence to promote a free exchange of ideas.

Listening. For enjoyment have the children listen while the poem "Young Cowboy," by Nona Keen Duffy, is read aloud. Ask them to listen for the rhyme and rhythm as well as for the information about the life of a cowboy. Allow free comment and discussion on whether the children would like to change places with this cowboy.

Listening to a poem

YOUNG COWBOY

I'm up at dawn
  Of every day,
I saddle my horse
  And ride away.

In rain and sun
  Through ice and snow,
I mount my horse
  And off I go!

In wind and dust,
  Through sleet or hail
I drive the cattle
  Down the trail.

I'm on the go
  From sun to sun
To get my chores
  And work all done!

Day in, day out,
  With little change
I rope and brand
  And ride the range!

NONA KEEN DUFFY

Enrichment Activities

Singing. Teach the children several typical cowboy songs and western folksongs, such as "Riding Round the Cattle," in *Animal Folk Songs for Children*, and "Rain or Shine" and "Good-bye, Old Paint," in *American Folk Songs for Children*, both collections by RUTH CRAWFORD SEEGER.

Learning western songs

Art and Construction. Boys who are clever with their hands might design and execute original western designs in leather. Wallets, bookmarks, or belts might be exhibited and later used for gifts.

Working with leather

Drawing. On brown wrapping paper or tagboard, outline a large map of the United States. As each story in this unit is read, have the children discuss the part of the country in which it happened. Help them to find and mark the location on the map. Ask different children to paint or draw the characters, buildings, or landscape characteristic of the region.

Making a picture-story map

The Rodeo (189–197)

Stories in Other Readers. Find these other cowboy stories for the children to read.

Good Times Today and Tomorrow, by ARTHUR I. GATES and others
"A Pony Called Lightning," pp. 257–272
"The Rodeo at the Fair," pp. 273–282

Beyond Treasure Valley, by EMMETT A. BETTS and others
"One Good Friend," pp. 216–223

Secrets and Surprises, by PAUL WITTY and IRMENGARDE EBERLE
"Prize Package," pp. 122–138
"On a Ranch" (whole unit), pp. 187–218

Our Good Neighbors, by WILLIAM H. BURTON and others
"On the Ranch," pp. 146–154

Enjoying other stories, songs, and records

Stories to Enjoy. The children may find out more about Danny in *A Ranch for Danny*, by CLYDE R. BULLA. Other good books are *Cocoa*, by MARGARET G. OTTO; *Cowboy Joe of the Circle S*, by HELEN RUSHMORE; *The True Book of Cowboys*, by TERI MARTINI. Good readers will enjoy *Texas Tomboy*, by LOIS LENSKI. An easy book is *Lance and Cowboy Billy*, by JACK HOLT and others. Have on hand *Book of Cowboys*, by HOLLING C. HOLLING; *Rodeo*, by DOROTHY BRACKEN; *Surprise for a Cowboy*, by CLYDE R. BULLA.

Poems to Enjoy. "The Cowboy's Life," by JOHN A. LOMAX, in *My Poetry Book*, by GRACE T. HUFFARD; "Open Range," by KATHRYN and BYRON JACKSON, in *Time for Poetry*, by MAY HILL ARBUTHNOT.

Music to Enjoy. "Home on the Range," in *Singing and Rhyming*, by LILLA BELLE PITTS and others; "America the Beautiful," in *Singing on Our Way*, by LILLA BELLE PITTS and others.

Records to Enjoy. Obtain any one of several good recordings of *The Grand Canyon Suite*, by Ferde Grofé. The children will enjoy hearing the horses' hoofs, and imagining the different pictures painted by the music. "Going West," by Frank Luther (PL 88028) on Decca LP is also enjoyable.

Enjoying films and filmstrips

Films to Enjoy. *Visit with Cowboys* (EBF), 1 reel, b&w/color. *Junior Rodeo Daredevils* (InstrFlms), 1 reel, b&w. *Life on a Cattle Ranch* (Coronet), 1 reel, b&w/color.

Filmstrips to Enjoy. *Pecos Bill Becomes a Cowboy* (CurriculumFlms), color.

The Harpers' Farm

Developing Readiness for Listening

"If you were going to visit a farm today, what are some of the things you would like to see? What are some of the things you would like to do? If you live on a farm, what do you like most about it? Dorothy Aldis has written a poem called 'The Harpers' Farm' which tells about some children who went to visit a farm. Listen, as I read it, to find out whether or not they had any of the experiences you think you would like to have."

Reading the Poem

After reading the poem to the pupils, encourage a spontaneous discussion. They may make comments such as: "I'd like to ride Bessie! I'd like to play in the hay! Weren't the kittens cunning! Mrs. Harper must like boys and girls!"

Rereading the Poem

Ask: "Did you notice, as I read, that the poet uses some words in her poem which make us feel as though we were really with the children? Listen for some of these words and phrases as I read the poem again." Read the poem in sections which lend themselves to discussion. Help the children to select such interesting expressions as "humping little hill," "misty summer heat," "gray and soft," "squeal and grab."

Related Reading Activities

Encourage the children to draw pictures to illustrate the parts of the poem that particularly appeal to them. Below their pictures have them copy the line or lines which they were illustrating. Mount these pictures on brown wrapping paper to make a mural about a farm.

Help the group to find poems which tell about life in different sections of the country and to add their favorites to their class poetry anthology.

325   *The Harpers' Farm* (198–199)

Perhaps the children will suggest writing original rhymes about their farm experiences. The rhymes might be illustrated and made into a book for the library table.

A Poem to Enjoy. "Farewell to the Farm," in *A Child's Garden of Verses*, by ROBERT LOUIS STEVENSON.

Stories to Enjoy. An easy book about farm life is *Ray and Stevie on a Corn-Belt Farm*, by JOAN LIFFRING. Better readers will like *Corn-Farm Boy*, by LOIS LENSKI.

Pages 200–207

The Horse Who Lived Upstairs

Joey was a city horse. During the day he pulled Mr. Polaski's vegetable cart and at night he was taken in an elevator to his stall on the fourth floor of a big brick building. Joey made many friends on his rounds, his master was kind to him, and he had a comfortable stall. But Joey was discontented. He longed for the country where he could sleep in a red barn and run about in a green meadow.

When Mr. Polaski decided to peddle vegetables from a truck, he took Joey to the country. The red barn and the green meadow were there, but Joey was kept so busy working that he could not enjoy them. The day Mr. Polaski came to get him was the happiest of Joey's life. "I am just a city horse," he said.

The children will enjoy this amusing story and observe that a change may not bring contentment.

Vocabulary

New Words: Page 200, *discontented, Polaski;* 201, *stall*;* 202, *interesting, ladies*, carrots;* 203, ——; 204, *poor;* 205, ——; 206, ——; 207, ——

Developing Readiness for Reading

Discussing story background

Meaningful Presentation of Vocabulary. "In the story 'The Rodeo,' do you remember that we said that city children usually do not have ponies. Do you remember why?" (There is no room for ponies in a big city.)

"Our next story is about a horse who lived in a city. This horse's name was *Joey*." Show the children the word *Joe*, which is familiar to them; then ask them to tell how the word is changed when *y* is added to it.

"Joey belonged to *Mr. Polaski*." Have the name pronounced several times by individual children and explain that it is a Polish name. "How many vowel sounds do you hear in *Polaski?* How many syllables are there?"

"Now Mr. Polaski sold fruit from a cart. What do you think Joey's job was? Whom might he meet on the street? Yes, and there were *ladies* and children who fed him *carrots*.

"Is there much room for a horse in the city? No, and there was something particularly *interesting* about Joey's *stall*. It was *upstairs*. How do you think Joey got there every night?" (He might have gone up in an elevator.) "Do you think that Joey was satisfied and contented in his upstairs stall? No, he was not. *Poor* Joey was *discontented*."

If necessary, illustrate the meaning of *discontented* with a pair of sentences such as the following:

Using clues
to attack words

The kitten was so *contented* that he purred and purred.
Because the dog was *discontented* at home, he ran away.

The children will readily unlock *upstairs*, an easy compound; *stall* will be recognized by analogy with *ball*.

Setting Up Reading Purposes. Ask, "Why might a horse like Joey be discontented?" Encourage the children to give their ideas. Write their suggestions on the chalkboard. "Let's read the story to see if our guesses are right. We'll find out whether Joey ever became a contented horse."

Reading the Story

Guided Reading

"Read the first page to find out why Joey was discontented." After the reading, ask: "Do you blame him for being discontented? Why or why not?

Page 200

"There were many things about his life in the city that Joey should have liked. Let's see what they were." After the reading, ask the children to read aloud specific sentences that tell what Joey had that should have made him happy.

Pages 201–202

　　　　The Horse Who Lived Upstairs (200–207)

"One day something happened that pleased Joey very much. Read this page to find out what it was. Do you think he'll be happy? Let's read to the end of the story to see.

"Why was Joey not as happy as he expected to be? Why were the picnic people unfriendly? What did Joey miss in the country? How did Joey feel when he saw Mr. Polaski? What did Joey say about the country? Did you like the way this story ended? Have you ever known a person who was a little like Joey?"

Rereading for Specific Purposes

Reading to check the realistic parts of the story

1. Have the children reread the story carefully to find all the parts in both the text and the pictures that could be true. Help them to describe and compare actual life in the city and in the country with what is told in the story.

Reading orally for interpretation

2. Have the children read the story aloud to another group. Have them show through their voices Joey's discontent, his excitement at moving to the country, his disillusionment there, and his happiness at returning to the city.

During the oral reading of the story the listeners should not have books in their hands but should enjoy listening to the reading.

Building Essential Habits and Skills

Comprehension and Study Skills

Illustrating main parts of the story

Main Idea. To give practice in expressing the main ideas of a story, have the children plan to illustrate one main idea from this story. The ideas listed here are suggestions.

1. Joey with the ladies from the apartment house nearby
2. Joey with the farmer's children
3. Joey in the barn
4. Joey at the picnic
5. Joey working with Mr. Polaski
6. Joey in the city in the summer

Have the children make their drawings or paintings without referring to the illustrations in the Reader. Ask them to give their own interpretation of the story, and expect illustrations like that at the top of the next page.

Joey working with Mr. Polaski

Joey at the picnic

Details. To give practice in recalling pertinent story facts, distribute copies of the following exercise:

Make an X beside each statement which is true. Use your book to look up things you don't remember.

In the city Joey was discontented because:

____X____ He didn't live in a red barn.
_____ He didn't like Mr. Polaski.
____X____ He didn't have a green meadow.
____X____ He lived upstairs.
_____ He worked too hard.
_____ He had no hat in summer.
____X____ He couldn't run about and be frisky.

In the country Joey was discontented because:

____X____ The barn was cold in winter.
_____ He had straw to sleep on.
_____ He didn't have an elevator.
____X____ He missed his friends.
____X____ He had to pull the cart and the plow.
____X____ The gruff old horse didn't like him.

329

Word Meaning. To check understanding of word meanings, give the children this exercise.

*have
run off*

Look at the first word. In the second column find its meaning. In the blank put the number 1. Find the meaning of the second word and in the blank put the number 2. Do the rest of the exercise the same way.

1. discontented	_9_	lunch under a tree
2. frisky	_3_	a green field
3. meadow	_2_	liking to run about and play
4. stall	_5_	a cage that lifts up anything
5. elevator	_10_	the noise of a horn
6. work horse	_4_	a pen for a horse
7. sunup	_7_	as it gets light
8. sundown	_1_	not happy
9. picnic	_6_	big, strong animal
10. honk	_8_	almost night

Recalling
the plural form
of nouns
ending in "y"

Structural Analysis. To review the plural form of nouns ending in *y*, proceed in the following way:

Write on the chalkboard the sentence: *The ladies patted Joey on the nose.* Ask, "How many ladies were there?" Elicit the fact that there could have been several, but that there were more than one. "Suppose only one lady patted Joey. How would we write that sentence?" Ask a volunteer to write, *A lady patted Joey on the nose.* "How is the word *lady* changed when we speak of more than one?" Have the two chalkboard sentences compared and discuss the changing of the *y* to *i* before adding *es*.

For additional group practice write on the chalkboard the words *pony, puppy, cherry, baby, country* (nouns ending in *y* preceded by a consonant). Ask the pupils to write the form of each word which means "more than one."

Perceiving
double consonants
in words

Syllabication. To teach the syllabic division of words containing double consonants, write on the chalkboard the following phrases:

interesting things will happen   *hot in summer*
gave him carrots   *had very little time*

Have the phrases read aloud. Underline the following words: *happen, carrots, summer, little*. Have them pronounced and ask the children how many syllables they hear in each.

Underscore the middle letters and say: "All these words have two consonants just alike in the middle. They are easy words to divide into syllables." Draw a vertical line to indicate the two syllables of *hap|pen*. Ask, "Who will divide the next word into syllables?" Continue until all the underlined words are divided. Then say, "Can you make a simple rule for dividing two-syllable words into syllables when there are two consonants just alike in the middle of the word?" Lead the children to state that *the first of the two consonants belongs with the first syllable, and the second consonant with the second syllable.*

Dividing words with double medial consonants

Offer further practice, using the words *butter, hurry, dollar, bunny, cotton, chatter, hammer, ladder, supper.*

Workbook
Pages 59 and 60.

Related Language Experiences

Listening. Read to the children one or more of the following stories about people or animals who were dissatisfied with their lot: *Copy-Kitten*, by Helen and Alf Evers; "The Bear Who Wanted to Be a Bird," in *Read Me Another Story*, compiled by the Child Study Association of America; *Pito's House*, by Catherine Bryan; and *Spotty*, by Margaret Rey.

Enjoying stories with similar themes

Have the children listen for the expressions of discontent and the resolution of each problem.

Letter Writing. If your school is in the city, the children might write letters to a third grade in the country and tell them something about life in a city.

Writing letters

Enrichment Activities

Drawing. Have the children add to the picture-story map of the United States. One way of carrying out the theme of this story would be to locate one or two large cities and have children sketch in some buildings on the map.

Adding to the picture-story map

Some children may also wish to make a mural showing Joey's life in the city and in the country.

Painting a mural

Stories from Another Reader. Have the children pick a favorite story from this reader and tell why they enjoyed it.

Lost and Found, by ROBIN PALMER
    All the city and country stories, pp. 57–212.

Stories to Enjoy. *Shoeshine Boy,* by JERROLD BEIM; *Big City,* by BERTA and ELMER HADER; *City Boy, Country Boy,* by MIRIAM SCHLEIN; more about Joey in *The Horse Who Had His Picture in the Paper,* by PHYLLIS McGINLEY; *Little Boy Brown,* by ISOBEL HARRIS; *The Little Carousel,* by MARCIA BROWN; *The Little House,* by VIRGINIA LEE BURTON; *We Live in the City,* by LOIS LENSKI.

Poems to Enjoy. Read this poem aloud to the children. Have them listen for the city scenes that are described and perhaps tell which horse they would prefer to be.

HORSES

I like a lot of people
    (Although it all depends)
But when it comes to horses
    I have some special friends.

There is a horse named Anna
    Who drove us through the Park.
I held the reins a minute
    We stayed 'til nearly dark.

There is a horse named Peter
    Who brings us daffodils
And little pots of tulips
    To fill our window sills.

There is the pickle wagon
    And one that carries grapes.
They both have friendly horses
    Of different size and shapes.

I met a horse on Broadway,
    And what do you suppose?
He put his head down gently
    And loved me with his nose.

MARCHETTE CHUTE

Also make available *All around the Town*, by PHYLLIS McGINLEY; *I Live in a City*, by JAMES S. TIPPETT; "Susie the Milk Horse," from *All Together*, by DOROTHY ALDIS; "The Milk-cart Pony," by ELEANOR FARJEON, in *Sung under the Silver Umbrella*, compiled by The Association for Childhood Education International; all the city and country poems in *Gaily We Parade* and *Bridled with Rainbows*, both by SARA and JOHN E. BREWTON.

Music to Enjoy. The children will enjoy learning songs about workers and city life, such as "The Oil Station Man," "The Lamplighter," "Will You Buy," all in *Singing and Rhyming*, by LILLA BELLE PITTS and others.

Bob Learns to Pitch

Pages 208–216

Bob's ambition was to join the neighborhood baseball team, but the boys said he was too small to play. Bob resolved that he would earn a place on the team. With his father's help, he read books on baseball and practiced until he could pitch a ball wherever he wanted it. When he was finally able to strike out Jack, he was accepted as a regular member of the team.

As the children read the story, they will appreciate the value of determination and perseverance.

Vocabulary

New Words: Page 208, *pitch*, team*, strike*;* 209, ——; 210, *read* (past); 211, *plate*;* 212, *batter*, thrown*;* 213, ——; 214, *felt*;* 215, ——; 216, ——

Developing Readiness for Reading

Meaningful Presentation of Vocabulary. "Do you ever watch baseball on TV? Have you ever seen a big-league baseball game? Do you know the names of any of the players?

Talking about baseball

How many of you play baseball? Can you tell a few things you know about playing baseball?"

Reading sentences from the chalkboard

After the children have offered their suggestions, write on the chalkboard such sentences as the following:

> *There are two <u>teams</u>.*
>
> *There is a home <u>plate</u>.*
>
> *The ball is <u>pitched</u> to the <u>batter</u>.*
>
> *Some balls are <u>thrown</u> low.*
>
> *You may <u>strike</u> out.*

Discuss the meanings of the statements. Point out the new words. Then say: "To learn about baseball rules, *you might read a book*. In this story, *Bob read a book about baseball*, and it helped him." Have the children read both sentences containing *read*. Lead them to observe that in the second sentence *read* sounds different from *read* in the first sentence, and that it tells about something that happened in the past.

Applying word-attack skills to words of lesson

Most children will be able to attack the new words independently through phonetic clues. If necessary, help the children to recognize *plate, strike, thrown*, by blending consonant blends with long-vowel phonograms; *team* through the sound of *ea; felt* through the sound of short *e; pitched* and *batter* through both phonetic and structural attack.

Setting Up Reading Purposes. "Today we shall read a true story about a boy who wanted to get on a baseball team. What would you have to be able to do before you could play on a team? Do you think Bob will make the team? Let us read the story to find out if the boys let him play."

Reading the Story

Guided Reading

Page 208

"Read page 208. Which boy in the picture is Bob? How do you know? What did he tell Jack?

Page 209

"This page tells us about Bob's plan to make the team. Read to find out what it was." After the reading, ask: "What was Jack's promise? What do you think about Bob's idea of getting some books? What did his Dad say? Is this true?

Teaching Finding New Neighbors
334

"Why do you think Bob felt he had the best father in the world? Do most boys and girls think this?

"What else did Bob's father do to help him?" After the reading, say, "Read aloud the part which tells what Bob's father said over the telephone." Discuss with the children that some fathers might like to do this but couldn't because of business or for other important reasons.

"Finish the story to find out if Bob made the team." After the reading, ask: "How did he do it? Why did Bob's father say, 'You're a good fellow, Jack, to give him a try.' Do you think Bob will be a successful player? Why?"

Page 210

Page 211

Pages 212–216

Rereading for Specific Purposes

Have the group reread the story silently to pick out key sentences which, when put together, will tell the whole story. The children may illustrate these sentences and arrange them in sequence on the bulletin board together with the pictures. When the pictures and sentences have been mounted on the

Reading to find main events; to arrange them in sequence

335   *Bob Learns to Pitch* (208–216)

bulletin board, have the group discuss whether or not the main events of the story are presented. If there are differences of opinion, the children may reread parts of the story.

Building Essential Habits and Skills

Comprehension and Study Skills

Evaluating information

Critical Reading. To strengthen the ability to recall accurately and clearly, give the children the exercise below. Discuss and check this exercise orally with the whole group.

Write <u>true</u> or <u>false</u> after each sentence. When you have finished, check each answer in the story. Mark it right or wrong on your paper. Then write down the number of the page on which the right answer is given.

About Baseball

The ball must go across the plate.   <u>true</u>   <u>page 211</u>

The ball must not be thrown above the batter's shoulders.
<u>true</u>   <u>page 213</u>

The ball should be thrown very low.   <u>false</u>   <u>page 213</u>

A pitch which does not go across the plate is a "ball."
<u>true</u>   <u>page 213</u>

The plate from which the players eat is called home plate.
<u>false</u>   <u>page 214</u>

Ball players can be big or little.   <u>true</u>   <u>page 215</u>

A pitch which is thrown in the right place is a "strike"
when a batter swings and misses.   <u>true</u>   <u>page 215</u>

Making inferences

Creative Reading. To give practice in reading between the lines, either distribute copies of the exercise below or write it on the chalkboard. A group discussion should follow.

Answer the questions by drawing a line under the right answer.

1. Where was it?

Bob pitched. Jack hit and ran.

at school   in the living room   <u>on the ball field</u>

Teaching *Finding New Neighbors*   336

2. What time was it?

> The clock was striking. The only light was given by the moon.

> <u>2 A.M.</u>   8 A.M.   1 P.M.

3. What place was it?

> Some were going up. Some were going down. Some talked. No one ran.

> on a train   <u>on the elevator</u>   in the barn

4. What was happening?

> The parade passed by slowly. The horses had silver trappings. Clowns were bouncing around. The elephants came last.

> a rodeo   <u>a circus</u>   a ranch

Word-Study Skills

Word Meaning. To check the understanding of baseball words, write the following words in a column on the chalkboard: *team, glove, batter, pitcher, baseball, plate.* In a different order write the definitions of the words. Have a child read a word in the column on the left and draw a line to its definition on the right.

Enriching word meaning; matching words and definitions

Bob Learns to Pitch (208–216)

Phonetic Analysis. 1. To check the ability to discriminate between short and long *ea*, write on the chalkboard two lists of words containing the vowel digraph *ea*. In one list write *easy, team, leak, east, speak, read, teacher, eagle, feast*. In the second list write *bread, head, heavy, read, feather, breakfast, ready, treasure*. Have the words in both lists pronounced and the *ea* underlined. Ask the children to recall the different pronunciations of the *ea* in each group. Expect the response that *ea* sounds like long *e* in the first group, like short *e* in the second group. Recall the two pronunciations of *read*.

2. To give practice in reading different words with *ea*, use the sentences below. Observe that the reader depends upon his knowledge of word meaning to decide how to pronounce *ea*.

> *Let us read about the sea.*
> *The beans were ready.*
> *He had a feather on his head.*
> *Bob was a player on the team.*

3. To teach recognition of the variant sounds of *o*, ask the children to leaf through this story to find words containing the letter *o*. As the children say the words, write them in columns according to the sound and the key word given at the top of each column below.

long o as in *no*	*short o* as in *lot*		*o* as in *for*
going	got	promise	important
almost	from	boxing	horse

Add to the lists as the children think of more words.

If children ask, point out that *o* has many other sounds besides the three listed on the chalkboard. Tell them that sometimes it has the same sound as other vowels, for example, in *come*, *o* sounds like short *u*, and *or* in *work* sounds like *ir* in *first*.

NOTE. Because the sound of *o* varies so much in different localities, the teacher should allow the accepted pronunciations of *o* with which the children are most familiar.

Structural Analysis. To recall the change in meaning when *er* is added to a verb, distribute copies of the exercise on page 339 or write it on the chalkboard.

Look at the first word. Next to it write what it is that the pitcher does. Finish the exercise in the same way.

pitcher ————
batter ————
hitter ————
player ————
striker ————
leader ————
swimmer ————
helper ————
reader ————

Think of some more <u>er</u> words that mean one who does something.

———— ———— ———— ————
———— ———— ———— ————

Write sentences with 5 of the words.

have run off

Workbook

Pages 61, 62, and 63.

Related Language Experiences

Discussion and Research. Encourage the children to talk about baseball players whom they admire and to exchange

Making a "Fair Play" chart

We Always Try
To wait our turn.
To play fair.
To be good winners.
To be good losers.

Bob Learns to Pitch (208–216)

information about the relative standings of the major baseball teams. Provide an opportunity for them to tell about interesting games or contests in which they have taken part. In discussing competitive games, emphasize the value of fair play. A chart about fair play on the playground might be composed. The one on the preceding page is merely a suggestion.

Sharing pictures
Suggest that the children find pictures of leading baseball players on the sport pages of newspapers. If some boys in the class have such a collection, encourage them to share the collection with the class. The children may also be interested to know that the Bob in this true story is Bob Feller, the famous pitcher.

Superior readers might be interested in making biographies of good baseball players and reporting on them to the class.

Enrichment Activities

Learning new games
Playing Games. A group may visit the physical-education instructor or the library to obtain some information about a

Teaching *Finding New Neighbors*

340

new game to play. Emphasize ways of learning about a new game—by asking, by reading, by trying, by practicing. Place the rules for the new game on a chart for future references. If possible, the group should learn a new indoor and a new outdoor game, and have time to play them several times.

Stories to Enjoy. *Giant in the Midget League,* by CARY JACKSON; *Pete's Home Run,* by MARION RENICK; *Hillbilly Pitcher,* by C. P. and O. B. JACKSON. Mature readers will enjoy *Out to Win,* by MARY GRAHAM BONNER, and *Baseball Pals,* by MATT CHRISTOPHER. An easy book is *Bats and Gloves of Glory,* by MARION RENICK. Enjoying literature and music

Music to Enjoy. "Ball Games," in *Merry Music,* by THERESA ARMITAGE and others.

El Burrito

Pages 217–223

Miguel, a Spanish-American boy, was devoted to the burro who hauled wood down the mountainside each day. When El Burrito became too old to work, his owner turned him out, but he gave Miguel permission to keep the animal if he found him. El Burrito came down from the mountain at last and carried the newspapers which Miguel wanted to sell. By the next summer the boy and the burro had earned enough to go camping together with a group from the village.

The children will feel the kindliness and good feeling for people and animals that are depicted in this story.

Vocabulary

New Words: Page 217, *El Burrito, Miguel, burro;* 218, ————; 219, ————; 220, *newspapers;* 221, ————; 222, ————; 223, ————

Developing Readiness for Reading

"Our next story is about another American boy, one whose parents or grandparents came from a country where people Discussing story pictures and related concepts

El Burrito (217–223)

speak Spanish. This boy would be called 'Michael' in English; in Spanish he is *Miguel* (mē gĕl')." Have the name pronounced by several children until it is familiar.

"Miguel lives in the southwestern part of this country." If a map of the United States is available, help the children find the region. Ask the children what other story characters lived here. Help them to recall Blue Cornflower, Dancing Cloud, and Swift Boy.

Show the picture on page 218. "Miguel has a friend. Do you know the name of this animal?" (A donkey or *burro*) Discuss the fact that the burro's owner uses the animal to carry wood from the neighboring mountain, and that Miguel is obviously fond of the burro. "Miguel called the burro *El Burrito*, which means 'The Little Burro.' "

Setting Up Reading Purposes. "Like many boys, Miguel wanted something very much. He was wondering how he could earn enough money to buy it. Have you ever wanted something very much?" Allow time for discussion. Then ask: "What do you want money for? Have you ever earned money yourself? How?" (Delivering *newspapers*, doing chores for Mother, etc.) "In this story Miguel found a new solution. Let's read the story to find out what it was."

Reading the Story

Guided Reading

Page 217 Have the children locate the story title, "El Burrito," in the table of contents and open their books to the correct page. Allow time for comments on the picture. Encourage discussion about the boy working beside his adobe house. Recall that such houses are found in the Southwest, where the weather is very dry. Ask: "Do people in other parts of the country have such houses? Why not?

Reading silently to answer questions "Read this page to find out why Miguel had no other children to play with." After the reading, ask: "Why did Miguel wish for a bicycle? Why did he watch for El Burrito every day?

Page 218 "Read this page to find why Miguel was worried." After the reading, ask: "What did Miguel do each day for the burro? Why do you think El Burrito's ears stood up? What do you think could have happened to the burro?

"Miguel finally thought of a good plan. Read two pages to find out what it was." After the reading, ask, "What kind of boy do you think Miguel was?" Have the children prove their answers by reading parts of the story orally. **Pages 219–220**

"How did Miguel find El Burrito?" After the reading, ask: "What did he do for the tired little burro? **Page 221**

"Finish the story to find out whether Miguel's plan worked out. Where did the boys go?" (Camping.) After the reading, ask: "Why was Miguel's plan a good one? Did people like El Burrito? Why did the little burro go camping with the boys?" **Pages 222–223**

Rereading for Specific Purposes

1. Ask: "What feeling did you get about the people in this story? Did they seem like kind and friendly people?" Help the children state some of the personal qualities of the story characters, such as Miguel's kindness to the burro and his thoughtfulness of his mother. Then have the children reread the story to find sentences that show how these qualities affected the actions of the story people. Have the sentences read aloud. *Skimming to locate ideas*

NOTE. If the children advance the idea that the burro's owner was cruel in turning him out, point out that the man was very poor and could not afford to feed an animal that could no longer work, and that the mountains probably afforded food and water for the burro.

2. Now have the children find all the kinds of work El Burrito did. Ask individuals to read aloud the parts that tell what he did. *Reading to give information*

Building Essential Habits and Skills

Comprehension and Study Skills

Specific Details. To practice recall of story facts, distribute copies of the exercise on the next page. *Recalling story details*

343   *El Burrito* (217–223)

Underline the correct statements.

1. Miguel was thinking

   how he could buy a burro.
   <u>how he could buy a bicycle.</u>
   how he could go to the village.

2. Miguel lived

   in a large city.
   in a tiny village.
   <u>far up the road from a village.</u>

3. Miguel did not see El Burrito

   for a week.
   for many, many days.
   <u>for three days.</u>

4. The burro was turned out because

   <u>he was too old to carry wood.</u>
   he was too old to carry newspapers.
   he was too old to live.

5. Miguel found the burro

   in the city.
   at the rodeo.
   <u>on the road.</u>

6. The burro took the place

   of the newspapers.
   <u>of the bicycle.</u>
   of his mother.

7. The boys and girls in the village

   <u>put flowers behind El Burrito's ears.</u>
   helped Miguel sell newspapers.
   did not like El Burrito.

8. Miguel took El Burrito camping because

   no one at home would take care of him.
   <u>the burro had helped earn money for the trip.</u>
   all burros like to go camping.

Creative Reading. To help the children translate new reading material into another medium, duplicate enough copies of the exercise below so that each child has a copy. Help slower children attack any words they do not know.

Read the story on this paper carefully. Then take a large piece of drawing paper and draw or paint a colorful picture about the things in the story. Be sure you put in everything.

Pedro and his family lived in a little mud house at the foot of some brown and gold mountains. Around the outside of the house there was a garden where Pedro's corn stood tall and his sister's squashes grew along the ground. In back of the yellow, flat-roofed house stood an orange tree and a lemon tree.

Next to the garden there was a river that came from the snow in the high mountains. There was very little water in it now because in this part of the country there was no rain all summer long. A little way to the east of Pedro's house, the land was so dry that no plants except cactus would grow.

Tonight the sunset was beautiful. The sun was a great red-gold ball. The brown and yellow mountains looked almost blue and pink.

It was almost time for supper. Pedro's mother was pounding out a flat corn cake on a stone. His sister put some yellow squashes in a basket to take to market in the morning. Pedro's father was setting down the little burro he had just finished making out of wood. He would sell that at the market too.

When you have finished your picture, check the story again.

Word-Study Skills

Word Meaning. To develop further the ability to attack hyphenated words, ask, "What does *empty-handed* mean?" Recall other hyphenated words presented previously: *co-pilot, snow-covered, half-closed, right-hand picket.* Ask individual children to use each of the words in a meaningful sentence.

Attacking hyphenated words

Phonetic Analysis. 1. To review variant sounds of *i*, write on the chalkboard the following words:

Recalling variant sounds of "i"

village	*lived*	*bite*
bird	*picked*	*decided*
first	*until*	*like*
silk	*girls*	*stirred*

Have the words pronounced and the sounds of *i* identified: long *i*, short *i*, *i* before *r*. Have the children rearrange the words, putting all the long-*i* words in one column, the short-*i* words in a second column, and the *ir* words in a third.

345

If children question the sound of *i* in *Miguel* and *Burrito*, tell them that *i* sometimes sounds like long *e*. They may observe the same sound in *gasoline, policeman, machine.*

Recalling the
variant sounds
of "e"
2. To recall the variant sounds of *e*, write the following sentences on the chalkboard and underline the words:

Miguel petted the burro.
Three days went by and Miguel did not see the burro.
Each day Miguel watched for the burro.
Miguel gave her the red leaves.

Direct the children to read the sentences silently and to think of the different sounds of *e* that they can hear and see in the underlined words. Lead a discussion of the differences in these sounds and help the pupils to summarize their knowledge of *e* sounds. They should be able to recognize the following:

Short *e*, as in *petted, red,* and *went.*

Long *e*, as in *three, see, each, leaves.* Recall the principle that in double vowels the first letter usually has its long sound and the second letter is silent.

The special sound of *e* followed by *r*, as in *her.*

The silent *e*, as in *gave.*

Have the children skim the story for other examples of the sounds of *e*. Write them in the appropriate columns on the chalkboard.

Arranging words
alphabetically
Alphabetizing. List the first names of the children in the group and ask the children to arrange them alphabetically.

Workbook

Pages 64, 65, and 66.

Related Language Experiences

Comparing
interpretations
Discussion. 1. When the children have finished the creative-reading exercise on page 345 of this manual, ask a few of them to exhibit their pictures before the rest of the group. Allow free discussion and comments and point out the differences in the pictures. Lead the children to conclude that it is possible for several people to carry out the same instructions

in very different ways, all of which may be correct and all of which may be pleasing.

2. Recall that Miguel's ancestors came to America from a Discussing origins of Americans Spanish-speaking country, perhaps Mexico. Ask the children to inquire at home about the country or countries from which their ancestors originally came. It there is time, have different children tell about customs their ancestors brought from their country which have been carried on in this country. Lead the children to understand that American people have diverse backgrounds and that we all profit from the many cultural contributions and ideas brought from other countries. Emphasize the fact that all of us are American, regardless of our country of origin.

Enrichment Activities

Co-ordinating Activity. Compare the life of a child living Collecting information in a village, such as Miguel's, with the life of a child on a ranch, in a big city, or in a small town, as described in the preceding stories in this unit. Collect or draw pictures for a display which will point up the variety of American life.

A Story in Another Reader. Here is another burro story. Enjoying literature and music

Friends and Fun, by ARTHUR I. GATES and others
   "The Burro That Had a Name," pp. 54–65

A Poem to Enjoy. This poem has a Spanish flavor. Read it to bring out the rhythm and the melody.

DAHLIAS

When I go riding
Up Rio de la Caza,
I call Jacobo
And he appears;

Saddles the pony,
And, slipping on the bridle,
He tucks two dahlias
Behind her ears.

EDITH AGNEW

Stories to Enjoy. Good books are *Burro Boy and His Big Trouble,* by LAURA BANNON; *Juanita* and *Pedro, the Angel of*

El Burrito (217–223)

Olvera Street, by LEO POLITI; *Nellie and the Mayor's Hat*, by CHARLOTTE BAKER; *Sarah's Idea*, by DORIS GATES; *The Hidden Burro*, by DELIA GOETZ. A good reference book is *The American Southwest* (a Golden Regional book). Good readers will like *My Pet Peepelo*, by ELLIS CREDLE, another story of a boy who needed to earn money. Slower readers will enjoy *The Fabulous Firework Family*, by JAMES FLORA.

A Record to Enjoy. "Rolito," by Frank Luther (DL 8021).

A Song to Enjoy. The mood of the story is caught very well by the song below. The children will enjoy learning and singing it.

EL BURRITO

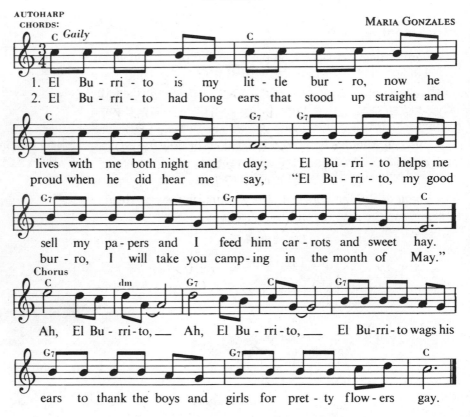

New Moon and the Dragon

New Moon, a Chinese-American girl, participated in the celebration of the Chinese New Year. Children will enjoy the story of this colorful custom which enriches American culture.

The story will deepen children's understanding and appreciation of the Chinese-American people. It will lead to discussion of other festivals and customs which were brought here by people of various countries.

Vocabulary

New Words: Page 224, *dragon, luck*, Chinese;* 225, ————; 226, *slippers*;* 227, *firecrackers*, balcony;* 228, *flag*;* 229, ————; 230, ————; 231, ————; 232, ————; 233, ————

Developing Readiness for Reading

Meaningful Presentation of Vocabulary. Ask the children to recall the names of children in stories recently read. Write several names as the children suggest them. Then write *New Moon* and tell them that "New Moon" is the name of a *Chinese* girl. Ask: "Do any Chinese people live in this country? Yes, and many are American citizens. Do you know where many Chinese live?" If background is needed, tell the children about the Chinatowns in large cities like New York and San Francisco. Show them pictures so that they may see that some of the houses have fancy roofs and *balconies.*

Discussing
story background

"Our story is about a little Chinese-American girl. She is getting ready for a very great feast, the Chinese New Year. The Chinese have a different calendar from ours, and so their New Year comes at a different time of year.

NOTE. The Chinese New Year is dependent upon the moon and is celebrated in late January or early February. The date of Easter, one of our holidays, also depends upon the moon. It occurs on the Sunday following the first full moon after March 21.

"Like all other people, the Chinese people like to have a good time, and their New Year's celebration certainly shows that." Suggest that the celebration usually lasts several days, that there is usually a New Year's parade in Chinatown with great *dragons* and *firecrackers,* and that the people send each other wishes for good *luck.*

Using phonetic
clues for the
new vocabulary

For the children who need extra help in word attack suggest a phonetic approach for the new words. Analyze *dragon, Chinese, slippers, flag,* through blending known elements; *luck* may be compared with *duck; firecrackers* is an easy compound.

Setting Up Reading Purposes. "Let us read this story to find out how New Moon celebrated the New Year and what a *dragon* had to do with it."

Reading the Story

Guided Reading

Page 224

Reading silently
to answer questions

"In this picture New Moon is in a store. What is she looking at? Let's read this page to find out what store it was and what interesting things there were to see." After the reading, ask: "Whose store was this? What was special on this day?

Page 225

"Read this page to find out what the Chinese believe brings good luck and why New Moon wanted a dragon head? What did she do to get ready for the New Year?

**Pages
226–227**

"Read two pages to find out what gifts New Moon received." After the reading, ask: "What preparations were made for the New Year? How did New Moon know when the New Year was starting?

Page 228

"Why did New Moon's mother want her to stay on the balcony? How did she help her father? How did New Moon feel about the flag? Do you think the balcony was a good place to watch all the things going on in the street? Why? What else might New Moon have seen besides Turtle Boy and his friends?"

Ask a child to reread the last sentence on page 228. "Is that true? Why?"

NOTE. Break the story here if the children are unable to read it all in one period.

**Pages
229–230**

"What is the subtitle? Do you remember what the dragon was supposed to bring? Read two pages to find out what New Moon's family did to get ready for the dragon." After the reading, ask: "What kinds of presents were hung out for the dragon? How could he reach New Moon's presents? How were New Moon, her mother, and the baby dressed? How did they know the dragon was coming?

"Finish the story to find out what happened when the dragon passed under New Moon's balcony." After the reading, ask: "How did the dragon look? Do you think you would have been frightened? Describe the parade. What happened after the parade had passed? What did you enjoy most during your visit with New Moon?"

Pages 231–233

Rereading for Specific Purposes

Say: "Sometimes authors use words so well that we feel as we are reading them that we actually can see what they are talking about. Close your eyes and try to see the picture that I shall read about." After the reading of one paragraph, let the children find other parts of the story that present good pictures. Have individual children take turns reading their chosen paragraphs aloud while the rest of the group listen with eyes closed.

Reading orally to present word pictures

Comprehension and Study Skills

Associating related ideas

Critical Reading. To strengthen the ability to use judgment, distribute copies of the exercise below. Some of the answers will vary according to the children's personal experience.

Read the phrases below carefully. Draw a line under each one that tells about things that both the Chinese and we do on a holiday.

1. Play with toys
2. Give presents to our friends
3. Get ready for a feast
4. Use bowls of fresh flowers
5. Put bowls of nuts and cakes on the table
6. Hang chairs with red silk
7. Wear gold rings
8. Wear silk slippers
9. Light firecrackers
10. Watch a parade from a balcony
11. Put up flags
12. Send letters to our friends to wish them a Happy New Year
13. Tie a present to a tape for a dragon to take
14. Dress in our best clothes
15. Have a feast

Testing story sequence

Sequence. To test the children's ability to recall story events in sequence, distribute copies of the following exercise:

Read again the part of the story called "The Dragon," on pages 229–233. Then read the sentences on this paper. Before the sentence that tells what happened first in the story, put the number 1. Before the sentence that happened next, put the number 2, and so on.

<u>6</u> After the parade Turtle Boy's family visited New Moon's house.

<u>5</u> The dragon made one last jump and moved on.

<u>3</u> They could already see the dragon down the street coming towards them.

_2_ Then New Moon put on her best silk suit to be ready to give the dragon his present.

_4_ The dragon rolled his eyes and took the present of fruit and money.

_1_ New Moon's mother tied the bag of fruit and money to a long red tape.

Word-Study Skills

Word Meaning and Recognition. To strengthen the ability to unlock new words through recognition of a part of the word, write on the chalkboard the following sentences:

Observing how words change

Many people came to <u>America</u> from <u>China</u>.

These <u>Chinese</u> people became <u>Americans</u>.

Have the sentences read aloud and call attention to the underlined words. Ask what parts are the same in *China* and *Chinese*, and in *America* and *American*, and have them circled. Call attention to the similarities in each pair of words and note that one word refers to the country whereas the other refers to citizens of the country. Point out that we also use *Chinese* or *American* when we talk about things pertaining to each country (Chinese bowls, American flag).

An interested group may wish to continue with the names of other countries. In preparation for the next unit help them attack such words as *Italy, Italian; Spain, Spanish; Sweden, Swedish.*

Phonetic Analysis. 1. To review the rule for sounding vowel digraphs, recall the principle that *when two vowels appear together in a word, the first vowel usually has the long sound and the second vowel is silent.* Illustrate with the following words: *eat, wait, road, painted, clean.* Ask the children to recall other words with these digraphs.

Reviewing vowel digraphs

Help the children look through the story to locate other examples. List the words on the chalkboard. If exceptions are noted, place them in a separate list. The following are among the exceptions that occur in this story: page 224, *pieces, head, great*; page 225, *believe, ready*; page 226, *breakfast.*

2. In a similar way review the two sounds of *ow*. Write *cow, flower, down,* and *now* on the chalkboard and have the words pronounced. Then write *throw, bowl, yellow,* and *below,* have the words pronounced, and help the children listen for the sound of *ow*.

Structural Analysis. To give practice in unlocking new words through recognition of structural changes, write on the chalkboard the following groups of words from the unit "Americans All":

board work

1. *own*	*lead*	*pitch*	*bat*
owner	*leader*	*pitcher*	*batter*
2. *pretty*	*silky*	*frisky*	*busy*
prettier	*silkier*	*friskier*	*busier*
3. *balcony*	*pony*	*carry*	*dry*
balconies	*ponies*	*carried*	*dried*

Have each group of words pronounced. Discuss how one word has been changed into another, as follows:

1. Recall the principle and use of *er* agent, meaning one who does something, in the first group of words.

2. Lead the children to observe the changing of *y* to *i* to add *er* in the second group of words.

3. Have the children note the changing of *y* to *i* before *es* and *ed* in the third group.

Syllabication. To give practice in recognizing syllables, duplicate the list of words below and direct the pupils to tell how many vowel sounds they hear and how many syllables they see in each word.

board work

shop	another	dust
hanging	children	presents
hurry	hiding	balcony
wonderful	began	follow
dragon	flag	luck
slippers	letters	flrecracker

Workbook

Pages 67, 68, 69, and 70.

Related Language Experiences

Background Chart. Have the children compose co-operatively a chart entitled "Americans All" with a list of the countries represented in their classroom. Encourage the children to tell of their own background and use this discussion period to develop further appreciation of others.

Dramatization. Let the children dramatize the story informally. They may play each scene several times with different children in the roles. Urge the listeners to be ready to offer specific suggestions for improvement.

Research. To give practice in finding and organizing information, have the children divide into groups with pupil leaders. Have each group select a phase of Chinese life which interests them, locate material about it, and make a report to the class. Help each group to set up its problem, to list specific questions, and to read to find the answers. Discuss possible sources of information, such as magazines, newspapers, and supplementary readers. Give individuals guidance in choosing material relevant to the topic which the group is investigating. Questions, such as those at the top of page 356, may be used for this research type of reading.

Making a chart

Dramatizing the story

Finding and reporting pertinent information

New Moon and the Dragon (224–233)

1. What is the date of the Chinese New Year?

2. What foods are most important to the Chinese?

3. What is a Chinese school like?

4. How does a Chinese-American boy or girl spend a day?

5. What games do Chinese children play? Which of their games are like ours?

6. What kind of work do people in China do? How is their work like ours?

7. What clothes do Chinese wear? How are they different from ours? Why?

8. What other days do Chinese celebrate?

Enrichment Activities

Making comparisons of the American ways of life

Co-ordinating Activity. Continue the bulletin-board display by adding information about the Chinatowns in large American cities. Encourage children to bring in Chinese objects and tell about them.

Making dragon heads

Art and Construction. If they wish, the children may make dragon heads of various shapes, colors, and designs either from paper bags, or papier mâché. Allow the children to look

at pictures of Chinese dragons and to use their imagination as to features and color.

Boys may be interested in making gay kites. Girls may wish to make fans with Chinese floral designs.

Drawing. To the picture-story map of the United States, have the children add pictures that show the influence of the Mexican and the Chinese parts of the American population.

Finishing the map

Stories to Enjoy. *Johnny Hong of Chinatown,* by CLYDE R. BULLA; *San Francisco Boy,* by LOIS LENSKI; *Tommy and Dee-Dee,* by YEN LIANG; *Peachblossom,* by ELEANOR LATTIMORE; *Chin-Ling, the Chinese Cricket,* by ALISON STILWELL.

Enjoying literature and music

Music to Enjoy. "Chinese New Year," in *Our Songs,* and "Chinatown," in *Merry Music,* both by THERESA ARMITAGE and others.

The Ice-Cream Man

Page 234

Developing Readiness for Listening

"Does a man ever come down your street selling ice cream? What do you call him? The poem I am going to read to you is about an ice-cream man. Listen to see if he is like the man who comes down your street."

Reading the Poem

After reading the poem, have children tell how this man is like (or unlike) the ice-cream man they know.

Rereading the Poem

Reread the poem, one stanza at a time, and discuss the meaning of the following lines:

Stanza 1. And brick's a blaze of heat,

Stanza 2. To see him fill the cones with mounds of cooling brown or white.

357

Stanza 3. From bottles full of frosty-fizz,
Stanza 4. His cart might be a flower bed

After the discussion read the poem once more while the children listen.

Related Activities

The children may draw their own illustrations for the poem or for any part of it. Have them copy below the picture the appropriate lines from the poem.

Encourage the children to write their own rhymes about the street vendors they patronize.

Read aloud other poems from Rachel Field's *Taxis and Toadstools*, especially "The Flower-Cart Man" and "Stores and Storekeepers."

Tell the children that Phyllis McGinley, who wrote "The Horse Who Lived Upstairs," also writes poems. Read from her *All around the Town* the poem for the letter *G*, "G's for the Gay Good-Humor Man."

Music to Enjoy. "The Ice-Cream Man," in *Singing on Our Way*, by LILLA BELLE PITTS and others.

All-Unit Activities

Culminating Activities

As a culmination of this unit, stress the unit theme, "Americans All." Ask the children to bring objects from other countries to share and exhibit. Play music from different parts of this country and Mexican or Chinese music. Help the children to write stories about how their parents or grandparents came to America. Stress how they benefited from this country and how they have contributed to the American way of life.

Continue collecting the children's original stories about living in a city, on a farm, or in a small town.

Putting On an International Program. In a group having a variety of foreign ancestors the children should be encouraged to appreciate their origins. The class might do research on accomplishments and specialties of different nationalities and their cultural contributions to life in this country. Such a study could culminate in an international program for the parents in which children with foreign ancestors might wear their national costumes, tell a story, recite a poem, sing a song, or do group folk dances from the various countries. The group may invite guests to tell about experiences they have had traveling in our own country. Films or filmstrips of contributions and customs of Americans with foreign origins may be shown.

Evaluating Activities

Word-Meaning Test (Workbook, p. 70). Distribute copies of the following test. Have the directions read silently and then orally.

Many different kinds of people live in America. They do different kinds of work. They have fun in different ways. But they are all Americans. The words below are from the stories you have read about "Americans All."

Put B before the words that make you think of Bob and the baseball games.

Put D before the words that make you think of Danny and the rodeo.

Put J before the words that make you think of Joey, the city horse.

Put M before the words that make you think of Miguel and El Burrito.

Put NM before the words that make you think of New Moon and the Chinese New Year.

D rodeo	D Pepper	J city horse
J elevator	J stall	NM balcony
J discontented	B pitch	D first prize
D grandstand	J Mr. Polaski	M El Burrito
B team	NM firecrackers	M camping
NM dragon	M newspapers	NM American flag
B baseball	D trick riding	B thrown low
M burro	B strike	NM silk slippers
B plate	M bicycle	D cow pony
NM drums	D pasture	D tapped Ginger

Comprehension Test. To check the children's recall of story facts in this unit, distribute copies of the following tests:

Write the correct answer after each question.

Who?

1. Who lived upstairs? _____ Joey _____
2. Who won a prize? _Danny and Judy_
3. Who sold vegetables on a city street? _____ Mr. Polaski _____
4. Who gave carrots to the horse? _____ ladies _____
5. Who owned Pepper? _____ Judy _____
6. Who gave Bob a try? _____ Jack _____
7. Who threw a firecracker at the edge of the balcony? _____ Turtle Boy _____
8. Who sold newspapers? _____ Miguel _____
9. Who learned to pitch? _____ Bob _____
10. Who paraded down the street? _____ the dragon _____
11. Who was riding Ginger? _____ Danny _____

What?

1. What did Danny and Judy get for a prize? belts
2. What did the ladies from the apartment give Joey? carrots
3. What did his dad do to help Bob? get books, practice with him
4. What did Miguel bring home to his mother? leaves
5. What was on the red paper New Moon got for the New Year? Good Luck
6. What tricks did the ponies do? trotted, turned, wheeled, backed, danced, bowed
7. What did Miguel wish he had? a bicycle
8. What did New Moon's father hang from the balcony? the American flag
9. What was inside the dragon? two men
10. What did Joey ride on to get to the fourth floor? an elevator
11. What did Bob learn from a book? things to make him strong
12. What did New Moon see in the sky? the new moon

Teaching *Finding New Neighbors*

360

Discuss the following questions, let the children answer in their own words, and on questions 1, 2, and 4, allow for differences of opinion.

Why?

1. Why did Miguel need El Burrito? —————————
2. Why did the Chinese children get presents? —————
3. Why did Judy and Danny win a prize? ——————
4. Why did the children throw firecrackers? ————
5. Why did Bob read the book? ———————————
6. Why did El Burrito's owner turn him out? ———————

7. Why was it hard for Danny to sit on the sidelines?
_____
8. Why could Judy go to the rodeo? —————————
9. Why was Joey discontented? ——————————
10. Why did Mr. Polaski give Joey up? ——————

Word-Study Test. To check the understanding of changing *y* to *i* when *es* is added to a word, give the children the following test:

Adding "es" to words ending in "y"

Finish each sentence with the correct form of the word at the right.

1. All the __ponies__ were in the pasture. pony
2. We heard the __babies__ crying. baby
3. The travelers went to many __cities__ . city
4. Jane ate three __candies__ . candy
5. People from many __countries__ came to America. country
6. Many __families__ live on farms. family

If children need more practice, give them the plural forms of other words ending in *y* and have them write the singular form of each word.

Syllables. To test recall of how to divide words into syllables, distribute copies of the exercise at the top of page 362.

Dividing words into syllables

361   All-Unit Activities

Mark the syllables in these words.

a|bout   afraid   again   ahead
along   around   away   alone

Mark the syllables in these words.

began	believe
slippers	Danny
sundown	driveway
grandstand	burro
Pepper	camping

type ✓

Helping the Individual Child

General Help. All through this unit the teacher will evaluate the work of the individual child. Is each child being challenged? Is the child having difficulty with this material? What is the difficulty? Use the tests in the "All-Unit Activities" to diagnose his difficulties. Check children's skills through the inventories on pages 67, 127, and 193. Give individual help to children showing needs.

Understanding
the main idea **Specific Help.** Group the children who have difficulty in determining the main idea of a story. Use one or more of the following techniques for helping them:

1. Read short paragraphs or stories to the group and encourage pupils to suggest titles for them. Lead them to see that a good title is one which tells the most about a story.

2. Read short stories and have the pupils retell the plot in one sentence.

3. Mount simple stories on tagboard with possible titles on the back of the sheet. Let the pupils read a story, illustrate it, choose the best title for the story, and write the title above the picture. In a group meeting have each child show his picture, read the name of the story, and retell it in three clear, concise sentences.

Enriching
word meaning *Word Meaning.* To help children who have trouble with meanings of words, encourage them to bring from home some old magazines with colored pictures that may be cut out

There will be many uses for these magazines, some of which are suggested here:

1. Let the group make a large word booklet for the library table. Have them collect different types of pictures and organize them according to descriptive words, such as *interesting, strange, frightening, beautiful, different, funny.*

2. Large action pictures may be cut out and mounted on sheets of paper. With the help of the teacher, the children may suggest phrases to describe the pictures. These phrases may be listed on the chalkboard and later printed under the picture by a member of the class. For example, "Bringing Milk," "Cutting Grass," "Getting the Mail."

Word Recognition. Children who need help in certain types of word-recognition activities may choose an assignment from the following items and clip or copy words that fit into each category: (*a*) Find words that end in *ing.* (*b*) Find words that end in *er.* (*c*) Find compound words. (*d*) Find pairs of words that rhyme.

Aiding word recognition

Phonetic Analysis. To review the sounds of *ow* and *ou*, recall the two sounds of *ow* as in *throw* and *cow*, and *ou* as in *house.* Have the pupils read the following sentences and place the words containing *ou* or *ow* in the proper column.

Reviewing "ou" and "ow"

1. The *flowers* are in the *round bowl.*
2. *How* do you go to *town*?
3. There is no *snow now.*
4. The little girl made a *bow* to the king. She wore a *bow* on her head.
5. She *counted* the *houses.* Many were colored *yellow.*
6. They had to go *out* of the yard and *around* the house.
7. The ball was *thrown* over the plate.

cow	throw	house
flowers	bowl	counted
how	snow	houses
town	bow	out
now	yellow	around
bow	thrown	

board work

Alphabetizing. For help in alphabetizing, mark envelopes, one with each letter of the alphabet. Let individual children cut out pictures of objects and classify them by putting them in the appropriate envelopes.

Alphabetizing

7. Riddle cards may be made by pasting a picture on one side of a card and writing a descriptive riddle on the other side. A child will read the riddle, guess the answer, and then turn over the card to verify his answer.

8. Clip and mount large pictures for the game of "Quick Look." Allow the group a few minutes to look at one picture. Then remove it from view. See how many pictured items can be recalled by the group. The items may be listed, read from the chalkboard, and then rechecked by a second look at the large picture.

Provision for Superior Readers. During the reading of this unit the better readers may wish to do outside reading to satisfy their curiosity about the people living in various parts of this country and about the customs which immigrants from other countries have brought with them.

If children are particularly interested in New Moon's way of life, have them try writing the characters for "good luck" which appear on page 226 of the Reader. Secure a copy of *You Can Write Chinese*, by Kurt Wiese, and encourage the children to write other words in Chinese. Allow the finished papers to be exhibited.

If it is possible, take the good readers to visit a museum to see Chinese fans, embroidery, pottery, jewelry, jade, porcelain, lacquer work, silks, etc. Emphasize the many cultural contributions the Chinese have made to the world.

In their enthusiasm to find out what happens next in a story, some superior readers may have a tendency to read carelessly or inaccurately. These children should be given interesting new story material to read. The teacher should then ask detailed thought questions about the story in order to check the children's comprehension.

Superior readers usually have a wide range of interests. One way of satisfying these interests is to provide for these children short stories, informative articles, news items, jokes, or stimulating information on current events cut from children's magazines or children's newspapers. Provide time for these children to discuss and share their ideas and conclusions with the rest of the class.

Make available a variety of anthologies of children's poetry. Ask the interested children to collect good poems related to the unit theme or to one facet of it in which they are particularly interested. The children might catalogue these poems alphabetically by author, either in a card file or in a list. For this unit the children might select categories such as the following: poems about farms or farm animals; poems about the West or cowboys; city poems about workers, traffic, houses; baseball poems; poems about horses. Collections that contain an especially good selection of such poems follow:

One Thousand Poems for Children, by Elizabeth H. Sechrist; *Sung under the Silver Umbrella*, compiled by The Association for Childhood Education International; *Very Young Verses*, by Barbara Geismer and Antoinette Suter; *The First Book of Poetry*, by Isabel J. Peterson; *Gaily We Parade*, by John E. Brewton; *A Small Child's Book of Verse*, by Pelagie Doane; *The Golden Flute*, by Alice Hubbard and Adeline Babbitt.

Suggest to the superior readers that they also collect other stories from the library that are related to the unit theme, such as those in *Told under the Stars and Stripes*, compiled by The Association for Childhood Education International.

All-Unit Activities

Unit VI · Days Everyone Likes

Introducing the Unit

Favorite holidays are the theme of this unit. "The Boy Who Believed" is a story about Columbus; "The Friendly Ghost" is a Halloween story that will be enjoyed at any time of the year; "Christmas with Stina Mor" takes us to Sweden; "Barney on TV" is a New Year story; "The Valentine Box" is about a familiar and popular school activity which every child enjoys. A Halloween and a Thanksgiving poem round out the unit.

The material of this unit offers an opportunity for developing an understanding of the meaning and origin of our holidays. During discussion with the group bring out the fact that some holidays, such as Thanksgiving Day, are national in character, whereas others, like Christmas, are celebrated in many countries of the world.

Some teachers will prefer to have these stories read at the time of year when they will best enrich the seasonal activities and interests of the group. Others will wish to have the children read them as part of a holiday unit.

The teacher will wish to collect pictures about holiday activities, stories, poems, and informational materials both to be read aloud to the children and to be read independently by them. Plan to have groups find out more about the background of holidays and allow them to use their information in projects or reports.

During the introductory discussion ask the children to name as many holidays as they can recall and list them on the chalkboard. Stimulate discussion about the ways in which some of the holidays are celebrated by the children and their families. Lead the children to realize that holidays are truly "Days Everyone Likes." Have them locate this unit in the table of contents and talk about the titles of the stories and poems. Suggest to the children that holidays usually honor the memory of a great man or a great event.

Talking about the unit theme

Story / Pages	Vocabulary / New Words	Developing Readiness	Reading the Story — Guided Reading	Rereading for Specific Purposes	Comprehension and Study Skills	Building Esse... / Word Mea...
The Boy Who Believed 235–240	Juan wharf ships Whiskers rats queen Columbus			Reading to make inferences	Critical Reading: recognizing cause-and-effect relationships (worksheet) — Workbook: 71, summarizing important story details; using context clues	Appreciati... scriptive lan... Recognizin... tonyms and ... nyms (work... Workbook... recognizing ... nyms; usin... trasting con... clues
The Friendly Ghost 242–251	ghost Julie Daisy Halloween screamed	New words are presented in context either written or oral. Children are encouraged to identify new words through comparison with known words and the use of phonetic and context clues.		Skimming to locate clues to solve the mystery	Organizing Information: classifying story facts according to the time they happened (worksheet) — Sequence: arranging the events of each night in the correct order — Main Idea: making titles for individual pages — Workbook: 74, drawing conclusions from new story material	Workbook... extending w... meanings; ... nizing silen... sonants
Christmas with Stina Mor 254–264	Stina Mor Anna post office postmaster package heavy sleigh wore crown America writing late		Silent and oral reading for comprehension and interpretation of story plot, mood, and characterization.	Reading orally to note changes in mood	Main Idea: selecting the main idea from story parts (worksheet) — Sequence: putting story facts into the right order (worksheet) — Workbook: 77, finding the main idea by answering riddles; 78, reading for specific information; 79, using a map to determine sequence	Learning ... ognize homo... (worksheet) Recognizi... words throu... text clues
Barney on TV 265–272	Barney Tilly Zipp Company born program Rover Shirley	Through discussion and exchange of ideas interest in the story is stimulated and background for understanding is developed. Purposes for reading are reached by the group with the teacher's guidance.		Reading orally for interpretation; recalling standards for good oral reading — Reading to find specific information for a letter	Critical Reading: evaluating ideas (worksheet) — Details and Sequence: identifying story dialogue (worksheet) — Workbook: 81, determining the validity of statements	
The Valentine Box 273–282	hearts Margaret envelope cap			Reading specific parts to make inferences	Sequence: arranging story events in order (worksheet) — Details: selecting details to prove a point — Workbook: 83, finding the main idea in new story material	Discrimin... between wo... with same a... ferent mean... (worksheet)
All-Unit Activities				Provision for less advanced readers: suggestions for improvement of oral reading; using the table of contents	Culminating Activity: Playing "Information Please" to identify story characters — Evaluation: story recall: remembering story-characters (worksheet) — Organizing Ideas: classifying details under holidays	Associatin... lated ideas Individua... playing "Fir... word that m... —"; atta... words throu... rhymes; a... ing related ... (worksheet) Provision ... perior reade... tacking new... (worksheet)

bits and Skills			Related Language Experiences	Enrichment Activities
Word-Study Skills				
Phonetic Analysis	Structural Analysis	Syllabication		
cognizing *qu* calling *wh* calling vowel digraphs rkbook: 73, attacking words with vowel digraphs a, *oa* and *ui*	Alphabetizing: practicing letter sequence; supplying missing letters		Making Plans: planning the unit activities (chart) Discussion: comparing conditions at the time of Columbus with conditions today Reporting: making a dramatized report	Co-ordinating Activity: publishing a class newspaper Science: learning about a compass; keeping a ship's log Collections: collecting information about different holidays Anthologies of Stories about Holidays Stories, poems, music, records, a filmstrip, and a picture
cognizing silent consos in words calling the variant sounds serving silent *g* rkbook: 75, recognizing nt sounds of c and g; usontext clues	Reviewing the suffix *ly* Finding root words (worksheet)	Practicing vowel sounds and syllables (chalkboard exercise)	Conversation: talking about being afraid; talking about Halloween Listening: to humorous ghost stories	Co-ordinating Activity Halloween party: planning a class party Stories in Other Readers Stories, poems, music, and a film
	Recalling comparative and superlative endings of adjectives (worksheet) Workbook: 80, recognizing the suffix *ly*		Discussion: talking about ethical values Choral Speaking: presenting Christmas poems Listening: hearing the poem "December" to appreciate the images	Co-ordinating Activity Art: illustrating scenes from the story Celebration: studying to put on an international Christmas program Stories in Other Readers Stories, poems, music, a film, filmstrips, and pictures
serving the long *e* sound calling consonant blends Vorkbook: 82, attacking words through phonetic	Reviewing the apostrophe as used in contractions and in the possessive Alphabetizing: playing an alphabet game	Recognizing syllables in words	Correspondence: writing a letter to a television station Dramatization: planning and presenting a TV program Discussion: comparing Barney's New Year celebration with New Moon's	Co-ordinating Activity Art: making a poster advertising Zipp products Stories
serving the effect of final t *e* on the last syllable in rkbook: 84, recognizing words through familiar dihs and context clues	Recalling compound words Alphabetizing: arranging names alphabetically	Reviewing *a* and *be* as syllabic divisions Observing *un* as a syllabic division Dividing words with *a*, *be*, and *un* into syllables (worksheet)	Creative Writing: rhymes for valentines Conversation: learning about the origin of Valentine's Day; discussing kindness to others	Co-ordinating Activity Construction: making valentines Planning a Valentine Party Stories in Other Readers Stories, a poem, and music
aluation: test for vowel ds dividual help: playing tball," "Baseball" with ren who need help with el digraphs rovision for superior readattacking new words ugh phonetic elements and ext clues (worksheet)	Evaluation: checking the ability to add the endings *ly*, *er*, *est* Workbook: 85, putting words from the unit in alphabetical order	Evaluation: recalling vowel sounds and syllables; checking syllables ending in silent *e*; checking vowel digraphs in syllables	Helping the individual child; improving creative writing through original rhymes Provision for superior readers; doing research on holidays to present a program	Culminating Activity: making a calendar of holidays

The Boy Who Believed

Juan was the boy who believed. He believed with Columbus that the world was round. He believed it so much that he gave his cat Gray Whiskers to Columbus to take with him on his first voyage.

Children reading this story may be reminded of the great explorations of today and will appreciate how important "believing" may be.

Vocabulary

New Words: Page 235, ————; 236, *Juan, wharf*, ships*;* 237, *Whiskers*, rats*;* 238, *queen*, Columbus;* 239, ————; 240, ————

Developing Readiness for Reading

Discussing related concepts

Meaningful Presentation of Vocabulary. "Our first story is about a boy who lived at the time of the great explorer, Christopher Columbus. Do you know what discovery Columbus made and when it was?" (October 12, 1492.) "Let's look at the globe to see where Columbus started and what route he took." Point out the Atlantic Ocean. "Before Columbus, people didn't dare to travel out into the Atlantic Ocean. They thought that the earth was flat and that they would fall over the edge into space if they went too far from land. Does anyone know why Columbus went on his daring voyage?" (He believed that the earth was round, and he wanted to find a shorter way to get to India.) "Columbus tried for a long time to find someone to give him money enough to outfit *ships.* Finally the *queen* of Spain helped him.

Using picture clues

"On pages 236 and 237 you see the ships tied to a *wharf* where they will be loaded. A boy is on the wharf. This boy's name would be 'John' in English but he is Spanish, so he is called *Juan* (hwän)." Tell the children that Juan's cat is named *Gray Whiskers.* "Is that a good name for a cat? Why? What makes you think that Juan was very fond of his cat?"

Using phonetic clues to attack new vocabulary

Whiskers and *wharf* may be attacked phonetically through the *wh* digraph. *Juan* begins with much the same sound although it is a different spelling. Better readers will attack *queen* and *ships* through the beginning sounds *qu* and *sh.*

Setting Up Reading Purposes. Have the children open their books to the story and read the title. "What do you suppose Juan believed?" Encourage the children to offer their own ideas. "You may read the whole story to yourselves to find out what Juan believed. Be ready to tell us whether or not you would have believed too."

NOTE. If this story is to be read early in the year, the teacher should ascertain whether the children are familiar with the following new vocabulary introduced earlier in this book: *touched* (p. 10), *arms* (p. 13), *present* (p. 15), *sure* (p. 80), *hard* (p. 108), *full* (p. 121), *interesting* (p. 202).

Reading the Story

Guided Reading

Pages 236–240

Observe the children as they read the story silently, making notations of word difficulties and reading habits that require correction. Help individuals if necessary.

After the children have finished reading the story, discuss such questions as the following:

Discussing the main idea of the story

What was it that Juan believed?

Would *you* have believed too? Why?

Bring out in the discussion the limited knowledge of the earth possessed by people in 1492, the superstitions, the dangers of long voyages in small sailing vessels, the courage required to believe in the strange man who dared to challenge accepted beliefs. Compare the voyage of Columbus with crossing the Atlantic Ocean today; with space travel.

Ask the questions below about details of the story. If there is disagreement or uncertainty, direct the children to prove their answers by referring to the text.

Recalling story details

1. In what year did Columbus sail? How long ago was it?
2. What interesting things were happening on the wharf?
3. What did the two men say about the ships?
4. What did Juan say to these men?
5. What did one man think would happen if the world were round?
6. How did Juan think that Gray Whiskers could help Columbus?

371   *The Boy Who Believed* (235–240)

Ask the children to open their books to find statements to help them answer the following questions. Suggest that they will have to read between the lines.

1. Why was Gray Whiskers interested?
2. Why did the men think the ships were sure to be lost?
3. Why did the men say the world was as flat as a pancake?
4. What do you learn about the men from this story?
5. What kind of boy was Juan?
6. What kind of man was Columbus?
7. Why was Juan willing to let Columbus have his cat?

Building Essential Habits and Skills

Comprehension and Study Skills

Recognizing
cause-and-effect
relationships **Critical Reading.** To develop greater skill in using judgment, distribute copies of the exercise below. Have each child decide which of the two reasons under each statement is the better. After the exercise is completed, call on individuals to explain their choices.

---

1. Juan did not go home because
    he was lost and could not find the way.
    <u>something interesting was happening at the wharf.</u>
2. The men said that the ships would be lost because
    <u>they believed the world was flat.</u>
    a great storm was blowing up.
3. The queen gave Columbus money for the trip because
    she was a very good woman.
    <u>she believed that Columbus was right.</u>
4. Juan was proud to give Gray Whiskers to Columbus because
    <u>he believed that Columbus would come back.</u>
    Gray Whiskers could not catch rats.

Word-Study Skills

Appreciating
descriptive
language **Word Meaning.** 1. To increase children's awareness of dramatic and descriptive language, present, one at a time,

the phrases from the story that are quoted below. As the children listen to each phrase, ask them to close their eyes and try to see the mental picture the phrase suggests to them. Let volunteers take turns expressing their ideas and reactions.

strange ships
fall off into a great, empty space
flat as a pancake
tall, dark man with gray hair
as if the queen were giving him a present

2. To call attention to synonyms and to antonyms, write on the chalkboard the following words:

Recognizing antonyms and synonyms

long—short
cellar—basement

Ask the children whether the words of the first pair have the same or different meaning. Ask the same question about the second pair of words. If the children need more practice, continue the lesson with other pairs of words, some of which have the same or similar meanings, some of which are opposite in meaning. To give independent practice in discriminating between synonyms and antonyms, distribute copies of the following exercise:

Read the first two words carefully. If they mean the same, write the letter *S* in the blank next to them. If they mean something different, write the latter *D* in the space.

S	ship—boat	D	empty—full
D	new—old	D	above—below
S	hunting—looking for	D	stay—leave
S	near—next to	S	dish—plate
D	lost—found	D	come—go
S	know—be sure of	S	hold—keep
S	round—like a ball	D	take—give

Phonetic Analysis. 1. To review the sound of *qu*, write on the chalkboard *quack*, *quick*, *quiet*, and have the words pronounced. Ask, "What new word in your lesson begins with the letters *qu?*" (*queen*) Ask the pupils if they have

Recognizing "qu"

observed that *q* never appears in a word without *u*. "Together *q* and *u* usually sound like *kw*."

Let the children discuss how knowing the sound of *qu* helps them to recognize the new words *quite* and *quail*. Have these words pronounced and used in sentences.

Recalling "wh"

2. To review the consonant digraph *wh*, write the new words *whiskers* and *wharf* on the chalkboard. Have them pronounced and the "blowing" sound of *wh* noted. Recall *whistled, which, white, wheels,* and *while*. Ask the children to pronounce these words and circle the *wh* in each one.

Give practice in listening for the *wh* sound by saying the list of unfamiliar words below, one at a time, pronouncing the *wh* sound distinctly so that the children will be sure to hear it. Have the children raise their hands each time they hear a word that begins with *wh*: *whale, wire, wheel, wise, wonder, whip, worry, wool*.

Recalling vowel digraphs

3. To strengthen recognition of vowel digraphs in one-syllable and two-syllable words, write on the chalkboard such words as these: *queen, feast, rain, load*. Have the words pronounced. Ask the children how many vowels they see in the words; how many vowel sounds they hear; how many syllables they hear. Lead them to recall that when double vowels appear in words, the first vowel is usually heard, the second silent. Call attention to the long sound of the first vowel in the digraphs just presented.

Then write *teacher, easy, reading, leaders, asleep, sailboat, suit, roadside*. Have the children pronounce the words, tell how many syllables they hear, and what vowel sound they hear in each syllable. For each double vowel or vowel digraph, have the children tell which vowel is silent and the sound of the one which is heard.

Alphabetizing

Alphabetizing. To discover if the children are able to recognize letters in alphabetical order and to give further practice in alphabetizing, write on the chalkboard this list of letters: *q, a, u, m, b, k, e, o, u, s*. Ask them to tell which letter comes first, which next, and so on, and have them rearrange the letters in correct sequence on their papers and on the chalkboard. Last, have them fill in the gaps with letters which have been left out.

Related Language Experiences

Making Plans. Encourage the children to suggest activities in which they would like to participate while they are reading the stories in this unit. Remember that it is important that the children engage in activities with a worth-while purpose and that they understand the purpose of what they are doing. Help them to record their plans on a chart as they are suggested and worked out, and to organize the committees. Refer to the chart frequently to check progress or to modify and supplement activities. A chart such as the following may be made:

Planning the unit activities

Fun for Red-letter Days

Learn about our national holidays.

Learn about our local holidays.

Read stories and learn poems.

Have a costume party.

Plan a holiday program.

Publish a class newspaper.

Discussion. An effective and stimulating way to initiate a discussion about Columbus and his undertaking is to read to the children the poem "Christopher Columbus," by ROSEMARY and STEPHEN VINCENT BENÉT, in *The First Book of Poetry*, by ISABEL J. PETERSON, or "The Boy Who Loved Maps," by RUTH CROMER WEIR, in *Holiday Round-Up*, by LUCILLE PANNELL and FRANCES CAVANAH.

Comparing Columbus's time with ours

Show a globe and have volunteers trace Columbus's voyage. Have the children tell how long it would take to make the same trip by flying over the Atlantic Ocean or by a fast ocean liner. Discuss the feelings one might have starting out on such a trip today as compared with the way the men felt about the trip in 1492.

Christopher Columbus

Lead the children to discuss the ideas about the world which people had in Columbus's time. Have them find the sentence or paragraph in the story which gives the clue as to why Columbus thought the world was round. Demonstrate this idea with the globe.

Making a dramatized report

Reporting. As an outcome of the discussion above, some children may be interested in making a dramatized report to the group. One child might pretend to be a sailor on the *Santa Maria*. Another child might pretend that he is the captain of a modern ocean liner or the pilot of an airplane. The children might compare the risks, preparations, supplies, possible events on the way, the time involved, the attitudes of the people going on the trip and of those staying at home. Some independent reading will help in preparing this report. *Columbus*, by Ingri and Edgar d'Aulaire, is informative and easy to read.

Better readers may find that one period in Columbus's life is particularly interesting to them. Help them in finding books and in organizing their information.

Enrichment Activities

Co-ordinating Activity. A useful activity for practicing all the language arts is the writing and publishing of a class newspaper. It will serve to record important happenings and activities in the classroom and will be an outlet for creative writing of all kinds. A rotating staff of editors, reporters, artists, and newsboys may be elected. The reporters might find news and other items of interest in and around the classroom. Under the teacher's guidance these items may then be written up and illustrated by one or more children. After a layout for the newspaper has been decided on and executed, a stencil may be cut and the sheets duplicated, printed, and finally distributed by the newsboys.

Publishing a class newspaper

A Columbus Day issue might consist of reports of interesting Columbus Day programs given in the school, personal news, and original stories and poems by all the children, as well as any regular columns on which the class will decide. This is an activity which can easily be continued during the remainder of the year and which will provide an impetus for individual written expression.

If there are no facilities for duplicating the paper, the children might arrange a bulletin-board newspaper by placing their articles and stories under appropriate headings.

Collections. Have the children find poems, stories, news clippings, and pictures related to each of the holidays of this unit. After each story is read, have the group assemble to give reports and reviews on the interesting material they have collected.

Collecting information

Science. Secure a compass or magnetize a needle to make a simple compass and have the children use it to determine directions. Refer to "A Compass Needle Is a Magnet," pp. 72–75, in *Science Everywhere*, by Gerald S. Craig and Marguerite W. Lembach, for information about a compass. The following·page shows one experiment which children may perform.

Learning about a compass

377   *The Boy Who Believed* (235–240)

Stories to Enjoy. Most third-graders will have no trouble reading *Columbus*, by INGRI and EDGAR d'AULAIRE; *The Columbus Story*, by ALICE DALGLIESH; *Heroes, Heroines, and Holidays*, by ELEANOR THOMAS and MARY G. KELTY, pp. 1–15; "On the Dock," by ALBERTA POWELL GRAHAM, in *Holiday Storybook*, compiled by The Child Study Association of America.

Collections of Holiday Stories to Enjoy. These collections may be used throughout the unit: *Big Meeting Day and Other Festival Tales*, by MAY JUSTUS and others; *The First Book of Holidays*, by BERNICE BURNETT; *Holiday Storybook*, compiled by The Child Study Association of America; *Red Letter Days: A Book of Holiday Customs*, by ELIZABETH HOUGH SECHRIST; *True Book of Holidays and Special Days*, by JOHN PURCELL; *Holiday Round-Up*, by LUCILLE PANNELL and FRANCES CAVANAH.

Poems to Enjoy. Read both of the poems on the next page to the children. Have the children listen for parts that particularly appeal to them and that they would like to memorize. The teacher may wish to have the children listen for the rhythm and the excitement in "Columbus." "Dark-eyed Lad Columbus" will especially appeal to the quiet, dreamy children. If there is time, these children may be encouraged to tell the class of their own ambitions and dreams. Creative children may wish to illustrate parts of the poems or write their own poems about Columbus.

COLUMBUS

Columbus sailed over the ocean blue
    To find the United States.
In three small ships he carried his crew,
    And none of the three were mates.

He found a land in the western seas,
    And Indians galore,
With jabbering parrots in the trees,
    And sharks along the shore.

He filled his pockets with sparkling stones
    And took to the mighty main,
With a couple of slaves, some nuts and cones
    For the glorious king of Spain.

Now this is the tale Columbus told,
    And most of the tale is true,
How he crossed the seas, a sailor bold,
    In fourteen-ninety-two.

                LEROY F. JACKSON

DARK–EYED LAD COLUMBUS

When the dark-eyed lad, Columbus,
    Saw the white sails dip and gleam,
Slanting, swaying down the harbor,
    In his heart he dreamed a dream.

"I will some day be a sailor!
    I will have a ship!" he cried.
"I will sail and sail the ocean
    Till I reach the other side."

So he dreamed and so he waited,
    And the dream came true, we know.
Now we name his name with singing,
    Dark-eyed lad of long ago!

             NANCY BYRD TURNER

Music to Enjoy. "Columbus," in *Singing and Rhyming,* by LILLA BELLE PITTS and others.

A Record to Enjoy. *Holidays for U. S.,* sung by FRANK LUTHER. 78 rpm, 10″ (Ginn).

A Picture to Enjoy. "The Return of Columbus," by Eugene Delacroix, in *Pictures to Grow Up With,* by KATHARINE GIBSON.

Filmstrip to Enjoy. *Columbus Day* (YoungAmerica), 25fr, color, one of HOLIDAY SERIES.

Page 241

Halloween

Developing Readiness for Listening

"Do jack-o'-lanterns and black cats remind you of a holiday? What else do you think of at Halloween time?" Encourage spontaneous discussion. "What kind of feeling does Halloween give you?" Expect such responses as "spooky," "scary," "frightening."

"I'm going to read you a poem called 'Halloween.' Listen for the pictures the poem suggests, and think about the way it makes you feel."

Reading the Poem

Have the children close their books and listen as you read the poem to them. Then have them tell what mental pictures they saw and how they felt as they listened to the reading.

Rereading the Poem

Ask the children to listen for interesting Halloween phrases as you read the first stanza, for example: "round as a jack-o'-lantern"; "trees blow black and bare"; "creeping with spooky giggles"; "chill ghostly air."

Read the second stanza, having the children point out such phrases as: "the haunted ground"; "bad black kitten."

Ask individual children, or the group as a whole, to read the poem aloud. Encourage them to give their listeners a true Halloween feeling.

Related Activities

Encourage the children to start a collection of holiday poems. Individual children may copy their favorites and others may illustrate them to make a book for the classroom library.

A Poem to Enjoy. The poem "Broomstick Time" will be enjoyed by the children because of its humor and Halloween spirit. Because of its brevity, it might be printed on a wall chart. After listening to the poem, the children may be encouraged to memorize or illustrate it.

BROOMSTICK TIME

On Hallowe'en the witches fly
Like withered leaves across the sky,
Each with a broomstick for a steed
That gallops at tremendous speed.
Although I don't approve of witches
Who wear tall hats and live in ditches,
Still I am glad there is a day
When broomsticks have a chance to play.

ROWENA BENNETT

Other Poems to Enjoy. "Hallowe'en," by ANNA MEDARY, "Hallowe'en," by HELEN WING, and "If You've Never," by ELSIE M. FOWLER, in *The Golden Flute*, compiled by ALICE HUBBARD and ADELINE BABBITT; "Black and Gold," by NANCY BYRD TURNER, and "Riddle: What Am I?" by DOROTHY ALDIS, in *Very Young Verses*, compiled by BARBARA PECK GEISMER and ANTOINETTE SUTER; "This Is Halloween," by DOROTHY BROWN THOMPSON in *Bridled with Rainbows*, by SARA and JOHN E. BREWTON.

Music to Enjoy. "A Goblin Lives in Our House," in *Singing on Our Way*, by LILLA BELLE PITTS and others; "Soon Comes the Day," "Five Little Pumpkins," "Goblins and Witches," all in *Singing and Rhyming*, by LILLA BELLE PITTS and others.

381

The Friendly Ghost

When Julie went to the country to visit her aunt and uncle, she felt homesick and strange. Uncle Fred took her a plate of apples at bedtime and left them beside the open window. Each night an apple disappeared mysteriously and Julie was sure a ghost had taken it. The appearance of a long white thing at the window confirmed her fears, until one moonlit night she discovered that the ghost was only her friend Daisy, Uncle Fred's white horse.

The children will enjoy sharing the mystery of the disappearing apples and will be amused at the solution. They will be interested too in Julie's feeling about the ghost.

Vocabulary

New Words: Page 242, *ghost, Julie;* 243, *Daisy*;* 244, *Halloween;* 245, *screamed*;* 246, ————; 247, ————; 248, ————; 249, ————; 250, ————; 251, ————

Developing Readiness for Reading

Talking about
related concepts

Meaningful Presentation of Vocabulary. Quote to the children the following two lines of the poem "Halloween":

"And we go creeping with spooky giggles
Through the chill ghostly air."

Recall that these lines are from the poem on page 241. Say: "Long ago some people believed that on *Halloween* the air was full of *ghosts* and witches. Do we still believe that? Do some children pretend to be ghosts on Halloween? What things do they do? Do these make-believe ghosts ever really scare anyone or do any harm?" Bring out during the discussion that these are friendly ghosts who never do any mischief but dress up only for fun.

Learning the new
vocabulary

On the chalkboard write the three names, *Julie, Ted,* and *Daisy.* Encourage the children to attack the names independently. Then tell them that Julie is a little girl who visited her aunt and uncle in the country. Ted and Daisy are two horses on the farm.

Using
phonetic clues
for word attack

If children have difficulty recognizing *screamed,* point out the *scr* and the vowel digraph *ea.*

Setting Up Reading Purposes. "Today's story is called 'The Friendly Ghost.' What do you think a friendly ghost might be?" Let the children discuss the possibilities. Then have them find the story in the table of contents and turn to the beginning page. Ask, "What is the first subtitle of the story?"

NOTE. If this story is read early in the year, it may be well for the teacher to ascertain whether the children know the new vocabulary taught previously in this book: *gentle* (p. 8), *afternoon* (p. 14), *remember* (p. 45), *swallow* (p. 80), *squeak* (p. 108), *shot* (p. 173), *pasture* (p. 194), *plate* (p. 211).

Reading the Story

Guided Reading

"Have you ever been away from home alone? How did you feel? This was Julie's first visit to the farm. Read the first two paragraphs silently to find out how Julie was feeling. Now finish the page to find out what kind of man Uncle Fred was. What did he bring Julie?

Page 242

Reading silently to answer questions

"Read this page silently to find out what Uncle Fred said to Julie. Why do you think he said these things?

Page 243

"Just as Julie felt better something happened to worry her again. What do you suppose it was? This page will tell you.

Page 244

After the reading, ask, "What would you do if you were Julie?

"Read the first paragraph to find out what Julie did. Yes, she screamed. Would you have done the same? What does 'shot down to the foot of the bed' mean? Finish the page to find out what Uncle Fred and Aunt Mary did and said." Pause for recall and ask, "What might eating apples have to do with seeing ghosts?

Page 245

"Let's find out what everyone thought about the ghost the next day. How did Julie feel about it when she went to bed the next night?" After the reading, ask: "What do you think happened to the apple? Why was it easy to talk about ghosts in daylight?

Pages 246–247

"What do you think happened the next night? Let's read the page. Was Julie braver on her second night? How would you feel? Now what do you think happened to the apples? This is a real mystery story, isn't it?

Page 248

"What is this subtitle? Who do you suppose the new friend is? Could it be the ghost? Finish the story to find out." After the reading, ask: "Did you guess who the ghost was? Why wasn't Julie as frightened on the third night?"

Rereading for Specific Purposes

Skimming to find clues to the story

Ask the children to reread the story silently to locate clues to the solution of the mystery which they may not have observed during the first reading. For example, the first paragraph on page 243 contains one clue; the first paragraph on page 247 contains another. Have the children write the page and paragraph of each clue they find. Have a discussion afterward so that they may share their ideas.

Building Essential Habits and Skills

Comprehension and Study Skills

Organizing story details

Organizing Information. To develop skill in classifying story facts, give the group copies of the following exercise:

Read each sentence. If it tells something that happened the first night, write 1 on the line before it; if it took place on the second night, write 2 before it; if on the third night, write 3 before it.

1 1. Julie asked Aunt Mary if there were ghosts in the old house.
2 2. She was too tired and happy to think about ghosts.
1 3. Julie felt homesick and strange.
2 4. She shot to the foot of the bed but did not scream.
1 5. Uncle Fred brought Julie three apples.
3 6. She went to bed by herself and went right to sleep.
1 7. When Julie heard a thump, thump at the window, she screamed.
3 8. Then she saw Daisy in the moonlight.
1 9. Aunt Mary and Uncle Fred came running.
2 10. A long white thing reached through the window.
1 11. Uncle Fred told Julie about Ted and Daisy.
3 12. The plate was empty.
2 13. There was only one apple left.
1 14. There were two apples left.

Sequence. To help children who need practice in putting story facts into the correct sequence, proceed as follows: After the preceding exercise has been completed by the children, put the sentences that tell about the events of the first night into one group, but not in the order of their occurrence. Do the same with the events of the second and third nights. If the exercise is to be done independently, each group of sentences may be duplicated and the children asked to number the sentences in sequence. For a slower group that needs more teacher guidance, print the exercise on tagboard and cut it into strips. The children may then rearrange the events in each group in the order in which they happened.

Arranging story events in order

Main Idea. To strengthen the ability to grasp main ideas, ask individual children to reread the story quickly, a page at a time, and to write a good title for each of the pages. Below are suggested titles.

Making titles

p. 242: Apples for Homesick Julie
p. 243: Two Horses
p. 244: Something at the Window
p. 245: A Ghost!
p. 246: The Mystery
p. 247: A Good Day
p. 248: Only One Apple!
p. 250: A Strange Sound
p. 251: Julie Solves the Mystery

When the children have finished the exercise, have them discuss their titles in the group. Ask the children to decide which titles are most satisfactory but allow for differences of opinion.

Word-Study Skills

Phonetic Analysis. 1. To call attention to silent consonants, write the word *ghost* on the chalkboard and have it pronounced. Ask: "What consonant is silent in this word?" (*h*) "Do you know other words in which consonants are silent?" Help the children list such words as *bought, bright, brought, frighten, high, light, neighbor, might, thought, through* (*gh*); *knife, knew, know* (*k*); *write* (*w*); *half* (*l*). Ask individual children to pronounce the words and identify the silent letter or letters.

Recognizing silent consonants in words

The Friendly Ghost (242–251)

2. To review the variant sounds of g, write on the chalk-board *games, eagle, flag, ghost, dragon, magic, signal, danger, giraffe, vegetables, strange.* Have the words pronounced and ask the children to observe the sound that g has in each word. Explain that, like *c,* g has a hard and a soft sound. Hard-g words are those in which g sounds as in *game;* soft g has the sound of g in *magic.* Tell the children that, like *c,* if g is followed by *e, i,* or *y,* it usually has a soft sound. Have the children say the words and rearrange them in columns under the words *Hard, Soft.* Have them attack new words with these sounds of g, as *gather, engineer, barge.* Check the children's understanding of the words by asking them to find the one that means "to collect," the one that means "a man who plans a bridge," the word that means "a boat."

3. Write *right, high, sign,* and expect the response that g is silent in these words. Draw from the children the generalization that g may have a hard sound, a soft sound, and no sound at all.

Structural Analysis. To review *ly* at the end of words, say: "One word in the title of our story ends in *ly.* What word is it? What root word can you find in *friendly?*" Have a volunteer underline the root word. Recall the meaning of the ending *ly.*

To give practice in the recognition and use of *ly,* distribute copies of the exercise below or write it on the chalkboard with suitable instructions. When the children have completed the exercise, ask them to tell the meaning of each word and then to use some of the words in sentences.

Read these words to yourself and circle the root word in each one.

quietly	proudly
strangely	bravely
suddenly	swiftly
slowly	quickly
loudly	strongly
gladly	brightly

Syllabication. To provide practice in listening to syllables, ask the pupils if they can tell how a vowel sound helps them recognize a syllable. They will probably say that every syllable has one vowel sound. Have the words below put on the chalkboard and ask the children to say them softly and tap the number of syllables. Let one child write the number beside each word. Ask them whether these words follow the rule: one vowel sound—one syllable.

team	*scream*	*ahead*
queen	*Daisy*	*goes*
squeak	*breakfast*	*ready*
afraid	*believe*	*loading*

If individuals have difficulty, help them to understand that certain vowels are silent in each of the words, and that the number of syllables is related to the number of vowel sounds they hear.

Workbook

Pages 74, 75, and 76.

Related Language Experiences

Conversation. Let the children talk about Julie's fear. Bring out in the discussion the fact that Julie was in a strange place, that she was homesick, and that her aunt had warned her that she might hear noises in the night, all of which might have made her more fearful. Help the children to understand that anyone would be frightened at seeing an unknown animal at the window at night, and that it is prudent to be cautious until one finds out the cause of the fright.

During the discussion bring out Julie's courage the last two nights in not calling for help, but handling her fear alone. Recall that Julie "found it easy to talk about ghosts in daylight." Ask, "What does that tell you about Julie?" (That she had common sense and didn't let her fear spoil her good time.) Discuss also the qualities that Julie showed by laughing at herself and her fear after the mystery had been solved.

Discussion. Continue the discussion of the different ways the children themselves celebrate Halloween and bring out the difference between having fun and doing harm to other people.

Listening. To develop the theme of a friendly ghost further, read aloud to the group humorous ghost stories such as "Horace, the Happy Ghost," by ELIZABETH IRELAND, in *Holiday Storybook*, published by The Child Study Association of America.

Enrichment Activities

Co-ordinating Activity. The Halloween issue of the class newspaper may contain original ghost stories, Halloween poems, articles on various aspects of Halloween, book reviews of Halloween stories, and records of various Halloween classroom activities, such as making masks, having a party, or playing Halloween games.

Halloween Party. If this story is read at Halloween time, let the children plan a class party. They may consult *Health and Safety for You*, by GRACE T. HALLOCK, ROSS L. ALLEN, and ELEANOR THOMAS, pp. 40–52, for suggestions. Some children may wish to present magic tricks described in *Spooky Magic*, by LARRY KETTELKAMP.

Stories in Other Readers. Ask individual children to use their spare time to prepare several Halloween stories to read aloud to the class. They will enjoy those listed below.

The New Friends and Neighbors, by WILLIAM S. GRAY and others
"Who Can Fool a Goat!" pp. 109–114

The New Streets and Roads, by WILLIAM S. GRAY and others
"A Halloween Surprise," pp. 35–41

Our Good Neighbors, by WILLIAM H. BURTON and others
"Halloween Fun," pp. 34–40

Magic Windows, by WILLIAM D. SHELDON and others
"A Halloween Story," pp. 107–114

Fun and Frolic, by PAUL WITTY and others
"The Ghost of a Pirate," pp. 230–240

Open Roads, by ULLIN W. LEAVELL and MARY LOUISE FRIEBELE
"Ghost in the Garden," pp. 158–165

Just Imagine! by WILLIAM S. GRAY and others
"The Stubborn Witch," pp. 197–203

Stories to Enjoy. *Georgie to the Rescue*, by ROBERT BRIGHT; *Danny's Luck*, by LAVINIA DAVIS; *Little Witch*, by ANNA BENNETT; *Proud Pumpkin*, by NORA S. UNWIN; *Pumpkin Moonshine*, by TASHA TUDOR; "The Giant Ghost," by ELIZABETH HOUGH SECHRIST, in *Holiday Round-Up*, by LUCILLE PANNELL and FRANCES CAVANAH.

Poems to Enjoy. The poem "Night Magic" will enrich the story just read. The children should be encouraged to express their reactions freely after the poem has been read to them.

NIGHT MAGIC

The apples falling from the tree
  Make such a heavy bump at night
I always am surprised to see
  They are so little, when it's light;

And all the dark just sings and sings
  So loud, I cannot see at all
How frogs and crickets and such things
  That make the noise, can be so small.

Then my own room looks larger, too—
  Corners so dark and far away—
I wonder if things really do
  Grow up at night and shrink by day?

For I dream sometimes, just as clear,
  I'm bigger than the biggest men—
Then Mother says, "Wake up, my dear!"
  And I'm a little boy again.

AMELIA JOSEPHINE BURR

Read aloud other Halloween poems in *Sing a Song of Seasons*, by SARA and JOHN E. BREWTON, pp. 65–71; "Halloween," by HARRY BEHN in *Time for Poetry*, by MAY HILL ARBUTHNOT.

Music to Enjoy. Halloween songs in *Singing on Our Way*, pp. 70–73, by LILLA BELLE PITTS and others.

A Film to Enjoy. *Georgie* (Weston), 1 reel, b&w/color.

Thanksgiving Day

Developing Readiness for Listening

"In late November, when all the crops have been gathered and the snow is already on the ground in many places, we celebrate another very important holiday. What do we call that day? Yes, Thanksgiving. What does the word *Thanksgiving* mean? Can you tell me why we give thanks on that day?"

During the discussion, bring out that Thanksgiving Day was first celebrated by the Pilgrims when they gave thanks for their first harvest in this country, and that we still continue to give thanks on this day.

"There are many happy Thanksgiving customs that we keep. What are some of the things that you and your family do every year? The poem 'Thanksgiving Day,' by Lydia Maria Child, tells some of the happy things about Thanksgiving in olden times.

"Listen carefully as I read it, and find out how this poet always spent Thanksgiving. Maybe you have felt the same way she feels in the poem."

Reading the Poem

The children should have their books closed as you read the poem. After reading it, encourage the children to comment freely and ask such questions as: "How do you think the author felt about Thanksgiving? What do you think made the sleigh ride such fun? How is your Thanksgiving different from this one? How is it the same?"

Rereading the Poem

"Open your books to page 252. Look at the picture. Do you think that it would be fun to ride in a sleigh to Grandfather's house? Close your eyes and listen as I read the poem again. What pictures do you see in your mind as I read each verse?"

Let individual children read single verses of the poem aloud. Remind them that they are reading aloud to give enjoyment to the listeners. At the end of each verse have the other pupils tell how the children in the poem felt. Bring out that they were happy, excited, impatient, cold, or hungry. If interest is still keen, have the children open their books and read the poem aloud in chorus. Suggest to the children that the poem should be read dramatically in order to bring out its spirit and enthusiasm.

Related Activities

Help the children make plans for a choral reading of the poem before an audience. Suggest that some of the children beat a soft rhythmic accompaniment with bells, triangles, and drums, as the others read the poem aloud. Stimulate interest in memorizing the poem.

Continue the discussion about Thanksgiving by talking with the children about their reasons for giving thanks. If there is interest, encourage the children to write original Thanksgiving prayers, stories, or poems.

Bring out that the poem treats an old-fashioned New England Thanksgiving, and that ever since the Pilgrims celebrated the first Thanksgiving in this country, certain traditions have been faithfully continued.

Stories to Enjoy. *The Thanksgiving Story*, by ALICE DAL-GLIESH; "The First Thanksgiving," by LENA BURKSDALE and "A New Pioneer," by DOROTHY CANFIELD, in *Holiday Storybook*, compiled by The Child Study Association of America; "The First Thanksgiving," by GRACE HUMPHREY, and "The Thanksgiving Stranger," by RUTH PLOWHEAD, both in *Holiday Round-Up*, by LUCILLE PANNELL and FRANCES CAVANAH.

Poems to Enjoy. "First Thanksgiving of All," by NANCY BYRD TURNER, and "Thanksgiving Magic," by ROWENA BENNETT, in *Sing a Song of Seasons*, by SARA and JOHN E. BREWTON; "If I Were a Pilgrim Child," in *Story-Teller Poems*, by ROWENA BENNETT; "When It's Thanksgiving," in *Up the Windy Hill*, by AILEEN FISHER; "The Pilgrims Came," in *For Days and Days*, by ANNETTE WYNNE; "The Magic Vine," author unknown, in *The Golden Flute*, compiled by ALICE HUBBARD and ADELINE BABBITT.

Music to Enjoy. "Over the River and through the Wood," and "He's a Big Fat Turkey," in *Singing on Our Way*, by LILLA BELLE PITTS and others.

Pages 254–264   Christmas with Stina Mor

Two Swedish children, unable to sell the straw goats they had made, were worried because they could not buy a Christmas gift for their mother. Perhaps their older brother would have sent a letter, they thought, as they stopped at the post office. There was no letter, only a heavy package for their neighbor, Stina Mor, which they delivered to her on their sled. The package, from Stina Mor's son in America, provided a happy Christmas for all of them.

Children will enjoy the story which depicts Christmas customs in another country. They will learn the value of giving up immediate pleasures in order to help others.

Vocabulary

New Words: Page 254, *Stina Mor;* 255, *Anna*, post office*;* 256, *postmaster*, package, heavy*;* 257, ————; 258, *sleigh, wore*, crown*;* 259, ————; 260, *America*, writing*;* 261, ————; 262, ————; 263, ————; 264, *late**

Developing Readiness for Reading

Meaningful Presentation of Vocabulary. "The story *Christmas with Stina Mor* (Stē′nà Mōōr) tells about a boy and girl who lived in Sweden. The boy's name was *Peter.* His sister was *Anna.* Their neighbor was *Stina Mor.* In Swedish this name means 'Mother Stina.' Why do you suppose the neighbor was called that? Who can tell us something about Sweden? Do you know where Sweden is? Let's look on the globe and find it. It is very cold there in the winter time. In our story people ride in *sleighs* over the snow. Can anyone tell us something about Swedish Christmas customs? Do you think that people give presents in gaily wrapped *packages?*"

Talking about related concepts

The new words *wore, crown,* and *late* may be attacked phonetically; *wore* and *late* have medial vowels lengthened by *e; crown* may be blended through its beginning blend *cr* and its known part, *ow. Post office* may be blended through familiar phonograms; *heavy* through the short sound of *ea. Postmaster* and *writing* are easily identified through familiar structural clues; *America* will be derived from the known word *American.*

Using phonetic and structural clues for word attack

Setting Up Reading Purposes. Encourage the children to describe briefly how Christmas is celebrated in their homes. Ask: "In what ways might people in Sweden have a Christmas celebration different from ours? How might their customs be like ours?" List on the chalkboard the ideas which children contribute. "I wonder if we are right. Let's read the story to see what Anna and Peter did at Christmastime."

NOTE. If this story is to be read early in the year the teacher should ascertain whether the children know the vocabulary introduced earlier in this book: *carried* (p. 14), *present* (p. 15), *glasses* (p. 38), *hardly* (p. 108), *sorry* (p. 149), *tapped* (p. 196).

Reading the Story

Guided Reading

Pages 254–264

The questions below may be written on the chalkboard or on a chart. Direct the children (1) to read the questions, (2) to read the story silently to find the answers, and (3) to be ready to read aloud the parts that answer the questions.

Reading silently to answer questions written on the chalkboard

Pages 254 and 255:

1. *What were Peter and his sister going to do with the straw goats?*
2. *Why were the two children not happy?*
3. *Why did they stop at the post office?*

Pages 256–261:

1. *Why did Peter and Anna decide to take Stina Mor's package?*
2. *What did the postmaster say about the package?*
3. *Where were the children in the sleigh going?*
4. *What did Anna think that the king would wear?*
5. *Why did the children have a hard time getting to Stina Mor's house?*

Pages 262–264:

1. *Who sent Stina Mor a surprise?*
2. *What surprise was in the package for Oscar's family?*
3. *What presents did Nils send his mother?*

Interpreting the story facts

After the silent reading, let the children read their answers to the questions and discuss the story further. "How did Anna and Peter show that they thought more about their neighbor's happiness than their own? How do we know that the postmaster was not right about Nils? How did the children prove that often when we help others we help ourselves? Why did Anna and Peter think that this would be the merriest Christmas ever?"

Rereading for Specific Purposes

Rereading orally to note changes in mood

Have the pupils find and read aloud parts which show that Anna and Peter were discouraged, thoughtful, sad, polite, helpful, happy, impatient, excited, merry. Help the pupils to express the way the children felt by the tone and pitch of their voices.

Building Essential Habits and Skills

Comprehension and Study Skills

Main Idea. To strengthen the ability to find the main idea in a part of the story, distribute copies of the exercise below. Have the children read each of the sentences under the subtitles and draw a line under the one which recalls most about that part of the story. Discussion may reveal some differences of opinion. If so, help the children reach an agreement.

Selecting main ideas

The Straw Goats

1. The children wanted to make their mother happy.
2. The straw goats got heavier every minute.
3. The children could not sell their straw goats.

Helping a Neighbor

1. Peter and Anna heard the sleigh bells.
2. The children took the package to Stina Mor.
3. Maybe the king wore a crown.

The Package from America

1. Mother had waited for Oscar to write to her.
2. Nils sent his mother a package.
3. This promised to be the merriest Christmas ever.

Sequence. To strengthen the ability to arrange story events in correct sequence, give the children copies of the exercise at the top of page 396.

Putting story facts into the right order

395

Christmas with Stina Mor (254–264)

Read the sentences on this paper. Put 1 before the sentence that tells what happened first in the story. Put 2 before the sentence that happened next, and so on.

_3_ On the way the children met their friends who were on the way to see the king.

_5_ Anna read the letter aloud to Stina Mor and found a letter from Oscar.

_1_ The children were unhappy because they had no present for their mother.

_2_ The postmaster had a package for Stina Mor.

_4_ Peter and Anna took the package to Stina Mor, although they too wanted to see the king.

_6_ The children were happy now because they had two presents for their mother.

Word-Study Skills

Learning to recognize homonyms

Word Meaning. To develop greater understanding of homonyms, write on the chalkboard the following pairs of words:

road, rode	*sea, see*	*son, sun*
no, know	*write, right*	*meet, meat*

Have the words pronounced and call the children's attention to the fact that the words in each pair sound alike but are spelled differently and have very different meanings. Ask the children to tell the meanings of the words in each pair and to use the words in sentences.

On the chalkboard write the following sentences:

The ship sailed out to ———.
Soon we could not ——— it any more.

see   sea

Ask the children to read the sentences to themselves, and to decide which word fits into each sentence. When all the

Teaching *Finding New Neighbors*   396

children understand that the use of a word is determined by its meaning in the sentence rather than by its sound, distribute copies of the following exercise:

Read each sentence and select the correct word to complete it. Write the word in the blank.

1. It was growing dark on the _road_ .
   Many children _rode_ on the sleigh.

           road   rode

- -

2. "It will be too bad if we have _no_ present for Mother," said Anna.
   The children did not _know_ that Nils and Oscar had sent the package together.

           no   know

- -

3. Oscar and Nils had gone to _sea_ many years before.
   The snow fell into the children's eyes so they could hardly _see_ .

           sea   see

- -

4. Oscar and Nils had remembered to _write_ letters to their mothers.
   The children were _right_ when they said it would be the merriest Christmas ever.

           write   right

- -

5. The big package for Stina Mor came from her _son._
   The _sun_ shines brightly on a summer day.

           son   sun

- -

6. The children could _hear_ the sleigh bells.
   They found out that the king would come _here_ very late.

           here   hear

Context Clues. To give practice in word recognition through use of context clues, ask the children to turn to page 256 and find the word *heavy*. Have a child read the paragraph in which this word appears. Ask, "How does the thought of the paragraph help you to know this word?"

Using context clues in word recognition

397

Christmas with Stina Mor (254–264)

Have children turn to page 258 and find the words *wore* and *crown*. Ask a child to read the paragraph containing them. "What one word helps you most to read the new words?"

Ask the children to turn to page 260 and read the paragraph containing *writing*. "What other word helps you most to know this word?" Have the children turn to page 264 and read the paragraph containing *late*. Ask, "What helps you to know this word?" If practice is needed, continue in this way with other words and discuss with the children the use of context clues plus phonetic and structural clues as ways of identifying new words.

Recalling "er" and "est" endings

Structural Analysis. To review the comparative and superlative forms of adjectives, distribute the worksheet below. Ask the children to read the first group of sentences and underline the root word common to all three. Discuss the meanings of the endings and recall the change from *y* to *i* before the ending. Then instruct the children to read all the sentences and to write the root word that is common to each group of three.

---

1. The package was heavy. _____
   It was heavier than they thought. _____
   It was the heaviest package in the post office. _____

2. This Christmas will be a merry one. _____
   It will be merrier than the last one. _____
   This Christmas will be the merriest ever. _____

3. The king's train was late. _____
   It was later than they thought. _____
   It was the latest it had ever been. _____

4. The postmaster said that Nils was lazy. _____
   He said that he was lazier than Oscar. _____
   He said that he was the laziest boy he knew. _____

5. It was easy to carry the straw goats to town. _____
   It was easier to carry them to town than back home. _____
   It was easiest to carry them when they sold well. _____

Workbook

Pages 77, 78, 79, and 80.

Related Language Experiences

Discussion. Have a discussion about Anna's and Peter's decision not to go with the school children. Raise questions such as: "How would Anna and Peter have felt if they had gone with the other children instead of getting the package? Why did they want to help Stina Mor?"

Discussing ethical values

Choral Speaking. Encourage the children to collect Christmas poems in books available in the school. Help the children select two or three which lend themselves to choral speaking and learn to read or say them for the class. "Long, Long Ago," in *Ring-A-Round*, by MILDRED P. HARRINGTON; "Why Do the Bells of Christmas Ring?" and "The Friendly Beasts," in *Very Young Verses*, by BARBARA PECK GEISMER and AN-TOINETTE SUTER, are poems that might be used.

Presenting poems

Listening. Read the poem "December" aloud to the children. This poem is so full of images that the children will find it easy to react to it and make it their own. Let them paint their feelings about it on colored construction paper.

Listening to a poem

DECEMBER

I like days
with a snow-white collar,
and nights when the moon
is a silver dollar,
and hills are filled
with eiderdown stuffing
and your breath makes smoke
like an engine puffing.

I like days
when feathers are snowing,
and all the eaves
have petticoats showing,
and the air is cold,
and the wires are humming,
but you feel all warm . . .
with Christmas coming!

AILEEN FISHER

Christmas with Stina Mor (254–264)

Enrichment Activities

Publishing
the Christmas
issue of the
newspaper

Co-ordinating Activity. If the newspaper is carried on for a longer time, be sure that each child in the room has had an opportunity to have some experience in several of the phases connected with putting it out.

The Christmas issue of the newspaper might consist of reports on Christmas customs of other lands as well as original poems and stories about Christmas.

Displaying
Swedish objects

Let the children help plan and arrange a display of objects made in Sweden, such as straw animals or figures, Christmas ornaments, carved animals, or Christmas cards and posters. Many of these are available in this country.

Illustrating
scenes from
the story

Art. Ask the children to select their favorite part of the story to illustrate. Have them close their books and use their own ideas in the drawings.

Having a
Christmas
celebration

Celebrating Christmas. If this story is read at Christmastime, it may contribute to the holiday activities. Emphasize that in different parts of the world Christmas is celebrated in different and yet similar ways.

Superior readers may be interested in reading further about the Christmas customs of different countries. This research might be done in small groups and shared with the rest of the class or with other classes. If there is time, some of the Swedish Christmas customs might be acted out, Swedish songs learned, stories and poems read aloud, and simple holiday food cooked.

Reading stories

Stories in Other Readers. There are so many charming Christmas stories that individual children may wish to read one and then retell it to the class in their own words. Help them to organize their thoughts so that the retelling will be smooth and logical.

Meet Our Friends, by WILLIAM H. BURTON and others
   "Burning the Greens," pp. 91–96

Our Good Neighbors, by WILLIAM H. BURTON and others
   "Merry Christmas Time," pp. 178–184

The New if I Were Going, by MABEL O'DONNELL
   "It Happened in Norway," pp. 22–62
   "It Happened in Lapland," pp. 64–88

Faraway Ports, by GERTRUDE HILDRETH and others
"Juan's Christmas Pinata," pp. 202–230

On We Go, by PAUL MCKEE and others
"Snipp and His Brothers," pp. 42–60

The New Streets and Roads, by WILLIAM S. GRAY and others
"The Traveling Christmas Party," pp. 114–122
"Paddy's Christmas," pp. 172–179

Stories to Enjoy. *The Christmas Anna Angel*, by RUTH SAWYER; *Noel for Jeanne Marie*, by FRANÇOISE SEIGNOBOSC (Françoise, pseud.); *Rosita*, by JEANNETTE BROWN; *Told under the Christmas Tree*, compiled by the Association for Childhood Education International; *With Bells On*, by KATHERINE MILHOUS; *More Favorite Stories Old and New*, by SIDONIE M. GRUENBERG.

Poems to Enjoy. *Christmas Bells Are Ringing*, compiled by SARA and JOHN E. BREWTON; "Golden Cobwebs," in *Story-Teller Poems*, by ROWENA BENNETT; "Till Christmas Comes," in *Up the Windy Hill*, by AILEEN FISHER; "Bundles," by JOHN FARRAR, "Long, Long Ago," Anonymous, and "Song," by EUGENE FIELD, all in *The Golden Flute*, by ALICE HUBBARD and ADELINE BABBITT; "The Postman Is a Happy Man" and "Great White World," in *For Days and Days*, by ANNETTE WYNNE.

Hearing poems and music

Music to Enjoy. *American Folk Songs for Christmas*, by RUTH SEEGER; "I Wish You a Merry Christmas" and "Hear the Christmas Bells," in *Singing on Our Way*, by LILLA BELLE PITTS and others; "Jolly Old Saint Nicholas," "Oh, Come, Little Children," and "Hark! the Herald Angels Sing," all in *Singing and Rhyming*, by LILLA BELLE PITTS and others.

A Film to Enjoy. *Christmas* (EBF), 1 reel, 5min, sd, color.

Filmstrips to Enjoy. CHRISTMAS SERIES: (1) *The Story of "Silent Night"*; (2) *The Tree and Other Traditions;* (3) *Santa Claus and Other Traditions* (JamHandy), each about 29frs. with captions, color. *Seasons and Festivals* (EyeGate), 23frs. with captions, color, in LITERATURE FOR CHILDREN Series.

Seeing a film, film-strips, and pictures

Pictures to Enjoy. "The Eve of St. Nicholas," and "The Twelfth Night Feast," by Jan Steen.

Barney on TV

Barney's dog had five puppies just as New Year's Day dawned. When Barney heard that the Zipp Oil Company would give prizes for the first babies born on New Year's Day, he reported this birth to the TV station. With five fathers of New Year babies, Barney took part in the TV program and astonished everyone by announcing the birth of five babies at his house. He not only received a prize of a box of dog food, but succeeded in finding homes for all the puppies!

The children will enjoy the humor of this story and share Barney's excitement and suspense.

Vocabulary

New Words: Page 265, *Barney, Tilly**; 266, *Zipp**, *Company, born**; 267, ————; 268, *program;* 269, *Rover**, *Shirley**; 270, ————; 271, ————; 272, ————

Developing Readiness for Reading

Talking about television

Meaningful Presentation of Vocabulary. "Do you enjoy watching television? What *programs* do you like especially well? Who sponsors them (pays to have them put on the air)? How do you know? (Commercials.) What products do you think the *Zipp Oil Company* might sponsor? In today's story a boy named *Barney Miller* is on a TV program."

Attacking new vocabulary through phonetic clues

The new words *Rover* and *Shirley* may be presented either in context during the guided reading, or taught here phonetically. *Barney, Rover,* and *Shirley* all contain familiar phonetic parts as well as vowels influenced by *r*. *Tilly, Zipp, program,* and *born* all have known parts which are easily blended.

Setting Up Reading Purposes. "Something happened on New Year's Day that gave Barney a big problem to solve. Then he discovered that he had a chance to appear on a TV program. And Barney had a real surprise for the audience. Let's read the story to find out what happened. Turn to the table of contents and find 'Barney on TV.' "

NOTE. If this story is to be read at New Year's time the teacher should ascertain whether the children know the vocabulary introduced earlier in this book: *afternoon* (p. 14), *remember* (p. 45), *shook* (p. 96), *circle* (p. 163), *swallowed* (p. 180), *read* (past) (p. 210), *newspapers* (p. 220), *slippers* (p. 226)

Reading the Story

Guided Reading

"Tilly had a surprise for Barney. Read this page to find out about the surprise." After the reading, ask: "What was the surprise? How many puppies were there? What color were they? Read the sentence aloud that tells when they were born. What does 'just as New Year's Day dawned' mean?

Page 265

Reading silently to answer questions

"Read two pages to find out the good idea that Barney had." After the reading, ask: "What were Barney and Chris going to do with the puppies? Do you think their mother should have let them keep all of them? Why couldn't Dick Harper take a puppy? Why couldn't Peanut Sanders have one? What did Barney mean by 'two sets of twins and one left over'? How do you think the man felt when he heard that?

Pages 266–267

"Read two pages to find out why Barney and Chris were worried." After the reading, ask: "How did Barney and Chris get to the TV station? How many other people were on the program? Why do you think that Barney's part would come at the end of the program? What names for the puppies did the boys think of?" (Rover, Shirley.) "What prizes did the fathers receive?

Pages 268–269

"Barney had a surprise on the program. Read two pages to find out what it was." After the reading, ask a child to read Mr. Casey's introduction of Barney and Barney's announcement of the puppies' names.

Pages 270–271

"Finish the story to see if Barney received a prize too." After the reading, ask: "What do you think Barney liked best about being on TV? Would you have liked being in Barney's place?"

Page 272

Rereading for Specific Purposes

1. Have the group prepare the story to read aloud to another group in the classroom or to another class. Help the

Reading orally for interpretation

children recall the standards for good oral reading and write their suggestions on the chalkboard, for example:

> *Read as if the people were speaking.*
> *Make everyone hear.*
> *Know all the words.*
> *Look up from the book now and then.*

Have the children practice reading the story in the group before they read it to others. Be sure that books are closed so that group members may listen and later make comments.

Rereading to find specific information for a letter

2. Have the children reread the first part of the story to find the specific information that Barney would need to write his letter to the TV station. Ask the children to write the information as sentences or phrases to help them remember important facts in sequence. They should keep their notes to use in writing the letters mentioned in "Related Language Experiences" of this lesson.

A list of questions on the chalkboard may be helpful in guiding the children in this activity.

> 1. *Who is Tilly?*
> 2. *When did Tilly have her puppies?*
> 3. *How many puppies are there?*
> 4. *What are they like?*

Building Essential Habits and Skills

Comprehension and Study Skills

Using judgment

Critical Reading. To develop greater skill in story interpretation, distribute copies of the exercise at the top of page 405. Have the children discuss their answers later, explaining their reasons for replying as they did. Some difference of opinion should be expected.

Identifying story dialogue

Details and Sequence. To strengthen the ability to recall story details, distribute copies of the exercise on the lower half of page 405. When the children have finished the exercise, let them check their answers in the book, give the page on which each sentence appears, and then number the quotations in the order in which they appeared in the story.

Are These Good Ideas?

After each sentence write <u>I think so</u> or <u>I do not think so.</u> Be ready to tell why you think as you do.

1. Mother didn't tell about the puppies until Barney and Chris woke up in the morning. ——————————

2. The puppies were by the furnace in the basement. _____

3. Barney and Chris could keep the puppies only six weeks. ——————————————————

4. Dick Harper could not have a puppy. ——————

5. Peanut Sanders could not have a puppy. ——————

6. Barney did not tell the gasoline-station man that the five babies were puppies. ——————————

7. Barney called the puppies Rover and Shirley. ———

8. Mr. Casey told the other fathers right away that the five babies were puppies. ——————————

9. The announcer talked about Zipp oil and gasoline. _____

10. The fathers were given play pens. ——————————

11. Barney was given a whole box of dog food. ———

Read each sentence. In the blank after each sentence write the name of the person who said it.

| Barney | Mother | Chris |
| The announcer | Mr. Casey | A father |

"Such tiny red puppies. How many may we keep?"
   <u>Chris</u>

"The Rovers are the boys. The Shirleys are the girls."
   <u>Barney</u>

"We now give a prize to Barney Miller. A whole box of dog food!" <u>the announcer</u>

"Jump into your slippers and come down." <u>Mother</u>

"There are two sets of twins and one left over."
   <u>Barney</u>

"Your part comes at the end of the program."
   <u>Mr. Casey</u>

"And I'll take whatever is left." <u>a father</u>

Word-Study Skills

Observing
the long "e" sound
of "ie"

Phonetic Analysis. 1. To make the children aware of *ie* in familiar words, write on the chalkboard *babies* and *puppies*. Then draw attention to the sound of *ie* in these words. Write on the chalkboard *ladies, prairie, believe, field, piece*. Have the children read the words aloud and underline the *ie* in each. They may note that the second letter gives the digraph its sound and the pronunciation of *ie* in these words is an exception to the rule.

To give independent practice, ask the children to write the words in sentences and underline each *ie* word.

Recalling
consonant blends

2. To review consonant blends with the children, write on the chalkboard the following words from the story: *program, prize, expressed, surprise, station, glasses, play, swallow, trying, cried*. Have the children take turns pronouncing each word and circling the consonant blend they hear. Have each child think of another word that contains the same blend as the word he has pronounced.

Reviewing
two uses of
the apostrophe

Structural Analysis. 1. To review the use of the apostrophe to show possession, write on the chalkboard *New Year's Day* and *Tilly's new family*. Help the children to recall that the apostrophe indicates "belonging to." Have the children use the phrases in sentences and give other examples of words with the apostrophe to show possession.

2. To recall the use of the apostrophe in a contraction, write on the chalkboard the sentences below. Have the children tell the words each contraction stands for and read each sentence aloud with the contraction and without it.

> *Chris didn't know.*
> *They're red with white feet.*
> *Their mother isn't here.*
> *I'm Mr. Casey.*
> *Don't you remember?*
> *Dad said we couldn't keep any.*
> *Oh, that's all right.*

Explain, if necessary, the difference in the use of the apostrophe in possessive forms and in contractions.

Teaching *Finding New Neighbors*

Alphabetizing. To give oral practice in alphabetizing, the children may enjoy playing some form of alphabet game. One possibility is to divide the group into two teams. The first child of one team gives a word beginning with *a*. The first child on the other team says a word beginning with *b*. The second child on the first team says a word beginning with *c*, and so on. Each time a child gives a right word he scores a point for his team.

Playing an alphabet game

A more challenging form of this game is to decide on a subject such as "Holidays," "Ships," "Farm," "Grocery-store," or "City." Proceed as above within the limits of the chosen subject.

Syllabication. To give practice in recognizing syllables, ask children to tell how many syllables they hear in the following words from the story: *Company, program, Casey, Rover, Shirley, Zipp, born, Barney, Tilly, gasoline, letter, five, together, only, animals.*

Recognizing syllables in words

Workbook

Pages 81 and 82.

Barney on TV (265–272)

Writing a letter

Correspondence. Have the children write a letter which Barney might have sent to Station WOZB. Help the children to write a concise but explicit letter using the notes which they made in rereading the story. If the children prefer, have them write a letter asking to appear on one of their own favorite television programs. Make sure that the letter form in all the letters is correct.

If a television studio is nearby, some of the children may wish to write letters asking for permission for the class to visit the studio. (See the illustration on the preceding page.)

Planning the TV program

Dramatization. The children will enjoy planning the program that took place on Saturday morning. Have different children try out for the parts. Committees may write commercials about Zipp oil and gasoline and submit their versions to the group, who may agree on the best one. After the program has been rehearsed, it may be presented to another group.

Comparing stories

Discussion. Compare New Moon's celebration of New Year with Barney's. How were they similar? How were they different? Have an interested group of children look more deeply into New Year's customs all over the world. They may give reports about their findings.

Enrichment Activities

Co-ordinating Activity. Plan and publish a New Year's issue of the newspaper. Have original New Year's stories and poems, as well as reports on classroom events and New Year's customs.

Publishing the newspaper

Art. Have some children draw a poster advertising Zipp products which can be shown on the TV program as the announcer gives the commercial. (See page 408.)

Drawing posters

The group doing research on New Year customs might illustrate them and display the pictures in the form of a frieze, an exhibit, or a book for the library table.

Stories to Enjoy. *Patrick and the Golden Slippers*, by KATHERINE MILHOUS; "Ring in the New," by LAURA HARRIS, "Twelve by Mail Coach," by HANS CHRISTIAN ANDERSEN, and "The Honorable New Year," by FRANCES CAVANAH, all in *Holiday Round-Up*, by LUCILLE PANNELL and FRANCES CAVANAH.

Reading stories

The Valentine Box

**Pages
273–282**

The valentine box at school was beautiful, but Jane dreaded the day of the party because she was new in the school and had made no friends. Would she receive any valentines from her classmates? On Valentine's Day Jane had an opportunity to help Margaret and thereby made a friend. The valentine party was a happy occasion after all.

The story will make the reader more aware of children's feelings in a new school, particularly on such special occasions as Valentine's Day.

Vocabulary

New Words: Page 273, *hearts;* 274, ———; 275, *Margaret;* 276, *envelope;* 277, ———; 278, ———; 279, ———; 280, *cap*;* 281, ———; 282, ———

Developing Readiness for Reading

Meaningful Presentation of Vocabulary. "Let us look at the table of contents. What holidays have the stories in this

Discussing story background

unit, 'Days Everyone Likes,' been about?" (Columbus Day, Halloween, Christmas, New Year's Day.) "And what is the name of the last story?"

Ask one child to read the title aloud. Some children may want to tell about especially pretty valentine boxes that they have had at school. Write on the chalkboard:

> *Put hearts on the box.*
> *Put the envelopes in the box.*

Have the sentences read aloud and the new words underlined. Be sure that the children identify *Margaret*, the new name in the story. The word *cap* will be recognized through phonetic clues.

Setting Up Reading Purposes. "Has anyone here ever gone to a new school? How did you feel? Did you miss your old friends? What do you suppose might happen to a new boy or girl on Valentine's Day? Have you ever worried that you might not get any valentines? Jane had just moved to Lakeside. She was worried that she would get no valentines. Do you think she was right to worry? Let's read this story to find out."

NOTE. If this story is to be read earlier in the year, the only unknown words would be *afternoon, carried* (p. 14), and *important* (p. 94).

Reading the Story

Guided Reading

Page 273

Reading silently to answer questions

Have the title and subtitle read aloud. Ask, "Why do you think Jane didn't want to go back to school after lunch?" After the reading, have one child read aloud the description of the valentine box and a second child read the two paragraphs that describe Jane's feeling.

Pages 274–275

"Read the next two pages to find out why Jane's mother wanted her to go to school in the afternoon and what happened on the way." After the reading ask, "Do you think Jane's valentines were pretty?" Have someone read the description orally. "How did Jane's mother help her protect her valentines from the snowstorm? What happened to Margaret's valentines? Why might the girls have a hard time picking them up?

"Finish this part of the story to find out whether the girls could save Margaret's valentines." After the reading, encourage discussion of the storm and of the girls' struggle. Ask different children to read the two pages orally, trying to make the listeners conscious of the storm and of the girls' shouts.

Pages 276–277

"What is the next subtitle? Finish the story to find out what is meant by 'The Snowstorm Valentine.'" After the reading, ask: "How did Jane feel when she saw that Margaret had no valentine for her? Was it a good idea to choose Jane to be the postman? Which of Jane's valentines do you think was her favorite? What happened that was even better than receiving valentines?"

Pages 278–282

Rereading for Specific Purposes

The children may reread the story silently, noting specifically the sentences listed below. Discuss the ideas which may be inferred from the text.

Making inferences

Page 274, paragraph 1, sentence 3: Why might being a quiet girl have something to do with making new friends?

Page 274, paragraph 3, sentence 2: Why did Jane's mother let Valentine's Day change her mind about keeping Jane at home?

Page 276, paragraphs 1, 2, 3: Why did Margaret say what she did when Jane offered to help?

Page 276, paragraph 7, sentence 2: What does this sentence mean?

Page 278, paragraph 1, sentences 1, 2: What does this sentence tell about the time?

Page 278, paragraph 3, sentence 1: Why did Jane speak quickly?

Pages 279–280: Find and read any sentence that tells what kind of boy Bill was.

Page 280, paragraph 3, sentence 2: Why did Miss Waters do this?

Page 282, paragraph 5: Why did Jane say this? Why do mothers want to know where their children are?

Page 282, paragraph 7: What did Jane get that was best of all?

411   *The Valentine Box* (273–282)

Building Essential Habits and Skills

Comprehension and Study Skills

Arranging
story events
in order

Sequence. To provide practice in recalling correct sequence of story events, distribute copies of the exercise below or write the sentences on the chalkboard to be copied by the children in the correct order:

Read all the sentences. Before the one that happened first put the number 1. Before the one that happened next put the number 2. Finish the rest of the sentences in the same way.

_4_ Bill was willing to help Jane.

_3_ Margaret's valentines were blown away.

_5_ Jane was asked to be postman.

_2_ Jane walked to school carrying her valentines.

_6_ Jane and her "snowstorm valentine" went out to play.

_1_ The class would have a valentine party but Jane was not happy.

Reading to prove
a point

Details. To develop skill in selecting details to prove a point, have the children write on their papers, "I know that Valentine's Day was cold, wet, and stormy because ———.

Ask the children to reread the story and find all the phrases or sentences that prove the above statement. For example, the children might copy down such phrases as "it was snowing hard," "needed something to keep the valentines dry," "wind was blowing the snow in circles and roaring through the trees," "looked at Margaret's wet rubbers," etc.

Word-Study Skills

Discriminating
between synonyms
and antonyms

Word Meaning. To give practice in discriminating between synonyms and antonyms, distribute copies of the independent exercise at the top of page 413.

Observing the effect
of final "e" on
the last syllable

Phonetic Analysis. Write the words *envelope* and *valentine* on the chalkboard and have the children tell how many syllables they hear in each word. Continue in the same way

Read the pair of words on each line. If they mean the same thing put S in the space. If they have different meanings put D in the space.

D	morning	evening
S	tiny	small
D	remember	forget
S	want	wish
D	later	now
S	nothing	none
S	racing	running
D	young	old
D	heavy	light
D	stand	sit
S	above	over
D	low	high

with *lemonade, decide,* and *Chinese.* Ask the children in what way all these words are alike. (The last syllable of each one ends in silent *e.*) Ask, "How does a silent *e* at the end of a word change it?" Circle the last syllable in each word. Lead the children to generalize that *in many two- and three-syllable words, the final e lengthens the vowel in the last syllable.*

For independent practice, have the children copy the words below on a piece of paper, say the words to themselves, and underline the syllable in each that is lengthened by the final *e,*

lemonade	envelope	valentine
decide	Chinese	jackknife
pancake	parade	surprise

Syllabication. 1. To review the syllabic division of words beginning with *a* and *be,* write on the chalkboard *across, above,* and *along.* Recall with the children that in these words the letter *a* is a syllable. Then have individual children divide the words into syllables by marking the *a.*

Reviewing "a" and "be" as syllabic divisions

2. Continue in the same way with words that begin with the *be* syllable. *Believe, began, below,* and *behind* are words that may be written on the chalkboard.

3. When the syllabic divisions are clear to all the children, write *uncover, untie,* on the chalkboard. Tell them that *un* is

Observing "un" as syllabic division

a syllable like *a* and *be*. Ask individual children to go to the chalkboard and underline *un* in each of the words.

4. To give independent practice in recognizing the syllabic divisions of words beginning with *a*, *be*, and *un*, distribute copies of the following exercise:

Draw a line through each word to divide it into syllables. Remember what you learned about *a*, *be*, and *un*. The first word is done for you.

a	cross	alone	away
believe	behind	below
untie	began	afraid
about	above	along

Put the right word from the list in each space below.

Please <u>untie</u> your apron, Mother, and come with me. Let's go <u>across</u> the street to the store. I am <u>afraid</u> to go there <u>alone</u>.

Recalling compound words

Structural Analysis. To review compound words, have the children recall the name of the town in which Jane lived. (Lakeside) Ask, "How do you suppose the town got its name?" Ask the children to identify the two parts of this compound word.

Ask the children to look for other compound words in the story. (*hatbox, maybe, afternoon, doorway, pocketbook, something, someone, snowman, peanut, cannot, snowstorm, anyway, anything, schoolroom, postman*) As the children find the words, write them on the chalkboard. Have the children identify the two parts of each.

Arranging words alphabetically

Alphabetizing. To review alphabetization, write on the chalkboard the proper nouns below which appear in this unit. Have the pupils identify each one. Then ask them to arrange the words alphabetically.

Daisy	*Anna*	*Uncle Fred*	*Peter*
Halloween	*Tilly*	*Zipp Company*	*Ned*
Oscar	*Queen*	*Columbus*	*Rover*
Barney	*Shirley*	*Postmaster*	*King*
Margaret	*Nils*	*Gray Whiskers*	*Julie*

Workbook

Pages 83, 84, and 85.

Related Language Experiences

Creative Writing. Lead the children to recall that Margaret did not have time to make a rhyme for Jane's valentine. If it is near Valentine's Day, ask the children to make rhymes suitable for Jane's valentine or for one of their own.

Making rhymes

Conversation. 1. Help better readers to read and tell about the origin of Valentine's Day.

Learning about St. Valentine

2. Recall the many acts of kindness described in the story. Point out that thoughtfulness of others helps one to make good friends. Ask the children to suggest ways in which one can show kindness to other people, not only on Valentine's Day but throughout the year.

Discussing kindness to others

Enrichment Activities

Co-ordinating Activity. Encourage the children to continue writing articles or news items for the class newspaper. Guide the children in selecting the best examples of creative writing and news reporting.

Publishing the newspaper

A Valentine's Day issue of the newspaper might consist of an article on the origin of the day and reports of various valentine customs that the children have found either from experience or study. There should be news reports on how the class celebrated the day, and original valentine poems, stories, and songs.

Art and Construction. If this story is read near Valentine's Day, have the children make valentines for one another. With the children's help, assemble pieces of lace paper, ribbon, gold and silver paper, as well as the usual school materials, and encourage the children to design and make their own valentines. Help them select the best of their original rhymes to write on the valentines.

Making valentines

Valentine Party. If the story is read or reread at Valentine's Day, help the children plan a valentine party with a valentine box, a postman, and simple refreshments. They

Planning a party

The Valentine Box (273–282)

may enjoy reading their original valentine verses as part of the program.

Enjoying stories and a poem

Stories in Other Readers. The children will enjoy reading about Valentine's Day and a story about helping others.

> *The New More Friends and Neighbors*, by WILLIAM S. GRAY and others
> "A Big Surprise," pp. 25–29
>
> *Story Caravan*, by WILLIAM D. SHELDON and others
> "Valentines for America," pp. 78–88
>
> *Open Doors*, by ULLIN W. LEAVELL and MARY LOUISE FRIEBELE
> "On Saturday Morning," pp. 24–31

Stories to Enjoy. *Appolonia's Valentine*, by KATHERINE MILHOUS; *Story of Valentine*, by WILMA PITCHFORD HAYS; "Valentine Box," by M. H. LOVELACE, in *Holiday Round-Up*, by LUCILLE PANNELL and FRANCES CAVANAH; "Juan Brings a Valentine," in *Holiday Storybook*, compiled by The Child Study Association of America.

A Poem to Enjoy. Girls will enjoy hearing this valentine poem. Some may wish to learn it and recite it in chorus.

MY VALENTINE

I have a little valentine
That someone sent to me.
It's pink and white and red and blue,
And pretty as can be.

Forget-me-nots are round the edge,
And tiny roses, too;
And such a lovely piece of lace—
The very palest blue.

And in the center there's a heart
As red as red can be!
And on it's written all in gold,
"To you, with Love from Me."

MARY CATHERINE PARSONS

Music to Enjoy. "When You Send a Valentine" and
"Father's Valentine," in *Singing on Our Way*; "Saint Valen-
tine's Day," in *Singing and Rhyming*, both by LILLA BELLE
PITTS and others.

Singing songs

All-Unit Activities

Culminating Activities

Playing "Information, Please." Write the names below
on slips of paper. Let each child draw one name and pantomime, dramatize, or give clues so that the others may guess
who he is. Have the child look through the unit to find out all
he can about the character he is to present.

Playing a game

Julie	Peter	Barney
Daisy	Anna	Tilly
Juan	Nils	Jane
Columbus	Oscar	Margaret
Stina Mor	Miss Waters	Mr. Casey
Jane's mother	Bill	Ned

Calendar of Holidays. Provide a large calendar of the current year on which the dates of holidays may be marked in
some special fashion. Include the holidays treated in the

Making
a holiday
calendar

stories of this unit and others with which the children are familiar. Have the children make riddles about the holidays and read them aloud for other members of the class to guess.

Evaluating Activities

Recalling story events **Story Recall.** To check the recall of story facts, distribute copies of the exercise below. Direct the children to read the sentences and to write after each the name of the character described in the sentence.

Who Was It?

1. She lost her valentines on the way to school. She carried them in a pocketbook. ___Jane___
2. He had a cat named Gray Whiskers. He gave the cat to Columbus. ___Juan___
3. She was afraid of ghosts and met a friendly one. ___Julie___
4. He put down his pencil and went to help Jane. ___Bill___
5. He was the announcer for the Zipp Oil Company's TV program. ___Mr. Casey___
6. Her son sent her a big package from America. ___Stina Mor___
7. He was on TV. He won a whole box of dog food. ___Barney___
8. They helped their neighbor before they had fun themselves. ___Peter___ and ___Anna___
9. He sent his mother a letter from America at Christmastime. ___Oscar___
10. He believed that the world was round. The Queen gave him three ships. ___Columbus___

Peter	Juan	Anna
Jane	Mr. Casey	Barney
Stina Mor	Oscar	Columbus
Bill	Julie	

Organizing details **Organizing Ideas.** To give practice in organizing details to fit a main idea, distribute copies of the exercise on page 419.

The words in the list below will make you think of one or more of the holidays you have read about. Put each word in the right column. Some words will remind you of two or three days. Write them under each day they fit.

HOLIDAYS

dinner	colored lights	Christmas trees
hearts	parties	presents
Columbus	spring	fall
frost	balls	turkey
first	play games	remember
pies	cakes	valentines
cakes	best suits	pretty dresses
evergreens	parades	clown
holly	surprises	winter
paste	ghosts	December
February	company	make-believe
October	ships	America
church	January 1	

Columbus Day	Halloween	Thanksgiving

Christmas	New Year's Day	Valentine's Day

Structural Analysis. To apply the ability to add the endings *ly, er, est,* distribute copies of the exercise at the top of page 420. Have the children read each sentence and the word which follows it; decide which ending to add to the word in order to complete the sentence; and then write the new word in the blank. Caution them that they will find

All-Unit Activities

some words ending in *y* and have them recall that the *y* is changed to *i* before the ending is added.

---

1. He held out his cat proudly . proud
2. Columbus was the bravest of all the men. brave
3. He was braver than those men who laughed at him. brave
4. Jane answered quickly . quick
5. Suddenly Julie knew that she saw Daisy and not a ghost. Sudden
6. The package was the heaviest that the postman had. heavy
7. She screamed very loudly when she thought she saw a ghost. loud
8. It was the merriest of all Christmas days. merry

Recalling vowel sounds and syllables

Syllabication. 1. To review vowel sounds and syllables, write on the chalkboard the words below. Have the children pronounce each word, tell the number of vowel sounds they hear and the number of syllables. (All words contain a single vowel in each syllable.)

program	*America*	*wharf*	*Tilly*
ships	*company*	*ghost*	*pitch*
writing	*Nils*	*Columbus*	*born*
Rover	*whiskers*	*postmaster*	*Anna*

Checking syllables ending in silent "e"

2. Present on the chalkboard the words below and have the children tell how many syllables they hear and see in each. Ask them to tell how all the words are alike. (All have final silent *e*.)

envelope	*awake*	*parade*
telephone	*valentine*	*beside*

Syllables with digraphs

3. Write the words below on the chalkboard and have the children tell how many syllables they hear and how the words are alike. (All have two vowels together, one silent and the other with a long sound.)

Halloween	*loading*	*screamed*	*waiting*
eaten	*queen*	*Daisy*	*reach*

Helping the Individual Child

Specific Help. 1. To help children who have trouble remembering and using phonetic and structural principles that have been taught, the teacher may initiate various drill games. Variations of the familiar game "Fish," in which children draw a word, and identify it or a part of it, are useful with some children.

Playing games to review phonetic and structural principles

To collect materials in order to construct a drill game, the teacher may utilize a group's current interests. Any simple sketch, such as a fruit tree with "apples" or "pears" with printed words on them, a flower garden, an animal that needs ears, eyes, or a tail on which words or letters are printed, a rocket that needs parts, etc., will serve to arouse interest. The teacher may say: "Find the word that contains ————; find the word that sounds like or rhymes with ————; find the word that means ————," and so on. The child who answers correctly then theoretically picks the fruit, ducks for the apple, climbs the mountain, takes off in an airplane, reaches Mars, pins the tail on the donkey, visits a country he likes, or any other goal that seems desirable.

2. Children of this age also usually enjoy team games such as football or baseball. A playing field may be sketched on the chalkboard or on tagboard and adapted to various purposes. One variation of baseball follows:

Playing a game to master vowel digraphs

To give extra practice in recognizing vowel digraphs, draw a baseball diamond on the chalkboard. Write one digraph (*ai, ea, oa, ee, oo,* or *ui*) at each base. A child who can write a word with the corresponding digraph at each base gets a home run.

The game of baseball may also be used to practice initial, medial, and final consonant sounds, consonant blends, and vowels.

Oral Reading. For those children who continue to have difficulty in expressing themselves effectively in oral reading, provide small-group practice to increase this skill, for example:

Improving oral reading

1. Select a story from the book which lends itself particularly well to oral reading and which presents no vocabulary difficulty.

421   All-Unit Activities

2. Discuss the story in detail. Call attention to words and punctuation marks which indicate how the material should be read. Recall how to express moods of the story with voices—how to show that you are excited, surprised, frightened, or sad. Read parts from the story to the children to illustrate the points brought out in the discussion.

3. Have each child select a paragraph from another story and practice it until he feels that he can read it satisfactorily before his group.

4. Have an informal reading party and let the children read their selections to others.

Using the table of contents

Table of Contents. Group those children who need further instruction in using the table of contents. During discussion, help the children to understand the purposes and uses of the table of contents. Provide exercises, such as the following:

1. Have the children turn to the table of contents. Direct them to list the titles and page numbers of stories which fall under certain classifications. Say: "If you were to choose stories from this book to recommend to a boy, which ones would you choose? Find the titles and page numbers of your choices. Which ones would you choose for girls?" Write the children's suggestions on the chalkboard.

2. Play "Find It Quickly" by giving the title of a story and having the children use the table of contents to locate the page number on which it starts. The child who finds the correct page number first suggests the next title to be located, and so on.

Improving auditory recognition, word attack, and creative writing

Rhymes. Children enjoy playing rhyming games and at the same time develop greater auditory acuity. The following simple techniques may be used with children who need such practice:

1. Provide opportunities to compose original rhymes, as:

> On the farm there is a pig.
> He's black and white and very big.
>
> My little brother's name is Fred
> He never likes to go to bed.

2. Let the children illustrate their original rhymes.

3. Encourage the children to compose and then to read original rhymes to the group. Suggest that they omit the last word of the rhyme, giving the opportunity for someone else to supply it.

4. Give each table or row one word, as *drink*. Allow three minutes and then count to see which group has found the greatest number of rhyming words.

Playing rhyming games

5. Play "Rhyming Riddles" in this way:

> I am little.
> I can fly and hum.
> I can give you something that rhymes with *money*.
> What do I give you? (*honey*)

6. Play "I am Thinking" in this way: A child says: "I am thinking of something in this room that rhymes with *look*. What is it?" (*book*)

7. List on the chalkboard several basic sight words on which practice is needed. Give a child a piece of colored chalk and say, "Underline a word that rhymes with *locket*." (*pocket*) When a second child takes a turn, give him a piece of chalk of a different color. At the end of the game have each child reread the words which he underscored with his color.

Provisions for Superior Readers. 1. To develop further the ability to associate related ideas, distribute the exercise below to the better readers. After the children have finished the

Associating related ideas

In each row underline the two words that go together.

1. wharf	program	slippers	ships
2. package	post office	rats	queen
3. team	ghosts	Halloween	bananas
4. Barney	write	sleigh	Juan
5. screams	heavy	letter	envelope
6. carrots	belt	blanket	buckle
7. write	Julie	crown	king
8. grass	ships	sleigh	pasture
9. stall	pitch	messenger	strike
10. America	minute	discontented	Columbus

All-Unit Activities

exercise, ask them to tell why they marked the words they did and what each relationship implies.

2. To develop further the ability to attack new words through phonetic elements and context clues, give better readers independent exercises, such as the one below. After the children have completed the exercise, take time to discuss the words, their meanings, and how the children attacked each one.

Read each new word. Write the correct word in each blank in the sentences below.

th—thirsty   thick   farther   gather   path   earth
1. If you're _thirsty_ get a drink of water.
2. A pretty, pink house stood a little _farther_ up the walk.
3. The shorter _path_ leads to the river.

sh—shadow   sharp   ashamed   flashlight   crash   rush
1. A _sharp_ knife will cut well.
2. The thief was _ashamed_ of stealing the money.
3. The children had to _rush_ so that they would not be late.

ch—check   choose   orchard   inches   ditch   porch
1. They could _choose_ their best picture to hang up.
2. There were twelve apple trees in the _orchard_ .
3. Mother put a swing on the _porch_ .

wh—whale   whisper   whirl
1. _Whisper_ me your secret so that no one will hear.
2. Fishermen try to catch _whales_ for oil and meat.

---

3. The children who read very well will enjoy stories about holidays other than those included in this unit, for example, *The Egg Tree*, by KATHERINE MILHOUS; *The Fourth of July Story*, by ALICE DALGLIESH; "The Little Cook's Reward," in *Treat Shop*, by ELEANOR M. JOHNSON and LELAND B. JACOBS, pp. 198–201.

4. Help a group of interested children plan to give a simple program for a patriotic holiday. Encourage the children to use their own ideas, guiding and suggesting only when neces-

sary. Make available books of poems, stories, and songs or informational books so that the children will be able to base an original play on historical fact. Have the program performed before the class.

5. Superior readers will be interested in reading about the origins and meanings of various holidays, and in reporting their findings to the class. A list of suggested topics follows:

Finding out about holidays

> Columbus
> Christmas Customs in Many Lands
> The Story of St. Valentine
> The Halloween Story
> The First Thanksgiving
> Washington's Birthday
> Why We Celebrate the Fourth of July

Unit VII · Old, Old Stories

Introducing the Unit

Most third graders revel in folk and fairy tales. The final unit in the book capitalizes upon this absorbing interest and presents favorite traditional tales: "The Cap That Mother Made," a Swedish tale; "The Traveling Musicians," by the Brothers Grimm; "The Lark and Her Young Ones," an Aesop fable; "The Lad and the North Wind," in play form; and a Danish tale, "The Princess Who Always Believed What She Heard." A poem, "Chanticleer," rounds out the unit.

The style of the stories and the comparatively few new words make it possible for the children to read them fluently and with enjoyment. These stories should be read for fun with major emphasis upon plot and the humor of certain situations. They should stimulate interest in wide reading of other traditional stories and acquaint children with their heritage of age-old folk and fairy tales.

To encourage wide reading of traditional stories throughout this unit, the teacher may display pertinent pictures and book jackets on the bulletin board, have on hand many collections of old stories and tales, and obtain many of the suggested records, films, and filmstrips.

Before the children begin to read the stories, find out what they know about traditional tales. Tell them that at one time the only way girls and boys could enjoy stories was by hearing someone tell them, for there were no books. Ask the children whether they had stories told to them before they were old enough to read. Ask individual children to tell some of these stories as they heard them. Call on individuals to tell briefly about their favorite fanciful tale or fable. If the children's experiences with traditional tales are limited, read several to them.

Discussing the theme of the unit

Have the children turn to the table of contents and read the names of the selections in this unit. Encourage discussion of the titles and the possible themes of the stories. Then have them turn to the unit in their books, look at the unit picture, and tell what they think is happening.

Story Pages	Vocabulary New Words	Developing Readiness	Reading the Story		Building Esse	
			Guided Reading	Rereading for Specific Purposes	Comprehension and Study Skills	Word Mea
The Cap That Mother Made 283–291	Anders tassel trade soldiers princess chain	New words are presented in context either written or oral. Children are encouraged to identify new words through comparison with known words and the use of phonetic and context clues.		Reading to plan a story activity	Comprehension Test: associating ideas with story characters (worksheet) Locating information: skimming for details Workbook: 86, organizing ideas for a dramatization	Word Rec tion: using clues to atta words Workbook enriching w meaning
The Traveling Musicians 292–298	musicians thieves			Skimming to find story sequence Preparing to read to an audience	Story Details: associating story events with related characters (worksheet) Critical Reading: using judgment to distinguish between fanciful and realistic material (worksheet) Workbook: 88, reading a picture map; following directions; 89, synonyms and antonyms	Interpreti phrases thre the use of s nyms
The Lark and Her Young Ones 300–302	lark			Reading for enjoyment	Critical Reading: using judgment; evaluating material (worksheet) Sequence: arranging events in sequence (worksheet)	
The Lad and the North Wind 303–309	lad north innkeeper cheese beat			Reading to present a play	Comprehension: testing comprehension skills; main idea; details; drawing conclusions (test) Recognizing sequence (test) Workbook: 91, expressing the main idea of a paragraph, detecting the mood of a situation	Recognizi words with meanings (sheet)
The Princess Who Always Believed What She Heard 310–317	lie princes Claus church			Reading for enjoyment Reading to retell parts of the story	Main Idea and Details: classifying ideas (worksheet) Critical Reading: discriminating between possible and impossible situations (worksheet)	Workbook 93, checkir meanings; ognizing wo multiple m
All-Unit Activities				Skimming the stories of the unit to prove statements Provision for superior readers: reading aloud old riddles	Comparing stories Recording story events (worksheet) Test for Details: recalling story facts in the unit (test) Summing Up: drawing conclusions and making inferences Helping the individual child: group inventory of growth in reading independence	Evaluatio checking ve lary preser the book by the game " ball" Workboo Vocabulary
Summarizing the Book					Critical Reading: evaluating and classifying the stories in the book (worksheet) Checking concepts gained Workbook: 95, summarizing the stories in the book; using the table of contents	

Developing Readiness (full vertical text): Through discussion and exchange of ideas, interest in the story is stimulated and background for understanding is developed. Purposes for reading are reached by the group with the teacher's guidance.

Guided Reading (full vertical text): Silent and oral reading for comprehension and interpretation of story plot, mood, and characterization.

| its and Skills | | | Related Language Experiences | Enrichment Activities |
| Word-Study Skills | | | | |
Phonetic Analysis	Structural Analysis	Syllabication		
ewing silent *k* in words cking new words with *k*	Recognizing compound words Reviewing hyphenated words	Reviewing how double consonant words are divided into syllables	Planning: the unit activities Conversation: talking about relative values Dramatization: dramatizing the story	Co-ordinating Activity: making dioramas Stories in Other Readers Stories, a poem, a song, records, films, and filmstrips
ning the sounds of *ew*	Observing plurals of nouns ending in *f*	Observing vowel sounds and syllables Workbook: 89, recognizing the number of syllables in words	Creative Writing: making animal rhymes Listening: listening to records and interpreting stories and music Discussion: talking about exaggerating	Co-ordinating Activity: modeling animals for the diorama Pantomiming the story Library: comparing different versions of the story Art: illustrating favorite scenes Stories, a poem, music, records, and filmstrips
lling the rule for vowel 'ns g long and short *ea* sheet) gnizing variant sounds kbook: 90, long and vowel sounds		Workbook: 90, reviewing principles of syllabication	Discussion: talking about lessons learned from stories Listening: hearing other fables Dramatization: acting out a fable	Co-ordinating Activity Recording: making a list of Stories Everyone Should Know Stories, a poem, a film, and filmstrips
ewing the consonant di-*th* gnizing three-letter ant blends *thr, str* gnizing silent con-s ing words with silent ants (worksheet)			Discussion: talking about preparations for the play Creative Writing: writing and presenting another old tale Writing: making programs for the play Listening: seeing and hearing "Music Stories"	Co-ordinating Activity Story Hour: reading and telling old stories Excursion: visiting the public library Seeing filmstrips
erving the sound of *au*; ewing *a* before *l, a* be-	Workbook: 92, alphabetizing		Conversation: talking about princesses Creative Writing: creating original stories	Co-ordinating Activity Completing the list, "Stories Everyone Should Know" Enjoying stories and an old rhyme
uation: generalizing vowel digraphs; check-wels influenced by *r* ing silent consonants; ing words with silent ants (worksheet)	Evaluation: reviewing plural forms of nouns, variant forms of verbs	Evaluation: syllabication test	Provision for superior readers: speech: articulating *d, p, t, k*	Culminating Activities: planning and presenting a story hour, a TV show Poetry Review

The Cap That Mother Made

Anders was very proud of the red-and-green cap with a blue tassel which his mother made for him. He refused to part with it, even though a big boy, Nils, offered his jackknife in trade, the princess gave him a chain of gold, and the king himself asked to trade his crown for the cap.

As they read the story, children will discuss the reason for Anders' behavior, and will understand that a simple gift fashioned by hand and given with genuine affection may have greater value to the recipient than more costly material possessions.

Vocabulary

New Words: Page 283, ———; 284, *Anders*, tassel*;* 285, *trade*;* 286, *soldiers, princess*;* 287, ———; 288, *chain*;* 289, ———; 290, ———; 291, ———

Developing Readiness for Reading

Discussing
the unit picture

Meaningful Presentation of Vocabulary. Have the children look at the unit picture on page 283. Say: "The boy in the picture is *Anders*. 'Anders' is a Swedish name and this is a Swedish folk tale. What is Anders wearing on his head?" (*a cap with a tassel*) "Who do you think the people at the table are?" (A king, a *princess*.) "In his hurry to get away Anders has lost something. What is it?" (*a chain*) "Why do you think Anders might be running away? There aren't any *soldiers* chasing him, but he seems to be holding on to his cap. Why might he do that?"

Using context and
phonetic clues
to attack the
new vocabulary

Most children will be able to attack the new words independently either through context or phonetic clues. The known parts of *Anders, tassel, princess,* and *chain* can be easily blended; *trade* follows the rule of the vowel lengthened by final *e*.

Setting Up Reading Purposes. "Let's turn to the story and read the title. Anders' mother had made the beautiful cap for him. Has anyone ever made anything for you? How did you feel about it? Would you ever trade it for something else? Let's read this story to see how Anders felt about the cap his mother had made him, and what adventures he had because of it."

Reading the Story

Guided Reading

Have the children read the entire story silently. Help individuals attack unfamiliar words as needed. Observe the children's reading habits and make note of those who read slowly, those who vocalize as they read, and those who point with the finger. Plan to give them the necessary help at a later time. Concentrate now on reading the story for enjoyment.

After the silent reading, ask: "In what ways did Anders prove that he was proud of his cap? What made Anders feel very sad? What did the princess want to trade for the cap? What did the king offer him? Do you agree with what Anders' brother said about him? How do you imagine Anders' mother felt about him? Would you have acted as Anders acted? Why or why not?"

Reading the entire story silently for enjoyment

Rereading for Specific Purposes

Have all the children in the group listen as one child reads a page orally. Tell them to think, while they listen, whether or not this would be a good story to dramatize, to make into a puppet show, or to make into a moving picture. After each page has been read, lead the children in discussing what could be done with it. Guide them to consider characters, conversation which could be developed from the story, setting, background, and costumes. After the entire story has been read by different individuals, have the children vote as to how to present it for an assembly, a parent group, or another group of children.

Rereading to plan a story activity

Building Essential Habits and Skills

Comprehension and Study Skills

Comprehension Test. To test the understanding of story facts, distribute copies of the exercise on page 432. After

Associating ideas with story characters

the children have finished the exercise, have them read the sentences aloud in the way the character might have spoken them.

Who Said?

The sentences below tell some of the things that were said in the story. After each sentence write the name of the person who was speaking.

Anders	king	Anders' brother
princess	queen	Anders' mother
Nils	soldier	old woman

1. "I'll trade my jacknife for your cap."   <u>Nils</u>
2. "Why don't you go to the king's ball?"   <u>old woman</u>
3. "You have good sense, little Anders."   <u>Anders' mother</u>
4. "He shall come to the ball with me."   <u>princess</u>
5. "You cannot go to the ball. You have no fine clothes."   <u>soldier</u>
6. "Surely, you will trade caps with me."   <u>king</u>
7. "You were a silly goose."   <u>Anders' brother</u>
8. "There isn't a cap in all the world finer than this one."   <u>Anders</u>
9. "You will want to lay your cap down when you eat."   <u>queen</u>

Skimming to find information

Locating Information. To increase the skill of quickly finding and recording story details, give the children the following instructions either orally or on the chalkboard: "On a piece of paper list the names of the people who wanted Anders' cap. Beside each name write the thing that person wanted to trade for it. Use your book to help you spell the names."

Word-Study Skills

Using various aids to word recognition

Word Recognition. To give practice in using a variety of clues to attack new words, have the children (1) locate the words below on the page indicated, (2) read the sentence in which the word appears, and (3) tell how they knew the word (by phonetic, structural, context clues, or a combination of these aids):

Page 284. *present* (initial blend, vowel sounds, context)
pieces (soft *c*)
Page 285. *wearing, shawl* (blending known parts)
enough (context)

Teaching *Finding New Neighbors*

Page 286. *soldiers* (context, blending)
              princess, messenger (blending)
Page 287. *through, thought* (consonant digraphs, blending)
Page 288. *candles, chain* (blending known parts, context,
              analogy)

Phonetic Analysis. To strengthen recognition of silent *k*, write the word *jackknife* on the blackboard. Call attention to the *k* in *knife*. Elicit the fact that it is silent. Ask the children to recall other words with silent *k*, such as *knew, know, knock*. Ask, "In what way are all these words alike?" Expect the response that the silent *k* is followed by *n*. Have the children recall the sound of *k* in such familiar words as *sky, kitten, market, week, blanket, king, silk, shook, kind*. Help the children attack the unfamiliar words *knot, knee,* and *knock* in sentences such as the following:

Margaret went down on one <u>knee</u> to untie the <u>knot</u> in the rope. There was a gentle <u>knock</u> at the door.

Structural Analysis. 1. To review compound words, have the children skim through the story to locate several examples. Have the children write them and circle each part of the compound. (*everyone, jackknife, cannot, doorway, ballroom, himself*)

2. To recall the use of the hyphen in compound words, write on the chalkboard the following phrases: *a red-and-green cap, well-dressed people*. Call attention to the hyphenated words. Recall the use of the hyphen to connect two or more words that express a single idea.

Syllabication. To practice dividing double-consonant words into syllables, write on the chalkboard the following words:

tassel	*nibble*	*slippers*	*peddler*
matter	*puppy*	*bottle*	*chatter*
sudden	*batter*	*pepper*	*pillow*

Ask the children to tell the number of syllables they hear in each word. Have them draw a vertical line through each word to separate the syllables. Call attention to the fact that these words are separated into syllables between the double consonants in the middle of the words. Have the

433   *The Cap That Mother Made (283–291)*

pupils observe the first syllable of each word and note that each one ends in a consonant, that the vowel comes between consonants, and that it has a short sound.

Then write on the chalkboard the words below and have the children copy and divide them into syllables. Have them notice the vowel sound in each first syllable.

silly	*hello*	*butter*	*supper*
office	*village*	*follow*	*pretty*
bunnies	*cellar*	*summer*	*suppose*

Workbook

Pages 86 and 87.

Related Language Experiences

Planning the unit activities

Planning. Discuss with the group which activities they would like to carry on during the reading of this unit. Explain that they will have a good opportunity to become familiar with other old stories; remind them that this is the last unit in the book. Plans such as the following may be made:

Our Plans

Listen to records.

Write group stories.

Have a story hour.

Put on plays.

Make dioramas.

Find old tales.

List our favorite stories.

Little Red
Riding Hood

Brer Rabbit

Conversation. Discuss why Anders' cap was his prized possession. To stress the concept of relative values, recall what Stina Mor wanted more than anything else for Christmas, a letter from her son. Guide the children in talking about other stories in which a person wanted something very much; for example, Bob who wanted nothing so much as to play on the baseball team. Let the children tell about things that they have which they would not want to trade.

Talking together

Dramatization. If the children have decided to make a play or a puppet show of this story, help them to enunciate clearly and to use appropriate tones of voice as they take turns playing the parts. This story may be played in five short scenes—*the home, the street, the king's palace, the ballroom, the home.*

Dramatizing the story

Enrichment Activities

Co-ordinating Activity. Discuss with the children how to plan models of their favorite old-story characters. Show them how to bend wire into various positions. Encourage the children to have their figures show action. Have them cover the wire frames with clay, as shown above, and then with paint. A group may wish to work together on one story, each child modeling one character. If there is enough space in the

Fashioning story characters from clay

The Cap That Mother Made (283–291)

classroom, the completed figures may be exhibited in large, open boxes which have been decorated to provide a background. These should be labeled with an explanatory paragraph.

Should the diorama boxes prove too space-consuming, the figures from each story may be effectively placed along the top of a bookcase or shelf. A mural may be painted by the children and tacked to the wall to serve as a common background for all the figures. Encourage the children to express their own ideas in executing some unifying theme, such as an enchanted forest, a storyland street scene, or imaginary castles.

Reading
independently **Stories in Other Readers.** The children will want to supplement their reading of traditional tales in other readers. This list is suitable for the entire unit.

Down Our Way, by ARTHUR L. BOND and others
"The Fox and His Bag," pp. 210–221

Good Times Today and Tomorrow, by ARTHUR L. GATES and others
"The Dress of Goose Feathers," pp. 245–254

Fun and Frolic, by PAUL WITTY and BARBARA NOLEN
"Wise Animals," pp. 244–272
"Foolish People," pp. 273–303

I Know a Story, by MIRIAM BLANTON HUBER and others

It Happened One Day, by MIRIAM BLANTON HUBER and others

After the Sun Sets, by MIRIAM BLANTON HUBER and others

The New More Friends and Neighbors, by WILLIAM S. GRAY and others
"The Man Who Kept House," pp. 210–217

The New Streets and Roads, by WILLIAM S. GRAY and others
"The Fairy Shoemaker," pp. 260–268
"The Turtle's Race," pp. 269–272
"The Golden Pears," pp. 273–276
"The Second Son's Trip," pp. 277–281
"The Fisherman and His Wife," pp. 287–297
"Mother Hulda," pp. 307–315

Story Caravan, by WILLIAM D. SHELDON and others
"The Real Princess," pp. 45–48
"The Purple Horse," pp. 49–59
"James the Huntsman," pp. 60–77

Enjoying literature
and music **Stories to Enjoy.** *The 500 Hats of Bartholomew Cubbins*, by DR. SEUSS; *Cinderella*, by CHARLES PERRAULT, illustrated by MARCIA BROWN; *East of the Sun and West of the Moon*, by PETER ASBJÖRNSEN; *Giants and Witches and a*

Dragon or Two, by PHYLLIS FENNER; *Golden Goose Book*, illustrated by L. LESLIE BROOKE; *Illustrated Treasury of Children's Literature*, by MARGARET MARTIGNONI; *Once Upon a Time*, by ROSE DOBBS; *Stone Soup*, illustrated by MARCIA BROWN; *Time for Fairy Tales*, by MAY HILL ARBUTHNOT; *Told under the Magic Umbrella*, compiled by The Association for Childhood Education International; *Story and Verse for Children*, by MIRIAM BLANTON HUBER.

A Poem to Enjoy. This is a good poem to learn for choral speaking.

THE FAIRY BOOK

When Mother takes the Fairy Book
    And we curl up to hear,
'Tis "All aboard for Fairyland!"
    Which seems to be so near.

For soon we reach the pleasant place
    Of Once Upon a Time,
Where birdies sing the hour of day,
    And flowers talk in rhyme;

Where Bobby is a velvet Prince,
    And where I am a Queen;
Where one can talk with animals,
    And walk about unseen;

Where Little People live in nuts,
    And ride on butterflies,
And wonders kindly come to pass
    Before your very eyes;

Where candy grows on every bush,
    And playthings on the trees,
And visitors pick basketfuls
    As often as they please.

It is the nicest time of day—
    Though bedtime is so near,—
When Mother takes the Fairy Book
    And we curl up to hear.

ABBIE FARWELL BROWN

The Cap That Mother Made (283–291)

A Song to Enjoy. "When Mother Takes the Fairy Book," in *The First Grade Book,* by LILLA BELLE PITTS.

Records to Enjoy. *Favorite Stories,* 33⅓rpm (RCA Camden); *Cinderella,* 78rpm, 2–10 (Disneyland).

Films to Enjoy. *Sleeping Beauty; Rumpelstiltskin* (EBF), ea 1 reel, 9min, sd, b&w, in FAIRY TALE CLASSICS series.

Filmstrips to Enjoy. These are suitable for the entire unit. TALES FROM GRIMM AND ANDERSEN series: *The Shoemaker and the Elves; The Wolf and the Seven Little Kids; Rapunzel; The Frog Prince; Spindle, Shuttle and Needle; Hans Clodhopper; The Princess and the Pea* (JamHandy), each about 26fr, with captions, color. *Folk Tales and Fairy Tales* (EyeGate), captions, 29fr, color.

Pages 292–298

The Traveling Musicians

The old tale of the donkey, the dog, the cat, and the rooster who set out for the city to become musicians is always a favorite with children. They enjoy the humor ot the animals' frightening the thieves away from the house in the wood, particularly the account of the thief who returned to the house late at night after the animals had established themselves there.

The story should be read for its plot and humor. Children will be amused by the thief's exaggerated account of his night visit to the house, and recall that people are often confused about actual happenings in time of stress.

Vocabulary

New Words: Page 292, *musicians;* 293, ————; 294, ————; 295, *thieves;* 296, ————; 297, ————; 298, ————

Developing Readiness for Reading

Discussing story background

Meaningful Presentation of Vocabulary. Say: "Have you ever heard the stories of 'Rapunzel,' 'Hansel and Gretel,' or

'Snow-White and the Seven Dwarfs'? Did you know that they were written down by two brothers, Wilhelm and Jakob Grimm? These brothers traveled widely and listened to the old stories that people had heard their fathers and grand-fathers tell. They collected all the stories in a book so that everyone could enjoy them.

"The story that we are about to read is called *The Travel-ing Musicians*. What is a musician?" (Anyone who has a talent for making music.) "These musicians traveled from place to place and they made very unusual music. They really used their heads when they saw some *thieves*. Can you tell what thieves are?"

Setting Up Reading Purposes. "Let's read the story 'The Traveling Musicians' to find out just how these musicians used their talents."

Reading the Story

Guided Reading

Have the children find the story title in the table of con-tents and turn to the page on which it begins. Say, "Read the first three pages to find out who the musicians were." After the reading, ask: "Why did they all get together? Where did they decide to stay when night came on?

Pages 292–294

"Read this page to find out what the animals saw in the house." After the reading, ask: "How might they have known that the men were thieves? Were they sure, or did they just think so?

Page 295

"Let us find out the animals' plan to scare the thieves away." After the reading, have different children read orally the sentences that tell what each animal did, interpreting the sounds as best they can.

Page 296

"The animals thought they were safe in their house, but they were mistaken. Finish the story to find out what hap-pened that night." After the reading, discuss the incidents as they actually occurred, and as the thief described them to his friends. Ask: "Why do you think he told such a story? Why were the animals able to win out against several men?"

Pages 297–298

The Traveling Musicians (292–298)

1. Ask the children to skim the story, two pages at a time, to determine the sequence of happenings in each part. Then have them read the groups of sentences below about each pair of pages. Have the sentences in each group numbered 1, 2, 3, to tell the order of events.

Pages 292–293: A donkey set out to become a musician.
<u>1</u>

A cat thought she might do well as a singer.
<u>3</u>

A dog looked very tired. <u>2</u>

Pages 294–295: Four animals went into the forest. <u>2</u>

The donkey saw food on a table. <u>3</u>

A rooster was afraid he would end up in a stew. <u>1</u>

Pages 296–297: Four animals sang together. <u>1</u>

One thief came back. <u>3</u>

Some thieves were frightened. <u>2</u>

Page 298: Four animals never did go to the city.
<u>3</u>

A thief told a strange story. <u>2</u>

The donkey kicked a thief. <u>1</u>

---

2. Have the children reread the story to plan how they might read it aloud to another group of children. They may decide to have one child read the narrative while other children take the parts of the story characters.

Once the plans are made, the children should practice their presentation and discuss ways of improving it before they appear before their audience.

Building Essential Habits and Skills

Comprehension and Study Skills

Story Details. To give practice in seeing relationships, distribute copies of the exercise at the top of page 441. Have a child read the directions aloud and be sure that each child in the group understands them.

Teaching *Finding New Neighbors*

Make a Dy if the sentence is about the donkey.
Make a Dg if the sentence is about the dog.
Make a C if the sentence is about the cat.
Make an R if the sentence is about the rooster.

<u>Dy</u> 1. He was growing old and could no longer work on the farm.

<u>R</u> 2. He told people that the sun would shine on washing day.

<u>C</u> 3. She could no longer catch rats.

<u>Dy</u> 4. He asked three other animals to become musicians.

<u>C</u> 5. She was a good night singer.

<u>R</u> 6. He was afraid that he would end up in a stew.

<u>Dg</u> 7. He could no longer go hunting.

<u>R</u> 8. From the treetop he saw a lighted house.

<u>Dy</u> 9. He peeped in the window because he was the tallest.

<u>C</u> 10. She went to sleep beside the fireplace.

<u>Dg</u> 11. He took a bite out of the thief's leg.

<u>Dy</u> 12. He kicked the thief as he ran across the yard.

<u>Dg</u> 13. The thief thought that he was a man with a knife.

<u>R</u> 14. "Put him in the stew," shouted the ghost.

<u>C</u> 15. The thief was sure that a woman jumped on him.

Critical Reading. To promote the ability to distinguish between fanciful and realistic material, distribute copies of the exercise below or read it aloud to the children. Direct the children to read the paragraphs and to put a *T* before the ones which *could be* true stories and an *M* before those which are make-believe stories.

Using judgment

  <u>T</u> 1. The donkey had worked hard. He was growing old. Soon he would not be able to work so hard. He would stay on the farm and eat. He would still sing "Ee-ah, ee-ah."

  <u>M</u> 2. The donkey sang "Ee-ah, ee-ah." He decided to run away. "Why don't you come with me?" he said to his friend the dog. "We could be musicians."

441   *The Traveling Musicians* (292–298)

T 3. The cat could catch rats. She lived on a farm with her master. She worked for him. At night she would roll up in front of his fire to sleep.

M 4. The cat looked sad and upset. She was in danger. "I do not know how I shall live," she thought. "I can sing. I will run away and be a musician."

M 5. The cat, the dog, the rooster, and the donkey set up housekeeping. They lived together in the little house and were so pleased they forgot about the thieves. They are still there until this very day.

T 6. The cat, the dog, the rooster, and the donkey all lived on the same farm. The farmer was good to them. He fed them every day. They all worked for him and were very happy.

Word-Study Skills

Interpreting phrases

Word Meaning. To increase the children's sensitivity to word meanings, write on the chalkboard the sentences below, which are taken from the story. Have the children read each sentence and suggest another way of saying the underlined phrase or phrases.

He had not gone far when he came upon a dog.
So I ran away, but what can I do for a living?
The dog said he was willing, and they went on together.
The cat was pleased and joined the party.
They saw a rooster crowing with all his might.
"With all my heart," said the rooster.

Learning the sounds of "ew"

Phonetic Analysis. 1. To teach the sounds of *ew*, put on the chalkboard the word *flew*, which appears in the story. Write other *ew* words on the chalkboard, such as *chew*, *blew*, *grew*, *threw*, *drew*, and draw from the children that in these words *ew* sounds like $\overline{oo}$ in *too*.

If the children are ready to make fine discriminations, lead them to observe the difference between the sound of *ew* in *grew* ($\overline{oo}$) and the sound of *ew* in *new* (long *u*). Write on the chalkboard the following list of words and help the children identify the sound of *ew* in each word: *new, blew, grew, mew, knew, flew.*

Structural Analysis. To introduce the plurals of nouns ending in *f* and *fe*, write on the chalkboard the following sentences:

Observing plurals of nouns ending in "f" and "fe"

> *The frightened thief ran to the door.*
> *Some thieves were sitting around a table.*

Have the sentences read aloud. Ask: "Which word means just one person? Draw one line under it. Which word means more than one person? Draw two lines under it. How has *thief* been changed to mean more than one?" Elicit the fact that the *f* is changed to *v* before the addition of *es.*

Write on the chalkboard the words *knife, leaf, calf,* and *wife,* and ask the children to write each word to mean more than one.

For independent practice, have the children use both the singular and plural forms of these words in written sentences.

Syllabication. Write the following words on the chalkboard: *traveling, donkey, rooster, musicians, henhouse, scare, cellar.* Have the children pronounce each word, tap the number of syllables they hear, and tell the number of vowel sounds they hear in the word.

Observing vowel sounds and syllables in words

Workbook

Pages 88 and 89.

Related Language Experiences

Creative Writing. After discussing the story, recall the rhyme on page 298:

Making rhymes

> "Cock-a-doodle-doo!
> Put him in the stew."

Suggest to the children that they make other rhymes beginning with the sounds produced by the animals in the story: Ea-ah, ee-ah; Bow-wow-wow; Mi-aow-ow; Cock-a-doodle-doo.

Listening. The children may want to listen to a recording of this story, *The Raggletaggletown Singers,* retold by Frank Luther.

Listening to records

443   *The Traveling Musicians* (292–298)

A group that enjoys music will like listening to *Cinderella*, a musical play by Prokofiev or to excerpts from a recording of Tchaikovsky's *Sleeping Beauty*. At first let the children just listen to the music. Have them listen once more with their eyes closed and choose a part which they particularly liked. Once they have become familiar with the music, some children may wish to write their own words to one of the passages or express their feelings about the music through creative dance or painting.

Talking together

Conversation. Discuss the thief's exaggerated account of his experience with the four animals. "Do people sometimes exaggerate? Is there a time to tell exaggerated stories? a time to report happenings accurately? Can you give us a good example?"

Enrichment Activities

Modeling animals

Co-ordinating Activity. Have the children model the animals from this story, as well as animal characters from other tales they may have been reading. Encourage interested children to use the clay figures in telling stories during story hour.

Reading another version of the story

Library. Another way of conducting the story hour at this time would be to ask a child to read to the class another version of this story, for instance, *The Traveling Musicians* by Hans Fischer. Encourage the children to compare the story and illustrations and to discuss the differences between the two versions.

Illustrating favorite scenes

Art. Suggest that the children draw or paint illustrations of favorite scenes from the story.

Enjoying other stories, songs, and records

Stories to Enjoy. *The Ugly Duckling* and *Red Rooster*, retold by EDNA BOUTWELL; *Tales from Grimm* and *More Tales from Grimm*, translated and illustrated by WANDA GÁG.

A Poem to Enjoy. Have the children learn the following old rhyme and pantomime it:

> The cock's in the wood pile a-blowing his horn,
> The bull's in the barn a-threshing of corn,
> The maids in the meadows are making of hay,
> The ducks in the river are swimming away.
>
> AUTHOR UNKNOWN

Music to Enjoy. "The Raggletaggletown Singers" and "Susie, Little Susie," in *Singing and Rhyming*, by LILLA BELLE PITTS and others.

Records to Enjoy. *Sleeping Beauty*, told by GUDRUN THORNE THOMSEN (American Library Association); *The Raggletaggletown Singers*, 78rpm (Lutherecord 1001), and *The Ugly Duckling*, 78rpm (Lutherecord 1002), both obtainable from Ginn and Company; excerpts from the Metropolitan Opera recording of *Hansel and Gretel*, 33⅓rpm, 2–12" (Columbia SL-102).

Filmstrips to Enjoy. PRIMARY GRADE STORIES: *Jack and the Beanstalk; Puss in Boots; Cinderella; The Four Musicians; Hansel and Gretel; Rumpelstiltskin* (YoungAmerica). ea about 50fr, with captions, color.

Enjoying filmstrips

Chanticleer

Page 299

Developing Readiness for Listening

This poem should be read after "The Traveling Musicians" for enjoyment of its humor and appreciation of its appropriateness to the theme of the story.

Discuss with the children which animals in the story were the best musicians. Lead them to recall and mimic the rooster's crow, "Cock-a-doodle-doo." Then direct the children to look at the illustrations on page 299 and enjoy the picture.

Ask: "What is the title of the poem? Yes, 'Chanticleer.' Do you know what *chanticleer* means? It is a very old name given to a rooster. It has a pleasing sound, hasn't it? Now close your books and listen while I read the poem."

Reading the Poem

Read the poem aloud. Ask if the children have ever been awakened by a rooster crowing. "Was it daylight? Did you think the crowing was a pleasant sound?"

445

Rereading the Poem

Read the poem again. Then encourage individual children to read it aloud for amusement and appreciation. Ask why they think the poem is appropriate to follow the story they have just read.

Related Activities

Discuss with the children the ideas in this poem, the words and phrases used to describe the rooster (*proud, shakes his comb, shakes his tail*). Repeat the last two lines of the poem and ask the children for their ideas on how the rooster knows the right time to crow. If there is time and interest in the group, talk about sunrises in the city and in the country and about early morning chores.

Have the children turn to the poem and look at the rhyming words. Point out to them that in this poem only the last word of every second line rhymes. Recall that some poems, such as "Home" in the Indian unit, have no rhyming words at all, only a certain rhythm and beauty of sound.

Encourage the interested children in the group to write poems on such subjects as roosters, farms, morning, sunrises, or imaginary talking animals.

Have the children illustrate original poems and stories or some they have enjoyed reading. Suggest that they use bright colors and make their pictures or designs interesting and bold. Exhibit the pictures on both sides of a folding screen, as shown on page 446. This might be set up near the library corner if there is room. Make arrows and signs pointing to the art exhibit and invite other children to see it.

Have a group member comment on the exhibit and write a review of it for the class newspaper.

A Song to Enjoy. "My Rooster," in *Singing and Rhyming*, by LILLA BELLE PITTS and others.

A Record to Enjoy. The children will be amused by "Hens and Roosters," from the *Carnival of Animals*, by CAMILLE SAINT-SAENS (Victor).

The Lark and Her Young Ones Pages 300–302

In this selection the children are introduced to a fable, a short story which teaches a lesson. The lark in this famous old fable helps her young ones learn that if one wants a job done, he must do it himself.

With the teacher's help, children will be able to make application of the fable to their own lives. They will enjoy reading or hearing other fables of Aesop, which are part of their literary heritage.

Vocabulary

New Words: Page 300, *lark*;* 301, ————; 302,

Developing Readiness for Reading

Meaningful Presentation of Vocabulary. Have the children locate the story in the table of contents and read the title aloud. Ask: "How did you know the word *lark*? What do you know about larks?" In the discussion bring out the fact that larks build their nests on the ground.

Unlocking a new word through context clues

447   *The Lark and Her Young Ones (300–302)*

Ask: "Who is the author of the story? Has anyone heard of Aesop before? He was a man who lived more than two thousand years ago and who taught people by telling animal tales called fables. Does anyone know what a fable is? It is a story that teaches a lesson. People told these fables again and again, long after Aesop had died. At last they were written down and printed in books. Since then people have learned many lessons from them."

Setting Up Reading Purposes. "What lesson do you suppose we can learn from a story about a lark and her baby birds? Let's find the story and read it to discover what Aesop is telling us."

Reading the Story

Guided Reading

Have the children read this story orally at sight. Before they begin to read, have them recall their standards for oral reading. Have all books closed except one. As each child in the group finishes reading a designated part, have him show the place to the next child who is to read.

After the reading, ask: "How did the mother lark know that it was time to leave? What lesson does the story teach? Read aloud the sentence that tells what the farmer learned. Can you think of a time when you should do a job yourself instead of leaving it to others?" Encourage spontaneous discussion. Ask: "Is there ever a time when this lesson might not be wise to follow? Why?"

Rereading for Specific Purposes

Have all the children reread the story silently for enjoyment. Ask them to restate the main idea of the story in their own words.

Building Essential Habits and Skills

Comprehension and Study Skills

Critical Reading. To strengthen the ability to evaluate material, distribute copies of the exercise at the top of page 449.

> Read each sentence. If you agree, write <u>Yes</u> in the space. If not, write <u>No</u>.
>
> 1. The lark should not have made her nest in a wheat field. _____
>
> 2. The mother lark should not have left her young ones alone. _____
>
> 3. The young larks should not have told what they heard. _____
>
> 4. Neighbors should help each other. _____
>
> 5. The aunts and uncles should have come at once.
>   _____
>
> 6. The farmers should not have waited for others.
>   _____
>
> 7. The larks should have left their nest as soon as the wheat was ready to cut. _____

After the children have done the exercise, have each sentence read aloud and discussed. Ask the children to give reasons for their answers.

Sequence. To strengthen the ability to recall correct sequence, direct the children to number the sentences below in the order in which the events occurred in the story.

Arranging events in sequence

> | | |
> |---|---|
> | 1 | The lark asked her young ones to listen for news about cutting the wheat. |
> | 2 | The farmer sent his son to ask the neighbors to cut the wheat. |
> | 5 | The lark said, "Uncles and aunts have to cut their own wheat." |
> | 3 | "There is no danger if the farmer waits for the neighbors," the lark said. |
> | 4 | "Run now and call your uncles and aunts," said the farmer. |
> | 6 | The farmer said, "I shall cut the wheat myself." |
> | 8 | The farmer had learned to do his work himself. |
> | 7 | The larks finally flew to a new home. |

Word-Study Skills

Recognizing variant sounds of "ea" and "ai"

Phonetic Analysis. 1. To review vowel digraphs, recall the rule for pronouncing two vowels together: the first vowel is usually long and the second is silent. Illustrate with the words *each, leak, paint, chain.*

Have the children skim the story to find the words which contain these two vowel combinations. Write the words on the chalkboard as the children dictate them. Then have the words pronounced. Underline those which follow the above rule (*wheat, each, leave, wait*) and if the children ask, note the exceptions to the rule (*hear, heard, learned, ready, again, said*).

Hearing two sounds of "ea"

2. To practice two sounds of the digraph *ea*, distribute copies of the following exercise:

Say the four words in each row across to yourself. Cross out the one word in each row that has a different sound of <u>ea</u> from the others.

easy	~~meadow~~	eagle	lead
meat	speak	breathing	~~ready~~
~~treasure~~	squeak	beads	teacher
team	wheat	~~head~~	each
beans	~~breakfast~~	beaver	eat
~~bread~~	leak	leaves	peanut

Recognizing variant sounds of "a"

3. To recall the variant sounds of *a*, list the following words: *cap, lark, came, trade, draw, farmer, family, also, camping, fall, straw, tassel.* Have the children pronounce each word, tell how many syllables they hear, and what sound of *a* they recognize in each word. The words in which *a* has the same sound may be arranged in groups. Children may supply more words to each group as they think of them.

Observe the individual responses to this exercise and arrange extra practice for those children who need it.

Workbook

Page 90.

Related Language Experiences

Conversation. Discuss the main idea of this fable: if you want a job done, do it yourself. Ask, "Can we think of some other stories we have read which teach a lesson?" Discuss such stories as "Christmas with Stina Mor," "The Cap That Mother Made," "Bob Learns to Pitch," and "New Shoes." Applying story concepts

Listening. If possible, obtain a copy of *The Sun and the Wind and Mr. Todd,* by Eleanor Estes and Louis Slobodkin, or read the children other fables by Aesop, such as "The Crow and the Pitcher" or "The Hare and the Tortoise." Have the children listen to the fables, draw the moral from them, and apply them to their own lives. Listening to other fables

Dramatization. Some children will enjoy acting out a fable, such as "The Hare and the Tortoise," for the rest of the group. A storyteller may express the moral at the end. Acting out a fable

Enrichment Activities

Co-ordinating Activity. Continue to encourage wide reading of folk and fairy tales throughout the unit and add clay people, animals, and houses to the diorama. Adding to the diorama

Recording. After the children have read and shared a number of stories—in their textbook, in supplementary readers, in collections of old tales—ask them to think of stories which everyone enjoys so much that they want to recommend them to all children of this age. Start a list of such stories and add other titles as the children continue their wide reading. Try to secure general agreement before placing any new title on the list.

A Story in Another Reader. Ask the children to draw the moral from this fable also.

> *The New Streets and Roads,* by WILLIAM S. GRAY and others
> "The Turtle's Race," pp. 269–272

Enjoying fables
and poems

Stories to Enjoy. *Aesop's Fables; Don't Count Your Chicks,* by INGRI and EDGAR D'AULAIRE.

A Poem to Enjoy. Sensitive children will enjoy this delicate poem.

LARKS[1]

Little larks
With pretty feet,
In the fields
They sit and eat,
Dancing, dancing daintily—
Among the stones
They look about
For tiny seeds
And pick them out,
Dancing, dancing daintily.

ROSE FYLEMAN

Enjoying films
and filmstrips

A Film to Enjoy. *Golden Ax* (EBF), 1 reel, 9min, sd, b&w. An Aesop fable pointing up the moral that honesty is the best policy.

Filmstrips to Enjoy. AESOP'S FABLES: *The Wolf in Sheep's Clothing; The Loud-Mouthed Frog; The Greedy Dog; The Mouse Who Boasted; The Mean Old Elephant; The Lion and the Goat; The Evil Spider* (CurriculumFlms), ea about 23fr, color.

[1]From *Picture Rhymes from Foreign Lands,* by Rose Fyleman. Copyright, 1935, by Rose Fyleman. Published by J. B. Lippincott Company.

The Lad and the North Wind

Pages
303–309

An old Norse tale, here retold in play form, relates how the North Wind blew away some meal which a poor lad was carrying home to his mother. The lad went up the mountain to the North Wind's home, to ask for his bowl of meal. On each of three occasions the North Wind gave him instead magic gifts, the first two of which were stolen from the lad by an innkeeper. With the third magic gift the lad was able to punish the innkeeper and to retrieve his stolen gifts.

After learning to read a story in play form, the children will enjoy presenting the play to another group in the school.

Vocabulary

New Words: Page 303, *lad**, *north**, *innkeeper**; 304, *cheese**; 305, ————; 306, ————; 307, ————; 308, *beat**; 309, ————

Developing Readiness for Reading

Meaningful Presentation of Vocabulary. Write the title *The Lad and the North Wind* on the chalkboard and ask a child to read it aloud. Both new words will be easily unlocked through phonetic analysis.

Write on the chalkboard the names of the characters, as listed on page 303, and have the names read aloud. Give assistance, if necessary, with the compound words *innkeeper* and *storyteller*. Ask: "What is an inn? What kind of work would an innkeeper do? What might a storyteller do in this play?"

Have the children turn to the page on which the story begins. Ask, "What do you notice that is different about the way this story is written?" Explain that they are to read a play. Have the children glance at various pages of the play and observe how the words to be spoken by each character are printed.

Present *cheese* by having the children blend its known parts and use it in a sentence. Present *beat* in a sentence and have a child show that affixing a consonant before *eat* would help unlock the word.

Introducing the story

Other ways of unlocking new words

Setting Up Reading Purposes. Say: "Today's story is another old tale that has been told and retold many times. It is a Norse tale. Who knows where a Norse tale comes from? This is another story of magic, and the North Wind is one of the main characters. Let's read this story to see what the North Wind could have to do with a lad."

Reading the Story

Guided Reading

Pages
303–309 When the children are familiar with the names of the characters in the play, have them read the play silently in preparation for oral reading. Help individual children to attack any words that cause difficulty. After the reading, discuss the play with the children, asking questions such as the following to stimulate thinking and interpretation.

Discussing the story What led the lad to the North Wind's door? Why should the North Wind be the one to help him?

Why did the lad blame the North Wind when his table-cloth and sheep did not perform magically at home?

Why do you think the North Wind finally gave the lad a magic stick?

How would you describe the way the North Wind treated the lad?

Do you think that this is a good play to read to some of our friends? Why?

Let different children take the parts of the story characters and read the play aloud. One child may be the narrator.

Rereading for Specific Purposes

Preparing to present the play Plan with the children what they should do before presenting the play to another group of children and list their suggestions on the chalkboard or on a chart like the one at the top of page 455.

Various children may choose to be stage managers, property men, the storyteller, and the four characters in the play. Each will then reread the story for a specific purpose.

After the rereading, allow time for children to report and discuss their plans and to practice their parts.

Teaching *Finding New Neighbors*

Getting Ready for the Play

Find out what properties we need.

Plan how the stage will look.

Try out for the parts.

Practice reading the play.

Building Essential Habits and Skills

Comprehension and Study Skills

Comprehension. To diagnose difficulties children may have in four phases of comprehension, distribute copies of the exercise below and that on page 456.

Testing comprehension skills

1. If you were to give this story another name, which of these would be best? Make X beside the best name.

Reading for the main idea

    ____ The Magic Sheep
    _X_ The Magic Presents
    ____ No Food

2. Draw a line under each kind of food that the magic tablecloth gave.

Reading for details

gingerbread	cheese	lemonade	squash
honey	sugar	fish	meat
molasses	beans	stew	cakes
hot bread	chicken	carrots	bananas

3. Make X beside the words you think are right.

Drawing conclusions

    Next time the lad will not
    ____ go to the North Wind.
    ____ take presents from the North Wind.
    _X_ show the innkeeper his treasures.

The Lad and the North Wind (303–309)

Put 1 beside the sentence that tells what happened first
in the story. Put 2 beside the sentence that tells what happened next. Proceed in this way with all the sentences.

   _6_ The North Wind gave the lad a stick.
   _3_ The innkeeper took the magic tablecloth.
   _1_ The lad asked the North Wind to give back his
        meal.
   _2_ The North Wind gave the lad a magic table-
        cloth.
   _5_ The innkeeper took the lad's magic sheep.
   _4_ The lad's next present was a magic sheep.
   _7_ When the innkeeper tried to take the stick, it
        beat him.
   _8_ The lad got back all his treasures.

Word-Study Skills

Word Meaning. To give practice in using words that are
spelled the same but have different meanings, distribute copies
of the exercise below. Help the children with any unfamiliar
words.

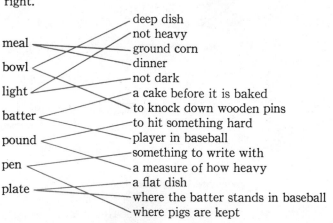

Each word at the left has two very different meanings.
From each word draw lines to its two meanings at the
right.

meal

bowl

light

batter

pound

pen

plate

deep dish
not heavy
ground corn
dinner
not dark
a cake before it is baked
to knock down wooden pins
to hit something hard
player in baseball
something to write with
a measure of how heavy
a flat dish
where the batter stands in baseball
where pigs are kept

Phonetic Analysis. 1. To recall *th,* present on the chalkboard the words below containing the digraph *th* in beginning, medial, and final positions. Have the pupils tell in what position the tongue is placed to produce the *th* sound. Point out that the two letters make only one sound.

Reviewing the consonant digraph "th"

As the children pronounce each word, have them tell whether the *th* is at the beginning, in the middle, or at the end of the word.

north	*thief*	*birthday*	*thought*
these	*cloth*	*mouth*	*their*
nothing	*feather*	*father*	*fourth*
thistle	*thumb*	*thin*	*breathing*

Point out that in *these, feather, father, their,* and *breathing, th* is voiced and that in the other words it is voiceless. Have the children practice pronouncing the words. Help them to hear both the voiced and the voiceless *th.*

2. To review *thr,* present on the chalkboard the words *throw, three, through.* Ask: "With what three letters do these words begin? How many sounds do you hear?" (Two.) Recall that the digraph *th* makes only one speech sound and lead the pupils to observe that *th* and *r* blend together into two sounds before the vowel in each word.

Recognizing three-letter consonant blends "thr" and "str"

Review the consonant blend *str* in *straight, straw, strike,* and *strange.* Lead the children to perceive *three* letter sounds in this blend. Ask them to suggest other words beginning with *thr* and *str.* If necessary, recall previous lessons in consonant digraphs and blends.

3. To develop further the children's awareness of silent letters in certain words, review the silent *k* in *know, knew,* and *knife.*

Perceiving silent letters in words

Continue by writing on the chalkboard the words *ghost, write, lamb, climb.* Ask the children to say the words aloud and to tell which letter they do not hear. Point out the silent *gh* in *sleigh, might, light, high.* If more teaching is necessary, have the children practice orally with other words (*frighten, brought, bought, bright, caught, high*).

To give practice in recognizing silent letters in words, distribute copies of an exercise like that on page 458.

The Lad and the North Wind (303–309)

In your books find these pages. On each page find the words that are asked for and write them in the spaces.

On page 45 find two words with silent *gh* and one with silent *k*.   caught   might   know

On page 136 find two words with silent *gh* and one with silent *k*.   light   brought   knife

On page 157 find three words with silent *gh* and one with silent *l*.   brought   high   frightened   could

On page 242 find three words with silent *gh* and one with silent *k*.   brought   might   light   knew

On page 285 find two words with silent *k* and one word with silent *l*.   jackknife   knew   couldn't

Should some children need more practice in recognizing silent consonants, have them skim the following pages for examples: p. 291 (*could, high, jackknife*); p. 293 (*listen, night*); p. 294 (*bright, night, light*); p. 295 (*walked*); p. 296 (*climbed, through, window*).

Workbook

Page 91.

Related Language Experiences

Discussion. Discuss with the children the preparations for presenting the play to another group in the classroom or to another class in the school. Allow sufficient time for assembling or making the simple properties and for the players to practice reading their parts. Keep the play simple, with the minimum of costumes and scenery.

Creative Writing. A group of superior readers may decide to choose a different old tale to rewrite into play form. Under the teacher's guidance and following the pattern of "The Lad and the North Wind," the children may create their own lines, rehearse in secret, and present their play as a surprise for the rest of the group.

Programs. Some members of the group may write invitations to another class to come to the play. Other members of the group may make a large chart or bulletin board display which will serve as a program. This might include an appropriate drawing, the title of the play, and the list of characters. If they prefer, the children may make individual programs for their guests.

The Lad and the North Wind

A play in one act by Vida Flygarn

Cast

The Lad	Jimmy Hudson
The Northwind	Charles Benton
The Innkeeper	Ray Bonano
The Mother	Kitty Bodky

Listening. Children will enjoy seeing and hearing *Music Stories*, a combination of filmstrips and records published by the Jam Handy Organization. Third graders will appreciate *Peter and the Wolf, Hansel and Gretel*, and *The Sorcerer's Apprentice*. On one side of each 12″, $33\frac{1}{3}$ rpm record, narration is combined with selected musical themes to correlate with individual filmstrip pictures. The reverse side of each record offers a full orchestral rendition of *Hansel and Gretel*, by Engelbert Humperdinck, *Peter and the Wolf*, by Sergei Prokofiev, and *The Sorcerer's Apprentice*, by Paul Dukas.

When the children have grasped the sequence and musical themes and moods of each story, they may listen to the records alone and plan to act out a story or create an original dance to fit one of them.

Enrichment Activities

Co-ordinating Activity. Continue to encourage wide reading of folk and fairy tales as the children read the stories in the unit and add to the display of clay figures in the dioramas.

Listing "Stories Everyone Should Know." Continue to add titles to the list of stories which was begun with the preceding story. Stimulate free discussion so that the children may agree on stories they recommend to other children. The following illustration is one example of a story chart.

Stories Everybody Should Know

Aesop — The Lion and the Mouse

Aesop — The Wind and the Sun

Grimm — The Three Feathers

Grimm — Snow White and Rose Red

Excursion. Let the group plan and take a trip to the public library to select other interesting folk and fairy tales. If possible, arrange with the librarian to tell a story to the group. Plan also to ask the librarian about other stories the children may want to read and consider adding to their list.

Story Hour. During the regular story hour, read aloud stories from the books listed under the first story in this unit. Allow individual children to conduct story hours, either reading or telling old tales.

Filmstrips to Enjoy. *Jack and the Beanstalk, Mr. Vinegar,* 24fr, and *Puss in Boots,* 30fr (CurriculumFlms); *Frog Prince* (JamHandy), 26fr, color.

The Princess Who Always Believed What She Heard

The king was disturbed because his daughter believed everything she heard, and he offered her hand and half his kingdom to anyone who could make her say, "It's a lie." After many princes and wealthy young men had tried without success, Claus, the son of a poor woodcutter, told the princess such tall tales that she finally exclaimed, "It's a lie!"

Children will enjoy the humor of this Danish tale. After reading it, they should discuss the difference between a tall tale, such as Claus told, and a deliberate lie. They should learn also the importance of developing a questioning attitude toward information they hear or read.

Vocabulary

New Words: Page 310, *lie**, *princes*;* 311, *Claus;* 312, ————; 313, ————; 314, ————; 315, ————; 316, *church*;* 317, ————

Developing Readiness for Reading

Meaningful Presentation of Vocabulary. Have the children turn to the table of contents, find the title of the last story in the book, and read it aloud. (*The Princess Who Always Believed What She Heard.*) After writing the title on the chalkboard, ask the children how they might be able to tell that this is an old tale. (It is about a princess. Old stories are often about princesses.) "What unusual thing does the title tell us about this princess?" (She always believed what she heard.) "What is strange about that? Do you always believe what you hear?" Mention briefly stories small children may tell about things they imagine; recall the exaggerated story told by the thief in "The Traveling Musicians."

"What do we call stories that could not possibly happen? Yes, they are often called 'tall tales.' Would you believe one of these tall stories? Why not?" (People tell them for entertainment.)

Talking about the story title

461   *The Princess Who Always Believed What She Heard* (310–317)

"Many years ago, when people had few books, they had to depend on storytellers for their entertainment. Usually there was a storyteller at every king's court; sometimes, too, storytellers traveled from court to court to tell their stories and to collect new ones. These storytellers told all kinds of stories. Some were true, some make-believe.

"A tall tale is an exaggerated story told for fun. When someone tells a tall story and pretends that he is telling the truth, we might call it a *lie*. Well, in the story we are about to read, a king had a daughter who believed all the tall stories and lies that anyone told her."

NOTE. If necessary, help children blend the new word *church* when they come to it in the story.

Setting Up Reading Purposes. "What do you suppose this king and a boy named *Claus* did to cure the princess of believing everything she heard? Let's read the story and find out."

Reading the Story

Guided Reading

"Read the first two pages to find out the king's plan and what happened first." After the reading, ask: "Why did Claus think he could win? What did the king think about Claus's chances? What do you think?

"Read the next two pages to find out what happened when Claus met the princess." After the reading, have one child read orally the tall tale that Claus told, and let another child read the princess's answer.

"Claus next told the princess two tall tales. Read two pages to find out what they were." After the reading, have the two tall tales read aloud. Ask: "Do you think the princess will say that the tale about the eggs is a lie? What would you say?

"Finish the story to find out if Claus finally succeeded." After the reading, discuss Claus's final story. Point out that this story differed from the tall tales in that it was actually an untruth about a person and therefore a deliberate and unkind lie. Ask: "Was it fair for Claus to tell a lie about the king? Why?"

Rereading for Specific Purposes

Have the children reread the parts of this story they liked best. Ask individual children to read their favorite parts aloud and to express their reasons for liking them. Reading for enjoyment

Ask the children to skim Claus's tall tales silently and retell them in their own words. After a child has told his version, encourage the listeners to comment on whether or not each speaker has given the important parts of a story. Reading to retell parts of the story

Building Essential Habits and Skills

Comprehension and Study Skills

Main Idea and Details. To provide practice in relating relevant details to the correct main idea, have the children recall the four tall tales which Claus told the princess, and write the subject of each story on the chalkboard, as follows: Recalling ideas

1. *Cabbages*	3. *Chickens*
2. *Barn*	4. *Church*

Then write the following exercise on the chalkboard or distribute copies of it: Classifying ideas

---

Read each phrase, decide which of the four tall tales on the chalkboard it tells about, and write the number of the right tale before the phrase. Before you hand in your paper, check your answers in the book and correct your paper.

  2   takes a cow years to walk through

  1   twelve workmen hiding from the rain

  3   a boat made of half a shell

  1   washed away by water leaking through a leaf

  4   sitting on the floor wearing a purple nightcap

  1   giant roots and great leaves

  4   no money for the poor

  2   too old to moo

  3   a meal for the whole village

  4   counting money that was covered with dust

  3   piled high as a castle wall

Critical Reading. To strengthen the ability to discriminate between possible and impossible situations, distribute copies of the following exercise to the children:

Write <u>Yes</u> or <u>No</u> after each sentence, and be ready to discuss your reasons for each answer.

What Would You Believe?

Would you believe

1. that the moon is made of green cheese? No
2. everything that anyone told you? No
3. that a princess could be beautiful? Yes
4. that chickens could be as white as snow? Yes
5. that hens can lay eggs as big as boats? No
6. that there are clouds in the sky? Yes
7. that a woodcutter could hang from the moon? No
8. that there could be an organ in a church? Yes
9. that it is fun to tell a tall story? Yes
10. that it is good to tell a lie? No

Word-Study Skills

Phonetic Analysis. To identify the sound of *au*, write on the chalkboard the word *Claus* and have it pronounced. Ask the children what sound the letter *a* has in this word. "With what other vowel is it used?" (*u*) Recall other words which contain these letters, for example, *caught, because.*

Reviewing
the sound of
"a" before "l"
and "w"

Recall the sound of *a* followed by *l*, as in the words *always, stall, ball, small, almost, call,* and *fall.* Then compare the above sound of *a* with the sound of *a* followed by *w*, as in *dawn, paw, shawl, saw, straw.* Help the children to make the generalization that the letters *au* may have the same sound as *a* followed by *l* or *w*.

Workbook

Pages 92, 93, 94, and 95.

Related Language Experiences

Conversation. Encourage spontaneous discussion about the princesses in other tales with which the children are familiar, for example, "The Sleeping Beauty," "The Princess and the Pea," "The Princess on the Glass Hill," and "The Twelve Dancing Princesses."

Talking
about princesses

Creative Writing. Ask the children to make up their own stories about a princess or a prince. They may enjoy working in groups of two or three as they develop the plot of the story. Select one child from each group to tell the original story to the group. Provide large sheets of ruled paper for each group. The stories may be written and illustrated on these and displayed. Encourage children to write large enough so that the stories may be read by the group. Later have the best stories developed into short plays or read at story hours.

Making up
original stories

Enrichment Activities

Co-ordinating Activity. Plan time for the pupils to continue their wide reading of folk and fairy tales and to put the finishing touches on the diorama. Be sure there are some magic touches, fairies, princesses, and castles.

Finishing
the diorama

Completing the List "Stories Everyone Should Know." Discuss the stories which the children have placed on their list. Decide whether any titles should be added to the list or removed from it. Plan to put the list in more permanent form: as an illustrated notebook or a large chart as shown on page 460.

Stories to Enjoy. Other Danish tales in *Thirteen Danish Tales,* by MARY C. HATCH; other tales of princesses, such as *The Plain Princess,* by PHYLLIS McGINLEY; "The Princess and the Pea," in *Fairy Tales and Stories,* by HANS CHRISTIAN ANDERSEN; *Princesses and Peasant Boys,* by PHYLLIS FENNER.

A Poem to Enjoy. Read the children the old verse below and ask them to listen for the impossibilities. Children who enjoy painting might try to illustrate one of the lines. Encourage children to make up their own absurd, tall stories in short sentences such as those in the poem.

> I saw a fishpond all on fire
> I saw a house bow to a squire
> I saw a parson twelve feet high
> I saw a cottage near the sky
> I saw a balloon made of lead
> I saw a coffin drop down dead
> I saw two sparrows run a race
> I saw two horses making lace
> I saw a girl just like a cat
> I saw a kitten wear a hat
> I saw a man who saw these too
> And said though strange they all were true.
>
> OLD RHYME

All-Unit Activities

Culminating Activities

Story Hour. Plan with the children how they may share their pleasure in reading old tales with other groups. Their plans may include:

Reading or dramatizing a story
Showing drawings of familiar stories for others to guess
Making riddles about well-known fairy-tale characters
Planning a TV quiz show about familiar folk and fairy tales

Discussing the Stories. Have the children turn to the table of contents and read the titles and authors of the stories in the unit. Ask them to select their favorites. Recall the stories by asking questions such as:

Which story was the funniest?
In which story did a boy show that he had good sense?
Which story taught the lesson, "Do it yourself"?
In which story did an innkeeper get what he deserved?
In which story were the tallest tales told?

Evaluating Activities

Vocabulary Test IV (Workbook, p. 96). To check the children's ability to recognize the new words of Units V, VI, VII, administer the test below. Direct the pupils to underline the word that you read in each row.

Checking recognition of the new words

1. team	thieves	<u>trade</u>	thief	those
2. prince	<u>plate</u>	program	poor	door
3. pepper	<u>picture</u>	paper	pitcher	<u>pasture</u>
4. <u>discontented</u>	dishes	different	decided	danger
5. <u>molasses</u>	minute	musician	moccasin	<u>messenger</u>
6. <u>wore</u>	world	wear	write	where
7. batter	balloon	Barney	buckle	<u>balcony</u>
8. <u>wharf</u>	wife	wolf	whiskers	whole
9. learns	hurts	<u>hearts</u>	heavy	rats
10. threw	<u>thrown</u>	three	through	throw
11. coming	carrots	camping	company	<u>Columbus</u>
12. sleigh	<u>slippers</u>	sled	Shirley	slide
13. Claus	clown	chain	<u>crown</u>	crow
14. brown	bow	poor	brave	<u>born</u>
15. wetting	<u>writing</u>	winning	working	wishing
16. hurt	howl	hearts	<u>heavy</u>	hunt
17. neighbor	meadow	noise	nearby	<u>newspaper</u>
18. elevator	<u>envelope</u>	enough	engineer	elephant
19. <u>screamed</u>	seemed	squirrel	steamed	secret
20. <u>listening</u>	interesting	nothing	<u>innkeeper</u>	sprinkling
21. lady	lad	lies	ladies	<u>lark</u>
22. <u>luck</u>	lick	lunch	duck	stuck
23. driver	danger	<u>dragon</u>	dancer	Danny
24. build	buckle	purr	<u>burro</u>	burn
25. <u>felt</u>	else	fell	flat	full
26. <u>green</u>	<u>queen</u>	squeak	quiet	guess
27. street	<u>straight</u>	scream	stick	<u>strike</u>
28. chair	<u>church</u>	chain	cheese	Chinese

467

Vocabulary Review. To provide a general check on the new words taught in the book, copy some words, phrases, or sentences on word cards and play the game "Football." Draw a football field on a large piece of paper with sections to represent ten yards each. A cardboard ball is placed on the fifty-yard line. If a child reads a card correctly, the ball is advanced ten yards toward the goal. If a child fails to read the card correctly, the ball is moved back ten yards toward his own goal. When a child crosses the opposite goal line, his score is six. If he reads the next card correctly, he adds one point to his score.

Football may also be played with two teams, each child reading one card. If a child fails, the ball goes to the other team. If the children are able to read most of the words or phrases, give the football to a team each time the other team makes a touchdown so that both teams remain active.

Test for Details. To evaluate recall of story facts in the unit, distribute copies of the following exercise:

Read the first sentence. On the line write the title of the story that sentence tells about. Continue in the same way with the rest of the exercise.

In Which Story Did It Happen?

1. A king wanted to trade caps with a boy.
   <u>The Cap That Mother Made</u>

2. A mother took good care of her babies.
   <u>The Lark and Her Young Ones</u>

3. A magic stick beat a thief.
   <u>The Lad and the North Wind</u>

4. A princess became the wife of a woodcutter's son.
   <u>The Princess Who Always Believed What She Heard</u>

5. Four animals decided to live together.
   <u>The Traveling Musicians</u>

6. A thief thought he saw a ghost on the roof.
   <u>The Traveling Musicians</u>

7. Gold popped from the mouth of a sheep.
   <u>The Lad and the North Wind</u>

Teaching *Finding New Neighbors*

Summing Up. To check the children's ability to think about the stories read, have a discussion about characters in the stories of this unit. Raise questions such as: Drawing conclusions; making inferences

How do you think Anders' mother felt about him? What makes you think so?

What kind of masters did the animal musicians have? Why do you think this?

Do you think the lark was foolish to build her nest in a wheat field? Why or why not?

What kind of person was the North Wind? Tell an incident from the story that makes you think as you do.

Why do you think Claus never told another lie after he had won the princess?

Skimming. In connection with the above exercise, allow the children to skim portions of the stories in the unit and to read excerpts which prove their points. Skimming to prove a point

Test on Syllabication. To test informally the understanding of the number of vowel sounds and the number of syllables, write on the chalkboard the words below which were introduced in this unit. Ask the children to pronounce each word; tell how many vowels they see; how many vowel sounds they hear; and therefore the number of syllables in the word. Recognizing syllables in words

Anders	*trade*	*chain*	*boats*
tassel	*church*	*lark*	*north*
princess	*keeping*	*cheese*	*lie*
beat	*innkeeper*	*lad*	*another*

Phonetic Analysis. To test informally the children's ability to generalize about vowel digraphs, ask the children to point out in the list above the words in which they see two vowels together (*beat, keeping, innkeeper, chain, cheese, boats, lie*) and to state a rule for pronouncing the words. Checking vowel digraphs

Have the children find words in which a vowel is followed by *r*, then state the generalization governing its pronunciation. Recognizing vowels followed by "r"

Structural Analysis. 1. To check the understanding of plural forms of nouns, write on the chalkboard the words at the top of page 470 and have them pronounced. Ask the pupils to go to the chalkboard and change each word to make it mean *more than one*, telling why they write the plural form as they do. Checking plural forms of nouns

469

thief	*soldier*	*wolf*	*lady*
prince	*leaf*	*musician*	*balcony*
knife	*church*	*wife*	*minute*

Reviewing
variant forms
of verbs

2. To review the principle of doubling the consonant before adding *ed* and *ing*, write on the chalkboard the words *mopping, tapped, trapping, stopped, running, stepping.* Have the pupils draw a line around the root word in the larger word and explain how the final consonant is doubled before adding *ing* and *ed.*

Then write *chewed, howled, drawing, beating* and have the pupils discuss the ending of each word and underline its root word.

To review the principle of dropping *e* before adding *ed* and *ing*, have the children add these endings to *scare, decide, trade, write, strike.*

Evaluating
growth

Self-evaluation. Help the children to see their growth in reading. Discuss what they have learned while reading *Finding New Neighbors.* Ask the pupils in what ways they read better now than they did when they finished the second grade. Guide the discussion to cover the growth in word recognition, silent and oral reading habits, comprehension skills, recreational and research reading.

Group Inventories. The inventories on pages 66, 67, 127, and 193 will serve as an informal check on the children's attitudes and general skills in reading and related activities. The chart on page 471 will help to determine the children's growth in reading independence during the year.

Testing
achievement

Achievement Tests. The *Third-Reader-I Achievement Test, Revised Edition,* which accompanies this GINN BASIC READER may be given when the book has been completed. Since this test has been carefully designed for diagnostic purposes as well as for measuring general achievement, individual results should be studied carefully.

Helping the Individual Child

Testing
silent consonants

Help for Slower Readers. To check the children's ability to recognize silent letters, or to give extra practice to the children who need help, distribute the exercise at the bottom of page 471.

INVENTORY OF GROWTH IN READING INDEPENDENCE	Alice	Ben	Mary	Tom
1. Can he follow printed directions?				
2. Does he carry out assignments with a minimum of teacher guidance?				
3. Does he persevere until he finishes an assignment?				
4. Is he able to work co-operatively in a group?				
5. Can he apply information gained in reading to other fields?				
6. Does he make ample use of the room library?				
7. Can he select pertinent information to answer questions?				
8. Is he able to reason about what he reads?				
9. Does he express his ideas succinctly and in logical sequence?				
10. Is he a good listener?				

Say the words below to yourself. In the blank before each word, write the silent consonant or consonants.

gh	thought	l	half	w	write	gh	sleigh
gh	high	h	ghost	gh	bright	t	listen
k	knife	l	talk	gh	caught	b	climb
gh	through	b	lamb	t	whistle	gh	frighten

Try to read these new words. Write the correct word in each blank.

1. Before you go into someone's house, always _knock_ at the door first.

    know   knock   knife   kneel

2. When the bell rings, your mother _answers_ the door.

    answers   asks   awake   adventures

3. Let's _weigh_ the chicken to see how heavy it is.

    tight   fright   weigh   pound

Provision for Superior Readers. Superior readers will be challenged by old riddles and will also enjoy reading them aloud to the group. Collect riddles such as the following, copy them, and keep them in a special envelope. Do not provide the answer until the children have had an opportunity to solve each riddle.

There was a girl in our town,
Silk an' satin was her gown,
Silk an' satin, gold an' velvet,
Guess her name, three times I've telled it. (Ann.)

In marble walls as white as milk,
Lined with a skin as soft as silk;
Within a fountain crystal clear,
A golden apple doth appear.
No doors there are to this stronghold,
Yet thieves break in and steal the gold. (An egg.)

Little Nanny Netticoat,
In a white petticoat,
And a red nose;
The longer she stands,
The shorter she grows. (A candle.)

Old Mother Twitchett had but one eye,
And a long tail which she let fly;
And every time she went over a gap,
She left a bit of her tail in a trap. (A needle and thread.)

Riddle me, riddle me, what is that,
Over the head, and under the hat? (Hair.)

Thomas a Tattamus took two tees,
To tie two tups to two tall trees,
To frighten the terrible Thomas a Tattamus!
Tell me how many T's there are in that. (Two—ThaT.)

AUTHORS UNKNOWN

Articulating
clearly words
ending in "d,"
"p," "t," "k" **Speech.** For practice in clear articulation, write on the chalkboard the words at the top of page 473. Call attention to the final sound in each word. Have the words pronounced, making sure that each child makes the others *hear* the final sound of the word.

Teaching *Finding New Neighbors*   472

lad	*sleep*	*sent*	*back*
wind	*tap*	*hot*	*ask*
stayed	*stop*	*feast*	*trick*
bread	*sheep*	*next*	*took*
behind	*pop*	*just*	*click*
reached	*keep*	*left*	*woke*
end	*drop*	*don't*	*dark*

Summarizing the Book

Discussing the whole book

Overview. To review the stories in the book, direct the pupils to turn to the table of contents. Have the names of the units and stories read. Encourage discussion of the units by asking questions, such as, "Which unit had the most exciting stories? the funniest stories? the most interesting stories? make-believe stories? fables?"

Discuss what a fable, an old story, a tall story, a true story, and a poem are. Let the children suggest definitions and then list their favorites from the book under those headings.

Ask the children to think about the stories and discuss questions such as the following:

Which stories were about wild animals? Which stories were about pets? Tell something that happened. Which animal would you most like to have as a pet? Why? Which stories took place in a city? Which happened in the country? Which stories were about the western part of our country? What would you like to do that some of these children did? In which stories did you learn something that you did not know? Tell about it. Which children would you most like to have as friends? Tell why. What kinds of things would you do when you played together? Which places would you like to visit?

Critical Reading. To help the children evaluate the stories in this book and group them in a new way, distribute an exercise such as the one on page 474. When the children have finished and have had time to think about the second part of each question, discuss the questions with them and the reasons for their answers. Allow for varying answers if the reasoning behind them is logical.

Thinking about stories read

Do You Remember?

Underline the titles that answer the first question in each box. Be ready to answer the second question later.

In which stories did animals play tricks? What tricks did each play?

Baby Bears	New Moon and the Dragon
Blue Cornflower	The Chimpanzee That Mopped
Maggie the Magpie	the Floor
Big Barby	The Friendly Ghost

In which stories did people help someone? How?

Bob Learns to Pitch	He-Who-Thinks-Well-and-Runs-
New Shoes	Quickly
Billy Tigertail	Strange Friends
The Boy Who Believed	El Burrito
	Christmas with Stina Mor

In which stories did people have problems? How did they solve them?

Barney on TV	Bob Learns to Pitch
The Valentine Box	El Burrito
How Percival Caught the Tiger	Blue Cornflower

In which stories were people afraid of something at first? What did they do about it?

A Dog of His Own	He-Who-Thinks-Well-and-
Big Barby	Runs-Quickly
Teeny and the Tall Man	The Friendly Ghost
Helping Hilda	Cowboys Are Brave

Poetry Review. Review with the children the poems that they enjoyed most, both in the Reader and in the Manual. Encourage individual children to recite poems they have memorized. Have choral readings of the poems that lend themselves to this activity. Help children complete and exhibit the poetry booklets of both favorite and original poems which they have compiled.

New Concepts. To check the understandings the children have gained through reading these stories, have them discuss what new neighbors they have met while reading this book. Let each child give a short talk, telling which character was his favorite neighbor and why.

Let the children play a game to review the story characters. Write on individual cards names such as Big Barby, Teeny, Hilda, Percival, Azor, Dancing Cloud, New Moon, Joey, Anna and Peter, and put them in a box. One child may "pull" a card, read, and call the name. He may choose someone to tell about the character. If no one can tell about it, the one who does the pulling may have another card. The names of the unknown characters may be written on the chalkboard. Provide time for the children to locate the unknown characters in the text.

Recalling stories and checking concepts gained

V

Index of Word-Study Skills

Outlining the Program
Objectives of: 49–51
Step in lesson plan: 60–61
Vertical program of: 20–24

Phonetic Analysis of Words
Consonants, developing auditory and visual recognition of
consonant blends: review of two-letter blends, 79–80, 406; *sp, tw,* 95; *cl, sw,* 152; *sl, st, sp, sm, sn,* 204; *qu,* 373–374; three-letter blends, *spr, str,* 95; *spr, scr, spl, str, thr,* 204; *thr, str,* 457
consonant digraphs: *ch, sh,* 119, 242, 424; *th* (voiced), 119, 457; *th* (voiceless), 119, 457; *sh, ch, ck* (final), 242; *kn,* 385, 433, 471; *wh,* 374, 424; *th, sh, ch, wh,* attacking new words with, 424
double medial: 330–331, 433, 434
silent: *gh, h, k, l, w,* 385; *g,* 386; *k,* 433; *k, b, gh* (review), 457; test, 471
variant sounds of: hard and soft *c,* 226, 285, 307; hard and soft *g,* 386
worksheets and independent exercises: 90, 152, 307, 424, 471
Vowels, developing auditory and visual recognition of
digraphs: definition of, 160; long and short *oo,* 142–143, 218; *ui,* 143; *ai, ea, ee, oa,* 160, 353, 374, 469; long and short *ea,* 160, 301, 338, 450; in syllables, 387, 420; exceptions, 301, 450; *ow* as in *throw,* 354
diphthongs: definition of, 284; *oi, oy,* 284; sounds of *ou,* 284, 301–302, 363; in new words, 302; *ow* as in *cow,* 354, 363
double vowels: see *digraphs*
long vowels: review of, 102, 103, 226, 251, 307; *y,* 102, 108–109; *a,* 170, 450, 464; *e,* 346; *i,* 216, 225, 345; *o,* 176–177, 338; *u,* 109; tests, 251, 307
silent vowels: 126, 160, 353
short vowels: review of, 102; *y,* 102, 103; *a,* 170, 450, 464; *e,* 346; *i,* 216, 226, 345; *u,* 293–294; tests, 251, 307; short vowel phonograms, 126
variant sounds of: *a,* 170, 450, 464; *a* followed by *l,* 464; *a* followed by *w,* 170, 464; *i,* 216–217, 345; *o,* 176–177; tests, 251, 307
worksheets and independent exercises: 103, 109, 176–177, 363, 413, 450

review of principles of dropping final *e* and doubling consonant before *ed* and *ing*: 205–206, 320–321, 470

Worksheets and independent exercises: 82, 154, 171, 179, 294, 302, 308, 309, 321, 339, 361, 386

Syllabication

Division of words into syllables: 272, 330–331, 362, 414, 433–434, 443

Division of words with double medial consonants: 330–331, 362, 433–434; deriving principle that the first of the two consonants belongs with the first syllable, and the second consonant with the second syllable, 330–331

Syllabic units: *a*, 271, 362, 413–414; *be*, 271, 362, 413–414; *un*, 413–414

Syllable as a word part containing one vowel sound: 206–207, 218, 227, 229; deriving principle that a syllable is a part of a word containing one vowel or speech sound, 233–234; test, 249–250

Syllables in words, recognizing: 249, 250, 271, 354, 362, 387, 407, 420, 443; tests, 307, 354, 469

in words with digraphs, 271, 387; test, 420

in words of two syllables ending in *e*, 412–413, 420

Worksheets and independent exercises: 249–250, 272, 362, 413, 414, 420

Alphabetizing

Alphabetical order:

meaning of, 171

arranging words in, 171–172, 248, 264, 346, 414

game, 407; test, 248

filling gaps in sequence, 263, 374

rearranging letters in sequence, 171, 248, 374

seeing words in relation to their place in the alphabet, 179, 263

Worksheets and independent exercises: 179, 248, 414

Methods of Using Word Analysis, applying phonetic and structural attack on new words

Analogy, using: 126, 218, 280, 433

Consonants and phonetic parts, blending: 143, 150, 152, 170, 177, 204, 242, 262–263, 280, 285, 302, 334, 386, 393, 402, 424, 430, 432, and whenever individual word attack is used

Context clues, using to check meaning of word analysis: 109, 170, 177, 218, 248, 263, 270, 272, 280, 293, 294, 302, 308, 321, 327, 338, 361, 374, 386, 397, 424, 432–433, and in every exercise where word analysis is used

Root words, identifying: *ly*, 144, 170–171, 386; *er*, as agent, 339; *er*, *est*, 262, 263, 309, 354; *ing*, 170, 320, 321; *ed*, 321

Phonetic elements, applying: 126, 143, 170, 177, 204, 218, 242, 262–263, 280, 293, 294, 302, 317, 321, 374, 386, 424, 432–433, 458, 464, and whenever individual word attack is used

using phonograms: 90, 126, 149–150, 200, 214, 223, 239, 259, 268, 334, 393

Structural analysis, using: 78, 144, 149–150, 154, 171, 179, 201, 202, 204–206, 223,

242, 262–263, 293, 294, 302, 317, 320–321, 327, 345, 361, 470, and whenever individual word attack is used

Syllabication: naming vowel sounds in syllables, 206–207, 218, 227, 233–234, 271, 387, 412–413, 420; using syllabication skills to pronounce unfamiliar words, 271–272

Vowel principles as helps in unlocking new words, using: 160, 170, 177, 226, 280, 290, 402, 430, and whenever individual word attack is used

Worksheets and independent exercises: 109, 152, 171, 177, 179, 272, 294, 309, 321, 361, 424, 458

Extending and Enriching Word Meaning

Context clues, using: 78, 114, 140–141, 157, 166, 200, 229–230, 248–249, 270, 293, 301, 308–309, 320, 327, 334, 353, 397–398, 424, and in every exercise where word analysis is used

Definitions of words, finding: 159–160, 169, 203–204, 270, 308–309, 330, 337, 345

Descriptive language: appreciating, 108, 142, 189, 372–373; action verbs, 231, 319–320, 363; proper adjectives, 353

Multiple meanings of words, understanding: 94, 293, 456

Phrase and sentence meaning: 142, 284, 442

Word relationships, recognizing:
classifying, 78–79, 142, 152, 353, 359, 423; test, 249
antonyms, 101, 118, 232, 373, 413
homonyms, 301, 396
synonyms, 216, 373, 413

Worksheets and independent exercises: 79, 102, 142, 169, 216, 232, 248, 301, 320, 330, 373, 396, 413, 423, 424, 456

Cumulative Vocabulary
for the First and Second Grades
and Third Reader, Level I

NOTE: The number 1 after a word indicates that it was introduced at the first-grade level; the number 2, at the second-grade level; and the number 3, in the Third Reader, Level I.

a[1]
Abel[2]
about[1]
above[3]
across[1]
afraid[2]
after[1]
afternoon[3]
again[1]
against[3]
ahead[2]
airplane[1]
all[1]
alligator[3]
almost[3]
alone[3]
along[2]
always[2]
am[1]
Ambrose[3]
America[3]
Americans[3]
an[2]
and[1]
Anders[3]
Andrew[3]
Andy[2]
angry[3]
animal[2]
Ann[2]
Anna[3]
announcer[2]

any[2]
apartment[2]
apple[1]
apron[3]
are[1]
arms[3]
around[1]
arrow[3]
as[1]
asked[2]
at[1]
ate[1]
aunt[1]
awake[3]
away[1]
Azor[3]

baby[1]
back[1]
bad[3]
bag[1]
baker[2]
balcony[3]
ball[1]
balloons[1]
banana[3]
bang[2]
Barby[3]
bark[2]
barn[1]
Barney[3]
baseball[2]

basement[2]
basket[1]
batter[3]
be[1]
beads[3]
beans[2]
beanstalk[2]
bear[1]
beat[3]
beautiful[2]
beaver[2]
because[2]
bed[2]
bee[1]
been[2]
before[2]
began[2]
behind[2]
believe[3]
bells[2]
below[3]
belt[3]
Ben[1]
best[2]
better[1]
Betty[1]
bicycle[1]
big[1]
Bill[2]
Billy[1]
bird[2]
birthday[1]

bite[3]
black[1]
blanket[3]
blew[2]
blocks[2]
blow[2]
blue[1]
boat[1]
Bob[2]
body[3]
book[1]
boots[3]
born[3]
bottle[3]
bought[2]
bounce[2]
bow[3]
bowl[2]
bow-wow[1]
box[1]
boys[1]
branch[3]
brave[3]
bread[1]
break[2]
breakfast[2]
breathing[3]
brick[3]
bright[2]
bring[1]
brook[1]
brothers[2]

brought[2]
brown[2]
bucket[3]
buckle[3]
buffalo[3]
bugs[2]
build[1]
bump[1]
bunny[1]
burn[2]
burro[3]
bus[1]
Bushy[2]
business[3]
busy[2]
but[1]
butter[2]
button[1]
buy(ing)[2]
buzzed[1]
by[1]

cabbage[1]
caboose[2]
cage[2]
cake[1]
call[1]
called[1]
came[1]
camp[3]
can[1]
candle[1]
candy[2]
cannot[1]
canyons[2]
cap[3]
car[2]
care[2]
carrot[3]
carry[3]
cart[2]
Casey[2]
castle[2]
cat[1]
catch[1]
caught[3]
cave[3]
cellar[2]
chain[3]
chair[1]

chatter(ed)[2]
cheese[3]
cherry[1]
chew[3]
chick[1]
chicken[3]
children[1]
chimney[2]
chimpanzee[3]
Chinese[3]
chipmunk[2]
chocolate[3]
Chris[2]
Chrissie Orne[3]
Christmas[2]
church[3]
circle[3]
circus[2]
city[2]
Claus[3]
cleaning[2]
click[2]
cliff[3]
climbed[2]
clinkety-clank[1]
clop[3]
close[3]
cloth[3]
clothes[2]
cloud[3]
clown[2]
cluck[3]
coat[2]
cock-a-doodle-doo[2]
cockatoo[3]
cold[1]
color[1]
colt[3]
Columbus[3]
come[1]
coming[2]
Company[3]
co-pilot[2]
corn[1]
corner[2]
cotton[2]
could[1]
count(ed)[2]
country[2]
cover[2]

cowboy[1]
coyote[3]
crawl[2]
cried[2]
crow[2]
crown[3]
crying[1]
cubes[3]
cubs[2]
cup[2]
curtains[3]
cut[2]

dad[3]
Daisy[3]
dance[1]
danger[3]
Danny[3]
dark[2]
David[2]
Dawn[3]
day[1]
decide[3]
deer[2]
Dick[1]
did[1]
different[2]
dig[2]
dinner[1]
discontented[3]
dishes[2]
do[1]
Doc[3]
doctor[3]
does[2]
dog[1]
dollar[2]
done[2]
donkey[2]
door[2]
dot[2]
down[1]
dragon[3]
dream[2]
dress[1]
drinking[2]
driver[2]
drop[1]
drum[1]
dry[2]

duck[1]
dust[3]

each[2]
eagle[3]
ear[1]
earn[2]
east[3]
easy[3]
eat[1]
Ebenezer[2]
edge[3]
eggs[1]
El Burrito[3]
elephant[2]
elevators[2]
Ella[3]
else[2]
empty[2]
end[3]
engine[2]
enough[2]
envelope[3]
even[3]
ever[2]
every[2]
express[2]
eyes[3]

face[2]
fall[2]
family[2]
far[2]
farm[1]
farmer[2]
fast[1]
faster[1]
father[1]
feast[3]
feather[1]
feed[3]
feel[3]
feet[3]
fell[2]
fellow[2]
felt[3]
fence[1]
field[2]
filled[3]
find[1]
fine[2]

finger[3]
finish[3]
fire[1]
firecrackers[3]
first[2]
fish[1]
five[2]
flag[3]
flash[2]
flat[2]
flew[2]
flies[2]
Flip[1]
floor[2]
flour[2]
flower[1]
fly(ing)[2]
follow[2]
food[2]
foot[1]
for[1]
forest[3]
found[1]
four[1]
fourth[2]
fox[1]
Fred[1]
fresh[3]
friend[2]
frighten[3]
frisky[1]
frogs[1]
from[1]
front[2]
Frost[3]
fruit[2]
full[3]
fun[1]
funniest[2]
funny[1]
furnace[2]

game[2]
garden[1]
gardener[2]
gasoline[2]
gate[2]
gave[2]
gentle[3]
get[1]

ghost[3]
giant[2]
ginger[2]
giraffe[3]
girls[2]
give[1]
glad[2]
glasses[3]
glove[2]
go[1]
goat[1]
gobble[1]
going[1]
goldfish[2]
gone[1]
good[1]
good-by[1]
goose[2]
got[2]
grandfather[2]
grandmother[2]
grandstand[3]
grass[2]
gray[2]
great[2]
green[1]
grew[2]
groceries[1]
ground[2]
grow[2]
Gruff[3]
guess[1]

had[1]
hair[2]
half[3]
hall[2]
Halloween[3]
hammer[2]
hand[2]
hang[3]
happen(ed)[2]
happy[1]
hard[3]
harp[2]
has[1]
hat[1]
hatch[3]
have[1]
hay[2]

he[1]
head[2]
hear[1]
heard[2]
heart[3]
heavy[3]
helicopter[2]
hello[3]
help[1]
hen[1]
her[1]
herd[3]
here[1]
hide[1]
high[2]
Hilda[3]
hill[1]
him[1]
himself[2]
his[1]
hit[3]
hold[2]
hole[2]
Hollyberrys[2]
home[1]
honey[1]
honked[2]
hoppity-hop[1]
Hoppy[2]
horn[2]
horse[2]
hospital[3]
hot[2]
house[1]
how[1]
howl[3]
hungry[2]
hunter[3]
hurry[1]
hurt[3]

I[1]
ice cream[1]
if[2]
I'll[2]
important[3]
in[1]
Indian[3]
innkeeper[3]
interest[3]

into[1]
is[1]
it[1]
Iva[3]

Jack[1]
Jane[3]
jar[3]
Jean[2]
Jerry[2]
jet[2]
jingle[1]
job[2]
Joe[2]
Johnny[2]
joins[2]
Josephine[3]
Juan[3]
Judy[3]
Julie[3]
jumped[1]
jungle[3]
just[1]

keep[2]
kick[3]
kind[2]
king[2]
kitchen[2]
kitten[1]
knew[2]
knife[3]
know[1]

lad[3]
ladder[2]
ladies[3]
lake[2]
lamb[1]
land[2]
lark[3]
Larry[3]
last[2]
late[3]
laughed[1]
lay[2]
lazy[2]
leader[3]
leak[2]
learn[1]
leaves[2]
left[2]

leg[3]
lemonade[3]
less[3]
let's[1]
letter[1]
lick[3]
lie[3]
lift[3]
light[2]
like[1]
lines[3]
lions[2]
listened(ing)[2]
little[1]
live(s, d)[2]
living[2]
load(ed)[2]
log[2]
long[2]
look[1]
looked[1]
lost[1]
loud[2]
low[2]
luck[3]
lumber[2]
lunch[2]

machine[2]
Mac's[1]
made[2]
Maggie[3]
magic[3]
magpie[3]
mailbox[2]
make[1]
man[1]
many[2]
Margaret[3]
market[3]
Mary[1]
matter[2]
may[1]
me[1]
meadow[3]
meal[3]
meat[3]
medicine[3]
men[2]
merry[2]

messenger[3]
met[1]
mew[1]
might[2]
Miguel[3]
Mike[2]
milk[2]
mill[1]
mind[3]
minute[3]
miss[1]
mitten[1]
moccasins[3]
molasses[3]
money[1]
monkey[1]
moo[2]
moon[3]
mop[3]
more[2]
morning[2]
most[2]
mother[1]
mountains[2]
mouse[1]
mouth[2]
moved[2]
Mr.[1]
Mrs.[1]
much[2]
mud[3]
muff[1]
Mulligan[2]
musician[3]
must[1]
my[1]

name[2]
Nan[1]
nearby[2]
nearer[2]
neck[3]
need[2]
neighbors[2]
nest[3]
never[1]
new[1]
newspaper[3]
next[1]
nibbles(d)[2]

night[1]
Nils[3]
no[2]
noise[1]
north[3]
nose[1]
not[1]
nothing[1]
now[1]
nuts[2]

of[1]
off[2]
oh[2]
oil[2]
old[1]
on[1]
once[2]
one[1]
only[3]
open(ed)[2]
or[2]
organ[1]
Oscar[2]
other[1]
our[2]
out[1]
over[1]
owl[2]
own[2]

package[3]
paint[1]
pan[1]
pancake[1]
paper[2]
parade[2]
park[2]
part[3]
party[1]
past[2]
paste[2]
pasture[3]
Pat[1]
Patsy[1]
paw[2]
pay[2]
peanut[2]
peddler[3]
peep[2]
Peggy[3]

pen[3]
pencil[3]
people[2]
Pepper[3]
Percival[3]
Peter[2]
pets[1]
picked[2]
picket[2]
picnic[1]
pictures[2]
pie[2]
piece[3]
Piffles[2]
piles[2]
pillows[3]
pilot[2]
pink[2]
pipe[2]
pitch[3]
place[2]
plant[1]
plate[3]
play[1]
please[1]
pocket[1]
Polaski[3]
pole[1]
policeman[2]
pond[2]
pony[1]
poor[3]
pop[1]
post office[3]
postman[1]
postmaster[3]
pot[3]
potatoes[3]
pound[3]
prairie[3]
prayer[3]
present[3]
pretty[2]
prince[3]
princess[3]
Pringle[3]
prize[2]
program[3]
promise[3]
proud[3]

puddle[1]
pull(ed)[2]
puppies[2]
puppy[2]
purple[2]
purr[3]
push[3]
put[1]

quack[1]
queen[3]
quick[2]
quiet[2]

rabbit[1]
raccoon[2]
race[1]
radio[2]
rain[1]
rain-maker[2]
ran[1]
ranch[2]
rats[3]
rattle[2]
rattlety-bang[2]
reach[2]
read[2]
read (past)[3]
ready[1]
real[2]
really[3]
red[1]
remember[3]
rhymes[2]
ride[1]
right[2]
ring[1]
river[2]
road[2]
roar[2]
robin[2]
rock[3]
rode[2]
rodeo[3]
rolled[1]
roof[2]
room[2]
rooster[1]
roots[3]
rope[2]
round[2]

Rover[3]
rows[2]
rubbers[2]
rumble[3]
run[1]
running[2]

sad[2]
said[1]
sailboats[2]
salad[2]
same[2]
sand[2]
sang[1]
sat[1]
Saturday[2]
save[3]
saw[1]
say[2]
scare[3]
scat[1]
school[1]
scream[3]
scrub[3]
sea[2]
seat[3]
secret[2]
see[1]
seeds[2]
seem[3]
seen[2]
seesaw[1]
sell[2]
Selma[3]
send[3]
sense[3]
sent[3]
set[3]
seven[1]
shall[1]
shawl[3]
she[1]
shed[2]
sheep[2]
shell[3]
shiny[2]
ships[3]
Shirley[3]
shoe[2]
shoemaker[2]

shook[3]
shoot[3]
shop[2]
shopkeeper[2]
shore[2]
short[2]
shot[3]
should[3]
shoulder[3]
shouted[2]
shovels[2]
show[2]
sick[3]
side[1]
sign[2]
signal[3]
silk[2]
silly[3]
silver[2]
sing[1]
singers[2]
sit[2]
six[3]
skin[3]
sky[2]
sled[1]
sleep[1]
sleigh[3]
slid[3]
slide[3]
slippers[3]
slow[3]
small[2]
smart[3]
smell[2]
smoke[2]
Snapp[2]
sneeze[3]
sniff[3]
Snipp[2]
Snook[3]
snow[1]
snowman[1]
snowplow[3]
Snurr[2]
so[1]
sofkee[3]
soft[2]
soldiers[3]
some[1]

something[1]
song[2]
Sonny[2]
soon[1]
sorry[3]
sound[2]
soup[2]
speak[3]
Speckles[3]
spend[2]
spider[3]
splash[1]
spoon[3]
spot[3]
spring[2]
sprinkler[1]
squash[2]
squeak[3]
squirrel[1]
stairs[2]
stall[3]
standing[2]
starfish[2]
start(ed)[2]
station[2]
stay[1]
steam[2]
step[1]
stew[3]
stick[2]
still[2]
Stina Mor[3]
stirred[2]
stone[2]
stood[3]
stool[3]
stop[1]
stopped[2]
store[1]
stories[2]
storm[2]
story[1]
stove[2]
straight[2]
strange[2]
straw[3]
street[1]
strike[3]
strong[3]
stuck[3]

such[2]
suddenly[3]
sugar[3]
suits[2]
summer[2]
sun[1]
supper[2]
suppose[2]
sure[3]
surprise[1]
Susan[1]
swallow[3]
sway[3]
sweet[3]
swift[3]
swim[2]
swing[3]
swish[3]

Tabby[2]
table[2]
tail[2]
take[1]
talk(ing)[2]
tall[2]
tap[3]
tape[2]
tassel[3]
teacher[3]
team[3]
Teddy[3]
Teeny[2]
telephone[1]
tell(ing)[2]
tents[2]
than[1]
thank[1]
that[1]
that's[2]
the[1]
their[2]
them[2]
then[1]
there[1]
these[2]
they[1]
thief[3]
thieves[3]
thin[3]
think[1]

this[1]
thistle[2]
those[3]
thought[2]
three[1]
threw[2]
through[2]
throw[2]
thrown[3]
thud[3]
thumb[2]
thump[2]
ticket[2]
tied[2]
tiger[3]
Tilly[3]
time[1]
Timothy[2]
tink-tinkle[1]
tiny[2]
tip[2]
tire[3]
to[1]
Toddle[2]
together[2]
told[2]
Tom[1]
tomorrow[1]
Tony[2]
too[1]
took[1]
top[2]
touch[3]
toward[3]
town[2]
toy[1]
track[2]
tractor[1]
trade[3]
trail[3]
train[1]
tra-la-la[2]
trap[3]
traveler[2]
treasures[2]
tree[1]
trick[2]
tried[2]
trip[2]
trotted[2]

truck[1]
trunk[3]
Tumble[3]
turkey[1]
Turners'[2]
turning[2]
turquoise[3]
turtle[1]
TV[2]
twelve[3]
twins[2]
two[1]

uncle[1]
under[2]
understand[3]
until[2]
up[1]
us[1]
use[2]

valentine[3]
vegetables[3]
very[2]
village[3]
visiting[2]

wagon[1]
waited[2]
walk[1]
walked[1]
wall[2]
want[1]
wanted[1]
warm[2]
was[1]
washing[2]
watched[2]
water[1]
waved[2]
way[2]
we[1]
wear[3]
wee[2]
week[3]
well[2]
went[1]
were[1]
west[3]
wet[2]
wharf[3]

what[1]
wheat[1]
wheels[2]
when[2]
where[1]
which[3]
while[2]
Whiskers[3]
whistle[3]
white[1]
who[1]
whole[3]
why[2]
wide[3]
wife[2]
wild[3]
will[1]
win[1]
wind[2]
window[1]
wing[3]
winter[2]
wishing[2]
with[1]
woke[3]
wolf[2]
woman[1]
women[3]
wonderful[1]
Woodfin[3]
woods[2]
word[3]
wore[3]
work[1]
worked[1]
world[2]
would[2]
write[3]
yard[2]
year[3]
yellow[1]
yes[1]
you[1]
young[3]
your[1]

Zeke[2]
Zipp[3]
zoo[3]
zoom[1]

485

VII

Bibliography for Teachers

TEACHING READING

ALMY, MILLY C. *Children's Experiences Prior to First Grade Reading* and *Success in Beginning Reading*. Bureau of Publications, Teachers College, Columbia University, 1949.

ANDERSON, I. H., and DEARBORN, W. F. *The Psychology of Teaching Reading*. The Ronald Press Company, 1952.

ARTLEY, A. STERL. *Your Child Learns to Read*. Scott, Foresman and Company, 1953.

BETTS, EMMETT A. *Foundations of Reading Instruction*. American Book Company, 1957.

BOND, G., and TINKER, MILES A. *Reading Difficulties: Their Diagnosis and Correction*. Appleton-Century-Crofts, Inc., 1957.

BOND, G., and WAGNER, E. B. *Child Growth in Reading*. Lyons and Carnahan, 1955.

BURROWS, ALVINA T. *What about Phonics?* Bulletin No. 57. The Association for Childhood Education International, 1951.

BURTON, WILLIAM H., and others. *Reading in Child Development*. The Bobbs-Merrill Company, Inc., 1956.

CARTER, H. L. J., and McGINNIS, D. J. *Learning to Read—A Handbook for Teachers*. McGraw-Hill Book Company, Inc., 1953.

Department of Elementary School Principals. *Reading for Today's Children*, Thirty-fourth Yearbook. The National Education Association of the United States, 1955.

DOLCH, EDWARD. *Methods in Reading*. The Garrard Press, 1955.

DOLCH, EDWARD. *Teaching Primary Reading*, 2nd ed. The Garrard Press, 1950.

DURRELL, DONALD D. *Improving Reading Instruction*. World Book Company, 1956.

GATES, ARTHUR I. *The Improvement of Reading*, 3rd ed. The Macmillan Company, 1947.

GRAY, L., and REESE, D. *Teaching Children to Read*, 2nd ed. The Ronald Press Company, 1957.

GRAY, WILLIAM S. *On Their Own in Reading*. Scott, Foresman and Company, 1948.

HARRIS, ALBERT J. *How to Increase Reading Ability*, 3rd ed. Longmans, Green & Company, Inc., 1956.

HESTER, KATHLEEN B. *Teaching Every Child to Read*. Harper & Brothers, 1955.

HILDRETH, GERTRUDE. *Readiness for School Beginners*. World Book Company, 1950.

McKEE, PAUL. *The Teaching of Reading*. Houghton Mifflin Company, 1948.

McKIM, MARGARET G. *Guiding Growth in Reading*. The Macmillan Company, 1955.

MONROE, MARIAN. *Growing into Reading.* Scott, Foresman and Company, 1951.

National Society for the Study of Education. *Reading in the Elementary School,* Forty-eighth Yearbook, Part II. The University of Chicago Press, 1949.

RUSSELL, DAVID H. *Children Learn to Read.* Ginn and Company, 1949.

RUSSELL, DAVID H. *Children's Thinking.* Ginn and Company, 1956.

TINKER, MILES A. *Teaching Elementary Reading.* Appleton-Century-Crofts, Inc., 1952.

WHEELER, ARVILLE. *The Teacher's Question and Answer Book for Better Reading.* Arthur C. Croft Publications, 1955.

YOAKAM, GERALD A. *Basal Reading Instruction.* McGraw-Hill Book Company, Inc., 1955.

TEACHING CHILDREN'S LITERATURE

ADAMS, BESS PORTER. *About Books and Children.* Henry Holt and Company, Inc., 1953.

ARBUTHNOT, MAY H. *Children and Books,* 2nd ed. Scott, Foresman and Company, 1957.

Association for Childhood Education International, The. *Adventuring in Literature with Children.* Association for Childhood Education International, 1953,

BETZNER, JEAN. *Exploring Literature with Children in the Elementary School.* Bureau of Publications, Teachers College, Columbia University, 1943.

DUFF, ANNIS. *Bequest of Wings: A Family's Pleasure with Books.* The Viking Press, 1944.

DUFF, ANNIS. *Longer Flight: A Family Grows Up with Books.* The Viking Press, 1955.

EATON, ANNE THAXTER. *Reading with Children.* The Viking Press, 1940.

FENNER, PHYLLIS. *The Proof of the Pudding: What Children Read.* The John Day Company, 1957.

HAZARD, PAUL. *Books, Children and Men.* The Horn Book, Inc., 1948.

LEWIS, CLAUDIA. *Writing for Young Children.* Simon and Schuster, Inc., 1954.

MARTIGNONI, MARGARET E. (editor). *The Illustrated Treasury of Children's Literature.* Grosset & Dunlap, Inc., 1955.

MARTIN, LAURA K. *Magazines for School Libraries,* rev. ed. The H. W. Wilson Company, 1950.

MEIGS, CORNELIA, and others. *A Critical History of Children's Literature.* The Macmillan Company, 1953.

SHEDLOCK, MARIE L. *The Art of the Story Teller.* Dover Publications, Inc., 1951.

SMITH, LILLIAN H. *The Unreluctant Years.* The American Library Association, 1953.

TOOZE, RUTH. *Your Children Want to Read.* Prentice-Hall, Inc., 1957.

GUIDING LANGUAGE EXPERIENCES

ANDERSON, VIRGIL A. *Improving the Child's Speech.* Oxford University Press, Inc., 1953.

APPLEGATE, MAUREE. *Helping Children Write.* Row, Peterson and Co., 1954.

Association for Childhood Education International, The. *Children and TV: Making the Most of It*, Bulletin No. 93. The Association for Childhood Education International, 1954.

Association for Childhood Education International, The. *When Children Write*, Bulletin No. 95. The Association for Childhood Education International, 1955.

BAKER, ZELMA W. *The Language Arts, the Child, and the Teacher*. Fearon Publishers, 1954.

BURGER, ISABEL B. *Creative Play Acting*. A. S. Barnes and Company, 1950.

BURROWS, ALVINA T., and others. *They All Want to Write*, rev. ed. Prentice-Hall, Inc., 1952.

Commission on the English Curriculum of the National Council of Teachers of English, The. *Language Arts for Today's Children*, Appleton-Century-Crofts, Inc., 1954.

DAWSON, MILDRED A., and ZOLLINGER, MARIAN. *Guiding Language Learning*. World Book Company, 1957.

DURLAND, FRANCES C. *Creative Dramatics for Children*. The Antioch Press, 1952.

HATCHETT, ETHEL LOUISE, and HUGHES, DONALD H. *Teaching Language Arts in Elementary Schools*. The Ronald Press Company, 1956.

HERRICK, V. E., and JACOBS, L. B. *Children and the Language Arts*. Prentice-Hall, Inc., 1955.

LEASE, R. G., and SIKS, G. B. *Creative Dramatics in Home, School and Community*, Harper & Brothers, 1952.

OGILVIE, MARDEL. *Speech in the Elementary School*. McGraw-Hill Book Company, Inc., 1954.

SHANE, HAROLD G. *Research Helps in Teaching the Language Arts*, Pamphlet. Association for Supervision and Curriculum Development, 1955.

STRICKLAND, RUTH. *The Language Arts in the Elementary School*, 2nd ed. D. C. Heath and Company, 1957.

TIDYMAN, W. F., and BUTTERFIELD, M. *Teaching the Language Arts*. McGraw-Hill Book Company, Inc., 1951.

VAN RIPER, CHARLES. *Helping Children Talk Better*. Science Research Associates, 1951.

WARD, WINIFRED. *Playmaking with Children from Kindergarten to High School*, 2nd ed. Appleton-Century-Crofts, Inc., 1957.

WATTS, A. F. *The Language and Mental Development of Children*. D. C. Heath and Company, 1947.

WITTY, PAUL, and BRICKER, HARRY. *Your Child and Radio, TV, Comics and Movies*. Science Research Associates, 1952.

ART, MUSIC, RHYTHMS, AND GAMES

ANDREWS, GLADYS E. *Creative Rhythmic Movement for Children*. Prentice-Hall, Inc., 1954.

Association for Childhood Education International, The. *The Arts and Children's Living*, Bulletin No. 2. The Association for Childhood Education International, 1945.

Association for Childhood Education International, The. *Music for Children's Living*. The Association for Childhood Education International, 1955.

AXLINE, V. *Play Therapy.* Houghton Mifflin Company, 1947.

BARKAN, MANUEL. *A Foundation for Art Education.* The Ronald Press Company, 1955.

BAUER, L. M., and REED, B. A. *Dance and Play Activities for the Elementary Grades,* Vol. 1. Chartwell House, Inc., 1951.

CHASE, ALICE E. *Famous Paintings.* The Platt & Munk Co., Inc., 1951.

D'AMICO, VICTOR E. *Creative Teaching in Art,* rev. ed. International Textbook Company, 1953.

ERDT, MARGARET H. *Teaching Art in the Elementary School.* Rinehart & Company, Inc., 1954.

EVANS, R., and BATTIS, E. *Childhood Rhythms: A Program of Rhythmic Activities for Children of Elementary School Age.* Chartwell House, Inc., 1955.

GERI, FRANK H. *Illustrated Games and Rhythms for Children,* Primary Grades. Prentice-Hall, Inc., 1955.

GIBSON, KATHARINE. *More Pictures to Grow Up With.* Studio Publications, 1942.

GIBSON, KATHARINE. *Pictures to Grow Up With.* Studio Publications, 1942.

HILL, W., MACKINTOSH, H. K., and RANDALL, A. *How Children Can Be Creative,* Pamphlet. United States Government Printing Office, 1954.

LOWENFELD, VIKTOR. *Creative and Mental Growth.* The Macmillan Company, 1947.

LOWENFELD, VIKTOR. *Your Child and His Art.* The Macmillan Company, 1955.

MURSELL, JAMES L. *Education for Musical Growth.* Ginn and Company, 1948.

SALISBURY, HELEN WRIGHT. *Finger Fun.* Cowman Publications, 1955.

SCHAEFER-SIMMERN, HENRY. *The Unfolding of Artistic Activity.* University of California Press, 1948.

COLLECTIONS OF STORIES, POEMS, AND SONGS

ALDIS, DOROTHY. *All Together.* G. P. Putnam's Sons, 1952.

ALLEN, MARIE LOUISE. *Pocketful of Rhymes.* Harper & Brothers, 1957.

ANDERSEN, HANS CHRISTIAN. *The Flying Trunk,* trans. by Lyda Jensen. Scott, Foresman and Company, 1951.

ARBUTHNOT, MAY HILL (compiler). *Time for Fairy Tales.* Scott, Foresman and Company, 1952.

ARBUTHNOT, MAY HILL (compiler). *Time for Poetry.* Scott, Foresman and Company, 1952.

ARBUTHNOT, MAY HILL (compiler). *Time for True Tales.* Scott, Foresman and Company, 1953.

ARMITAGE, THERESA. *Merry Music.* C. C. Birchard Company, 1953.

ARMITAGE, THERESA. *Our Songs.* C. C. Birchard Company, 1953.

ASBJORNSEN, PETER C. *East of the Sun and West of the Moon.* The Macmillan Company, 1953.

Association for Childhood Education International, The. *Sung under the Silver Umbrella.* The Macmillan Company, 1935.

Association for Childhood Education International, The. *Told under the Blue Umbrella.* The Macmillan Company, 1933.

Association for Childhood Education International, The. *Told under the Christmas Tree*. The Macmillan Company, 1948.

Association for Childhood Education International, The. *Told under the Green Umbrella*. The Macmillan Company, 1930.

Association for Childhood Education International, The. *Told under the Magic Umbrella*. The Macmillan Company, 1946.

Association for Childhood Education International, The. *Told under Spacious Skies*. The Macmillan Company, 1952.

Association for Childhood Education International, The. *Told under the Stars and Stripes*. The Macmillan Company, 1945.

BARROWS, MARJORIE. *Read-Aloud Poems Every Young Child Should Know*. Rand McNally & Company, 1957.

BARROWS, MARJORIE. *200 Best Poems*. Whitman Company, 1938.

BENNETT, ROWENA. *Story-Teller Poems*. The John C. Winston Company, 1948.

BREWTON, JOHN E. (compiler). *Gaily We Parade*. The Macmillan Company, 1940.

BREWTON, JOHN E. (compiler). *Under the Tent of the Sky*. The Macmillan Company, 1937.

BREWTON, SARA, and BREWTON, JOHN E. (compilers). *Bridled with Rainbows*. The Macmillan Company, 1949.

BREWTON, SARA, and BREWTON, JOHN E. (compilers). *Christmas Bells Are Ringing*. The Macmillan Company, 1951.

BREWTON, SARA, and BREWTON, JOHN E. (compilers). *Sing a Song of Seasons*. The Macmillan Company, 1955.

BROOKE, L. LESLIE (compiler). *Golden Goose Book*. Frederick Warne & Co., Inc.

BROWN, HELEN A., and HELTMAN, HARRY J. (compilers). *Let's Read-Together Poems*. Row, Peterson and Co., 1949.

BURNETT, BERNICE. *The First Book of Holidays*. Franklin Watts, Inc., 1955.

Child Study Association of America, The. *Holiday Storybook*. Thomas Y. Crowell Company, 1952.

Child Study Association of America, The. *More Read to Yourself Stories: Fun and Magic*. Thomas Y. Crowell Company, 1956.

Child Study Association of America, The. *Read Me Another Story*. Thomas Y. Crowell Company, 1949.

CHUTE, MARCHETTE. *Around and About*. E. P. Dutton Company, 1957.

CHUTE, MARCHETTE. *Rhymes about the City*. The Macmillan Company, 1946.

CHUTE, MARCHETTE. *Rhymes about the Country*. The Macmillan Company, 1941.

CHUTE, MARCHETTE. *Rhymes about Ourselves*. The Macmillan Company, 1941.

COATSWORTH, ELIZABETH. *The Littlest House*. The Macmillan Company, 1940.

COATSWORTH, ELIZABETH. *Summer Green*. The Macmillan Company, 1948.

DALGLIESH, ALICE. *Once upon a Time*. Charles Scribner's Sons, 1938.

DEPEW, OLLIE (compiler). *Children's Literature by Grades and Types*. Ginn and Company, 1938.

DOANE, PELAGIE (compiler). *A Small Child's Book of Verse*. Oxford University Press, Inc., 1948.

DOBBS, ROSE (editor). *Once upon a Time: Twenty Cheerful Tales to Read and Tell*. Random House, Inc., 1950.

EDEY, MARION, and GRIDER, DOROTHY. *Open the Door.* Charles Scribner's Sons, 1949.

FENNER, PHYLLIS (compiler). *Giants and Witches and a Dragon or Two.* Alfred A. Knopf, Inc., 1943.

FENNER, PHYLLIS. *Princesses and Peasant Boys: Tales of Enchantment.* Alfred A. Knopf, Inc., 1944.

FERRIS, HELEN (compiler). *Favorite Poems Old and New.* Doubleday & Company, Inc., 1957.

FIELD, RACHEL LYMAN. *Taxis and Toadstools.* Doubleday & Company, Inc., 1926.

FISHER, AILEEN. *Up the Windy Hill.* Abelard-Schuman, Inc., 1953.

FYLEMAN, ROSE. *Picture Rhymes from Foreign Lands.* J. B. Lippincott Company, 1935.

GAY, ZHENYA. *Jingle Jangle.* The Viking Press, 1953.

GEISMER, BARBARA PECK, and SUTER, ANTOINETTE BROWN (compilers). *Very Young Verses.* Houghton Mifflin Company, 1945.

GLENN, MABELLE, and others. *Tuning Up.* Ginn and Company, 1943.

GRIMM, JAKOB, and GRIMM, WILHELM. *More Tales from Grimm,* trans. and il. by Wanda Gág. Coward-McCann, Inc., 1947.

GRIMM, JAKOB, and GRIMM, WILHELM. *Tales from Grimm,* trans. and il. by Wanda Gág. Coward-McCann, Inc., 1936.

GRUENBERG, SIDONIE (compiler). *Favorite Stories Old and New,* rev. ed. Doubleday & Company, Inc., 1955.

GRUENBERG, SIDONIE (compiler). *More Favorite Stories Old and New.* Doubleday & Company, Inc., 1948.

HARRINGTON, MILDRED P. *Ring-a-Round.* The Macmillan Company, 1930.

HATCH, MARY C. *Thirteen Danish Tales.* Harcourt Brace and Company, 1947.

HUBBARD, ALICE, and BABBITT, ADELINE (compilers). *The Golden Flute.* The John Day Company, 1932.

HUBER, MIRIAM BLANTON (editor). *Story and Verse for Children,* rev. ed. The Macmillan Company, 1955.

HUFFARD, GRACE T., and others. *My Poetry Book,* rev. ed. The John C. Winston Company, 1956.

JUSTUS, MAY, and others. *Big Meeting Day and Other Festival Tales.* E. P. Dutton & Co., Inc., 1950.

LANDECK, BEATRICE (compiler). *More Songs to Grow On.* Edward B. Marks Music Corp., 1954.

LANDECK, BEATRICE (compiler). *Songs to Grow On.* Edward B. Marks Music Corp., 1950.

LEAR, EDWARD, and others. *Book of Nonsense.* E. P. Dutton & Co., Inc., 1927.

LOVE, KATHERINE I. *Pocketful of Rhymes.* Thomas Y. Crowell Company, 1946.

MARTIGNONI, MARGARET (editor). *Illustrated Treasury of Children's Literature.* Grosset & Dunlap, Inc., 1955.

McEWEN, CATHERINE S. *Away We Go.* Thomas Y. Crowell Company, 1956.

McFARLAND, WILMA. *For a Child.* The Westminster Press, 1947.

McGINLEY, PHYLLIS LOUISE. *All around the Town.* J. B. Lippincott Company, 1948.

MILNE, A. A. *Now We Are Six.* E. P. Dutton & Co., Inc., 1950.

MILNE, A. A. *When We Were Very Young.* E. P. Dutton & Co., Inc., 1950.

MITCHELL, LUCY SPRAGUE. *Another Here and Now Story Book.* E. P. Dutton & Co., Inc., 1945.

MITCHELL, LUCY SPRAGUE, and STALL, DOROTHY. *Our Country.* D. C. Heath and Company, 1945.

PANNELL, LUCILLE, and CAVANAH, FRANCES (compilers). *Holiday Round-Up.* Macrae Smith Company, 1950.

PETERSON, ISABEL J. (compiler). *The First Book of Poetry.* Franklin Watts, Inc., 1954.

PITTS, LILLA BELLE, GLENN, MABELLE, and WATTERS, LORRAIN E. *The First Grade Book* (OUR SINGING WORLD). Ginn and Company, 1957.

PITTS, LILLA BELLE, GLENN, MABELLE, and WATTERS, LORRAIN E. *Singing and Rhyming* (OUR SINGING WORLD). Ginn and Company, 1957.

PITTS, LILLA BELLE, GLENN, MABELLE, and WATTERS, LORRAIN E. *Singing on Our Way* (OUR SINGING WORLD). Ginn and Company, 1957.

PURCELL, JOHN. *True Book of Holidays and Special Days.* Childrens Press, 1955.

RICHARDS, LAURA E. *Tirra Lirra.* Little, Brown and Company, 1955.

ROBERTS, ELIZABETH MADOX. *Under the Tree.* The Viking Press, 1930.

ROBINSON, THOMAS PENDLETON. *In and Out.* The Viking Press, 1943.

SECHRIST, ELIZABETH H. (compiler). *One Thousand Poems for Children.* Macrae Smith Company, 1946.

SECHRIST, ELIZABETH H. *Red Letter Days, a Book of Holiday Customs.* Macrae Smith Company, 1940.

STEVENSON, ROBERT LOUIS. *A Child's Garden of Verses.* Charles Scribner's Sons, 1955. (Copyright 1905, reset 1955)

THOMAS, ELEANOR, and KELTY, MARY G. *Heroes, Heroines, and Holidays.* Ginn and Company, 1952.

THOMPSON, BLANCHE J. (editor). *Silver Pennies.* The Macmillan Company, 1925.

TIPPETT, JAMES S. *I Know Some Little Animals.* Harper & Brothers, 1941.

TIPPETT, JAMES S. *I Live in a City.* Harper & Brothers, 1927.

UNTERMEYER, LOUIS (compiler). *This Singing World.* Harcourt, Brace and Company, 1923.

UNTERMEYER, LOUIS (compiler). *The Magic Circle.* Harcourt, Brace and Company, 1952.

WERNER, JANE (compiler). *The Golden Book of Poetry.* Simon and Schuster, Inc., 1949.

WYNNE, ANNETTE. *For Days and Days.* Frederick A. Stokes Company, 1919.

STORIES TO READ

NOTE. Titles marked with * are for below-average readers, with ** for average readers, with *** for better readers. Those marked with *** are suitable for the teacher to read to the group.

**AGNEW, EDITH J. *The Gray Eyes Family.* Friendship Press, 1952.

*ANDERSON, CLARENCE W. *Blaze Finds the Trail.* The Macmillan Company, 1950.

**AULAIRE, INGRI D', and AULAIRE, EDGAR D'. *Columbus.* Doubleday & Company, Inc., 1955.

**AULAIRE, INGRI D', and AULAIRE, EDGAR D'. *Don't Count Your Chicks*. Doubleday & Company, Inc., 1943.

*BAILEY, CAROLYN SHERWIN. *Country-Stop*. The Viking Press, 1942.

**BAKER, CHARLOTTE. *Nellie and the Mayor's Hat*. Coward-McCann, Inc., 1947.

**BANNON, LAURA. *Burro Boy and His Big Trouble*. Abingdon Press, 1955.

*BANNON, LAURA. *When the Moon Is New*. Albert Whitman & Company, 1953.

*BEATTY, HETTY B. *Little Owl Indian*. Houghton Mifflin Company, 1951.

**BEIM, JERROLD. *Shoeshine Boy*. William Morrow and Company, Inc., 1954.

*BEMELMANS, LUDWIG. *Madeline's Rescue*. The Viking Press, 1953.

***BENNETT, ANNA E. *Little Witch*. J. B. Lippincott Company, 1953.

*BILL, HELEN E. *The Shoes Fit for a King*. Franklin Watts, Inc., 1956.

**BLACK, IRMA SIMONTON. *Maggie: a Mischievous Magpie*. Holiday House, 1949.

***BLEEKER, SONIA. *Indians of the Longhouse*. William Morrow and Company, Inc., 1950.

***BLEEKER, SONIA. *Pueblo Indians: Farmers of the Rio Grande*. William Morrow and Company, Inc., 1955.

***BLEEKER, SONIA. *The Seminole Indians*. William Morrow and Company, Inc., 1954.

***BLOUGH, GLENN O., and CAMPBELL, M. H. *When You Go to the Zoo*. McGraw-Hill Book Company, Inc., 1955.

***BONNER, MARY GRAHAM. *Out to Win*. Alfred A. Knopf, Inc., 1947.

*BRACKEN, DOROTHY. *Rodeo*. The Steck Company, 1949.

**BREWSTER, BENJAMIN. *The First Book of Cowboys*. Franklin Watts, Inc., 1950.

***BREWSTER, BENJAMIN. *The First Book of Indians*. Franklin Watts, Inc., 1950.

**BRIDGES, WILLIAM. *Zoo Babies*. William Morrow and Company, Inc., 1953.

***BRIDGES, WILLIAM. *Zoo Doctor*. William Morrow and Company, Inc., 1957.

*BRIDGES, WILLIAM. *Zoo Pets*. William Morrow and Company, Inc., 1955.

*BRIGHT, ROBERT. *Georgie to the Rescue*. Doubleday & Company, 1956.

***BROCK, EMMA L. *Kristie's Buttercup*. Alfred A. Knopf, Inc., 1955.

***BROCK, EMMA L. *Plug-Horse Derby*. Alfred A. Knopf, Inc., 1955.

**BRONSON, WILFRED S. *Coyotes*. Harcourt, Brace and Company, 1946.

**BROWN, JEANETTE P. *Rosita: A Little Girl of Puerto Rico*. Friendship Press, 1948.

**BROWN, MARCIA. *Cinderella*. Charles Scribner's Sons, 1954.

*BROWN, MARCIA. *The Little Carousel*. Charles Scribner's Sons, 1946.

**BROWN, MARCIA. *Stone Soup*. Charles Scribner's Sons, 1947.

**BROWN, PAUL. *Pony School*. Charles Scribner's Sons, 1950.

**BROWN, PAUL. *Sparkie and Puff Ball*. Charles Scribner's Sons, 1954.

**BROWN, PAUL. *War Paint, an Indian Pony*. Charles Scribner's Sons, 1936.

*BRUNHOFF, LAURENT DE. *Babar's Fair Will Be Opened Next Sunday*. Random House, Inc., 1955.

**BRYAN, CATHERINE, and MADDEN, MABRA. *Pito's House*. The Macmillan Company, 1943.

**BUFF, MARY, and BUFF, CONRAD. *Dancing Cloud, the Navajo Boy*. The Viking Press, 1957.

**BUFF, MARY, and BUFF, CONRAD. *Hah-Nee of the Cliff Dwellers*. Houghton Mifflin Company, 1956.

**BULLA, CLYDE ROBERT. *Eagle Feather*. Thomas Y. Crowell Company, 1953.

**BULLA, CLYDE ROBERT. *Johnny Hong of Chinatown*. Thomas Y. Crowell Company, 1952.

*BULLA, CLYDE ROBERT. *A Ranch for Danny*. Thomas Y. Crowell Company, 1951.

**BULLA, CLYDE ROBERT. *Surprise for a Cowboy*. Thomas Y. Crowell Company, 1950.

*BURTON, VIRGINIA LEE. *The Little House*. Houghton Mifflin Company, 1942.

*CHANDLER, EDNA WALKER. *Cowboy Sam and the Fair*. Beckley-Cardy Company, 1953.

*CHANDLER, EDNA WALKER. *Cowboy Sam and Freddy*. Beckley-Cardy Company, 1951.

**CLARK, ANN NOLAN. *Blue Canyon Horse*. The Viking Press, Inc., 1954.

**CLARK, ANN NOLAN. *In My Mother's House*. The Viking Press, 1941.

***CLARK, ANN NOLAN. *Little Navajo Bluebird*. The Viking Press, 1943.

**CLEARY, BEVERLY. *Henry and Ribsy*. William Morrow and Company, Inc., 1954.

***COATSWORTH, ELIZABETH. *Dog Stories*. Simon and Schuster, 1953.

***COATSWORTH, ELIZABETH. *The Peddler's Cart*. The Macmillan Company, 1956.

**CREDLE, ELLIS. *My Pet Peepelo*. Oxford University Press, Inc., 1948.

**CROWLEY, MAUDE. *Azor*. Oxford University Press, Inc., 1948.

**CROWLEY, MAUDE. *Azor and the Blue-eyed Cow: A Christmas Story*. Oxford University Press, Inc., 1951.

**CROWLEY, MAUDE. *Azor and the Haddock*. Oxford University Press, Inc., 1949.

*DALGLIESH, ALICE. *Bears on Hemlock Mountain*. Charles Scribner's Sons, 1952.

**DALGLIESH, ALICE. *The Columbus Story*. Charles Scribner's Sons, 1955.

***DALGLIESH, ALICE. *The Fourth of July Story*. Charles Scribner's Sons, 1956.

**DALGLIESH, ALICE. *The Thanksgiving Story*. Charles Scribner's Sons, 1954.

***DARLING, LOUIS. *Chickens and How to Raise Them*. William Morrow and Company, Inc., 1955.

*DAUGHERTY, JAMES. *Andy and the Lion*. The Viking Press, 1938.

**DAVIS, LAVINIA R. *Danny's Luck*. Doubleday & Company, Inc., 1953.

**DEARBORN, FRANCES R. *How the Indians Lived*. Ginn and Company, 1927.

**DE LA ROCHE, MAZO. *The Song of Lambert*. Little, Brown and Company, 1956.

**ESTES, ELEANOR, and SLOBODKIN, LOUIS. *The Sun, the Wind, and Mr. Todd*. Harcourt, Brace and Company, 1943.

**EVERS, HELEN, and EVERS, ALF. *Copy-Kitten*. Rand McNally & Company, 1957.

*FATIO, LOUISE. *The Happy Lion*. McGraw-Hill Book Company, Inc., 1954.

*FATIO, LOUISE. *The Happy Lion Roars*. McGraw-Hill Book Company, Inc., 1957.

*FISCHER, HANS. *Pitschi*. Harcourt, Brace and Company, 1953.

**FISCHER, HANS. *The Traveling Musicians*. Harcourt, Brace and Company, 1955.

*FLETCHER, HELEN, and DECKTER, JACK. *The Puppet Book*. Greenberg: Publisher, 1947.

**FLETCHER, SYDNEY E. *American Indian*. Grosset & Dunlap, Inc., 1954.

***FLETCHER, SYDNEY E. *Big Book of Cowboys*. Grosset & Dunlap, Inc., 1950.

***FLETCHER, SYDNEY E. *Big Book of Indians*. Grosset & Dunlap, Inc., 1950.

*FLORA, JAMES. *The Fabulous Fireworks Family*. Harcourt, Brace and Company, 1955.

***FORBUS, INA B. *The Magic Pin.* The Viking Press, 1956.

*GÁG, WANDA. *Nothing at All.* Coward-McCann, Inc., 1941.

***GANNETT, RUTH STILES. *My Father's Dragon.* Random House, Inc., 1948.

***GATES, DORIS. *Sarah's Idea.* The Viking Press, 1938.

**GEISEL, THEODOR (pseud. Dr. Seuss). *And to Think That I Saw It on Mulberry Street.* Vanguard Press, Inc., 1937.

**GEISEL, THEODOR (pseud. Dr. Seuss). *The 500 Hats of Bartholomew Cubbins.* Vanguard Press, Inc., 1938.

***GEISEL, THEODOR (pseud. Dr. Seuss). *If I Ran the Zoo.* Random House, Inc., 1950.

**GOETZ, DELIA. *The Hidden Burro.* William Morrow and Company, Inc., 1949.

**GOUDEY, ALICE E. *Here Come the Bears!* Charles Scribner's Sons, 1954.

**GOUDEY, ALICE E. *Here Come the Elephants!* Charles Scribner's Sons, 1955.

**GOUDEY, ALICE E. *Here Come the Lions!* Charles Scribner's Sons, 1956.

***GRANT, BRUCE. *The Cowboy Encyclopedia.* Rand McNally & Company, 1951.

*HADER, BERTA, and HADER, ELMER. *Big City.* The Macmillan Company, 1947.

*HADER, BERTA, and HADER, ELMER. *Lost in the Zoo.* The Macmillan Company, 1951.

*HADER, BERTA, and HADER, ELMER. *The Mighty Hunter.* The Macmillan Company, 1943.

*HARRIS, ISOBEL. *Little Boy Brown.* J. B. Lippincott Company, 1949.

***HOFSINDE, ROBERT. *Indian Sign Language.* William Morrow and Company, Inc., 1956.

***HOLLING, HOLLING C. *Book of Cowboys.* The Platt & Munk Co., Inc., 1937.

***HOLLING, HOLLING C. *Book of Indians.* The Platt & Munk Co., Inc., 1935.

*HOLT, JACK, and COGGINS, CAROLYN. *Lance and Cowboy Billy.* Whittlesey House, McGraw-Hill Book Company, Inc., 1950.

*IPCAR, DAHLOV. *World Full of Horses.* Doubleday & Company, Inc., 1955.

***JACKSON, C. PAUL. *Giant in the Midget League.* Thomas Y. Crowell Company, 1953.

**JAGENDORF, MORITZ. *The First Book of Puppets.* Franklin Watts, Inc., 1952.

*KEPES, JULIET. *Five Little Monkeys.* Houghton Mifflin Company, 1952.

***KETTELKAMP, LARRY. *Spooky Magic.* William Morrow and Company, Inc., 1955.

**KIENE, JULIA. *The Step-by-Step Cookbook for Boys and Girls.* Simon and Schuster, 1956.

**KINGMAN, LEE. *The Magic Christmas Tree.* Farrar, Straus and Cudahy, Inc., 1956.

*KRAUSS, RUTH. *The Backward Day.* Harper & Brothers, 1950.

**LA RUE, MABEL G. *Dicky and the Indians.* Ginn and Company, 1948.

*LA RUE, MABEL G. *Tiny Toosey's Birthday.* Houghton Mifflin Company, 1950.

**LATTIMORE, ELEANOR. *Peachblossom.* Harcourt, Brace and Company, 1943.

***LENSKI, LOIS. *Corn-Farm Boy.* J. B. Lippincott Company, 1954.

*LENSKI, LOIS. *Cowboy Small.* Oxford University Press, Inc., 1949.

***LENSKI, LOIS. *San Francisco Boy.* J. B. Lippincott Company, 1955.

***LENSKI, LOIS. *Texas Tomboy.* J. B. Lippincott Company, 1950.

*LENSKI, LOIS. *We Live in the City.* J. B. Lippincott Company, 1954.

*LIFFRING, JOAN. *Ray and Stevie on a Corn-Belt Farm.* Follett Publishing Company, 1956.

*McCLUNG, ROBERT. *Major.* William Morrow and Company, Inc., 1956.

**McGINLEY, PHYLLIS. *The Horse Who Had His Picture in the Paper.* J. B. Lippincott Company, 1951.

**McMEEKIN, ISABELLA. *The First Book of Horses.* Franklin Watts, Inc., 1949.

**MARKS, MICKEY KLAR. *Fine Eggs and Fancy Chickens.* Henry Holt and Company, Inc., 1953.

***MARRIOTT, ALICE. *Indians on Horseback.* Thomas Y. Crowell Company, 1948.

**MARTINI, TERI. *The True Book of Cowboys.* Childrens Press, 1955.

**MARTINI, TERI. *The True Book of Indians.* Childrens Press, 1954.

**MILHOUS, KATHERINE. *Appolonia's Valentine.* Charles Scribner's Sons, 1954.

**MILHOUS, KATHERINE. *The Egg Tree.* Charles Scribner's Sons, 1950.

**MILHOUS, KATHERINE. *Patrick and the Golden Slippers.* Charles Scribner's Sons, 1951.

**MILHOUS, KATHERINE. *With Bells On.* Charles Scribner's Sons, 1955.

***MOON, GRACE. *Chi-Weé.* Doubleday & Company, Inc., 1925.

**MOON, GRACE, and MOON, CARL. *One Little Indian.* Albert Whitman & Company, 1950.

*MORDVINOFF, NICHOLAS (pseud. Nicolas). *Bear's Land.* Coward-McCann, Inc., 1955.

*NEWBERRY, CLARE T. *Lambert's Bargain.* Harper & Brothers, 1952.

**OLDS, ELIZABETH. *Feather Mountain.* Houghton Mifflin Company, 1951.

**OTTO, MARGARET G. *Cocoa.* Henry Holt and Company, Inc., 1953.

**PACK, ELIZABETH. *Kee and Bah, Navajo Children.* American Book Company, 1940.

***PECK, LEIGH. *Don Coyote.* Houghton Mifflin Company, 1942.

**PELS, GERTRUDE. *Easy Puppets.* Thomas Y. Crowell Company, 1951.

***PISTORIUS, ANNA. *What Dog Is It?* Wilcox & Follett Co., 1951.

*POLITI, LEO. *Juanita.* Charles Scribner's Sons, 1948.

*POLITI, LEO. *Pedro, the Angel of Olvera Street.* Charles Scribner's Sons, 1946.

***RENICK, MARION R. *Bats and Gloves of Glory.* Charles Scribner's Sons, 1956.

**RENICK, MARION R. *Pete's Home Run.* Charles Scribner's Sons, 1952.

*REY, HANS A. *Curious George.* Houghton Mifflin Company, 1941.

*REY, HANS A. *Curious George Takes a Job.* Houghton Mifflin Company, 1947.

**REY, MARGARET, and REY, HANS A. *Spotty.* Harper & Brothers, 1945.

***ROUNDS, GLEN. *Buffalo Harvest.* Holiday House, 1952.

*ROWAND, PHYLLIS. *George.* Little, Brown and Company, 1956.

**RUSHMORE, HELEN. *Cowboy Joe of Circle S.* Harcourt, Brace and Company, 1950.

**SAWYER, RUTH. *The Christmas Anna Angel.* The Viking Press, 1944.

*SCHLEIN, MIRIAM. *City Boy, Country Boy.* Childrens Press, 1955.

**SCHLEIN, MIRIAM. *Elephant Herd.* William R. Scott, Inc., 1954.

*SCHLOAT, G. WARREN, JR. *The Wonderful Egg.* Charles Scribner's Sons, 1952.

*SEIGNOBOSC, FRANÇOISE. *Noël for Jeanne-Marie.* Charles Scribner's Sons, 1953.

**SELSAM, MILLICENT E. *Egg to Chick.* International Publishers Co., Inc., 1946.

**SHANNON, TERRY. *Little Wolf, the Rain Dancer.* Albert Whitman & Company, 1954.

*SMILEY, VIRGINIA K. *Little Boy Navajo.* Abelard Schuman, Ltd., 1954.

*STERNE, EMMA G. (pseud. Emily Broun). *A Ball for Little Bear, An Ojibway Legend.* E. P. Dutton & Co., Inc., 1955.

**STILWELL, ALISON. *Chin-Ling the Chinese Cricket.* The Macmillan Company, 1947.

**TOUSEY, SANFORD. *Indians of the Plains.* Rand McNally & Company, 1940.

*TUDOR, TASHA. *Pumpkin Moonshine.* Oxford University Press, Inc., 1938.

*UNWIN, NORA S. *The Proud Pumpkin.* E. P. Dutton & Co., Inc., 1953.

*WEIL, TRUDA. *Animal Families.* Childrens Press, 1947.

**WHITE, BESSIE F. *A Bear Named Grumms.* Houghton Mifflin Company, 1953.

**WIESE, KURT. *You Can Write Chinese.* The Viking Press, 1945.

**YEN LIANG. *Tommy and Dee-Dee.* Oxford University Press, 1953.

*YLLA. *Two Little Bears.* Harper & Brothers, 1954.

**ZIM, HERBERT S. *Alligators and Crocodiles.* William Morrow and Company, Inc., 1952.

**ZIM, HERBERT S. *Big Cats.* William Morrow and Company, Inc., 1955.

***ZIM, HERBERT S. *Elephants.* William Morrow and Company, Inc., 1946.

**ZIM, HERBERT S. *Monkeys.* William Morrow and Company, Inc., 1955.

**ZIM, HERBERT S. *Parrakeets.* William Morrow and Company, Inc., 1953.

OTHER READERS AND TEXTBOOKS

BETTS, EMMETT A., and WELCH, CAROLYN M. *Beyond Treasure Valley.* American Book Company, 1953.

BETTS, EMMETT A., and WELCH, CAROLYN M. *Down Singing River.* American Book Company, 1949.

BETTS, EMMETT A., and WELCH, CAROLYN, M. *Over a City Bridge.* American Book Company, 1953.

BOND, GUY L., and others. *Down Our Way.* Lyons and Carnahan, 1954.

BOND, GUY L., and others. *Just for Fun.* Lyons and Carnahan, 1954.

BOND, GUY L., and others. *Once upon a Storytime.* Lyons and Carnahan, 1954.

BOND, GUY L., and others. *Stories from Everywhere.* Lyons and Carnahan, 1954.

BURTON, WILLIAM H., BAKER, CLARA B., and KEMP, GRACE K. *Meet Our Friends.* The Bobbs-Merrill Company, Inc., 1950.

BURTON, WILLIAM H., BAKER, CLARA B., and KEMP, GRACE K. *Our Good Neighbors.* The Bobbs-Merrill Company, Inc., 1950.

CRAIG, GERALD S., and LEMBACH, MARGUERITE W. *Science Everywhere.* Ginn and Company, 1954.

GATES, ARTHUR I. *It Is a Big Country.* The Macmillan Company, 1953.

GATES, ARTHUR I., HUBER, MIRIAM B., and SALISBURY, FRANK S. *Friends and Fun.* The Macmillan Company, 1951.

GATES, ARTHUR I., HUBER, MIRIAM B., and SALISBURY, FRANK S. *New Friends and New Places.* The Macmillan Company, 1957.

GATES, ARTHUR I., HUBER, MIRIAM B., and SALISBURY, FRANK S. *Today We Go.* The Macmillan Company, 1957.

GATES, ARTHUR I., and PEARDON, CELESTE C. *Good Times Today and Tomorrow.* The Macmillan Company, 1951.

GATES, ARTHUR I., and PEARDON, CELESTE C. *Good Times Tomorrow*. The Macmillan Company, 1951.

GRAY, WILLIAM S., MONROE, MARION, and ARTLEY, A. STERL. *Just Imagine*. Scott, Foresman and Company, 1953.

GRAY, WILLIAM S., and others. *Tall Tales*. Scott, Foresman and Company, 1953.

GRAY, WILLIAM S., and others. *The New Friends and Neighbors*. Scott, Foresman and Company, 1956.

GRAY, WILLIAM S., and others. *The New More Friends and Neighbors*. Scott, Foresman and Company, 1956.

GRAY, WILLIAM S., and others. *The New Streets and Roads*. Scott, Foresman and Company, 1956.

HALLOCK, GRACE T., ALLEN, ROSS L., and THOMAS, ELEANOR. *Health and Safety for You*. Ginn and Company, 1954.

HILDRETH, GERTRUDE, and others. *Faraway Ports*. The John C. Winston Company, 1958.

HILDRETH, GERTRUDE, and others. *The Story Road*. The John C. Winston Company, 1958.

HUBER, MIRIAM B., SALISBURY, FRANK S., and O'DONNELL, MABEL. *After the Sun Sets*. Row, Peterson and Co., 1953.

HUBER, MIRIAM B., SALISBURY, FRANK S., and O'DONNELL, MABEL. *I Know a Story*. Row, Peterson and Co., 1953.

HUBER, MIRIAM B., SALISBURY, FRANK S., and O'DONNELL, MABEL. *It Happened One Day*. Row, Peterson and Co., 1953.

JOHNSON, ELEANOR M., and JACOBS, LELAND B. (editors). *Treat Shop*. Charles E. Merrill Books, 1954.

LEARY, BERNICE E., REICHERT, EDWIN C., and REELY, MARY K. *Skipping Along*. J. B. Lippincott Company, 1953.

LEAVELL, ULLIN W., and FRIEBELE, MARY LOUISE. *Open Doors*. American Book Company, 1957.

LEAVELL, ULLIN W., and FRIEBELE, MARY LOUISE. *Open Roads*. American Book Company, 1957.

McKEE, PAUL, and others. *Come Along*. Houghton Mifflin Company, 1957.

McKEE, PAUL, and others. *Looking Ahead*. Houghton Mifflin Company, 1957.

McKEE, PAUL, and others. *On We Go*. Houghton Mifflin Company, 1957.

O'DONNELL, MABEL. *The New Friendly Village*. Row, Peterson and Co., 1950.

O'DONNELL, MABEL. *The New If I Were Going*. Row, Peterson and Co., 1956.

SHELDON, WILLIAM D., and AUSTIN, MARY C. *Magic Windows*. Allyn and Bacon, Inc., 1957.

SHELDON, WILLIAM D., and AUSTIN, MARY C. *Story Caravan*. Allyn and Bacon, Inc., 1957.

SHELDON, WILLIAM D., AUSTIN, MARY C., and DRDEK, RICHARD E. *Fields and Fences*. Allyn and Bacon, Inc., 1957.

SHELDON, WILLIAM D., AUSTIN, MARY C., and DRDEK, RICHARD E. *Town and Country*. Allyn and Bacon, Inc., 1957.

SMITH, NILA BANTON. *In New Places*. Silver Burdett Company, 1945.

WITTY, PAUL, and EBERLE, IRMENGARDE. *Secrets and Surprises*. D. C. Heath and Company, 1955.

WITTY, PAUL, and NOLEN, BARBARA. *Do and Dare*. D. C. Heath and Company, 1955.

WITTY, PAUL, and NOLEN, BARBARA. *Fun and Frolic*. D. C. Heath and Company, 1955.

WITTY, PAUL, and PALMER, ROBIN. *Lost and Found*. D. C. Heath and Company, 1955.

YOAKAM, GERALD, HESTER, KATHLEEN, and ABNEY, LOUISE. *Children Everywhere*. Laidlaw Brothers, Inc., 1947.

YOAKAM, GERALD, HESTER, KATHLEEN, and ABNEY, LOUISE. *Making Storybook Friends*. Laidlaw Brothers, Inc., 1947.

YOAKAM, GERALD, HESTER, KATHLEEN, and ABNEY, LOUISE. *Stories We Like*. Laidlaw Brothers, Inc., 1947.

A few books that are no longer being published are included in this bibliography because of their value to teachers and their availability in many schools and libraries.

AUDIO–VISUAL MATERIALS

Unit I · Pets and Playtime

Films

Five Little Pups (Cornell). 1 reel, b&w/color.

Let's Visit a Poultry Farm (Coronet). 1 reel, sd, b&w/color.

Peppy, the Puppy: Background for Reading and Expression (Coronet). 1 reel, sd, b&w/color.

Polly, the Parrot: Background for Reading and Expression (Coronet). 1 reel, sd, b&w/color.

Seven Little Ducks (Bailey). 1 reel, sd, b&w/color.

Shaggy, the Coyote: Background for Reading and Expression (Coronet). 1 reel, sd, b&w/color.

Filmstrips

The Adventures of Pete and His Dog (JamHandy). 26fr, color.

Aubel and Leman (CurriculumFlms). 25fr, color.

Buying a Pet (JamHandy). 11fr, color.

Chickens on the Farm (JamHandy). 23fr, color. (THE FARMER'S ANIMAL FRIENDS series.)

Feeding the Animals (EBF), color. (LIFE ON THE FARM SERIES.)

Gathering Eggs (EBF), color. (LIFE ON THE FARM SERIES.)

Lost Dog (PopScience). 40fr, color.

Paul's Puppy (EBF). 46fr, color. (PET STORIES series.)

Peggy's Parakeet (EBF). 46fr, color. (PET STORIES series.)

Record

Little Red Hen, by Frank Luther. (Decca.)

Unit II · At the Zoo

Films

Black Bear Twins, Second Edition (EBF). 1 reel, b&w.
Elephants (EBF). 11min, sd.
Flipper, the Seal (Coronet). 1 reel, sd, b&w/color.
Monkeys (EBF). 1 reel, sd, b&w/color.
Rikki, the Baby Monkey (EBF). 1 reel, sd, b&w/color.
Tommy, the Lion (YoungAmerica). 1 reel, sd, b&w.
The Zoo (EBF). 1 reel, sd, b&w/color.
Zoo Animals of Our Storybooks (Coronet). 1 reel, b&w/color.

Filmstrips

ALL AROUND THE ZOO series: (1) *The Animal Kingdom Is Big;* (2) *Arriving at the Zoo;* (3) *Mealtime at the Zoo;* (4) *Animal Health and Hygiene;* (5) *Animal Habits;* (6) *Fun for Everybody* (ClassroomFlms). Color.
Elephants in Africa (EBF). 46fr, color. (THE AFRICAN LION series.)
King of Beasts (EBF). 50fr, color. (THE AFRICAN LION series.)
Larger Animals of Africa (EBF). 47fr, color. (THE AFRICAN LION series.)
Let's Go to the Zoo (JamHandy). 12fr, color.

Record

Carnival of Animals, by Camille Saint-Saens. 33⅓ rpm, 12″. (Columbia—CL-720.)

Unit III · Just for Fun

Film

Georgie (Weston). 1 reel, b&w/color.

Filmstrips

Gingerbread Boy (CurriculumFlms). 38fr, color.
Rudy and Trudy Bear (CurriculumFlms). Color.

Records

"Tame Bears," by Edward Elgar in *Listening Program*, Vol. II. (RCA Victor.)
"Of a Tailor and a Bear," by Edward MacDowell in *Listening Program*, Vol. III. (RCA Victor.)

Unit IV · Indian Children

Films

Boy of the Navajos (Coronet). 1 reel, sd, b&w/color.
Boy of the Seminoles—Indians of the Everglades (Coronet). 1 reel, sd, b&w/color.
The Hopi Indians (Coronet). 1 reel, sd, b&w/color.
Hopi Indian Village Life (Coronet). 1 reel, sd, b&w/color.
Hopi Indian Arts and Crafts (Coronet). 1 reel, sd, b&w/color.

Filmstrips

How the Indians Lived: *Woodland Indians (Iroquois)*; *Plains Indians (Dakota)*; *Southwest Indians (Hopi)*; *Southwest Indians (Navajo)* (JamHandy). Ea 35fr, color.

Indians of the Northeastern Woodlands—Hunter from the Longhouse (SVE). 32fr, color. (Adventures with Early American Indians series.)

Indians of the Southwest—Pueblo Dwellers and Apache Raid (SVE). 32fr, color. (Adventures with Early American Indians series.)

Records

Music of the Sioux and the Navajo. (Folkways—401.)

Music of the American Indians—Southwest. (Folkways—420.)

The Pueblo Indians in Story, Song, and Dance, Soundbook. (Book-Records Inc.—4095.)

Unit V · Americans All

Films

Junior Rodeo Daredevils (InstrFlms). 1 reel, b&w.

Life on a Cattle Ranch (Coronet). 1 reel, b&w/color.

Visit with Cowboys (EBF). 1 reel, b&w/color.

Filmstrips

Orello, the Donkey (CurriculumFlms). Color.

Pecos Bill Becomes a Cowboy (CurriculumFlms). Color.

Records

Going West, sung by Frank Luther. (Decca—PL 88028.)

Cowboy Ballads, sung by Cisco Houston. (Folkways—22.)

The Grand Canyon Suite, by Ferde Grofé. 33⅓ rpm, 12″. (Victor LM—1004.)

Rolito, sung by Frank Luther. (Decca—DL 8021.)

Unit VI · Days Everyone Likes

Films

Christmas (EBF). 1 reel, 5min, sound, color.

Georgie (Weston). 1 reel, b&w/color.

Filmstrips

Columbus Day (YoungAmerica). 25fr, color. (Holiday Series.)

The Story of "Silent Night" (JamHandy). 29fr, color. (Christmas Series.)

Santa Claus and Other Traditions (JamHandy). 27fr, color. (Christmas Series.)

Seasons and Festivals (EyeGate). 23fr, color. (Literature for Children series.)

The Tree and Other Traditions (JamHandy). 29fr, color. (Christmas Series.)

We Visit Sweden (EyeGate). 24fr, color.

Films

Rumpelstiltskin (EBF). 1 reel, 9min, sd, b&w. (FAIRY TALE CLASSICS series.)
Sleeping Beauty (EBF). 1 reel, 9min, sd, b&w. (FAIRY TALE CLASSICS series.)

Filmstrips

AESOP'S FABLES: *The Wolf in Sheep's Clothing*; *The Loud-mouthed Frog*; *The Greedy Dog*; *The Mouse Who Boasted*; *The Mean Old Elephant*; *The Lion and the Goat*; *The Evil Spider* (CurriculumFlms). Ea about 25fr, color.
Frog Prince (JamHandy). 26fr, color.
Jack and the Beanstalk (CurriculumFlms). 24fr, color.
Mr. Vinegar (CurriculumFlms). Color.
Folk Tales and Fairy Tales (EyeGate). 29fr, color. (LITERATURE FOR CHILDREN series.)
MUSIC STORIES series: *Peter and the Wolf*; *Hansel and Gretel*; *The Nutcracker*; *Peer Gynt*; *The Firebird*; *The Sorcerer's Apprentice* (JamHandy). Ea about 30fr, color. This series includes both filmstrips and records.
PRIMARY GRADE STORIES—SET A: *Jack and the Beanstalk* (50fr); *Puss in Boots* (50fr). SET B: *Little Red Riding Hood* (40fr); *The Gingerbread Boy* (34fr). SET C: *Cinderella* (47fr); *The Four Musicians* (51fr); *The Boy and the North Wind* (45fr). SET D: *Hansel and Gretel* (52fr); *The Lion and the Mouse* (38fr); *Rumpelstiltskin* (50fr) (YoungAmerica). All four sets color.
TALES FROM GRIMM AND ANDERSEN series: *The Shoemaker and the Elves* (26fr); *The Wolf and the Seven Little Kids* (26fr); *Rapunzel* (29fr); *The Frog Prince* (26fr); *Spindle, Shuttle, and Needle* (29fr); *Hans Clodhopper* (28fr); *The Princess and the Pea* (22fr) (JamHandy). Color.

Records

Cinderella. (Disneyland.)
Favorite Stories. (RCA Camden.)
Hansel and Gretel, by Engelbert Humperdinck, recorded by The Metropolitan Opera Company. (Columbia—SL 102.)
"Hens and Roosters," from *Carnival of Animals*, by Camille Saint-Saens. $33\frac{1}{3}$ rpm, 12". (Columbia—CL 720.)
Sleeping Beauty, told by Gudrun Thorne Thomsen. (American Library Association.)
The Raggletaggletown Singers, sung and recorded by Frank Luther. 78rpm (LUTHERecord 1001. Ginn.)
The Ugly Duckling, sung and recorded by Frank Luther. 78rpm (LUTHERecord 1002. Ginn.)

VIII

Directory of Publishers

ABELARD-SCHUMAN, LTD., 404 Fourth Avenue, New York 16, New York.

ABINGDON PRESS, 150 Fifth Avenue, New York 11, New York.

ALLYN AND BACON, INC., 150 Tremont Street, Boston 11, Massachusetts.

AMERICAN BOOK COMPANY, 55 Fifth Avenue, New York 3, New York.

THE AMERICAN LIBRARY ASSOCIATION, 50 East Huron Street, Chicago 11, Illinois.

THE ANTIOCH PRESS, Yellow Springs, Ohio.

APPLETON-CENTURY-CROFTS, INC., 35 West 32nd Street, New York 1, New York.

THE ASSOCIATION FOR CHILDHOOD EDUCATION INTERNATIONAL, 1200 Fifteenth Street, N.W., Washington 5, D.C.

THE ASSOCIATION FOR SUPERVISION AND CURRICULUM DEVELOPMENT, 1201 16th Street, N.W., Washington 6, D.C.

A. S. BARNES AND COMPANY, 11 East 36th Street, New York 16, New York.

BEACON PRESS, INC., 25 Beacon Street, Boston 8, Massachusetts.

BASIL BLACKWELL AND MOTT, LTD., 49 Broad Street, Oxford, England.

BINFORDS AND MORT, PUBLISHERS, 124 N.W. 9th Avenue, Portland 9, Oregon.

THE BOBBS-MERRILL COMPANY, INC., 730 North Meridian Street, Indianapolis 7, Indiana.

THE BOOK HOUSE FOR CHILDREN, Tangley Oaks, Lake Bluff, Illinois.

BUREAU OF PUBLICATIONS, Teachers College, Columbia University, 525 West 120th Street, New York 27, New York.

CAPITOL PUBLISHING COMPANY, INC., 737 Broadway, New York 3, New York.

CHARTWELL HOUSE, INC., 112 East 19th Street, New York 3, New York.

CHILDRENS PRESS, INC., Jackson Boulevard and Racine Avenue, Chicago 7, Illinois.

COWARD-MCCANN, INC., 210 Madison Avenue, New York 16, New York.

COWMAN PUBLICATIONS, INC., 747 North Seward Street, Los Angeles 38, California.

ARTHUR C. CROFT PUBLICATIONS, 100 Garfield Avenue, New London, Connecticut.

THOMAS Y. CROWELL COMPANY, 432 Fourth Avenue, New York 16, New York.

THE JOHN DAY COMPANY, INC., 62 West 45th Street, New York 36, New York.

DODD, MEAD & COMPANY, INC., 432 Fourth Avenue, New York 16, New York.

DOUBLEDAY & COMPANY, INC., 575 Madison Avenue, New York 22, New York.

DOVER PUBLICATIONS, INC., 920 Broadway, New York 10, New York.

E. P. DUTTON & CO., INC., 300 Fourth Avenue, New York 10, New York.

FARRAR, STRAUS AND CUDAHY, INC., 101 Fifth Avenue, New York 3, New York.
FEARON PUBLISHERS, 2450 Fillmore Street, San Francisco 15, California.
FOLLETT PUBLISHING COMPANY, 1010 West Washington Boulevard, Chicago 7, Illinois.
THE GARRARD PRESS, 119–123 West Park Avenue, Champaign, Illinois.
GINN AND COMPANY, Statler Building, Boston 17, Massachusetts.
GROSSET & DUNLAP, INC., 1107 Broadway, New York 10, New York.
HARCOURT, BRACE AND COMPANY, 750 Third Avenue, New York 17, New York.
HARPER & BROTHERS, 49 East 33rd Street, New York 16, New York.
D. C. HEATH AND COMPANY, 285 Columbus Avenue, Boston 16, Massachusetts.
HENRY HOLT AND COMPANY, INC., 383 Madison Avenue, New York 17, New York.
THE HORN BOOK, INC., 585 Boylston Street, Boston 16, Massachusetts.
HOUGHTON MIFFLIN COMPANY, 2 Park Street, Boston 7, Massachusetts.
INTERNATIONAL TEXTBOOK COMPANY, 1001 Wyoming Avenue, Scranton 9, Pennsylvania.
ALFRED A. KNOPF, INC., 501 Madison Avenue, New York 22, New York.
J. B. LIPPINCOTT COMPANY, East Washington Square, Philadelphia 5, Pennsylvania.
LITTLE, BROWN AND COMPANY, 34 Beacon Street, Boston 6, Massachusetts.
LONGMANS, GREEN & CO., INC., 55 Fifth Avenue, New York 3, New York.
LOTHROP, LEE & SHEPARD COMPANY, INC., 419 Fourth Avenue, New York 16, New York.
LYONS AND CARNAHAN, 2500 Prairie Avenue, Chicago 16, Illinois.
MCGRAW-HILL BOOK COMPANY, INC., 330 West 42nd Street, New York 36, New York.
DAVID MCKAY COMPANY, INC., 55 Fifth Avenue, New York 3, New York.
THE MACMILLAN COMPANY, 60 Fifth Avenue, New York 11, New York.
MACRAE SMITH COMPANY, 225 South 15th Street, Philadelphia 2, Pennsylvania.
WILLIAM MORROW AND COMPANY, INC., 425 Fourth Avenue, New York 16, New York.
THE NATIONAL COUNCIL OF TEACHERS OF ENGLISH, 704 South Sixth Street, Champaign, Illinois.
THE NATIONAL EDUCATION ASSOCIATION OF THE UNITED STATES, 1201 16th Street, N.W., Washington 6, D.C.
THOMAS NELSON & SONS, 19 East 47th Street, New York 17, New York.
OXFORD UNIVERSITY PRESS, INC., 114 Fifth Avenue, New York 11, New York.
PANTHEON BOOKS, INC., 333 Sixth Avenue, New York 14, New York.
PEARN, POLLINGER, AND HIGHAM, 76 Dean Street, Soho, London, W. 1, England.
THE PLATT & MUNK CO., INC., 200 Fifth Avenue, New York 10, New York.
PRENTICE-HALL, INC., 70 Fifth Avenue, New York 11, New York.
G. P. PUTNAM'S SONS, 210 Madison Avenue, New York 16, New York.
RAND MCNALLY & COMPANY, P.O. Box 7600, Chicago 80, Illinois.
RANDOM HOUSE, INC., 457 Madison Avenue, New York 22, New York.
RINEHART & COMPANY, INC., 232 Madison Avenue, New York 16, New York.
THE RONALD PRESS COMPANY, 15 East 26th Street, New York 10, New York.
ROW, PETERSON AND CO., 1911 Ridge Avenue, Evanston, Illinois.
SCIENCE RESEARCH ASSOCIATES, 57 West Grand Avenue, Chicago 10, Illinois.

WILLIAM R. SCOTT, INC., 8 West 13th Street, New York 11, New York.

SCOTT, FORESMAN AND COMPANY, 433 East Erie Street, Chicago 11, Illinois.

CHARLES SCRIBNER'S SONS, 597 Fifth Avenue, New York 17, New York.

SIDGWICK & JACKSON, LTD., 1 Tavistock Chambers, Bloomsbury Way, London, W.C. 1, England.

SILVER BURDETT COMPANY, Park Avenue and Columbia Road, Morristown, New Jersey.

SIMON AND SCHUSTER, INC., 630 Fifth Avenue, New York 20, New York.

THE STECK COMPANY, Ninth and Lavaca Streets, Austin 6, Texas.

SUMMY-BIRCHARD PUBLISHING CO., 1834 Ridge Avenue, Evanston, Illinois.

TRANSATLANTIC ARTS, INC., Hollywood-by-the-Sea, Florida.

UNITED STATES GOVERNMENT PRINTING OFFICE, North Capitol and H Streets, N.W., Washington 25, D.C.

UNIVERSITY OF CALIFORNIA PRESS, Berkeley 4, California.

THE UNIVERSITY OF CHICAGO PRESS, 5750 Ellis Avenue, Chicago 37, Illinois.

VANGUARD PRESS, INC., 424 Madison Avenue, New York 17, New York.

D. VAN NOSTRAND COMPANY, INC., 120 Alexander Street, Princeton, New Jersey.

THE VIKING PRESS, 625 Madison Avenue, New York 22, New York.

FREDERICK WARNE & CO., INC., 210 Fifth Avenue, New York 10, New York.

FRANKLIN WATTS, INC., 699 Madison Avenue, New York 21, New York.

THE WESTMINSTER PRESS, Witherspoon Building, Philadelphia 7, Pennsylvania.

ALBERT WHITMAN & COMPANY, 560 West Lake Street, Chicago 6, Illinois.

WILCOX & FOLLETT CO., 1000 West Washington Boulevard, Chicago 7, Illinois.

THE WILLIAM-FREDERICK PRESS, 313–315 West 35th Street, New York 1, New York.

THE H. W. WILSON COMPANY, 950–972 University Avenue, New York 52, New York.

THE JOHN C. WINSTON COMPANY, 1010 Arch Street, Philadelphia 7, Pennsylvania.

WORLD BOOK COMPANY, 313 Park Hill Avenue, Yonkers 5, New York.

THE WORLD PUBLISHING COMPANY, 2231 West 110th Street, Cleveland 2, Ohio.

DISTRIBUTORS AND PRODUCERS OF AUDIO–VISUAL AIDS

(Bailey)   Bailey Films, Inc., 6509 Longpre Ave., Hollywood 28, Calif.

(Barr)   Arthur Barr Productions, 6211 Arroya Glen, Los Angeles 42, Calif.; 1265 Bresee Ave., Pasadena 7, Calif.

(Cornell)   Cornell Film Company, 1501 Broadway, New York 36, N.Y.

(Coronet)   Coronet Films, Coronet Bldg., Chicago 1, Ill.

(CurriculumFlms)   Curriculum Materials Corp., 1319 Vine Street, Philadelphia 7, Pa.

(Dowling)   Pat Dowling Pictures, 1056 S. Robertson Blvd., Los Angeles 35, Calif.

(EBF)   Encyclopædia Britannica Films, Inc., 1150 Wilmette Ave., Wilmette, Ill.

(EyeGate)   Eye Gate House, Inc., 2716 Forty-first Ave., Long Island City 1, N.Y.

(FilmAssociates)   Film Associates of California, 10521 Santa Monica Blvd., Los Angeles 25, Calif.

(FosterFlms)   Foster Films, 6 Kneeland Ave., Binghamton, N.Y.

505

(Frith)   Frith Films, 1816 N. Highland, Hollywood 28, Calif.

(GatewayProd)   Gateway Productions, Inc., 1859 Powell St., San Francisco 11, Calif.

(Heidenkamp)   Heidenkamp Nature Pictures, 538 Glen Arden Dr., Pittsburgh 8, Pa.

(InstrFlms)   Instructional Films, Inc., 1150 Wilmette Ave., Wilmette, Ill.

(IntlEducMatlsCorp)   International Education Materials Corporation, 625 Madison Ave., New York 22, N.Y.

(JamHandy)   The Jam Handy Organization, 2821 E. Grand Blvd., Detroit 11, Mich.

(PopScience)   Popular Science Filmstrips, McGraw-Hill Text-Film Department, 330 West 42nd St., New York 36, N.Y.

(SVE)   Society for Visual Education, Inc., 1345 W. Diversey Parkway, Chicago 14, Ill.

(TompkinsFlms)   Tompkins Films, 960½ Larrabee St., Los Angeles 46, Calif.

(WestonWoods)   Weston Woods Studios, Inc., Westport, Conn.

(YoungAmerica)   Young America Films, McGraw-Hill Book Company, Text-Film Department, 330 West 42nd St., New York 36, N.Y.

RECORDINGS

Columbia Records, 799 Seventh Avenue, New York 19, New York.

Decca Records, Inc., 50 West 57th St., New York 19, New York.

Folkways Record and Service Corporation, 117 West 46th St., New York 36, New York.

Ginn and Company, Statler Building, Boston 17, Massachusetts.

Radio Corporation of America (RCA Victor), Educational Sales Department, Camden, New Jersey.

story books, 252–253; dioramas, 133, 436, 451, 460, 465; dragon heads, 357; "Fair Play" chart, 339–340; frieze, 409; hand puppets, 219, 228, 237; holiday calendar, 417–418; Indian chart, 82–83, 286; Indian costumes, 286; Indian dictionary, 264, 287; Indian dolls, 274; Indian mural, 274; Indian objects, 266; Indian play, 296; invitation cards, 185; leather products, 323; lion charts, 162; masks, 388; mobiles, 155; movie, 207, 208; murals, 146, 155, 162, 173, 182, 303, 304, 325, 331, 436; peace pipe, 303; picture dictionary, 250; picture map, 287, 311; picture-story map, 323, 331, 356; play programs, 459; pocket chart, 82–83, 286; puppet theater, 220; puzzles, 162; scenery, 228; succotash, 274; tachistoscope, 132–133, 190; toy papier mâché horse, 85; valentines, 415; vowel chart, 170; word wheel, 191; for patriotic holiday program, 424–425; for publishing class newspaper, 377, 388, 400, 409, 415; for puppet shows, 219, 227, 228, 237, 244; for quiz program, 154–155; for story hour, 228; for Valentine party, 415–416; for zoo exhibit, 145–146; for zoo party, 185. *See also* Charts, Programs, *and* Projects

Directory of publishers, 503–505

Discussions, 96, 122, 144, 175, 188, 208, 234, 245, 246–247, 248, 255, 273, 277, 285, 291, 300, 303, 322, 325, 339–340, 347, 357–358, 371, 375–376, 384, 390, 399, 402, 408, 427, 430, 454, 461–462, 467; for background, 149, 289–290, 326–327, 349–350, 367, 409–410, 438–439; introduction to, 62; of questions and answers, 282; of text in review, 473–475; of related concepts and experiences, 72, 87, 88, 89–90, 98, 104, 112, 114, 120, 138, 157, 165–166, 200, 213, 223, 238–239, 264, 267, 279, 297–298, 316–317, 333–334, 341–342, 355, 370, 382, 393, 447–448, 458; to compare interpretations, 346–347; to form judgments, 218

Displays, 72, 82, 84, 97, 111, 129, 146, 182, 252, 255, 347, 356, 400, 459, 466. *See also* Exhibits

Dramatic play, 44, 133, 165, 183, 219, 220, 227

Dramatization, 44, 104, 240, 275, 295, 311, 355, 408, 435, 451, 454, 458–459

Drawing, 83, 92, 145, 146, 154, 155, 165, 182, 185, 202, 225, 237, 277, 280, 286, 323, 325, 328, 331, 345, 347, 356, 400, 409, 444. *See also* Illustrating

Enrichment activities, 17, 33–35, 55, 62–64. *See under this heading throughout the lesson plans*

Enunciation, 92, 110, 154, 180, 274, 435; game, 180

Evaluation, 12–13, 37, 65; by children, 120, 150, 244, 274, 355, 470; informal analysis, 66, 67, 92, 122, 126–128, 192–193, 251–252, 362, 469, 470, 471; of oral reading, 192–193; of reading habits, 250; of test results, 53, 123–126, 186–189, 248–250, 359–362, 418–420; of text, 473–474. *See also* Tests *and* Activities, all-unit

Excursions, 97, 144–145, 210, 365, 460

Exhibits, 104–105, 121, 145–146, 162, 173, 266, 277–278, 304, 358, 409, 436, 447, 474. *See also* Displays

Eye-voice span, improvement of, 194, 309–311

Films to enjoy, 64, 89, 97, 111, 122, 148, 164, 165, 276, 289, 303, 324, 389, 401, 438, 452

Filmstrips to enjoy, 64, 86, 97, 111, 122, 135, 148, 212, 266, 276, 289, 297, 324, 380, 401, 438, 445, 452, 459, 460

Finding New Neighbors, 46; description of, 52; function of, 52; lesson plans for, 69–475; summarizing, 473–475. *See also* Program, third year

Folk tales, 438–440, 460; Danish, 461–466; fables, 447–448, 451–452; Indian, 288; Norse, 453–454; Swedish, 430–431

Following directions, 101, 154, 180, 207, 241–242, 307–308, 344–345, 359, 432, 440–441; giving directions, 303

Framing, introduction to, 56; word parts, 251, 317; words, 129, 166, 205, 243, 290

Games, alphabet, 407; baseball, 421; "Beanbag Toss," 189–190; chart of, 341; clapping, 206–207, 218, 234; drill, 189, 421; "Find It Quickly," 422; "Fish," 421; "Football," 468; guessing, 175; "Going on a Trip," 180–181; "I Am Thinking," 423; "I Packed My Suitcase and Took—," 180–181; Indian, 278, 303; "Information, Please," 417; learning new games, 340–341; listening, 180–181; "Listening for Vowel

Sounds," 227; "Look and Find," 132; phonetic analysis, 421; "play parrot," 180; "Quick Look," 364; research on, 208; to review story characters, 475; rhyming, 422–423; "Stop and Go," 132; structural analysis, 421; syllable, 206–207, 218, 234; vocabulary, 468; vocabulary review, 189–190; word, 132, 203–204, 308–309; word-recognition, 189–190, 364, 468

Generalizations, 77, 160, 170, 206, 207, 226, 246–247, 320, 321, 331, 346–347, 374, 386, 413, 464, 469

Grouping, 47, 53, 62, 66, 92, 128, 172, 175, 180, 192–193, 227, 250, 362, 385, 421–423, 465

Guided reading, step in lesson plans, 57–58; suggestions for, 90, 115, 167, 201, 282, 350. *See under this heading throughout the lesson plans*

Habits, reading. *See* Reading habits

Highlights, description of, 56; of lesson plans, 72, 89, 98, 105, 113, 138, 149, 156, 165, 174, 200, 213, 222, 229, 238, 258, 267, 279, 289, 297, 326, 333, 341, 349, 370, 382, 392, 402, 409, 430, 438, 447, 453, 461

Holidays, 367; calendar of, 417–418; Christmas, 392–401; Columbus Day, 370–380; Halloween, 380–389; New Year's Day, 402–409; summarization of origin and meaning of, 425; Thanksgiving, 390–392; Valentine's Day, 409–417

Illustrating, 83, 92, 96, 104, 110, 120, 121, 132, 133, 155, 162, 174, 181, 202, 225, 234, 237, 241–242, 264, 273, 277, 287, 325, 326, 328, 335, 377, 379, 381, 399, 400, 409, 444, 447, 465, 466. *See also* Painting *and* Pictures

Independent reading, 49, 64; sharing, 123; stimulating, 127–128. *See also* Stories in other readers *and* Stories to enjoy

Index of word-study skills, 476–479

Individual differences, provisions for, 38–41, 61, 65–67, 92; general suggestions, 38–40, 126–128, 189, 250–251, 308–309, 362; specific suggestions, 40–41, 66, 128–133, 192–195, 251–253, 309–311, 362–365, 421–425, 470–473; vertical program of, 10

Information, arousing interest for, 135; books for, 266, 275, 296, 303; collecting related, 377; locating, 83, 104, 111, 269, 311, 355,

376–377, 432; organization of, 140, 260–261, 283, 285, 293, 300, 355–356, 377, 384; securing, 121, 133, 182, 195, 261, 266, 274, 285, 296, 303, 340–341, 425

Informational books, 266, 275, 296, 303

Interests, reading, 29–31, 44–45, 127–128; chart of, 236–237; motivation of, 133, 191–192, 195, 209–210, 427

Interpretation of moods, 107, 175, 180, 220, 240, 292, 295, 328, 391, 394–395, 411, 422, 454

Inventory of progress, 65; of growth in attitudes toward reading, 66; of growth in reading independence, 470, 471; of growth in reading skills, 67; of oral reading abilities, 193; of reading interests, 191–192; of word-attack skills, 127

Labels, objects, 304, 311, 436; picture, 129, 304

Language experiences, related, 31–33, 61–62. *See under this heading throughout the lesson plans*

Lesson plans, character of, 55; examples of, 57–58; steps in, 55–56; for Third Reader I, 69–475

Letter writing, 322, 331, 404, 408

Library corner, activities for, 182, 252–253, 287; chart, 236–237; committees for, 111, 227, 228, 244, 287; construction of, 208–209; donating of books for, 209; management of, 219, 227–228; story hours, 195, 210, 227, 228, 237, 275, 444, 460, 466; use of, 72, 122, 191–192, 208–210, 244, 264, 274. *See also* Stories in other readers

Listening, development of skills, 61–62, 96, 111–112, 120–121, 147–148, 172, 175, 180–182, 184–185, 235–236, 245, 277, 323, 325, 328, 331, 357–358, 388, 389, 390–391, 416–417, 443–444, 445, 451, 459; for descriptive parts, 214; games, 180–181; to visualize poetry, 87–88, 164–165, 234, 273, 380–381, 399

Literary appreciation, 51, 52, 175, 181–182, 197–253, 331, 399, 427–475. *See also* Poems to enjoy *and* Stories to enjoy

Main idea, reading for, 48, 60; associating events with subtitles, 292; choosing titles, 215–216, 231, 232, 362, 385, 455; choosing subtitles, 77, 93; classifying related ideas,

513

54–55, (I) 123, 124, (II) 186, (III) 305–306, (IV) 467; vertical program of, 20–22

Voice, use of, 62, 75, 92, 107, 116, 158, 180, 194, 219, 227, 274, 295, 328, 395, 422, 435. *See also* Speech training

Vowel sounds, chart, 170; digraphs, 143–144, 160, 161, 218, 301, 338, 353, 374, 406, 450, 469; diphthongs, 284, 301–302, 354, 363, 442–443; lengthened by silent *e*, 108–110, 393, 412–413; long, 102–103, 108–110, 176–177, 225–226, 307; principles of, 108–110, 160, 226, 232–233, 271, 346, 353, 374, 406, 413, 450, 469; review of, 102–103, 160, 161, 170, 225–226, 232–233, 374; short, 102–103, 177, 225–226, 307; silent, 108–110, 160, 226, 353, 374, 470, 471; variant sounds, 170, 176–177, 216–218, 251, 301, 338, 345–346, 450, 464, 469

Word-analysis, encouraging independent word-attack, 170, 177, 262–263, 272; tests, 125–126. *See also* Index of word-study skills, Phonetic analysis, *and* Structural analysis

Word meaning, 24–25; list of skills, 49; antonyms, 101–102, 118, 232, 373, 412, 413; classifying, 152, 249; enriching, 94, 116, 129, 159–160, 216, 217, 250, 337, 362–363, 372–373, 446; extending, 169, 250, 293; finding descriptive words (adjectives), 108, 189, 363; games, 203–204; homonyms, 301, 396–397, 456; hyphenated words, 243, 345; interpreting phrases, 78–79, 318–319, 442; mastering difficult words, 78, 95; matching words with meaning, 114–115, 169, 186, 330, 337; recognizing descriptive action words (verbs), 231, 319–320, 363; synonyms, 216, 217, 373, 412, 413; tests, 186, 249; use in word-attack, 293, 353; using context clues, 78, 270

Word recognition, list of skills, 50; checking, 123, 124, 305–306, 467; developing independence in, 130–131, 157, 170, 382, 424, 432–433; games, 189–190, 364, 468; improvement of, 118, 128–133, 363; look-alike words, 131; methods of word attack, 73, 78, 95, 345–346, 353, 398, 432–433; practice, 284; tests, 248–249; using context clues, 248–249, 397–398, 424, 432–433

Word-study skills, 60–61; index of, 476–479; list of, 49–51, 61; vertical program of, 20–22

Workbook, use of, 53–55, 61. *See under this heading throughout this manual*

Worksheets, for independent practice, 79, 82, 90, 93, 94, 100, 101, 102, 103, 107, 108, 109, 117–118, 124, 125, 126, 131, 141, 142, 151, 152, 159, 161, 168, 169, 171, 176–177, 179, 186, 188, 203, 215, 216, 217, 225, 231, 232, 241, 248–249, 250, 251, 261–262, 270, 272, 281, 283, 291, 292, 294, 300, 301, 302, 306–307, 308, 309, 319, 320, 321, 329, 330, 336–337, 339, 344, 352, 353, 359, 360, 361, 362–363, 372, 373, 384, 386, 395, 396, 397, 398, 405, 412, 413, 414, 418, 419–420, 423, 424, 432, 440, 441, 442, 448, 449, 450, 455, 456, 458, 463, 464, 471, 474

Writing, 61, 62, 93, 96, 104, 110, 133, 145, 185, 195, 237, 252–253, 295, 303, 331, 358, 408; Chinese, 364; Indian picture, 295, 296; introduction to, 62, 63. *See also* Creative writing

Illustrations by Warren Buckley, Paul Granger, Robert Magnusen, and Kenneth MacKellar, Inc.

Finding
New Neighbors

REVISED EDITION

- •DAVID H. RUSSELL
- •GRETCHEN WULFING
- •ODILLE OUSLEY

GINN AND COMPANY | BOSTON · NEW YORK · CHICAGO · ATLANTA
DALLAS · PALO ALTO · TORONTO · LONDON

Acknowledgments

Grateful acknowledgment is made to the following authors and publishers for permission to use and adapt copyrighted materials:

Abingdon Press for "Speckles and the New Boy," adapted from *Speckles Goes to School* by Grace Berquist, copyright, 1952, by Pierce and Smith, and published by Abingdon Press.

Thomas Y. Crowell Company for "The Rodeo," adapted from *A Ranch for Danny* by Clyde Robert Bulla, copyright, 1951, by Clyde Robert Bulla. Adapted and reprinted by permission of the publishers, Thomas Y. Crowell Company, New York.

Doubleday & Company, Inc., for the poems "The Animal Store" and "The Ice-Cream Man," from *Taxis and Toadstools* by Rachel Field, copyright, 1926, by Doubleday & Company, Inc.; and for "Teeny and the Tall Man," adapted from *Teeny and the Tall Man* by Julian Meade, copyright, 1936, by Julian R. Meade, adapted and reprinted by permission of Doubleday & Company, Inc.

E. P. Dutton & Company, Inc., for "The Friendly Ghost" by Elizabeth Yates, adapted from the book *Spooks and Spirits and Shadowy Shapes*, copyright, 1949, American Book Company, adaptation used by permission of E. P. Dutton & Company, Inc., publishers; for the poem "Tiger," from the book *Stories to Begin On* by Rhoda W. Bacmeister, copyright, 1940, by E. P. Dutton & Company, Inc.; and for "The Little Cat That Could Not Sleep," adapted from *The Little Cat That Could Not Sleep* by Frances Margaret Fox, copyright, 1941, by E. P. Dutton & Company, Inc.

Alfred A. Knopf, Inc., for "Helping Hilda," adapted and reprinted from *Kristie and the Colt* by Emma L. Brock, by permission of Alfred A. Knopf, Inc. Copyright, 1942, 1945, 1947, 1949, by Alfred A. Knopf, Inc.

J. B. Lippincott Company for "He-Who-Thinks-Well-and-Runs-Quickly," adapted from *Indian Hunting Grounds* by Caroline D. Emerson, copyright, 1938, by J. B. Lippincott Company.

The Macmillan Company for "Baby Bears," adapted from *Baby Bears* by E. Charushin, copyright, 1944, by The Macmillan Company; and for "Little Fox of the Forest," adapted from *Little Fox* by Katharine Keelor, copyright, 1932, by The Macmillan Company; both by permission of the publishers.

Phyllis McGinley for "The Horse Who Lived Upstairs," adapted from *The Horse Who Lived Upstairs* by Phyllis McGinley. Adapted and reprinted by permission of the author. Copyright, 1944, by Phyllis McGinley. Published by J. B. Lippincott Company.

McGraw-Hill Book Company, Inc., for the poem "Halloween," reprinted by permission from *The Little Whistler* by Frances Frost, published by McGraw-Hill Book Company, Inc., copyright, 1949, by McGraw-Hill Book Company, Inc.

William Morrow and Company, Inc., for "The Chimpanzee That Mopped the Floor," adapted from *Zoo Babies* by William Bridges, copyright, 1953, by William Bridges, by permission of William Morrow and Company, Inc.

Oxford University Press, Inc., for "Azor," adapted from *Azor* by Maude Crowley, copyright, 1948, by Oxford University Press, Inc. Adapted and reprinted by permission of the author and Oxford University Press, Inc.

2

American Junior Red Cross News and Rose Leion for adaptations of "Billy Tigertail" and "El Burrito" (Little Burro), copyrighted by the American National Red Cross.

Carol Ryrie Brink for "The Boy Who Believed," adapted from her story in *Come to Storyland*, published by The Saalfield Publishing Co.

Dodd, Mead & Company, Inc., for "New Shoes," from *Tell Them Again Tales* by Margaret and Mary Baker, copyright, 1934, by Dodd, Mead & Company, Inc.

Ginn and Company for "Blue Cornflower" by Ann Nolan Clark, adapted from *The Great Idea* in *The Children's Bookshelf*.

Harcourt, Brace and Company, Inc., for "Cowboys Are Brave," adapted from *Two and Two Are Four* by Carolyn Haywood, copyright, 1940, by Harcourt, Brace and Company, Inc.; and for "The Princess Who Always Believed What She Heard," adapted from *Thirteen Danish Tales* retold by Mary C. Hatch, copyright, 1947, by Harcourt, Brace and Company, Inc.

Holiday House for "Maggie the Magpie," adapted from *Maggie: A Mischievous Magpie* by Irma Simonton Black, copyright, 1949, by Holiday House; and for "How Percival Caught the Tiger," adapted from *How Percival Caught the Tiger* by Percival Stutters, copyright, 1936, by Holiday House. Both by permission of the publisher.

Jack and Jill and the authors for the following stories: an adaptation of "The Valentine Box" by Maud Hart Lovelace; "Big Barby" by Zillah K. Macdonald; and "Bob Learns to Pitch" by Worthen C. Cornish. All copyrighted by The Curtis Publishing Company.

Little, Brown and Company for the poem "Some Fishy Nonsense," from *Tirra Lirra* by Laura E. Richards.

G. P. Putnam's Sons for "The Lad and the North Wind," adapted from *Popular Tales from the Norse* by George Webbe Dasent; and for the poems "The Harpers' Farm," from *Hop, Skip and Jump* by Dorothy Aldis, copyright, 1936, courtesy of G. P. Putnam's Sons; and "In Spring in Warm Weather," from *All Together* by Dorothy Aldis, copyright, 1952, courtesy of G. P. Putnam's Sons.

Story Parade, Inc., for "Barney on TV," adapted from *Barney Broadcasts* by Eda and Richard Crist, copyright, 1954, by Story Parade, Inc. Adapted and reprinted by permission.

The Viking Press, Inc., for "The Doctor at the Zoo," from *Big Zoo* by William Bridges, copyright, 1941, by William Bridges and Desider Holisher, adapted and reprinted by permission of The Viking Press, Inc., New York; for "Home," from *In My Mother's House* by Ann Nolan Clark, copyright, 1941, by Ann Nolan Clark, reprinted by permission of The Viking Press, Inc., New York; and for "The Eagle Hunt," from *Dancing Cloud* by Mary and Conrad Buff, copyright, 1937, by Mary Marsh and Conrad Buff, adapted and reprinted by permission of The Viking Press, Inc., New York.

Albert Whitman & Company for "New Moon and the Dragon," from *Young Americans from Many Lands* by Anne Merriman Peck and Enid Johnson, copyright, 1935, by the publisher, Albert Whitman & Company.

Yale University Press for "Chanticleer" by John Farrar, from *Songs for Parents*, copyright, 1942, by Yale University Press.

Special acknowledgment is made to Nora Burglon for "Christmas with Stina Mor" and to Henry R. Fea for "A Dog of His Own," stories not previously published; and to Vida F. Aygarn for her adaptation of "The Lad and the North Wind."

ILLUSTRATIONS BY Carl Bobertz, Edward Bradford, André Dugo, Phoebe Erickson, William S. Gillies, Barbara Latham, Margo Pisillo, John Polgreen, Ray Quigley, Fred Scott-Wood, Kate Seredy, George Withers, and Cleveland L. Woodward

Stories in This Book

Pets and Playtime

At the Zoo

Just for Fun

Indian Children

Americans All

Days Everyone Likes

Old, Old Stories

7

Big Barby

Making Friends with Barby

When Father first brought Barby home,
the children were afraid of her because
she was so big. She looked as big as an
elephant to the twins.

"She's big, but she's gentle," said
Father to the four children. "I bought
her because she is gentle."

8

Just then Barby turned her big head, and the twins were afraid. Peggy ran behind Mary. When Barby moved about, Pat took hold of Father's hand.

"You need not be afraid of Barby," said Father. "Andrew, you may show her the way around the place."

Andrew was a little afraid, but he said, "Come, Barby." He took the big horse into the barn and out.

"Let her learn the way to the drinking place," said Father. "Take her around the yard, Andrew. Let her get used to you and the farm."

9

So Andrew took Barby to the drinking place and let her have a drink. Then he took her into the shed where the wagon had been put.

The other children thought Andrew was very brave because he did not look afraid.

"Does Barby like sugar?" Mary asked. She took some sugar out of her pocket and gave it to Andrew.

"Hold your hand out flat," Father said. He showed Andrew how to hold the sugar for Barby.

"Don't be afraid and don't pull your hand back when she touches it," he said.

10

Andrew put his hand under Barby's nose. He could feel her mouth soft and wet as it touched his hand. Andrew was afraid, but he did not move. Then the sugar was gone.

"She took it," Andrew said. He had a brave, pleased feeling.

"Let me give her some sugar," said Pat.

"Let me," said Peggy.

"No," said Father. "Let her get used to Andrew first. One at a time."

It was not many days before Barby was a real pet. She was never tied. She came at the children's call. She would look for sugar in their pockets.

Riding to School

"School starts tomorrow," said Andrew.

"I want to go to school," said Peggy. "I'm six years old."

"Oh, it's too far for you to walk," said Mother. "It's a long way to school and a long way home! It's too far for you and Pat to walk."

"But not too far to ride," Father said. "Barby will take you all to school. That is why I bought her."

So the next morning Barby learned something new. She learned the way to school. Father showed her how to go. The four children rode on her wide back.

12

Andrew sat in front, holding fast to Barby. Behind him sat the six-year-old twins. Mary came last. She put her arms around the twins. They took hold of Andrew.

Clop, clop, clop. Barby went down the side road to the highway.

Clop, clop, clop. Barby stepped with care because of the stones in the road.

Clop, clop, clop. Down the hill to the brook and up the long hill on the other side, Barby went with her load.

When they reached the schoolhouse, Father helped the children down. Then he took Barby home again.

In the afternoon when school was out, Father and Barby were waiting to take the children home.

After that, Barby knew the way. Father never came with her again. She would carry the children right to the schoolhouse steps.

Mary would always slide off Barby's wide back first. Then she would hold up her arms to catch Peggy. Next Pat would slide down, and last of all Andrew.

Then Barby would start home—clop, clop, clop. In the afternoon she would come back to get the children. All winter and through the spring Barby carried them to and from school.

When summer came, Father took Barby to a field on the far side of the farm. The children did not see her for a long time.

14

"When is Barby coming back?" the twins asked. "We want to ride on Barby."

"You shall ride again when school starts," Father told them.

One day the twins had a birthday party. They were seven years old. They had presents and a cake with seven candles.

While the children were eating the cake and ice cream, something happened.

"Look!" called one boy.

The twins turned around quickly. There was the big horse at the window.

"Barby has come to our party," said Peggy.

15

"Barby wants some cake," said Pat, holding some out on his hand.

But Barby did not take the cake. She turned away from the window.

Then Father called, "Barby is asking you to come out. She has some birthday presents for you."

When the children ran outdoors, they saw two frisky colts near Barby.

"Twin colts!" said Pat.

"A colt for each of us," said Peggy.

"Good Barby," said Mary. She petted the horse's soft nose.

"Someday your colts will help you carry us to school," said Andrew.

Zillah K. Macdonald

16

In Spring in Warm Weather

Little colts caper and kick up their heels.
They race toward their mothers when
  ready for meals.
Wobbly kneed calves stand close to the
  barn
Out of the wind where it's sheltered and
  warm.
Woolly lambs, all of them, know right
  away
That the first thing to do is to learn how
  to play.
New kittens are mewing, new mice try to
  squeak,
New birds in their nests will fly in a week—
In spring, in warm weather, all over our
  farm
There's hardly a baby that hasn't been
  born.

Dorothy Aldis

17

Speckles and the New Boy

Can Speckles Help?

Jerry left his wagon outside and went into the henhouse. He put his hands under his little hen to pick her up.

"Speckles," he said, "I'm going to take you to school. Miss Baker asked if any of us had a setting hen we could bring to school. Will you be good and sit on eggs and hatch chicks?"

"Cut-cut-a-cut," said Speckles.

Jerry took Speckles outside and put her into the box waiting in his wagon. Then he started down the road to school.

18

"Cluck, cluck, cluck," said Speckles, as the wagon rattled along.

"I knew you wanted to set, Speckles," said Jerry. "I knew it when you wouldn't get off your nest. So I told Miss Baker I would bring you to school today."

It was easy to talk to Speckles. Jerry wished it were just as easy to talk with the boys and girls at the new school.

"You will like school, Speckles," he said. "I want you to be good and hatch the chicks. Then the boys and girls may stop calling me the new boy."

19

When Jerry brought Speckles into the schoolroom, everyone ran to look at her.

"A hen! The new boy brought a hen!" Ann's mouth flew open round like an O.

Bob tripped and bumped into Jerry, who dropped the box.

Out flew Speckles. Round and round she ran under tables and chairs. Away she flew straight for an open window.

"Catch her!" Jerry called. "She will fly out the window!"

Tony put the window down with a bang. The little speckled hen flew to Miss Baker's table. Papers fell to the floor.

20

" Cut-cut-cut-a-cut," said Speckles.

She flew off the table and ran into a corner. There Jerry picked her up.

" Don't be afraid, Speckles," he said.

Miss Baker had a pen ready for Speckles. Its gate was just big enough for a boy to get through. There was straw on the floor.

Inside the pen was a low box with straw in it. There were some brown eggs in the box. This was to be Speckles' nest.

Jerry put Speckles in the pen and petted her. Ann sprinkled feed on the straw. Bob set a pan of water in the pen.

21

Speckles ran to hide behind the nest. Then she walked around inside the pen. Her feathers looked shiny in the sun.

" She's pretty," said Jean.

" She's beautiful," said Dot.

Speckles ate the chicken feed and took a drink of water. But she did not go to the nest.

" Miss Baker, will Speckles ever sit on the eggs ? " asked Ann.

" Jerry, you have helped your father with the hens," said Miss Baker. " Can you tell us why Speckles doesn't go to the nest ? "

" If we were more quiet —," Jerry said.

Right away the room was still.

Soon Speckles stepped up to the nest. She put her head to one side and looked at it. Then she jumped into the nest.

" How long does it take for a chicken's eggs to hatch ? " Jean asked.

"About three weeks," said Miss Baker.

22

Watching and Waiting

The next morning Speckles jumped off the nest and ran about.

"Speckles left the nest," said Mike.

"Now the eggs will get cold," said Jean. "Why did she leave the nest?"

"She has to eat and drink," said Jerry.

Miss Baker said, "Jean, you may give Speckles her chicken feed today. And, Mike, you may give her some water."

Speckles stepped about in the straw and ate the chicken feed. Then she ran to get a drink. Soon she was back in the nest.

"It's about time!" said Ann.

23

Day after day went by. Speckles was a good little hen now. Each day she left the nest just long enough to eat a little chicken feed and drink some water. Her feathers lost their shiny look.

On week days the children took turns caring for Speckles. They gave her food and water and cleaned her pen. On the days when there was no school, Miss Baker and Jerry took care of her.

Jerry counted the days until the time for the chicks to hatch. He didn't know three weeks could be so long. But he was happy because the children liked Speckles.

On the morning of the last day Miss Baker said, " Jerry, will you please see if the eggs are hatching ? "

Jerry hurried into the pen. With gentle hands he took his little hen off the nest and looked at the eggs. " There—there isn't one egg that's hatching," he said sadly.

24

In the afternoon Jerry looked at the eggs again. In some he could see round holes. He put his head down to one egg.

"Peep, peep, peep, peep," he heard. Sounds were coming from the eggs.

"Some of them are hatching," Jerry said. He was so happy he wanted to shout.

"How long do you think it will take for all the chicks to hatch?" asked Miss Baker.

"Until dark or after," said Jerry as he put Speckles back on the eggs.

"Then we must wait until tomorrow to see the chicks," said Miss Baker. "It's time to go home now."

Next morning little yellow heads were
peeping out from under Speckles. Jerry
set her on the floor of the pen. Twelve
little chicks were in the nest.

Jerry picked up a chick. It was as soft
as silk. He was very gentle as he set it
on the floor.

" Cluck, cluck, cluck," called Speckles.

" Peep, peep, peep," said the chicks.

One by one Jerry took the chicks out
of the nest and set them on the floor.

All the chicks ran to Speckles. She sat
down, and they crawled under her.

" Jerry, please bring out one little chick
so we can see it better," said Miss Baker.

Jerry picked up a yellow chick, and the
children took turns feeling its soft down.

26

" We have waited a long time for you," said Ann as she petted the chick.

The next afternoon Jerry put Speckles and her twelve chicks into the big box. He set it in his wagon and started home.

Then he heard Bob and Tony calling his name. So he waited for them to catch up with him.

" Jerry, may we pull Speckles home ? " asked Bob.

" Yes," said Jerry, feeling happy. He was not the new boy any longer. Speckles and her chicks had brought him friends.

Grace Berquist

27

Cowboys Are Brave

All day long the children had played they were cowboys. They raced across the yard and back again. Round and round the barn they went.

They were trying to catch the thief who was always taking their horses.

As the four children ran they shouted, " Bang ! Bang ! Bang ! "

Teddy called, " To horse, boys ! "

28

Peter cried, "Let's get that thief!" But by dinner time the horse thief had not been found.

After dinner Peter said, "Do you know what we must do tonight?"

"What?" asked Jane.

"We must sleep in the barn," he went on. "Then if the horse thief comes again, we can catch him."

"That's right," said Teddy.

"Yes, let's sleep in the barn," said Jane. "It will be fun."

"I like the barn," said Susan.

"Susan," said Peter, "you had better not sleep in the barn, because you are too little. You would be afraid."

"No, I would not," said Susan.

"Yes, you would," said Teddy. "You would be afraid of the noise the coyotes make in the night."

"I will not be afraid," said Susan. "I want to sleep in the barn, too."

She began to cry.

"Oh, all right," said Peter. "But if you are afraid, you cannot be a cowboy. Cowboys have to be brave. That horse thief might come any time."

The children hurried into the house and asked if they might sleep in the barn. It was a warm night, so Mother and Father said they might. It would be fun sleeping in the hay.

When they were ready for bed, the children took their blankets out to the barn. The two little dogs went with them.

What good beds the hay made with the blankets for covers! Soon the children were sleeping.

"Whoo-hoo-hoo!" called an owl.

Teddy woke and heard, "Whoo-hoo! Whoo-hoo-hoo!" He was afraid.

"Maybe it's a coyote," he thought.

Reaching for his shoes, he picked them up and walked out of the barn. Then he ran fast until he reached the side door of the house. It was open.

Quickly Teddy climbed the stairs and crawled into his bed.

After a while Jane woke and sat up straight. It was very dark. She could hear a noise over her head. She thought it was a mouse. Jane wished that she were in the house where there wasn't any mouse near her bed.

The noise was louder now, too loud for a mouse. It might be a coyote!

Jane left her shoes behind as she ran out of the barn. Through the flower garden and up to her room she ran and hopped into bed.

How good it was to be in her own bed! It was soft and warm.

32

In the night it rained. The sound of the rain on the roof of the barn woke Peter. A door was banging in the wind. It scared him. He wished that it would stop. Bang, bang, bang went the door.

It was raining more now. Peter was cold. He wished that he were in the house. Bang ! Bang !

He looked around in the dark barn. He couldn't see the other children. He guessed they were sleeping.

Quiet as a mouse, he walked to the door and looked out at the falling rain. Then he hurried across the garden to the house.

When Peter reached his room, he pulled off his wet clothes and crawled into the good dry bed.

Just before morning a farmer's dog began to howl. The sound woke Susan.

Bow-wow-ow-ow-ow! She heard it again.

" Teddy," she said, " is that a coyote ? " There was no sound.

" Teddy! Peter! " she called. " Jane! "

Bow-wow-ow-ow! The dog's howling was all she heard.

Susan sat up. The sun was just coming up. There was a little light in the barn. She looked around her and saw that the others were gone. She was alone!

Just as Susan was afraid she would be scared, she looked down. There were the two little dogs.

She was not alone after all. The dogs were right there, sleeping near her. She could reach out and touch them. So why be afraid of a coyote ?

Susan picked up the little dogs and put them next to her. They were warm and soft.

The howling had stopped now. Soon Susan went to sleep again.

The next time she woke, there was Mother standing in the doorway of the barn.

" Good morning, Susan," she said. " Were you afraid ? "

" No, Mother," said Susan. " I'm a cowboy. Cowboys are brave."

Carolyn Haywood
35

Maggie the Magpie

Maggie was a pet magpie. She was a very pretty bird, much bigger than a robin. Her feathers were shiny black and snow white. Her tail was long and beautiful.

When the sunlight touched her black feathers, they looked green and blue and purple. As she flew, there was a flash of white.

Maggie liked to play with bright shiny things, like tinkling bells. And being a magpie, Maggie liked to chatter.

36

Mr. and Mrs. Wood thought Maggie was a very smart bird. She would ride on Mr. Wood's shoulder, chattering softly. She could make so many sounds that she learned to talk somewhat like Mrs. Wood.

When Maggie talked, she always bobbed her head. The things she could say best were, "Come here, Maggie. Come here. Hello! Hello!"

Most of the time the door of Maggie's cage was open. She could fly in and out just as she pleased. She could fly about the yard in the summer. But at night she always came into the house to sleep in her cage.

The two children who lived next door
were great friends of Maggie the magpie.
Timothy thought she was a very smart
bird. Betty thought she was beautiful.

One afternoon Timothy and Betty were
helping Mr. Wood in his garden. Maggie
was sitting on Timothy's shoulder and
chattering softly to herself.

Mrs. Wood had been busy in the kitchen.
Now she came out into the yard, carrying
a basket of cakes, four glasses, and a bowl
of ice cubes. She set these on the table
under a big tree.

"Hello, hello," called Maggie, flying out of the garden and over to the table. Then she saw the cakes and picked one up.

"Go away, Maggie!" cried Mrs. Wood, waving her hand at the magpie.

Maggie flew off with the cake. But as soon as Mrs. Wood went into the house to get the lemonade, Maggie flew back. She could not keep away from the bright shiny ice cubes.

She picked up an ice cube, and flew away with it. One by one she carried the ice cubes off and put them in a pile under a tree.

39

When Mrs. Wood came out with the lemonade, work stopped in the garden. Mr. Wood and the children were ready for the cold lemonade. They hurried out of the garden and washed their hands. Then they joined Mrs. Wood in the yard.

"Look at this bowl," said Mrs. Wood. "The ice cubes are gone, and the bowl is tipped over."

"What could have happened?" asked Mr. Wood.

Just then Maggie began to call, "Come here, come here," from across the yard.

40

"Oh, look over there," said Timothy. "Maggie is calling us."

"She has something for us to see," said Betty.

"The ice cubes," said Mr. Wood.

"Come here, come here," called Maggie, walking up and down in front of a small pile of shiny ice cubes.

"Maggie!" cried Mrs. Wood. "Back to the cage for you!"

"Oh, let her stay here," said Mr. Wood. "It will be fun to watch her when she sees the ice cubes getting smaller and smaller.

"Maggie doesn't know what will happen to them out here in the sun. I'll get some more ice cubes for the glasses of lemonade."

Irma Simonton Black

The Animal Store

If I had a hundred dollars to spend,
   Or maybe a little more,
I'd hurry as fast as my legs would go
   Straight to the animal store.

I wouldn't say, " How much for this or
     that ? " —
   " What kind of a dog is he ? "
I'd buy as many as rolled an eye,
   Or wagged a tail at me !

I'd take the hound with the drooping ears
    That sits by himself alone;
Cockers and Cairns and wobbly pups
    For to be my very own.

I might buy a parrot all red and green,
    And the monkey I saw before,
If I had a hundred dollars to spend,
    Or maybe a little more.

Rachel Field

43

A Dog of His Own

The Coyote

Ben lay in bed with his eyes wide open, listening. There were no sounds of cars or buses. It was quiet in his room and just as quiet outside.

After living in a big city, Ben had moved with his mother and father to the country. He could not get used to the quiet and the dark at night.

Now as he listened he heard a very strange noise. " Wah-wah-wah-o-o ! Wah-wah-wah-o-o ! "

44

Ben sat up in bed, calling, "Mother! Dad! What's that?"

"It's a coyote, Ben," his father called from another room. "We must see that the coyotes don't get our chickens."

Ben lay back in bed. He was still scared. But he tried to remember what he had heard about coyotes.

Ben remembered that coyotes caught small animals and birds. They could run very fast, and they howled at night. But they were afraid of people.

"Just the same," thought Ben, "I wish I had a big dog—the biggest kind of dog there is!"

The next morning at breakfast Ben said, "Dad, let's get a big dog. That would keep coyotes away from our chickens."

"All right, Ben," said his father. "I don't know of anyone who has puppies to sell just now. You might ask about it at school this morning."

45

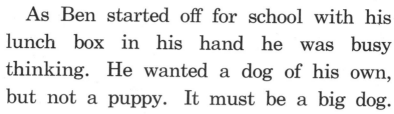

As Ben started off for school with his lunch box in his hand he was busy thinking. He wanted a dog of his own, but not a puppy. It must be a big dog.

Ben had to go over hills and across a long meadow to reach school. For much of the way he could not see any houses.

After climbing the first long hill, he turned to look back. Then he started down toward the woods. That was when he saw the coyote. What if it caught up with him!

The coyote was a long way off, but it was watching Ben with bright eyes. Ben watched the coyote.

First it was on one hill, then it was on a hill much nearer. Its nose and ears were turned toward him. It did not run like other animals he had seen.

Ben made himself go on. He whistled and bumped his lunch box against his leg to make a noise.

As he came to the woods he tried to be brave. But he could not watch the coyote when he got under the trees.

When Ben reached the first trees, he started to run. He ran as fast as he could, his lunch box banging against his legs. He did not stop until he was through the woods and in the meadow. Then he looked around for the coyote. It was gone.

He did not tell the boys and girls at school about the coyote, but he did ask Miss Gray about a dog.

" Does anyone know where Ben might get a dog ? " she said to the children. " He wants one very much."

48

May Wheeler, a quiet little girl, said, " If Ben would come over to our place, I think my mother would give him a puppy. My dog, Frisky, has puppies."

Ben said, " Thanks, May. I'll tell my dad." He did not say that he wanted a big dog. A puppy would not do. She might ask why he wanted a big dog.

When school was out, Ben started home across the meadow. He looked at the hills, but he did not see the coyote. When he came to the woods, he began to whistle and run. There was no sign of the coyote.

After school the next afternoon Ben and his father went to see the puppies. But Ben still wanted a big dog.

He said, " Puppies are so little, Dad. I do want a big dog."

May Wheeler was in the yard when Ben's father stopped the car in the driveway.

" Hello," she said. " The puppies are in the barn."

A Puppy or a Big Dog?

There were four puppies on a warm, soft blanket in a bed of hay. Ben sat down to get nearer to them. He watched the four puppies rolling and playing together on the blanket.

One of them came over to him. Its short tail was sticking straight out. It tried to nibble at his fingers.

Ben knew that he could not go home without that black puppy.

"Dad," he said, "this is the one for me. See how he bites my finger."

Ben's father looked at the puppy and asked, " What are you going to call him ? "

" I don't know," said Ben. He decided it would have to be a very fine name for this wonderful puppy—his very own.

The next morning, after Ben waved to his mother and started down the hill toward the woods, the coyote was there.

He shouted, but the animal did not go away. It came nearer, and Ben ran all the way to school.

He decided that he would have to tell his father to take the puppy back. He must have a big dog.

When Ben got home that night, he hurried to the barn to look at the puppy. It ran toward him on its short legs and chewed at his shoes.

How soft and warm it was when he picked it up! Its ears were like silk. As he petted the puppy it tried to nibble and bite first his thumb, then a coat button.

"I'll wait until after supper to take you back," said Ben.

He carried the puppy outside and set it down in the grass, but the grass was so long the puppy could not run about.

"I think you would like to go up on the hill to play," he said. "The grass is short there."

Along the fence, through the gate, and up the hill he ran with the puppy in his arms. At the top of the hill he sat down and put the puppy on the ground near him. The grass was short enough here for the little dog to move about.

The puppy looked around, chewed some grass, and barked at an airplane as it flew overhead. Then the puppy jumped high in the air to catch a black bug.

"You're smart," said Ben. "I think you want to fly like that airplane. I'm going to call you Jet."

Just then Ben saw the coyote. It was sitting on the next hill. Its yellow eyes were watching the puppy.

Quickly Ben found a stone and jumped up. Down the hill he ran straight at the coyote. He wasn't afraid any more.

"You old coyote!" he shouted as he threw the stone. "You needn't think you will get my puppy."

The coyote turned and ran away.

When Ben carried his puppy down the hill again, he did not look behind him. "You don't have to be afraid of coyotes," he told the puppy. "You have me to take care of you."

That night the coyote howled again. "Wah-wah-wah-o-o-o!"

Ben just laughed to himself and rolled over so that he could see the basket where the puppy was sleeping.

"Who wants a big dog?" he asked. "My Jet is the best dog in the world."

Henry R. Fea

54

At the Zoo

Teeny and the Tall Man

Teeny was happy. She and the Tall Man had come to the big zoo.

The Tall Man was Teeny's neighbor and friend. His real name was Mr. Bush, but he was so very tall that Teeny called him the Tall Man.

Teeny and Mr. Bush liked the big zoo. There they could see animals from jungles and other places all over the world.

This afternoon Teeny and the Tall Man stopped first in front of the big cage where the monkeys lived. Some of them had come from a jungle far away. Teeny had seen the monkeys many, many times, but she was glad to see them again.

One little monkey was eating a stick of candy. Two other monkeys were playing together.

An old monkey looked at Teeny as if he knew her and would like to talk to her. Teeny looked him straight in the eye.

" I think he wants to tell me a secret," she said.

57

"He's a white-nose monkey," said Mr. Bush. "He's very friendly. He likes to have people always watching him, just like some children I know."

"What children?" Teeny asked.

Mr. Bush laughed. "Oh, you know how some children always show off and say, 'Look at me, look at me!' Then when you look, you don't see anything but what you have seen all along.

"The white-nose monkey is like that. He is forever trying to be a clown."

As Mr. Bush walked over to the next cage he said, "See the monkeys with the very long tails and legs? They are called spider monkeys."

"Because they have long legs like spiders?" Teeny asked.

"That's right," said Mr. Bush.

Teeny knew about spiders. Sometimes spiders would be near enough to touch, but she wasn't afraid of them at all.

58

"I hear that spider monkeys make good pets," said Mr. Bush. "And they can do many tricks. They can reach for things with their tails. They can ride a pony. Now let's look at some other animals."

Teeny knew all the animals, but they looked different when she walked along listening to her tall friend.

There was the lion who roared so loudly.

There was the brown bear who liked to sleep in his stone house all winter.

There was the elephant with his long trunk, looking as if he had a tail at each end of his body.

And then there was the giraffe!

Mr. Bush looked up at the animal that was almost three times as tall as he was.

"Now, Teeny," he said, "this is what I call a real somebody! Look at his long legs and his long neck. I don't suppose you see anybody who looks like a giraffe?"

Teeny was laughing, but she did not say anything.

"Come, now, Teeny, don't you see anybody?" said Mr. Bush.

"Well, you do, just a little, Mr. Bush," Teeny said. "But I think he's a very fine giraffe!"

"I'm glad I look like a giraffe with a long neck and not like an elephant with a trunk," said Mr. Bush.

60

Then he asked, " Do you know what a wonderful animal the giraffe is ? He is so tall that he could eat dinner off my head.

" I have always heard that the giraffe knows the right way to eat his hay and vegetables. He does not put too much in his mouth at once. He does not drop hay all over things and make loud noises.

" I have heard of just one giraffe that liked to play tricks on people."

" What did he do ? " asked Teeny.

" Well, once upon a time that giraffe looked out of his cage. Way down on the ground he saw a woman with a new spring hat. It had pretty flowers on it.

" The flowers made the giraffe think of the flowers where he had lived before he came to the zoo. So he reached out and ate the flowers before the woman knew what he was doing. They were almost as good as hay and vegetables."

" That was the end of the hat," said Teeny, laughing.

"Oh, but I must tell you that this animal is very different from me in one way," said Mr. Bush.

"What way?" asked Teeny.

"The giraffe never talks, and I haven't stopped talking."

"But talking is fun," said Teeny.

"Yes, it is fun," said the Tall Man. "Well, Uncle Giraffe, good-by to you. I'll be seeing you again before long."

They went out of the zoo and down the walk through the park. Teeny began to think some more about Mr. Bush and the giraffe.

She decided that her tall friend did not care if people thought he looked like that funny animal with the long neck.

"If Mr. Bush looks like a giraffe," she thought, "I guess I look like a white-nose monkey. And I don't care because he's such a friendly animal."

Julian Meade

63

The Chimpanzee That Mopped the Floor

Josephine was just a baby when she was found alone in the jungle. How hungry and afraid she was, for she was lost!

The man who found Josephine took her home with him. The man's wife liked the baby chimpanzee. She said, "I am going to name her Josephine. She can live in our house. She can sleep in the big chair outdoors. She can play in the yard all day."

64

So the man's wife gave Josephine some warm milk and put her to bed in a chair.

Every day she played in the yard, and she grew bigger and bigger.

Sometimes she would go into the house to watch the people at work. If someone was mopping the floor, Josephine would try to catch the mop. She would slide on the wet floor.

She liked the kitchen too. She wanted to try the different kinds of food.

People were always saying, " No, no, Josephine! You go out and play in the yard."

At last the man and his wife decided to move to another house. It was such a small house that there was no room in it for a chimpanzee. They wanted to find a good home for her. So they gave her to a zoo in the city.

Living in the zoo was different from living in a house. Now Josephine did not play outdoors all day long. She did not sleep in a big chair.

Every morning her cage was opened. Josephine played in the hall while the keeper mopped the floor.

First he got a bucket of warm water. Josephine climbed on a chair to watch the water splashing into the bucket. Then she followed the keeper down the hall to get the mop.

Sometimes as the mop went swish, swish, swish across the floor Josephine caught it. Then she swished the mop around, just as if she were trying to help.

66

"Why don't you give Josephine a mop and bucket of her own?" someone asked the keeper one morning. "She can mop the floor for you while you do something else."

The keeper thought it would be fun to see what would happen. So he found a short stick and tied a cloth on the end of it. Then he put some warm water in a little pan.

"You're my helper, Josephine," he said. "You mop the floor with this cloth. I'll wash the windows."

That was the first time Josephine ever had a mop and a pan of water all her own. First she licked the pan. Then she licked the cloth. Then she put the mop in the water and got it all wet.

At last she began to swish her own little mop around on the floor!

Josephine didn't do a very good job of mopping the floor. She mopped just one little spot. Then she wet the mop and washed the same spot all over again.

68

At last Josephine emptied the water on the floor and put the pan on her head like a hat.

After that, the keeper didn't tell her she could be his helper any more. He mopped the floor himself.

Sometimes people asked the keeper why he didn't let Josephine help him.

He always said, "Josephine is the cleanest little chimpanzee I ever saw. She uses a big pan of water to mop one little spot. I don't let her help me because I would have to spend all morning carrying pans of water to her."

William Bridges

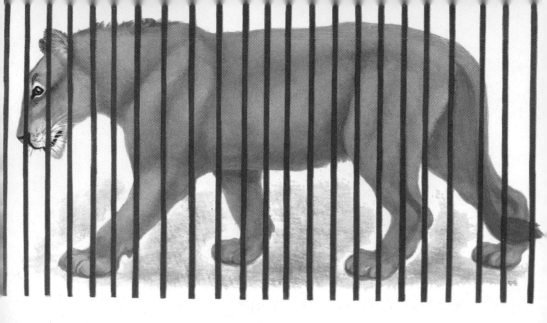

Strange Friends

Something was the matter with the mother lion at the zoo. Around and around her cage she walked as if she were looking for something.

When the keeper brought pieces of meat for her dinner, she was not hungry. She ate less and less and went on walking up and down the cage.

Now and then she lay down, but she did not sleep long. Soon she was walking again, making almost no sound with her big soft paws.

The mother lion was not sick. She was sad because her two babies were no longer with her. They had gone to another zoo, but she had no way of knowing that. She looked for them in every corner of the cage, but she could not find them.

The keeper knew that mother animals are sad if something happens to their babies. He was very kind to the mother lion. He brought her the best pieces of meat, but she ate less every day.

He knew that she would get thinner if she did not eat and sleep enough. She might be very sick if she could not learn to get along without her babies.

One morning as the keeper was cleaning the cages he saw a little dog come into the zoo. How thin and hungry the small dog looked!

Now dogs are not wanted in the zoo. They might scare the wild animals. So the little dog could not stay.

The keeper picked up the little dog and gently put him outside the gate. Then he went back to his work.

Before long he had some work to do near the mother lion's cage. There was the little dog again! He stood looking into the cage at the mother lion.

The keeper was surprised to see the lion stop walking around and come to the front of the cage.

She did not roar or spring at the walls of her cage. She stood still, as if the dog were an old friend. It was very strange.

72

The keeper knew that he must not let a dog stay with the wild animals. Once more he took the little fellow to the gate and put him outside. When he came back, the lion was walking around and around her cage again.

Would she never stop walking? Would she never be hungry again? The keeper did not know what to do for the mother lion.

The sun was high in the sky by the time he had cleaned all the cages. He watched some children come through the gate.

The children stopped at each cage to look at the animals. They saw the tiger and the tiger kittens eat their dinner. They watched the great white bear and her cub splash about in the water.

After a little while the keeper heard the children give a great shout. He left his work and ran as quickly as he could to see what had happened.

There inside the lion's cage was the same little dog. No one had seen him come back to the cage. No one had seen him crawl through the fence. But there he was, trying to make friends with the sad mother lion.

Everyone stood very still to watch what would happen. The little dog seemed to say, "I know how sad you are. I am sad, too. Let us be friends."

The mother lion walked across her cage. She sniffed and sniffed the strange animal from head to tail.

74

The mother lion seemed to know that the little dog needed a friend. She lay down and began to lick him just as she had licked her two babies. Soon the dog and the lion were sleeping side by side.

When dinner time came, the lion let the dog eat some of her meat. She was hungry, too, and ate a good dinner herself.

After that, the dog and the lion were great friends. They were happy because they needed each other. And no one tried to take the little dog away again. From that day he had a home with the wild animals in the zoo.

Gretchen Wulfing

75

Wonderful Day

We went to the zoo,
And we saw a cockatoo.

The spotted leopard padded
Around and round his cage,
And the lordly lion roared
Like a giant in a rage.
The tall and thin giraffe
Spread his legs to eat his hay.
The polar bear stayed in his pool,
Keeping cool that way.
The seals and golden pheasants,
All the beasts and birds were fun.
We ate our lunch beside a pond,
But the day seemed just begun
When—

—we wandered through the zoo
And we saw the kangaroo!

David H. Russell

76

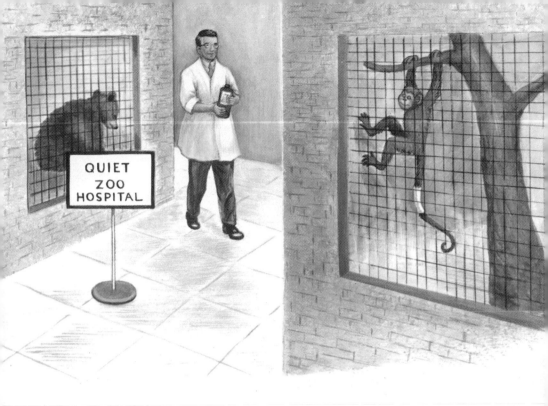

QUIET
ZOO
HOSPITAL

The Doctor at the Zoo

A Strange Job

Many people who come to the zoo never see the animal hospital. It is far away from the cages. Sick animals need to be in a quiet spot far from the other animals.

The animal doctor has a strange job at the zoo hospital. But he may give a sick animal the same kind of medicine that doctors give to sick people.

77

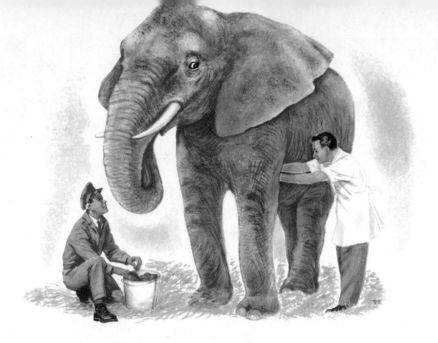

A wonderful new kind of medicine was a big help when an elephant at the zoo was sick. The keeper got a bucket of potatoes and began to give them to the elephant one by one. That was to keep her busy while the doctor was giving her the medicine. Then it would not seem to hurt much.

The elephant ate the potatoes happily. She did not pull away when the doctor put the medicine into her leg. She went right on eating potatoes.

The medicine made the elephant well.

When animals are sick, they cannot tell the doctor how they feel. Most of them do their best to keep him from finding out. But one day the doctor had a surprise.

The great white cockatoo was brought to the hospital because its wing was hurt.

The keeper liked the cockatoo best of all the birds in his care.

"Will he be O.K., Doc?" asked the keeper.

"I think so," said the doctor, and he began to take care of the cockatoo's wing.

"O.K., Doc," said the cockatoo. "O.K., Doc." All the time the doctor was working, the cockatoo was saying, "O.K., Doc."

Medicine for a Mountain Lion

One day a mountain lion was sick and needed some medicine. The doctor put the medicine inside some big pieces of meat.

Then he thought of a way to make the animal swallow the meat quickly, so he would not know there was medicine in it.

"We threw one piece of meat into his cage," said the doctor. "The mountain lion took it at once and began to chew.

"Just at that time we threw in another piece. When the animal saw the next piece, he swallowed the first one and jumped for the new one.

"We didn't let him chew long before we threw in still another piece.

"We threw in one piece of meat after another, until we got to the last one. Then we wanted to make sure that the lion would gobble it quickly. He needed the medicine in all the pieces of meat."

"The lion was starting to chew the last piece. I was afraid he would bite into the medicine and not swallow it," the doctor went on with his story.

"Then I saw a man working near the cage. He had a long stick in his hand. I took the stick and touched the piece of meat with the end of it. I made the mountain lion think I was trying to take the meat away.

"That worked! The animal backed away and swallowed the piece of meat without chewing it. And that's how we got him to take all his medicine!"

A Sick Monkey

The zoo doctor knows about the ways of all the different animals. Sometimes this helps him to take care of them when they are sick.

One time a new monkey came to live in the zoo. He had been brought on a boat from a country far across the sea.

The men on the boat did not know what to feed the monkey. When he reached the zoo, he was so thin and sick that he was put in the hospital.

The doctor was sure that the monkey needed food, but he would not try to eat. When beautiful soft bananas were placed before him, he would not touch them.

At last the doctor went into the cage. He sat down and took the monkey in his arms. Then he rubbed a piece of banana over the animal's paws. He knew that monkeys like to keep very clean.

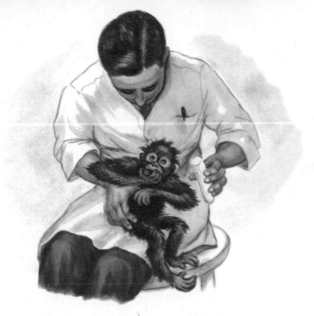

The monkey looked at his paws as if he wanted to wash them clean. Then he began to lick the banana off.

Once more the doctor rubbed banana on the monkey's paws. Again the animal licked them. The doctor did this until all of the banana was gone.

After three days of this kind of feeding, the monkey was better. Soon he could eat his food without help.

You can see that the doctor in the zoo has to know much about animals. And he must be ready to use many tricks.

William Bridges

The Little Cat
That Could Not Sleep

Once there was a little cat who wanted to stay awake all night. So she walked around and around, waving her tail.

After supper, when her mother and the other kittens were sleeping, she walked out of the barn and up the hill to the house. There Little Cat found the big dog sleeping on the step.

"Not I!" thought Little Cat. "I shall stay awake all night."

Soon all the animals on the farm were sleeping. The horses, the cows, and the sheep were all sleeping. Little Cat thought, "Not I! I shall really stay awake all night."

But Little Cat found out that it was not much fun to stay awake all night by herself. There was no one for her to talk with. So she started down the road to visit the animals in the zoo. Surely she would find some other animal there who liked to stay awake all night.

On the way she saw a robin in a tree. The robin was sleeping with his head under his wing. She saw two rabbits sleeping in the grass, and a squirrel sleeping in a tree by the roadside. By this time it was getting dark.

When Little Cat reached the zoo, all was quiet. The lion lay with his head on his paws, breathing up, breathing down, breathing up, breathing down.

Little Cat opened her eyes wide and walked away fast.

Little Cat visited the deer, but they too were sleeping soundly. Some were sleeping with their legs under them. Some were sleeping with their heads straight out. But all the deer were sleeping, sleeping, sleeping . . .

"Isn't anyone in the zoo staying up tonight?" thought Little Cat. "Well! Well! That's strange!" And she walked on, waving her tail in the air.

The sky grew darker and darker. The stars came out one by one. Little Cat went to see the elephants. The elephants were sleeping standing up.

87

They stood first on one foot, then on
another foot, on one foot and then on
another . . . moving and swaying.

Little Cat, watching them, began to
purr.

"This is really fun!" she thought,
purring happily.

Then Little Cat sat down on the ground
and watched some more. Her bright eyes
were wide open.

She watched the elephants swaying and
moving, standing first on one foot, then
on another. One foot, another foot, one
foot, another foot . . .

88

Next thing Little Cat knew she was purring and purring, and moving her head to keep time with the elephants. They still were swaying, rocking, swaying, rocking, with their long trunks reaching to the ground.

Now it was dark, and the stars were bright. The elephants were still swaying . . . one foot, another foot, one foot, another foot . . .

And before she knew it, Little Cat was sleeping soundly.

Frances Margaret Fox

89

Tiger

There's a tiger in a cage, in the zoo,
And his stripes run up and down
 and sort of round and round,
And his stripes are black and orange,
 In the zoo!

When the tiger wants his dinner,
 in the zoo,
The keeper hears him roar,
 and he opens up the door,
And he gives him meat to eat, meat to eat,
 In the zoo!

Then the tiger has a grin on his chin,
 in the zoo,
And he whiffles with his nose,
 and he washes off his toes,
And he jumps up on a shelf
 and goes to sleep,
 In the zoo!

Rhoda Bacmeister

90

Helping Hilda

How Hilda Helped

Hilda was the greatest little helper in the world. She began helping when she got up in the morning. She helped all through the day and stopped only when she climbed into her bed at night.

She helped her mother and her father at home in the city. Now she was visiting her Aunt Selma in Little River, and she was helping her.

Hilda could make beds without dropping the covers on the floor more than once. She could dry the dishes and break only one or two cups.

She could carry a bag of vegetables along the village street without dropping more than one or two things. She was a great help to everyone.

" Are you coming with me to the market, Hilda ? " Aunt Selma asked one day. " When we come back, I will make gingerbread."

" Oh," cried Hilda, " gingerbread ! May I help make it ? "

" Why, yes," said Aunt Selma. " There are some things you could do to help."

" If you don't mind, I will stay at home and do the cleaning. Then I'll be ready to help with the gingerbread."

Aunt Selma didn't mind, but she was a little surprised. Hilda liked to go to market better than anything else.

"All right, Hilda. There will not be many groceries to carry home. I can do it," said Aunt Selma. Then she walked away toward the village with her bag over her arm.

Feeling important, Hilda ran into the living room. She swished here. She swished there. Only one book fell on the floor, but a bowl rolled around as if about to fall.

All the time Hilda was singing happily, " Gingerbread, gingerbread, molasses and brown sugar, eggs and milk and flour and eggs and sugar, molasses and ginger, ginger, ginger ! Tra-la-la ! Tra-la-la ! "

" Now I'll need an apron," sang Hilda, hopping into the kitchen and feeling more important than ever.

She tied on Aunt Selma's big apron and said to herself, " I'll just get out all the things to make the gingerbread. What a help it will be! First, the milk." She carried the milk to the table.

" Butter." She put it on the table.

" Ginger." She opened the can of ginger and sniffed a big sniff, such a big sniff that she wanted to sneeze.

" Eggs next," said Hilda as she put the open can of ginger on the table.

She took some eggs out of a bowl. She was holding them in her hands while she tried to keep from sneezing. It was the ginger sneeze.

" A-a-a, a-a-a," cried Hilda, " a-a-a, a-a-a, CHEW ! "

The sneeze shook Hilda all over. It shook her head. It shook her hair. It shook her shoulders and her arms. It shook her hands. Away flew one of the eggs. Down on the floor it fell, the shell breaking into many pieces.

" Oh, my," said Hilda. " I'll have to pick it up."

Hilda put the other eggs on the table. It was easy to pick up the shell, but the white and yellow moved away. She tried to pick them up with a spoon. The egg went this way and that. Her fingers could not get it into the spoon.

96

Slowly Hilda backed away as the egg slid over the floor. Hilda backed, and the egg slid after her. It slid away from the table and to the back door. It grew smaller and smaller as it slid along until there was only a little piece of it left.

"Guess I'll have to scrub the floor."

Hilda mopped the floor and scrubbed it and dried it. She scrubbed until the egg was all washed away.

"There! That will help Aunt Selma," said Hilda. "She will not have to scrub the floor. Now the molasses."

Molasses for Gingerbread

Hilda carried the molasses bottle to the table and tried to turn the top. Just then Nils came across the kitchen. Nils was Aunt Selma's white cat. He rubbed against Hilda's legs.

She tried to turn the bottle top. She pulled and turned. And flip! Off the top came. The bottle tipped over, and the molasses began to run out slowly. It ran over the table and down on the floor. It ran over Nils' paws—the sticky brown molasses.

98

Nils did not like molasses. He did not
like it to eat. He did not like it on his
feet. He jumped high in the air. He ran
across the kitchen. He climbed up the
kitchen curtains and down again. Then
he went behind the stove.

Hilda stood with her hands in the air
as the drops of molasses flew from the
feet of Nils all over and up and down.
All around on the floor, all over the
curtains, all over the stove, all over Aunt
Selma's apron!

"Nils!" she cried. "Why, Nils, Nils! There is molasses on everything. Come let me wash it off your feet."

She pulled Nils from under the stove and put him on a stool. She scrubbed his feet with the scrubbing cloth as well as she could.

Nils moved so fast that she was not sure which foot she had just washed, but at last all four feet were clean. Then she put Nils out the back door and said, "Now scat while I clean up the kitchen."

"I think I had better scrub the floor again," said Hilda to herself.

And she did. She scrubbed all the sticky spots that she could find. She washed the molasses bottle, which was very sticky.

"I'll have to wash the curtains too, I guess, and Aunt Selma's apron," and she put them in a pan of water. "Aunt Selma will be glad to have this done for her. The curtains and the apron will be clean. Where is the top of the molasses bottle?"

"Hello, there," and in walked Aunt Selma, back from her marketing. "Oh, you have been helping!"

101

" Yes," said Hilda, crawling out from under the table. The top of the molasses bottle was in her hand. Her face was red. There was molasses on it.

" Yes," she said again as she washed the bottle top with the scrubbing cloth. " I have been getting things ready for the gingerbread, and cleaning up a little, too —the egg and the molasses, you know.

" I have washed Nils' paws and scrubbed the kitchen floor. After I did it once, I had to do it all over again. Am I a big help to you, Aunt Selma ? "

" Oh, Hilda," said Aunt Selma, and she was laughing, " you are the best helper in this big wide country. I don't know what I would do without you ! "

Hilda was pulling her foot from a sticky place on the floor.

" Now what more can I do to help ? " she asked.

Emma L. Brock

New Shoes

Once upon a time, on a market day, a peddler came to Forest Hill. Nobody had ever seen him before. Nobody knew his name or where he lived or what his business was.

All that was strange enough, but there was something stranger still. The peddler carried a big bag over his back and a stool under his arm.

When he came to the market place, he began to call, " New shoes for old ! "

Farmer Gruff and all the good people of Forest Hill came hurrying round him.

" New shoes for old ! " they cried. " We cannot have heard right ! Who would be silly enough to take our old shoes and give us new ones in their place ? "

But that was the way it was. The peddler's business was giving new shoes for old.

It did not take Farmer Gruff long to kick his way to the front.

" There are some old shoes for you ! " he said.

" They're kicked through," said the peddler.

"What if they are?" shouted Farmer Gruff. "Give me some new ones for them. That was your promise."

"Yes, that was the promise," said the peddler. He pulled some new shoes out of his bag. The farmer sat on the stool to try them on. They were just right.

Away went the farmer, laughing to himself to think that anyone could be so silly as the peddler. He did not see that the peddler was laughing, too!

The peddler had many callers that day. There was busy Mrs. Friendly, who was always hurrying about to help people.

There was Tommy Tumble, who *would* walk through puddles and stay out of school.

There was pretty Patsy Painter, who was always running to the looking glass to see herself. And there were many others.

One by one they sat on the stool, and the peddler gave them fine new shoes.

Everyone went away very much pleased —at first! But some were not happy very long, for there was something strange about the new shoes. When Farmer Gruff wanted to kick the dog, he found he could not move his foot. It stuck fast to the floor.

He tried to kick the dog with the other foot, and that stuck to the floor, too.

"Help! Help!" he shouted.

"What's the matter?" cried his wife, running in from the kitchen.

"Matter!" cried the farmer. "A thief of a peddler gave me some new shoes, and now I cannot kick the dog!"

"And a very good thing, too," said Mrs. Gruff. "You are far too quick to get angry and kick things."

"But I'm stuck to the floor!" shouted the farmer. "I cannot move!"

"Have you tried to do anything but kick the dog?" asked his wife.

"No!" he shouted. "And I shall kick it as soon as I can lift my feet."

"Then I guess you will have to stand where you are until you want to do something better," said Mrs. Gruff.

That is just what happened. As soon as the farmer stopped wanting to kick the dog and thought about milking the cow, he could lift his feet again.

Tommy Tumble did not find anything strange about his shoes until the next morning. It was time for school, but he wanted to go swimming. The new shoes did not let him go. They took him straight to school, and on the dry side of the road.

107

"I'll tell my mother!" cried Tommy.

The new shoes gave a squeak, squeak, squeak. They squeaked just as if they were laughing at him. When he remembered what his mother always said, he thought it would be better not to tell her.

"It's hard, very hard," he sniffed. "I don't like being good!"

When market day came round again, everybody hurried to the market place. There were Farmer Gruff and Tommy Tumble. There was Patsy Painter, who could not stand in front of a looking glass all day, and there were all the others.

They had come to tell the peddler in angry words what they thought about him.

They were going to make him give back their old shoes—all but little Mrs. Friendly. She said she had never had such wonderful shoes before. She had baked a chocolate cake for the peddler's dinner.

But the peddler did not get their angry words or the chocolate cake. He never came back to Forest Hill. He must have laughed a little whenever he remembered the good day's work he had done there.

Margaret and Mary Baker

Baby Bears

One day in a country far, far away a man came home with two baby bears in his hat. He had found them alone in the forest.

When his wife, Iva, saw the bears in his hat, she put up her hands in great surprise. The man laughed and emptied the bears on an old coat.

And there the baby bears lived. They had warm milk to drink when they were hungry. They went to sleep every night on the old coat.

By summer the bears were bigger than cats, and then they grew to be as big as small dogs. As they grew bigger, they played many tricks.

They liked to pull feathers out of Iva's best pillows. Soft white feathers would fly about everywhere. Soon the pillows would be as flat as pancakes.

One of the bears would tip over a soup bowl on the table. The hot cabbage soup would run all over the table and down on the floor.

The other bear liked to hide things. Iva wouldn't miss a pan or a spoon until she was in a hurry to get dinner. Then she would have to crawl under a chair or a table, looking for the pan or spoon.

At last Iva could stand it no longer and put the bears out of the house.

" Run along," she said. " Have all your fun outdoors."

So the two bears started living outdoors.

111

You would think the bears would have run into the forest, but they never did. Iva's house was their home. If they were afraid of something, they ran into the house and lay down on the old coat.

" What have you done now ? " Iva would say.

The bears would look as gentle as lambs. Then each would try to hide behind the other, and they would peep out at her with their bright brown eyes.

Soon a neighbor would come to the door and say, " Your bears, Iva, have been digging up seeds in my garden."

" Oh, me ! " Iva would cry. " I wish there was a way to sell these bears to the circus in the city."

Well, going to the city was easier said than done. In the spring the roads were just like rivers. In the summer there was too much work to do, so no one would be riding to the city then. In the winter there was too much snow on the roads.

The bears had to stay on in the village.

One day that summer a hunter happened to come to the village and hear about Iva's pet bears.

The hunter went straight to Iva's house. He thought she would be happy to show him the bears. But she told him to look for them outside.

The hunter walked through the streets of the village, looking for the bears. But he could not find them anywhere.

" Well," he thought, " they must have run away into the forest."

113

Just then a big brick fell under the hunter's nose. It came down with a loud bang. He jumped quickly away and looked up at the nearby roof.

There were two brown bears. They were very busy taking bricks out of a chimney. The bears took turns pulling out bricks and letting them slide off the roof.

The hunter ran into the house to tell Iva what was happening.

Iva came outside and cried, "Get off that roof!"

114

The bears stopped pulling out bricks. They climbed down quickly and quietly.

That night three neighbors came to see Iva. The bears had stopped up their chimneys with bricks. When the fires were made, all the smoke came back into the house.

Iva started to cry. " See for yourself," she said to the hunter. " See what they do. When they were little, they did baby tricks. Now I cannot put up with them. Please take them away with you."

The hunter put ropes around the bears' necks and took them out of the village. When they came near the forest, he took off the ropes so that the bears could run into the forest.

The bears did not run away. They were afraid of the strange forest and stayed near the man. When he started down the road, they followed him.

The hunter saw that the bears would not leave him, so he took them to the city to sell them to the circus.

The owner of the circus was happy to have bears that could do so many tricks. He could sell more tickets to the circus. And the bears were very happy in their new home.

For a while they missed Iva and the village, the feather pillows, and the brick chimneys. But they soon found that it was more fun doing tricks for all the children who came to see the circus.

E. Charushin

117

How Percival Caught the Tiger

Percival Summers went to the jungle to trap wild animals for the circus. He had some brave jungle boys with him.

One day they were walking through the jungle looking for tracks of wild animals.

All at once Percival saw a tiger.

The tiger saw Percival.

Percival was so scared he jumped right out of his shoes.

The boys and Percival ran as fast as they could until they were out of danger. Then they sat down to think.

118

Percival thought and thought. He wanted to catch that tiger.

He called his brave boy Joe and said, " What in all this world do tigers like best to eat ? "

Joe thought and thought.

At last he said, " The things that tigers like best in all this world are baked sweet potatoes covered with brown sugar and butter."

Percival was very much surprised.

He sent two boys to a faraway village for a big basket of sweet potatoes. The others made a cage with a big trap door in the top.

When the boys came with the sweet potatoes, Percival baked them all. When they were done, he cut them open and put a stone inside each one. Then he closed them again so they would look all right to the tiger. He covered the potatoes with brown sugar and butter.

Percival and his brave boys went to the
jungle. They carried the cage, the sweet
potatoes, and a long rope.

They put the sweet potatoes where the
tiger would be sure to find them.

They waited.

Pretty soon they heard the tiger roar.
He sniffed the sweet potatoes and began
to eat them.

He was in such a hurry he swallowed
them whole and never knew there was a
stone in each one.

120

His body began to hang down and down, until it was hanging right down on the ground, because he was so full of whole sweet potatoes and stones.

The tiger was so full that he couldn't move or turn around. Percival and his boys could go near him without danger. They tied his back legs together with the long rope and threw one end over a branch of a tree.

They pulled him into the air. The tiger didn't like that. He kicked and kicked until the branch was about to break. Stones fell from his mouth. They fell and fell until the tiger was empty again.

The brave jungle boys got the big cage, let him down into it, and closed the door. They named him Sweet Potato and sent him to the circus.

And that is how Percival caught the tiger.

Percival Stutters

Azor

Azor Talks with Larry

Azor could play ball pretty well. He could swim pretty well. And he could mind his own business, as you will see.

But there was one strange thing about Azor. Animals talked to him. They really did. It was no silly baby talk. The things they told him were important things.

It wasn't Azor who thought there was anything strange about it. It was other people.

122

Big boys laughed at him and called him a baby. Little boys laughed at him. And nobody believed him, but Pringle, and Pringle was only three.

One of the animals who told him things was Larry, the big black-and-white cat who lived next door. Larry didn't like anyone much. He didn't like the woman who owned him. He didn't like any of the people in town or any of the other animals. He sat on his front steps and watched everything with half-closed eyes.

Larry did like Azor. He thought Azor had sense. Azor never threw things at him or ran after him, the way the other boys did. Azor had sense enough not to call him silly names, as the girls did.

So the morning after Mrs. Woodfin lost the silver earring that had been her grandmother's, Larry came out of his yard when he saw Azor leaving for school.

" That earring," he said, " is behind the fourth right-hand fence picket in Mrs. Snow's yard, if you want to know."

" Thank you," said Azor.

After school Azor walked down to Mrs. Snow's house and got the earring. Then he took it to Mrs. Woodfin's house. She wasn't home, but at suppertime she came to Azor's house and gave him a dollar.

" You are a good boy, Azor," said Mrs. Woodfin. " You hunted for my earring when you could have been playing with the other boys."

124

"I didn't go hunting for it," said Azor. "Larry told me where it was, and I just went and got it."

Everybody was in the living room, so they all heard and didn't believe him.

His mother told him to stop telling stories to Mrs. Woodfin at once!

His father said he was too old for this kind of thing. And his big brother told him not to be a baby.

Azor only said, "He really did," and went outside.

Ambrose Tells Azor a Secret

Larry wasn't the only one who told him things. There was Ambrose Frost too.

Ambrose was Mr. Frost's horse. In the winter he pulled the sidewalk snowplow, and in the summer he pulled Mr. Frost's vegetable wagon. So he was around town more than half the year. Ambrose knew everybody, and everybody knew Ambrose.

One day there was a big snowstorm. As soon as it stopped snowing, Azor went out to shovel snow off the walk.

Across the street Chrissie Orne was
shoveling, too. Pringle was making a
snowman.

Chrissie Orne's walk was shorter than
Azor's, so when he had finished his own
shoveling, he came over to help Azor.
Pringle came, too, and started a new
snowman in Azor's yard.

After a while Chrissie Orne's mother
sent him to the corner store for some
baking chocolate. While Chrissie Orne
was gone, the postman came along and
handed Azor a big letter.

When he opened it, there was a valentine. It was a picture of a girl with yellow hair. She was sitting in a red boat.

While he was looking at the valentine, Pringle hopped over through the snow. Her eyes were bright blue. The sun made her hair look like shiny molasses candy.

"Who's it from, Azor, who's it from?" she asked.

Azor turned it around and around. He looked at the back and at the front and under the red paper. But he found nothing.

"I don't know," he said. "It has no name on it."

So Pringle went back to her snowman.

128

Just then Ambrose came back, pulling the plow. He had to stop in front of Azor's house while Mr. Frost lighted his pipe, and he stood watching Azor and the valentine.

"I see you got one from Ella Snook," he said at last. Then Mr. Frost finished lighting his pipe, and they went on up the street.

"Ambrose says it's from Ella Snook," Azor called to Pringle.

"Maybe he saw her mail it," she said.

The next day in school Azor knew why Ella Snook looked at him and laughed. When it was time to go home, he went over to her.

"Thank you for the valentine," he said. "I didn't send you one because I didn't think you were going to send me one."

"How did you know it was from me?" Ella Snook asked. "I didn't put my name on it. Anyway, I didn't send you any."

"Yes, you did," said Azor. "Ambrose told me."

David was sitting nearby, and he heard. Soon everybody was laughing at Azor.

"Mr. Frost's Ambrose!" they said.

130

"A HORSE!" they laughed.

"He says he TALKED to him!" they howled.

"He never talks to me," Abel Frost said, "and he's my grandfather's horse!"

Miss Burns said, "Abel! Children! Children! Quiet!"

So they had to stop. But when they got outside, they began to laugh at Azor again, so he said good-by and started across the schoolyard.

On the sidewalk near the gate he met Ambrose with the plow. Ambrose looked over his shoulder as he went by and said, "If they knew more, they would say less."

And Azor started to whistle.

That day Azor promised himself that after this he would mind his own business.

"Now I see where my big mouth gets me," he said as he went whistling up the street.

Maude Crowley

131

Some Fishy Nonsense

Timothy Tiggs and Tomothy Toggs,
They both went a-fishing for pollothywogs;
  They both went a-fishing
  Because they were wishing
To see how the creatures would turn into
    frogs.

Timothy Tiggs and Tomothy Toggs,
They both got stuck in the bogothybogs;
  They caught a small minnow,
  And said 't was a sin oh!
That things with no legs should pretend
    to be frogs.

132   *Laura E. Richards*

Indian Children

Little Fox of the Forest

One Winter Night

Little Fox came running down the hill with his dog. He was dressed in winter clothes. He carried a bow and arrows and a wild turkey.

On the snow-covered ground were the tracks of a squirrel, but nothing else was stirring. The raccoon and the chipmunk were sleeping in their holes. The frog pond was covered with ice.

Little Fox gave his owl call to tell his mother he was coming. When he reached a small bark house near one end of the Indian village, he told the dog to stay outside. Then he went into the house.

Singing Water, his mother, was at home alone. His father was away on a long hunt. Little Fox was helping his mother by hunting with bow and arrows. This was his first turkey.

Singing Water took the turkey and said, " Someday you will be a great hunter like your father. Now a stew is ready for our supper, but first will you get the water and firewood for the night? Then I have a surprise for you."

Little Fox put away his bow and arrows. Then he hurried to get water and wood, for he wanted to see the surprise. He was hungry too, and the stew smelled good.

After Little Fox brought in the wood and water, he asked, "What is it, Mother? Is it some new moccasins?" He looked down at his old moccasins.

"No, it is this little bag to hang around your neck. You can now carry the stone knife your father made for you."

"I feel like a man when I can carry my own knife," said Little Fox. "I will skin all the rabbits after this."

"Watch what you say, Little Fox. It is harder than you think," said his mother.

It was growing dark now at the end of that short winter day, but the fire inside the house gave light enough.

Singing Water took steaming hot stew out of the big bowl on the fire and put it into a smaller bowl. She and Little Fox sat by the fire and ate the stew from this bowl. With it they had corn cakes that were baked on hot stones.

Little Fox could hear his dog sniffing outside. He called him in and gave him some of the stew. Then the dog lay down by the fire. They were all three warm and happy.

"Mother, tell me about the Little People. Do they ever go out on a cold night like this?" asked Little Fox.

137

"No, Little Fox," said his mother. "That is why we can talk about them in the winter. They are all covered up in ice and snow."

Just then the wind shook the house. The deerskin door blew wide open.

"What was that?" asked Little Fox.

Singing Water touched the bag that was hanging from shell beads around her neck.

"Do not be afraid," she said. "This will keep away everything bad. The medicine man gave it magic. The magic is against everything bad."

Singing Water pulled the skin across the doorway. Then she sat down by the fire and began to tell a story about the Little People.

She told how a woman once gave help to them. After that, there was always firewood at her door, because the Little People wanted to thank her.

138

Soon Little Fox grew tired and crawled into his bed. Beaver skins made it soft.

The wind blew harder and harder. It shook the bark house. Something hit Little Fox on the head and bounced off.

" What was that, Mother ? " he called.

Then he saw that a basket hanging on the wall had tipped over. The falling nuts were hitting him.

139

Home from the Hunt

Many cold days went by. Warm days like spring followed. The bear and her cubs came out. The raccoon and the small chipmunk looked out of their holes.

Little Fox's father had been gone more than four weeks. Singing Water was afraid that something had happened to the hunters. She went to the older men of the village to ask what they thought.

These older men talked together. What should be done? Should they send out young men to find the hunters? What help should they send?

140

Every day Little Fox climbed the highest tree on the highest hill to look for the hunting party. One day he saw the hunters far down the river.

"They are coming!" he called from the treetop.

At once all the people ran out of the houses.

"My father and all the other hunters are in a boat up the river a long, long way," Little Fox shouted. "I see them from the tree."

Some young men went out in their boat
to pilot the tired hunters home.

Little Fox watched the two boats as
they came nearer the shore.

The hunters' boat was full of skins.
There were beaver, deer, bear, and fox
skins — piles and piles of them. There
would be enough skins to make new
clothes and beaded moccasins for all.

The hunters were bringing fresh deer
meat and piles and piles of meat that had
been dried in the sun. There would be a
feast for everyone! It was the greatest
hunt the village could remember.

Singing Water and others had hurried to make good fires when they first saw the men. Now the fresh meat was placed on poles over the fires. When it was ready, there was a great feast.

That night after the feast the hunters told stories of all that they had seen and done. Little Fox and all the village were glad to have them at home again.

Katharine Keelor

143

Blue Cornflower

Blue Cornflower was playing with her brother, Strong Boy. This was the last week she would be at home for a long time.

Her home was in a big Indian village where the houses were made of mud bricks. These mud bricks had been dried in the sun.

Long ladders were used to reach the houses. Blue Cornflower had to climb four ladders up from the ground to get home.

The house where Blue Cornflower lived was the highest one of all. It seemed to her that it reached almost to the sky.

Blue Cornflower was seven years old, and it was time for her to go to the Big Rock School for Indian children.

Blue Cornflower's father and mother were sad because their little girl was going away, but they wanted her to go to school.

Her mother made her a new dress with a red belt. She tied silver flowers and blue beads to her ears. Her father made high white boots of soft deerskin for her.

145

When the day came for Blue Cornflower to go away, her mother gave her some paper bread. It had been made with water, honey, and flour stirred into a paste and baked as thin as paper. Her grandmother gave her a bright red shawl to keep her warm.

Strong Boy wanted to give her his lamb, but Blue Cornflower could not take a lamb to school with her.

Blue Cornflower's grandfather told her to remember the ways of her people. Grandfather was a medicine man. He knew many stories about the moon and the stars. He knew when to plant corn. He knew all the ways of his people.

A big car came to take Blue Cornflower to school. She had on her new dress with the red belt, the red shawl, and the white deerskin boots. She had never been in a car before. It went so very fast that it seemed to her to be flying like an eagle.

In the car were other children going to the Big Rock School. The driver of the car was very kind to them.

After a long trip they reached the school. There were trees and grass in the yard. There were straight-up-and-down brick houses.

Inside the brick school there were no sheepskins on which to sit. There was a furnace, but no fireplace. There were chairs and tables and a radio. Machines were used to make things. The place was not like home.

Everyone was very kind, but Blue Cornflower was homesick. She did not understand the new ways.

One night at bedtime Blue Cornflower saw the new moon peeping in at her window. She knew that when the new moon comes before the snow, it is feather-planting time for the Indians.

They believe that if they tie a prayer wish to a feather, it will fly to Those Above. It will fly just as an eagle flies up to the sky.

Blue Cornflower remembered what her grandfather had told her. She knew the ways of her people, but what could she do?

148

The people in the big brick school buildings did not know about feather-planting time. Her kind grandfather was far away. He could not bring her eagle feathers and help her to plant them.

Blue Cornflower was very sad. Her grandfather was a medicine man. But would he understand that she could do nothing about feather-planting time?

One of the teachers was sorry that Blue Cornflower was homesick. That day she took the little girl home with her.

"Take off your pretty shawl, Blue Cornflower," she said. "You may look at the pictures in this book. When I come back, I will tell you a story." Then the teacher went out.

Blue Cornflower did not hear her go. She had seen a feather, a beautiful feather, on the teacher's hat!

Quickly she pulled it off. Now where could she find a colored prayer stick?

She hunted and hunted around the room. She could not find a prayer stick.

When the teacher came back, Blue Cornflower looked as if she wanted to cry, but Indian girls do not cry.

The teacher saw her pretty feather in Blue Cornflower's hand. Her hat looked strange without its feather. But she did not care, because she was sorry for the homesick little Indian girl.

" What is the matter ? " she asked.

" I need a stick, teacher, a stick with color, please," Blue Cornflower said. But she would not tell why she needed it.

The teacher thought and thought. Where was she to find a colored stick ?

At last she thought of something. She brought out a new blue pencil and some bright red tape.

Blue Cornflower tied the feather to the pencil with the bright red tape. It made a beautiful prayer stick.

Softly she said her prayer wish to it:

"Winter snows, sleep!
Growing time, come soon,
That I may go back to my
mother's house."

Quickly she ran out under the stars to plant her beautiful prayer stick.

Blue Cornflower was happy. Those Above would hear her prayer wish. Now she could tell her grandfather that she had remembered the ways of her people.

Ann Nolan Clark

151

Home

This is my mother's house;
My father made it.
He made it with adobe bricks;
He made it strong;

He made it big;
He made it high;
My mother's house,
I live in it.

This is my mother's house;
My mother plastered it
With brown clay;
On the outside
My mother plastered it.

The inside walls are white;
My mother made them white;
The floor is smooth;
My mother made it smooth,
For me to live there.

In my mother's house
There is a fireplace;
The fireplace holds the fire.
On dark nights the fire is bright;
On cold nights the fire is warm.
The fire is always there,
To help me see,
To keep me warm.

In my mother's house
There are the grinding stones;
The big, flat holding stone,
The small rubbing stone;
The grinding stones,
My mother's grinding stones.

On the floor
Beside her stones
My mother kneels,
And with her hands
She grinds the corn;
Yellow corn and blue corn
My mother grinds
For me to eat.

In my mother's house
All day
I play and work;
All night
I sleep.

The walls come close around me
In a good way.
I can see them;
I can feel them;
I live with them.

This house is good to me,
It keeps me;
I like it,
My mother's house.

Ann Nolan Clark

The Eagle Hunt

On Black Cliff

Dancing Cloud knew that Wildhorse, his father, needed some eagle feathers for the feather dance. One May morning Dancing Cloud jumped on his horse and rode to find Swift Boy, his best friend.

"Let us hunt eagles," said Dancing Cloud. "I remember that I saw an eagle's nest halfway up Black Cliff."

"I too have seen it," said Swift Boy. The two boys rode across the dry open country to the canyon and Black Cliff.

156

While Swift Boy waited below, Dancing Cloud climbed the cliff on the side where the climbing was not hard. When he got to the top, he took his rope and tied to it an old can, which he had brought along.

Dancing Cloud lay down on the ground and looked over the high cliff. Far below him he could just see a tiny piece of the eagle's nest, which stuck out over a rock.

Dancing Cloud began to let down the rope. Down, down, went the can. It stopped just outside the nest. With a shout Dancing Cloud moved it in and out. The can banged against the rocks. It would have frightened anything.

The boys watched, one on top of the cliff, one below. The old eagles were not to be seen. They must be away looking for food.

After a short time a baby eagle was scared by the noise. It sat on the edge of the nest and looked around.

Then the little eagle fell over the edge. It could not fly very well. Partly falling and partly flying, it dropped down toward Swift Boy.

But the young eagle did not fall all the way to the ground. It caught on a rock that stuck out far above Swift Boy's head. The boys could not see it any more.

Dancing Cloud banged the can again. Another young eagle came out. It too dropped over the edge.

Swift Boy thought, "At last we have one." But that bird caught on the rock where its brother had stopped.

Dancing Cloud banged the can again and again. No more birds came out, so he climbed down the cliff by the way he had climbed up.

"What shall we do now?" he asked Swift Boy. "How can we get up to that rock?"

For a long time the two boys tried to find a way to climb to the rock. The sun was low in the sky when at last Dancing Cloud shouted, "A trail, a trail!"

Up the trail the boys climbed, putting their feet into every little hole. Once Dancing Cloud almost fell, but he caught himself just in time. At last the two reached the edge of the rock where the birds were hiding.

"Look, a cave!" said Dancing Cloud. "The young eagles must be hiding in the cave." It was black and frightening.

"I saw something move inside the cave," said Swift Boy. He was afraid.

159

Dancing Cloud was really afraid, but he crawled into the cave and found a young eagle there. It tried hard to get away from him. He caught it by the leg and pulled it out.

" Tie its legs," said Dancing Cloud. " I saw the other eagle in the back of the cave. I'll get that one too."

" One eagle is enough," said Swift Boy.

" I want the other," said Dancing Cloud, and in he crawled again.

When his eyes were used to the dark, he could just see the other eagle. He caught it by the leg and soon brought it out into the light.

" You tie this one too," he said. " I saw something else in the cave. I think it was a jar. I am going back into the cave to get it."

" Oh, no ! " cried Swift Boy. " If it is a jar, the Dawn People live in the cave. They would be angry if we touched it."

"But the jar is near the front of the cave. The Dawn People live far back where it is dark," said Dancing Cloud.

He went again into the cave. He was very much frightened. The Dawn People might be angry, but he took the jar and crawled out with it.

The jar seemed to be filled with sand. The boys turned the sand over with a stick and saw something blue. The jar was half full of beautiful blue stones!

"Turquoise! Real turquoise!" cried Dancing Cloud. "What fine belts and rings the stones will make!"

161

Home with the Treasure

Dancing Cloud and Swift Boy filled their pockets with the beautiful turquoise stones. It was all right to take them, they thought, because the Dawn People never came out of their caves.

Quickly the boys picked up the eagles and hurried down the trail to the ground. They were glad to get on their horses and ride away from the canyon toward home. More than once they looked back, afraid that the Dawn People were angry.

It was suppertime when they got home. Swift Boy took half of the turquoises and one of the eagles. He rode off quickly so that he would get home before dark.

Dancing Cloud showed his father the baby eagle. Then out of his pockets he took the blue stones.

" Where did you get the turquoises ? " asked Wildhorse. " They look very old."

162

Dancing Cloud told his father about the cave and the jar. " Will the Dawn People be angry because we took the turquoises ? " he asked.

" Quiet, boy," said Wildhorse. " The Dawn People will not be angry if you do not think and speak badly of them."

" Swift Boy and I want belts with silver circles and buckles on them," said Dancing Cloud. " Do you think Big Arm would make belts for us with some of these stones ? "

" Yes," said Wildhorse, " and Big Arm will be glad to have some of the turquoises to pay for his work."

163

The next day the boys rode to the home of Big Arm. He told them that the turquoises were very old. No one had found stones like them for many years.

Swift Boy and Dancing Cloud had many happy days with Big Arm. They helped him hammer out some silver for their belts and buckles. The finished belts with turquoises in the circles were beautiful.

Dancing Cloud said, " I am glad we went to Black Cliff to hunt eagles." He did not even speak of the Dawn People.

164   *Mary and Conrad Buff*

He-Who-Thinks-Well-and-Runs-Quickly

Crying Coyote

One summer morning an Indian boy stood alone on the prairie. As far as he could see on every side, there was this great rolling land covered with high green grass.

Every summer the buffaloes came in big herds across the prairie. It was then that the buffalo hunts took place. Even now a hunt had started.

Crying Coyote had been sent out to watch, and to let the hunters know when he saw buffaloes coming. He had been picked from all the boys because he ran so swiftly.

The older boys said that running was all Crying Coyote could do. They laughed at him.

He had been named Crying Coyote because as a baby he was afraid. He had cried out at the barking of a coyote at night. How he wished for another name!

From his watching place the boy heard a low rumbling sound. Quickly he put his ear to the ground.

The rumbling grew to the thud, thud, thud of faraway feet. Crying Coyote jumped up and ran to the top of a little hill. From there he could see far, far across the prairie to the east.

From the hilltop the thud of buffalo feet sounded nearer and nearer.

166

Far out across the prairie clouds of
smoke filled the air. The boy knew that
some hunters had gone far to the east
to drive the buffaloes toward the west.
These men had lighted fires in the grass
to frighten the herd of buffaloes.

The animals would turn and run from
the fire and smoke. They would run
toward the west away from the strange
red danger.

To the west hunters waited near a big pound or trap. This trap had been set up where trees grew along a river.

Branches and tree trunks had been piled together to make a fence. In the east side a gateway had been left open.

Thud, thud, thud! The rumbling of the buffalo feet grew louder and louder.

Now Crying Coyote could see the leaders of the herd. More and more buffaloes came. They looked like tiny spots headed west toward the trap.

168

Crying Coyote threw a wolf skin high into the air. It was a signal to the men near the pound that all was well. Four times he threw his wolf skin. Then on swift moccasins he ran toward the pound.

The hunters were hiding behind two lines of rock piles leading toward the pound. They were waiting to drive the buffaloes the last little way into the pound.

Thud, thud, thud came the sound of feet behind Crying Coyote. The herd was so near to him that he was afraid.

169

But now Crying Coyote was near a rock pile. Quickly he jumped behind it. His friend Black Eagle was there, too.

" Is the herd a big one ? " he asked.

" The prairie to the east is covered with buffaloes ! " said Crying Coyote.

Suddenly the leader of the herd raced by the rock pile where the two boys were hiding. Down toward the pound the great animal went. The other buffaloes followed behind the leader.

Someone gave a signal. From behind the lines of rock piles jumped men and boys. They waved skins in the air and shouted at the buffaloes.

The frightened animals ran faster. They pushed against one another. Black Eagle and Crying Coyote ran with the men, driving the buffaloes on.

All at once one young buffalo ran back from the herd. With his great head and horns he came straight toward Crying Coyote.

It seemed as if the boy were taking root. He could not move. He was in great danger, but Black Eagle jumped quickly to save him. Black Eagle threw his wolf skin into the buffalo's face and against the horns.

171

It stopped the animal long enough for Black Eagle to pull his friend behind a pile of rocks. Crying Coyote fell to the ground, very much frightened.

" You should stay with the women until the hunt is over," said Black Eagle. " You're no hunter ! You're just a crying baby ! "

Crying Coyote was very sad. He could not help it. The buffalo had come so quickly. He had had no time.

Then he thought, " Black Eagle had time to think ! Why did I stand still, while he threw the wolf skin ? "

Now the leader of the herd was inside the pound, and the other buffaloes were pushing against him. He began to circle round and round inside the fence. Other frightened animals joined him. Round they circled in a cloud of dust.

Men and boys herded in the last buffalo. Then they threw logs across the opening.

Saving the Hunt

With their bows and arrows ready the hunters waited for the signal to start the shooting.

Suddenly an arrow shot up into the air, through the cloud of dust. Up and up it went, as if it were shot from a giant's bow. It was Great Bear's signal for the shooting to start. Great Bear was Crying Coyote's father.

Arrows flew through the air like swift flying birds. Buffalo after buffalo fell.

Crying Coyote did not join in the shooting. He went alone to the far side of the big pound. Black Eagle had called him a baby, who should stay with the women !

Through the cloud of dust Crying Coyote watched, but he did not shoot. He was so near the buffaloes that he could almost put his hand on their great backs.

Crying Coyote saw one buffalo stop running in circles. It stood pawing the ground and digging up grass. Then it ran at the side of the pound and pushed against the branches and tree trunks.

Crying Coyote ran toward the spot. The other hunters were far away at the other side of the pound. There was no one else nearby.

Down came the branches and tree trunks as the buffalo pushed at them.

174

Crying Coyote shouted to drive the animal back, but it did no good. If one buffalo ran away, the boy knew that the herd would follow and be lost.

Crying Coyote ran toward the animal and waved his wolf skin. The buffalo still pushed against the side of the pound.

Then another tree trunk fell from its place. It fell across Crying Coyote's leg, holding him to the ground. The buffalo was almost upon him.

At first the boy was very much afraid. Then all at once he knew he must save the hunt. It was his father's hunt. He must work quickly.

Crying Coyote picked up his bow and put an arrow in place. With a quick pull he shot from where he lay.

One, two, three arrows he shot into the body of the buffalo.

The animal stood over Crying Coyote for a minute. Then it fell. Its body lay against the tree trunk.

The boy shouted, but no one could hear. No one could see with the dust flying.

He could not move, but he was happy. The body of the buffalo had blocked the opening in the log fence. No other animal could get through it. He, Crying Coyote, had saved the hunt.

176

Great Bear's Messenger

It was Black Eagle who found Crying Coyote at last. He shouted to the men to come quickly. Many hands pulled the buffalo and the tree trunk off Crying Coyote, and helped him to his feet.

For a minute the world seemed to go round, and he sat down quickly, not knowing where he was. Black Eagle gave him water from a buffalo horn.

Then Crying Coyote saw that Great Bear, his father, stood before him.

"What has happened?" asked Great Bear, looking at his son.

The boy did not speak, but Black Eagle said very quickly, "A buffalo pushed through the logs at this place. See, the buffalo is shot and blocks the opening. No other animal got through."

"And who shot the animal?" asked Great Bear. "What arrows are these?"

177

" The arrows are Crying Coyote's," said Black Eagle proudly.

" The boy did well," said the hunters. " He saved us many animals ! "

At first Great Bear did not speak, but he stood looking at his son.

" Go," he said at last. " Carry word to our people that there has been a great hunt. Tell them to move the tents to this spot so that the women may dry the meat and dress the hides. Great Bear sends the word."

Crying Coyote looked at his father in surprise. Then he began to understand.

Crying Coyote was to be the messenger. It was as if Great Bear said to all the world, " My son is no longer a baby and afraid. I am proud of him. Before all the people I make him my messenger. No longer shall he be called Crying Coyote. His name shall be He-Who-Thinks-Well-and-Runs-Quickly."

Crying Coyote got to his feet. His body no longer shook from his fall. Straight and tall he stood. His eyes met Black Eagle's. The older boy looked at him proudly. Crying Coyote was very happy, but he would not show it.

Without a word the boy turned and started down the trail. It was a half day's run across the prairie to the Indian tents.

The sun was going down, but there was still some daylight left. There would be a moon that night to show the way when the sun was gone. Swiftly and proudly the boy ran along the trail.

Caroline D. Emerson

Billy Tigertail

Billy Tigertail opened his eyes and was surprised to find the morning so quiet.

Then he remembered why it was so very still. His father, Buffalo Tigertail, and his big brother, Dick, were gone. They had gone to hunt the alligator in the dark waters near their camp.

Billy remembered how last night he had watched his father and brother load their things in the boat. He had even asked if he might go with them.

"You are too young to hunt the alligator," Buffalo Tigertail had said. "There is great danger in alligator hunting. But someday you will be man enough to put on the wide belt and go with us to hunt the alligator."

Now Billy sat up and rubbed his eyes. He had heard the soft sound made by a spoon. His mother was stirring the *sofkee* in the pot steaming over the fire. Little Patsy was at play nearby.

It was time to get up. A breakfast of *sofkee*, made of corn meal and vegetables, waited for him. How good it smelled!

Billy Tigertail lived with his family in the Indian camp. The houses stood on piles above the ground. Nearby was the highway leading into town. In front of the camp were the dark still waters where the alligators lived.

When Billy was eating his breakfast of *sofkee*, his mother said, " You must stay home and take care of Nan and Patsy while I go to town to get cloth. I need it to make aprons to sell."

" Why cannot Patsy take care of little Nan ? Then I could go to town with you," said Billy. " Patsy is six years old, and anyway, all Nan does is sleep in her bed that swings under the roof ! "

Mother laughed softly and asked, " Who would feed the little girls if they were left alone ? "

182

" The *sofkee* pot is always on the fire, and the *sofkee* is always ready to eat," said Billy.

" Now, now," said his mother. " Show me that you can take good care of our home for this whole day. And Father may take you on his next hunt for the alligator." Then she walked to the highway to take the bus into town.

After Billy waved good-by to her, he worked in his vegetable garden. Patsy was busy making rows of mud pies.

183

Suddenly he heard little Nan crying. So he climbed up to her swinging bed and gave her some milk.

Gently he rocked the bed. All was quiet now. Only the leaves on the trees were rattling in the wind and making a noise like rain.

"Ow-eee!" A cry came from Patsy! Where was she? Over there by the fireplace, where she had set up a row of mud pies. Billy ran to her.

Patsy was holding up a little brown hand. It was covered with hot corn meal from the *sofkee* pot.

"Patsy!" cried Billy, "why did you put your hand right in the pot? Don't you know how to eat with the *sofkee* spoon?"

"I know," cried Patsy, "but I tripped, and my hand fell in. Ow-eee!"

"Don't cry," said Billy. "I will take care of it." He got some grass and cleaned the hot corn meal off Patsy's hand.

184

Billy knew about a plant that would help Patsy's hand. Once when he had hurt his thumb, his mother had used leaves from this plant on it. Quickly he cut open one of the plant's green leaves and let the yellow part run out. Gently he rubbed it over Patsy's hand.

"It is better, isn't it, little Patsy?" asked Billy, and Patsy stopped crying.

"Come!" said Billy. "We will eat some *sofkee*. After that, we will play very quietly near Nan. Then I can keep an eye on her while she sleeps."

185

All the time they played, Billy was thinking about one thing. What would his mother say when she found out that Patsy had burned her hand? She might think that he had not cared for her well. Then he would never go alligator hunting!

When his mother came home, the first thing Billy said was, "Patsy burned her hand in the *sofkee* pot."

"I tripped and fell against the *sofkee* pot," said Patsy.

Her mother touched the little hand gently. "Who took such good care of your burned fingers?" she asked.

"Billy did, and all the hurt is gone," Patsy said.

186

Mother handed Billy a brown paper bag and said, " You have earned this present."

"A belt! A belt like the one Father wears," said Billy. "Oh, thank you, Mother, thank you."

" I will make it beautiful with many colored beads," said his mother. " You have been a man today, so you should wear a man's belt! "

Just then shouts were heard far away. " They have come back! " cried Billy.

He ran to the edge of the dark water, and there was Father piloting his boat through the water to the shore.

187

Over the dark water near the camp the boat moved slowly. Billy could see Dick sitting on a big alligator.

"What a good hunt you have had!" said his mother. "We will sell the alligator hide, but the tail will make some wonderful new *sofkee*."

They waited until Buffalo and Dick had put on clean clothes. Then they all sat down to a supper of chicken and sweet potatoes.

While they ate, Mother told how Billy had cared for Patsy's hand after it had been burned in the *sofkee*.

"It is good, my son," said Buffalo. "I think you are big enough to go with us on our next hunting trip!"

Billy was too happy to speak, but his black eyes were so bright that everyone knew how proud he was.

Rose Leion

Americans All

The Rodeo

Danny was riding Ginger in the big parade. It would have been great fun if only Judy had been there to ride with him.

Judy lived with her grandfather on a ranch over the mountain. She and Danny went to the same school, so they had fun riding and teaching their ponies to do tricks together.

Then Judy's grandfather had been sick, and she had no more time to ride with Danny before the rodeo.

Now the parade was almost over. The riders lined up across the ring. A cowboy clown with a nose like a cherry got off his donkey and took a bow. The clown made everyone laugh, and the parade ended.

Danny took Ginger outside and tied him up. Then he joined his family who had tickets for the grandstand.

It was hard for Danny to sit in the grandstand while his friends got ready for the children's trick riding. He and Judy were to do trick riding together, but last week she had said that she could not come to the rodeo.

191

Danny watched cowboys roping and riding wild horses. A cowboy from his own ranch stayed on a horse that tried to throw him.

Danny thought the rodeo was great, but he wanted to be in it, not on the side lines. He wanted to show what Ginger could do. There wasn't a smarter cow pony in the whole show.

Just then someone called, " Danny ! "

He turned and cried, " Judy ! "

" Are Pepper and I in time to ride with you in the rodeo ? " Judy asked.

"I — I don't know," said Danny. "The trick riding will be starting soon."

"Why don't you ask Mr. Hill?" said Danny's father. "He is taking care of the trick riding."

"All right, Dad, we will," said Danny. "Come along, Judy. Let's hurry and find Mr. Hill."

As they climbed out of the grandstand Danny asked, "How did you get here? I thought you couldn't come."

"Grandfather is better and said Pepper and I could come after all."

"There's Mr. Hill over by the gate," said Danny. "Let's go."

He began to run, Judy following right behind. When they reached the gate, they asked if they might be in the children's trick riding.

"Glad to have you," said Mr. Hill, "but you will be at the very end."

"Thank you, Mr. Hill," said Danny.

As Mr. Hill walked away Danny turned to Judy and said, " We haven't done our tricks for a long time."

" We can try them out now," Judy said. " We can go to that pasture over there."

While Danny and Judy rode Ginger and Pepper around the pasture Mr. Hill was in the rodeo ring. The trick riding had started. Children from ranches far and near took part.

First a little boy rode a pony across the ring and jumped over a low gate.

Next came a girl on a beautiful gray horse. He told how old he was by lifting his foot three times.

Next came a boy who rode two ponies at the same time. Like a circus rider he stood up, with one foot on the back of each pony.

Mr. Hill called out, "And last we have Judy and Danny riding Pepper and Ginger ! "

194

Judy and Danny rode out into the ring together. Danny tried not to look up at the grandstand. He tried to think only of his riding.

He played follow-the-leader with Judy. When Pepper trotted, Ginger trotted, too. When Pepper turned around, Ginger turned around. The ponies walked in step as they turned, wheeled, backed, and danced.

195

Riding up in front of the grandstand, Danny said quietly, "Together, now!"

He tapped Ginger on the neck. Judy tapped Pepper on the neck. The ponies bowed together. Judy and Danny took off their hats.

People in the grandstand stood up and shouted. Danny thought it was the most noise he had ever heard.

He and Judy waited by the gate and listened.

Over the radio Mr. Hill was announcing the winners of rodeo prizes. "And in the boys' and girls' trick riding." He looked at the paper in his hand.

"First prize goes to Judy and Danny," Mr. Hill went on.

Judy and Danny rode out to get their prizes. Mr. Hill gave them each a belt with a gold buckle.

"I always wanted a belt with a gold buckle," said Judy. "Grandfather will be so pleased. I must hurry home and show it to him."

"I'll always keep this belt," said Danny. "Thank you, Mr. Hill."

What a great day this had been after all!

Clyde Robert Bulla

197

The Harpers' Farm

We always drive along until
We reach a humping little hill,
And on the other side of this
The farm should be and there it is,
Waiting for us, white and neat
In the misty summer heat.
And here we are and here we are,
Climbing quickly from the car
And asking may we ride the horse,
And Mrs. Harper says, " Of course."
And asking are there any new
Kittens, and she says, " A few."
And asking may we go and play
Hide-and-seek up in the hay.
And in the corner of the loft
There are the kittens, gray and soft,
With tongues just learning how to drink
And little ears all lined with pink.

198

Then Mrs. Harper calls, " Yoo hoo ! "
And so we run (we always do)
Out the barn and through a gate
And find some cookies on a plate.
And there is also lemonade
In a pitcher in the shade.
And after that we always climb
On Bessie's back, one at a time,
And Mrs. Harper laughs at us,
But it seems very dangerous,
Stuck so high up in the sun
Looking down at everyone.
We squeal and grab each other's clothes.
We hang on with our knees and toes
And say, " Giddap," and Bessie does,
And such a gallop never was !
Then we get off her all alone,
Her tail a rope for sliding down.
And soon it's late and time to go,
So we tell Mrs. Harper so.
" Thanks for the lemonade," we say,
And wave good-by.   And drive away.

Dorothy Aldis

199

The Horse Who Lived Upstairs

There was once a horse named Joey who was discontented. He was discontented because he didn't live in a red barn, and he didn't live in a green meadow where he could run about and be frisky.

Joey lived upstairs in a big brick building in a great city. He worked for Mr. Polaski, who had fruits and vegetables to sell to city people. Joey pulled the vegetable wagon through the city streets.

And in a great city there isn't room for barns or meadows.

200

So every night when Joey came home, he stepped into an elevator, and up he went to his stall on the fourth floor of the big brick building. It was a fine stall and Joey had everything he needed. He had hay to eat, water to drink, and fresh straw to sleep on.

He even had a window to look out of. But still Joey was discontented.

It wasn't that he had to work hard. Mr. Polaski was kind to him and brought him home at five every day.

In the winter Joey had a blanket to wear on his back to keep him warm.

In the summer Mr. Polaski got him a hat to wear on his head to keep off the hot sun.

And every day many interesting things happened. Sometimes he met a policeman who gave him sugar. Sometimes ladies from an apartment house nearby patted him on the nose and gave him carrots.

He saw the children playing in the playgrounds and the parks.

But still Joey was discontented.

202

"This is no place for a horse," Joey used to say to the work horse who lived in the next stall to him. "We city horses don't know what real living is. I want to move to the country and sleep in a red barn and run about in a green meadow."

So how happy he was when one day Mr. Polaski said to him, "Joey, I think I could sell more vegetables if I had a truck. I will miss you, Joey, but you will like it very much on the farm where I am going to send you."

The next morning a big truck rolled up. Joey got inside, and away he went to the country.

"Good-by, Joey," called his friend, the work horse. "Have a good time on the farm."

When Joey reached the country, sure enough, there was the red barn, and there was the green meadow.

" This is the place for me!" cried Joey to himself. But poor Joey!

The barn was cold in winter and hot in summer. He didn't have a blanket, and he didn't have a hat. And he had very little time to run about in the green meadow. He had to spend the day pulling carts and the plow.

The farmer worked from sunup to sundown. So did Joey.

There were children, but they climbed on his back when he wanted to eat. And in place of the friendly work horse, there was a gruff old gray horse, who looked down his nose at Joey because Joey knew so little about a farm.

One day, when he wasn't pulling a plow, Joey saw some people having a picnic in the meadow. He decided to join them, for they looked as if they came from the city. He thought they might have some sugar in one of their pockets.

204

When he reached the spot, they had gone for a walk. So he ate up their lunch.

When they came back, they were very angry, and Joey had to stay in his stall all afternoon. He didn't even have a window to look out of.

Poor Joey missed his friends, the policeman and the ladies who patted him on the nose and gave him carrots. He missed all the interesting things in the city.

"I don't think I should live in the country after all," said Joey. "I am now more discontented than ever."

Next day he heard the honk of a horn. He looked from the door of the barn, and there was Mr. Polaski getting out of a truck!

"I have come for Joey," Mr. Polaski told the farmer. "I cannot get some parts for my truck, so I think I will sell fruit and vegetables from my wagon again."

My, but Joey was happy!

206

He went back to the city with Mr. Polaski and got into the elevator, and up he went to the fourth floor of the big brick building. There was his stall, and there was the window for him to look out of. And there was the friendly work horse.

"Glad to see you back, Joey," said the work horse. "I have missed you. The policeman has missed you. The ladies have missed you, and so have the children in the playgrounds and the parks. Tell me, how did you like the country?"

"The country is all right for country animals," Joey said, "but I guess I am just a city horse."

And he was never discontented again.

Phyllis McGinley

207

Bob Learns to Pitch

Bob wasn't very big. When the neighbor boys got up a baseball team, they said he was too small to play.

" What we need is a good pitcher," said Jack. " You aren't big enough for a pitcher."

"All right, Jack," said Bob, " but I'm going to make the team before the end of the summer. If I strike you out, will you let me play on the team ? "

Jack laughed and said, "Yes, Bob, if you can strike me out, I promise to let you play on the team."

That night Bob had a talk with his father. "Dad, where can I get some books on baseball pitching?" he asked.

His father laughed. He had been a fine baseball player when he was a boy.

"A pitcher has to have a strong arm," he said. "And you cannot get a strong arm from just reading books, Bob."

" You read a book about boxing, Dad,"
said Bob. "And you box with a man
downtown. Wouldn't a book tell me how
to make my arm strong ? "

" Why, yes," said his father. " I guess
you're right, but you would have to do
what the book said."

The next night Bob's father brought
home two books.

" Here's a book about another Bob," he
said. " He is a great pitcher. The book
shows just how he holds the ball. This
other book shows you things to do that
will make you strong."

Bob began to look at the pictures in
the books. Then his father pulled out
something that he had been hiding under
his coat. It was a baseball glove.

" For me, Dad ? " Bob asked.

His father handed the glove to him.
Bob thought he had the best father in
the world.

The next night, when his father got home, Bob said, "I read that book about the other Bob. It said his father used to go out with him and catch the ball. That was how he learned to pitch it across the plate to just the right spots. Will you help me, Dad?"

His father said, "You wait a minute." He went into the house, and Bob could hear him calling up someone. He said, "I'm not coming downtown tonight. I'm busy at home."

After that, he helped Bob every night. They would go out in the driveway, and Bob would pitch and pitch.

At last he could put the ball where he wanted it almost every time.

"That's the way to do it, Bob," his father would say. "A good pitcher knows how to put the ball where he wants it."

When they were through pitching, Bob's mother would have some chocolate ice cream ready for them.

One night Bob asked his father, "Now do you think I'm good enough to strike out Jack?"

"Well," said his father, "what did you read about pitching to a batter?"

"I read that I should watch the batter," Bob said. "I should find out if he can hit a ball thrown low better than a ball thrown high, or a ball thrown very near him better than a ball thrown far away."

"That's right," said his father. "Now you need to watch Jack. He's a good batter, but maybe he can hit one kind of pitch better than another kind."

212

Bob knew the things a pitcher must know. He knew that the ball has to go across the plate where the batter stands. It must not be above his shoulders or too low.

If a pitch doesn't go over the plate just right, it is called a "ball." But a pitch thrown in the right place is a "strike," even if the batter doesn't swing at it.

Well, Bob watched Jack. And he soon saw that Jack could hit balls thrown high better than low balls. So Bob worked at throwing low pitches.

After he had worked about four weeks, his father felt of his arm one night.

"Bob, your arm is much stronger," he said. "Why don't you try to pitch to Jack now?"

Bob was pleased that his father thought his pitching was good. But could he strike out Jack? He thought and thought about it after he went to bed. He felt his arm. At last he said to himself, "Tomorrow I'm going to try."

The next day he went to the baseball field. "Jack," he said, "I think I can strike you out now."

Jack laughed, but he said, "All right. If you can, I guess you may play on the team. I promised that." He picked up a bat and stood at the plate.

Bob put on his glove and threw the first ball. Jack gave a hard swing with his bat and missed it.

He said, "I'm not warmed up, I guess."

214

Bob threw again, and Jack took another swing, missing the ball. This time he looked surprised and laughed a little.

Bob threw another low one. S-s-wish! Jack's bat made a sound like wind. He had missed three times.

"Say, you're good, Bob," said Jack. "How did you do it?"

"Well," said Bob, "I read some books, but my dad helped me most."

Just then there was a noise behind a pile of lumber. The boys turned around. There was Bob's father!

He was on his way home from work and had been watching the boys play ball.

He thought they wouldn't see him, but he had stepped on an old pan left near the lumber and it had rattled.

" That was a good job, Bob," he said. " And you're a good fellow, Jack, to give him a try."

Jack still looked a little surprised.

" You're all right, Bob," he said. " You can play on the team for sure."

Bob walked home with his father. He was swinging his glove and thinking, " Dad is proud of me." It made him feel good, and when they got home, Mother had big dishes of ice cream ready for them.

216

Worthen C. Cornish

El Burrito

As Miguel worked in the garden he was busy thinking. How could he earn enough money to buy a bicycle? And wasn't it about time for El Burrito to be coming along?

El Burrito was a little brown burro that carried wood down from the mountains to the village. Miguel watched for him to go past every day.

Miguel lived in a tiny house far up the road from the village, so he had no one to play with. The other children lived down in the village.

When Miguel saw El Burrito coming, he picked up a carrot and waited for the little burro. El Burrito stopped for a minute to eat the carrot and to be petted. Then he followed his owner slowly along the road, his head down, his ears standing up straight and proud.

One day El Burrito did not go past the little house where Miguel lived. Three days went by, and still no small brown burro with great soft eyes.

Now on the fourth day Miguel said to himself, " I must find out what could have happened to El Burrito."

Miguel put on his shoes and his big hat. He walked down to the village and asked about El Burrito.

No one knew what had happened to the little burro. But everyone knew that his owner had turned him out.

Someone said, " Have you not heard? El Burrito is too old to carry wood. His owner is very poor. He has no money to feed a burro that cannot work."

" I will look for El Burrito," said Miguel.

" If you find him, keep him," said the burro's owner.

" Thank you," said Miguel, starting home.

" But, Miguel," said his mother when he told her what had happened, " if you find El Burrito, what will you do with him? "

" I will think of something," said Miguel.

On Saturday morning Miguel walked up the mountain. He looked everywhere for the little brown burro.

Miguel found only trees with yellow and red leaves. So he picked pretty red leaves and took them home.

"You have not come home empty-handed," said his mother as she put the leaves into a blue jar.

"I have been thinking of El Burrito," said Miguel. "You know I could not sell newspapers because I had no bicycle to carry them over the mountain. Maybe I could use the burro in place of a bicycle. Then I could save enough money to go camping next summer."

That afternoon Miguel was getting a squash off the low roof for his mother when he saw a little cloud of dust down the road. Soon a tired little burro could be seen, walking slowly toward Miguel.

"El Burrito!" shouted Miguel, running down the road toward him.

Miguel took the burro into the yard and gave him food and water. Then Miguel cleaned his coat until it was like silk. As Miguel worked, he decided what he and El Burrito would do.

221

After school the next week Miguel took El Burrito to the newspaper station. There the bags on the burro's back were filled with newspapers.

So old El Burrito took the place of a bicycle and helped Miguel to sell newspapers. That was easy work after all the years of carrying wood.

Everyone had a friendly word and a bite to eat for El Burrito. The boys and girls put so many flowers behind the straight, proud ears that it looked as if they were growing there. And El Burrito liked his job and all his new friends.

222

The following summer, when Miguel went camping, El Burrito's bags carried corn and dried meat and beans and even a pan and a tent. The food and other things were for the campers to use.

The little burro had helped Miguel to earn more than enough dollars to pay for his camping trip, so he went along too. What would a camping trip be without a burro like El Burrito?

Rose Leion

New Moon and the Dragon

Good-Luck Wishes

On her way home from school New Moon went into her father's shop. She always liked to look at the beautiful silks and the long pieces of painted glass hanging about the shop. The glass tinkled in the wind. She always stopped for a minute at the table of Chinese toys.

Today New Moon saw another wonderful thing. It was a dragon head, painted red and green and yellow. It had a great mouth and big round eyes and red balls at the top.

224

To all Chinese children the dragon is wonderful. On the first day of the New Year he comes out from a secret hiding place and parades through the streets. People give him presents, for they believe he will bring good luck.

"I wish I could have a dragon head," said New Moon.

"Well, we shall see," said Father.

On the day before the New Year began, Mother was busy getting food ready for the feast. New Moon helped to dust and clean.

The chairs for the uncles and aunts who were coming to dinner were covered with bright red silk.

225

Chinese bowls filled with nuts and cakes were put on tables. There were bowls of fresh flowers too. Red papers with good wishes for the New Year were placed near the pictures of the grandfather and grandmother. These letters on the red papers said, "Good luck." 福喦

The next morning when New Moon came to breakfast, Mother and Father were waiting to give presents to the children. New Moon could hardly wait to open them. First of all there was money tied in red paper, one piece for New Moon and one for her baby brother.

In a little box New Moon found a gold ring. It would take the place of a baby ring, which was now too small for her.

In a bigger box were Chinese slippers made of silk. New Moon slipped them on. With the ring and slippers she felt like a lady.

226

But she stopped being a lady when Father handed her the last present. It was a dragon head! New Moon played that she was a dragon. Her baby brother kicked with his tiny feet and laughed at her.

Then New Moon heard the noise of firecrackers outside. She ran out on the balcony. The New Year was starting!

Down on the street some boys were lighting firecrackers, shouting, and racing around.

" Good luck, Turtle Boy," called New Moon to one of the boys.

227

"Good luck, New Moon," Turtle Boy called back. "Do you want a firecracker?"

He lighted one and threw it so that it went off at the edge of the balcony. New Moon shouted and laughed. She wanted to join the boys, but she heard Mother call, "Stay on the balcony, New Moon."

Soon Father came out. "You may help me put up the American flag, New Moon," he said.

So New Moon helped to hang the big American flag just so over the balcony. She was very proud of the flag, for she was an American.

228

The Dragon

Up and down the street people were hanging out presents for the dragon. Some of the presents were fruit and money tied up in red paper.

Mother tied a little bag of fruit and some money to a long piece of red tape.

" New Moon," she said, " when the dragon comes to us, you shall give him our presents. You will let them down over the balcony until the dragon takes them."

In the street were many boys and men. From the windows and balconies women and little girls were watching. New Moon saw Turtle Boy just below, still shooting off firecrackers.

" I am going to follow the dragon when he comes out," called Turtle Boy. He threw a firecracker and ran up the street.

" Come, New Moon," said her mother. " It is time to put on your best dress."

New Moon and her mother put on their most beautiful silk suits. New Moon was proudly wearing her silk slippers and new ring.

When New Moon went back to the balcony, she heard far up the street the sound of Chinese drums.

"Oh, Mother, Mother," she cried, "the dragon is coming!"

Mother hurried out to the balcony with the baby in her arms. He was dressed in red silk.

Now they could see the dragon as he danced along. He was colored red and yellow and green. The red balls on his head waved, and his great ears moved up and down.

He stopped not far away to take a present which was let down from a balcony. The drums rolled, the dragon danced.

Then the dragon came on toward New Moon's house. Silk flags, red, blue, and gold, waved as they were carried past. A boy let go a silver balloon, and it sailed away.

New Moon let their present down over the balcony. It was swinging on the end of the red tape.

The great dragon's head reached up below her. His green eyes rolled. His mouth opened and closed. He jumped up and took the fruit and the money. Then he began to dance.

There was a man inside the dragon's head, holding it up and dancing with it. There was another man inside the tail, making it wave and turn. New Moon knew that very well, but just the same she was a little frightened.

The dragon made one last jump, and the parade moved on. Drums rumbled, and flags waved. New Moon saw her father and her uncle and Turtle Boy walking behind the dragon.

She watched until the parade had gone far down the street and she could only hear the drums.

After the parade Turtle Boy and his father and two uncles came to New Moon's house. The whole family sat down to a feast that lasted a long time.

Just before New Moon went to bed, Mother took her out on the balcony for one last look. The street was very quiet, because nearly everyone was inside feasting. Up in the sky above the houses New Moon saw bright stars and the new moon.

"See, Mother," she said. "There I am up in the sky."

"So you are," said Mother. "Happy New Year and good luck, New Moon!"

Anne Merriman Peck and Enid Johnson

233

The Ice-Cream Man

When summer's in the city,
    And brick's a blaze of heat,
The Ice-Cream Man with his little cart
    Goes trundling down the street.

Beneath his round umbrella,
    Oh, what a joyful sight,
To see him fill the cones with mounds
    Of cooling brown or white,

Vanilla, chocolate, strawberry,
    Or chilly things to drink
From bottles full of frosty-fizz,
    Green, orange, white, or pink.

His cart might be a flower bed
    Of roses and sweet peas,
The way the children cluster round
    As thick as honeybees.

234

Rachel Field

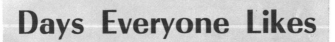

Days Everyone Likes

235

The Boy Who Believed

Juan sat on the end of a wharf, kicking his brown legs. In his arms was a big gray cat. The sunlight danced on the blue sea. It was a fine summer day in the year 1492.

Something interesting was going on near the wharf. Three ships were being made ready for a long trip. They were not big ships or new ones, but they interested Juan very much.

Gray Whiskers, the cat, was interested, too. She tried to jump out of Juan's arms. She wanted to go hunting for rats on the strange ships.

" Those old ships are not good for a long trip," said a man who stood nearby, watching the loading of them.

" No, they are not very good ships," said another man, " and they are full of rats, but it does not matter. They are sure to be lost."

" Why are they sure to be lost ? " asked the first man.

The other man laughed. "Don't you know?" he said. "There is a strange fellow who thinks that the world is round! He is to sail with these three ships. When he reaches the end of the world, his ships will fall off into a great empty place."

Juan stood up with the big gray cat in his arms.

"Our queen believes that Columbus is right," he said. "She has helped him get the ships for the trip."

"The queen is a very good woman," said the man who had laughed. "But look at the sea, boy! Tell me if you see anything round about that? The sea is flat, flat as a pancake!"

"Yes, but look again," cried Juan. "Look at the ship that is sailing away. Only the top of its sail can be seen. It is this which makes Columbus think the world is round."

"Tell me, boy," said one man. "If the world is round, how can people stay on the other side of it? Why don't they fall off?"

"I do not know," said Juan. "That is what Columbus is going to find out. When he comes back, he will tell us."

The men on the wharf laughed — all but one. He was a tall, dark man with gray hair. He was listening to the talk.

"So you believe that Columbus will come back?" the first man asked Juan.

"Yes," said Juan. He was still holding Gray Whiskers in his arms.

"That is fine talk," the man went on. "But you would not even let your cat go along to catch rats on his ship. You know you would never see her again."

"I should be proud if my cat could help this man Columbus," said Juan.

The tall, dark man on the wharf walked over and touched the boy's shoulder.

"I am Columbus," he said. "Would you send your cat with me?"

"Yes," said Juan at once, "for I know that you will come back."

"It may be a long time, my boy," said Columbus. "But I will come back."

"Then take my cat," said Juan. "Gray Whiskers is a good cat, and they say that your ships are full of rats."

Columbus looked into the boy's eyes. Then as if the queen were giving him a present, he took Gray Whiskers from Juan's arms.

Carol Ryrie Brink

Halloween

The moon is round as a jack-o'-lantern;
The trees blow black and bare;
And we go creeping with spooky giggles
Through the chill ghostly air.

Whose shadow is that on the haunted
    ground?
Who's hiding behind that tree?
Oh, down the tree runs my bad black
    kitten,
And the shadow is only me!

Frances Frost

241

The Friendly Ghost

What Happened to the Apples?

Julie had come to visit Aunt Mary and Uncle Fred. She knew them, for they had visited her home in the city. But this was the first time she had gone to their farm.

She felt homesick and strange as she looked around her room before she got ready for bed. She wished she could go home tomorrow. She wished— Julie didn't want to cry.

There was a light tap on the door. " May I come in, Julie ? I have something for you." It was Uncle Fred.

" Ye-es," Julie said, swallowing quickly. " I have brought you some apples. You might get hungry in the night." Uncle Fred set a plate, holding three red apples, on the little table by the window. " They are from our own trees."

242

Uncle Fred looked out the window of the small ground-floor bedroom. "I used to have this room when I was a boy," he said. "I always liked it because I could watch the horses and cows in the pasture. How would you like to ride one of the horses sometime, Julie? Their names are Ted and Daisy."

"Oh, that would be fun!" she said.

"Ted is the gentle one," Uncle Fred said, "but Daisy is all right if she likes you."

"How shall I know if Daisy likes me?"

"Oh, you will know all right. She will come right up to you."

After Uncle Fred left the room, Julie felt better. She thought that the days ahead would be great fun. She had just hopped into bed when Aunt Mary came in to say good night.

" Sleep well, Julie, and don't be afraid if you hear noises in the night. An old house squeaks now and then."

" Are there ghosts here ? " asked Julie.

" Oh, no ! " said Aunt Mary. " Why are you thinking about ghosts ? It's not time for Halloween ? "

Long after Aunt Mary left the room, Julie thought about ghosts. Everything was quiet — or almost quiet, with just a squeak or two. But Julie couldn't sleep.

She sat up and reached for an apple. Just then she heard a thump, thump, outside the window. Right in front of her eyes the curtains at the window moved, very slowly. Something long and thin and white was there.

244

Julie screamed and pulled the pillow over her head. Then she shot down to the foot of the bed.

Aunt Mary and Uncle Fred heard her screams and came running down the stairs. They turned on the light in Julie's room and threw back the bed covers.

"It was a ghost, I know it was," Julie said.

Aunt Mary put her arms around Julie and said, "You know, Julie, there are no such things as ghosts."

Uncle Fred laughed. "Well, I guess I know one little girl who shouldn't eat apples before she goes to sleep."

"But I d-didn't eat an apple," Julie said. "I was just g-going to."

"That's funny," Uncle Fred said, "for I'm sure I put three apples on the plate, and now there are only two."

"Maybe you ate one yourself, Fred," said Aunt Mary. "But never mind. Let's all get back to bed."

At breakfast the next morning they all laughed about the Halloween ghost. Even Julie found it easy to talk about ghosts in daylight. Uncle Fred said it must have been a dream. No one could understand why only two apples were on the plate.

At last Aunt Mary said, "Maybe you ate one in your sleep, Julie."

That first day in the country was a busy one for Julie. She had fun digging in the garden. She saw the tractor and other farm machines. She helped Aunt Mary make a salad for lunch. It was an apple and carrot salad.

246

She sat on the pasture gate for a while and watched the two farm horses. She liked brown Ted, but she liked the white horse, Daisy, even better. By the end of that first day she was so full of sun and wind and good times that she was ready for bed.

Aunt Mary said to Julie, " No Halloween ghosts tonight ! "

Julie was too tired and happy to think about ghosts. She lay in bed with her eyes almost closed, remembering all the wonderful things she had done that day.

Suddenly she opened her eyes wide as she heard a thump, thump. The curtain began to move at the window, and the long white thing that she had seen the night before reached through the window.

Julie didn't take time to scream. She shot under the bed covers and pulled them down around her at the foot of the bed.

In the morning Aunt Mary found her there with the blankets every which way.

Julie told her what had happened. "It was a ghost," she said. "I know it was."

"But, Julie, there aren't any such things as ghosts," said Aunt Mary.

Then she looked at the plate on the table by the bed and said, "Why, Julie, you ate another apple!"

Julie looked at the table for the first time that morning, and her eyes grew big and round. There was only one apple left on the plate.

A New Friend

That afternoon Uncle Fred took the two horses up to the house and asked Julie which one she would like to ride.

" I should like to ride Daisy," Julie said.

Uncle Fred shook his head. " Daisy doesn't make friends quickly, but maybe she will be all right with you."

He lifted Julie onto the white horse's back. Then he got on brown Ted, and together they rode off. Uncle Fred was surprised when he saw how gentle the white horse was with Julie.

249

" I think you have been making up to my Daisy on the quiet," Uncle Fred said.

Julie shook her head and ran her hand down Daisy's neck. She wanted to show that she wasn't afraid of everything.

They rode around the pasture and down the road. Julie listened to the farm sounds as they rode along — the mooing of the cows, the quacking of the ducks, the honking of a goose, the buzzing of bees, the frogs in the pond.

That night Julie went to bed by herself. She was sure now that she must have been dreaming, for she knew there couldn't be any ghosts in such a wonderful place.

No one believed she did not eat the apples. Maybe she really did eat them in her sleep!

Julie was so tired and happy that she went right to sleep. Sometime in the night she heard a strange sound and opened her eyes.

Moonlight was filling the room, and Julie could see that something had put its head in the window. She sat up in bed and opened her mouth to scream. Then suddenly she saw who it was. It was her friend Daisy !

" Hello, Daisy," she said softly. " Would you like this apple ? "

Julie looked down at the plate, but it was empty !

" I guess you do like apples," she said, " and you make a very good Halloween ghost."

Elizabeth Yates

251

Thanksgiving Day

Over the river and through the wood,
  To Grandfather's house we go ;
    The horse knows the way
    To carry the sleigh
Through the white and drifted snow.

Over the river and through the wood,
  Oh, how the wind does blow !
    It stings the toes
    And bites the nose
As over the ground we go.

Over the river and through the wood,
  To have a first-rate play.
    Hear the bells ring,
    " Ting-a-ling-ding ! "
Hurrah for Thanksgiving Day !

Over the river and through the wood,
   Trot fast, my dapple-gray!
     Spring over the ground
     Like a hunting hound!
   For this is Thanksgiving Day.

Over the river and through the wood,
   And straight through the barnyard gate.
     We seem to go
     Extremely slow,
   It is so hard to wait!

Over the river and through the wood,
   Now Grandmother's cap I spy!
     Hurrah for the fun!
     Is the pudding done?
   Hurrah for the pumpkin pie!

Lydia Maria Child

Christmas with Stina Mor

The Straw Goats

It was growing dark on the road leading toward the purple hills. This was the day before Christmas, but the boy and girl walking along the snow-covered road were not happy.

Each of them had a straw goat. They had made the goats and carried them in their arms all the way to town. Now they pulled them along by their horns.

"This morning I was sure it would be easy to sell them," said Peter. "They looked so fine to me then."

254

"Maybe they seemed fine only because we made them," said Anna.

In the land where the children lived, everybody had a straw goat for Christmas. People might do without a Christmas tree but never without a goat.

"Now that we did not sell our goats, what shall we do for a Christmas present for Mother?" Peter asked.

Anna thought of all the things their mother had done for them that year.

"It will be too bad if we have no present for her at all," she said.

They had reached the village post office. Peter said, "Let's stop here and see if there is any mail."

They were thinking of the same thing. Their older brother, Oscar, had gone to sea many years before. Maybe he had thought to send a letter to his mother this Christmas. The letter would be the best present they could bring her.

Helping a Neighbor

The postmaster was busy with the mail.
He looked up over his glasses.

" No, there is no mail for you," said he,
" but there is a package for Stina Mor."

Stina Mor was their neighbor. Everyone
called her Stina Mor (Mother Stina).

" We could take it to her," said Peter.

" No," said the postmaster quickly, " not
without your sled. The package is big and
heavy."

Peter and Anna went along with their straw goats, which seemed to grow heavier with every step. The goats' tails made little lines in the snow.

" If we cannot carry that package, I'm sure Stina Mor cannot," Peter said.

"After her fall down the cellar stairs, she cannot walk as far as the post office," said Anna. " And she has no one at all to help her."

" Let's go home and get our sled," said Peter, " and take Stina Mor's package to her."

" What a surprise it will be for her, getting a big package like that ! " said Anna.

The two began to run. The straw goats no longer seemed heavy.

Soon Anna and Peter were at home. While Peter got his strong sled out of the shed, Anna ran in to tell their mother where they were going.

It was starting to snow. They had not gone far when they heard the jingle of sleigh bells behind them. Then a sleigh went past and stopped. It was filled with children from their room in school.

"Come along with us," the children called. "We have just heard that the king is coming through our town on the express. We are going to the station to sing Christmas songs for him."

Anna and Peter had never seen the king. Anna had read that he sometimes wore a crown — just such a crown as the kings in stories wore. How fine it would be to sing to the king!

258

But if they went in the sleigh, they would not have time to get Stina Mor's package. The post office would close at five. It would not open again until after Christmas. Stina Mor might not have any Christmas presents at all if they did not get the package.

"We cannot go with you this time," they called. "We are sorry."

Another and another sleigh went past. Anna could hardly keep from crying. It would be so wonderful to see the king!

259

At the door of the post office Peter said, "We have come for Stina Mor's package."

"There is a letter for her, too," said the postmaster. "It's from that lazy son of hers in America. It's about time he is writing to his mother."

Peter thought of their brother, Oscar, who had gone to sea and did not write letters to their mother any more. Was that why she looked so sad at times?

The postmaster brought the package and letter to the door. The package was so heavy that Peter and Anna together could hardly get it upon the sled.

260

"What do you suppose can be in it?" asked Anna.

"If that lazy son of Stina's sent it," said the old postmaster, "it might be nothing but a great stone." He hurried back into the warm post office.

Peter and Anna could not walk fast on the snow-covered road. The snow fell into their eyes so they could hardly see.

The package made the sled do strange things. It would slide first to one side, then to the other. Anna had to go behind to push and to hold the package in place. At last they got it to Stina Mor's house.

Peter tapped on the door. Stina Mor opened it, letting a warm light out into the dark.

"Merry Christmas," said Peter. "We have a post-office package for you."

"It may be from America!" Stina Mor said quickly.

"And here is a letter too," said Anna.

The Package from America

While Stina Mor looked around for her glasses the two brought in the package.

"Is the letter from Nils?" Stina Mor asked. "Is it from my son in America?"

"It is," said Anna.

"Please read it for me," said Stina Mor. "I cannot find my glasses."

Anna took off her mittens, opened the letter, and began to read:

"Merry Christmas to you, Mother! You will be glad to know that I have a fine job at last. I am sending you a box of Christmas presents.

"My old neighbor, Oscar, is no longer sailing the seas. He is working where I am. We make parts for helicopters. The letter inside this one is from him. Will you give it to his mother?"

Anna gave a happy cry. "The letter Mother has been wanting for so long!"

"Go on," Stina Mor said. "What more does it say in the letter from Nils?"

Anna read —

"Oscar has put some packages for his family in the box I am sending."

"We must open the big box at once," Stina Mor said.

Peter and Anna could hardly wait while they helped take the paper off the big package. Inside there were many smaller packages. There was a box from Oscar for them and one for their mother.

263

Stina Mor was looking over her presents. " I can use this warm coat and this shawl and these slippers," she said. " But Nils doesn't know that I no longer eat sweets. You may take that box home with you."

She gave them a box of chocolates.

" Oh, thank you ! " cried Anna. " Now we have two presents for Mother."

On the way home Peter said, " The box of candy will be a present from us. We earned it partly, didn't we ? "

Just outside their own house they met the sleighs full of children again. " The king's train is very late," they called. " So we are going back later."

" We can go with you then," Peter and Anna said.

As they hurried into the house they were laughing. They had been sad about the straw goats ! And now it promised to be the merriest Christmas ever !

Nora Burglon

Barney on TV

Tilly had her puppies just as New Year's Day dawned. They were red with white paws, and there were five of them. But Barney Miller and his little brother Chris didn't know about it until their mother woke them in the morning.

"Tilly has something to show you," she said. "Jump into your slippers and come down."

"Puppies!" shouted Barney and Chris together. Half a minute later they were down by the furnace in the basement, looking at Tilly's new family.

265

" Such tiny red puppies," said Chris. " How many may we keep ? "

" Don't you remember ? Mother and Dad said we couldn't keep any. As soon as they're six weeks old, we must find homes for all five of them."

" Dick Harper wants a puppy," Chris said.

" The Harpers have two cats."

" Peanut Sanders — " began Chris.

Barney shook his head. " His mother doesn't like animals in the house. The Harpers and Sanders are out, but in six weeks we may think of somebody."

Later that morning Barney went down to the store for a bottle of milk. On his way home he went past the Zipp Oil station. He remembered something he had heard on TV. The Zipp Oil Company was giving prizes for the first babies born on New Year's Day. Nothing had been said about the kind of babies to be born.

266

There was a man at the gasoline station, so Barney stopped and said, "We had some new babies just born today. What do I do to get a prize?"

"Write to the TV station, Zipp Oil Company program. Babies? Twins?"

"Yes," said Barney. "There are two sets of twins and one left over."

Before the man could say any more, Barney was racing toward home. He wanted to write to the TV station.

Two days later Barney got a letter. He was to come to station WOZB on Saturday afternoon at two.

Barney read the letter over and over again. Would he look and sound all right on TV ? Chris said that he sounded as good as the boy from the moon on the TV program and looked better.

By the time Saturday came, Barney was too busy trying to find homes for Tilly's puppies to care how he sounded.

Chris went with Barney to the TV station. They took a downtown bus to the building and went up to the top floor in an elevator.

Five New Year's Day fathers were there, waiting for the Zipp program to start. Another man, who wore glasses, came over and talked with Barney.

" I'm Mr. Casey," said the man. " Your part comes at the end of the program. Please sit down over here."

268

As the boys sat down Chris said, " What if he asks the puppies' names ? "

" Quick ! " said Barney. " Think up some names ! "

" Rover, Shirley," began Chris.

Just then the show went on the air. There was a picture of a Zipp Oil Company station, and the announcer started talking about Zipp oil and gasoline. After that, he gave play pens to the fathers of the babies born on New Year's Day.

Barney did not listen to the program. He was trying to think of names for the puppies. He needed five names in a hurry.

Somehow, Rover was the only one he could think of. He thought of Rover, Rover, over and over again. He could not ask Chris to help because no one could talk while the program was on the air.

Then Mr. Casey called to Barney, and he stood up.

"And now, friends," said Mr. Casey, " a young man is here to tell us about five New Year babies at his house. Yes, five babies! Mr. Barney Miller, are you still sure you counted right ? "

" Yes, Mr. Casey," said Barney. " There are five down in our basement, and they're red with white feet."

270

The fathers on the program expressed great surprise. One dropped his hat on the floor, and it rolled in a circle.

Mr. Casey hurried to say, "Tilly is a dog, and her babies are puppies. What are their names, Barney?"

Barney swallowed such a swallow that he was sure it was heard on every TV set. "Rover," he said. "And — and Shirley. The Rovers are the boys. The Shirleys are the girls. And if anybody has a good home for them, I'll be glad . . ."

"I'll buy a Shirley!" cried one father.

"A Rover for me!" said another father.

271

Mr. Casey said, "*Shhh-shhh!*" But another father called out, "A Rover here!"

"I'll buy a Shirley!" cried the fourth.

"And I'll take whatever is left," shouted the last one.

Mr. Casey waved his arms, and a man brought in a heavy box which he put on a chair. The chair tipped over, and cans bounced off, rolling on the floor and banging against chairs and feet.

Above the noise the announcer shouted, "We now give a prize to Barney Miller. A whole box of dog food! Be with us next Saturday, friends, for another Zipp Oil Company program!"

Mr. Casey turned to Barney. "Thanks," he said. "Thank you very much, Barney."

"Oh, that's all right," Barney said. "If Tilly ever has New Year puppies again, I'll write you a letter."

Eda and Richard Crist

The Valentine Box

At the New School

The valentine box was beautiful. The children had made it by covering a big hatbox with red paper. They had pasted white hearts on the sides.

The box sat on a table, looking bright and important. Most of the children could hardly wait for the party, but Jane did not have a " party " feeling.

As she started home to lunch she was glad it was snowing hard. Maybe her mother would not let her go back to school in the afternoon.

273

Jane was afraid she wouldn't get any valentines. She was new in the town of Lakeside. Being a quiet girl, she found it hard to make friends in the new school.

In the doorway at home Jane took off her boots and carried them into the house.

"What a day!" her mother said. "If this was not Valentine's Day, I would telephone the school and keep you home. But I'm going to let you take this old pocketbook to carry your valentines. You will need something to keep them dry."

Jane and her mother had made the valentines together, writing rhymes for them. One was a train with an engine and caboose. A red heart popped out of the little caboose. The engine had wee hearts on the sides.

After lunch Jane put on her winter coat and her high boots. Then she dropped her valentines in the pocketbook and started back to school.

274

Across the street three other children were going to school together. They were pushing one another into the snow and shouting.

The storm was wild now. The wind was blowing the snow in circles and roaring through the trees. Jane wished she had a muff to keep her hands warm.

As she reached the corner by the school she heard someone behind her cry, "Oh! Oh!"

Turning around, Jane saw Margaret, a girl from her room at school. Bright papers were flying about her head.

275

"My valentines!" cried Margaret.

"I'll help you pick them up," Jane said as she ran after an envelope.

"We can never, never find them," said Margaret.

"Yes, we can," said Jane. "Look, here's one, and here's another!"

Margaret caught three, and Jane a fourth on a picket fence. It was like a game. The wind joined in the fun. It blew one valentine heart on top of a stop sign at the corner.

"I'll get it," said Jane, "before it blows out into the street."

"There goes one more," said Margaret. The envelope danced over the snow as easily as the down of a thistle. She and Jane tumbled after it, but the wind blew it always ahead of them. Back at the school the bell began to ring.

"Jane!" cried Margaret. "Go back to school. You will be late."

"No later than you will be," Jane said. "I'm going to catch that valentine if it's the last thing I do."

The valentine blew on until it landed, like a helicopter, on the head of a snowman. He was a wonderful snowman, standing alone in front of an apartment house. He had pink cotton ears and a peanut nose.

"Sorry, Mr. Snowman," said Margaret as she reached for the envelope. "You cannot have this valentine for a hat."

Then she took Jane's hand, and they raced to school.

277

The Snowstorm Valentine

The hall was warm and very quiet. The doors on each side were closed. Margaret and Jane shook the snow off their coats.

Together they counted valentines: one for Miss Waters, one for Tony, others for Johnny, Mac, Susan, Dot, Bill, Andy. The girls saw that there wasn't one for Jane.

"It's too bad they're wet," Jane said quickly. "Mother gave me a — Why, where is it? I must have dropped it while I was running after valentines."

278

"Let's go right back," Margaret said.

"No," said Jane. "Anyway, not now. We had better tell Miss Waters first."

They hurried to their room and told Miss Waters what had happened. "Did you have anything important in the pocketbook, Jane?" she asked.

"My valentines," said Jane.

Miss Waters looked down at Jane's boots. "You're warm and dry," she said. "There's time enough for you to run back and take a look."

"May I go along to help hunt?" Margaret asked. "It was because of me that Jane lost the pocketbook."

Miss Waters looked at Margaret's wet rubbers and said, "Your feet must be wet. You had better stay here and get warm and dry. But Bill might like to help Jane look for her pocketbook."

"Sure," said Bill, putting down his pencil.

He put on his boots and his warm coat
and cap. Then he and Jane went out
into the snow.

As they went up the street she told him
how the valentines had zoomed up into the
air like airplanes, and Bill laughed. Soon
they reached the snowman and there, at
his feet, was the pocketbook.

When Jane and Bill came back to the
schoolroom, Jane dropped her valentines
into the box. Then Miss Waters asked
her to be the postman.

Jane lifted the cover from the red valentine box and took out the envelopes, one by one, calling the names: " Andy — David — Margaret — Dot — Johnny — Nan — Tony — "

Four times there were valentines for Jane. The fourth one was big, and the envelope was made from school paper.

The valentine was the picture of a funny snowman wearing an envelope for a cap. There were pictures of two girls, one on each side of the snowman. And below it Jane read the words in red pencil.

For My Snowstorm Valentine

Margaret said, " I made it while you were looking for the pocketbook. I didn't have time to make up a good rhyme."

" It's wonderful ! " Jane said.

After the valentine box the children played games. Then they had cakes and little pink candy hearts.

When the party was over, Jane and Margaret walked home together. It had stopped snowing, the wind had gone down, and the afternoon sun was out. " Can you come over to my house ? " Margaret asked.

" Let's ask my mother," Jane said.

So they stopped at her house, and Jane said, " Mother, this is Margaret, my snowstorm valentine."

Her mother laughed with them as the girls told her how they had run after valentines in the snow. After that, the two new friends went out to play. Living in Lakeside was going to be fun.

Maud Hart Lovelace

Old, Old Stories

The Cap That Mother Made

There was once a little boy called Anders. One day his mother gave him a present, a cap that she had made herself.

The cap was red, all but one little part. That was green because there were not enough red pieces to finish it. And the tassel was blue.

Anders put the cap on his head. His family told him he looked very fine in it.

So Anders put his hands in his pockets and went out for a walk. He wanted everyone to see his new cap.

Soon Anders met Nils, a big boy, much bigger than he. Nils was so big that he was wearing high boots and carrying a jackknife.

When Nils saw Anders' fine new cap, he stood still to look at it. Then he went up to Anders to feel it and to play with the blue tassel.

"I'll trade my jackknife for your cap," he said.

Anders knew that it would be a fine thing to own a jackknife. But he couldn't part with the cap, even for the knife.

"I'm sorry, Nils," he said. "I cannot trade my cap."

Off went Anders down the road. Soon he met an old woman wearing a shawl. She said, "Little boy, you look very fine. Why don't you go to the king's ball?"

"I think I will," said Anders. "With this cap on my head I look fine enough to visit the king."

285

So he walked on until he came to the king's castle. Two soldiers were standing at the gate. One of them asked, "Where are you going?"

"I am going to the king's ball," said Anders.

"You cannot go to the king's ball," said the soldier. "You have no fine clothes."

"My cap is as good as any fine clothes," said Anders. And he told them how his mother had made the red-and-green cap.

Still the soldiers would not let him through the gate.

Just then the princess happened to go past the gate. She saw Anders standing there looking very sad. So she said to the soldiers, "What is the matter? Why don't you let this little boy come to the king's ball?"

One of the soldiers said, "The king's messenger announced that the ball is for those who are well-dressed."

286

"But he has a cap with a tassel," said the princess. "That will do just as well. He shall come to the ball with me."

The princess took Anders through the great gate and up the wide stairs.

Anders and the princess stood in the doorway to the ballroom for a minute. Then they walked across the room. Women in beautiful silk dresses and men in fine suits of silk and cloth of gold turned to look at Anders. They must have thought he was a king's son.

At the far end of the ballroom was a long table lighted by many candles. There were gold cups and silver plates filled with cakes and fruits. The princess sat on a gold chair next to the queen, and Anders sat on another gold chair.

"You will want to lay your cap down when you eat," said the queen, and she reached out to take it off his head.

"Oh, I can eat just as well with it on," said Anders, holding it with his hands.

"I will give you some cakes for the cap," said the princess.

Anders only shook his head. He would not give up his cap even for a princess.

Then the princess put cakes and fruit into his pockets, and she put her own gold chain around his neck.

"I thank you for the cakes and fruit and the beautiful chain," Anders said. "But I cannot give away the cap my mother made, not even for a chain of gold."

Just then the king himself came into the ballroom, followed by six soldiers. The king wore clothes of beautiful blue silk. On his head was a great gold crown. He looked kindly at Anders.

" That is a fine cap you have," he said.

" Yes, it is," said Anders. " My mother made it for me, but everyone tries to take it away from me."

" Surely you will want to trade caps with me," said the king.

289

He took off his gold crown. At the
same time he reached for the cap with
the blue tassel.

Anders said not a word. He jumped
from his chair and ran across the ballroom
floor. Down the hall he flew, as if his feet
had wings, and through the gate, before
the soldiers could stop him.

Half of the cakes and fruit fell out of
his pockets. The gold chain fell from his
neck.

But he still had his cap! He had the
cap his mother had made! He was
holding fast to it as he ran home.

There Anders told his family all that had happened to him.

He told them that everyone had liked his red-and-green cap and had tried to get it away from him. He told how the king had wanted to trade his crown for the little cap.

Then Anders' big brother said, " You were a silly goose not to trade. Think of the things you could buy if you were king. You could buy high boots and a jackknife all your own. You could buy a cap even finer than this one, a cap with a feather."

" No, I wasn't silly ! " cried Anders with flashing eyes. " There isn't a cap in all the world finer than this one my mother made for me ! "

" You have good sense, little Anders," said his mother. " If you had a crown of gold, you could not look so fine as you do in your cap with the blue tassel."

A Swedish Tale

The Traveling Musicians

There was once an old donkey that could no longer work on the farm. So one morning he started for the city. " There," he thought, " I may do well as a musician."

He had not gone far when he came upon a dog, who looked very tired.

" What is the matter, my good friend ? " asked the donkey.

" Oh, me ! " said the dog. " I am old and can no longer go hunting. What can I do for a living ? "

"Listen!" said the donkey. "I am going to the great city to be a musician. Why don't you come with me?"

The dog said he was willing, and they went on together.

Before long they saw a cat sitting in the road. Her face was sad.

"Good morning, my good cat," said the donkey. "What is the matter with you?"

"Oh, me!" said the cat. "How am I to live when I can no longer catch rats?"

"Come, come," said the donkey. "Why not go with us to the great city? You are a good night singer, and you will do well as a musician."

The cat was pleased and joined the party.

As they were going past a farmyard they saw a rooster on the roof of a henhouse. He was crowing with all his might.

"Good for you!" the donkey called. "Upon my word, you make a fine noise! Tell me, what is all this about?"

"Why," said the rooster, "I was just saying that we shall have bright sun for our washing day. But no one has sense enough to thank me. I'll end up in a stew."

"Anything will be better than staying here and ending up in a stew," said the donkey. "Come with us, Mr. Rooster."

"With all my heart," said the rooster. So the four traveled on together.

When night came on, they went into the forest to sleep. The rooster flew to the top of a tree, looked out on all sides, and saw a light.

"There must be a house no great way off," he called. "I see a light."

"If that is so, we had better go there," said the donkey, "for this place is not the best in the world."

The four hurried toward the spot where the rooster had seen the light.

The donkey, who was the tallest, walked up to the house and peeped in.

"What do you see?" asked the rooster.

"I see a table loaded with all kinds of good things," said the donkey, "and some thieves are sitting around it."

"That would be a good place for us to stay," said the rooster. "Let's scare the thieves away."

The donkey stood with his front feet against the window. The dog got on his back, and the cat climbed on the dog's shoulders. The rooster flew up and sat upon the cat's head.

The donkey sang, " Ee-ah, ee-ah."

The dog howled, " Bow-wow-wow."

The cat mewed, " Mi-aow-ow."

The rooster crowed," Cock-a-doodle-doo ! "

Then they all pushed through the window and tumbled into the room.

296

The thieves had been frightened enough when they heard the singing, but now they were sure some great giant was after them. They ran away as fast as they could.

Late that night one of the thieves, who was braver than the others, went to see what was going on in the house. He found everything quiet, so he went into the kitchen.

The thief picked up a candle and started toward the fireplace to light it. The cat was sleeping by the fire. She woke up and opened her eyes. Seeing the thief, she jumped on his back.

The frightened thief ran to the door. There the dog took a bite out of his leg.

As he ran across the yard the donkey kicked him and the rooster began to crow with all his might.

The thief hurried back to his friends and told them how a woman had jumped on him. Then a man behind the cellar door had cut his leg with a knife.

In the yard a black giant had hit him with a great hammer. And on the roof had sat a ghost with wings, shouting:

" Cock-a-doodle-doo !
Put him in the stew."

After this the thieves were afraid to go back to the house.

The musicians were so pleased with their new home that they never went to the city. They lived together in the little house, and there they are to this day.

Wilhelm and Jacob Grimm

Chanticleer

High and proud on the barnyard fence
Walks rooster in the morning.
He shakes his comb, he shakes his tail
And gives his daily warning.

"Get up, you lazy boys and girls,
It's time you should be dressing!"
I wonder if he keeps a clock,
Or if he's only guessing.

John Farrar

The Lark and Her Young Ones

A lark once had her nest of young ones in a wheat field. Each day she had to leave them alone while she hunted bugs and seeds.

Each day she asked the young larks to listen for news about cutting the wheat. Then away she flew, singing a happy song.

One day while the young larks were alone the farmer came to look at his wheat. "It is high time," he called to his son, "that our wheat is cut. Go tell all our neighbors to come in the morning and help us cut it."

When the mother lark came, her children told her what they had heard.

300

" There's enough time," said she. " If the farmer waits for his neighbors to help him, there is no danger. The wheat will not be cut tomorrow."

The next day the farmer came again. The day was warm, and the wheat was ready to cut, but nothing had been done.

" There is not a minute to be lost," he said to his son. " If the neighbors will not help us, we must call in others. Run now and call all your uncles and aunts. Tell them to be here tomorrow morning to cut the wheat."

The young larks told their mother what the farmer had said.

"If that is all," she said, "then do not let it frighten you. The uncles and aunts will have wheat of their own to cut. But listen to what you hear the next time."

The next day while she was away the farmer came as before. He found that the wheat was almost ready to fall from the stalks.

"We cannot wait for help any longer," he said to his son. "When the sun comes up tomorrow morning, I shall cut the wheat myself."

When the young larks told their mother what they had heard, she cried, "Then it is time to be off! If the farmer has decided to do the work himself, the wheat will really be cut." And away the lark family flew to a new home.

The next day the farmer came and cut the wheat. He had learned that if he wanted a job done, he must do it himself.

An Aesop Fable

The Lad and the North Wind

The Players

THE NORTH WIND   THE INNKEEPER

THE LAD   THE MOTHER

THE STORYTELLER

THE STORYTELLER. Once upon a time a poor lad was on his way home with a bowl of meal. The North Wind was blowing so hard that it sent the meal flying far and wide. The lad was cold and hungry and angry. He ran up the mountain and tapped at the North Wind's door.

303

THE NORTH WIND. Who-ooo! What do you want? Whoo-ooo!

THE LAD. I want my meal. My mother and I are poor and hungry.

THE NORTH WIND. I'm sorry, lad, I cannot give back your meal. It flew far and wide. But I'll give you a magic tablecloth. Ask it for food when you are hungry, and you will eat a fine dinner.

THE LAD. Oh, thank you, North Wind. I'll take it right home to my mother.

THE STORYTELLER. By now it was getting dark. The lad's home was far away. So he stayed at an inn that night and showed the innkeeper his tablecloth.

THE INNKEEPER. A tablecloth! Whoever heard of a tablecloth giving food.

THE LAD. I'll show you how it gives food. Watch now. Cloth, cloth, give us our dinner. See! What did I tell you? There is hot bread, honey, cheese, beans, squash, fish, and meat on the table.

THE INNKEEPER. What a feast that magic cloth gave us! Let's eat, and then you shall have the best bed in the inn.

THE STORYTELLER. Now the innkeeper was a thief. In the night while everyone was sleeping he took the magic cloth and put in its place an old cotton cloth. The next morning the lad carried the old cloth home.

THE LAD. Look! Look, Mother! See what the North Wind gave me. I say, "Cloth, cloth, give us food," and there on the table is a feast for a king.

305

THE MOTHER. I don't see any food, not even a wee piece of cheese.

THE LAD. The magic did not work. The North Wind tricked me.

THE STORYTELLER. The lad climbed the mountain again to see the North Wind.

THE NORTH WIND. What do you want now ?

THE LAD. I have come for my meal.

THE NORTH WIND. I cannot give you the meal, but I'll give you a magic sheep. When you need money, just say, " Sheep, sheep, give money." The sheep will open its mouth and gold will pop out.

THE STORYTELLER. Down the mountain went the lad leading his magic sheep. Once again he stopped at the inn for the night and showed the magic sheep to the innkeeper. Click, click, click, out popped some money.

THE LAD. See, Mr. Innkeeper, how my sheep gives money.

306

THE INNKEEPER. Gold! Wonderful! Now go to bed, lad, and sleep well.

THE STORYTELLER. That night the innkeeper took the magic sheep and left another in its place. The next morning the lad hurried away, leading the sheep behind him. When he reached home, he tried to show his mother how the magic worked.

THE LAD. Sheep, sheep, give money.

THE MOTHER. I don't see any money.

THE LAD. Oh, sheep, please give money.

THE STORYTELLER. This was not a magic sheep. No money dropped from its mouth. So the lad went back to see the North Wind.

307

THE NORTH WIND. Who-ooo-ooo is there?

THE LAD. I have come for my meal. My mother is hungry and I am angry.

THE WIND. I have no meal, but I have a magic stick. If you want to use it on a thief, just say, " Beat, stick, beat." It will keep on beating the thief until you say, " Stick, stop beating."

THE STORYTELLER. The lad took the stick and hurried to the inn. The innkeeper thought that the stick was full of magic like the wonderful tablecloth and sheep. So in the night he tried to trade another stick for the magic one. But the lad woke up just in time to see him.

THE LAD. Beat, stick, beat.

THE STORYTELLER. The stick began to beat the innkeeper.

THE INNKEEPER. Oh, lad, save me! Make your stick stop beating me. I'll give you back everything and never take anything again.

THE LAD. Stick, stop beating.

THE STORYTELLER. How happy the lad was when the innkeeper gave back the magic tablecloth and the sheep. As soon as it was light the lad set out for home with his treasures. Down the mountain he went, whistling happily.

THE LAD. The North Wind is a good fellow after all. These presents are treasures.

THE STORYTELLER. And this is the end of our play made from an old story.

Adapted by Vida F. Aygarn

309

The Princess Who Always Believed What She Heard

Once upon a time there was a beautiful young princess who always believed everything she heard.

The king said that anyone who could make the princess say, " It's a lie," should win the princess and half his lands.

All the princes thought this would be easy. They came from far and near and tried to make the beautiful princess say, " It's a lie."

310

When one prince said, "The moon is made of green cheese," she said, "How I should like to have a piece of green cheese —cut very thin."

And so on and on it went, until every prince had tried. Then other young men took their turn, and each thought he would win the princess, but not one did.

By now the king's messenger had come to a far place where a poor woodcutter and his son, Claus, lived.

When Claus heard the news, he said to himself, "No one can tell a better tall story than I."

Then and there he put on his best clothes, told his father good-by, and hurried off to the castle.

The king looked at Claus and said, " I do not think you can win. You live far from the castle and understand little of the ways of the world."

" I can tell a story that even the princess
will not believe," said Claus.

" Well, you may try," said the king.

So Claus took the princess for a walk in
the kitchen garden and said, " What big
cabbages and tall beanstalks are growing
here ! "

" The king feeds many mouths," said
the princess.

" But your cabbages are nothing like
my father's, which have giant roots and
great leaves," said Claus. " Once we were
building a new barn. There were twelve
men working on it.

312

"Suddenly it rained so hard that the roof leaked. The workmen ran to hide under a giant cabbage. They were keeping dry until a man put his knife through one of the leaves to see if the rain was over. Then so much water leaked in upon them that they were washed away!"

"What a big cabbage!" the princess said, and that was the end of the cabbages.

Claus was not to be put off in this way. He talked about the fine barn.

"The king's house must have a king's barn," said the princess.

313

"But you should see my father's barn," said Claus. "Why, our barn is so big that it takes a cow years and years to walk through it. She comes out so old that she cannot moo any more."

"That is a great barn!" the princess said, and that was the end of the barn.

So Claus took the princess to the king's chicken yard, and here he said, "You have beautiful chickens, as white as snow."

"The king's chickens have something to crow about," said the princess.

"But they are not so fine as my father's," said Claus. "Why, their eggs are so big they make a meal for the whole village. When we saw a shell in half, we have two boats."

"What big eggs!" said the princess.

"But that is not all!" cried Claus. "Our hens lay twelve cartloads a day. They are piled high as a castle wall, even higher, if we don't keep our eyes open."

314

Claus stopped for a minute and then went on, " One day we had a pile that reached up to the moon, and I was on top of it. When I tried to climb down, the load fell over. There I was, hanging from the moon.

" I would be hanging there still, if I had not thought quickly and found a cloud. I tried to let myself down on it, but the cloud did not reach far enough. So I had to jump off the tip of that cloud and fly down."

Claus stopped talking for a minute and looked at the princess, but she did not say anything. So he went on with his tall story.

"Where should I land but on a church roof! When I looked in the church, your father was there. He was sitting on the floor, listening to the organ as he counted his money. He had an old purple nightcap on his head, and his pockets were filled with gold and silver. The money had been there so long that it was covered with dust.

"All the people in the church gave money to the poor. But not the king. He gave nothing."

316

"Stop!" cried the princess, looking very angry. "It's a lie! My father is a kind man. He helps the poor, and he always wears his best crown in church."

"I am sure that is so," said Claus, the woodcutter's son. "But little does it matter, for I have made you say, 'It's a lie!' Now I'll be a prince, and you will be my wife."

That's just what happened in the great castle. And never again did Claus or anyone else ever tell lies — which was very right.

Mary C. Hatch

317

To the Teacher

Third Reader, Level I, *Finding New Neighbors*, follows *Around the Corner*, the Second Reader, Level II, of the GINN BASIC READING SERIES. This Third Reader is designed to be read during the first half of the third year.

This Third Reader introduces 335 new words and maintains all the words taught at the first-grade and second-grade levels of this series except 11 proper nouns and 2 sound words. Variant forms are not counted as new when they are formed by adding *s*, *es*, *ed*, *ing*, *er* (comparison), *est*, *er* (agent), *y*, or *ly* to known words. These inflectional variants include those formed by dropping the final *e*, doubling the final consonant, or changing *y* to *i* before the endings. Also not counted as new are possessive forms of known words, contractions in which the apostrophe represents the omission of one letter only, compounds of which each part is a known word, and words which are parts of known compounds.

New Words in This Book

UNIT I

7 . . .

---

8 Barby
gentle
9 Peggy
Andrew
10 brave
sugar
touches
11 feel
12 six
years
wide
13 arms
clop
14 afternoon
carry
slide
15 presents
16 colts

---

17 *Poem*

---

18 Speckles
setting
hatch
19 cluck
nest
easy
20 . . .
21 pen
straw
feed
22 chicken
weeks
23 . . .
24 . . .
25 . . .
26 twelve
27 . . .

---

28 thief
Teddy
29 Jane
30 coyotes
blankets
31 woke
32 . . .
33 scared

34 howl
alone
35 . . .

36 Maggie
magpie
37 smart
shoulder
hello
38 glasses
cubes
39 lemonade
40 . . .
41 . . .

42 *Poem*
43 . . .

---

44 eyes
45 Dad
remember
caught
46 meadow
toward

47 whistled
against
leg
48 . . .
49 . . .
50 fingers
bites
51 decided
52 chewed
53 . . .
54 . . .

UNIT II

55 zoo

---

56 jungles
57 . . .
58 spider
59 trunk
end
body
60 giraffe
almost
neck

318

61 vegetables
62 . . .
63 . . .

---

64 chimpanzee
mopped
Josephine
65 . . .
66 bucket
swish
67 cloth
68 licked
spot
69 . . .

---

70 pieces
meat
less
71 sick
thinner
wild
72 stood
73 tiger
74 seemed
sniffed
75 . . .

---

76 *Poem*

---

77 doctor
hospital
medicine
78 potatoes
hurt
79 cockatoo
wing
Doc
80 swallow
sure
81 . . .
82 bananas
83 . . .

---

84 awake
85 really
86 breathing
87 . . .
88 swaying
purr
89 rocking

---

90 *Poem*

UNIT III

91 . . .

---

92 Hilda
only
Selma
93 village
market
mind
94 important
molasses
95 apron
sneeze
96 shook
shell
spoon
97 slowly
slid
scrub
98 bottle
Nils
99 feet
curtains
100 stool
which
101 . . .
102 . . .

---

103 peddler
Forest
business
104 Gruff
silly
kick
105 promise
Tumble
106 stuck
107 angry
lift
108 squeak
hard
109 words
chocolate

---

110 Iva
111 pillows
112 . . .
113 hunter
114 brick
115 . . .
116 . . .
117 . . .

118 Percival
trap
danger
119 sweet
sent
closed
120 whole
121 hang
full
branch

---

122 Azor
Larry
123 believed
Pringle
half
124 sense
Woodfin
125 . . .
126 Ambrose
Frost
snowplow
127 Chrissie Orne
finished
128 valentine
129 Ella
Snook
130 send
131 . . .

---

132 *Poem*

UNIT IV

133 Indian

---

134 bow
arrows
135 stew
136 moccasins
knife
skin
137 . . .
138 beads
bad
magic
139 tired
hit
140 should
young
141 . . .
142 fresh
feast
143 . . .

144 Strong
mud
145 belt
boots
146 shawl
moon
147 eagle
understand
148 prayer
those
above
149 teachers
sorry
150 pencil
151 . . .

---

152 *Poem*
153 . . .
154 . . .
155 . . .

---

156 cliff
cloud
swift
157 below
frightened
edge
158 partly
159 trail
cave
160 jar
Dawn
161 filled
turquoise
162 . . .
163 speak
circles
buckles
164 even

---

165 prairie
buffaloes
herds
166 rumbling
thud
east
167 west
168 pound
leaders
169 signal
lines
170 suddenly
171 pushed
save
172 women
dust

319

320